Regulation

The International Library of Essays in Law and Legal Theory
Second Series
Series Editor: Tom D. Campbell

Titles in the Series:

Freedom of Speech, Volumes I and II
Larry Alexander

Privacy
Eric Barendt

Comparative Legal Cultures
John Bell

Contract Law, Volumes I and II
Brian Bix

Corporate Law
William W. Bratton

Law and Democracy
Tom Campbell and Adrienne Stone

Legal Positivism
Tom D. Campbell

Administrative Law
Peter Cane

International Trade Law
Ronald A. Cass and Michael S. Knoll

Sociological Perspectives on Law, Volumes I and II
Roger Cotterrell

Intellectual Property
Peter Drahos

Family, State and Law, Volumes I and II
Michael D. Freeman

Natural Law
Robert P. George

The Creation and Interpretation of Commercial Law
Clayton P. Gillette

Competition Law
Rosa Greaves

Chinese Law and Legal Theory
Perry Keller

Constitutional Law
Ian D. Loveland

Law and Legal Interpretation
D. Neil MacCormick and Fernando Atria

Human Rights
Robert McCorquodale

Anti-Discrimination Law
Christopher McCrudden

Medical Law and Ethics
Sheila McLean

Mediation
Carrie Menkel-Meadow

Environmental Law
Peter S. Menell

Criminal Law
Thomas Morawetz

Law and Language
Thomas Morawetz

Law and Anthropology
Martha Mundy

Gender and Justice
Ngaire Naffine

Law and Economics
Eric A. Posner

Japanese Law
J. Mark Ramseyer

Restorative Justice
Declan Roche

Justice
Wojciech Sadurski

The Rule of Law
Frederick Schauer

Regulation
Colin Scott

War Crimes Law
Gerry Simpson

Restitution
Lionel D. Smith

Freedom of Information
Robert G. Vaughn

Tort Law
Ernest J. Weinrib

Rights
Robin West

Welfare Law
Lucy A. Williams

Regulation

Edited by

Colin Scott

Australian National University, and London School of Economics

ASHGATE
DARTMOUTH

Published by
Dartmouth Publishing Company
Ashgate Publishing Limited
Gower House
Croft Road
Aldershot
Hants GU11 3HR
England

Ashgate Publishing Company
Suite 420
101 Cherry Street
Burlington, VT 05401-4405
USA

Ashgate website: http://www.ashgate.com

British Library Cataloguing in Publication Data
Regulation. – (International library of essays in law and
legal theory. Second series)
1. Legislation
I. Scott, Colin
342

Library of Congress Cataloging-in-Publication Data
Regulation / edited by Colin Scott.
p. cm. — (International library of essays in law and legal theory. Second series)
Includes bibliographical references.
ISBN 0-7546-2182-0 (alk. paper)
1. Delegated legislation. 2. Law—Philosophy. I. Scott, Colin (Colin D.) II. Series.

K3178 .R44 2002
340'.1—dc21

2002074710

ISBN 0 7546 2182 0

Printed in Great Britain by The Cromwell Press, Trowbridge, Wiltshire

Contents

Acknowledgements vii
Series Preface ix
Introduction xi

PART I THE CHARACTER OF REGULATORY LAW

1 Edward L. Rubin (1991), 'The Concept of Law and the New Public Law Scholarship', *Michigan Law Review*, **89**, pp. 792–836. 3
2 Gunther Teubner (1984), 'After Legal Instrumentalism? Strategic Models of Post-regulatory Law', *International Journal of the Sociology of Law*, **12**, pp. 375–400. 49
3 Boaventura de Sousa Santos (1985), 'On Modes of Production of Law and Social Power', *International Journal of the Sociology of Law*, **13**, pp. 299–336. 75

PART II LEGAL THEORIES OF STATE AND MARKET

4 Douglass C. North and Barry R. Weingast (1989), 'Constitutions and Commitment: The Evolution of Institutions Governing Public Choice in Seventeenth-Century England', *Journal of Economic History*, **49**, pp. 803–32. 115
5 P.P. Craig (1991), 'Constitutions, Property and Regulation', *Public Law*, pp. 538–54. 145
6 Tony Prosser (2000), 'Public Service Law: Privatization's Unexpected Offspring', *Law and Contemporary Problems*, **63**, pp. 63–82. 163
7 Wernhard Möschel (2001), 'The Proper Scope of Government Viewed from an Ordoliberal Perspective: The Example of Competition Policy', *Journal of Institutional and Theoretical Economics*, **157**, pp. 3–13. 183

PART III REGULATORY RULES

8 J.M. Black (1995), '"Which Arrow?": Rule Type and Regulatory Policy', *Public Law*, pp. 94–117. 197
9 Robert Baldwin and Keith Hawkins (1984), 'Discretionary Justice: Davis Reconsidered', *Public Law*, pp. 570–99. 221
10 John Braithwaite and Valerie Braithwaite (1995), 'The Politics of Legalism: Rules Versus Standards in Nursing-Home Regulation', *Social and Legal Studies*, **4**, pp. 307–41. 251

11 Julia Black (1998), 'Talking About Regulation', *Public Law*, pp. 77–105. 287

PART IV ORGANIZATIONS AND INSTITUTIONAL VARIETY

12 Jonathan R. Macey (1992), 'Separated Powers and Positive Political Theory: The Tug of War Over Administrative Agencies', *Georgetown Law Journal*, **80**, pp. 671–703. 319
13 Karen Yeung (1999), 'Quantifying Regulatory Penalties: Australian Competition Law Penalties in Perspective', *Melbourne University Law Review*, **23**, pp. 440–75. 353
14 Christine Parker (2000), 'Reinventing Regulation within the Corporation: Compliance-Oriented Regulatory Innovation', *Administration & Society*, **32**, pp. 529–65. 389
15 Carol A. Heimer (1996), 'Explaining Variation in the Impact of Law: Organizations, Institutions, and Professions', *Studies in Law, Politics and Society*, **15**, pp. 29–59. 427
16 Peter Vincent-Jones (1999), 'The Regulation of Contractualisation in Quasi-markets for Public Services', *Public Law*, pp. 304–27. 459
17 Erich Schanze (1995), 'Hare and Hedgehog Revisited: The Regulation of Markets That Have Escaped Regulated Markets', *Journal of Institutional and Theoretical Economics*, **151**, pp. 162–76. 483

PART V ACCOUNTING FOR REGULATION

18 David Schneiderman (2000), 'Constitutional Approaches to Privatization: An Inquiry into the Magnitude of Neo-Liberal Constitutionalism', *Law and Contemporary Problems*, **63**, pp. 83–109. 501

Name Index 529

Acknowledgements

The editor and publishers wish to thank the following for permission to use copyright material.

Cambridge University Press for the essay: Douglass C. North and Barry R. Weingast (1989), 'Constitutions and Commitment: The Evolution of Institutional Governing Public Choice in Seventeenth-Century England', *Journal of Economic History*, **49**, pp. 803–32. Copyright © 1989 Economic History Association. Published by Cambridge University Press.

Elsevier Science Ltd for the essays: Gunther Teubner (1984), 'After Legal Instrumentalism? Strategic Models of Post-regulatory Law', *International Journal of the Sociology of Law*, **12**, pp. 375–400. Copyright © 1984 Academic Press Inc.; Boaventura de Sousa Santos (1985), 'On Modes of Production of Law and Social Power', *International Journal of the Sociology of Law*, **13**, pp. 299–336. Copyright © 1985 Academic Press, Inc.

Georgetown University Law Center for the essay: Jonathan R. Macey (1992), 'Separated Powers and Positive Political Theory: The Tug of War Over Administrative Agencies', *Georgetown Law Journal*, **80**, pp. 671–703. Copyright © 1992 Georgetown Law Journal.

Carol A. Heimer (1996), 'Explaining Variation in the Impact of Law: Organizations, Institutions, and Professions', *Studies in Law, Politics and Society*, **15**, pp. 29–59. Copyright © 1996 Carol A. Heimer.

Michigan Law Review Association for the essay: Edward L. Rubin (1991), 'The Concept of Law and the New Public Law Scholarship', *Michigan Law Review*, **89**, pp. 792–836.

J.C.B. Mohr (Paul Siebeck) Tübingen for the essays: Wernhard Möschel (2001), 'The Proper Scope of Government Viewed from an Ordoliberal Perspective: The Example of Competition Policy', *Journal of Institutional and Theoretical Economics*, **157**, pp. 3–13. Copyright © 2001 Mohr Siebeck; Erich Schanze (1995), 'Hare and Hedgehog Revisited: The Regulation of Markets That Have Escaped Regulated Markets', *Journal of Institutional and Theoretical Economics*, **151**, pp. 162–76.

Tony Prosser (2001), 'Public Service Law: Privatization's Unexpected Offspring', *Law and Contemporary Problems*, **63**, pp. 63–82. Copyright © 2001 Tony Prosser.

Sage Publications Inc. for the essay: Christine Parker (2000) 'Reinventing Regulation within the Corporation: Compliance-Oriented Regulatory Innovation', *Administration & Society*, **32**, pp. 529–65. Copyright © 2000 Sage Publications, Inc.

Sage Publications Ltd for the essay: John Braithwaite and Valerie Braithwaite (1995), 'The Politics of Legalism: Rules Versus Standards in Nursing-Home Regulation', *Social and Legal Studies*, **4**, pp. 307–41. Copyright © 1995 Sage Publications Ltd.

David Schneiderman (2000), 'Constitutional Approaches to Privatization: An Inquiry into the Magnitude of Neo-Liberal Constitutionalism', *Law and Contemporary Problems*, **63**, pp. 83–109. Copyright © 2001 David Schneiderman.

Sweet & Maxwell Ltd for the essays: P.P. Craig (1991), 'Constitutions, Property and Regulation', *Public Law*, pp. 538–54. Copyright © 1991 Sweet & Maxwell and Contributors; J.M. Black (1995), '"Which Arrow?': Rule Type and Regulator Policy', *Public Law*, pp. 94–117. Copyright © 1995 Sweet & Maxwell and Contributors; Robert Baldwin and Keith Hawkins (1984), 'Discretionary Justice: Davis Reconsidered', *Public Law*, pp. 570–99; Julia Black (1998), 'Talking About Regulation', *Public Law*, pp. 77–105. Copyright © 1998 Sweet & Maxwell and Contributors; Peter Vincent-Jones (1999), 'The Regulation of Contractualisation in Quasi-markets for Public Services', *Public Law*, pp. 3047–27. Copyright © 1999 Sweet & Maxwell and Contributors.

University of Melbourne, Law School for the essay: Karen Yeung (1999), 'Quantifying Regulatory Penalties: Australian Competition Law Penalties in Perspective', *Melbourne University Law Review*, **23**, pp. 440–75.

Every effort has been made to trace all the copyright holders, but if any have been inadvertently overlooked the publishers will be pleased to make the necessary arrangement at the first opportunity.

Preface to the Second Series

The first series of the International Library of Essays in Law and Legal Theory has established itself as a major research resource with fifty-eight volumes of the most significant theoretical essays in contemporary legal studies. Each volume contains essays of central theoretical importance in its subject area and the series as a whole makes available an extensive range of valuable material of considerable interest to those involved in research, teaching and the study of law.

The rapid growth of theoretically interesting scholarly work in law has created a demand for a second series which includes more recent publications of note and earlier essays to which renewed attention is being given. It also affords the opportunity to extend the areas of law covered in the first series.

The new series follows the successful pattern of reproducing entire essays with the original page numbers as an aid to comprehensive research and accurate referencing. Editors have selected not only the most influential essays but also those which they consider to be of greatest continuing importance. The objective of the second series is to enlarge the scope of the library, include significant recent work and reflect a variety of editorial perspectives.

Each volume is edited by an expert in the specific area who makes the selection on the basis of the quality, influence and significance of the essays, taking care to include essays which are not readily available. Each volume contains a substantial introduction explaining the context and significance of the essays selected.

I am most grateful for the care which volume editors have taken in carrying out the complex task of selecting and presenting essays which meet the exacting criteria set for the series.

TOM CAMPBELL
Series Editor
Centre for Applied Philosophy and Public Ethics
Charles Sturt University

Introduction

In assembling this collection I have endeavoured to identify key journal essays which seek to reconceptualize or problematize law in regulatory settings. The scholarly literature defines regulation in different ways for different purposes. Lawyers have tended towards a definition which emphasizes sustained oversight by reference to rules, whereas scholars in other disciplines have extended the set of activities covered by the term to include all interventions by government to steer the economy and, the broadest of definitions, all mechanisms of social control (cf. Black, 2001a; Daintith, 1997, pp. 3–5). The interest in this volume in concepts of law in regulation has led me to adopt the narrow definition generally, but with some reference both to other forms of government intervention and other forms of social control.

Scholarship among regulation specialists remains a growth industry with important contributions from disciplines as diverse as economics, political science, sociology, law, anthropology and management studies (Noll, 1985). The diversity of the literature is sometimes masked by the relative success of economic theories of regulation which focus on market-like behaviour of politicians, bureaucrats and businesses. The economic approach is well represented in a number of standard texts in regulation (Baldwin and Cave, 1999; Ogus, 1994). A number of the central themes of investigation for economic theories, such as the normative basis for regulation and deregulation (Keeler and Foreman, 1998), have yielded little new understanding of law, nor have they been much influenced by legal research. From the perspective of this volume, economic theories of regulation are significant to the extent that they generate or elaborate distinctive conceptions of law. I suggest that these theories tend to share with 'public interest theory' an instrumental conception of law as a neutral technology for implementing policy choices. Consequently, they have contributed less than might have been anticipated to a project of rethinking law to meet the challenges of a regulatory age. Accordingly, alternative theories which place regulatory law at their centre have considerable prominence in this volume.

The Character of Regulatory Law

The study and theorization of law in both civilian and common law jurisdictions has placed considerable emphasis on the generality of legal norms, whether contained in codes, judgments or legislation. Paradigmatic legal rules within these traditions have been those which have applied to all society with a relatively low degree of specificity as to what the norms require. The nineteenth-century revolution in government in industrializing nations entailed significant departures from the principles of generality of law, with the introduction of quite specific rules and the development of specialized enforcement bureaucracies, particularly in safety-critical domains such as factories, food manufacture and retailing, and transportation (Carson, 1979; Paulus, 1974; MacDonagh, 1961). This tendency creates a significant dilemma for law, in that it is displaced to some extent by the new requirements of particular regulatory regimes, but not wholly dispensed with. The 'persistence of legalism' in contemporary governance arrangements provides legal scholarship with one of its most interesting challenges (Murphy, 1997, pp. 148–53).

The British constitutional scholar, Albert Venn Dicey, responded to deviation from the generality of legal norms and concomitant extension of bureaucratic discretion with alarm. He gave an influential series of lectures on the topic at Harvard Law School in the early years of the twentieth century attacking collectivism and outlining his concerns that contemporary administrative developments challenged his conception of the rule of law (Dicey, 1914; cf. Hayek, 1982, vol. 1, pp. 141–44). Horwitz has suggested that Dicey's 'praise for a lost age of laissez-faire individualism was warmly received in the only Western society where that doctrine continued to dominate public philosophy' (Horwitz, 1992, p. 226). Dicey's legacy, in both policy and academic circles, is a certain scepticism as to the appropriateness of delegation of power to administrative agencies both in the United States and Commonwealth countries (Duxbury, 1995, pp. 149–58; Arthurs, 1979). The first essay in this volume, by Edward L. Rubin (Chapter 1), outlines the potential for reconceptualizing law for an administrative (or regulatory) age. Rubin's call for a 'new public law' squarely addresses the necessity for regulatory law scholars to address what goes on within administrative bureaucracies if they are to contribute meaningfully to the policy discourse with a distinctive legal voice.

The problems presented to law by the administrative revolution in government have been most clearly elaborated by scholars working within the German tradition. Jürgen Habermas observed the 'materialization' of law as the demands of the German welfare state forced legislatures to specify more minutely in legal rules the requirements of regimes of welfare and social regulation (Habermas, 1996, ch. 9). Building on Niklas Luhmann's hypothesis of the functional differentiation of political, economic and social sub-systems, Gunther Teubner has suggested that an instrumental conception of law as servant to the intent of the legislature or the requirements of the economic system cannot be sustained. In Chapter 2 Teubner sets out his diagnosis of the 'regulatory crisis' which emerges from recognizing the limits of instrumental conceptions of regulatory law. It is in this essay that Teubner set legal scholars down the path of investigating 'proceduralization' as a solution to the problem that norms originating from the political or economic system cannot be reliably translated into the legal system (Black, 2000, 2001b; Prosser, 1999).

A related, but distinct critique of legal instrumentalism derives from the theory of legal pluralism with its emphasis on the variety of sources of norms, particularly within colonial and developing economies (Neves, 2001). Legal pluralism has had particular purchase on regulatory scholarship because of perceptions of 'fragmentation' of authority associated with the development of the regulatory state (Cotterrell, 1992, pp. 161–66). This pluralist perspective on law in contemporary societies is represented in Chapter 3 by Boaventura de Sousa Santos and provides one of the foundations for the elaboration of 'de-centring' of regulation both as empirical observance and as a governance strategy (Black, 2001a; cf. Scott, 2001).

Legal Theories of State and Market

There are a number of theoretical perspectives which have as one of their concerns the appropriate balance between state and market in contemporary societies. Some reject the distinction between state and market, pointing out the importance of traditional state law (property rights, contracts and so on) and even of regulatory law in constituting markets (Llewellyn, 1925 cited in Duxbury, 1995, p. 325; Shearing, 1993; Hunt, 1993, ch. 13). Legal theorization of the state–market relationship has been dominated by questions of the appropriate content and interpretation of constitutions. The contrasting normative structures to be found within constitutions or other aspects of legal institutions is a somewhat neglected variable in explaining variety in capitalist arrangements (Daintith, 1997, pp. 7–8).

As noted above, Dicey saw the incursion of collectivist, discretionary law into market activities as, above all, a constitutional issue, although the peculiarities of the British constitution have substantially inhibited the development of a constitutional theory of the state–market relationship. By contrast, Supreme Court jurisprudence in the United States did elaborate a constitutional theory to delimit the legitimate boundaries of state action with legal norms (Siegel, 1984). The constitutional literature on the legitimate boundaries of regulation has focused centrally on the property rights of citizens and viewed state incursion on those rights as a matter requiring justification (Daintith, 1998; Epstein, 1985). Among the most powerful applications of the property rights conception has been an economic approach which sees constitutions, and subconstitutional rules, as solutions to the significant problem of creating credible commitment of governments to create a stable market environment so as to foster investment by businesses. In Chapter 4, Douglass North and Barry Weingast deploy the property rights approach to develop an institutional account of the success of the processes of industralization in eighteenth- and nineteenth-century Britain. Within this approach the constitution is seen as a regulator of government. This literature is significant not least because it has underpinned programmes of research and institutional reform in developing countries overseen by the World Bank (Levy and Spiller, 1996).

Recent developments in governance in industrialized commonwealth countries, and notably programmes of privatization and re-regulation, have caused legal scholars to examine afresh some of the older doctrines governing regulatory relationships (Taggart, 1995). Chief Justice Hale's theory of the relationship between property rights and state activity, developed in the eighteenth century (Hale, 1787), was influential in the development of nineteenth-century American doctrines governing the constitutional legitimacy of regulation. In Chapter 5 Paul Craig contrasts the constitutional significance of property rights in the United Kingdom and the United States, arguing that Hale's doctrine explicitly recognizes that the ownership of private property can carry with it public obligations. The significance of this theory for contemporary economic regulation is elaborated by Tony Prosser (Chapter 6) in which he argues that policies of privatization in European Union countries have generated a new set of principles which he gathers together under the rubric of 'public service law'. This doctrinal development is an unintended consequence of public policy initiatives in regulation.

While American constitutional theory underpins a certain regulatory conservatism, this may be contrasted with the German position where scholars within the Freiburg School, in particular, attempted explicitly to theorize a stronger role for the state in regulating or ordering markets. The 'ordo-liberal' theory was extremely influential in recasting state–market relations after the Second World War (Vanberg, 1998). In Chapter 7 Wernhard Möschel examines the distinctive features of the ordo-liberal theorization of the state–market relationship, showing how it manages to reconcile a strong role for the state in regulating markets with a conception of the rule of law. Within this perspective, law is not an instrument for protecting citizens from the state, but rather a mediator between the interests of the state in ordering a competitive market and the interests of businesses in pursuing their economic activities unhindered.

Regulatory Rules

Turning from high-level justifications for the regulatory role of the state to the micro-level of regulatory regimes, we find that greatest emphasis in the legal regulation scholarship is placed on rules and norm types (Diver, 1983). Functionalist accounts of which types of rule are best suited to particular regulatory objectives sit somewhat uneasily with the anxious challenges to instrumental theories of regulatory law noted in Part I of this volume. As Julia Black notes (Chapter 8), processes of rule-making have tended to be neglected in the wider literature on regulation. The making of rules, and thus the consideration of appropriate rule types, is a job for legal scholarship. Many regulatory rules are open-textured and invite bureaucrats to exercise wide discretion in reaching decisions. This is precisely the tendency in regulatory law which so worried Dicey. More recent scholarship, building on the work of Kenneth Culp Davis (1969), has sought to link choice of rule types with the development of broader norms of institutional decision-making which take proper account of the problem of regulatory discretion (Pratt, 1999; Rubin, 1997). The emphasis of Chapter 9 by Robert Baldwin and Keith Hawkins lies in securing a systematic understanding of regulatory discretion in its many different contexts and using this as the basis for reconceptualizing the problem of discretion as multilayered and amenable to a variety of solutions well beyond Davis' own proposals for structuring and checking discretionary power.

Scepticism about the capacity of rules to secure regulatory outcomes has tended to be reasoned inductively from empirical research into regulatory regimes (Baldwin, 1990; Lange, 1999; McBarnet and Whelan, 1991). John and Valerie Braithwaite (Chapter 10) question the effectiveness of attempts to provide for optimal provision in rule-making and to constrain discretion. They suggest that attention to the precision of rules in one part of a regulatory regime may affect the overall reliability of the regime in generating particular outcomes. Thus they argue for the potential of a more context-specific set of principles for the deployment of different rule types. An underdeveloped theme of this literature is the contingency of law within regulatory settings upon the relationships between the various actors (Reichman, 1992). The context of 'regulatory conversations' between actors within regulatory regimes is the theme of Chapter 11 by Julia Black. Recognizing that such conversations about rules are both an inevitable and necessary part of the way that the meaning of a regulatory regime is constructed, Black argues for a form of proceduralization within which attention is paid to the commitment of actors, access to the process, the distribution of authority and accountability of those involved. The positions of the various actors can be adjusted to secure compliance with these principles for the 'regulation' of regulatory regimes. Black has subsequently elaborated on these arguments to develop a more theoretical basis for 'proceduralization' within regulatory regimes which is targeted at the twin problems of effectiveness and legitimacy of regulation (Black, 2000, 2001b; see also Croley, 1998).

An alternative approach to understanding rules within regulatory regimes uses comparative analysis across similar domains in different jurisdictions to secure a better understanding of both variation and the conditions under which the deployment of rules may be effective.

Important studies comparing the United Kingdom and the United States (Vogel, 1986), the United Kingdom and Japan (Vogel, 1996) and the United States and Japan (Kagan, 2000) have used measures of 'formalism' as one of their key variables. In emphasizing the formalistic tendencies in American regulation in both rule-making and enforcement – a style labelled as 'adversarial legalism' by Kagan (2000) – this research suggests that regulatory practice in general and the conception of regulatory law in particular in the United States is rather exceptional. Japan and the United Kingdom have, historically, shared a tendency towards informal state–industry relations which has fed through into contemporary legal relations (although such informalism has come under significant pressures in many policy domains in recent years). Discussion of such variety leads us into the discussion of institutions in Part IV.

Organizations and Institutional Variety

It is frequently assumed that regulation is simply what regulatory agencies do. By contrast, a regimes analysis demonstrates that the regulatory functions of standard-setting, monitoring and enforcement are often widely dispersed among a variety of actors (Hood, Rothstein and Baldwin, 2001, ch. 2). A key question, therefore, is how to explain and justify variety in the institutional forms of regulation. The regulatory agency model has been of particular importance in the United States and has been theorized as a response to the weaknesses of court-like adjudication in addressing 'polycentric' issues (Fuller, 1978). A cultural reluctance to assign wide powers to regulatory agencies arguably creates a greater urgency in understanding institutional variety in regulation in Europe (Hancher and Moran, 1989). New institutionalism is an important theoretical strand in contemporary theory in sociology, economics and political science which has been deployed in the investigation of regulation. However it has, to date, been fairly marginal in generating new theorizations of regulatory law (Cooney, 1996; Black, 1997; Suchman and Edelman, 1996).

The economic form of new institutionalism, exemplified by North and Weingast in Chapter 4, has perhaps had the greatest impact on legal regulation scholarship. The literature on the containment of agency discretion (characterized as the risk of 'bureaucratic-drift') represents a sophisticated application of theories originating in transaction cost economics to regulatory institutions (Horn, 1995; Mashaw, 1997). The capacity of the theory for the development of normative theories of institutional design is exemplified by Jonathan R. Macey's essay (Chapter 12). Macey challenges the argument that Congress can effectively deploy a variety of rule types to control or 'hardwire' what agencies may do, and shows that both the executive and the judiciary have means to subvert congressional intent.

A further important question of institutional variety is concerned with approaches to enforcement. A wide variety of approaches to enforcement have been identified in empirical analyses (Braithwaite, Walker and Grabosky, 1987). A key variable is the legal basis for enforcement and what we might call the 'cultural effects' of deploying criminal law, administrative law or private law, for example. In the United Kingdom, criminal law has been widely deployed to create offences of strict liability in regulatory domains (Richardson, 1987). In those jurisdictions and domains where criminal law is routinely used to control regulatory wrongdoing there is some evidence of a clash of cultures between the regulatory instrumentalism of the particular regime on the one hand, and the traditional culture of the criminal law on the other (Scott, 1995). This tension can be viewed through the lens of Teubner's theory of reflexive law as a problem of communication between a political system concerned to legislate for regulatory offences with criminal law, and an autonomous legal system concerned to protect the integrity of the criminal law (represented as both a concern with only applying sanctions to morally wrong conduct, and providing appropriate procedural protection to those processed within the criminal law system). The underlying debate in criminal law theory is outlined and applied to the case of competition law enforcement in the essay by Karen Yeung (Chapter 13). For Yeung, one way of resolving the issue is to assess the nature and appropriateness of criminal law penalties as a means of reconciling the competing views on the appropriateness of the 'regulatory crime' paradigm.

Whilst the effectiveness of rigid enforcement or 'regulatory unreasonableness' has often been questioned by the empirical literature (Ayres and Braithwaite, 1992; Bardach and Kagan, 1982), equally, conventional conceptions of the 'rule of law' are challenged by more discretionary patterns of regulatory rule-making and enforcement. A key example in the United States is that of the Environmental Protection Agency's Project XL, a programme of environmental regulation which permits firms to offer superior environmental performance in return for oversight which is less onerous than the conventional system of minute regulation by permit (Freeman, 1997, p. 55ff). Chapter 14 by Christine Parker demonstrates that attention to 'compliance orientation' within regulated firms provides a possible solution to the effectiveness versus 'rule of law' debate. A key to this institutional approach to regulatory innovation is the capacity of compliance officers within firms to secure a cultural orientation to meeting the expectations of regulatory regimes (whether defined in terms of narrow rule adherence or, more broadly, in terms of outcomes). The questions of the role of professionals and the reception of regulatory and private law within organizations are central issues in Carol Heimer's essay (Chapter 15), which examines the conditions under which organizations receive and act upon changed legal norms in the regulatory setting of medical practice. Heimer is thus able to develop some hypotheses as to when regulatory law is likely to be effective.

Beyond agency regulation, regulatory scholarship has identified the potential for alternative forms of ordering to classical command and control (Baldwin, 1997). One basis for such analysis is recognizing that legal authority is but one form of power and, although the state may have a near monopoly of such power, other key sources of power – information, wealth, and organizational capacities – are widely dispersed (Daintith, 1997, pp. 30–34; Scott, 2001). Lawrence Lessig's influential attempt to meet the challenge of control of cyberspace uses an alternative analytical frame for analyzing the potential for different forms of control. He posits the existence of four basic 'modalities of regulation' oriented to law, social norms, markets and architecture (Lessig, 1999a, 1999b). Within Lessig's schema, law equates to the classical hierarchical control of regulation, social norms to the informal social control of the community (Posner, 2000), and markets to competitive pressures as constraints on action (Murray and Scott, 2002). The concept of architecture extends beyond the design of buildings to encompass the design of other artifacts – notably, computer software. In the difficult world of cyberspace the architecture of software provides a key means by which firms control what users can and cannot do, and this technology can be turned to public-regarding purposes through its harnessing by the state. In this way, Lessig extends the well-established capacities of physical design to control behaviour (Shearing and Stenning, 1985). In practice, alternative modes of regulation are often hybrids of two or more modalities. Thus, in Lessig's terms, tax incentives combine law with markets (Ogus, 1998), self-regulation forms a hybrid of norms and law and contractual governance resembles a hybrid of markets and law (Collins, 1999; Freeman, 2000b; Teubner, 1998). In Chapter 16 Peter Vincent-Jones directly addresses the issue of unresponsiveness of regulatory regimes and the problem of control by asking to what extent hybrid forms of contractual governance provide better solutions than command and control regulation.

Market behaviour may cause traditional regulation to be avoided by actors who can adjust their affairs or location so as to fall outside the scope of a regime. In Chapter 17 Erich Schanze argues that this may be efficient and, where this is so, should be supported by the courts. This 'regulatory bifurcation' is reminiscent of a model of regulatory reform under which only part of a market is regulated and the remainder left to market forces (Ayres and Braithwaite, 1992, ch. 5). In other contexts, the predominance of non-state ordering may indicate a breakdown in formal governance requirements, with (often undesirable) private ordering mechanisms effectively competing for business with the state. This is particularly true for societies with less well-developed state apparatus, as with Russia (Frye, 2000), but examples of the phenomenon are also to be found in more developed state systems, such as Japan, which have permitted organized crime to prosper (Milhaupt and West, 2000).

Accounting for Regulation

Fragmentation of state authority and diffusion in regulatory technique has generated particular problems for administrative law theory in adapting traditional conceptions of accountability to legislatures and courts and of the rule of law to meet these new governance forms (Rubin, 1989; Scott, 2000). Legal scholars have endeavoured to work out new conceptions of public law which address the increasing importance of self-regulation by firms and locate the phenomenon within a (revised) constitutional theory (Black, 1996). They have sought to adapt thinking about public law so that it meets the challenge of recognizing that the participation of private actors in public decision-making in regulatory spheres is both normal and inevitable (Freeman, 2000a). These issues are addressed both by Edward Rubin in Chapter 1 of this volume and, more fully, in the volume in this series on *Administrative Law* edited by Peter Cane.

More pressing, perhaps, than the recognition of fragmentation of regulatory authority within states is the linkage of private power and globalization in contemporary regulatory governance (Braithwaite and Drahos, 2000). The problems presented to legal theory associated with sovereignty and identifying the legitimate boundaries of state action are particularly acute in developing countries which are caught between the twin economic powers of multinational enterprise and international organizations such as the World Bank and the IMF. This challenge requires the reconceptualization of the issues discussed in Part II of this volume to take into account dilutions of national sovereignty (Aman, 2001; Slaughter, 2001). The potential for such an approach, taking Latin America as its case study, is provided in the final chapter by David Schneiderman.

Conclusion: Future Directions for Problematizing Law in Regulation

This volume attests to the rich variety of scholarship which addresses problems of legal and regulatory theory. A number of theoretical and analytical approaches which problematize conceptualizations of law have been developed, which could be deployed to elaborate upon discussion of established questions and develop novel questions. I make no pretence here to set out a coherent research agenda for regulatory law. Rather, I highlight some trends emergent in the literature. Questions deserving of elaboration include the reshaping of legal conceptions of accountability, the squaring of instrumental regulatory models with competing conceptions of the rule of law, the role of law in models of ordering which displace to command and control regulation, and reflexive conceptions of law as both regulating social and economic fields and being regulated by their relations with other subsystems.

Much of the newer literature is focused on institutional questions and, in contrast with earlier literature on the character of regulatory law and on the state–market relationship, is often informed by empirical observation, either at first-hand or at one remove or both. Key new themes include: understanding the role of discourse (Black, 2002); rhetoric and networks in constructing regulatory fields and relationships (Maher, 2002); the role of emotions in shaping and mediating regulatory relations (Lange, 2002); the potential for 'meta-regulation' as an overarching strategy of indirect control (Grabosky, 1995; Parker, 2002); the role of law within fragmented conceptions of governance, such as the Foucauldian 'governmentality' model (Hunt, 1993); and competing conceptions of globalization and organizationally-focused observations of regulatory regimes (Parker, 2002). International trends in governance tend to accentuate the contingency of the meaning of regulatory law upon both narrow and broader environmental conditions, and make it more urgent that legal theory should respond with ways of making sense of such regulatory diffusion (Picciotto, 2002).

References

Aman, Alfred C. (2001), 'The Limits of Globalization and the Future of Administrative Law: From Government to Governance', *Indiana Journal of Global Legal Studies*, **8**, pp. 379–400.

Arthurs, H.W. (1979), 'Rethinking Administrative Law: A Slightly Dicey Business', *Osgoode Hall Law Journal*, **17**, pp. 1–45.

Ayres, Ian and Braithwaite, John (1992), *Responsive Regulation: Transcending the Deregulation Debate*, Oxford: Oxford University Press.

Baldwin, Robert (1990), 'Why Rules Don't Work', *Modern Law Review*, **53**, pp. 321–37.

Baldwin, Robert (1997), 'Beyond Command and Control', in Keith Hawkins (ed.), *The Human Face of Law*, Oxford: Oxford University Press.

Baldwin, Robert and Cave, Martin (1999), *Understanding Regulation*, Oxford: Oxford University Press.

Bardach, Eugene and Kagan, Robert (1982) *Going By the Book: The Problem of Regulatory Unreasonableness*, Philadelphia: Temple University Press.

Black, Julia M. (1996), 'Constitutionalising Self-Regulation', *Modern Law Review*, **59**, pp. 24–56.

Black, Julia M. (1997), 'New Institutionalism and Naturalism in Socio-Legal Analysis: Institutionalist Approaches to Regulatory Decision Making', *Law and Policy*, **19**, pp. 59–93.

Black, Julia M. (2000), 'Proceduralizing Regulation: Part I', *Oxford Journal of Legal Studies*, **20**, pp. 597–614.

Black, Julia M. (2001a), 'Decentring Regulation: The Role of Regulation and Self-Regulation in a "Post-Regulatory" World', *Current Legal Problems*, pp. 103–46.

Black, Julia M. (2001b), 'Proceduralizing Regulation: Part II', *Oxford Journal of Legal Studies*, 21, pp. 33–58.

Black, Julia M. (2002), 'Regulatory Conversations', *Journal of Law and Society*, **21**, pp. 163–96.

Braithwaite, John and Drahos, Peter (2000), *Global Business Regulation*, Cambridge: Cambridge University Press.

Braithwaite, John, Walker, John and Grabosky, Peter (1987), 'An Enforcement Taxonomy of Regulatory Agencies', *Law and Policy*, **9**, pp. 323–51.

Carson, W.G. (1979), 'The Conventionalization of Early Factory Crime', *International Journal of the Sociology of Law*, **7**, pp. 37–57.

Collins, Hugh (1999), *Regulating Contracts*, Oxford: Oxford University Press.

Cooney, Mark (1996), 'Legal Sociology and the New Institutionalism', *Studies in Law, Politics and Society*, **15**, pp. 85–101.

Cotterrell, Roger (1992), *The Sociology of Law*, London: Butterworths.

Croley, Steven P. (1998), 'Theories of Regulation Incorporating the Administrative Process', *Columbia Law Review*, **98**, pp. 1–86.

Daintith, Terence (1997), *Regulation (Chapter 10)*, in *International Encyclopedia of Comparative Law*, Tübingen: Mohr Siebeck.

Daintith, Terence (1998), 'State Power', in Peter Newman (ed.), *The New Palgrave Dictionary of Economics and the Law*, London: Macmillan.

Davis, Kenneth Culp (1969), *Discretionary Justice: A Preliminary Inquiry*, Baton Rouge: Louisiana State University Press.

Dicey, Albert Venn (1914), *Lectures on the Relation Between Law and Public Opinion*, London: Macmillan.

Diver, Colin (1983), 'The Optimal Precision of Administrative Rules', *Yale Law Journal*, **93**, pp. 65–109.

Duxbury, Neil (1995), *Patterns of American Jurisprudence*, Oxford: Oxford University Press.

Epstein, Richard A. (1985), *Takings: Private Property and the Power of Eminent Domain*, Cambridge, MA: Harvard University Press.

Freeman, Jody (1997), 'Collaborative Governance in the Administrative State', *UCLA Law Review*, **45**, pp. 1–98.

Freeman, Jody (2000a), 'Private Parties, Public Functions and the New Administrative Law', *Administrative Law Review*, **52**, pp. 813–58.

Freeman, Jody (2000b), 'The Contracting State', *Florida State University Law Review*, **28**, p. 155.

Frye, Timothy (2000), 'Rackets, Regulation and the Rule of Law', *Journal of Law, Economics and Organization*, **16**, pp. 478–502.

Fuller, Lon L. (1978), 'The Forms and Limits of Adjudication', *Harvard Law Review*, **92**, pp. 353–409.

Grabosky, Peter N. (1995), 'Using Non-Governmental Resources to Foster Regulatory Compliance', *Governance*, **8**, pp. 527–50.

Habermas, Jürgen (1996), *Between Facts and Norms: Contributions to a Discourse Theory of Law and Democracy*, Cambridge: Polity Press.

Hale, Matthew (1787), 'De Portibus Maris', in *Hargrave's Collection of Tracts*, Dublin.

Hancher, Leigh and Moran, Michael (eds) (1989), *Capitalism, Culture and Regulation*, Oxford: Oxford University Press.

Hayek, Friedrich A. (1982) *Law, Legislation and Liberty: A New Statement of the Liberal Principles of Justice and Political Economy*, London: Routledge.

Hood, Christopher, Rothstein, Henry and Baldwin, Robert (2001), *The Government of Risk*, Oxford: Oxford University Press.

Horn, Murray (1995), *The Political Economy of Public Administration*, Cambridge: Cambridge University Press.

Horwitz, Morton J. (1992), *The Transformation of American Law 1870–1960*, Oxford: Oxford University Press.

Hunt, Alan (1993), *Explorations in Law and Society: Towards a Constitutive Theory of Law*, London: Routledge.

Kagan, Robert A. (2000), 'Introduction: Comparing National Styles of Regulation in Japan and the United States', *Law and Policy*, **22**, pp. 225–44.

Keeler, Theodore E. and Foreman, Stephen E. (1998), 'Regulation and Deregulation', in Peter Newman (ed.), *The New Palgrave Dictionary of Economics and the Law*, London: Macmillan.

Lange, Bettina (1999), 'Compliance Construction in the Context of Environmental Regulation', *Social and Legal Studies*, **8**, pp. 549–67.

Lange, Bettina (2002), 'The Emotional Dimension in Regulation', *Journal of Law and Society*, **29**, pp. 197–225.

Lessig, Lawrence (1999a), *Code: And Other Laws of Cyberspace*, New York: Basic Books.

Lessig, Lawrence (1999b), 'The Law of the Horse: What Cyberlaw Might Teach', *Harvard Law Review*, **113**, pp. 501–48.

Levy, Brian and Spiller, Pablo (eds) (1996), *Regulation, Institutions and Commitment*, Cambridge: Cambridge University Press.

Llewellyn, Karl (1925), 'The Effect of Legal Institutions Upon Economics', *American Economic Review*, **15**, pp. 665–83.

Maher, Imelda (2002), 'Competition Law in the International Domain; Networks as a New Form of Governance', *Journal of Law and Society*, **29**, pp. 111–37.

McBarnet, Doreen and Whelan, Christopher (1991), 'The Elusive Spirit of the Law: Formalism and the Struggle for Legal Control', *Modern Law Review*, **54**, pp. 848–73.

MacDonagh, Oliver (1961), *A Pattern of Government Growth: The Passenger Acts and Their Enforcement 1800–1860*, London: MacGibbon and Kee.

Mashaw, Jerry L. (1997), *Greed, Chaos and Governance: Using Public Choice to Improve Public Law*, New Haven, CT: Yale University Press.

Milhaupt, Curtis J. and West, Mark D. (2000), 'The Dark Side of Private Ordering: An Institutional and Empirical Analysis of Organized Crime', *University of Chicago Law Review*, **67**, pp. 41–98.

Murphy, Tim (1997), *The Oldest Social Science? Configurations of Law and Modernity*, Oxford: Oxford University Press.

Murray, Andrew and Scott, Colin Scott (2002), 'Controlling the New Media: Hybrid Responses to New Forms of Power', *Modern Law Review*, **65**, pp. 491–516.

Neves, Marcelo (2001), 'From the Autopoiesis to the Allopoiesis of Law', *Journal of Law and Society*, **28**, pp. 242–64.

Noll, Roger G. (ed.) (1985), *Regulatory Policy and the Social Sciences*, Berkeley: University of California Press.

Ogus, Anthony (1994), *Regulation: Legal Theory and Economic Theory*, Oxford: Oxford University Press.

Ogus, Anthony (1998), 'Corrective Taxes and Financial Impositions as Regulatory Instruments', *Modern Law Review*, **61**, pp. 767–88.

Parker, Christine (2002), *The Open Corporation: Self-Regulation and Democracy*, Melbourne: Cambridge University Press.

Paulus, Ingeborg (1974), *The Search for Pure Food*, London: Martin Robertson.

Picciotto, Sol (2002), 'Introduction: Reconceptualizing Regulation in the Era of Globalization', *Journal of Law and Society*, **29**, pp. 1–11.

Posner, Eric A. (2000), 'Law and Social Norms: The Case of Tax Compliance', *Virginia Law Review*, **86**, pp. 1781–819.

Pratt, Anna C. (1999), 'Dunking the Doughnut: Discretionary Power, Law and the Administration of the Canadian Immigration Act', *Social and Legal Studies*, **8**, pp. 199–226.

Prosser, Tony (1999), 'Theorising Utility Regulation', *Modern Law Review*, **62**, pp. 196–217.

Reichman, Nancy (1992), 'Moving Backstage: Uncovering the Role of Compliance Practices in Shaping Regulatory Policy', in K. Schlegel and D. Weisburd (eds), *White-Collar Crime Reconsidered*, Boston, MA: Northeastern University Press.

Richardson, Genevra (1987), 'Strict Liability for Regulatory Crime: The Empirical Research', *Criminal Law Review*, pp. 295–306.

Rubin, Edward L. (1989), 'Law and Legislation in the Administrative State', *Columbia Law Review*, **89**, pp. 369–426.

Rubin, Edward L. (1997), 'Discretion and its Discontents', *Chicago-Kent Law Review*, **72**, pp. 1299–336.

Scott, Colin (1995), 'Criminalising the Trader to Protect the Consumer', in Ian Loveland (ed.), *Frontiers of Criminal Law*, London: Sweet & Maxwell.

Scott, Colin (2000), 'Accountability in the Regulatory State', *Journal of Law and Society*, **27**, pp. 38–60.
Scott, Colin (2001), 'Analysing Regulatory Space: Fragmented Resources and Institutional Design', *Public Law*, pp. 329–53.
Shearing, Clifford (1993), 'A Constitutive Conception of Regulation', in John Braithwaite and Peter Grabosky (eds), *Business Regulation in Australia's Future*, Canberra: Australian Institute of Criminology.
Shearing, Clifford D. and Stenning, Philip C. (1985), 'From the Panopticon to Disney World: The Development of the Discipline', in Anthony N. Doob and Edward L. Greenspan (eds), *Perspectives in Criminal Law*, Toronto: Canada Law Book Inc.
Siegel, Stephen A. (1984), 'Understanding the *Lochner* Era: Lessons From the Controversy Over Railroad and Utility Rate Regulation', *Virginia Law Review*, **70**, pp. 187–263.
Slaughter, Anne-Marie (2001), 'The Accountability of Government Networks', *Indiana Journal of Global Legal Studies*, **8**, pp. 347–67.
Suchman, Mark C. and Edelman, Lauren B. (1996), 'Legal Rational Myths: The New Institutionalism and the Law and Society Tradition', *Law and Social Inquiry*, **21**, pp. 903–41.
Taggart, Mike (1995), 'Public Utilities and Public Law', in Philip Joseph (ed.), *Essays on the Constitution*, Wellington: Brookers.
Teubner, Gunther (1998), 'After Privatization: The Many Autonomies of Private Law', *Current Legal Problems*, **51**, pp. 393–424.
Vanberg, Viktor J. (1998), 'Freiburg School of Law and Economics', in Peter Newman (ed.), *The New Palgrave Dictionary of Economics and the Law*, London: Macmillan.
Vogel, David (1986), *National Styles of Regulation: Environmental Policy in Great Britain and the United States*, Ithaca, NY: Cornell University Press.
Vogel, Steven Kent (1996), *Freer Markets, More Rules: Regulatory Reform in Advanced Industrial Countries*, Ithaca, NY: Cornell University Press.

Part I
The Character of Regulatory Law

[1]

THE CONCEPT OF LAW AND THE NEW PUBLIC LAW SCHOLARSHIP

Edward L. Rubin *

I. Introduction

This article is an attempt to identify the nature of an emerging field of legal scholarship known as "New Public Law." "New," of course, is a dangerous term. Our society's image of itself as forward looking and its tendency to market itself to itself through claims of novelty has spawned a range of phrases from the New Deal to the New Criticism to various new, improved laundry detergents. One does not hear very many positive comments about the "old" these days. The argument that old ways of doing things are better has become an emblem of mistaken thought, and the elderly have been demoted from a source of experience and wisdom to just one more underrepresented group. As a result, it is very easy to make grandiose and ultimately unjustified claims for minor changes by slapping the word "new" on them.

But there is something truly new about New Public Law; something which promises to revitalize legal scholarship by enabling it to deal with the central features of our present-day legal system. Most legal scholarship, of course, is about the present; the problem is it tends to be restricted to an increasingly secondary legal institution, namely, the judiciary. Our legal system is dominated by legislatures and administrative agencies and consists primarily of the huge volume of statutes and regulations they produce. It is difficult to gaze on this vast, recent, rapidly developing, disorganized sprawl. One is tempted to be a legal tourist, wandering among the historic, well-documented edifices at the center and ignoring the formless suburbs that comprise the major portion of the new metropolis. This is the choice that legal scholarship has made thus far.

There is nothing wrong or insignificant about this scholarship, and we should not abandon it. Judicial decisionmaking remains an important aspect of our legal system, and the current analysis of it is a worthwhile enterprise. But it is simply less important than it used to be, and the continued concentration of attention on it abandons increasingly large areas of potential inquiry. The New Public Law

* Professor & Associate Dean, University of California, Berkeley. B.A. 1969, Princeton; J.D. 1979, Yale. — Ed.

scholarship represents an effort to expand the boundaries of legal scholarship until they are once again coterminous with the boundaries of law, as they were before the administrative state evolved.

This enterprise involves much more than a shift in subject matter. The conceptual structure of existing legal scholarship is simply unsuited to an analysis of the administrative state. Legal scholars have not restricted their efforts to judicial decisionmaking because of some quixotic desire to reject the modern world; on the contrary, they are fully cognizant of its character and regularly discuss the way it affects their area of study. Their tendency to remain within the confines of that area, as established during the past century, springs from an uncertainty about the way to conceptualize the administrative apparatus. Instead legal scholars consign it to other disciplines, such as political science or public policy. Statutes, regulations, and administrative action are not regarded as "law"; they are law of course, in common parlance and in practical effect, but they are not amenable to the conceptual system of existing legal scholarship.

A new conceptual system cannot be developed out of thin air, however, or instituted by fiat. If legal scholars are to address the realities of the administrative state, they must do so with the skills available to them and within their present institutional structures. Change is possible, but anything more than incremental change in an academic discipline is unlikely, and recommendations that demand more condemn themselves to irrelevance. To put the matter another way, a New Public Law scholarship that deals with our administrative state must continue to be recognizable as law to existing legal scholars. Such an adaptation of legal analysis may not be possible, but it is certainly worth trying.

The emerging New Public Law scholarship represents such an attempt. This article discusses the changes in the law that have motivated it, the conceptual structure that it has developed in response to those changes, and the way in which that conceptual structure, despite its novelty, remains recognizable as legal scholarship.

II. Legal Scholarship and Society's Concept of Law

Calls for a new mode of legal scholarship or legal education based on the realities of our modern state are far from new, of course. Indeed, they began at the same time that law schools themselves began[1]

1. *See, e.g.*, W. Chase, The American Law School and the Rise of Administrative Government 46-59 (1982); *see generally* R. Stevens, Law School: Legal Education in America from the 1850s to the 1980s 39-84 (1983).

and have continued unabated to the present day. A crescendo of sorts was reached during the legal realist movement, with the work of Harold Laswell and Myers McDougal being particularly notable in its demand for policy analysis and empirical observation.[2] Given the regularity with which this demand has been sounded, it seems surprising that it remains so unrequited and that any effort to respond to it could be described as new. Commentators, apparently at a loss for an explanation, tend to attribute the lack of change to the baneful influence of Harvard Law School.[3] A more convincing explanation, however, is conceptual; legal scholars have continued to write about law the way they do because of their conception of law. Change will not come until that conception changes; as long as new approaches are defined as law-and-something else, rather than as law, the very characterization necessarily proclaims their marginality.

But why should legal scholars alter their conception of law? The most obvious response is that society's conception of law has changed and that legal scholars must keep pace. That claim, however, contains an often-overlooked complexity that is responsible for much of the disjunction between our legal scholarship and our legal system. Very few intellectual disciplines must reconceptualize their methodology because of an underlying change in their subject matter. For example, the past fifty years have seen cataclysmic historical events — World War II, the Cold War, the end of colonialism, and so forth. But these events generally are not regarded as demanding a change in the methodology of historical studies. Quite the contrary, we would look to our established methodology as a way to understand the events that have occurred.

There are two caveats to the observation, but neither comes close to the complete negation of it that apparently obtains in legal scholarship. First, events that occur in the underlying subject of study may produce a change in methodology by disproving some widely held belief. The classic example is Einstein's Theory of Relativity, which altered so many scientific theories about physical reality.[4] But this

2. Lasswell & McDougal, *Legal Education and Public Policy: Professional Training in Public Interest,* 52 YALE L.J. 203, 207-17 (1943); McDougal, *The Law School of the Future: From Legal Realism to Policy Science in the World Community,* 56 YALE L.J. 1345 (1947); *see also* Gellhorn, *The Law Schools' Responsibility for Training Public Servants,* 9 U. CHI. L. REV. 469 (1942); Keyserling, *Social Objectives in Legal Education,* 33 COLUM. L. REV. 437 (1933).

3. *See* W. CHASE, *supra* note 1, at 23-83; R. STEVENS, *supra* note 1, at 51-64; Schlegel, *Langdell's Legacy or, The Case of the Empty Envelope* (Book Review), 36 STAN. L. REV. 1517, 1524-25 (1984).

4. For Kuhn, Einstein's theory is a classic example of a paradigm shift from one basic conception of the world to another. T. KUHN, THE STRUCTURE OF SCIENTIFIC REVOLUTIONS 97-101 (1962). Kuhn is not particularly interested, however, in the distinction between the content

occurs less often than one might suppose; more typically, the event disproves a particular theory within the existing methodology. Einstein's theory, epochal though it was, did not really transform the methodology of modern physics. The content changed, but the discipline proceeded in much the same way as it had before.[5] Moreover, even this fairly limited effect of methodology is not necessary but contingent; it depends on whether the event in question disproves rather than confirms existing methodological approaches. The development of the Watson-Crick DNA model, for example, was as significant for molecular biology as Einstein's theory was for theoretical physics. But it had no methodological implications at all; Watson and Crick achieved it using the existing methodology, and it only confirmed that methodology's effectiveness.[6]

The second caveat is that methodologies do change, and these changes are often linked to broader patterns. But the patterns tend to be intellectual ones, related to our general conception of methodology, rather than events in the underlying subject matter. The methodology of history has changed from a narrative of public events to an analysis of socioeconomic relationships, and this change can be traced to a specific period of time. But the events that produced this change were intellectual, not historic; they can be attributed to Adam Smith or Auguste Compte much more directly than to Napoleon or Wellington. Moreover, once the change has occurred, the new methodology is equally applicable to events before the change. The historical writing of classical authors exemplifies the premodern narrative style, but it would be absurd for modern historians to view socioeconomic methods as inapplicable to Greek or Roman history.

Thus, the idea that alterations in society's conception of law require a new legal theory must depend upon some feature of legal theory that distinguishes it from other academic disciplines. This distinguishing feature is most readily identified as the prescriptive

and the methodology of science, an issue on which he has been criticized. *See* Lakatos, *Falsification and the Methodology of Scientific Research Programmes* in CRITICISM AND THE GROWTH OF KNOWLEDGE 91, 178 (T. Lakatos & A. Musgrave eds. 1970). It is unclear how a change in world-view correlates with a change in method. Perhaps the most notable methodological change that Einstein's overthrow of Newtonian mechanics produced was the stochastic model of physical phenomena, a model which made Einstein himself distinctly uncomfortable. *See* N. BOHR, *Discussion with Einstein of Epistemological Problems in Atomic Physics*, in ATOMIC PHYSICS AND HUMAN KNOWLEDGE 32, 56 (1958); W. HEISENBERG, PHYSICS AND BEYOND 62-69 (1971).

5. With the exception of the change described in note 4, *supra*, the mode of generating and verifying empirical data did not really change, even in response to a change as large as Einstein's revision.

6. For an account of this event, see J. WATSON, THE DOUBLE HELIX (1968).

quality of legal scholarship.[7] While the declared purpose of most natural and social sciences is to discover observed events, and the purpose of most humanistic studies is to interpret artistic productions, the declared purpose of legal scholarship is to frame recommendations to responsible decisionmakers. This does not mean that the only criterion for judging legal scholarship is whether its recommendations are adopted. Like other fields, law constitutes a self-sustaining discipline, whose participants are capable of evaluating their own efforts. What it means is that the concept of recommendation, or prescription, structures the entire discipline, and that evaluation will be based on whether or not the work provides a reasonable or imaginative recommendation.

Because prescription is the structuring purpose of legal scholarship, that scholarship must develop a mode of discourse appropriate to its prescriptive enterprise. It must, in other words, speak explicitly to the decisionmakers who constitute the audience for its prescriptions. It must address the issues that these decisionmakers confront, speak in terms that are meaningful to them, and frame proposals that they can conceivably implement. Again, these principles only structure the discourse and are not necessarily literal requirements. Although it may be gratifying for a legal scholar to have her recommendations adopted, the quality of her work will not be judged by its adoption, but by its logic, creativity, and judgment, when viewed as a set of recommendations.

Because of the prescriptive quality of legal scholarship, changes in the way our society conceives and uses law demand changes in the scholarship's methodology. Not all changes are equally profound, of course. Just as new discoveries in natural sciences can transform the content of an entire field without altering its methodology, some changes in the legal system do not require any corresponding changes in legal scholarship. In 1937, for example, the Supreme Court changed its entire theory of the Constitution.[8] That shift provided a

---

7. The discussion is based on Rubin, *The Practice and Discourse of Legal Scholarship*, 86 MICH. L. REV. 1835 (1988).

8. *See, e.g.*, West Coast Hotel v. Parrish, 300 U.S. 379 (1937) (upholding state regulation of women's wages, and overruling substantive due process decision in Adkins v. Children's Hosp., 261 U.S. 525 (1923)); United States v. Carolene Prods. Co., 304 U.S. 144 (1938) (upholding state regulation of filled milk and rejecting substantive due process rationale); Olsen v. Nebraska, 313 U.S. 236 (1941) (upholding state law fixing maximum fee, and explicitly denying precedential value of prior substantive due process decision in Ribnik v. McBride, 277 U.S. 350 (1928)). For the view that these decisions represented a transformation of the Constitution, equivalent in effect to the Civil War Amendments, see Ackerman, *Constitutional Politics/Conventional Law*, 99 YALE L.J. 453, 486-515 (1989); Ackerman, *The Storrs Lectures: Discovering the Constitution*, 93 YALE L.J. 1013, 1044-72 (1984).

topic of debate among constitutional scholars for several decades, but it did not require a different approach to scholarship; the Court's new theory could be subjected to the same techniques of case analysis as the old one.

The changes that have occurred in our social conception of law over the course of the past century are of a different order. They have changed the meaning of law in its entirety because they have created a new group of legal decisionmakers. These decisionmakers, primarily legislators and administrators, are now the principal law-creating officials in our society, and thus the most appropriate audience for legal scholars. To the extent that legal scholars fail to structure their works as recommendations to these decisionmakers, they will restrict the significance of their endeavors.

Legal scholars, however, need not change. They can opt for the limited significance that results from continuing to underemphasize legislative and administrative lawmaking. Because scholarly success is determined within the academy, and not by the decisionmakers whose lawmaking function is ignored, the system can perpetuate itself. This is particularly true because legal scholars, as faculty members, control entry into a lucrative profession. If those who rejected Einstein's theory, and insisted on the truth of Newtonian mechanics, controlled entry into civil engineering, they too might still grace our campuses some ninety years after their ideas ran into conceptual difficulties.[9]

Thus, although the transformation of our legal system ought to produce changes in a prescriptive discipline such as legal scholarship, that transformation will not compel the change. The legal academy has enough autonomy to retain its premodern attitudes. Change requires a new conception of law; scholars must not only think differently about what counts as law, but they must think differently about the essence of law itself. To explore the parameters of the process more fully, it is necessary to consider the old and new conceptions of law in greater detail.

III. The Old Concept of Law

A century ago, when law schools first appeared as graduate programs in American universities[10] and legal scholarship took shape as

9. Civil engineering could be performed perfectly well on the basis of Newtonian mechanics, since relativistic effects do not appear at the velocities and energy levels involved. Our hypothetical Newtonians could not analyze the behavior of elementary particles, of course, but they might respond that the study of these particles was not physics, but quantumology, and consign it to a separate department of the university.

10. During the 1820s, and again in the 1850s and 1860s, a number of American colleges established affiliations with private law schools. *See* R. Stevens, *supra* note 1, at 5-28. These

an academic discipline, law was conceived as the special province of the judiciary. The judiciary both declared the law and applied it to particular cases. Law meant the common law, the body of rules which defined crimes and governed interactions between private citizens.[11] Sophisticated observers recognized, of course, that the legislature could make law and that the Constitution served as the organic law of the nation. The general view, however, was that both ordinary legislation and the Constitution belonged to the realm of politics, and were somehow distinct from the process by which courts declared and applied the law.[12] These distinctions may seem artificial and incoherent today, but they were entirely meaningful to the attorneys and judges who comprised the legal community a century ago.

The common law that judges declared and implemented possessed a number of distinguishing features that sprang from the judiciary's institutional position and conceptual orientation. Much of this is familiar but, as Melvin Eisenberg's recent study suggests, it is too subtle and complex for easy generalizations.[13] For present purposes, however, a few features that distinguish the judge-made law of the previous century can be identified.

To begin with, traditional common law was regarded as embodying a set of transcendental principles, that is, principles that were not simply the enacted rules of a particular regime but general legal principles that applied to all societies.[14] Fault, intent, consent, causation, property, responsibility, and various other concepts were seen as universal elements of any developed legal system. This belief has an undeniable intellectual appeal, but it also rested on a strong institutional basis. As a result of our revolution we rejected the King of England, the statutes of England, the taxes of England, even the judges of England, but we did not reject the judge-made law of England.[15] The only

---

law schools were pure trade schools — somewhat similar, one gathers, to the present-day truck driving schools that advertise on late-night television. The development of law school as a three-year graduate program was the work of Charles Eliot, as President of Harvard, and Christopher Langdell, as Dean of the Law School. *See id.* at 36-37; *see also* Chase, *The Birth of the Modern Law School,* 23 AM. J. LEGAL HIST. 329 (1979). The new structure required the study of law to become an academic discipline as well as training for a profession.

11. *See* G. GILMORE, THE AGES OF AMERICAN LAW 41-67 (1977); L. FRIEDMAN, HISTORY OF AMERICAN LAW 354-56 (1973).

12. *See* R. STEVENS, *supra* note 1, at 39-42.

13. M. EISENBERG, THE NATURE OF THE COMMON LAW (1988).

14. *See* G. GILMORE, THE DEATH OF CONTRACT 35-44 (1974) (discussing Williston); Grey, *Langdell's Orthodoxy,* 45 U. PITT. L. REV. 1, 5, 11-15 (1983); White, *The Impact of Legal Science on Tort Law, 1880-1910,* 78 COLUM. L. REV. 213, 220-21 (1978).

15. *See* 1 J. KENT, COMMENTARIES ON AMERICAN LAW 472-73 (2d ed. 1832):

> The common law of England has been assumed, or declared by statute, with the like modifications, as the law of every state. . . .
>
> The best evidence of the common law is to be found in the decisions of the courts of

basis for this continued fealty to the laws of a deposed sovereign was that these laws were not the political acts of a particular regime but law itself — general or transcendental principles that were valid in all societies.

As our democracy evolved, the idea of a transcendental law was infused with the newer one that judges, unlike the legislature or the chief executive, were appointed officials who could exercise lawmaking power only when they were discovering general principles, rather than expressing their own policy preferences. Alexander Bickel christened this same concern "the counter-majoritarian difficulty" in the case where a court overturns an enacted statute on constitutional grounds.[16] The justification for such actions generally turns on some appeal to the Constitution itself, but common law judges, who were equally unelected, had no positive law on which they could rely; the legitimacy of their lawmaking role in a democratic government had to derive from the inherent validity of the laws that they declared — from its relationship to general principles.

Second, judge-made law must develop incrementally. Because of the institutional structure of the judiciary, judges cannot initiate lawmaking opportunities. They do have the power to select among the opportunities presented, even at the trial level, but they are limited to the range of cases presented to them. Moreover, this phenomenological position as a decisionmaker is contextualized within the case. To borrow Gadamer's image, the facts presented by the case create the horizon of judges' legitimate decisionmaking power.[17] While judicial notice, the Brandeis brief, and the more sociological style of contemporary legal reasoning allows some lateral expansion of this horizon, judges still have no independent fact gathering or general lawmaking powers. They are on the safest and most legitimate ground when they

> justice, contained in numerous volumes of reports, and in the treaties and digests of learned men, which have been multiplying from the earliest periods of English history down to the present time.

Kent also allows "English statutes passed before the emigration of our ancestors" to be part of the common law of the United States. *Id.* at 473. Presumably, this is because these statutes serve as a basis for judicial decisions. Clearly, contemporary English statutes would not be treated one same way.

16. *See* A. BICKEL, THE LEAST DANGEROUS BRANCH 16-23 (1962). Not all of Bickel's concerns apply to judicial lawmaking. For example, Bickel believed that the judiciary's power to declare enacted laws unconstitutional might weaken the democratic process because legislators would rely on the courts to correct their mistakes. *Id.* at 21-22. This is not a significant problem in common law, because legislation clearly supersedes it. But Bickel's basic concern about lawmaking by officials who are not subject to public scrutiny and control is fully applicable.

17. H. GADAMER, TRUTH AND METHOD 269-74 (G. Barden & J. Cumming trans. 2d ed. 1975). *See id.* at 269 ("Every finite present has its limitations. We define the concept of 'situation' by saying that it represents a standpoint that limits the possibility of vision. Hence an essential part of the concept of situation is the concept of 'horizon.' ").

restrict themselves to the range of situations that the case presents. This necessitates an incremental decisionmaking style, one that proceeds by fact-specific stages rather than by broad generalizations.[18] When courts, even constitutional courts, veer too far from this ideal, their decisions become suspect. The *Roe v. Wade* opinion,[19] with its judicial statute about trimesters, is a familiar example. While the challenge to this case is largely a political and moral one, its legitimacy certainly was impaired by the universal agreement that the Supreme Court wrote a poor opinion.[20]

The combination of transcendental principles with incremental decisionmaking tends to generate another characteristic of the judge-made law: its reliance upon analogy. Eisenberg indicates that analogy is not an independent technique but a mode of reasoning that must be guided by overarching rules or principles.[21] The converse is true as well; in traditional common law analysis, principles were typically brought to bear upon the case at hand through the medium of analogy. The reason is that these principles are found in the specific, situation-contained cases that form the arena of judicial reasoning. If cases serve as the only arena for the actuation of these principles, then they are the primary and most important source of law. To discard the use of analogy, one would need unmediated access to the principles themselves. This is possible when the transcendental principles have some independent source; the claim of divine revelation, for example, rejects established bodies of doctrine in favor of direct communication with the Almighty. Closer to home, constitutional courts sometimes reject a line of precedent by going back to the original words of the Constitution.[22] In the common law, however, no recognized authority establishes the guiding principles. These principles are most authoritatively established through their appearance in decided cases, much as artistic genius is actuated exclusively through specific works of art.[23] This

18. *See* E. LEVI, AN INTRODUCTION TO LEGAL REASONING 16-17 (1948).

19. 410 U.S. 113 (1973).

20. Negative assessments of the Court's opinion are legion. *See, e.g.*, Ely, *The Wages of Crying Wolf, A Comment on* Roe v. Wade, 82 YALE L.J. 920 (1973); Epstein, *Substantive Due Process by Any Other Name: The Abortion Cases*, 1973 SUP. CT. REV. 159; Henkin, *Privacy and Autonomy*, 74 COLUM. L. REV. 1410 (1974); Lupu, *Untangling the Strands of the Fourteenth Amendment*, 77 MICH. L. REV. 981, 998-99 (1979); Regan, *Rewriting* Roe v. Wade, 77 MICH. L. REV. 1569 (1979).

21. M. EISENBERG, *supra* note 13, at 83-96.

22. A notorious example is Board of Regents v. Roth, 408 U.S. 564, 576-78 (1972), where the Court suddenly found that the word "property" in the due process clause had significance for the doctrine that had not been previously recognized.

23. I. KANT, CRITIQUE OF JUDGMENT 46-50 (J. Bernard trans. 1951).

compels judges to take prior cases very seriously and leads naturally to an analogical approach.

Finally, the common law is characterized by a mode of argument which can be referred to as process justification. The decisionmaker justifies her decision by setting forth the steps she used to reach it. In a typical judicial opinion, the judge begins by characterizing the facts of the case at hand and then compares this characterization with the conclusions of prior cases. By pointing out similarities and differences between these prior cases, guided by the principles that transcend each case but find expression in it, the judge will then reach a conclusion about the proper way to decide the case at hand. If this conclusion is subject to significant challenges, from one of the parties or otherwise, the judge will typically consider each challenge in order and explain why it is not persuasive. This process argument is not psychological but conceptual. The judge is not trying to recreate her actual thought patterns, but to justify her conclusion by showing that it proceeds from accepted sources by legitimate, properly argued steps.

While process reasoning is obviously compatible with an incremental, analogical approach, it is not necessarily limited to that approach. Mathematical proofs also employ process reasoning, although they generally do not rely upon analogy or incrementalism. The necessary link seems to be between process reasoning and transcendental principles. If one begins with general principles, then truth is to be found by reasoning from those principles deductively. There is no independent criterion for testing the validity of the endpoint; one must trace the path back to the principles with which one began. The process becomes more complicated, at least in theory, if one does not possess unmediated access to those principles, and must discern their contours from their contextualized expressions. This precludes pure deduction, as in mathematics, and compels reliance on techniques such as analogy.

The common law, of course, has not remained unaltered since the age of formalism. In fact, its distinctive features, as identified above, have been significantly modified by the political and conceptual events of this century.[24] Most notably, common law decisionmaking no longer makes a strong claim to transcendental principles, although residual traces of this claim can still be found in judicial language.[25]

24. *See* Farber & Frickey, *In the Shadow of the Legislature: The Common Law in the Age of the New Public Law*, 89 MICH. L. REV. 875 (1990); Strauss, *Review Essay: Sunstein, Statutes and the Common Law — Reconciling Markets, the Communal Impulse, and the Mammoth State*, 89 MICH. L. REV. 907 (1990).

25. Legal realism and critical legal studies have expended much of their energy in establishing the political, rather than transcendental, nature of legal principles. *See, e.g.*, R. UNGER,

The more frequent claim is that the principles which animate judicial decisionmaking are transpolitical; although they may not be universally true, they are true for our culture because they reflect a consensus that crosses existing political boundaries. This is sufficient to establish the legitimacy of judicial lawmaking in the face of Bickel's countermajoritarian concern. It does not explain why the common law of another nation, such as England, would have authoritative force, but by the twentieth century, America's common law was sufficiently indigenous to render such an explanation unnecessary.

Along with the reinterpretation of guiding principles of common law as transpolitical rather than transcendental came the cautious use of other modes of reasoning in judicial decisionmaking. Policy sometimes displaced analogy; instead of looking to prior decisions as authority, judges would look to statutes, executive proclamations, or public opinion.[26] This policy orientation was linked to the change in the perceived provenance of the animating principles. If the principles were merely transpolitical, and not transcendental, they could be embodied in sources other than judicial decisions. One might find these principles reflected in particular legislative actions or particular expressions of popular opinion. The problem, of course, was to separate the transpolitical from the contingently political, the policy of the public at large from the policy of the Democratic or Republican party.[27] For this reason, public policy had to be invoked with care, and only in the context of proper judicial analysis. Nonetheless, it was an available source of authority, and allowed the common law to reflect broad social and political developments. These modifications produce the flexibility and continued vitality of common law results.

IV. The New Concept of Law

The growth of the administrative state and the associated or parallel developments in social attitudes have brought with them a new

Knowledge and Politics (1975); Cohen, *Transcendental Nonsense and the Functional Approach*, 35 Colum. L. Rev. 809 (1935). By now, the point has been fully assimilated into our legal consciousness. *See* B. Ackerman, Reconstructing American Law 6-22 (1984).

26. *See* M. Eisenberg,, *supra* note 13, at 29-31.

27. The crucial factor is consensus. One reliable guide to consensus is a statute which, despite its partisan provenance, becomes the law of the land upon enactment. *See* Farber & Frickey, *supra* note 24, at 892-93, 898-99. Another guide is social attitudes that seem to the judge to be broadly, albeit not universally, held. *See* M. Eisenberg,, *supra* note 13, at 14-26; Greenwalt, *Policy, Rights, and Judicial Decision*, 11 Ga. L. Rev. 991, 1004-05 (1977); Wellington, *Common Law Rules and Constitutional Double Standards: Some Notes on Adjudication*, 83 Yale L.J. 221, 226-29 (1973). The dangers and inconsistencies of relying on each of these sources are obvious, even to judges; the point is merely that judges aspire to transpolitical, rather than contingently political, sources for their policy determinations.

conception of law, and a concomitant change in judicial attitudes and methods. Scholars frequently speak of the judge who ventures beyond the bounds of the common law for principles of legal decisionmaking and implements his conclusions by extensive, specially designed remedial orders.[28] In recent years, the emphasis on the judge's role as an interpreter of statutes has grown, again rejecting the boundaries of common law to deal with the judge's function in the modern state.[29] All this writing, however, gravely underestimates the changes that have occurred because it continues to focus on the judge. The most notable change that the administrative state has effected in our legal system is that judges are no longer our primary lawmakers. Legislators and administrators now fill that role. Consequently, any body of writing that focuses on judges is likely to overlook the truly distinctive features of law in the modern state. Those features can only be perceived by considering the lawmaking functions of legislators and administrators, and investigating what law means to these decisionmakers.

At the outset, one must recognize that the advent of legislators and administrators as our primary lawmakers is just one part of the larger set of changes produced by the administrative state. Administrators have also become our primary adjudicators,[30] and to the extent that adjudication continues to make law, that lawmaking process will occur within the administrative agency as well.[31] The Presidency has changed character, becoming much more of a coordinating and direc-

28. *See, e.g.*, D. HOROWITZ, THE COURTS AND SOCIAL POLICY 4-9 (1977); Chayes, *The Role of the Judge in Public Law Litigation*, 89 HARV. L. REV. 1281, 1284 (1976); Fiss, *The Supreme Court, 1978 Term — Foreword: The Forms of Justice*, 93 HARV. L. REV. 1, 2-3 (1979); Resnick, *Managerial Judges*, 96 HARV. L. REV. 374, 376-78 (1982).

29. *See, e.g.*, G. CALABRESI, A COMMON LAW FOR THE AGE OF STATUTES 2 (1982); Aleinikoff, *Updating Statutory Interpretation*, 87 MICH. L. REV. 20, 62-66 (1988); Eskridge, *Dynamic Statutory Interpretation*, 135 U. PA. L. REV. 1479 (1987); Macey, *Promoting Public Regarding Legislation Through Statutory Interpretation, An Interest Group Model*, 86 COLUM. L. REV. 223, 226-27 (1986); Posner, *Statutory Interpretation — In the Classroom, In the Courtroom*, 50 U. CHI. L. REV. 800, 801-02 (1983); Sunstein, *Interpreting Statutes in the Regulatory State*, 103 HARV. L. REV. 405, 412-13 (1989).

30. For an extensive discussion of the failure of legal scholarship to deal with administrative adjudication, see W. CHASE, *supra* note 1, at 12-22. Chase's account focuses heavily on historical contingencies, particularly the domination of the Harvard Law School method. In his view, things might have gone quite differently had Ernst Freund, the hero of his account, prevailed in his plans at the University of Chicago, instead of being defeated by Joseph H. Beale and Felix Frankfurter, *id.* at 46-59, 94-135. There is poignance to the story Chase relates, but it seems difficult to believe that such large trends turned on the personal influence of a few academics.

31. For a discussion of the way in which administrative adjudication requires a reinterpretation of the adjudicative process, see J. MASHAW, BUREAUCRATIC JUSTICE 14-17 (1983); J. MASHAW, DUE PROCESS IN THE ADMINISTRATIVE STATE 12-15 (1985); Rubin, *Due Process and the Administrative State*, 72 CALIF. L. REV. 1044 (1984); Van Alstyne, *Cracks in "The New Property": Adjudicative Due Process in the Administrative State*, 62 CORNELL L. REV. 445 (1977).

tion-setting office for the executive agencies and perhaps the independent agencies as well.[32] Other forms of control, besides formal lawmaking, have arisen or expanded in importance. All these developments are relevant to legal scholarship; for the present however, the most important development, because it represents the very essence of our new governmental system, is that legislators and administrators make the vast bulk of our laws. As a result, the entire concept of law has been transformed. The general character of this transformation has been explored by Bruce Ackerman,[33] and by Philippe Nonet and Philip Selznick,[34] among others. For present purposes, the concern is with the way that our society's dominant conception of law itself has changed since the common law era.

Legislators and administrators live in a regime of positive law, not transcendental or even transpolitical legal principles. For legislators, the law is an instrumentality by which they achieve their political or ideological goals. For administrators, some law is a set of explicit instructions from the legislature, ranging from the incredibly vague to the unbelievably detailed, but always proceeding from a definite source and having some specific purpose. The remaining law consists of the rules the administrators promulgate, and is analogous to legislation; it implements specific purposes, theoretically the purposes of the authorizing statute, but often as political or ideological as the legislature's.[35] Courts intercede in this modern lawmaking process, but less often than the casebooks would suggest and almost always in a supervisory capacity. They declare that the administrators have violated a governing statute, or that the legislature has violated the Constitution, but they always point to a positive legal enactment of our own nation rather than invoking transcendental principles. Legislators and administrators, in their day-to-day activities, see law as an instrumentality, a means of achieving specific purposes.

Secondly, the development of law in our modern legal regime is not necessarily incremental. Sometimes it is: statutes are amended, agencies redirected by legislative oversight, regulations amended by

32. *See generally* E. CORWIN, THE PRESIDENT: OFFICE AND POWERS 1787-1984, 84-191 (R. Bland, T. Hindson, J. Peltason eds. 5th ed. 1984); R. NATHAN, THE ADMINISTRATIVE PRESIDENCY (1983); R. NEUSTADT, PRESIDENTIAL POWER (1960); Bruff, *Presidential Power and Administrative Rulemaking,* 88 YALE L.J. 451 (1979).

33. B. ACKERMAN, *supra* note 25.

34. P. NONET & P. SELZNICK, LAW AND SOCIETY IN TRANSITION (1978).

35. *See generally* E. BARDACH, THE IMPLEMENTATION GAME: WHAT HAPPENS AFTER A BILL BECOMES A LAW (1977); M. DERTHICK, NEW TOWNS IN-TOWN: WHY A FEDERAL PROGRAM FAILED (1972); I. PRESSMAN & A. WILDAVSKY, IMPLEMENTATION (2d ed. 1979); B. RADIN, IMPLEMENTATION, CHANGE, AND THE FEDERAL BUREAUCRACY: SCHOOL DESEGREGATION POLICY IN H.E.W. 1964-68 (1977).

the agencies, and interpretations of existing laws and regulations altered by shifts in administrative strategy. But at other times, major policy initiatives are undertaken: a new statute, a major change in executive policy, even a comprehensive regulation. The degree of change is thus the decisionmaker's choice, rather than being fixed by the decisionmaking process itself. To continue Gadamer's image, the regulatory state adds another dimension to the case-situated position of legal decisionmakers. It enables them to rise out of specific situations to an altitude where comprehensive planning over a wide area of legal terrain can occur. As a consequence, detail may be lost, but that is a specific problem that the decisionmakers may try to solve when operating at that altitude. This additional dimension allows for general declarations of law, designed to implement broad, comprehensive policies.

Because of this instrumental and potentially comprehensive approach, the development of law no longer relies upon analogy. Stated most starkly, and with only slight exaggeration, prior legislation has no binding effect on current enactments whatsoever. It may serve as a source of information; a conscientious, public-oriented legislator will look at prior laws to determine whether a particular legislative strategy is effective, while a venal, public-choice legislator will look to these laws to see whether a particular strategy got its sponsors clobbered in the last election. But neither legislator will regard prior law as a source of authority for a new enactment. The policy judgments that control their enactments, unlike the principles that control judicial decisions, are not perceived as being expressed through the medium of prior enactments.[36] Because these policies are contingent and instrumental, rather than transcendental, legislators can have direct access to them, and they are not necessarily expressed in prior statutes.

For administrators, the governing statute is of course an authority, but this is the authority of hierarchy and direct command, not the analogical authority of parallel decisions. Administrators also decide on the basis of policies; these may come from the statute, or from nonstatutory political or ideological considerations. But they have a definite source, and need not be sought in prior regulations. Modern law develops by adding new enactments, and replacing or amending old ones, but not by analogy from prior laws. Thus, it has no need of the

---

36. In narrative accounts of legislative drafting and design, politics and policy figure prominently, but prior law is hardly ever mentioned. *See, e.g.*, S. Bailey, Congress Makes a Law: The Story Behind the Employment Act of 1946 (1950); S. David, With Dignity: The Search for Medicine and Medicaid (1985); E. Redman, The Dance of Legislation (1973).

elaborate theory of overruling that Eisenberg has explicated for the common law.[37]

Finally, modern legislative and administrative law is distinguished from the common law by its mode of justification. Instead of process justification, where the decisionmaker traces an idealized path from source to conclusion, legislators and administrators use what may be described as cause-and-result justification. They take action because a problem exists,[38] and their choice of action is based on the expected effects. This mode of justification is set forth in the preamble of virtually every statute. The "Whereas" clause states the problem — "Whereas the legislature finds that there exists a lack of affordable rental housing within its jurisdiction . . ." — and the "hereby enacts" clause states the expected result — "the legislature hereby enacts a general limitation on rents, so that more rental units will be offered at affordable rates." It would seem irrelevant, and peculiar, for a statute to explain how the legislature figured out the provisions it enacted.[39] This is not simply because of Bismark's observation that anyone who loves law or sausage should not watch either being made. The legislature could readily present a sanitized version of its thought process, if that were deemed important. But it is not: statutes are regarded as instrumentalities, designed to achieve particular results, and they are justified by a perceived need to achieve results in a given area, and by the results that they achieve.

This then is the conception of law that emerged from our modern, administrative state. In some sense it simply describes the lawmaking functions of legislators and administrators, as opposed to judges, and it emphasizes the shift from common to statutory law. But it also

37. M. EISENBERG, *supra* note 13.

38. This is the mode of thought that Max Weber identified as purposive-rational, and that he specifically linked to modern bureaucratic institutions. *See* M. WEBER, ECONOMY AND SOCIETY (G. Roth & C. Wittich eds. 1978). For an incisive discussion of Weber's approach, see 1 J. HABERMAS, THE THEORY OF COMMUNICATIVE ACTION 143-271 (T. McCarthy trans. 1981).

39. The growing criticism of using legislative history as a guide to interpretation is based on the perceived irrelevance of any effort to recreate the thought process of the legislature. While speeches and committee reports generally attempt to justify the statute's provisions in terms of the results to be achieved, they sometimes do advance purported descriptions of the legislative thought process. Because these descriptions have no legitimate function, they have come to be perceived as conscious efforts to manipulate subsequent interpreters of the statute. *See, e.g.*, Begier v. IRS, 110 S. Ct. 2258, 2267 (1990) (Scalia, J., concurring); Blanchard v. Bergeron, 109 S. Ct. 939, 946 (1989) (Scalia, J., concurring); *In re* Sinclair, 870 F.2d 1340, 1341-44 (7th Cir. 1989) (Easterbrook, J.); Stoddard v. Board of Governors, 868 F.2d 1308, 1311 (D.C. Cir. 1989) (Buckley, J.) (quoting Board of Governors v. Dimension Fin. Corp., 474 U.S. 361, 373-74 (1986)); Natural Resources Defense Council v. EPA, 822 F.2d 104, 113 (D.C. Cir. 1987) (Starr, J.); Easterbrook, *The Role of Original Intent in Statutory Construction*, 11 HARV. J.L. & PUB. POL'Y. 59 (1988); Starr, *Observations About the Use of Legislative History*, 1987 DUKE L.J. 371. There has been no similar attack on judges explanations of their decisions as a guide to interpretation.

represents our society's view of what "law" really is. Thus, legal decisions in other institutions, such as courts, tend to be assimilated into the dominant view. In preadministrative America, lawmaking by legislatures was regarded as an appendage to the common law, a way of overruling particularly unpopular decisions, asserting or waiving governmental rights, or enforcing judicial decrees.[40] Of course, legislatures did many other things as well — they appropriated funds, imposed taxes, approved treaties, acquired and distributed government property, and so forth, but these things were generally not viewed as law. Conversely, our modern view of judge-made law is that it consists of the incremental articulation of a general plan in situations where such an approach makes sense on policy grounds.[41] The common law authority of courts is established by tradition, but we tend to explain it in a similar manner. Moreover, that explanation — that conception of law — has been internalized by judges themselves. When they feel obligated to provide an explicit justification for a decision, they often rely on the type of policy argument that serves as the basis of legislation, rather than the principles and analogies of common law.[42]

V. THE OLD LEGAL SCHOLARSHIP

Legal scholarship in the premodern era was not identical to the old concept of law described above. But because it was a prescriptive scholarship addressed to judges, it needed to adopt a mode of argument which was consistent with judicial reasoning. Thus, one of the basic tasks of legal scholars was to discern the general principles embedded in the common law. The best medium for doing so were treatises, those magisterial surveys that marshalled thousands and thousands of judicial decisions, set them in neat rows and files, discerned their general pattern and articulated it as a principle of law. These treatises came to be viewed as the apotheosis of legal scholar-

40. *See, e.g.*, 1 J. KENT, *supra* note 15, at 464.

41. This is an essentially positivist approach, implying that judicial power derives from positive enactments of the legislature. *See, e.g.*, H.L.A. HART, THE CONCEPT OF LAW 121-32 (1961); H. KELSEN, GENERAL THEORY OF LAW AND THE STATE 58-64 (1945); J. RAZ, THE AUTHORITY OF LAW 181-97 (1979). When the legislature enacts a judicially enforced statute whose terms are vague, the courts are empowered to fill in the gaps by judicial lawmaking.

42. *See* M. EISENBERG,, *supra* note 13, at 26-37; Chayes, *supra* note 28; Fiss, *supra* note 28; Lyons, *Justification and Judicial Responsibility*, 72 CALIF. L. REV. 178 (1984). They may also rely on moral principles, *see* M. EISENBERG, *supra* note 13, at 14-26, and the legitimacy of their policy orientation has been questioned, *see* Dworkin, *Hard Cases*, 88 HARV. L. REV. 1057 (1975). But as an empirical matter, the tendency of modern courts to speak in policy terms seems clear.

ship, the aircraft carriers of the scholarly fleet.[43] The surest route to preeminence was to write one, and the authors of the leading treatises are still well-known by law-trained people — synonymous with the subject matter, nearly — while their equally learned contemporaries are long-forgotten.

The relationship between the treatises and judicial decisions are a classic example of what Eisenberg refers to as the responsiveness of common law.[44] While treatises were not authority per se, they became acceptable citations as crystallizations of the principles embodied in a line of cases. They thus provided judges with a pastor, although not a Pope — an indirect expression of the general truth that could be confirmed by the individual act of examining the precedents. The treatise writers responded by proudly filling their footnotes with "citing treatise" citations, and this became further evidence of their quasi-canonical status.

Law review articles could fulfill this same function, sometimes cautiously, as the germ of a future treatise chapter, sometimes with startling originality, as Warren and Brandeis did with the right to privacy.[45] More often, however, articles related to another feature of the common law, namely its incrementalism. As the common law developed on a case-by-case basis, the law reviews responded, first with case notes, soon thereafter with more detailed analyses. These articles depended on the case for their conceptual horizon, and they also depended on it for their subsequent significance. As long as the case represented a current statement of the law and a guiding precedent for other decisions, its attendant article was of significance; as the case faded in importance, to be replaced by others, the article faded into the dim obscurity of law school libraries. Of course, many articles had greater aspirations, establishing a somewhat higher altitude, and thus defining a broader conceptual horizon than the cases that inspired them. But even these generally remained in contact with the underlying case law, providing a greater, but essentially parallel perspective, like a spotter plane above advancing troops.

The reasoning of legal scholarship was not identical to judicial reasoning; it relied more on principles and less on analogy, and it was not as painstaking in its process arguments. But because it was prescrip-

43. Simpson, *The Rise and Fall of the Legal Treatise: Legal Principles and the Forms of Legal Literature*, 48 U. CHI. L. REV. 632, 670-71 (1981).

44. M. EISENBERG,, *supra* note 13, at 12-13.

45. Warren & Brandeis, *The Right to Privacy*, 4 HARV. L. REV. 193 (1890). On the influence of this famous article, see Gordon, *Right of Property in Name, Likeness, Personality and History*, 55 NW. U. L. REV. 553 (1960); Kalven, *Privacy in Tort Law — Were Warren and Brandeis Wrong?*, 31 LAW & CONTEMP. PROBS. 326 (1966).

tive scholarship addressed to judges, it was compelled to adopt an approach congruent with judicial reasoning.[46] Analogies were regularly invoked, not with the same urgency but as important evidence. To demonstrate that a particular conclusion was justified, and another mistaken, scholars often traced the proper path of argument by process reasoning. They often criticized the reasoning in certain cases more harshly than the judges, because scholars were not bound by rules of precedent or authority, and did not feel obligated to grant prior decisions the same deference that judges did. But their analysis largely mirrored the judicial approach. Their invocation of principles was more direct, but different only in degree.

Legal scholars used judicial reasoning not simply as a technique, however, but as a system of meaning. Because the scholarship defined its role as offering prescriptions to judges, the system of judicial reasoning seemed like the law itself. Statutory and administrative lawmaking were defined out of the discipline, banished to the nether world of policy.[47] Judicial reasoning — the incremental, analogical, process argumentation indirectly guided by general principles — was assumed to be the only methodology of law. That was what legal scholars meant by the well-worn slogan, thinking like a lawyer, that they used as a basis for bedeviling their first-year classes.

Legal scholarship has changed, of course, since the classic era of treatise writing and common law analysis. Treatises have waned in their importance, to the point that they are more often regarded as guides for students and practitioners than as major scholarly achievements.[48] Law review articles and books, even those that represent the standard mode of scholarship, now invoke policy arguments and social science insights more often than they present close arguments from lines of doctrine. But most of this work continues to be directed largely to judges, and its modes of argument have changed only to the degree that the judges' arguments themselves have changed. Policy, for example, is considered a way of informing the judicial decisionmaking process, a means of redirecting the incremental, analogical flow of doctrine. It is recognized, but placed within a judicial framework, just as judges themselves do as a matter of institutional necessity. Explicit policy analysis, unconnected with the judicial

46. This phenomenon can be termed a "unity of discourse" between judges and scholars. Rubin, *supra* note 7, at 1859-65.

47. *See* W. CHASE, *supra* note 1, at 46-76; R. STEVENS, *supra* note 1, at 51-64.

48. There are exceptions of course. The most notable, in recent years, is L. TRIBE, AMERICAN CONSTITUTIONAL LAW (2d ed. 1988) which set forth a highly developed, controversial theory of the Constitution. See also J. WHITE & R. SUMMERS, UNIFORM COMMERCIAL CODE (3d ed. 1988), whose views have been a factor in the scholarly debate within its field.

decisionmaking process, is consigned to other disciplines, such as economics or political science.

The shift in basic lawmaking functions from judges to legislatures and administrators might have rendered this judicial orientation untenable for a prescriptive discipline like law. Recommendations about law, after all, should be addressed primarily to those responsible for lawmaking. But the prescriptive character of legal scholarship does not require that the success of a work be measured by its real-world impact. Rather, prescription serves as a framework of meaning, establishing guidelines for creating and evaluating scholarly endeavors. The work is judged by its quality as a prescription, not by its actual effect. This internal value system, a characteristic legal scholarship shares with virtually every other discipline, gives the field its coherence. But it also enables legal scholars to continue addressing a decisionmaker who has been demoted to a subsidiary status, despite the explicitly prescriptive nature of their discourse.

Legal scholarship, to be sure, contains a number of new trends — most notably critical legal studies and the economic analysis of law. These two rather disparate movements share a desire to distance themselves from standard legal scholarship, employing other disciplines to build new intellectual constructs. Nonetheless, both movements have remained bound to the judicial orientation of standard scholarship. This is surprising given their aspirations and their rhetoric, but it indicates how alluring the siren-song of the judicial framework seems to be.

The judicial orientation of critical legal studies is the result of its origins. There is a radical tradition in American thought — one that is somewhat apologetic about its debt to Marxism, but intellectually coherent nonetheless.[49] This tradition could have been focused directly on the legal order, both as a critique of existing arrangements for the governance of society and as a blueprint for new laws that would achieve more justice and equality. Instead, the critical legal studies movement was formed from a mixture of this radical tradition and a complex, philosophic argument that legal doctrine is inherently incoherent.[50]

49. *See, e.g.*, C. BEARD, AN ECONOMIC INTERPRETATION OF THE CONSTITUTION (1913); G. KOLKO, THE TRIUMPH OF CONSERVATISM (1963); A. ROCHESTER, THE POPULIST MOVEMENT IN THE UNITED STATES (1943).

50. *See, e.g.*, Dalton, *An Essay in the Deconstruction of Contract Doctrine*, 94 YALE L.J. 997 (1985); Freeman, *Legitimizing Racial Discrimination Through Antidiscrimination Law: A Critical Review of Supreme Court Doctrine*, 62 MINN. L. REV. 1049 (1978); Kelman, *Interpretive Construction in the Substantive Criminal Law*, 33 STAN. L. REV. 591 (1981); Klare, *Judicial Deradicalization of the Wagner Act and the Origins of Modern Legal Consciousness, 1937-1941*, 62 MINN. L. REV. 265 (1978); Peller, *The Metaphysics of American Law*, 73 CALIF. L. REV. 1151

The incoherence argument presents a number of difficulties. To begin with, it never developed a sufficient conception of coherence, and thus was limited to responsive criticism, rather than formulating a comprehensive critique.[51] Second, it was attacking something of a straw person; legal realism had already criticized the coherence of legal doctrine rather effectively,[52] and most sophisticated defenders of doctrinal coherence probably recognized that doctrine as an uneasy practical accommodation by the time critical legal studies took shape.[53] This attenuates the linkage between the coherence argument and the political motivation of critical legal studies. That linkage is necessarily forged by the argument that law's claim to coherence is a means of defending the status quo and suppressing people's emancipatory instincts.[54] But if law no longer relies heavily on coherence arguments, its social injustice must spring from sources other than its claim to intellectual coherence.

The most serious problem with the incoherence argument, however, is that it applies almost exclusively to judges.[55] Judges are the only public officials whose lawmaking authority is even arguably derived from the conceptual coherence of law. They are, or were, the

(1985); Singer, *The Player and the Cards: Nihilism and Legal Theory*, 94 YALE L.J. 1 (1984); Tushnet, *Following the Rules Laid Down: A Critique of Interpretivism and Neutral Principles*, 96 HARV. L. REV. 781 (1983).

51. *See, e.g.*, Stick, *Can Nihilism Be Pragmatic?*, 100 HARV. L. REV. 332 (1986).

52. *See* B. ACKERMAN, *supra* note 25, at 6-22. For leading legal realist criticisms, see, for example, J. FRANK, LAW AND THE MODERN MIND (1930); Bingham, *What Is the Law?*, 11 MICH. L. REV. 1 (1912); Cohen, *Property and Sovereignty*, 13 CORNELL L.Q. 8 (1927).

53. The relationship between critical legal studies and legal realism is explored in Peller, *supra* note 50, at 1219-59; Tushnet, *Critical Legal Studies: An Introduction to Its Origins and Underpinnings*, 36 J. LEGAL EDUC. 505 (1986). In essence, Peller and Tushnet perceive a similarity in the critical enterprises of the two movements, although they regard the critical legal studies attack as the more thoroughgoing. The difference they perceive between these movements is that legal realism had a more optimistic, constructive tone. In fact, critical legal scholars find the proposals of the realist school just as lacking as they find the structure of the common law.

54. *See, e.g.*, M. HOROWITZ, THE TRANSFORMATION OF AMERICAN LAW 1780-1860 (1977); R. UNGER, THE CRITICAL LEGAL STUDIES MOVEMENT 5-14 (1986); Dalton, *supra* note 50. The theoretical basis of this claim is provided by critical theory. *See* J. HABERMAS, KNOWLEDGE AND HUMAN INTERESTS (J. Shapiro trans. 1971); M. HORKHEIMER & T. ADORNO, DIALECTIC OF ENLIGHTENMENT (J. Cumming trans. 1972).

55. The same is often true of two recent movements roughly allied with critical legal studies, namely radical feminism and critical race theory. *See, e.g.*, Austin, *Sapphire Bound!*, 1989 WIS. L. REV. 539 (plea for listening to minority women's voices, followed by analysis of the reasoning in a judicial decision); Ehrenreich, *Pluralist Myths and Powerless Men: The Ideology of Reasonableness in Sexual Harassment Law*, 99 YALE L.J. 1177 (1990) (proposing pluralist, nonsexist concept of discrimination, then analyzing a judicial decision); Matsuda, *Looking to the Bottom: Critical Legal Studies and Reparations*, 22 HARV. C.R.-C.L. L. REV. 323 (1987) (recommending a new legal consciousness, then exemplifying it with a judicially structured argument for reparations); West, *Jurisprudence and Gender*, 55 U. CHI. L. REV. 1 (1988) (proposing a feminist conception of law, and applying it to rape and abortion cases).

ones who claimed that they were simply extrapolating the transcendental principles that inhere in the body of decided cases. Legislators and administrators, our primary lawmakers, see themselves as implementing public policy that is derived from other sources. The coherence of the enactments they produce is of minor importance, either morally or practically. At most, it is a heuristic, a way to make enacted law easier to understand and implement.[56]

The critical legal studies attack on coherence, therefore, deconstructs very little as far as modern legislative and administrative enactments are concerned. As a result, the linkage between the attack and the political motivation of the movement dissolves in this arena. While some critical legal studies writers have focused on other legal decisionmakers,[57] the movement has generally leveled its attack on an outmoded justification by a subsidiary legal institution, and thus failed to articulate a radical critique of our basic legal structure. The reason for this diversion of attention is that critical legal studies, like traditional scholarship, remains bewitched by the judiciary. For traditionalists, judges seem like the only officials worth speaking to; for the crits, these same judges seem like the only officials worth criticizing. The whole movement smacks of an almost adolescent rebellion against the most familiar and convenient authority figure, rather than a comprehensive attack on social injustice.

Law and economics explicitly adopts an interdisciplinary framework, a framework which has been directed toward policy analysis since its very inception. One would have thought that this would have naturally and effortlessly led to the analysis of legislative and administrative actions, and to the exploration of whether these actions were economically efficient. Instead, the legal scholars who inaugurated the field focused their attention, once again, on the judiciary. Guido Calabresi used economics to analyze common law liability rules.[58] This

56. *See* Trubek, *Where the Action Is: Critical Legal Studies and Empiricism*, 36 STAN. L. REV. 575 (1984). Trubek perceives an empiricist theme to critical legal studies, a study of "relations among legal ideas, social beliefs, action, and order," *id.* at 603, that is directed to generating a new legal consciousness. He observes, however, that the movement has been notably averse to empirical research. *Id.* at 615-18. He connects this to the overemphasis on ideology, the unproved assumption of CLS scholars that deconstructing ideology will lead to social change. *Id.* at 610-15. But a further explanation is that CLS has mounted an attack on legal rules within the arena of judicial doctrine. Trubek's own description indicates this; he identifies the empiricism of CLS in its willingness to look at doctrine from the outside, as an observer of its social role. *Id.* at 586-600. But what is being looked at is "doctrine" — judge-made or judge-interpreted rules.

57. *See, e.g.*, Frug, *The City as a Legal Concept*, 93 HARV. L. REV. 1057 (1980) (legislators, among others); Simon, *Visions of Practice in Legal Thought*, 36 STAN. L. REV. 469 (1984) (lawyers); *see also* C. MACKINNON, TOWARD A FEMINIST THEORY OF THE STATE (1989).

58. Calabresi, *Some Thoughts on Risk Distribution and the Law of Torts*, 70 YALE L.J. 499 (1961); Calabresi, *Does the Fault System Optimally Control Primary Accident Costs?*, 33 LAW &

was followed, more fatefully, by Richard Posner, who quickly moved from a promising analysis of regulation to the fantastic claim that common law was economically efficient.[59] With that, the entire approach became bound, almost inextricably, to the analysis of judicial decisionmaking.

It is widely maintained now that Posner was wrong, that he misdescribed the common law and failed to understand its meaning.[60] More significantly, however, this argument, right or wrong, simply overlooked the real value of economics. Economics is an analytic tool, deriving its philosophic origin from utilitarianism, which allows us to determine whether particular strategies are economically efficient. Adam Smith used the method to critique the regulatory system of the guilds,[61] and Alfred Kahn used it to critique the regulatory system of the New Deal.[62] The question legal scholars could have asked is whether particular sets of laws were efficient, and if not, what laws should be enacted in their place. Perhaps they would have concluded that the enforcement of private agreements was the most efficient in a wide variety of contexts. Perhaps they would also have concluded that courts were the most efficient mechanisms for enforcing these agreements. But the starting point of this analysis would have been our predominant set of laws, namely, the laws enacted by the legislatures and administrative agencies. Instead, law and economics proceeded backwards. It began with the common law doctrines and tried to justify those doctrines in economic terms. It thus confined itself to judicial decisionmaking, a limitation which it has only recently and intermittently escaped.[63]

CONTEMP. PROBS. 429 (1968); *see* Calabresi & Melamed, *Property Rules, Liability Rules, and Inalienability: One View of the Cathedral,* 85 HARV. L. REV. 1089 (1972).

59. R. POSNER, ECONOMIC ANALYSIS OF LAW 25-191 (2d ed. 1977); R. POSNER, THE ECONOMICS OF JUSTICE 254-67, 282-99 (1981); Posner, *A Theory of Negligence,* 1 J. LEGAL STUD. 29 (1972); Posner, *The Ethical and Political Basis of the Efficiency Norm in Common Law Adjudication,* 8 HOFSTRA L. REV. 487 (1980).

60. *See, e.g.,* K. SCHEPPELE, LEGAL SECRETS 248-65 (1988); Cooter & Kornhauser, *Can Litigation Improve the Law Without the Help of Judges?,* 9 J. LEGAL STUD. 139, 154-56 (1980); Cooter, Kornhauser & Lane, *Liability Rules, Limited Information, and the Role of Precedent,* 10 BELL J. ECON. 366 (1979); Kornhauser, *A Guide to the Perplexed: Claims of Efficiency in the Law,* 8 HOFSTRA L. REV. 591, 610-39 (1980); Michelman, *A Comment on Some Uses and Abuses of Economics in Law,* 46 U. CHI. L. REV. 307 (1979).

61. A. SMITH, THE WEALTH OF NATIONS (1776).

62. A. KAHN, THE ECONOMICS OF REGULATION: PRINCIPLES AND INSTITUTIONS (rev. ed. 1988).

63. Again, there are a number of works that use law and economics to analyze other topics, *see, e.g.,* Ehrlich & Posner, *An Economic Analysis of Legal Rulemaking,* 3 J. LEGAL STUD. 257 (1974); Scott, *Rethinking The Regulation of Coercive Creditor Remedies,* 89 COLUM. L. REV. 730 (1989). What is striking, given the discipline from which it draws its inspiration, is law and economics' continued emphasis on judicial decisions.

Other themes, of course, arise in law and economics, critical legal studies, and even traditional scholarship. All these fields are complex and they include hundreds, thousands, and, in the case of traditional scholarship, tens of thousands of separate works. The point is not to caricature the literature, but to identify its major theme or project — the intellectual inquiry that serves as an organizing principle, and to which scholars in the field devote their attention. This central theme is judicial decisionmaking. Despite all the methodological innovations of recent decades, legal scholarship still defines its primary area of concern, its concept of what really counts as law, in relation to the judiciary. Given the scholarship's prescriptive aspirations, the changes in our legal structure demand a new approach.

VI. The New Scholarship

This brings us to the New Public Law. At present, the effort is indeed quite new, but it is also too diffuse to possess established boundaries. Many of the best examples of this scholarship were written without conscious recognition that they represented a qualitative break with the past, and certainly without any sense that they were part of a movement. What follows is an effort to define the distinctive features of this work and provide a framework for its further development.[64]

To create a public law scholarship that is truly new, scholars must address themselves to the legislators and administrators who make the law, not to the judiciary. Law means something different to these decisionmakers, and this is the conceptual change to which legal scholars must adjust. The purpose of the reorientation is not only to influence legislators and administrators, but to think differently about the law itself. For a prescriptive discipline like law, the intended audience serves as a structuring principle for the discourse; thus, the test of a scholarly work is whether it presents a well-reasoned prescription, not whether its recommendations are followed. The main reason to

64. Given the volume of legal scholarship, developing an exhaustive list of works in a particular field, even a newly emerging one, would be a daunting task. A few exemplary works of New Public Law scholarship which will provide concrete examples of the general category, are as follows: B. Ackerman & W. Hassler, Clean Coal/Dirty Air, or How the Clean Air Act Became a Multibillion Dollar Bail-Out for High Sulphur Coal Producers and What Should Be Done about It (1981); S. Breyer, Regulation and Its Reform (1982); Meidinger, *The Development of Emissions Trading in U.S. Air Pollution Regulation*, in Making Regulatory Policy 153 (K. Hawkins & J. Thomas eds. 1989); Diver, *The Optimal Precision of Administrative Rules*, 93 Yale L.J. 65 (1983); Lehman, *Social Irresponsibility, Actuarial Assumptions and Wealth Redistribution: Lessons About Public Policy From a Prepaid Tuition Program*, 88 Mich. L. Rev. 1035 (1990); Rabin, *EPA Regulation of Chlorofluorocarbons: A View of the Policy Formation Process*, in Making Regulatory Policy, *supra*, at 133; Sunstein, *Paradoxes of the Regulatory State*, 57 U. Chi. L. Rev. 407 (1990).

shift the audience from judges to legislators is to produce a new set of questions and a new mode of analysis that enables one to deal with the realities of our modern legal system in a way that is conceptually impossible if one thinks of oneself as addressing a judge. By making this shift, one changes each of the features of the law from its judicial to its legislative and administrative version, and thereby generates a new way of thinking about law itself.

First, legislators and administrators do not see law as an embodiment of general principles, but as an instrumentality for achieving policy goals. The task of the New Public Law is to identify these instrumentalities, to develop a theory for translating policy into law. Law, a term which must be taken to include administrative regulations, is the medium in which policy directives are expressed. It is not the only medium, to be sure: many less formal devices are employed, including memoranda, verbal orders, negotiations, legislative hearings, and sub rosa threats. But most major legislative or administrative initiatives are embodied in a set of formally enacted rules.

The New Public Law scholarship attempts to answer a new set of questions: Which rules work best in general? Which work best for particular purposes? Under what circumstances is specificity desirable, and under what circumstances is it counterproductive? What is the best mechanism for enforcing various provisions? How important is public participation for achieving the purpose and how can such participation be secured? These inquiries suggest an approach to law whose components are not doctrinal arguments, nor translations of public policy into doctrine, but legislative and administrative techniques, and the translation of policy into those instrumentalities.

Perhaps the largest part of this inquiry involves the question of enforcement. This is one aspect of a statute or regulation, but it requires a perspective on the whole of modern governance. At the outset, one must choose between alternative enforcement mechanisms, that is, between courts and agencies.[65] The old scholarship's concern with courts has yielded some writing on this topic, but a consistent analysis of the relative virtues of the two institutions, as means of implementing public policy, is still needed. The issue must be analyzed

65. The question is often framed in terms of whether we ought to regulate a particular area or leave it unregulated, which of course means it would be regulated by the courts. *See, e.g.*, S. Breyer, *supra* note 64, at 156-83; B. Mitnick, The Political Economy of Regulation: Creating, Designing and Removing Regulatory Forms (1980); A. Stone, Regulation and Its Alternatives (1982). This elides the choice of substantive standards with the choice of enforcement mechanisms, particularly because there are a variety of substantive standards that can only be enforced by agencies in our system. The somewhat narrower question that focuses directly on the enforcement issue is whether we should choose a court or an agency to enforce a rule that could, in constitutional and practical terms, be assigned to either one.

from the legislature's perspective — an analysis that incorporates Kelsen's basic insight that in a regime of positive law, all judicial authority results from a grant of jurisdiction by the legislature.[66]

If the courts are chosen as the means of enforcement, the discussion will tend to converge with existing scholarship. Nonetheless, the questions will be asked from a different perspective. How should the legislature allocate the burden of proof in order to achieve certain goals? Should it authorize attorneys' fees or punitive damages? Should it create per se violations? These questions are reasonably familiar, but they are being viewed from the opposite side. The scholar would be addressing the legislator, and recommending ways to implement its goals, rather than addressing the judge, and recommending ways to understand the legislature.

This bears directly on the question of statutory interpretation. In prescriptive scholarship, the scholar must generally address one decisionmaker, as a rational or quasi-rational audience, and treat other decisionmakers as external forces. The legal literature on statutory interpretation, like most other legal literature, speaks to the judge and treats the legislature as an outside force whose goals and meaning must be guessed at, assumed, or counterfactually constructed.[67] The new approach addresses the legislature and treats the judiciary as an outside force. The question in that case is how to draft a statute that will be interpreted by the courts in the manner one desires.[68] This is

66. *See* H. KELSEN, *supra* note 41, at 274-78; *see also* J. RAZ, THE CONCEPT OF A LEGAL SYSTEM (2d ed. 1980). Whether there is a higher law is not directly relevant, in part because we have codified our higher law in a positive albeit general form, but mainly because that higher law would not preclude the legislature from deciding whether to preserve or displace common law. In other words, Kelsen accurately describes the structure of a modern state, even if he fails to provide a satisfactory theory of law.

67. For example, Cass Sunstein's recent discussion begins with the modern approach to interpretation:

> The meaning of a statute inevitably depends on the precepts with which interpreters approach its text. Statutes do not have pre-interpretive meanings, and the process of interpretation requires courts to draw on background principles. These principles are usually not "in" any authoritative enactment but instead are drawn from the particular context and, more generally, from the legal culture. Disagreements about meaning often turn not on statutory terms "themselves," but instead on the appropriate interpretive principles.

Sunstein, *supra* note 29, at 411-12 (footnote omitted). This approach was originally developed with respect to literary or religious texts whose origins lie in the remote and, at some level, incomprehensible past. *See* R. PALMER, HERMENEUTICS 33-40, 75-83 (1969). That is not a defect of Sunstein's analysis; it is an inevitable attribute of any work that addresses the interpreter, whether judge, reader, or stage director, rather than the creator.

68. From this perspective, Sunstein's insight in the previous note might be restated as follows:

> The effect of a statute inevitably depends on the precepts with which subsequent interpreters approach its text. Statutes do not have inevitable effects, because the process of interpretation permits courts to draw on background principles. These principles cannot be prescribed by the legislature but instead will unavoidably be drawn from the particular context of the interpreter, and more generally, from the legal culture of a future time. The interpret-

not an easy question, because of the inherent uncertainty of language, the political differences between courts and legislatures, the need for flexibility as circumstances change, and a variety of other factors. But a responsible legislator must address this question, and it merits a developed theory.

If the legislature chooses an administrative agency as the means of enforcement — a situation that is increasingly the norm — the issues multiply in their complexity and their unfamiliarity. Unlike courts, which are generally just given instructions by the legislature, agencies are frequently created or restructured by a regulatory statute. Even if the existing administrative structure is retained, the legislature has many more options when it assigns enforcement to an agency, the most notable being reliance on the agency's rulemaking power. The legislature can choose to rely heavily on this power by drafting a statute that consists of a few hortatory declarations, or it can choose to preclude this power, either directly or by drafting rules of crushing specificity, or it can choose any intermediate position. Legal scholarship contains a number of articles discussing whether courts should hold the first type of enactment void,[69] but it offers little guidance about which type is the best means of implementing social policy. This is a major task for the New Public Law.[70]

Another set of questions involves administrative strategies. When agencies issue regulations, they are also creating law as a means of implementing social policies. Many of the questions that apply to legislation apply to these regulations as well. But agencies combine enforcement activities with rulemaking, so another range of questions arises. For example, should the agency strive for full compliance, should it single out the worst offenders, or should it select examples at

ers will disagree about the meaning of the statutory terms themselves because of differences in their interpretive principles.

The term "effect" has been substituted for "meaning" in the first and second sentences because texts almost always have meaning for their creators; the problem is that the creators cannot control the reader's construction of meanings, although the construction is based upon the text, and determines the effect of the text's creation.

69. *See, e.g.*, Farina, *Statutory Interpretation and the Balance of Power in the Administration State*, 89 COLUM. L. REV. 452, 476-88 (1989); Merrill, *Standards — A Safeguard for the Exercise of Delegated Power*, 47 NEB. L. REV. 469 (1968); Schoenbrod, *The Delegation Doctrine: Could the Court Give It Substance?* 83 MICH. L. REV. 1223 (1985); Schwartz, *Of Administrators and Philosopher-Kings: The Republic, the Laws, and Delegations of Power*, 72 NW. U. L. REV. 443 (1977).

70. For some rare examples, see Diver, *supra* note 64; Ehrlich & Posner, *supra* note 63.

random?[71] Should it mediate, educate, or punish?[72] Should it rely on an hierarchical or decentralized structure? These decisions may not seem like law, but they can be prescribed by administrative rules, or even by legislation. Presently, they count as law only from the conceptual perspective of legislators and administrators. They do not embody general, transcultural principles, but simply implement a policy goal. If scholars are to address these decisionmakers, they need to conceptualize law in these terms.

A second feature of the New Public Law scholarship is a comprehensive or global approach, derived from the frequency of a similar approach in the legislative and administrative realm. Because legislators and administrators are not limited to case-by-case adjudication, they can adopt as broad a perspective as they choose, dealing with an entire area, or with a series of related (or even unrelated) areas. Legal scholars can begin by discussing how broad such perspectives should be. But more importantly, they must adopt a similar perspective and speak to the concerns of legislators or administrators. From the higher altitudes at which these decisionmakers sometimes operate, scholars can survey an entire subject area, not on a case-by-case basis, but in terms of general, long range plans. They can anticipate issues, telling decisionmakers which are likely to arise, instead of responding to those that have arisen and have been addressed by a decided case. They can attempt to develop comprehensive plans, rather than discerning general patterns from preexisting legal events. In short, they can adopt the legislature's basic temporal orientation toward the future, in place of the judiciary's orientation toward the past.

Underlying this is a basic institutional difference between the two groups of decisionmakers. Judges do not initiate the cases they decide; where they have some flexibility, they are generally in the position of responding to the issues brought to them by adversary parties. Legislators and administrators are subject to no such constraint. While they sometimes act in response to the importuning of interest groups,

71. The pathbreaking work in identifying these issues, within the context of legal scholarship, was K. DAVIS, DISCRETIONARY JUSTICE (1969). Davis's view is that the legislature should constrain discretion in the enforcement process, in the interest of justice and political accountability. His moral outrage at an inevitable situation, however, obscures most of the interesting questions. The inquiry has been continued by political scientists. *See, e.g.*, E. BARDACH & R. KAGAN, GOING BY THE BOOK, THE PROBLEM OF REGULATORY UNREASONABLENESS (1982); M. BROWN, WORKING THE STREET 21-36 (1988); Scholz, *Discretion and Enforcement Efficiency: Problems of Complexity, Contingency, and Corruption*, in ADMINISTRATIVE DISCRETION AND PUBLIC POLICY IMPLEMENTATION 145 (D. Shumavon & H. Hibbeln eds. 1986).

72. The use of mediation as a tool has received some attention. *See* Koch & Martin, *FTC Rulemaking Through Negotiation*, 61 N.C. L. REV. 275 (1983); Comment, *Negotiated Rulemaking: An Analysis of the Administrative Issues and Concerns Associated with Congressional Attempts to Codify a Negotiated Rulemaking Statute*, 4 ADMIN. L.J. 227 (1990).

they must necessarily choose among a vast array of such importunings. They cannot possibly respond to every claim that is cognizable in their terms, as the judiciary does. Moreover, legislators and administrators often show considerable initiative, the President's legislative program being the obvious example. The New Public Law scholarship must display similar initiative, because of its need to frame prescriptions and because of the conceptual model of its audience. It must anticipate issues, and propose statutory or administrative solutions, rather than responding to events and recommending alternative judicial reasoning.

The thinking process, the mode of reasoning, of the New Public Law scholarship is different as well. In framing recommendations, scholars are not searching for solutions which are intellectually coherent with a pattern of previous decisions, but for solutions that effectively achieved specific goals. This reorientation is generated by the shift from analogical to instrumental thinking that characterizes modern legislative and administrative decisionmakers. When addressing these decisionmakers, scholars should not treat prior enactments as authority, but rather as a source of data. The crucial question is to determine what worked in the past, why it worked, and whether it can be improved; or alternatively, what failed in the past, why it failed, and whether it can be avoided.

Legislators and administrators, after all, are decisionmakers who are explicitly authorized to change the law. In fact, the ideal way for them to fulfill their responsibilities may be to review regularly the enactments of their predecessors, and determine which ones should be altered or abolished. Sunsetting provisions certainly have this goal in mind.[73] Whether or not they are an effective device, and how methodical and comprehensive the review should be, are themselves important questions for legal scholars. At a less general level, these questions indicate a general attitude toward substantive law. The scholar's task, in large measure, is to carry out this review of existing legislation. Government decisionmakers must respond to crises, their operational responsibilities, the complex dynamics of their institutional setting and the blizzard of political demands in which they live; they therefore are rarely able to review existing legislation in a precise and thoughtful manner. But scholars can do so, and they can then

73. For discussions in legal literature, see G. CALABRESI, *supra* note 29, at 59-65; Adams, *Sunset: A Proposal for Accountable Government,* 28 ADMIN. L. REV. 511 (1976); Note, *Zero-Base Sunset Review,* 14 HARV. J. ON LEGIS. 505 (1977). A much more extensive discussion appears in *Sunset Act of 1977, Hearings Before the Subcomm. on Intergovernmental Relations of the Senate Comm. on Governmental Affairs,* 95th Cong., 1st Sess. (1977).

bring significant problems or possibilities to the decisionmakers' attention. This review is necessarily structured by a search for effective social policy, not for an intellectually coherent legal structure.

A somewhat deeper way the New Public Law scholarship involves a different mode of argument is the shift from process justification to cause-and-result justification. Process justification has been central to legal scholarship for so long that it seems like the essence of the discipline, the sinews of any legal argument. In fact, it soon appears rather quaint when one is addressing a legislator or administrator. These decisionmakers respond to perceived problems in the operation of existing law, not to the lack of coherence in these laws, or their failure to reflect a general principle. They judge their efforts by the effects produced. To speak to them, legal scholars need to employ the same mode of analysis. This not only means discussing causes and results, but arguing in terms of these phenomena.

All of the foregoing attributes of the New Public Law scholarship are derived from the structure of that scholarship, that is, its choice of audience and topic. A further question is whether this scholarship requires or implies any particular methodology. While this question must in some sense be answered by time, the approach is general enough to include a number of existing methodologies, such as critical legal studies and law and economics. In fact, one might argue that these methodologies are intrinsically more congenial to the New Public Law, and have been applied to judicial decisions at the expense of their true analytic capabilities. Hence, the new legal scholarship is at least as capacious as the old one, and probably more so. The only methodology that would be excluded would be the one that was peculiar to traditional scholarship, that is, the doctrinal analysis of legal cases. In its place would be a new vocabulary of government planning and strategy on which the varied insights of existing intellectual movements could be brought to bear.

VII. The New Public Law Scholarship: An Example

In 1989, Congress enacted and the President approved the Financial Institutions Reform, Recovery and Enforcement Act, or FIRREA.[74] The purpose of this legislation is to resolve the savings-and-loan crisis, a social debacle consisting of the failure of 500 banking institutions, the insolvency of a federal insurance fund (the FSLIC), and a remaining exposure that is variously estimated at $100 to $500

74. Pub. L. No. 101-73, 103 Stat. 183 (1989) (codified in scattered sections of 12 & 15 U.S.C.).

billion.[75] FIRREA is a complex statute, which is not easily summarized. In essence, it reorganizes the entire regulatory structure of the savings-and-loan, or thrift, industry, establishes an independently funded agency to administer failed institutions (the Resolution Trust Corporation), places primary regulation of surviving savings and loans in an office within the Treasury Department (the Office of Thrift Supervision), confers extensive new enforcement powers on these agencies, including cease and desist orders, civil penalties, and criminal penalties, and imposes a range of substantive regulations on the surviving savings-and-loan institutions.

Prior to the enactment of FIRREA, virtually nothing about the statute had appeared in legal literature, although the issue had been brewing for at least a decade.[76] Since then, a few pieces have been published in practitioner-oriented journals, like the *Business Lawyer*, but little else has appeared.[77] This apparent lack of interest clearly does not stem from FIRREA's unimportance. The Act represents a major reorganization of the financial services industry, involves sums of Department of Defense proportions, and may well determine whether we reach the end of this millennium without a fiscal Armageddon. In the most pragmatic terms, FIRREA will occupy a great deal of the time of a great many lawyers. A significant proportion of the attorneys in major and midsize firms will have some contact with it, and a sizable number will be devoting their lives to it for the next five or ten years. In all likelihood, the graduates of leading law schools will spend more time on FIRREA in the near future than they will spend on the entirety of tort law.

The lack of legal literature about this statute and its attendant is-

75. *See generally* H.R. REP. No. 54, 101st Cong., 1st Sess., *reprinted in* 1989 U.S. CODE CONG. & ADMIN. NEWS 86; E. KANE, THE S & L INSURANCE MESS: HOW DID IT HAPPEN? 1-22 (1989).

76. The thrift problem has been extensively discussed in the business and economic literatures. *See, e.g.*, F. BALDERSTON, THRIFTS IN CRISIS (1985); R. BRUMBAUGH, THRIFTS UNDER SIEGE (1988); A. CARRON, THE PLIGHT OF THRIFT INSTITUTIONS (1981); N. EICHLER, THE THRIFT DEBACLE (1989); E. KANE, *supra* note 75; E. KANE, THE GATHERING CRISIS IN FEDERAL DEPOSIT INSURANCE (1985); P. PILZER, OTHER PEOPLE'S MONEY: THE INSIDE STORY OF THE S & L MESS (1989).

77. Clark, Murtagh & Corcoran, *Regulation of Savings Associations Under the Financial Institutions Reform, Recovery and Enforcement Act of 1989*, 45 BUS. LAW. 1013 (1990); Gail & Norton, *A Decade's Journey from "Deregulation" to "Supervisory Reregulation": The Financial Institutions Reform, Recovery, and Enforcement Act of 1989*, 45 BUS. LAW. 1103 (1990); Gail, *Highlights of the Financial Institutions Reform, Recovery and Enforcement Act of 1989 (FIRREA): What Foreign Banks Should Know*, 24 INTL. LAW. 225 (1990). One piece appears in a university-sponsored journal: Malloy, *Nothing to Fear but FIRREA Itself: Revising and Reshaping the Enforcement Process of Federal Bank Regulation*, 50 OHIO ST. L.J. 1117 (1989). Professor Malloy teaches at Fordham, Professor Norton at Southern Methodist University; the other authors are practicing attorneys.

sues can more reasonably be explained by legal scholars' belief that it lacks intellectual interest. FIRREA does not embody any general principles of law, nor does it contain any well-structured legal arguments. It is a law, in common parlance, but it does not involve any of the characteristics that most legal scholars recognize as law. This will change, of course, once the statute is construed by the courts; while statutory interpretation does not partake of common law's transcendental imagery, it at least displays the mode of reasoning that is familiar, significant, and interesting to legal scholars. And should any portion of the statute — even a small, insignificant portion — be declared unconstitutional, an ecstatic outpouring of scholarly attention is certain to occur.

From the perspective of the New Public Law scholarship, however, FIRREA is a fascinating and immensely significant study, as significant to legal scholarship as it is to the nation in general. The statute can be seen as an instrumentality for implementing public policy, in particular, the policy of resolving the savings-and-loan crisis and avoiding economic catastrophe. This raises a number of major questions. For example, is an independent and independently funded agency like the Reconstruction Trust Company the best way to administer failed savings and loans? This points to a theory about the kind of governmental organizations that most effectively carry out specific types of tasks. More generally, should administration of this statute have been divided up among a series of new agencies, new units, and preexisting agencies, as opposed to being unified in one of the three (and, if so, which one)? Another major question is whether the panoply of enforcement mechanisms in the statutes will provide effective supervision of the industry. The previous regime has been criticized as overly timid,[78] but the source of this timidity is uncertain, so we do not know whether FIRREA simply presses a few more weapons into the trembling hands of an inveterate poltroon. Alternatively, perhaps the previous regime was too aggressive and scared away good managers and good money with its intemperance. FIRREA also suggests a variety of more substantive questions: for example, are capital adequacy standards the best way to avoid risk, or should we rely on some market mechanism by reducing deposit insurance? All these questions emerge from shifting the perspective to view law as a means of implementing public policy.

The New Public Law would also shift the temporal horizon of the scholarship. For the past ten years, at the very least, everyone in-

78. *See, e.g.,* E. KANE, *supra* note 75, at 63-120.

volved in the financial services industry has anticipated a crisis of some sort.[79] If legal scholars had abandoned the incremental approach that characterizes judicial reasoning, they might have focused on the problem as it developed, and proposed legislative or administrative solutions at that time. These proposals would then have been available to both public decisionmakers and the scholarly community when FIRREA was being debated, just as scholars' proposals about judicial decisionmaking are available to judges when the next related case is being decided. Instead, legal scholars said virtually nothing about FIRREA when all the major decisions were being made, and their contributions will necessarily be limited to secondary adjustments and interpretations of the statute now that it has been enacted.

The change involved is conceptual, as well as temporal. FIRREA, like most modern lawmaking, is social planning; it looks toward the future, and attempts to structure and control a part of our society in a coordinated way. Congress is not declaring a right and establishing a passive enforcement mechanism that will adjudicate people's claim to that right. It is empowering an administrative agency — actually a group of agencies — and instructing them to implement a plan. For legal scholars to participate in this process of modern lawmaking, either by advancing new proposals or by criticizing existing ones, they must think in terms of social planning. Any number of important legal articles could have been written about the way to design a savings-and-loan statute, and the way to capture specific plans in legal language, but the whole issue lies beyond the conceptual horizon of most existing legal scholarship.

In discussing and analyzing these plans, scholars could make use of prior law, not as analogy or precedent, but as a source of data. Congress has been regulating parts of the financial services industry for over a century,[80] and regulating the thrift industry in a comprehensive fashion for nearly half a century.[81] As a result of these efforts, a vast amount of information is available about the effectiveness of various statutory provisions, from their general concept to their specific language. To make use of this information, prior statutes must be re-

79. The financial issues were all fully canvassed by Carron in 1981, *see* A. CARRON, *supra* note 76; indeed, they were already quite familiar to policymakers at that time. *See* S. Rep. No 378, 96th Cong., 2d Sess. 3-5, *reprinted in* 1980 U.S. CONG. & ADMIN. NEWS 238-40 (committee report accompanying the Depository Institutions Deregulation and Monetary Control Act of 1980, P.L. 96-221, 94 Stat. 732).

80. The oldest of the existing regulatory statutes is the National Bank Act, ch. 106, 13 Stat. 99 (1864) (codified as amended at 12 U.S.C. § 1-216).

81. Federal Home Loan Bank Act, ch. 522, 47 Stat. 725 (1932) (codified as amended at 12 U.S.C. §§ 1421-1449); National Housing Act, ch. 847, 48 Stat. 1246 (1934) (codified as amended in scattered sections of 12 U.S.C.).

garded as a source of data, not as a source of authority. Congress has plenary authority to replace these statutes; indeed, given the seriousness of the crisis, it probably has a responsibility to do so. But it has an equal responsibility to learn from past experience; we should not make the same mistakes in 1989 that we made in 1980, 1965, or 1933.

Had legal scholars found the savings-and-loan crisis to present important issues, had they addressed it in planning terms, and had they used prior law as a source of data, they would have been in a position to advance the kinds of recommendations to which prescriptive scholarship aspires. To justify these recommendations, in a way that would make sense to the decisionmakers who are being addressed, at least in theory, these proposals would need to be justified in terms of their results.

The arguments that legal scholars would advance to justify their recommendations are reasonably apparent. If they recommend a particular regulatory structure, they must argue for it in terms of its ability to manage failed savings and loans, while avoiding further failures. An argument for a comprehensive agency or for the subordination of all the different agencies to the Treasury Department or the President would need to be justified in these terms; a traditional approach, arguing that these solutions could be derived from our theory of government, would seem chimerical to public policymakers. The same is true for the recommendation of various enforcement mechanisms. While familiar question about constitutional and moral constraints undoubtedly limit what a government agency can do, those constraints only establish outer boundaries. The choices made within those boundaries must be justified by their real world effects.

VIII. Can Legal Scholars Do It?

The major objection raised in law schools to the claim that legal scholarship must change is not conceptual, but pragmatic. One component of this objection involves the training and background of legal scholars: "Other academics are trained to do *X;* we would just be amateurs, dabbling in areas that possess a sophisticated theory of their own, and that demand specialized, rigorous training."[82] Legal scholars also assert they lack the institutional resources needed for this new approach to law, such as grants, graduate students, and access to data processing faculties.[83] Finally, if legal scholars develop a new ap-

82. *See, e.g.,* Friedman, *The Future of Law and Social Sciences Research,* 52 N.C. L. Rev. 1068 (1974); Schuck, *Why Don't Law Professors Do More Empirical Research?,* 39 J. Legal Educ. 323 (1989).

83. *See, e.g.,* Friedman, *The Law and Society Movement,* 38 Stan. L. Rev. 763, 774-79

proach directed to legislators and administrators, its intended audience may not pay attention and the entire effort will be fruitless.

The first two of these concerns reflect a misunderstanding of the New Public Law. As existing examples of New Public Law scholarship suggest, the idea is not to transform legal scholarship into public policy or social science, but to develop a new approach based on a new conception of law. Although the relationship between law and other disciplines would change, the structure of legal academics — the training and institutional organization — would remain.[84] In other words, the New Public Law is not an abandonment of the field, but a reinterpretation of it to enable it to fulfill its self-declared purposes.

This can be seen most clearly by examining the relationship of the New Public Law scholarship to other fields, most notably public policy and social science. This scholarship, which focuses on planning and treats law as an instrumentality for achieving defined purposes, certainly overlaps substantially with public policy research.[85] But even if one insists on maintaining the distinction between law and policy, a vast field remains for legal scholars to occupy. Once the policy analysis is complete, a means must be found to implement the choice that the analysis has generated. In the regulatory area, legislatures act largely by passing laws, and administrators often act by passing regulations. This means more than simply stating the policy in legal language. It involves what might be called the fine structure of the statute or regulation, the myriad of decisions that must be made below the level of the basic policy choice. Many of the questions discussed above would be included in this category — the choice of enforcement

(1986); Schuck, *supra* note 82; Trubek, *A Strategy for Legal Studies: Getting Bok to Work*, 33 J. LEGAL EDUC. 586, 587-89 (1983); Trubek, *The Place of Law and Social Science in the Structure of Legal Education*, 35 J. LEGAL EDUC. 483, 484 (1985) [hereinafter Trubek, *The Place of Law and Social Science*].

84. Undoubtedly, the number of applicants with advanced degrees in other fields, and the attractiveness of such applicants to law school admissions committees, will increase. This is an incremental change, however, and affects the tone of the law school, rather than altering its structure.

85. In fact, there is probably no intellectually meaningful argument for distinguishing between these fields in the first place. The first law schools to appear on university campuses were pure trade schools staffed by practicing lawyers, and functioned as a substitute for apprenticeship. *See* R. STEVENS, *supra* note 1, at 7-10. The theoretical study of law and the incorporation of public policy perspectives was far removed from these institutions. When law schools developed as true university departments, with a faculty consisting of full-time academics, there were several attempts to integrate professional training for private practice with policy analysis. *See id.* at 39-42; W. CHASE, *supra* note 1, at 46-59. These efforts seemed to have foundered on a variety of institutional realities, but also on a formalist conception of law that excluded public policy. That conception was persuasive at the time but no one believes it any more. *See* B. ACKERMAN, *supra* note 25, at 6-22.

mechanisms, the design of new mechanisms, the nature of the instructions given to those entities, and so forth.

These problems are preeminently legal questions; to the extent that legal scholars do not address them, virtually no one will. To be sure, a public policy and political science literature on implementation is developing,[86] but it tends to focus on the administrative level only. More significantly, it represents only one small area within the general scope of these disciplines, whereas it is one of the central questions for the legal field. In general, one might distinguish the elements of a statute or regulation on the basis of its discourse. The policy choice emerges from internal discussions among members of the decisionmaking body; this can reasonably be regarded as the realm of public policy research, if one chooses to preserve that distinction. But once that choice is made, it must be implemented by instructions issued to an enforcement mechanism, whether court or agency. This is legal scholarship's domain, a fact which no one doubts when the enforcement mechanism is a court, as it necessarily was in most premodern statutes. The emphasis on judicial decisionmaking obscured the statute's character as a legislative instruction. In the modern administrative state, the instruction is generally issued to an agency,[87] but it remains a declaration of the law and a subject that legal scholars should address.

The skills we associate with legal training are the ones needed for this purpose. These include a close attention to language, an understanding of the relationship between linguistically stated rules and institutional behaviors, an ability to translate fact situations and other data into a legal framework, an understanding of the relationship between normative or political choices and systems of rules, and an ability to apply general principles to specific situations. Of course, all these skills must be adapted to a new environment. New skills must be acquired, such as a deeper understanding of power relationships and nonjudicial institutions, while some existing skills, such as reasoning from precedent, are no longer needed. But the general range of techniques that would be needed are recognizable as "legal" ones.[88]

86. *See supra* note 35.

87. *See* F. HAYEK, LAW, LEGISLATION AND LIBERTY: RULES AND ORDER 124-44 (1973); T. LOWI, THE END OF LIBERALISM 105-07 (2d ed. 1979); Diver, *supra* note 64, at 76-77; Rubin, *Law and Legislation in the Administrative State*, 89 COLUM. L. REV. 369, 375-80 (1989).

88. These skills, it should be noted, are not those associated with "skills training," but those involved in the study and practice of law as a totality. Skills training involves what Habermas refers to as strategic action, that is, action designed to affect people's behavior (to get them to do what the actor wants), 1 J. HABERMAS, *supra* note 38 at 273-337. For a general description of skills training, see Grossman, *Clinical Legal Education: History and Diagnosis*, 26 J. LEGAL EDUC. 162 (1974); *see also* Gaubatz, *Moot Court in the Modern Law School*, 31 J. LEGAL EDUC.

In fact, the New Public Law could aspire to the heroic stance that legal academics adopted in the formalist era. As the field develops, scholars should be able to articulate general theories covering large segments of their subject area. One can imagine a theory about when private causes of action are effective, what kinds of agencies can implement specific programs, how statutory language can be used to control adjudicatory behavior, or which enforcement strategies an agency should use in particular circumstances. We might even see a revival of the treatise, with its comprehensive treatment of recognizable divisions within the general area of study. Part of the reason treatises flourished was that legal scholars were occupying and organizing new territory — new in the sense that it had not been previously discussed within the framework of their formalist theory. The New Public Law might serve as the impetus for similarly comprehensive efforts.

The same can be said about the relationship of legal scholarship to social science. Clearly, many of the tasks involved in New Public Law scholarship call for insights and techniques from social science disciplines. The structure of enforcement mechanisms, for example, must be informed by political science analysis of these institutions. Other aspects of this scholarship would depend even more heavily on social science. To use prior law as a source of data, one must rely on studies of the law's effects; while such studies sometimes appear in legal literature, they are more commonly performed by political scientists, economists, and sociologists, using techniques that are characteristic of those fields. Similarly, the cause-and-result justification of recommendations would depend upon these fields. Because the prediction of results requires extrapolation from existing data, using models, controlled experiments, attitude surveys, and the like, the methodological component of this effort is likely to be fairly complex.

While all this social science can appear to be a daunting prospect to academics whose training consisted of reading appellate decisions, law professors, in theory, are able to perform social science studies. Some have,[89] and most probably could with a combination of self-training, collaborative efforts, and the collegial assistance generally available on a university campus.[90] But the essential task of legal

87 (1981). Legal skills are those involved in any legal activity including policymaking (instrumental action in Habermas' terminology) and the general effort to understand a legal system (hermeneutic action).

89. For a few examples, see D. Chambers, Making Fathers Pay: The Enforcement of Child Support (1979); G. Hawkins & F. Zimring: Deterrence: The Legal Threat in Crime Control (1973); M. Lawrence, J. Snortum & F. Zimring, Social Control of the Drinking Driver (1988).

90. In addition, empirical research need not consist of technical studies and statistical analysis. Simply getting out of the law school and talking to the folks about whom one is generalizing

scholars is not to generate data; rather, it is to make use of data in framing recommendations.[91] Public decisionmakers, many of whom have only legal training, and many of whom have even less, do this all the time in designing laws and regulations. It could thus be considered an inherently legal task, at least in the context of the modern state. Certainly, it is not duplicative of other disciplines. While social scientists are often willing to advance prescriptions based upon their research, they do not often engage in a sustained application of research results to the problem of drafting statutes or regulations.[92] If legal scholars do not pursue this inquiry, it will not be done, which is often the case at present. Such an assignment of responsibility makes sense, for if generating research data is the work of social scientists, determining the meaning of that data for our problems of governance is the work of the legal community.[93]

The legal scholar, moreover, need not passively receive other people's studies. Legislatures and administrative agencies commission research, and legal scholars could generate needed research as well by suggesting useful lines of inquiry to social scientists. This requires planning — the scholar must identify a problem, sketch a long-term solution, and decide what research is needed to indicate the advisability of that solution. Judicially oriented scholarship is unlikely to frame questions that seem meaningful to social scientists, but New Public Law scholarship would be a different matter. There are also possibilities for collaborative work between social scientists and legal scholars; this would make more sense to both scholars if the temporal structure of their approach were roughly congruent. In the end, legal scholars need to learn to work with social scientists and make use of

can be a valuable source of information and can serve as the basis of important empirical studies. *See, e.g.*, Getman, *Contributions of Empirical Data to Legal Research*, 35 J. LEGAL EDUC. 489 (1985); Trubek, *The Place of Law and Social Science*, *supra* note 83, at 483-84.

91. The failure of prior efforts to incorporate empirical research into legal scholarship is certainly chastening. *See* R. STEVENS, *supra* note 1, at 131-41; Schlegel, *American Legal Realism and Empirical Social Science: The Singular Case of Underhill Moore*, 29 BUFFALO L. REV. 195 (1980). But one problem seems to have been that legal scholars were committed to generating empirical research, rather than to using it. Of course, gathering data without a clear sense of purpose is a quagmire, as Schlegel indicates. But even gathering data with that sense of purpose can be a quagmire for legal scholars, given the institutional realities. *See* Getman, *supra* note 90. The starting point, rather, is to perceive the relevance of empirical research, to use what is available, and to confess ignorance as to the rest (rather than speculating about it, as legal scholars tend to do). Once that point is reached, the legal scholar can consider whether she should undertake the effort to gather the missing data herself.

92. Drafting exemplary statutory or regulatory language is simply not part of social science methodology, even when the work would lead logically to this result from a legal scholar's point of view.

93. *See* M. Galanter, Presentation, "The Future of Law and Social Sciences Research," at Assessment Conference: Developments in Law & Social Sciences Research, 52 N.C. L. REV. 969, 1060 (1974) (real problem with empirical study of law is conceptual, not institutional).

their results, not to transform themselves into members of a different discipline.

The third pragmatic objection to the New Public Law scholarship is that legislators and administrators will not listen to it. We are persuaded that judges listen, that they possess the quality of responsiveness to scholarship that Eisenberg describes. This is partially because the scholars' mode of reasoning is so precisely attuned to their own, but also because we view judges as public-oriented decisionmakers. Legislators and administrators seem more political and less intellectual; more important perhaps, their staffs consist of people other than recent law school graduates. A New Public Law scholarship directing recommendations to them might seem — despite all its modernity and intellectual significance — to be a voice crying in the wilderness.

But just as the first two objections represent a misunderstanding of the New Public Law scholarship, this objection represents a misunderstanding of prescriptive scholarship in general. Of course legislators and administrators will not always, or even often, follow the recommendations of legal scholars. In some cases, they have their own ideas; in others, their actions may well be determined by political considerations. But as stated above, the test of prescriptive scholarship is not whether decisionmakers embrace it as a complete solution to the issues they confront. The test, rather, is whether its orientation serves as a structuring principle for scholarly evaluations of each others' work and thereby provides a framework for the cumulative development of a prescriptive discipline.

Both prescriptive and descriptive scholarship represent efforts to achieve understanding; according to our rules of scholarly discourse, description is an effort to understand the present condition of the subject, and prescription is an effort to understand its potentialities.[94] Because prescription is phrased in terms of concrete recommendations, it may seem purposeless unless those recommendations are acted upon. Yet description is even more remote from action, and we recognize its value in terms of our goal of understanding. Prescription contributes to understanding as well, particularly when we are studying a dynamic

94. This appears to run counter to Habermas' distinction between strategic (or instrumental) discourse and hermeneutic discourse. *See* 1 J. HABERMAS, *supra* note 38, at 284-95. But the crucial question is one of intentionality. Statements framed as a prescription can be hermeneutic (*i.e.*, directed toward understanding) if they are intended and structured to achieve an understanding of the proper course of action, that is, an autonomous agreement by the other party that the recommended course of action is desirable. In fact, given the phenomenological perspective that lies at the base of Habermas' approach, the inherent intentionality of all thought would tend to efface any normative distinction between prescription and description, provided that both are intended to reach an autonomous, mutual agreement, rather than using the recipient of the communication as a means to an end.

subject that is shaped by social action. Thus, a scholarly discourse that enables us to frame prescriptions for ordinary governmental action is not only a means of improving the specific actions discussed, but a means of understanding government in general. This general understanding may in turn enable us to improve the governmental process, in ways that are quite distinct from the adoption of specific scholarly prescriptions.

Real-world influence is satisfying, however, and most legal scholars would probably be loath to abandon it as a potential reward or validation of their work. But they do not need to do so; the idea that legislators or administrators are deaf to scholarly arguments, while judges attend to them, misconceives the way in which scholarly ideas exercise practical effects. To expect that the scholar will frame a recommendation and some government official, whether judge or legislator, will then implement it in the precise form in which it was advanced is a chimera spawned by a conception of authority, not influence. That sort of immediate and complete response is what superiors expect from their subordinates, or better still, what parents expect from their children: "When I say that the market is the best mechanism for setting utility rates, I expect you to deregulate at once, and I don't want you fooling around with political considerations or alternative policies!" Even superiors and parents often find their expectations frustrated; anyone who defines scholarly influence in terms of an equivalent level of obedience will be more frustrated still and will probably conclude that no such influence exists. In fact, the mechanism of influence is more varied and less determinate. In some cases recommendations create general moods, from which decisionmakers distill approaches to specific problems. Or these recommendations insinuate themselves into the decisionmaker's world view, to reappear in forms that neither the decisionmaker nor the scholar could predict. They may act as catalysts, clarifying and mobilizing thoughts that the decisionmakers have long possessed, but never acted on. Or they may shape decisions that have already been made, providing direction and detail.

Because of the complexity and subtlety of this process, scholarly influence can readily coexist with political motivation. To be influenced by scholars, legislators need not be Platonic guardians. If they give some thought to the public interest, if they sometimes base their actions on their sense of what is best for the nation rather than for themselves, they will be open to the variety of channels through which scholars can address them.[95] Moreover, scholarly influence may not even require this dilute form of explicit public interest. The way decisionmakers construct their conceptions of political advantage may itself provide a channel for prescriptive discourse. Decisionmakers may believe that they can maximize their chance for reelection or reappointment by simply following the express commands of special interest groups, but they may also believe that they will obtain political advantage by achieving the results those groups desire. Once political advantage is constructed in this way, policy-based scholarship will seem relevant, however indirectly. Going further, once a body of prescriptive scholarship exists, it may influence the legislators' estimation of political advantage.

IX. Is It Law?

One further aspect of the New Public Law scholarship that produces a lurking sense of unease is whether or not such scholarship really involves "law." The depth of legal scholars' commitment to a judicial orientation suggests that there is something definitional about that orientation, something that goes beyond a conscious choice of topic to one's self-image as an academic. The reason biologists ignore nature poetry in their scholarly work is not because they regard poetry as invalid; if asked, they would answer that poetry is simply not "biology." The scholarly aversion to addressing legislators and administrators may spring from similar sources. It is not easy to respond to this concern, because it relies on a somewhat elusive conception of law. For present purposes, an answer can be provided by distinguishing three possible meanings of the term: that law is a system for controlling people, specifically officials who wield state power; that law is a conceptual system with an inherent logic; and that law is a moral system, embodying widely held or transcendental values. This article will conclude by briefly considering whether the New Public Law qualifies as "law" according to each of these three meanings.

One of the great benefits of law is the rule of law, and a principal virtue of a rule of law is the control it exercises over government officials. When we speak of our society as one of laws, we are not thinking of its ability to manage the economy or to preserve public order,

95. Public choice theory asserts that legislators and administrators never adopt this perspective, *see, e.g.,* M. Fiorina, Congress: Keystone of the Washington Establishment (1977); D. Mayhew, Congress: The Electoral Connection (1974); Peltzman, *Toward a More General Theory of Regulation,* 19 J.L. & Econ. 211 (1976). But most observers take the view that these officials respond to a variety of motivations. *See, e.g.,* R. Fenno, Congressmen in Committees (1973); J. Kingdon, Agendas, Alternatives and Public Policies (1984); A. Maass, Congress and the Common Good (1983); W. Muir, Legislature (1982).

but of the controls that are imposed on power-holding individuals.[96] This is an instrumental concept of law; the argument is that law serves as the best means for achieving equity or justice.

This view of law explains legal scholars' concern with the judiciary for two different reasons. First, the judiciary is assigned the task of imposing law on other branches of government. If an agency oversteps its jurisdiction, if an administrator cancels peoples' benefits because he thinks they are ugly, if a legislature curries electoral favor by infringing on constitutional rights, the courts are supposed to intercede and say: "We forbid you to do this because it violates the law." Second, the judiciary, in this supervisory role, and in the other roles such as adjudicating between private parties, is itself constrained by law. Judges (have no popular mandate and no supervisors besides other judges; their actions are constrained only by the law itself and it is only through fealty to law that they avoid the charge of uncontrolled discretion. These two legal roles are related, of course; judges are the chosen agent to impose the law on others because they themselves are bound by it in an immediate and unalloyed manner.

Legislators and administrators, one might argue, are of less concern to legal scholars because they are supervised by judges, and because their own actions, while they remain within judicially established boundaries of lawfulness, are controlled by popular mandates, not by law. This was a persuasive argument in 1840, but, as a practical matter, it ignores the reality of the administrative state. The vast bureaucratic apparatus of our modern state has obliterated Montesquieu's neat categories of governmental functions. Judicial supervision remains important, but it is no longer adequate to ensure that powerful government officials obey the law. These officials are too numerous, their tasks are too technical and their ongoing responsibilities too comprehensive to be controlled by a few hundred law-trained judges. Under FIRREA, for example, small armies of administrators, in at least four major administrative agencies, will wield extensive power over savings-and-loan institutions, including the power to restructure or eradicate these institutions within relatively brief periods of time. The federal judiciary will not be able to ensure the lawfulness of this enterprise in any realistic sense. In addition, the multiple layers of the bureaucratic system are too thick to be controlled by elected officials. FIRREA mandates that the ongoing administration of savings-and-loan institutions be moved from an independent agency to the Treasury Department. This is congruent with formalist views

96. *See* F. HAYEK, *supra* note 87, at 3-5, 24-31; T. LOWI, *supra* note 87, at 92-129.

that independent agencies are unconstitutional, but the practical difference it makes in terms of popular control is questionable; the only elected official with direct authority over the numerous operations-level administrators under the new organization will be the President of the United States.

The use of law as a means of controlling government officials thus becomes an argument for a New Public Law, not against it. If we want the rule of law, we must secure it through recommendations to legislators and administrators. We must ensure equity and justice by the way we design statutes and the way we structure our administrative system, not through eighteenth-century bromides about judges and elections. Law is to be found in the administrative mechanisms that control the discretion of operations-level personnel, in the resolution of turf battles between administrative agencies, in the heavy, three-ring binders that contain the operations manuals for a veritable infinity of governmental functions, and in the day-to-day practices of several million federal and state employees sitting at metal desks behind shoulder-high acoustic partitions. Unless scholars have a legal theory that articulates controls at this mundane level, they cannot contribute fully to establishing the rule of law.

As a conceptual system, the appeal of judicial lawmaking is its intellectual coherence. Common law fits together in a fashion which permits deductive arguments at a preempirical level. Other areas, including constitutional law, at least aspire to this same coherence and thus encourage and respond to similarly theoretical arguments. Assessing this perceived coherence is a complex task, but one cannot deny its appeal.

The response here is fairly obvious however. Legal scholarship cannot choose its topics on the basis of their aesthetic qualities unless it is willing to be condemned to a subsidiary role. There are undoubtedly regularities in the legislative and administrative realm, but they are approximate, empirically grounded ones, not the celestial music of the formalist's dreams. That may make the field less entrancing, but it does not make it any less important. Our society is too pragmatic, and the demands of modern governance are too insistent, for us to abandon intellectual inquiry into a field because of the unappetizing quality of the results.

Going further, our society's dominant intellectual system is heavily empirical in its designation of value. We have an independent, empirically based set of criteria for assigning significance to particular inquiries or fields, and we then seek whatever regularities or truths (as we define them) we can discover about each field, on the basis of our operative methodologies. We do not begin with a methodological definition of value, which then confers significance on those fields to which it can be applied. Thus, it is intellectually indefensible for legal scholars to begin with an a priori definition of truth, and then restrict their inquiries to fields where those truths can be observed. Undoubtedly, our judgments of significance are theory-laden, but the theory is self-consciously different from our systems of evaluation. We can say, quite definitively, that the administrative system is important because of its impact on society. It is then incumbent upon scholars to develop the best theories, both descriptive and prescriptive, for that system, even if those theories seem less satisfactory than those in other fields.

Finally, there is the moral component of law. Common law and other judicially developed areas seem to express a normative perspective which statutes and administrative regulations lack.[97] To the extent that legal scholarship constitutes an exploration of those norms, a New Public Law would lie beyond its boundaries.[98] Of course, we would want to impose our norms on the administrative state, but that process could only be implemented by morally cognizant actors, in other words, the judiciary. This sensibility is probably one reason why legal scholars tend to regard the administrative system through judicial eyes.

One difficulty here involves the status of the norms that purportedly inform judicial decisionmaking. If these norms are regarded as deontological, one would need some moral theory that would generate

97. The most forceful modern exponent of this view is Ronald Dworkin. As a consequence, he develops a normatively based theory of law derived almost exclusively from judicial decisionmaking. *See* Dworkin, *supra* note 42. In R. DWORKIN, LAW'S EMPIRE (1986), he does discuss legislation, but he seems to view it as a secondary illustration of his judicially based model.

98. In discussing the law-and-society movement, Lawrence Friedman argues that one can readily adopt a "scientific" or social science approach to an inherently "nonscientific" topic, that is, the legal scholar can study normative systems, just as sociologists of religion study religious beliefs. Friedman, *supra* note 83, at 764-66. Epistemologically, the point is certainly true, if only because there is probably no area, including astronomy, particle physics, or animal behavior that is inherently "scientific." The term refers to our attitude toward the subject matter, not some inherent trait that the subject possesses. But at the more specific level, Friedman raises a major problem about the disjunction of methodology and subject matter. If one is studying a normative system, it is possible, of course, to employ social science methods, as Friedman suggests. But the use of these methods distances the scholar from her subject matter. If one regards the subjects as equals, one will tend to join their normative debates, rather than just studying them from afar. This tendency is validated by current thinking about social science methodology. *See, e.g.*, H. GADAMER, *supra* note 17, at 235-74; C. GEERTZ, THE INTERPRETATION OF CULTURES (1973); 1 A. SCHUTZ, COLLECTED PAPERS 48-66 (1962); C. TAYLOR, THE EXPLANATION OF BEHAVIOR (1964); P. WINCH, THE IDEA OF A SOCIAL SCIENCE 72-109 (1958); Winch, *Understanding a Primitive Society*, 1 AM. PHIL. Q. 307 (1964). The social science approach, although theoretically applicable to normative behavior, is much more comfortable when applied to instrumental behavior, that is, when the subjects themselves recognize the methodological relevance of social science to their own activities because they are trying to achieve a goal, rather than express a norm.

them But the norms implicit in the common law, or other judicially established fields, are too specific to be intrinsic elements of any moral theory our society would regard as persuasive.[99] In general, we tend to justify common law norms by instrumental arguments,[100] which raises the possibility that these norms, however homologous in structure with true deontological propositions, are no better at achieving our true, deontological norms such as equality and justice than are a variety of purely instrumental mechanisms. To redeem the deontological status of common law norms, one would need to invoke a second-level norm, to the effect that instrumentalities achieve a preferred status when they are stated in normative discourse. But this too must be related to a general moral theory, or it is nothing more than a bald assertion that common law is superior to statutory law. It is doubtful that we have such a moral theory.

Indeed, the reverse may be the case. Habermas' argument,[101] echoed by critical legal studies scholarship,[102] is that the claim to deontological moral status, like the claim to objective truth, is a form of oppression unless that claim is an aspirational one which explicitly opens itself to hermeneutic evaluation. To be sure, common law has a hermeneutic structure because it abjures unmediated access to its guiding principles in favor of contextualized expression. But that structure does not apply to any second-order claim to the superiority of normative discourse. Indeed, the discourse of social theory and public policy enables us to evaluate the ability of normatively stated propositions to achieve our underlying values. The common law's claim to independent moral status is little more than an assertion of unjustified authority.

In fact, the whole notion that judicial decisionmaking necessarily produces justice, or is more likely to produce justice than some other

99. *See* Summers, *Two Types of Substantive Reasons: The Core of a Theory of Common-Law Justification,* 63 CORNELL L. REV. 707 (1978). Summers provides a list of deontological norms or "rightness reasons" in common law; it includes conscionability, punitive desert, justified reliance, restitution for unjust enrichment, comparative blame, due care, and relational duty. *Id.* at 718-19. These are highly specific legal standards; while Summers may be correct in claiming them as a basis for judicial decisions, it would be hard to view them as a justification for the common law itself.

100. For example, one might justify the norm of "conscionability" by arguing that it achieves equality, or autonomy; it would be hard to claim that we have a moral position that supports conscionability per se. This makes conscionability an instrumentality for achieving some deeper norm, even if Summers is correct in doubting that it can be reduced to a purely instrumental social policy. *See* Summers, *supra* note 99, at 778-82. In fact, many observers feel that there is a fairly strong tendency to justify all judicial decisionmaking in policy terms. *See* Farber & Frickey, *supra* note 24, at 876-77; Strauss, *supra* note 24, at 917.

101. *See* J. HABERMAS, *supra* note 54, at 87-90; J. HABERMAS, *Technical Progress and the Social Life World,* in TOWARD A RATIONAL SOCIETY 50 (1971).

102. M. HOROWITZ, *supra* note 54; R. UNGER, *supra* note 54, at 5-14.

mechanism, is a myth. This is not to say that it is false. It is a myth in the sense that it encapsulated a world-view, and provided a system of meaning through which we could live and, in this case, govern ourselves. Whether this system was desirable or undesirable remains an open question; the point is simply that the judicial approach is not law, but a particular concept of law that was engendered by a particular worldview. It no longer represents a comprehensive worldview, but continues to thrive as a more particularized claim. Some scholars may find this claim to be an adequate justification for focusing their efforts on judicial decisionmaking. For most scholars, however, that focus is a product of habit and conceptual orientation, not a well-developed normative position.

The modern, administrative state has its own myth, its own normative system of meaning. This myth is that the welfare of our society, and the essential, deontological norms in which we believe, are achievable by governmental action. It further claims that the performance of our government can be improved, that there are techniques of governance that can be discovered, adopted, and applied. The New Public Law enables legal scholarship to participate in this enterprise, and indeed, to play an essential role that is not available to any other academic discipline. One can, of course, reject the New Public Law by rejecting this myth. But as the administrative state continues and expands, this rejection will increasingly condemn legal scholars to fatalistic irrelevance or dyspeptic reaction.

[2]

*After Legal Instrumentalism? Strategic Models of Post-regulatory Law**

GUNTHER TEUBNER
European University Institute, Florence

1. Concepts, Models, Theories

1.1 Concepts of law

To construct "Rechtsbegriffe" (concepts of law) raises suspicion in the scientific community of today. When legal theorists dealing with the function of law in the welfare state present ambitious intellectual constructs, such as instrumental versus expressive law (Ziegert, 1975), autonomous versus responsive law (Nonet & Selznick, 1978), substantive versus reflexive law (Teubner, 1982) purposive versus procedural law (Unger, 1976; Wiethoelter, 1982, 1984), they have to face accusations of violating the basic norms of scientific discourse. Special zeal in this policing function is demonstrated by authentic legal sociologists (e.g. Black, 1972; Blankenburg, 1984). In the name of science and with the sharpened tools of modern social science methodology, they charge the construction of "Rechtsbegriffe" with being against the letter and spirit of the canons of social research methodology.

To begin with minor offences, conceptualisations are too vague and operationalisations extremely cloudy. The phenomenon in question is not identified properly. Is the law itself formal, substantive, reflexive? Or is it legal consciousness (of whom? the profession? the law professors?)? Are we dealing with theories about law, general principles behind the law, or with doctrinal construction within the law? Is it law in the books which is supposed to unfold an autonomous logic of development, or is it law in action (Friedman, 1984)? In addition, there is operational negligence: how are broad

*First published as *E.U.I. Working Paper No. 100,* April 1984.

concepts to be translated into precise measurement procedures for empirical research? How is one to decide whether, at a certain historical time, law was formal, or material, or procedural, or reflexive? (Rottleuthner, 1983*a*, p. 15; 1983*b*).

A more grave offence in the eyes of the science police, is that those constructs do not appear to produce theories in the sense of a generalised set of assumptions from which testable hypotheses could be derived. Rather, they represent vague "concepts", ideal–typical configurations of legal elements revealing some obscure sort of legal rationality. Worse, they are too speculative: they seem to be interested in ideas, rather than in facts. How far are they concerned about a methodologically sound empirical proof of their broad generalisations? Worst of all, they are hopelessly normative since they not only analyse a certain potential development in law but argue more or less openly for a conscious realisation of this potential. In short, rather than being good theories about law, these are bad ideologies for lawyers. No question, they serve the function of 'covering the social interests behind such rhetoric by some quasi-distanced meta-theory'. And, if not intentionally, they do this at least subconsciously via a "projection" of normative purposes and similar "pathologies" (Blankenburg, 1984).

Legal theorists in turn might defend their "Rechtsbegriffe" rather defensively. One way is to adapt their constructs as far as possible to meet the rigid standards of social science methodology. Normative elements are either denied or reduced or at least neatly detached from the core analytical–empirical elements. Outright speculations are transformed into more technical hypotheses disciplined by their theoretical derivation. And those hypotheses are formulated so that they can be tested by elaborate empirical methods (see Rottleuthner, 1983*a*, *b*). Unfortunately, as a result of this tailoring the intellectual constructs are pruned of much of their explanatory and creative power.

Another defensive ploy is to play the game of soft science as against hard core science. In this one might protect "Rechtsbegriffe" by referring to the relative weakness of scientific methods in regard to the complexity of their object (Hayek, 1972), to a non-empirical logic of theoretical reasoning (Alexander, 1982), to the inherent normative qualities of scientific research activities (the German Werturteilsstreit), to pragmatism and legal naturalism (Selznick, 1973), or to "anything-goes"-pluralism (Feyerabend, 1975). Unfortunately, in this game of soft science one loses many of the insights of modern theory of science.

1.2 Theory or strategy?

In contrast to the defensive arguments, I will try a more offensive defence of formal, substantive, instrumental, expressive, reflexive, etc. law. In my view, it is a grave error to subsume "Rechtsbegriffe" under the specific logic of scientific inquiry since, in the strict sense they are not scientific theories but are strategic models of law. Strategic models are, at the same time, both more *and* less than scientific theories. They incorporate sociological theories of law but transform these into legal constructions of social reality. In addition they incorporate normative evaluations and strategic considerations. My thesis is *they represent legal "internal models" of law in society, their main function being to use the self-identity of law to produce criteria for its own transformation*. In this sense, legal theory does not only form part of the subject matter of the scientific enquiry, it also forms part of the legal system and thus orients legal practice. What appears, for orthodox legal sociology, to be the private vice of legal theorists might turn out to be their public virtue: the ability of legal theory to produce normative criteria for a conscious self-transformation of the law.

For this interpretation of how and why legal theory constructs its "Rechtsbegriffe" I rely on the following four intellectual traditions.

(1) *General model theory* (Stachowiak, 1965, 1973). This theory develops an understanding of scientific theories, legal doctrines and political action programmes as being the internal models of specific social systems and explains the differences between them in terms of their purpose, function, and social context. The crucial point is that internal models do not function as passive receivers of external information but as active designers of the system's environment. More particularly, this theory permits the distinction between different sub-models within legal models of reality and the analysis of the relations between them (empirical, prospective and operative sub-models) [Teubner, 1978; see below subheading 1.3].

(2) *Cybernetic theory of adaptive systems* (Buckley, 1968). This approach identifies "internal models" of external reality as being the main adaptive mechanisms which map parts of the environmental variations and constraints into the internal organisation as structure. Thus, the evolution of complex adaptive systems to higher levels depends on the successful mapping as a selective matching of system and environment.

(3) *The concept of self-reflection of a social system* (Luhmann, 1981*a*, p. 126; 1981*b*, p. 419). The main function of self-reflection is the use of a system's identity for its self-substitution. Especially, to define legal theory as the law's reflective theory identifies its function for orienting legal transformation.

(4) *Theory of self-referential systems* (Maturana, 1970, 1975; Varela, 1979; Zeleny, 1981; Hejl, 1982*a, b*). Concepts of self-observation and self-consciousness of systems are developed in which systems can be seen to represent themselves and to interact with those representations. In the case of law, this leads to the necessity of a social orientation within the law (in the sense of a consensual description of experience), in which the social

situation of the producers of the description is always presupposed. Consequently it makes no sense to attempt a critique of lawyers' ideologies in the name of science, but rather one should formulate those constructs in terms of competing social models according to the social context in which they were created.

What is the relation of strategic models to scientific theories? As stated above, concepts of formal and substantive law are not to be identified as theories. However, they are not unscientific uncontrolled ideologies as our science police suspects (Blankenburg, 1984). Rather, they incorporate sociological theories and must be compatible with scientific developments. To use a somewhat ironical formulation, they are "more or less empirical theories with practical intentions" (Rottleuthner, 1983*b*). In particular, if the models ascribe certain social functions to law, they have to deal with sociological theories about relations of law and society. If legal "formality", for example, means setting a framework for autonomous economic and social action, further if "materiality" means social guidance through law and "reflexivity" means a generalised form of legal control of social self-regulation (Teubner, 1982, p. 252), then obviously, sociological theories have something to offer.

Nevertheless, it would be erroneous to describe this relation as a contrast between lawyers' ideology and social reality. There is no direct access to social reality, there are only competing system models of reality (Stachowiak, 1973, p. 97). Therefore, one has to see this as a problematic relation between legal and social models of reality; each having its own rightful claims. There is a fundamental difference between the analytical–empirical environment of science, the perception of which is due to more or less severe restrictions, and the world constructions of legal theory which have quite different restrictions.

The same holds true for the dynamics of motives. The motives and value premises of legal constructions of reality are different from those of scientific constructions (e.g. scientific rationality, experience orientation, scientific discourse procedures). That means we have to accept different "cognitive conditionings" (Stachowiak, 1973, p. 97) as premises of operational processes in law and in science. In short, the differences between scientific theories and strategic models refer to the selection of the model variables, the procedures of model construction, the methods of testing, the criteria of certainty and the requirements for success.

This implies complications for the relationship between scientific theories about law and strategic models in law. Historical accounts of legal developments or empirical sociological analyses are not — as some would argue — intrinsically superior to legal conceptualisations of law in society, due to their closer access to social reality. A higher degree of isomorphy (structural and material approximation of model and original) is not yet an argument for the superiority of an alternative model. In particular, science cannot authoritatively define models of external reality. Science produces only hypothetical models which can be tested in their capacity for strategic purposes. Science can serve only as stimulation, not as notification (Habermas, 1976, p. 107).

In a precise sense, therefore, one cannot speak of an incorporation of theories into legal models, or of a legal reception of sociology. Rather, one has to see them as competing constructions of reality which allow for comparison of their relative strength.

It is possible to see this relation as a problem of power: who has the power to force a construction of reality upon others? (Hejl, 1982*a*, p. 320). However, I prefer to see it as a problem of compatibility, of possibilities of analogisation and of mutual learning. Legal history and legal sociology produce results which may be either rejected by lawyers or which may lead to profound changes in legal model construction. At best, there is a productive mutual penetration in the sense of scientific "subsidies" (Luhmann, 1981*a*, p. 134) of grand concepts of law in legal theory. In sum, it is the precarious double character of legal models influenced by internal legal "ideologies of legitimacy" and external sociological "functional analyses" which forms our understanding of specific types of legal rationality.

How are these models to be tested? When we label them as legal "models" and not as theories, we have their action orientation in mind. If their function is to produce criteria for the self-transformation of law, they go beyond scientific theories which are tested by empirical falsification of hypotheses. At the same time they are more than just choices of direction or strategies for the law. We are dealing with competing intellectual constructs that contain different empirical assessments of society, as well as their normative evaluation and subsequent strategic decision. The premises, structures and consequences of all these models can be analysed and discussed. The *experimentum crucis* takes place only when they re-enter social reality. Since there exist no scientifically accepted laws of socio-legal development it is only legal practice which can decide on the success of those competing models. The models can be tested if they are institutionalised and exposed to the competitive markets of scientific discourse, to legal doctrinal controversies, to conflicts of social movements, and to institutional decisions. Experience can be gained only in the form of social experiments in which those legal models are tried out.

1.3 Elements of strategic models of law

What determines the selectivity of such strategic models? In terms of general model theory (Stachowiak, 1965, 1973) models are intentionally defined by three elements:

(1) projective element: models are always representatives of originals which, in turn, may be models themselves;

(2) selective element: models represent in principle only specific attributes of the original;
(3) pragmatic element: models are not defined *per se*; they fulfill their representation function (a) for certain subjects, (b) within a given time interval, and (c) restricted to certain intellectual or factual operations.

The extension of such a concept is extremely wide. By varying and recombining the three elements, however, a meaningful model typology can be formed. This typology ranges from graphical and technical models, via semantic models at different levels, (among which there are even poetical and metaphysical models) to scientific models (theories in the narrower sense) and planning and decision models (Stachowiak, 1973).

Now, it would be too easy to subsume our "grand concepts" of law under one of these model types, e.g. the "socio-normative" model or the "imperative" model (Stachowiak, 1973, p. 234). This would not take into account that in strategic models qualitatively different model operations take place, different in regard to the choice of attributes and the method of their symbolic manipulation. In other words, we are faced with selections in different dimensions which cannot be accommodated within one model type. This suggests that they may be thought of as complex models composed of three sub-models: an empirical, a prospective, and an operative sub-model. Thus, one gets close to the construction of planning models in politics which differ from scientific models in the above-named elements, i.e. projective, selective, and pragmatic elements (Stachowiak, 1973, p. 269). The parallel is obvious. However, it needs some re-formulation in order to grasp the specific properties of strategic models of law as opposed to general planning models.

The *empirical* sub-model is the model type with the largest distance from action orientation. The degree of selectivity is rather low, as well as the transformation of the original data into other symbolic systems. The empirical sub-model concerns the social fields regulated by law, i.e. empirical theoretical statements about social structures, functions and development tendencies in the regulated areas, and interrelations between legal norms and social structures. The *prospective* sub-model defines the dimension of normative evaluation and strategic goals. It refers to fundamental principles which justify the specific way that legal norms should govern human actions. It has to do with statements about the purposes of law, means–end-relations, and evaluations of legal and social consequences. The *operative model*, finally, is closely oriented to action and shows the strongest degree of manipulation of the original data. It has to do with the internal conceptual and procedural structure of law and the systematisation of doctrine.

We do not gain an adequate understanding of those sub-models if we see their relation simply as additive, as a mere cumulation of otherwise independent empirical, normative, and strategic elements. Rather, we have to take into account their mutual interdependence. All three sub-models are highly selective and the problem is how to define their criteria of selectivity. The thesis is: *criteria of selectivity are to be found in a circular relation, in the mutual limitation of the three sub-models.* If we want to understand why certain assumptions about the social world within these models differ from scientific theories in terms of testing procedure and criteria of certainty we have to see that they are determined by the normative and strategic context of the prospective and operative sub-models. And if we want to understand what makes the difference between a "concept" of, for example, formal law and a mere technical recommendation of normative generality and conceptual precision, then we have to realise that such a "concept" is informed by underlying theoretical assumptions and normative evaluations which are formulated in the empirical and prospective sub-model.

To sum up, when in legal theory "grand concepts" are produced such as formal, substantive, reflexive law, they do not represent external scientific theories but internal strategic models of law. Strategic models are highly selective legal constructions of social reality. Their selectivity is defined by the social context and the criteria of selectivity result from the mutual limitation of their empirical, prospective, and operative sub-models. The ultimate test is re-entry into social reality. Their social function is the self-identification of the legal system as a criterion for its own transformation.

2. Competing Strategic Models in the Regulatory Crisis

All these elements of our definition can be identified if one looks at emerging concepts in the current socio-legal discussion of the regulatory crisis in the modern welfare state (Mayntz, 1979; Mitnick, 1980; Reich, 1984). Regulatory law — the most ambitious, modern, goal-oriented, sociologically informed type of law representing a political mechanism of social guidance — is said to be in a deep crisis, or at least in a state of institutional failure. Out of this diagnosis emerge three concepts of law which deserve the name of strategic models. They all use the identity of law as a criterion for its post-instrumental transformation. But they differ widely in regard to the empirical, prospective, and operative sub-models and their interaction with each other. Depending on what problems of regulatory law in relation to regulated fields are perceived as relevant, and how positively or negatively the instrumentalisation of law through the political system is evaluated, very different types of solutions are arrived at.

2.1 Implementation

The implementation approach represents a strategic model in the empirical dimension of which the crisis of regulatory law is identified as a problem of effectiveness (e.g. Mayntz, 1980). The starting point is the guidance intention of the political system and law is analysed as ineffective insofar as it turns out to be an unsuitable instrument for fulfilling those intentions in social reality.

Background theories are theories of societal guidance through political processes (e.g. Etzioni, 1968). These are closely related to the prospective dimension. A society is envisaged in which the political system takes over the responsibility of unresolved social problems of society. Compensatory state intervention is supposed to react against the undesirable side-effects of the modernisation processes. The normative goal is an increase in social welfare through democratic processes and political decisions. Law is politicised in the sense that it serves as one of the main mechanisms towards the realisation of the welfare state. It belongs to the inherent logic of this model that, in its operative dimension, the crisis of regulatory law is to be cured by *increasing its instrumental effectiveness* (Clune, 1983). If the problem of regulatory law is its implementation, then effective implementation mechanisms have to be designed. The point will then be to strengthen the cognitive, organisational and power based resources in such a way that the law can cope in practice with its control function. In this sense, legal doctrine will have to shift from being primarily concerned with juridical conflict resolution to more of a legal policy orientation (Nonet & Selznick, 1978). Legal science will see itself as a part of the social sciences, which produce control-knowledge (Ziegert, 1975). Law would then primarily be social technology (Podgorecki, 1974). Economic and sociological analyses will be brought in, with a view to efficiency. This means, at the same time, that the law must take into account its own implementation in social reality and the social consequences (implementation research and consequence control, e.g. Waelde, 1979, Mayntz, 1980).

2.2 Re-formalisation

In the diagnosis of the regulatory crisis, the selection of attributes for the empirical sub-model is quite different. The crisis is mainly identified with the economic and social costs which regulation creates. State interventionist law is supposed to be one of the main obstacles to reaching the goal of allocative efficiency. Background theories are various liberal and neo-liberal theories, the concept of "interventionist constructivism" being a prominent and ambitious example (Hayek, 1972). In the prospective dimensions the maximisation of freedom is the main normative goal. This function of law is to define a general framework for social freedom insofar as it establishes a sphere for autonomous activity and fixed boundaries for the property rights of private actors.

In the operative dimension, strategies aim at a certain *de-legalisation*, an ordered retreat of the law for the "occupied" areas of social life, either by a complete withdrawal of its regulatory function ("de-legalization" in the strict sense), or by concentrating its forces on the secure bastions of formal rationality ("re-formalization", Grimm, 1980). In this connection, particular interest attaches to the re-privatisation of state tasks and also to the abandonment of interventionist constructivism in favour of general law, in a conception of law as a set of rules of the game (Hayek, 1973; Hoppmann, 1972; Mestmaecker, 1978).

2.3 Control of self-regulation

As alternative solutions transcending the distinction between formal and substantive law, strategies are discussed that amount to a more abstract, more indirect control through the law. The law is relieved of the burden of direct regulation of social areas, and instead given the task of the active control of self-regulatory processes (e.g. Bohnert & Klitzsch, 1980). Empirically, the crisis of regulatory law is identified as an incompatibility of the internal logics of different social systems. It has been demonstrated that regulatory law programmes obey a functional logic and follow criteria of rationality and patterns of organisation which are poorly suited to the internal social structure of the regulated spheres of life (Pitschas, 1980, p. 150). In consequence, law as a medium of the welfare state either turns out to be ineffective or it works effectively but at the price of destroying traditional patterns of social life (Habermas, 1981, II, p. 531).

Scientific background theories are as a rule current macro-social theories: either the theory of functional differentiation or variants of critical theory or diverse attempts at a selective accommodation between them. Prospective orientations of those concepts are highly diverse according to the range of macro-theories to which they are connected. However, they have in common the normative problem of how to achieve social integration; how to define the identity of society, given the ubiquitousness of disruptive conflicts between the different rationalities of highly specialised social sub-systems (Habermas, 1975; Luhmann, 1982). Clearly, this social integration cannot be achieved by the state imposing unified norms on society. Nonetheless, social integration is still seen as a political problem in which the legal–political system — however indirectly — plays a critical role.

In the operative dimension, "proceduralization" is offered as a formula for the role of the law in promoting and controlling the setting up of "social systems with a learning capacity" (Wiethoelter, 1982, 1984; *cf.* also Mayntz, 1983*b*; Brueggemeier, 1982, p. 60). The empirical basis is in a whole variety of new forms of non-directive legal interventions (Winter, 1982, p. 9). This approach emphasises the design of self-regulation mechanisms, combining competition, bargaining, organisation and countervailing power (Hart, 1983, p. 22).

There are essentially three issues at stake: (a) the guarantee of life-world autonomy by an "external constitution" (Habermas, 1981, II, p. 544); (b) structural preconditions of effective self-regulation, for instance, by way of "external decentralization" of public tasks (Lehner, 1979, 178ff, Gotthold, 1983) or in the sense of internal reflection of social effects (Teubner, 1982; Hart, 1983); and (c) canalisation of inter-system-conflicts through "procedural regulation" (Mayntz, 1983*b*; Streeck & Schmitter, 1984) or "relational programs" or neo-corporatist mediation processes (Willke, 1983,

p. 62), or by semi-formal procedures of "practice as a discovery method" (Joerges, 1981, 1983), or by an institutionalised co-ordination of different system rationalities (Scharpf, 1979; Assmann, 1980; Ladeur, 1982, 1984).

3. Self-referentiality as the Criterion?

Is there a reasonable way to choose between those competing strategic models? As we said earlier, the ultimate test for success is the effect of their re-entry into social reality. But this does not exclude evaluating them in terms of higher or lower plausibility. In my view, a plausible choice can be made: that of concentrating intellectual attention and institutional energy on the third strategy, the legal control of social self-regulation. I find criteria of plausibility in the theory of self-referential systems.

Why make use of the theory of self-referential systems? This newly developed theory has been formulated by biologists (Maturana, 1970, 1975; Maturana, Varela & Uribe, 1974; Varela, 1979; Zeleny, 1981) and transferred to the social sciences (Hejl, 1982*a*, *b*; Luhmann, 1981*a*, 1984*a*, *b*; Teubner and Willke, 1984). There is not as yet general agreement that it is a fruitful paradigm. Thus, we shall use it in a more experimental manner as a strictly heuristic device. What follows for our problematic law and society relation if we reformulate them in terms of self-referentiality? What hypotheses, what recommendations for political–legal action are implied?

The message of self-reference can be clearly distinguished from older versions of systems theory. While classical notions of system concentrated on the internal relations of the elements, searching for emerging properties of the system ("the whole is more than the parts"), modern theories of "open systems" reject the "closed system approach" and stress the exchange relations between system and environment. One *leitmotiv* is requisite variety (Ashby, 1975, p. 207). How can the system cope with an over-complex environment? Another is contingency theory (Lawrence & Lorsch, 1967): how can we explain internal structures as a result of environmental demands? A third one is the input/output model (Easton, 1965): in what way are inputs processed into outputs through an internal conversion process? These are the guiding questions of the open system approach.

In a sense, the theory of self-referential systems seems to return to the concept of a closed system, even to a radical concept of closure. *A system produces and reproduces its own elements through the interaction of its elements* (Maturana *et al.*, 1974, p. 187) — by definition, a self-referential system is a closed system. However, what makes the theory more promising than both its forerunners is the inherent relation of self-referentiality to the environment. Self-referential systems, being closed systems of self-producing interactions, are, necessarily at the same time, open systems with boundary trespassing processes (Hejl, 1982*b*, p. 57). And it is precisely the linkage between internalising self-referential mechanisms and externalising environment exchange mechanisms which makes the concept of self-reference more fruitful and more complex than its predecessors with their somewhat sterile alternative of closed versus open systems.

If we are using self-referentiality as the criterion to judge competing strategic models of post-instrumental law, two directions of analysis seem to be fruitful. One concerns the question what effective *limits* the self-referential structure of social systems sets to legal intervention. The second direction of analysis concerns the *social knowledge* which is necessary if law acting within those limits seeks to cope with self-referential structures of the regulated areas. Thus, we arrive at the following theses if we reformulate the premises of the competing strategic models in terms of that theory.

(1) *The regulatory trilemma.* The implementation strategy will ultimately run aground on the internal dynamics of self-referential structures of both the regulating and the regulated system. Without taking into account the limits of "structural coupling", it inevitably ends in a trilemma: it leads to either "incongruence" of law and society, or "over-legalisation" of society, or "over-socialisation" of law. Moreover, the models of causal linearity which the implementation strategy is using seem to be insufficient as social knowledge to be required for the "regulation" of autopoietic systems.

(2) *Social self-closure.* The re-formalisation strategy neglecting in its turn the need of self-referential systems to externalise, develops no obstacles against the dynamics of social self-closure. An increase in sub-system rationality may be the result, but with possibly disastrous effects in regard to the co-ordination with the system's environment.

(3) *Response to self-referentiality.* In contrast, the third strategic model seems to be compatible with self-referentiality. As we have seen, for the control of self-regulation, theorists have developed a broad range of rather diverse recommendations about the way to "proceduralise" the law. Now, in the light of self-referentiality, what seem to be obviously heterogeneous recommendations, can be interpreted as complementary strategies. The maintenance of a self-reproductive organisation needs societal support. The recommendations can be read as strategies to make compatible the self-referentiality of various social sub-systems. "Proceduralisation" represents society's response to the needs of self-referentiality: "autonomy", "externalisation", and "co-ordination".

If we translate our problem of legal regulation into the language of self-reference a decisive difference becomes apparent. Models of regulation and of implementation, even if they are developed in the open system framework, deal with the implicit assumption of basal linearity. This means, that they see the relation between the regulating systems (politics and law) and the regulated system (functional sub-system, organisation, interaction) as a relation between environment and system in which the regulating systems maintain and control the goals and the processes of the regulated systems. Deviant behaviour is supposed to be controlled and corrected by the regulated system. This holds true even for recent reformulations of implementation theory (Mayntz, 1979, p. 55; 1983*a*, p. 7; Bohnert & Klitzsch, 1980, p. 200). While it is true that they abandon a purely instrumentalist model and take into account autonomy in the regulated area and complicated interaction processes in the implementation field, they still have no adequate concept of what constitutes the autonomy of the regulated system. They still conceive of the regulated system as *allopoietic*, as dependent on the actions of the regulating system.

In contrast, a theory of self-reference would define the regulated area as a system consisting of elements which interact with each other in such a way that they maintain themselves and reproduce elements having the same properties as a result of repeating the self-producing interaction (Hejl, 1982*b*, p. 56). They are systems that keep their reproductive organisation constant. To be sure, their concrete structures can be influenced and changed by regulation, but only within the limits of that reproductive organisation (see Maturana, 1975). Any external regulatory influence which leads to a new internal interaction of elements not maintaining its self-reproductive organisation, is either irrelevant or leads to the disintegration of the regulated system (*cf.* Hejl, 1982*b*, p. 58).

The picture becomes more complicated if we take into account that the regulating systems, politics and law, are themselves self-reproductive systems. We have then to reformulate the hierarchical relation of regulation into a circular interaction between three self-referential systems (law, politics and regulated sub-systems). The limits of regulation are then defined by the threefold limits of self-reproduction. *A regulatory action is successful only to the degree that it maintains a self-producing internal interaction of the elements in the regulating systems, law and politics which is at the same time compatible with self-producing internal interactions in the regulated system.* This threefold compatibility relation may be called "structural coupling" (Maturana, 1974). Thus, we can formulate the *regulatory trilemma*: if regulation does not conform to the conditions of the "structural coupling" of law, politics, and society, it is bound to end up in regulatory failure. There are three ways regulation can fail:

(a) *"Incongruence" of law, politics and society.* The regulatory action is incompatible with the self-producing interactions of the regulated system. However, the regulated system reacts by not reacting. Since the regulatory action does not comply to the relevance criteria of the regulated system, it is simply irrelevant for the elements' interactions. The law is ineffective as it creates no change in behaviour. However, the self-producing organisation remains intact, in law as well as in society. This is what one might call the symbolic use of politics and law (Edelman, 1964).

(b) *Over-legalisation of society.* Again, the concrete self-producing interactions within law, politics and within society are not compatible with each other. In this case, however, the regulatory action influences the internal interaction of elements in the regulated field so strongly that their self-production is endangered. This leads to disintegrating effects in the regulated field, well-known under the heading of "colonialization" (Habermas, 1981, p. 542). The regulatory programmes obey a functional logic and follow criteria of rationality which are poorly suited to the internal social structure of the regulated spheres of life. Law as a medium of the welfare state works efficiently, but at the price of destroying the reproduction of traditional patterns of social life.

(c) *"Over-socialization" of law.* A third type of regulatory failure should be taken into account. Once again incompatibility of self-production is the result of regulation, but in this case with the difference that the self-producing organisation of the regulated area remains intact while the self-producing organisation of the law is endangered. The law is "captured" by politics or by the regulated sub-system, the law is "politicized", "economized", "pedagogized" etc. with the result that the self-production of its normative elements gets overstrained. Overstrain of the law in the welfare state may be the effect of its political instrumentalisation (Luhmann, 1984*a*), but it may also result from the law's "surrender" to other sub-systems of society at the cost of its own reproduction (Nonet & Selznick, 1978, p. 76). The "over-socialization" of law may take many forms.

All in all, these three types of regulatory failure which each show very distinctive features have one thing in common. In each case, regulatory law turns out to be ineffective because it overreaches the limitations which are built into the regulatory process: the self-referential organisation of these systems, either the regulated field, or politics of the law itself. The effects are likewise problematic, being either irrelevance or regulation or disintegrating effects in the self-reproductive organisation of law, politics, or society.

Up to now we were concerned with the effective limits which the self-referential organisation of regulated social areas sets to the implementation strategy. Now we focus on the question of social knowledge. The question is: does the implementation strategy apply adequate internal models of social reality in order to cope successfully with the self-referential organisation of the regulated sub-systems? As we have seen above, the implementation strategy works with purely instrumentalist models which differ more or less only to the degree of their complication and refinement. In its most simple form a political goal or a political programme is defined as purpose and the question is scrutinised if legal norms as means do reach this purpose. It becomes more complicated if one enriches the factual situation in the implementation field in order to assess the chances for realisation more successfully. Another possibility is to ask for side-effects and dysfunctional consequences. Basically, however, the model is limited to linear causality: the goal determines the programme, the programme determines the norm, the norm determines changes of behaviour, those changes determine the desired effects.

It would be erroneous to insist that such models of linear causality are bound to fail totally if applied to self-referential systems. The basal circularity of self-reference does not mean that any contact between systems is excluded. Rather, a limited mutual "understanding", is possible, but in a very complicated fashion. For "understanding" one social system has to internalise the self-referentiality of the other. This is a complicated process which makes plausible how limited causal models are for the intervention into self-referential systems. The simple model of "political goal — legal norm — social effects" would have to be enriched with social knowledge about how self-referential systems receive regulatory information and how they process it according to their autonomous rules of internal interaction. This presupposes profound knowledge about general regularities of a self-closed structure and its effects in particular cases which is generally not at hand. Law would have to store social knowledge about the general self-referential circularity in different social sub-systems and their particular effects, a knowledge which even for social science is not available.

It is precisely this lack of social knowledge which was the reason why Renate Mayntz (1983*a*), the leading researcher in implementation in West Germany, demanded a theoretical re-orientation of the whole of implementation research. According to Mayntz, implementation research is at present not in a position to develop coherent middle range theories about political programmes and their social effects in the implementation field. It runs aground on the complexities of the regulated area. What is possible is at best conceptualisation, typologies, and particular cases studies. It is the non-generalisable case study which seems to be the only method available to collect knowledge about causal relations in the implementation fields. Cautious inductive conclusions from established experience to future regulations determine the potential and limits of causal models in regulatory law.

What did we gain up to now from using the concept of self-referentiality? We utilised it as the criterion to judge the potential and limits of the implementation model. It led us to the regulatory trilemma as the basic limitation of the implementation strategy and within this limitation to the limited use of linear causal models. If it is true that instrumental law runs massively aground on the structures of self-referentiality, so that its absolute and relative limits are easily reached, then the question emerges if and how at all law can cope with self-referential systems. Would this not mean that law has to retreat to its own basal circularity concentrating on internal interaction of its own elements — norms, decisions, doctrines — and leaving outside effects to whatever their fate might be? This is by no means only a rhetorical question. Perhaps it was the hidden wisdom of "autonomous law" which did not care for ethical, political, economic and social considerations. However, before one indulges in a resigned new justification of the old formalism, one should scrutinise strategic models of post-instrumental law, which compete with the implementation model to see if they are better suited to respect the absolute limits of self-referentiality and to produce norms within these limits that are not *a priori* counter-productive. Again, we are using self-referentiality as the criterion in two directions: (1) limits of self-production, and (2) social knowledge required for coping with self-reproductive organisation.

4. Three Dimensions of Reflexive Law: Some Illustrations

It seems there are needs of self-referential systems which all stem from the necessity of maintaining their basal circularity. Regulatory processes can interfere positively and negatively with those needs. They can sabotage them, they can neglect them, or they can support, even facilitate them. The external support of self-referentiality is precisely the place at which one should localise recent efforts to translate the intentions of regulatory law into "reflexive" models of the control of self-regulation.

At first sight, they seem rather diverse and heterogeneous. But they are seen to support each other if one re-interprets them in the light of self-referentiality. One way to interpret them is rather modest and only negative: they can be read so as to avoid the regulatory trilemma and to design legal interventions in such a way that the self-referential structures of law, politics, and society are not infringed. Another interpretation is more ambitious and more positive: they attempt to define certain basic needs of self-referential systems and to design a law which is responsive to those needs.

To be sure, self-referentiality is a highly abstract concept. If it is supposed to serve as a criterion to judge the social adequacy of legal interventions, everything depends on its re-specification in concrete contexts (Joerges, 1983, p. 14). Thus, one of the most important tasks for this theory will be to identify the concrete mechanisms of self-referential closure and openness and the linkage between them (see as an important step into this direction, Luhmann, 1984*a*, p. 8).

4.1 Autonomy: school law

Juergen Habermas (1981, p. 552), in his discussion of recent trends of juridification, develops a remarkable sensitivity in this direction. His ambivalent attitude toward legal welfare state interventions in the "life-world" can be interpreted as reflecting the dilemmatic structure of law in its double capacity to infringe and to facilitate self-productive interactions in the spheres of socialisation, social integration and cultural reproduction. Habermas considers legal regulations as "destructive to the very nature of such relations'' (Blankenburg, 1984, p. 7). This is only one aspect. However, Blankenburg misses the crucial point when he interprets Habermas as postulating the need ''to keep any sort of legal regulation out of interactions that need spontaneous social communication". This is to misrepresent Habermas as a partisan of a naive communal de-legalisation movement. Habermas has a strongly normative interest in the law as such, especially in its emancipatory potential as a universalisation mechanism (Habermas, 1962, pp. 91 and 242; 1963, p. 82; 1973, p. 123; 1976, p. 260; 1981, pp. 322, 364 and 522). In the case of welfare state law he searches for criteria which would allow one to distinguish at least analytically between the law's capacity to guarantee freedom and its capacities to destroy it (Habermas, 1981, pp. 534ff). He comes up with the distinction between law as medium and law as institution, the test being the justifiability through moral norms of the ''life-world''. As a medium, law is a functional socio-technological steering instrument through which the sub-systems of economy and politics are ''colonizing'' central areas of cultural reproduction, social integration, and socialisation. Only when law is restricted to an ''external constitution'' of the ''life-world'' spheres, can it serve as an ''institution'' facilitating rather than disintegrating ''consensus oriented procedures of conflict regulation'' (Habermas, 1981, pp. 546 and 544).

In our interpretation, this concept of law as ''institution'' shows signs of adequacy to self-referential structures within certain social contexts. Take the example of school law which Habermas uses. By protecting children's and parents' basic rights against the school administration, the law tends to free the education process from bureaucratic and administrative constraints. However, as a medium it is, in itself, in conflict with the form of pedagogic action if it is not restricted to the mere ''frame of a legal school constitution''. In the past the function of the ''school constitution'' was to secure its freedom from administrative pressure. And its future function could be — if we may extrapolate from Habermas' argument — to defend it against those bureaucratic processes which translate the ''economic system imperative to de-couple the school system from the basic right of education (Bildung) and to close-circuit it with the occupation system'' (Habermas, 1981, p. 545). It is only within such a sphere of autonomy protected by a legal ''external constitution'' that the educational system has a chance of defining on its own in what respect it will depend upon its environment in self-referential processes. An external constitution thus facilitates internal reflection on the basic orientation of education: balancing environmental demands of performance — knowledge, skills — against its proper social functions — ''Bildung'', learning how to learn (see Luhmann & Schorr, 1979, p. 18).

Of course, this is a precarious process. It is a paradoxical technique: fire to fight fire. And there are no guarantees against burning down the whole area, against an almost total legalisation and judicialisation (Blankenburg, 1984, p. 24). But at the same time there is no reason to believe that a blind automatism is at work. Rather, it is a matter of political commitment and careful institutional design. Habermas himself shows this sensitivity to the problem by sympathising with the paradoxical suggestion of Simitis and Zenz (1975, p. 51): to dejudicialise legalised conflicts.

Such a retreat of the law from a regulation of whole life areas to the mere guarantee of their autonomy has effects not only for the areas concerned but for the law itself. If the law is relieved from its regulatory function, it is relieved at the same time in its constructing models of social reality. Such a law concentrating on securing social autonomy need not utilise ambitious models of causal relation between legal norm and social effects. It suffices to develop a very general and rather vague understanding of self-regulatory processes in the social areas concerned. Since its function is the enablement of freedom within delimitated autonomous areas no knowledge is needed about their internal processes.

As useful as the concept of the external constitution is, there are two points which show the necessity of reformulating the argument. One is its generalisation and re-specification; the other shows that an external constitution in this sense is a necessary but not a sufficient condition for "reflexive law".

The effect of legalisation processes disintegrating reproductive structures is not limited to the spheres of the "life-world". Any social system with a self-referential structure can be endangered by outside interferences in the self-productive interaction of its elements (Hejl, 1982*b*, p. 58). Even the "systems" of economy and politics can be paralysed by legalisation. This is again a problem of self-referentiality. Economic and political processes will be paralysed if their self-productive and reproductive capacities are infringed. Thus, the concept of "colonialisation" needs to be generalised and applied to any inter-system relations.

This is the point at which the crucial task of re-specification begins for a theory of self-referentiality to define for any social system the specific self-productive mechanisms that need to be shielded from outside interference, whether it be a great functional system (politics, economy, education, religion, family, etc.), or be it a large organisation or a small interaction. Of course, in this operation one abstracts from the difference between system and life-world which is crucial for Habermas' normative intentions. However, those intentions need not be given up; they can be re-introduced at a more general level through the concept of responsiveness to human needs, which would cut through the system/life-world difference and be applicable to any social system.

4.2 Externalisation: corporate social responsibility

This re-specification is necessary if "reflexive" legal action is to go beyond the mere securing of autonomy (see Teubner & Willke, 1984). Autonomy is a necessary, but not a sufficient precondition of self-referential processes. It does not guarantee their success. Self-referentiality is a precarious structure. It is always in danger of self-closure and self-referential systems need outside support to develop certain externalisations. The political system, for example, tends to operate too selectively and tends to concentrate on the complicated games of politics, thereby neglecting problems of its social environment (Luhmann, 1981*a*, p. 57). In a similar way, the economic system works selectively via the language of monetary action and is not able adequately to re-translate its environmental consequences into its own language (Willke, 1982).

Insofar as systems cannot develop sufficient externalisation on their own, outside pressures are needed to impose structures on them which avoid self-closure. This is not to say that law or politics are the only, or even the main, outside mechanisms of enforcing externalisation. Law can serve only as one among other compensatory institutions of society which compensate for the self-reference of social systems. Compensatory institutions have to operate under the double constraint of integrating environmental demands into the system while not disintegrating its conditions of self-production and reproduction.

"Corporate social responsibility" is a good case in point (see Teubner, 1983, p. 34; 1984). If it is meant to go beyond a managerialist ideology and to be taken seriously as a compensatory institution which builds social side-purposes into economic actions (Willke, 1982, p. 17), then a powerful outside pressure which is supported by political–legal measures is necessary. However, it has been demonstrated again and again how easily "external" regulations run aground on the regulatory trilemma (Stone, 1975, p. 93; 1984). The most promising approach seems to be "internal" regulation: strategic intervention into certain characteristics of the organisation's decision-making process; the so-called structural, as opposed to the duty-approach (Teubner, 1983, p. 48; 1984; Wedderburn, 1984). Their success, however, depends upon their taking into account the self-referential structure of economic organisations. For example, they have to follow what Krause calls a "profit-threatening strategy" (Krause, 1984).

As the example shows, this poses problems of power. Political and social power is needed to exert external pressure on established social systems to externalise their self-reference. The imposition of an "external constitution"; the re-distribution of property rights to hitherto excluded constituencies; the redesign of decisional procedures all constituting the core elements of "reflexive law", aim at a power change within the sub-system in question and demand strong power support from outside (Teubner, 1982, p. 254, 273 and 276).

Historical examples — the legal institutionalisation of collective bargaining and of co-determination of labour — show that the role of law in influencing power relations is not simply marginal. Rather, law is one of the major mechanisms to change social power relations inside the organisation (I.D.E.,

1979). Formalising property rights which are backed by the sanctioning power of the state clearly does not create social power, but it stabilises social power rendering it, to a certain degree, independent from fluctuations of shifting power and market relations.

Thus, reflexive law depends on political power relations, and in this respect does not differ from regulatory law. In situations of social power relations, the success of both legal forms depends on the extensive use of political power resources. There is, however, a decisive difference. The difference concerns the strategic use of power as a limited resource. Regulatory law, working with detailed regulation and a sophisticated implementation machinery, is bound to liquidate a large amount of socio-political power. Techniques of reflexive law, however, tend to minimise that liquidation by restricting themselves to certain strategic organisational and procedural key-variables. Galanter (1974) makes this point very clearly. Concerned with the problem of how to use the law to reduce social inequality in conflict situations, he considers a whole range of strategic variables (legal rules, institutions, lawyers, parties). Under the perspective of effectiveness he clearly prefers organisational variables over material legal rules. It makes for a more economic use of the scarce power resources to concentrate them on the strategic changes of the organisation rather than dispersing them in permanent regulatory efforts.

It should be stated clearly, however, that power equalisation is not the primary aspect of "reflexive law". As important as it is in the public control of private government (Macaulay, 1983) it does not make sense to tie the concept of "reflexive law" too closely to power-equalisation within social sub-systems, especially private organisations. The minimisation of power is not a reasonable normative end in itself, it is an instrumental device for achieving certain social goals. Strategies of power-equalisation make sense only if those goals are expected to be achieved through symmetrical power relations. This is not immediately apparent. Power-equalising strategies are well suited to situations of zero-sum-games: gains in power on the one side mean losses of power on the other. The optimal state is a precarious power-equilibrium. The law's role in private organisations would be to control misuse of power and to stabilise the equilibrium. This is the classical view of the law's role toward power. However, a change from equilibrium models to growth models of organisations would drastically change the law's relations to power: "The division of power is not the thing to be considered but that method of organization which will generate power" (Lammers, 1967). In a growth model, power is seen not as a constant but as a variable phenomenon. In consequence, power-equalisation only amounts to a "distributive–regressive" solution of the organisation problem while the "productive–progressive" solution would be an increase of collective need satisfaction through *mutual power-increase* and power distribution (Hondrich, 1975, p. 55).

Within this perspective, power is not primarily seen as a source of inequality and injustice but as a social instrument for an effective transfer of decisions. The task of the law then is still to control power abuses, but the central problem becomes rather to design institutional mechanisms that mutually increase the power of members and leadership in private organisations. Lammers, for example, concludes in "Power and participation": "Managers and managed in organisations can, at the same time, come to influence each other more effectively and thereby generate joint power as the outcome of a better command by the organisation over its technical, economic and human resources'' (Lammers, 1967, p. 201).

That means, among other things, that power-equalisation is not suited to use as a criterion for distinguishing between conservative and progressive forms of ''reflexive law'', centrist and radical views of decentralisation (Unger, 1983). More even, being bound to static equilibrium models, power-equalisation appears itself as a conservative strategy. If we are looking for normative criteria to judge social institutions, responsiveness to human needs (Hondrich, 1975) is the case in point and not neutralisation of power. Dynamic, flexible institutions with strong asymmetric power relations can, under certain conditions, be more responsive to human needs than self-closed, power-symmetrical, equilibrium institutions.

More important than the issue of power is the question what kind of social knowledge is necessary for the law in order to intervene in self-referential systems successfully. What is the use of increasing power resources if the cognitive resources are lacking, or if they are so insufficient that they guide power resources into the wrong direction? Indeed, reflexive law clearly needs more and different social knowledge from a law which restricts itself to an ''external constitution''. This might suggest that reflexive modes of social guidance overload the cognitive competences of the law. However, it should be seen as well that the reality models needed in a reflexive law have considerably lower requirements than those needed in comprehensive planning models of regulatory law. As in the case of power resources, reflexive forms of law aim at an ''economic'' use of cognitive resources. A profound ''understanding'' of the total self-referential structures and processes in the implementation field is not necessary. As Hayek (1972, 1973) has demonstrated convincingly in his critique of constructivist interventionism, even science is not in a position to achieve such a profound understanding of particular processes in complex structures, much less then politics or law. The ''economic'' advantage of reflexive law is that it requires only general knowledge of self-referentiality and need not control specific effects. It is sufficient to restrict ''understanding'' to the strategic structures according to which reflexion processes take place within the social sub-system concerned, since reflexive law intends only to change those general forms of procedure and organisation. If it is true, for example, that in the economic system, reflexion takes place at the general level of monetary policies, then it would be sufficient to use social knowledge about the banking sector and its political processes in their general structure in order to achieve changes. One would not need models for the total economic system and its particular processes. Another example: if the reflexion centre of an economic organisation can be localised in its board system then corporation law could utilise rather simple models about internal decision making in order to influence reflexion processes through norms of organisation and procedure.

4.3 Co-ordination: concerted action

Up to this point, we have discussed how law reflects two basic needs of self-referential sub-systems: the need for autonomy and the need for externalisation. A third dimension becomes apparent if one takes into account that not only social sub-systems but also the encompassing society as a whole constitutes a self-referential system. The interaction of the functional sub-systems, politics, economy, law, education, religion, family, etc. can be seen as a self-producing interaction between elements of a larger system. Each of these sub-systems contributes to the maintenance of societal self-reference. The law's contribution in this respect is the resolution of inter-system-conflicts. Helmut Willke (1983) has developed a concept of a legal programme aiming at this function: the "relational programme". As opposed to the typical programmes of formal law (conditional programme) and of instrumental law (purpose programme), the function of relational programmes is to make compatible different purposes and rationalities of social sub-systems by committing political and social actors to discursive procedures of decision-making. He identifies the emergence of this new type of legal programme in diverse inter-system-coordination mechanisms, such as the Concerted Action (Konzertierte Aktion) or the Science Council (Wissenschaftsrat) in the German Federal Republic.

One promising mode for understanding the working of such "relational programmes" can be found in the theory of "black-boxes" developed in the context of cybernetics (Glanville, 1979). Self-referential system — social systems like law, politics and regulated sub-systems — are "black boxes" in the sense of being mutually inaccessible to each other. One knows the input and the output, the conversion however remains obscure. Now, black box techniques do not aim at shedding light onto this obscure internal conversion process, but circumvent the problem by an indirect "procedural" activity. They concentrate not on the internal relations within the black box, but on the interrelation between the black boxes. Black boxes become "whitened" in the sense that an interaction relation develops among them which is transparent for them in its regularities. So law still can not intervene directly into the economy, legal access however consists in the relation between law and economy. This seems to be the peculiarity of relational programmes which regulate internal processes in systems indirectly so that they concentrate on the relations between the systems. That means again drastically decreasing the requirements of the cognitive capacities of law and politics, since they do not any longer attempt directly to influence economic action but to influence only "concerted action", the internal structure of which is for them much more transparent.

It is crucial that between the interaction relation and the regulated system, in our example, between concerted action and economy, consists a dense connection which is the source for guidance effects. This is to be expected from two mechanisms. One is the commitment of economic actors to the concerted action and the other is that the concerted action as such develops cognitive modes of the economy which may be more adequate than those of politics and of the law. The whole way of thinking is quite close to what Lindblom called the combination of social knowledge and interaction (Lindblom and Cohen, 1979). According to Lindblom one has to give up concepts of comprehensive social planning since they are utopian and unrealistic and has to replace them by more realistic models in which limited and strategic knowledge is combined with social interaction, that is in our concept the interaction among the two black boxes in order to reach guidance effects within one of the black boxes.

Autonomy, externalisation and co-ordination — these are three dimensions in which reflexive law responds to the basic needs of self-referential systems. These dimensions have been analysed by different legal theorists with the intention of pointing out the developmental tendencies of post-instrumental law. With the concept of self-referentiality I have tried to demonstrate that they represent complementary rather than competing approaches. "Proceduralization" of the law (Wiethoelter, 1982, 1984), as opposed to formalisation and to materialisation is one formula which captures what they have in common. Another, with slightly different nuances is the "constitution of organization" (Brueggemeier, 1982) as opposed to the constitution of status and of contract. A third one would be "relational programme" or "reflexive law", stressing the aspect of legal prerequisites for social self-regulation (Teubner, 1982; Willke, 1983, 1984). Clearly, those formulae invite misunderstanding (Blankenburg, 1984). If they are arbitrarily separated from their theoretical background (functionalist or "critical" macro-theories) and are equated with just any type of procedural and organisational law, for example, in a stratified society, they become rather meaningless. It is then easy to ask: what's new?

More serious questions have to be raised about the relation of procedural elements to formal and material elements in post-instrumental law. Again, in any type of law all these three elements can be identified, though with different weight and different functions. After all, classical "formal" law had specific content and specific procedures (Teubner, 1982, p. 252; Wiethoelter, 1984). What are the material orientations of post-instrumental law?

The answer can be only very tentative. Material orientations of procedural law aim at nothing less ambitious than a bridging of functionalist and critical approaches to social theory. Wiethoelter argues explicitly for an understanding of "proceduralisation" as "the problem of the justification of 'reasonable' practical actions under 'system' — conditions''. The goal is to create a ''forum, in which transformations of society are dealt with reconstructively and prospectively'' (Wiethoelter, 1984). I think I agree with the general intention. I would, however, prefer to point to the limited potential of practical philosophy beyond the sphere of morality in personal interaction and to stress the aspect of enhancing specific learning capacities in decentralised social sub-systems. These learning capacities should be oriented toward re-introducing the consequences of social sub-systems into their own reflexion structure. Setting such a context of discovery — would that satisfy our need for a material orientation of reflexive law?

References

Alexander, J.C. (1982) *Theoretical Logic in Sociology*, Vol. 1. *Positivism, Presuppositions and Current Controversies*. University of California Press: Berkeley.

Ashby, W.R. (1975) *An Introduction to Cybernetics*. Chapman and Hall: London.

Assmann, H.-D. (1980) *Wirtschaftsrecht in der Mixed-Economy., Auf der Suche nach einem Sozialmodell fuer das Wirtschaftsrecht*. Athenaeum: Frankfurt.

Black, D. (1972) Book Review: Philip Selznick, Law, Society and Industrial Justice, 1969. *American Journal of Sociology* **78**, 709.

Blankenburg, E. (1984) The poverty of evolutionism. A critique of Teubner's case for ''reflexive law''. *Law and Society Review* **18**, 273.

Bohnert, W. and Klitzsch, W. (1980) Gesellschaftliche Selbstregulierung und staatliche Steuerung. Steuerungstheoretische Anmerkungen zur Implementation politischer Programme. In *Implementation politischer Programme* (Mayntz, R., Ed.). Athenaeum: Koenigstein.

Brueggemeier, G. (1982) Wirtschaftsordnung und Staatsverfassung'' — ''Mischverfassung des demokratischen Interventionskapitalismus'' ''Verfassungstheorie des Sozialstaates''. Drei Modelle der Verflechtung von Staat and Wirtschaft? In *Rechtsformen der Verflechtung von Staat und Wirtschaft* (Gessner, V. & Winter, G., Eds). Westdeutscher Verlag: Opladen.

Buckley, W. (1968) Society as a complex adaptive system. In *Modern Systems Research for the Behavioural Scientist* (Buckley, W., Ed.). Aldine Publ. Co.: Chicago.

Clune, H. (1983) The political origins and political process of regulation: what we can learn from a positive political analysis. In *Reflexive Law and the Regulatory Crisis* (Trubek, D. Ed.). Madison.

Easton, D. (1965) *A Systems Analysis of Political Life*. Wiley: New York.

Edelman, M. (1964) *The Symbolic of Use of Politics*. University of Illinois Press: Urbana.

Etzioni, A. (1968) *The Active Society. A Theory of Societal and Political Processes*. Free Press: New York.

Feyerabend, P. (1975) *Against Method. Outline of an Anarchistic Theory of Knowledge*. Atlantic Highlands Humanities Press: London.

Friedman, L. (1984) Legal culture and the welfare state. In *Dilemmas of Law in the Welfare State* (Teubner, G., Ed.). Walter de Gruyter: Berlin, New York.

Galanter (1974) Why the ''haves'' come out ahead: speculations on the limits of legal change. *Law and Society Review* **9**, 95.

Glanville, S.R. (1979) The form of cybernetics: whitening the black-box. In *General System Research — A Science, a Methodology, a Technology* (Society for General System Research, Ed). Conference Papers, Houston.

Gotthold, J. (1983) Privatisierung oder Entbuerokratisierung kommunaler Sozialpolitik. In *Abschied vom Recht?* (Voigt, R., Ed.). Suhrkamp: Frankfurt.

Grimm, D (1980) Reformalisierung des Rechtsstaats als Demokratiepostulat. *Juristische Schulung,* **20**, 704.

Habermas, J. (1962) *Strukturwandel der Oeffentlichkeit*. Luchterhand: Neuwied.

Habermas, J. (1963) *Theorie und Praxis. Sozialphilosophische Studien*. Luchterhand: Neuwied.

Habermas, J. (1973) Zum Begriff der politischen Beteiligung (1958). In *Kultur and Kritik* (Habermas, J., Ed.). Suhrkamp: Frankfurt.

Habermas, J. (1975) *Legitimation Crisis*. Beacon: Boston.

Habermas, J. (1976) *Zur Rekonstruktion des Historischen Materialismus*. Suhrkamp: Frankfurt.

Habermas, J. (1981) *Theorie des kommunikativen Handelns*. Suhrkamp: Frankfurt.

Hart, D. (1983) Contract and consumer protection: organizing countervailing power — on the development of substantive and reflexive elements in modern contract law. In *Reflexive Law and the Regulatory Crisis* (Trubeck, D., Ed.). Madison.

Hayek, F. A. (1972) The theory of complex phenomena. *Studies in Philosophy, Politics and Economics*. Simon and Schuster: Chicago.

Hayek, F. A. (1973) *Law, Legislation and Liberty* Vol. 1. *Rules and Order*. University of Chicago Press: Chicago.

Hejl, P. M. (1982*a*) *Sozialwissenschaft als Theories selbstreferentieller Systeme*. Campus: Frankfurt.

Hejl, P. M. (1982*b*) Die Theorie autopoietischer Systeme: Perspektiven fuer die soziologische Systemtheorie. *Rechtstheorie* **13**, 45.

Hondrich, K. O. (1975) *Menschliche Beduerfnisse und soziale Steuerung*. Rowoblt: Reinbek.

Hoppmann, E. (1972) *Fusionskontrolle*. Mohr: Tuebingen.

I.D.E. (1979). Industrial Democracy in Europe. *Industrial Research Group: Industrial Democracy in Europe*. Oxford University Press: Oxford.

Joerges, C. (1981) *Verbraucherschutz als Rechtsproblem*. Recht und Wirtschaft: Heidelberg.

Joerges, C. (1983) Regulatory law, private government and self-regulation. In *Reflexive Law and the Regulatory Crisis* (Trubek, D., Ed.). Madison.

Krause, D. (1984) Corporate social responsibility: interests and goals. In *Corporate Governance and Directors' Liability* (Hopt, K. J. & Teubner G., Eds). Walter de Gruyter: Berlin, New York.

Ladeur, K.-H. (1982) Verrechtlichung oder Oekonomisierung des Rechts? In *Rechtsformen der Verflechtung von Staat und Wirtschaft* (Gessner, V. & Winter, G. Eds). Westdeutscher Verlag: Opladen.

Ladeur, K.-H. (1984) *Abwaegung. Ein neues Paradigma des Verwaltungsrechts*. Campus: Frankfurt.

Lammers, C. J. (1967) Power and participation in decision-making in formal organizations. *The American Journal of Sociology* **73**, 201.

Lawrence, P. R. & Lorsch, J. W. (1967) *Organization and Environment: Managing Differentiation and Integration*. Harvard University: Boston.

Lehner, F. (1979) *Grenzen des Regierens*. Athenaeum: Koenigstein.

Lindblom, C. & Cohen, D. (1979) *Usable Knowledge. Social Science and Social Problem Solving*. Yale University Press: New Haven, London.

Luhmann, N. (1981*a*) *Politische Theorie im Wohlfahrtsstaat*. Olzog: Muenchen.

Luhmann, N. (1981*b*) *Ausdifferenzierung des Rechts. Beitraege zur Rechtssoziologie und Rechtstheorie*. Suhrkamp: Frankfurt.

Luhmann, N. (1982) *The Differentiation of Society*. Columbia University Press: New York.

Luhmann, N. (1984*a*) The self-reproduction of the law and its limits. In *Dilemmas of Law in the Welfare State* (Teubner, G., Ed.). Walter de Gruyter: Berlin, New York.

Luhmann, N. (1984*b*) *Soziale Systeme. Grundriss einer allgemeinen Theorie*. Suhrkamp: Frankfurt.

Luhmann, N. & Schorr, K.-E. (1979) *Reflexionsprobleme im Erziehungssystem*. Klett-Cotta: Stuttgart.

Macauly, S. (1983) Private Government. In *Reflexive Law and the Regulatory Crisis* (Trubke, D., Ed.). Madison.

Maturana, H. R. (1970) *Biology of Cognition*. Illinois: Urbana.

Maturana, H. R. (1975) *Autopoietic Systems. A Characterization of the Living Organization*. Illinois: Urbana.

Maturana, H. R., Varela, F. E. & Uribe, R. (1974) Autopoiesis: the organization of living systems. *Bio Systems* **5**, 187.

Mayntz, R. (1979) Regulative Politik in der Krise? In *Sozialer Wandel in Westeuropa* (Matthes, J., Ed.). Campus: Frankfurt.

Mayntz, R. (1980) Die Implementation politischer Programme. In *Implementation politischer Programme* (Mayntz, R., Ed.). Athenaeum: Koenigstein.

Mayntz, R. (1983*a*) *Implementation politischer Programme II*. Westdeutscher Verlag: Opladen.

Mayntz, R. (1983*a*) The changing conditions of effective public policy — a new challenge for policy analysis. *Policy and Politics* **11**, 123.

Mestmaecker, E.-J. (1978) *Die sichtbare Hand des Rechts. Ueber das Verhaeltnis von Wirtschaftsordnung und Rechtssystem*. Nomos: Baden-Baden.

Mitnick, B. (1980) *The Political Economy of Regulation Creating, Designing and Removing Regulatory Forms*. Columbia University Press: New York.

Nonet, P. & Selznick, P. (1978) *Law and Society in Transition*. Harper and Row: London.

Pitschas, R. (1980) Soziale Sicherung durch fortschreitende Verrechtlichung? In *Verrechtlichung* (Voigt, R., Ed.). Athenaeum: Koenigstein.

Podgorecki, A. (1974) *Law and Society*. Routledge and Kegan Paul: London.

Reich, N. (1984) The regulatory crisis — does it exist and can it be solved? *Government and Policy* **177**.

Rottleuthner, H. (1983) *Theorien der Rechtsentwicklung zwischen Empirie und Geschichtsphilosophie*. Typoscript: Berlin.

Rottleuthner, H. (1984) *Rechtssoziologische Studien zur Arbeitsgenists–barkeit*. Nomos: Baden Baden.

Scharpf, F. (1979) Die Rolle des Staates im westdeutschen Wirtschaftssystem: Zwischen Krise und Neuorientierung. In Schriften des vereins für Socialpolitik, N.F. Bd. 102, Staat und Wirtschaft (v. Weizsäcker, c.c., Ed.) Berlin.

Selznick, P. (1973) Rejoinder to Donald Black. *American Journal of Sociology* **78**, 1266.

Simitis, S. & Zenzy, G. (1975) (Eds). *Familie und Familienrecht*. Suhrkamp: Frankfurt.

Stachowiak, H. (1965) Gedanken zu einer allgemeinen Theorie der Modelle. *Studium Generale* **18**, 432.

Stachowiak, H. (1973) *Allgemeine Modelltheorie*. Springer: Wien, New York.

Stone, C. D. (1975) *Where the Law Ends. The Social Control of Corporate Behaviour*. Harper: New York.

Stone, C. D. (1984) Public interest representation: economic and social policy inside the enterprise. In *Corporate Governance and Directors' Liability* (Hopt, K. J. & Teubner, G., Eds). Walter de Gruyter: Berlin, New York.

Streeck, W. & Schmitter. Ph. C. (1984) Commuity, market, state — and associations? The prospective contribution of interest governance to social order. *E.U.I. Working Paper No. 94*, Florence.

Teubner, G. (1978) Generalklauseln als sozio-normative Modelle. In *Generalklauseln als Gegenstand der Sozialwissenschaften* (Luederssen, K. *et al.*) Nomos: Baden-Baden.

Teubner, G. (1982) Substantive and reflexive elements in modern law. *Law and Society Review* **17**, 239.

Teubner, G. (1983) Corporate responsibility als Problem der Unternehmens-verfassung. *Zeitschrift fuer Gesellschafts-und Unternehmensrecht.* **11**, 34.

Teubner, G. (1984) Corporate fiduciary duties and their beneficiaries. A functional approach to the legal institutionalization of corporate responsibility. In *Corporate Governance and Directors' Liability* (Hopt, K. J. & Teubner, G., Eds). Walter de Gruyter: Berlin, New York.

Teubner, G. & Willke, H. (1984) Kontext und Autonomie. Gesellschaftliche Selbststeuerung durch reflexives Recht. *Zeitschrift fuer Rechtssoziologie* **6**, 4.

Unger, M. (1976) *Law in Modern Society. Toward a Criticism of Social Theory*. Free Press: New York.

Unger, M. (1983) The critical legal studies movement. *Harvard Law Review* **96**, 563.

Varela, F. J. (1979) *Principles of Biological Autonomy*. North Holland: New York.

Waelde, T. (1979) *Juristische Folgenorientierung. "Policy Analysis" und Sozial kybernetik.* Athenaeum: Koenigstein.

Wedderburn, K. W. (1984) The legal development of corporate responsibility. In *Corporate Governance and Directors' Liability* (Hopt, K. J. & Teubner, G., Eds). Walter de Gruyter: Berlin, New York.

Wiethoelter, R. (1982) Entwicklung des Rechtsbegriffs. In *Rechtsformen der Verflechtung von Staat und Wirtschaft* (Gessner, V. & Winter, G. Eds). Westdeutscher Verlag: Opladen

Wiethoelter, R. (1984) Materialization and Proceduralization in Modern Law. In *Dilemmas of Law in the Welfare State* (Teubner, G., Ed.). Walter de Gruyter: Berlin, New York.

Willke, H. (1982) *Gesellschaftliche Kriterien oekonomischer Rationalitaet*. Typoscript: Koeln.

Willke, H. (1983) *Entzauberung des Staates*. Athenaeum: Koenigstein.

Winter, G. (1982) Literaturbericht zum Thema. In *Rechtsformen der Verflechtung von Staat und Wirtschaft* (Gessner, V. & Winter, G., Eds). Westdeutscher Verlag: Opladen.

Zeleny, M. (1981) (Ed.) *Autopoiesis: A Theory of the Living Organization*. Reidel: New York.

Ziegert, K. (1975) *Zur Effektivitaet der Rechtssoziologie. Die Rekonstruktion der Gesellschaft durch Recht*. Enke: Stuttgart.

Date received: April 1984

[3]

*On Modes of Production of Law and Social Power**

BOAVENTURA DE SOUSA SANTOS
University of Coimbra, Portugal

Introduction

For many years law was identified with the law of the state, the law produced by the legislature or the higher courts and distributed by the lower courts, the police, the prison system and a myriad of state regulatory agencies to be consumed by all ordinary citizens. Legal philosophy first, and Anglo–American social anthropology and sociology later, led to the conclusion that there were in society many more legal orders than those recognised as such by the state. During my field work in the squatter settlements of Rio de Janeiro (Brazil) in 1970, I came to the conclusion that the *favela* in which I lived had its own internal legal system, distinct from the Brazilian official legal system (Santos, 1977). It was a situation of legal pluralism, a concept coined by legal philosophers and historians of the end of the nineteenth century and beginning of the twentieth century and, later, elaborated upon by legal anthropology and sociology (Abel, 1979; Bohannan, 1967; Bobbio, 1942; Carbonnier, 1979; Del Vecchio, 1957; Ehrlich, 1936; Fitzpatrick, 1983; Galanter, 1981; Hooker, 1975; Macaulay, 1983; Moore, 1978; Nader, 1969). In this my work as in the work of other researchers along the same lines, I soon identified two major problems: firstly, the conception of a plurality of legal systems within the same political space could lead to a relative neglect of the state law as a central form of law in our societies [1]; secondly, once the concept of law was disengaged from the concept of the state, the identification of a plurality of laws would know no limit with the result that, if law is everywhere, it is nowhere [2].

As far as social power or power in society is concerned, the dominant view for many years was that the social power that really mattered was identical with political power and that political power was identical with state power.

*An earlier version of this paper was presented at the University of Madison-Wisconsin, November 1983 and to the European Conference on Critical Legal Studies, Coimbra, March 1985.

Conservative political philosophy, the sociology of organisations and, more recently, Foucault (1976; 1977; 1980) have shown that there are in society other important sources of social power besides the state. But again two problems are posed: firstly, if there is a multitude of forms of power operating in society, how to establish the specificity and the centrality of state power? Secondly, are all forms of power equivalent? And, if power is everywhere, it is anywhere? [3]

In this paper I will try to answer some of these questions. My main thesis is that

> capitalist societies are *political* formations or configurations which are constituted by four basic modes of production of political power articulated in specific ways. These modes of production generate four basic forms of power which, though interrelated, are structurally autonomous. Concomitantly, capitalist societies are *legal* formations or configurations which are constituted by four basic modes of production of law articulated in specific ways. These modes of production generate four basic forms of law which, though interrelated, are structurally autonomous.

As we approach the end of the twentieth century, our conceptions about the nature of capitalism, the state or the law are increasingly confusing and self-contradictory. In my view, this is due to three main factors. Firstly, we continue to analyse the complex processes of social transformation of our time in terms of the concepts originated or consolidated in the nineteenth century—such as the conceptual distinctions state/civil society, politics/economy, public/private — whose adequacy is reaching a breaking point. Secondly, the nation–state has predominated as both the unit of analysis and the research logic, which has prevented us from grasping both the autonomy of structures and processes in smaller social units (the infra-state logic) and the autonomy of global movements at the level of the world system (the supra-state logic). Thirdly, because it is based on the social experiences of core societies (that is, the advanced capitalist countries) our social theory is bound to produce spurious generalisations. As a consequence, our conceptual frameworks tend to be less than adequate for comparative analysis. The more general the social theory, the more likely it will be based on the social experiences of the advanced capitalist countries and biased in their favour (the bias of centrecentrism).

In recent times two conflicting arguments have been presented about the nature of capitalist development. One basically argues "that capitalism has never historically operated in the mode its ideology dictates because it cannot and that, as a consequence, the final triumph of capitalist values will be the sign of the final crisis of capitalism as a system" (Wallerstein 1980, p.374). The other argument, presented by Hirschman (1977) is that capitalism cannot be criticised for being repressive, alienating, or one-dimensional in contrast with its basic values, because capitalism has indeed accomplished what it was expected to accomplish, namely "to repress certain human drives and proclivities and to fashion a less multifaceted, less unpredictable and more 'one-dimensional' human personality'' (1977, p.132). In other words, ''capitalism was supposed to accomplish exactly what was soon to be denounced as its worst feature'' (1977, p.132). Thus, the survival of capitalism is premised upon the denial of its ideology, in one case, and upon the tireless fulfillment of it, in the other.

Similar conflicting arguments can be found in the recent work on the nature of the capitalist state. While some authors have shown the tendency for the state to intervene and to penetrate more and more in the civil society and to do so in an increasingly authoritarian way—what has been described as the ''regulatory state'', ''authoritarian statism'', ''surveiled democracy'', ''liberal corporatism'', ''friendly fascism'', or ''fascism with human face''—other authors (and even the same authors) have converged in the idea, seemingly inconsistent with the previous one, that the state is increasingly inept to perform the variety of tasks—facilitative and repressive, legitimation oriented and accumulation oriented—expected from it by an economic and social structure dominated by monopoly capital. According to this idea, the state lacks either the financial resources (the argument of the fiscal crisis), or the institutional capacity (the argument of the inadequacy of state bureaucracy to adapt to a fast-changing economic environment) or still it lacks the mechanisms that in civil society steer the action and account for efficiency (the argument of the lack of market signals). The state emerges in these analyses as both an all-engulfing leviathan and as a failing structure (to the point that a theory of the failure of the state is already being called for: Jänicke, 1980).

Finally, in the field of law, there have also been put forward in recent times conflicting arguments as to the nature of the role of law and particularly of the rule of law in our fast-changing societies. While some authors have described (and also prescribed: Hunt, 1981) the increasing centrality of law in our societies as a civilizational asset, the unqualified human good attributed to the rule of law by E. P. Thompson (1975), other authors have, on the contrary, described (and sometimes prescribed: Bankowski & Mungham, 1976) the fast decline of law in late capitalist societies either because it has been encircled and even emptied by other forms of social control (Foucault's argument of the rise of disciplinary power-knowledge) or because its formal rationality is unfit for a social engineering based on particularistic, flexible regulation (Poulantzas' (1978b) and Offe's argument (1984, p. 252)) or still because it has been over-used and over-extended to the point of risking degeneration (Habermas' (1982) and most recent Teubner's argument (1983)).

One striking thing about these arguments is that all of them seem to have a grain of truth; all sound true in that they uncover a specific aspect of social transformation in our time. But they also sound unconvincing or even utterly wrong in their claim of generality. It is not my intention to offer here a thorough critique of all these positions. I will concentrate on the arguments dealing specifically with state power and law and even here I will remain, so to say, at an archeological level as I will simply try to show that the difficulties with these arguments lie deeply in the conceptual framework within which they operate.

I will start by criticising some of the concepts which in my view have become epistemological obstacles to the advancement of social knowledge. They are, above all, the conceptual distinction between state and civil society and also some of its corollaries, such as the separation of the economic realm from the political realm; the reduction of political power to state power; the identification of law with state law; and finally, the separation of law from politics. I designate all these conceptions as a 'conceptual orthodoxy' to signal that their predominance in social thought is compatible with their theoretical bankruptcy. [4]. I will then present the outline of an alternative conceptual framework, which, I hope, will open up a new scientific agenda. I also suggest that my alternative will enable us to direct our research strategies towards solving some old questions which are being asked again today with increasing political drama, for example, by decreasing order of generality: the question of the pathology of modernity as recently reformulated by Habermas (1982); the question of the decline of law and particularly, of the rule of law; and finally the question of deregulation or delegalisation, the so-called regulatory crisis.

State and civil society

It has been said that the dualism state/civil society is the greatest of all dualisms in modern western thought (Gamble, 1982, p.45). In this conception the state is a contrived reality, an artificial, modern creation, when compared with civil society. In our century no one has expressed this idea better than Hayek: "Societies form, but states are made" (1979, p.140). The modernity of the nineteenth century constitutional state was featured in its formal organisation, its internal unity, its absolute sovereignty in a system of states and above all in its unified and centralised legal system, conceived as the universal language through which the state communicated with civil society. In contrast with the state, civil society was viewed as the realm of economic life, of spontaneous social relations guided by private, particularistic interests.

However, the dualism state/civil society was never unequivocal and, indeed, it was from the start pregnant with contradictions and bound to be in permanent crisis. To begin with, the principle of the separation state/civil society encompassed both the idea of a minimum state and of a maximum state, as state action was simultaneously conceived as a potential enemy of individual freedom and as the condition of its exercise. The state as a contrived reality was the necessary condition of the spontaneous reality of civil society. Eighteenth century thought is saturated with this contradiction since its proclamation to free economic activity from the corporatist regulations of the ancient régime by no means involves the conclusion that modern economy will dispense with enlightened state action [5].

This is particularly evident in the work of Adam Smith (1937) for whom the idea that commerce generates freedom and civilisation goes hand in hand with the defence of political institutions that secure a free and civilized commerce. The state is assigned a very active and indeed a crucial role in creating the institutional and legal conditions for the expansion of the market [6]. As Billet has justly said from the first to the last chapter of *An Inquiry Into the Nature and Causes of the Wealth of Nations* "one is struck by the idea, crucial to Adam Smith's thought, that the character of a nation's political institutions and practices decisively affects its capacity for sustained economic development" (1975, p.430). Comparing Portugal and Spain with Britain, Adam Smith considers the despotic nature of the former states, their "violent and arbitrary government" as responsible for their stagnant economies and relative poverty:

> Industry is there neither free nor secure and the civil and ecclesiastical governments of both Spain and Portugal are such as would be alone sufficient to perpetuate their present state of poverty (Smith, 1937; p.509).

Still more striking is that for Smith despotism may be either the result of an arbitrary government, ruling by force and unrestrained by institutional or legal constraints, or the result of a weak government, an unstable authority incapable of maintaining law and order and of performing the regulative functions required by the economy (Billet, 1975, p.439; Viner, 1927, p.218).

The idea of the separation of the economic from the political, based on the state/civil society distinction and expressed in the *laissez faire* principle, seems to be fraught with two insoluble contradictions. The first contradiction is that, given the particularistic nature of interests in civil society, the principle of *laissez faire* cannot be equally valid for all possible interests. Its internal coherence is premised upon an accepted hierarchy of interests, candidly implied in John Stuart Mill's dictum that "every departure from *laissez faire*, unless required by some great good, is a certain evil" (1921, p.950). The discussion of the principle always takes place in the shadow of the discussion of the interests to which the principle is to be applied. Thus, the same legal measure may be object of opposing but equally consistent interpretations. To give an illustration, the joint stock legislation of 1825–65 was viewed by some as a good example of *laissez faire* in that it removed restrictions on the mobility of capital, and by others as a clear violation of *laissez faire* in that it accorded privileges to corporate enterprises which were denied to the individual entrepreneurs (Taylor, 1972, p.12). This explains why Victorian England has been portrayed by some as the age of *laissez faire* and by others as the embryo of the welfare state [7].

The second contradiction concerns the mechanisms by which the principle of *laissez faire* is socially activated. Nineteenth-century England witnessed not only the growth of legislation on social and economic policy but also the rise of an amalgam of new state institutions such as the Factory Inspectorate, the Poor Law Board, the General Board of Health, etc. Interestingly enough, some of the laws and institutions were intended to carry out *laissez faire* policies. As Dicey noticed "sincere believers in *laissez faire* found that for the attainment of their ends the improvement and the strengthening of governmental machinery was an absolute necessity" (1905, p.306). This means that to a great extent *laissez faire* policies were carried out through active state intervention. In other words, the state had to intervene in order not to intervene.

In view of all this the question emerges: if the state/civil society distinction was so pregnant with contradictions why was it so widely accepted, so self-evident and even commonsensical?

Before trying to answer this question I would like to illustrate breifly the weight of this conceptual orthodoxy within Marxism itself as this will be linked to the further development of my argument. Leaving aside the English and French liberal political theory of the eighteenth century and focusing solely on the nearest background of Marx's thought, the German context, it should be emphasised that, according to Hegel (1981), civil society is a transitional stage in the development of the idea, the final stage being the state. The family is the thesis, civil society is the antithesis and the state is the synthesis. Civil society is the "system of needs", the destruction of the unity of the family and the atomization of its members; in sum, the realm of particularistic interests and of egotism, a stage to be superseded by the state as the ultimate unifier of interests, the universal idea, the most final completion of moral consciousness (1981, p.140). There are thus two threads in Hegel's thought about the state and civil society. One, very much subsidiary of the English and French liberal thought, is the conceptual distinction between state and civil society in terms of contradictory entities. The other, distinctively Hegelian, is the idea that the concept of civil society is not on an equal foot (on the same speculative level) with the concept of the state. It corresponds to a lesser developed stage of consciousness actually to be subsumed by the state and as such the dichotomy state/civil society as two autonomous self-identical concepts, is thus theoretically untenable. Though this latter thread, in spite of its mystifactory content, is in my view still today most crucial to understanding of the historical social processes of capitalist societies, it was abandoned in the philosophical and historical controversies that followed Hegel's work. The reification of the dichotomy state/civil society was soon accomplished, mainly through the writings of Lorenz von Stein II (e.g. 1888).

In spite of the brilliant rescue attempt undertaken by Max Adler (1922), I think that Marx accepted the reified version of the state/civil society distinction. He inverted it but didn't supersede it. He discovered that the allegedly 'natural' laws of classical economy hid social relations of exploitation which the state, only apparently neutral, had the function to guarantee.

Rather than the universal social interest, the state represented the interest of capital in reproducing itself. However, interested as he was in meeting the classical economy on its own ground, Marx ended up trapped in the separation between economy and politics, and tended to reduce politics and law to state action. He could not see the real (and not merely metaphorical) sense in which the 'economic relations' were not only social relations but also distinctively political and legal in their structural constitution. The metaphor of the economic base grounding the political and legal superstructure is thus not a complete distortion of Marx's thought as can be demonstrated by its remarkable resilience in light of the subsequent attempts to reconstruct the question it meant to address. I will mention very briefly one of such attempts, by far the most influential within the western Marxism of the last 20 years. I am referring to the French structuralist Marxism of Althusser and his group—with its theory of relatively autonomous instances (the economic, the political, the ideological), the concept of over-determination and the principle of economic determination in the last instance. The bias of economism is still present in this school and it is rather visible in the work of Poulantzas (1978a), without any doubt the most brilliant analyst of law and politics in this school. In his analysis of the relation of property as one of the elements of the economic instance he emphasises that "it should be noted that it belongs strictly to the region of the economic and that it should be clearly distinguished from the juridical forms with which it is invested i.e. from juridical property" (1978a, p.26). And he criticises Maurice Godelier for ignoring that "the relations of production and the productive forces belong to the same combination/structure of the economic whereas private (juridical) ownership of the means of production belongs to the superstructure" (1978a, p.67) [8].

How to explain the self-evidence of the conception of the economic as a separate and autonomous realm and of the correspondent conception of the political and legal as an exclusive attribute of the state? How to explain the persistence of the state/civil society dichotomy in spite of its internal contradictions and permanent crises?

As with any other social doctrine this conceptual orthodoxy has a shred of truth. In feudalism, necessary labour (that is, the labour required for the subsistence of the serfs) and surplus labour (that is, the labour peformed by the serfs to guarantee the subsistence and accumulation of the feudal lords) were separate both in time and in space. Because the feudal lords did not own the means of production they had to rely on the political and legal institutions of the state to extract from the serfs the surplus labour. In a way, since the feudal lords had no private ownership of the means of production, their social power was most directly linked to their private ownership of the state. In capitalism, on the contrary, necessary and surplus labour take place within the same labour process given the control over the latter by capitalists as an attribute of their ownership of the means of production. Once the state guarantees the enforcement of the law of property, class relations occur and reproduce by themselves in the private realm of the factory. It seems, therefore, that the externality of the state *vis à vis* the relations of production is the correlate of the conceptualisation of production relations as an economic, private affair between private individuals within the civil society.

On further reflection, this derivation is not logically necessary. Without questioning the externality of the political and legal institutions of the state *vis à vis* the production relations, it should be equally logical to conceive these relations inside the factory as a set of political and legal social processes taking place outside the state, under the direct control of capital. And indeed it would not be difficult to detect, inside the factory, legislative bodies, power blocks, coalitions, legal regulations, dispute settlement mechanisms, positive and negative sanctions, police surveillance, etc. Why was this alternative conceptualisation of factory reality not adopted? Why was this extreme variety of social processes lumped together in the amorphous concept of "economic relations?"

In my view the separation of the economic from the political made possible both the naturalisation of capitalist economic exploitation and the neutralisation of the revolutionary potential of liberal politics—two processes that converged to consolidate the capitalist model of social relations.

If by an exercise of imagination we compare social relations across time, it is in the field of political relations, the relations in the public place, that capitalist societies represent most unequivocally a civilisational progress. For the first time in history, the state has become truly public, that is, not the private possession of any specific group [9]. The universalisation of citizenship through equal civil and political rights, made the state, in all its theoretical attributes, the ultimate consubstantiation of the democratic ideal of equal participation in social affairs.

If, on the contrary, we take production relations in capitalist societies, the picture is almost the negative of the previous one. We may still grant to capitalism a tremendous progress in terms of technology of production but concerning the social relations in production we are led to conclude with Meiksins Wood that "in no other system of production is work so thoroughly disciplined and organised, and no other organisation of production is so directly responsive to the demands of appropriation" (1981, p.91). This unprecedented control over production is what Marx called the despotism of the workshop (1970) and Braverman the degradation of the labour process (1974).

It is my view that the dichotomy economy/politics made these two pictures imcomparable or incommensurable. It kept them separate in such a way that the political form of social relations could not become the model for the economic form of social relations. Confined to the public place, the democratic ideal was neutralised or strongly limited in its emancipatory potential. On the other hand, the conversion of the public place into the exclusive site of law and politics performed a crucial legitimation function in that it convincingly obscured the fact that the law and the politics of the capitalist state could only operate as part of a broader political and legal configuration in which other contrasting forms of law and politics were included.

In the periphery of the world economy, that is, in the colonies first and in the less developed, peripheral countries later, the shred of truth of the dichotomy state/civil society was even thinner. There civil society was from the start a product of the state in the most direct sense. More so than in the metropolitan countries, the creation of the labour force was an administrative issue for the colonial state or for the quasi-state colonial companies. Moreover, the persistence of pre-capitalist modes of production, submitted to capital through market mechanisms but autonomous in terms of the organisation of production, called for the direct political control of surplus appropriation and thus for a certain privatisation of state power and state functions as illustrated in *coronelismo* (in Brazil) and *caudilhismo* (in Spanish speaking Latin America).

Thus, both in the core and in the periphery of the world economy, the conceptual orthodoxy I have been criticizing has become today an epistemological obstacle calling for a theoretical alternative.

A structural map of capitalist societies

When we compare capitalist societies with feudal societies, one of the most striking features of capitalist societies is the extent to which power relations are institutionalised and juridified and particularly the extreme diversity of institutional and legal forms in which social life is moulded. The political nature of power is not the exclusive attribute of any given form of power, it is rather the global effect of the combination of the different forms of power and of the modes of production thereof. Similarly, the legal regulation of social relations is not the exclusive attribute of any form of normative order, it is rather the end result of the combination of the different forms of law and the modes of production thereof.

I distinguish in society four structures upon which four primary clusters of social relations are grounded. These structures I call *the householdplace*, the *workplace*, the *citizenplace*, and the *worldplace*. For clarification purposes I will resort to systems language and say that these places are the organising matrix of four systems, the domestic system, the production system, the sovereignty system, and the world system.

The social relations clustered around the householdplace are constitutive of the mutual obligations imposed on family members and consist mainly of the relations between husband and wife and between either and the children and more generally of kinship relations [10]. The social relations clustered around the workplace are constitutive of the labour process and consist of both the relations of production at the level of the enterprise (between direct producers and appropriators of surplus value) and the relations in production (between workers and management and among workers) [11]. The social relations clustered around the citizenplace are constitutive of the so-called public sphere and consist of the relations between citizens and the state. The social relations clustered around the worldplace are the relations among the nation-states as they integrate the world economy.

To see the worldplace as an internal (national) structure of social relations needs a brief explanation. For a long time social theory treated the nation-state, conceived as an insulated, self-contained social structure, as the privileged unit of analysis. In the last two decades, due mainly to dependency theory and the link it established between development and underdevelopment, the impact of international conditions was added to the scientific agenda. However, in the most important work produced so far in this area, that of Wallerstein (1980), the emphasis on world dynamics has been so dominant that the specificity of national conditions becomes almost irrelevant. This is particularly true of those social conditions that are traditionally most identified with territorial boundaries, such as law and politics. In my view, a proper balance must be found between the old and the new perspective not for the sake of eclecticism, but rather because capitalist development, being as worldwide as it is uneven, depends on the existence of sovereign national-states to reproduce such international unevenness. The balance is achieved in my scheme by conceptualizing the worldplace as an internal structure, that is, as the organising matrix of the pertinent effects of world conditions upon the internal workplace and citizenplace and, through these, upon the householdplace. Such pertinent effects are determined by the position a given society occupies in the world system, a position which is, in turn, determined by the extent to which such society is able to manipulate in its favour the fluctuations of the world economy.

The four structural places identified are complex in their internal constitution. Each consists of five structural elements, namely, a unit of social practice, an institutional form, a mechanism of social power, a form of law, and a mode of rationality (as shown in Fig. 1). As to the unit of social practice, it is the family in the householdplace, the class in the workplace, the individual in the citizenplace and the nation in the worldplace. The institutional form is marriage/kinship in the householdplace, the factory in the workplace, the state in the citizenplace and international agencies and bilateral/multilateral agreements in the worldplace. The mechanism of social power is patriarchy in the householdplace, exploitation in the workplace, domination in the citizenplace and unequal exchange in the worldplace. The form of law is domestic law in the householdplace [12], production law in the workplace, territorial law in the citizenplace and systemic law in the worldplace. Finally, the mode of rationality is affection-maximising in the householdplace, profit-maximising in the workplace, loyalty–maximising in the citizenplace and effectivity–maximising in the worldplace [13].

The four places are structurally autonomous though articulated and interpenetrated in different ways. Given the internal complexity of the four

Structural places \ Elementary components	Unit of social practice	Institutional form	Mechanism of power	Form of law	Mode of rationality
Householdplace	Family	Marriage/ kinship	Patriarchy	Domestic law	Affection maximising
Workplace	Class	Factory	Exploitation	Production law	Profit maximising
Citizenplace	Individual	State	Domination	Territorial law	Loyalty maximising
Worldplace	Nation	International agencies; bilateral/ multilateral agreements	Unequal exchange	Systemic law	Effectivity maximising

Figure 1. A structural map of capitalist societies.

structural places, most of the relations among them can only be established at the empirical level and tend to be different in core and in peripheral societies. At the theoretical level, using Erik Wright's model of determination (1979), the most that can be said is that: the workplace tends to establish the structural limits of the transformation of the householdplace and the citizenplace; the householdplace tends to determine ranges of outcomes in both the workplace and the citizenplace within a structurally limited range of possibilities, and it also mediates the relations between these two structural places; the citizenplace tends to reproduce social relations inside the workplace and the householdplace; the worldplace mediates the relations between the workplace and the citizenplace; the structural relations between the worldplace and the householdplace occur through the workplace and the citizenplace [14].

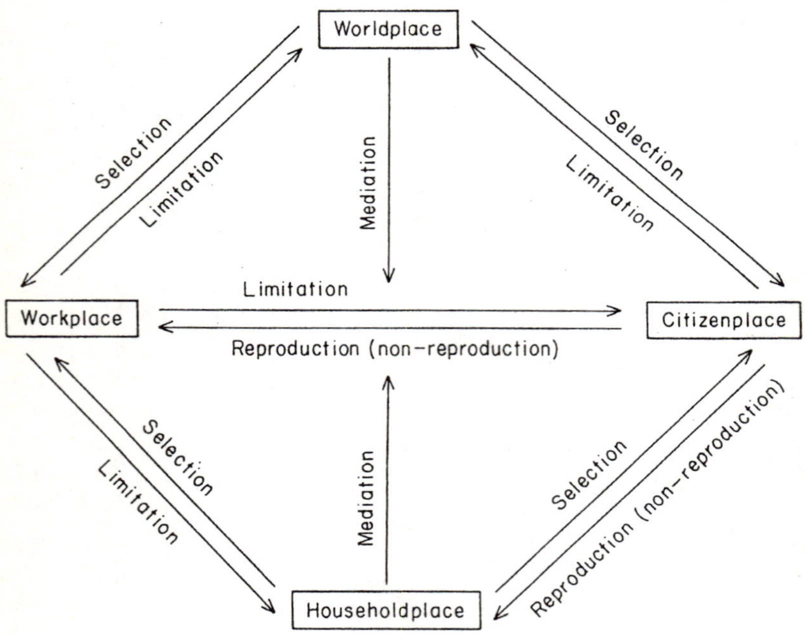

Figure 2. Structural relations (core countries).

Beyond this the structural relations among the four clusters of social relations tend to differ in core and in peripheral societies. In core societies the workplace and the citizenplace tend to establish the limits of the transformation of the worldplace while the latter selects among possible developments within the former (Fig. 2). In peripheral societies, on the contrary, the worldplace tends to establish the limits of transformation of both the workplace and the citizenplace, while these select among possible developments of the worldplace

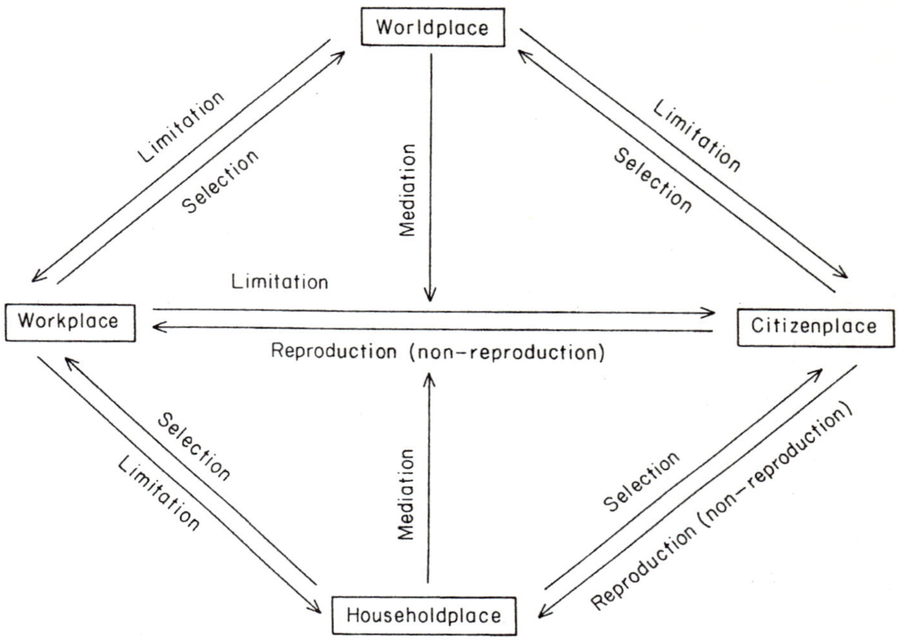

Figure 3. Structural relations (peripheral countries).

(Fig. 3). Thus, the weaker the worldplace position of a given society the greater the probability that its workplace and citizenplace and, through them, its householdplace will be affected by the workplace and the citizenplace of a core society [15].

To call these places structural means to see them not only as the most basic clusters of social relations, but also as being structurally autonomous. There are other clusters of social relations, but they occupy intermediate positions among the householdplace, the workplace, the citizenplace, and the worldplace and as such they lack structural autonomy. They are heterogeneous in their internal texture, for they combine elements of all or some of the structural places. For instance, the health, or the education system are clusters of social relations located between the householdplace, the workplace, and the citizenplace. Similarly, multinational corporations are heterogeneous clusters of social relations in our societies as they integrate elements from three structural places. For instance, multinational corporations, as an institutional form, combine elements of the factory, of the state, and of international agencies. As modes of rationality they combine profit maximising with loyalty maximising and effectivity maximising (Fig. 4) [16].

I will now provide this model with some historical concreteness, concerning

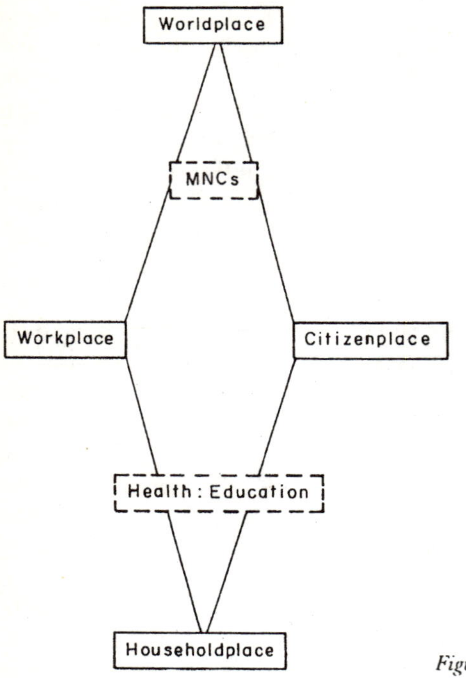

Figure 4. Heterogeneous clusters of social relations.

in particular the institutional forms, the forms of law and the mechanisms of social power.

I will argue that the hidden basis of capitalist development lies, firstly, in a complex articulation between different modes of production of political power and centred around four political institutions: marriage/kinship, the factory, the state, and international agencies/bilateral and multilateral agreements; and secondly, in a socially constructed suppression of the political and legal character of the social relations inside all institutions except the state: social relations inside marriage/kinship are transformed into effective necessities, natural predispositions, mutual protection and management of emotions, social relations inside the factory are transformed into technical necessities, organisational innovations, industrial relations, and scientific management; and social relations inside international agencies and agreements are transformed into relations among sovereign countries, new international economic order, external debt, or, at the most, into a 'rudimentary', non-coercive form of law (international law).

Starting with a historical example and restricting myself for now to the workplace and the citizenplace, I will review Marx's analysis of the emergence of the factory acts in nineteenth-century England in the first volume of *Capital* (Chapter 10) and offer a partial re-interpretation.

The crucial role of the state and state legislation in the creation of the labour force required by the emerging capitalist mode of production is today well documented. This is a long historical process that in England lasted from the fifteenth to the eighteenth century. As Marx puts it in the *Grundrisse* "the annals of English legislation contain the bloody handwriting of coercive measures employed to transform the mass of the population, after they had become propertyless and free, into free wage labourers" (1973, p.769). Marx analyses then in *Capital* the "bloody legislation against vagabondage" at the end of the fifteenth century and during the whole sixteenth century throughout Europe (1970, p.734).

These were laws that created the labour force and were an essential factor of so-called primitive accumulation. Once this stage was concluded and the labour force was created one would think that capitalist relations of production would develop by themselves. In capitalism, as I already mentioned, "surplus labour and necessary labour glide one into the other" (Marx 1970, p.236) and as a result "the dull compulsion of economic relations" (Marx 1970, p.737) operates by itself making superfluous any direct intervention of the state in the appropriation of the surplus labour by capitalists. Indeed, this is only part of the picture. Firstly, because the "dull compulsion of economic relations" was in fact constituted by the state law of property and the law of contract. Secondly, because whenever the economic compulsion failed (as in the case of destruction of machinery or of strikes) its operation could only be restored by state coercive intervention. And, thirdly, because the state intervention in the reproduction of the labour force went much beyond coercive measures against workers in exceptional situations. The factory acts on the working day are a good illustration of such an intervention [17].

Marx emphasises that given "the passion of capital for an unlimited and reckless extension of the working day" (1970, p.298) "the factory legislation was the first conscious and methodical reaction of society against the spontaneously developed form of the process of production" (1970, p.480). Were these laws against the interests of capital? "No", Marx replies, because the "unrestricted waste of human life" (1970, p.475) resulting from the "unnatural extension of the working day" (1970, p.266) would in the end paralyse the mechanism of exploitation. But the truth of the matter is that capitalists fought as much as they could against the promulgation of the factory acts and they used the most diverse devices to evade their enforcement once they were passed [18]. On the contrary, workers fought for those laws and Marx concluded that "the establishment of a normal working day is the result of centuries of struggle between capitalist and labourer" (1970, p.270), the product of a "protracted civil war" (1970, p.299).

Marx's analysis of the factory acts suffers from a certain ambiguity. If the factory acts furthered the interests of capital, why did capitalists fight against them? Why did the workers fight for them? If they were in favour of the interests of capital, were they necessarily detrimental to the interests of the workers?

These questions were not adequately answered by Marx. Neither were they answered in most analyses of the New Deal legislation, and they are still not being answered in the current discussions of the rise and demise of the welfare state or of the regulatory state.

In my view, the factory acts symbolise *an historical turning point in the articulation of citizenplace and workplace*, a process that laid out the structural foundations for class compromises in core societies and for their non-viability or instability in peripheral or semi-peripheral societies. The factory acts were an absolute gain for the workers at the level of the citizenplace. The corresponding absolute loss for capital at that level was, however, compensated for by the gains it did obtain at the level of the workplace within the new parameters established by the laws. Marx and social historians of the period emphasise that the factory acts contributed decisively to the restructuring of capital: they accelerated the transition from the manufacture system to the factory system and they changed the conditions of competition in favour of the most productive and technically advanced factories and industries. The gains for capital were thus an increase in the control over the social relations in the workplace through the intensification of the labour process (speed-ups, introduction of piece-wages, mechanisation, etc.). These gains could not be generalised to all capitals and capitalists. They were allocated to those that could convert the losses in the citizenplace into gains in the workplace. All others would disappear or be proletarianised. For those capitalists that succeeded, the loss in the citizenplace was compensated for or neutralised by the gain in the workplace. For the workers the inverse was true.

But the most important feature of this transaction is that, due to the autonomy of the structural places, it remained invisible, it remained below the threshold of social consciousness. This game of gains and losses was socially constructed not as a positive sum game between the workplace and the citizenplace but as two separate zero sum games—one in the workplace, the other in the citizenplace—whose results could not be measured one against the other. Gains for workers and losses for capital in the citizenplace; gains for capital and losses for workers in the workplace. That is, the gains and losses were not compensated for at the same level, nor were they perceived as results of reciprocal developments and as such their structural combination remained hidden. Capital's loss of political power within the citizenplace could not be measured against its gain of political power in the workplace. Its loss of control over territorial law could not be measured against its gain of control over production law.

The incommensurability of gains and losses was crucial to consolidate and legitimate capitalist social relations because it reinforced the differences between the workplace and the citizenplace. It made clear that the distribution of social power and legal competence to the workers in the citizenplace could never expand to the workplace in the same way or by the same process, and that this fact would not be conceived as the result of a political decision but rather as the technical consequence of the structural autonomy of the two places. In other words, under capitalist social relations, the worker would always be less a citizen of his or her factory than of his or her country; moreover, such a discrepancy would be considered to be not only inevitable but also natural.

The fact that the worker's gains were obtained in the citizenplace was important in itself. They were translated into territorial law, a form of law based on rights. Given their institutional separation from the workplace, rights are relatively stable entitlements. They are not strictly tied up to the fluctuations of the economic cycle. This lack of reciprocity with production reinforced the mode of rationality of the citizenplace, which I have called loyalty-maximising, and by the same token stabilised its mechanism of power which I have called domination (that is, coercion plus hegemony). However, this relative stability was obtained through a process which simultaneously obtained the consent of the workers to be subjected, within the workplace, to production law, a form of law based not on rights but on interests. And since interests are defined by the rationality of profit maximising and satisfied through the mechanism of exploitation, they are precarious entitlements, strictly tied up to the fluctuations of production and as unstable as production itself.

In other words, the factory acts legitimated the state before the workers-as-citizens and, by the same process, they legitimated the factory before the workers-as-a-class-of-wage-labourers. This laid out the structural foundation for the types of class compromises that were later on achieved most notably by social democracy in the core countries.

It is by now clear that in my view the ideological nature of law in capitalist societies does not lie in the discrepancy between law in books and law in action, as is commonly assumed, but rather in a well-knit social construction that converts territorial law into the exclusive form of law, suppressing thereby domestic law, production law, and systemic law, without which territorial law could not operate as it does in our society. Legal doctrine, no matter how critical, has done nothing since the nineteenth century but consolidate and legitimate this suppression of dimensions of the legal formation. Capitalism in this sense is less than democratic, not because the law of the citizenplace is less than democratic, but rather because this form of law, no matter how democratic, must coexist with the more despotic law of production, a relation increasingly mediated by (also less than democratic) domestic law and systemic law.

This explains why all the attempts to create industrial citizenship, under conditions of capitalist appropriation of the means of production are always bound to fail whenever they come into conflict with the logic of profit maximising [19].

What is characteristic of capitalist societies is that the primacy of the political (much more prominent than in feudal societies) manifests itself in a fragmented and asymmetric way. Capitalist societies are indeed segmented societies, as anthropologists would say, organised according to the principle that the political and legal forms of the citizenplace set the boundaries for all the other clusters of social relations, somehow operating like revolving doors through which other forms of political power and law circulate in society.

Marx was acutely aware of the changes in the regulation of labour taking shape in his time and indeed he established the material base for the articulation among different political and legal forms when he distinguished between the division of labour in society at large and the division of labour in the workshop and related one to the other:

> The division of labour in the workshop implies concentration of the means of production in the hands of one capitalist; the division of labour in society implies their dispersion among many independent producers of commodities... in a society with capitalist production, anarchy in the social division of labour and despotism in that of the workshop are mutual conditions the one of the other (1970, p.355–6).

But he failed to see in these changes the dynamics of the articulation among political and legal forms and institutions throughout society. When he uses the terms political and legal in the context of the workplace he does so in an analogical or metaphorical sense. The forms of cooperation set in motion by capitalist production are such that "that a capitalist should command on the field of production is now as indispensable as that a general should command on the field of the battle" (1970, p.330). However, this power of command is not merely a technical function, it is rather and at the same time a "function of the exploitation of a social labour process" (1970, p.331). The political analogy is taken to the extreme when Marx says that:

> This power of Asiatic and Egyptian kings, Etruscan theocrats, etc., has in modern society been transferred to the capitalist, whether he be an isolated or, as in joint-stock companies, a collective capitalist (1970, p.334).

As to the legal analogy or metaphor, the factory code is conceived as a "caricature", a code

> in which capital formulates like a private legislator and at his own good will, his autocracy over his workpeople, unaccompanied by the division of responsibility, in other matters so much approved of by the bourgeoisie, and still unaccompanied by the still more approved representative system... (1970, p.424).

The main point of my argument is that the power of command in the workshop is not political power in any metaphorical sense. It is as political as the power of the citizenplace, the power of the householdplace or the power of the worldplace. They are different in their forms as they derive from different modes of production (exploitation, domination, patriarchy and unequal exchange) but this does not alter their political nature. On the contrary, such nature is not an attribute of any of them taken separately, it is rather the aggregate effect of the articulations among them.

Similarly, the factory code is not law in any metaphorical sense. It is law, just as the law of the state is law. Moreover, the fact that it is unhampered by the representative system of the citizenplace doesn't make it a caricature. The despotic law of production is a necessary condition of democratic territorial law.

The idea of conceiving regulation of labour in the factory as a form of law was originally hinted at by the Austrian Marxists, particularly by Max Adler in *Zuchthaus und Fabrik* (n.d.) and K. Renner's *The Institutions of Private Law and Their Social Functions* (1976). Adler is mostly concerned with the functional and structural relations between the prison and the factory, thus inaugurating a line of research that was later on pursued by the Frankfurt School through Rusche & Kirchheimer, *Punishment and Social Structure* (1968), and most recently by Foucault's *Discipline and Punish* (1977) and Melossi's & Pavarini's *The Prison and The Factory* (1981) [20]. Closer to my concerns here is K. Renner's political and legal conception of the organisation of production.

K. Renner is best known for his theory of property. According to him, the law of property, originated in the Roman law as "a person's all-embracing legal power over a tangible object" (1976, p.81), changed completely its social function in the transition from feudalism to capitalism when the means of production became an object of private appropriation. While previously, property rights granted to the proprietor a mere control over things, with the emergence of capitalism and the private appropriation of the means of production, the control over things was transformed, subreptitiously as it were, into a control over people, that is, a control over the workers operating, through the contract of labour, the means of production:

> In the eyes of the law, the property-subject is related to the object only, controlling matter alone. But what is control of property in law, becomes in fact man's control of human beings, of the wage-labourers, as soon as property has developed into capital. The individual called owner sets the tasks to others, he makes them subject to commands and, at least, in the initial stages of capitalist development, supervises the execution of his commands. The owner of a *res* imposes his will upon *personae*, autonomy is converted into heteronomy of will (1976, p.106).

According to Renner, the most relevant aspect of this transformation is that the right of ownership assumes a new social function without any change in the norm itself. As the literal formulation of the norm does not change, the change in its social function remains ideologically hidden.

This social theory of property is complemented with a political and legal conception of the organisation of production, a lesser known aspect of Renner's work but particularly relevant for my argument here. In his view, the regulation of labour inside the factory, under the command of capital, is a delegated public authority since "the institution of property leads automatically to an organisation similar to the state" (1976, p.107). Accordingly, "the factory is an establishment with its own code with all the characteristics of a legal code" (1976, p.115). Renner sharply criticises lawyers and legal doctrine for not taking in due account this legal reality:

> we see further that this regulation of power and labour remains concealed to the whole of bourgeois legal doctrine which is aware of nothing but its most formal, general and extraneous limitations (1976, p.114).

But in spite of pointing in the right direction, Renner should be criticised on three accounts. Firstly, he takes too far the identification of law and power of the state with law and power of the factory. He fails to recognise the structural differences between state and factory as two institutional forms and, consequently, the structural differences between the two forms of law and social power through which they operate. In my view, such differences and their articulation is what characterises capitalist societies most specifically. Secondly, Renner conceives power and law in the factory as exclusively coercive. It is true, as I have already mentioned, that production and labour are as tightly organised and disciplined in capitalism as never before. This, however, does not mean that such organisation and discipline are only made effective through coercion. Thirdly, Renner neglects the historical specificity of capitalism as when he says that "the employment relationship is. . . a public obligation to service, like the serfdom of feudal times" (1976, p.115). This is obviously not true. What differentiates capitalism from feudalism is precisely the privatisation of the political power over production which separates the control over production from the performance of public functions and communal services typical of feudalism (Brenner, 1977; Wood, 1981, p.86).

In recent times, Michael Burawoy has presented the most forceful argument in favour of a broad political conception of the labour process. Resorting to the Gramscian concept of hegemony, Burawoy shows that the specificity of the capitalist organisation of production is that it must elicit, in order to be efficient, the active consent and the participation of workers in their own exploitation (1979, p.27). This conception is rendered by the idea of the factory as an 'internal state', an idea that, as we saw, goes back to Renner at the same time that it echoes explicitly Selznick's theory of industrial justice (1969). Burawoy's main thesis is that the despotic form of production relations in the phase of competitive capitalism has evolved, in the phase of large corporations and trade unionism, into an hegemonic form, resting "on a limited participation by representatives of labour in the government of industry" (1979, p.110). This evolution is captured by the concept of the 'internal state' by which he means:

> the set of institutions that organise, transform or repress struggles over relations in production and relations of production at the level of the enterprise (1979, p.110).

The most important among such institutions are the collective bargaining and grievance procedures.

I would like to qualify this stimulating analysis of the labour process with two critical observations. Firstly, though Burawoy, in contrast with Selznick, emphasises that the politics of production are subjected to the logic of securing and obscuring the extraction of surplus value, he takes too far, in a direction opposite to Renner, the identification of the politics of production with global politics or, in my conception, the politics of the workplace with the politics of the citizenplace. The structural difference between the two lies precisely in the presence in one of them of the logic of securing and obscuring the extraction of surplus. Such is the difference, which in my view, accounts for the despotic nature of the political and legal forms of the workplace [21]. This by no means contradicts the presence of hegemonic or consent components, which, as we well know after E.P. Thompson (1975) and Douglas Hay (1975), were also present in the despotic laws of the *ancien régime*. Coercion and consent, though present in both the workplace and the citizenplace, are different in their form and in their mode of production and combine according to different logics in the two structural places [22]. There are different hegemonies in society (family hegemony, state hegemony, factory hegemony, world hegemony) and they are not necessarily congruent.

The second critical observation is that, due to the relative collapsing of the different power forms, Burawoy neglects the central question of the articulation among them. Moreover, neither he nor Meiksins Wood, who has also in recent times argued in favour of the political character of production relations (1981), conceptualises in adequate terms the specificity of state law. Burawoy accepts implicitly the base/superstructure framework and Wood relapses into it, ending up by hesitantly locating part of state law in the base and part in the superstructure (1981, pp.79,80) [23].

In this section I have argued that the social reproduction of capitalist relations lies, firstly, in a complex articulation between four different modes of production of political power and law centred around four political institutions: marriage/kinship, factory, state, and international agencies/agreements; and, secondly, in a social construction that suppresses the political and legal character of social relations inside all institutions except the state.

This argument was developed with reference to the workplace and the citizenplace. With some adaptations, it could also be developed with reference to the householdplace. Since the 60s, women's studies have drawn our attention to the multiple forms of sexual discrimination. One of the most promising lines of research concentrates on the legal non-intervention in the private sphere in order to show the extent to which women are subjected to primary (as opposed to secondary) social control. According to Tove Stang Dahl and Annika Snare, "the significant factor is not so much what the law says but what it defines as outside the limits of its jurisdiction" (1978, p.17).

"Coercion of privacy" is the concept used by the two authors to illustrate the persistence of women's subordination in spite of the laws passed to eliminate some forms of sexual discrimination. In my view, coercion of privacy and primary social control is the realm of domestic law. Even if territorial law has eliminated some forms of discrimination, the social position of women remains 'unequal' because while the male worker occupies a subordinate position in production law but a superordinate position in domestic law, the female worker occupies a subordinate position in both kinds of law.

The argument presented in this section could also be extended to the social relations among nations in the worldplace, but that would be another paper.

Towards a new scientific agenda

The structural autonomy of the householdplace, the workplace, the citizenplace, and the worldplace is what distinguishes capitalist societies from all previous ones. This is, however, the product of a long historical process. As an illustration, in the early stages of capitalist development the structural elements of the citizenplace collapsed in many respects with those of the workplace [24]. This was due, in part, to the fact that the state was, particularly on the continent, an important organiser of production [25]. This complex intertwining of the coercive apparatus of the state with that of production prompted Adler's (n.d.), Rusche's & Kirchheimer's (1968) argument of the close functional relationship between the prison and the factory. From another perspective, looking at models of organisation of the citizenplace and the workplace, we should be reminded of Weber's (1948) and Hobsbawm's (1975) arguments that given the incapacity of the pre-capitalist family-based industries to establish the organisational model for the large enterprises emerging in the eighteenth century, such a model was sought in the military organisation and in the emerging state bureaucracy, a transplant particularly evident in the case of railways.

The autonomy of the structural places was accomplished differently and in different degrees in different countries. Today, looking at trends in the post-war period through the analytical windows opened up by the theoretical framework presented here, we witness a subtle but quite evident process of structural approximation or interpenetration between the workplace, the householdplace and the citizenplace. This is, however, a very different process from that observed in earlier times. It is different in at least two respects: firstly, it takes place under the increasing mediating pressure of the worldplace; secondly, it assumes different and combined forms in core and peripheral societies.

In core countries, in view of their capacity to influence global patterns of development in their own favour we have witnessed an increasing interpenetration between the householdplace, the workplace and the citizenplace, under the pulling effect of the citizenplace. Two different processes preside over this development: *the delegation process* and *the proliferation process*. By *delegation* I mean the process whereby the citizenplace transfers its mechanism of social power, entrusting it to the workplace and the householdplace. This delegation of power, a kind of indirect rule, is illustrated in most social policies of advanced capitalist countries in recent times. For instance, the so-called 'deregulation' of the economy in the U.S.A. implies a transference of policies of domination from the citizenplace to the workplace. Similarly, the idea that some of the social services and social security benefits, until now provided by the state, should in the future be provided by the family implies a transference of policies of domination from the citizenplace to the householdplace. These strategies enable the citizenplace to duplicate itself in the workplace and the householdplace without any formal expansion of its institutions or laws and indeed through some institutional reductions (programme and budget cuts) What I call *proliferation*, on the other hand, is a more complex process and consists in the increasing structural homology or isomorphism between the institutional and legal forms of the citizenplace and those of the workplace and the householdplace. In this process, there is no formal delegation of power but simply the social reproduction of citizenplace forms outside the citizenplace.

When we compare the transformations in the workplace, the citizenplace, and the householdplace in recent decades we are struck by the parallel developments in production law, in territorial law, and in domestic law. The development towards a more bureaucratic and technocratic form of regulation of the labour process, as documented by Braverman (1974), Edwards (1979) and Clawson (1980) among others, runs parallel to a similar development in territorial law and in the administration of justice, as documented by Habermas (1962), Luhmann (1972), Unger (1976), Nonet & Selznick (1978) and Heydebrand (1979) and runs also parallel to a similar development in domestic law and family life as documented by Donzelot (1977), Barrett (1980, p.227) and Hartman (1981) [26]. But even more striking is the fact that in the three structural places, these developments are combined with others of an apparently contradictory nature. In the workplace, Elton Mayo's idea of work humanisation (1933) and, more recently, the ideas of workers' participation and job enrichment are structurally homologous with those in the citizenplace of the 'back to the community' movement, delegalization, and informal justice (Abel, 1982; Santos, 1980) and also with the ideas in the householdplace of the family as an informal and egalitarian community ('open families', 'free communes'), delegalised mainly through the avoidance of official marriage and the acceptance of its partial and temporary nature. Moreover these opposing developments seem to be combined in the three structural places according to a similar logic.

However, we should caution ourselves against overstressing such parallel developments. Since the structural places remain autonomous, there are always contradictory developments, the articulation of which should also be investigated. As an illustration, it should be noted that in the early 1970s the enthusiasm for the ideas of work humanisation and workers' participation waned (Clegg & Dunkerley, 1980, p.513) while the ideas of community services and of informal justice continued to be advocated, often with additional enthusiasm. This discrepancy is not due to a time lag between the citizenplace and the workplace. Because production law is based on interests and these are defined by the rationality of profit maximising, its normative orientations are much more unstable than those of territorial law which is based on rights as defined by the rationality of loyalty maximizing [27]. Industrial sociologists have drawn our attention to the cycles of control of workers and to their close tuning to the production cycle (Ramsay, 1977). Due to the economic recession of the '70s the power relations within the workplace changed in favour of capital. The workers' challenge of the control of the labour process by management decreased as the coercive apparatus of production law increased (the dismissal coupled with the threat of prolonged unemployment and the perspective of decreasing welfare payments). The hegemony component of the production relation may have lost, in this process, some of its weight. The extent to which the relative loss in factory hegemony was compensated for by a relative increase in state hegemony (made possible by the changes in the citizenplace referred to above) should be investigated.

The analysis of the combination among these parallel and contradictory developments should alert us to the possible refractions within the citizenplace, the workplace and the householdplace resulting from the evermore complex role of the state in the new forms of work control made possible by the recent changes in the organisation of production, the new productive order which some call the third age of the factory (Gaudemar, 1980) or, in Italy, the 'diffuse factory' (Coriat *et al.*, 1980, Sabel, 1982, p.209) Such changes in the organisation of production deepen the relations between the workplace and the householdplace. Through the new forms of the "putting out system" (piece work done at home) the family becomes again a site of production—the home-factory—and domestic law is put at the service of production law.

In peripheral societies recent trends are much more diversified and it is questionable that they can be brought together under a general tendency. Nevertheless, as peripheral societies become more and more vulnerable to fluctuations of the world economy which they cannot steer in their favour, a trend is discernable toward an increasing structural approximation of the workplace, the householdplace and the citizenplace, which, in contrast with what happens in core societies, is occurring under the pulling effect of the workplace. As the citizenplace is increasingly the site of negotiation of dependance, the pertinent effects of the worldplace upon the citizenplace in the peripheral societies are so pervasive that the citizenplace becomes in itself little more than a pertinent effect of the worldplace. The permanent offices of the IMF in the Palacio do Planalto (government palace) in Brazil stand as a dramatic illustration of this interpenetration of the citizenplace with the worldplace. But the pressure of the worldplace is also manifested in the articulation between the citizenplace and the workplace. The workplace of peripheral societies tends to distinguish itself from that of the core societies in at least two ways—firstly, the greater despotism in social relations in view of the existence of the industrial reserve army; secondly, the high degree of internal incoherence and fragmentation in view of the persistence of precapitalist modes of production (the peasant economy) formally subjected to the capitalist mode of production. The combined effect of these two characteristics upon the citizenplace is manifesting itself, through the mediation of the worldplace, by the increasing responsiveness of the state to the coercion demands of the workplace. The wider order of labour is more and more dependent upon the combination of the criminal law of the citizenplace with the criminal law of the workplace. The external weakness of the peripheral state (due to its position in the world system) is combined with the internal repressive strength against the exploited classes. This explains why Offe's argument (1983) on the compatibility of capitalism and democracy is increasingly restricted to the core countries (and even there it seems to lose steam).

The presence of the workplace *in* the householdplace is equally imposing in peripheral societies. The changes in the organisation of production mentioned above are particularly drastic in such societies. The decomposition and recomposition of the labour force which is under way on a world scale takes many forms. In general, it can be described as the 'return of variable capital' since its main objective consists in undermining the already precarious stability of the wage relation (Rojas, 1984; Santos, 1985). The wage becomes an unstable and occasional source of income and the mechanisms for the institutionalisation of the capital/labour conflicts (collective bargaining, etc.), no matter how limited, are neutralised. Under such circumstances, the household is called upon to supplement the low and occasional wage income of the individual worker through other wage and non-wage incomes (peasant economy, informal sector, petty commodity production, underground economy). Thus, the householdplace assumes production functions and becomes the centre of a complex income pool that guarantees the reconstitution of the labour power spent in the workplace.

The analysis of these different movements in the core and in the periphery and of their combinations, as hypothesized in my conception, could open, I suggest, a new scientific agenda on the question of law and politics on a world scale. This conception can also provide at least the beginning of an answer to some of the old questions put forward at the outset of this paper.

The decline of law

I will start with the question of the crisis of law or of the decline of law. For most authors, the decline of law is a direct consequence of the overuse of law for social engineering purposes, that is, the overlegalisation of social reality, or, for German authors, the rematerialisation of law (Teubner, 1983; Voigt, 1980), or, still, for Habermas, the internal colonisation of the life world (1982). This argument is usually made in conjunction with the argument of the functional inadequacy of law to regulate certain continuing (multiplex, as social anthropologists would say) relations among citizens or between citizens and the state, or with Poulantzas' argument according to which the power block holding government is increasingly unstable to rule by general legal provisions (1978b, p.218). The global effect of these conditions is a legitimation crisis coupled, in Habermas (1962), with a motivation crisis.

In my view, all these theories have a grain of truth. Their major limitation consists in restricting their analysis to what in my conception is only one dimension, though a very important one, of the legal configuration of capitalist societies. As a result they fail to recognise the changing articulations among territorial law, domestic law, production law, and systemic law. Just as an illustration, it is not surprising that Teubner finds a good example of what he calls reflexive law in labour laws because they respect the autonomy of the subsystem of production (1983, p.276). The mystification in this conception lies in conceiving 'reflexiveness' as an exclusive attribute of state labour laws, instead of analysing the social processes by which the workplace, the householdplace, and the citizenplace combine to define the global regulation of labour according to a specific borderline between production law, domestic law and territorial law, a borderline that changes across times and societies [28].

What is in decline is not law but rather the law of separation between state and civil society. But this cannot be conceived as a pathological phenomenon, as when Habermas speaks of the pathology of modernity, because, as I have argued, it is inscribed in the organising matrix of capitalist societies. To be fully coherent, Habermas should speak of modernity as pathology rather than of the pathology of modernity. Indeed, one must agree with Hirschman that capitalism cannot be blamed for accomplishing what it was always supposed to accomplish (1977, p.132).

There is no legitimation crisis, therefore, as far as the legal formation in its totality is concerned. Both production law and systemic law have never been so hegemonic, particularly in core countries. It is also mystifying to speak of deregulation. What is at stake is what I have described as processes of delegation and proliferation, that is to say, different forms of substitution of territorial law for production law, domestic law, or systemic law. Deregulations are reregulations.

The decline of Foucault

A much broader question—though it also touches upon the issue of the decline of law—is raised by Foucault in his theory of the dominant forms of social power in contemporary societies (1976, 1977, 1980). Foucault's major thesis is that, since the eighteenth century, the power of the state, what he calls the juridical or legal power has been confronted with and gradually displaced by another form of power which he calls disciplinary power. The latter is the dominant form of power in our time and is generated by the scientific knowledge produced by human sciences as it is applied by professions in institutions, private or public: in schools, hospitals, barracks, prisons, families, factories.

I will briefly summarise Foucault's characterisation of his two forms of social power: juridical (or state) power is based on the theory of sovereignty; it is power as a right possessed or exchanged; it is a zero-sum power; it is centrally organised and exercised from top down; it distinguishes between legitimate and illegitimate power exercise; it applies to autonomous pre-constituted recipients or targets; it is based on a discourse of right, obedience, and norm. In contrast, disciplinary power has no centre; it is exercised throughout society; it is fragmented and capillary; it is exercised from bottom up constituting its own targets as vehicles of its exercise; it is based on a scientific discourse of normalisation and standardisation produced by the human sciences.

Though Foucault is rather confusing about the relation between these two forms of power [29], it is clear that according to him they are incompatible and that the scientific, normalising power of the disciplines has become the most pervasive form of power in our society.

From the standpoint of the theory of social power and law which I have been presenting here, Foucault's view must be criticised on two accounts.

On the one hand, although Foucault is correct in positing the existence of power forms operating outside the state, he goes too far in stressing their dispersion and fragmentation. He is left with no theory of the hierarchy of power forms and consequently with no theory of social transformation. He obscures the central role of the power forms of the citizenplace and the work-place in our societies, domination and exploitation, respectively.

On the other hand, it must be noted that, in other respects, Foucault does not go far enough. He takes the conventional critical wisdom about the state for granted, in that he conceives state power and law as a monolithic entity and reduces it to the exercise of coercion [30]. This leads him to overstate the mutual incompatibility of juridical power and disciplinary power and to overlook the subtle interpenetrations between them.

I will illustrate this circulation of meaning between the two forms of power by looking at the distinction between law as a normative command and law as a scientific description of regularities among phenomena. This distinction has been so reified in our cultural paradigms, since Aristotle at least, that it has obscured the fact that, very often, social processes, acting as symbolic melting pots, create configurations of meaning in which elements of both conceptions of law are present in complex combinations.

Indeed, the idea that law as normative is also somehow law as scientific, has a certain tradition in modern social thought which goes back at least to Giambattista Vico. In 1725, Vico wrote in *Scienza Nuova* contrasting philosophy with law:

> Philosophy considers man as he ought to be and is therefore useful only to the very few who want to live in Plato's Republic and do not throw themselves into the dregs of Romulus. Legislation considers man as he is and attempts to put him to good use in human society (1953, pars. 131–2).

The idea of creating a social order based on science, that is, a social order in which the commands of law are emanations of scientific findings on social behaviour, is paramount in the eighteenth and nineteenth centuries from Montesquieu and Saint-Simon to Bentham, Comte and Durkheim. The same is true of certain currents of legal theory. As David Trubek has recently written, "During the classical age jurists presumed to transcend the uncertainty of philosophical speculation for the hard and sure world of science" (1983, p.67). In all these trends scientific law is contained, in a recessive form, in the normative law.

But this interpenetration has also occurred in the opposite direction. Within the workplace and concerning production law, many models of organisation of production have been offered, most prominently the model of scientific management, whose normative claims are presented in the form of scientific claims. This is well illustrated in a quotation of Taylor, the father of Taylorism: "best management is a true science, resting upon clearly defined laws, rules and principles" (1911, p.1, in Clegg & Dunkerley 1980, p.87). More generally, the sociologists of the professions have shown how professional privileges derived from scientific knowledge legitimate decisions in which scientific judgements glide into normative judgements, a process very well documented in the medical professions [31].

All these interpenetrations show that the distinctions are increasingly blurred, that the normative and the normalising are less far apart than Foucault assumes. I suggest that this is in part the result of the processes of delegation and proliferation I mentioned above.

Conclusion

In this paper I have presented the outline of an alternative to the conceptual orthodoxy centred around the state/civil society dichotomy. The scientific process developed here is best described as having originated in the following exercise. Let us suppose that we forget all the old concepts we have been using for classifying society. How will we then make sense of reality? This is not an easy task since orthodoxy has multiple ways of vindicating its influence on the common sense of social scientists, no matter how self-conscious. One keeps falling back into the old conceptual bric-a-brac.

The main scientific purpose of this alternative conception consists in demonstrating that the recognition of the centrality of state power and law is compatible with the recognition of the multiplicity of forms of power and forms of law in capitalist societies. This was done by subjecting such a multiplicity to a principle of structuration, and by relativising the state in two different directions: toward the inside, through the structural autonomy of social relations in smaller political and legal spaces (the householdplace and the workplace); toward the outside, through the structural autonomy of social relations in bigger political and legal spaces (the worldplace).

So far I have only developed the structural side of this theoretical framework. But, as I said, structures are nothing more than sedimented clusters of social relations. This means that structure and action are not just intimately related; they are the two sides of any form of social practice. In view of the structural analysis presented here, there are at least two ways in which the relation between structure and action can be explored.

Firstly, to demonstrate the theoretical bankruptcy of the orthodoxy crystallised in the state/civil society dichotomy should be conceived as a first analytical step to be followed by a second and equally important one which will account for the presence of such dichotomy in our common sense, and, thus, for the ways in which such dichotomy constitutes our cognitive everyday practice, the social perceptions and the social experiences of lawyers, politicians, social scientists and the people in general. The epistemological break with common sense does not eliminate it as a social phenomenon; it simply creates the conditions to convert it into a theoretical object of its own. Throughout this paper I emphasised the crucial ideological function of the commonsensical reduction of law and politics to the realm of the state. The analysis of the structure of a given legal configuration should be complemented by the analysis of the social configuration of the legal *habitus* in which such structure circulates [32]. These two analytical steps call for different methodological and even epistemological concerns but they should be viewed as different moments of a global scientific strategy. Taken together, they are the meeting ground of structuralism and phenomenology.

The second and broader path through which the relation between structure and action can be explored consists in the analysis of the articulation among the units of social interaction and of the cultural constellations condensing their life experiences. As will be remembered (see Fig. 1), according to my structural map, people are human configurations of familes, classes, individuals, and nations combined in different ways in view of their specific locations in each one of the structural places. Moreover, people may also be, permanently or transitorily, heterogeneous units of social practice (intermediate between the structural places) as when they are students, clients, or patients. Indeed some people stay so long (or so deep) in such intermediate social relations that these become the dominant place of their life experiences.

The internal diversification and heterogeneity of our cultural and ideological constellations is the mirror image of the human configurations that activate and transform them. Class ideologies coexist with individual ideologies, family ideologies and with national ideologies as much as class struggles coexist with individual struggles, family struggles and national struggles. The global profile emerging from the combination among different ideologies and struggles is historically contingent and differs in core and peripheral societies.

The empirical investigation of all these working hypotheses constitutes another and equally important scientific agenda. The elaboration of a map of structural places would be of no interest if there were no travellers to use it.

Acknowledgement

The socio-legal community of Madison offered me a uniquely stimulating environment to discuss the issues raised in this paper: special thanks to David Trubek and Erik O. Wright. I am also thankful to Richard Abel, Yves Dezalay, Kim Economides, Maureen Cain, Fernando Ruivo, Maria Leitão Marques and Virginia Ferreira for their detailed comments on an earlier version of this paper.

Notes

1 In "The Law of the Oppressed" I described the structural differences between the the law of the *favela* (Pasargada law, as I called it) and the Brazilian official law and conceived the articulation between the two as an "interclass legal pluralism ... structured by an unequal relationship of exchange in which Pasargada law is the dominated part" (1977, p.89). However, this articulation was not grounded on a broader social theory that would account for the different modes of production of law from which they derived. Though his analysis is restricted to the so-called Third World, Fitzpatrick (1983, 1984) has presented so far the most stimulating and successful attempt to develop a social theory of legal pluralism.

2 This problem raises another one, the problem of the concept of law. After a long and inconclusive debate over the analytical status of the concept of law (known as the Gluckman-Bohannan debate) legal anthropologists reconstructed their *empirical object* in terms of 'disputes' and 'dispute settlement mechanisms'. This reconstruction had a strong impact on legal sociology, though it didn't solve the basic problem of defining the adequate support of a sociological theory of law, that is, the problem of the *theoretical object* (Santos, 1977, p.10; Cain & Kulcsar, 1982). Although the vast majority of legal sociologists avoids confronting this problem, the solutions, whenever made explicit, oscillate between a broad (Santos, 1977, p.10) and a narrow (most recently, Macaulay, 1983, pp.57–8) concept of law. In the latter case, legal pluralism is conceived in functionalist rather than in structuralist terms: "A social theory cannot assume that public government has a monopoly on those functions the theory assigns to the legal system" (Macaulay, 1983, p.57). Such a conception, however, calls for a 'structural equivalent' to law broad enough

to fill the gap between law-as-structure and law-as-function. In Macaulay's case this is provided by the concept of 'private government.'

3 In the Weberian tradition the sociology of organisations must be credited with the most sustained effort to develop typologies of forms of power. However, lacking in general a social theory of power relations it has failed to "distribute" such typologies in society. Its most serious limitation is thus its claim to generality, the attempt to develop models equally valid for all clusters of social relations. It misses in its descriptive flatness the rich processes of segmentation and structuration which contradictorily separate and combine different forms of power or different types of organisations. A good overview is given by Clegg & Dunkerley (1980).

4 In my view the crisis of western thought opened up by the collapsing of religious orthodoxy in the sixteenth century remained unresolved until the nineteenth century when a new symbolic matrix, centred around the ideas of the state and of the rule of law, finally emerged. At the beginning of the nineteenth century Saint-Simon could still speak of a spiritual crisis as the deep cause of the social turmoil in the European societies of the time. In his and in Comte's view, modern science should become the nucleus of the new orthodoxy. It seems, however, that science was only able to perform such a role as part of an overarching orthodoxy based on the idea of the state and of the law. As evidence of this new orthodoxy stands the fact that the state and the law were by far the social phenomena that offered greatest resistence to their conversion into objects of social scientific inquiry. For a long time and without resorting to any form of censorship, the state and the law managed to suppress any form of knowledge other than the closed-circuit, intimate knowledge they were able to produce through consecration institutions (such as law schools) and organic intellectuals (such as lawyers), a kind of self-knowledge known as normative political science or legal science. In these studies, rather than objects, state and law were indeed subjects of knowledge personified in lawyer's writings.

5 This is very clearly the case of the Scottish enlightenment thinkers whom the nineteenth century thought converted into doctrinaires of *laissez faire*—which they were not, or were only retrospectively, that is, *vis à vis* the corporatist regulations of the feudal state. They were indeed keenly aware that modern economy would lead to the emergence of a state with an incommensurably higher potential to influence the lives of people than that of the feudal state. This explains why they were so concerned with developing political arrangements that would prevent the abuse of power "les grands coups d'authorité" in Montesquieu's words.

6 There has been some debate about the role of political and legal institutions in A. Smith's thought. Against what is becoming a widely accepted view (Viner, 1927; Billet, 1975; Samuels, 1979), Hirschman tends to minimise such a role. But he also recognises that "it appears that Smith advocated less a state with minimal functions than one whose capacity for folly would have some ceiling" (1977, p.104).

7 In this light it would not be surprising if the crisis of the welfare state or the crisis of regulation, as currently discussed, were conceived by some as the return to the age of the *laissez faire* and by others as the embryo of a new more authoritarian state form.

8 These formulations, which first appeared in 1968, were by far the most influential. The evolution of Poulantzas' thought on this issue can be traced in his last book (1978b).

9 Until the eighteenth century the privatisation of state power was achieved by

multiple means. One of the most pervasive was the sale of offices (Swart, 1949).

10 I am aware of the difference between 'household' and 'family'. They do not necessarily coincide. The structural place is defined in terms of the household in order to stress the sharing relationship (above all, the income-pooling practices). But since the institutional and ideological reproduction of the household occurs mainly through the concept of family (the social unit based on kinship or biological ties), I use the latter to define the elementary components of the householdplace. With similar purposes, Michele Barrett speaks of 'households' and of 'familial ideology' "as terms that avoid some of the naturalism and mystification engendered by the 'family' " (1980, p.199). (See also Donzelot, 1977.)

11 For the distinction between relations of production and relations in production, see Burawoy (1979).

12 Domestic law is here restricted to the household. Y. Dezalay, in an important paper on disciplinary councils in enterprises, uses the term 'domestic order' in a broader sense, as "the complex and durable interactions inside a restricted group that shuns judicial interventions" (1985, p.4). Thus conceived, domestic order includes both domestic law and production law as used in this paper.

13 All the structural elements are internally complex and allow for internal fragmentation, assymetry and contradiction. This is obviously the case of the state as an institutional form but it is equally true of territorial law (Santos, 1980, p.381).

14 The modes of determination used here are derived from Wright (1979, p.15). Erik O. Wright distinguishes among different modes of determination. *Structural limitation* "constitutes a pattern of determination in which some social structure establishes the limits within which some other structure or process can vary, and establishes probabilities for the specific structures or processes that are possible within those limits". *Selection* "constitutes those social mechanisms that concretely determine ranges of outcomes, or in the extreme case specific outcomes, within a structurally limited range of possiblities". Reproduction/non-reproduction "implies that the reproducing structure *prevents* the reproduced structure from changing in certain fundamental ways". *Mediation* "defines a mode of determination in which a given social process shapes the consequences of other social processes" (1979, pp.15–29). Given the topic of this paper, I am not concerned here with the dynamic aspect of this model of determination and that is why I do not consider two other modes of determination mentioned by E.O. Wright: *transformation* and *limits of functional compatibility*.

15 Though the structural relations between the householdplace and the other structural places remain the same in the core and in the periphery of the world system the concrete roles played by the household and the nature of its elementary components are quite different in these two types of societies. This has to do with the articulation in peripheral societies of the capitalist mode of production with pre-capitalist work relations and with the fact that women are above all involved in activities which are not typically capitalist (Meillassoux, 1975; Saffioti, 1977: 33; Women and National Development, 1977; Rogers, 1981). More on this later.

16 The heterogeneous clusters are particularly unstable forms since they reflect the effects of contradictory developments in the four structural places. Moreover, their specific locations in the *continua* among the structural places also change over time. For instance, multinational corporations originated as heterogeneous clusters belonging both to the workplace (they organised production relations) and to the

worldplace (their specific presence in any given country was both the cause and the effect of the country's location in the world economy). However, due to their expanded capacity to manipulate in their favour the whole political 'environment' and to assume quasi-sovereignty functions MNCs have gradually incorporated citizenplace features in their structure, a form of heterogeneity particularly evident in the peripheral societies.

The European Economic Community is another instance of structural changes in a given cluster of social relations over time. The EEC originated as an institutional and legal form of the worldplace of each one of the countries integrating it. In recent times, however, it has gradually evolved into an heterogeneous form occupying an intermediate location between the citizenplace and the worldplace. On the one hand, certain EEC regulatory agencies have become, through the preemption clause, quasi-state apparatus of each one of the community members, particularly with reference to the common agricultural policy. On the other hand, through the supremacy clause established by the community court, the EEC legislation is also, within certain limits, the constitutional law of each one of the country members. Within the reach of this clause the EEC legislation has ceased to be systemic law to become territorial law. The internal diversity of this legislation and of its articulations with the different territorial laws is so great that it probably constitutes a new form of legal pluralism of its own.

17 As late as 1949 Kahn-Freund could say that:

> the regulation of hours of work by legislation or collective agreements was the earliest and remains the most notable restriction of the command power which is the concomitant of the ownership of means of production (in Renner, 1976, p.161).

18 Marx describes in great detail the different forms of resistance against the laws: frontal violation; the relay system making it difficult for factory inspectors to detect violations; restriction of the inspectors' access to the factories; wage cuts; changes in the legal concept of 'child' (what Marx calls "capitalist anthropology": 1970, p.280); the use of the 'economic crisis' as a justification for not enforcing the laws; the denial of responsibility; the negotiation over the range and degree of violation. See also Carson (1979).

19 The history of this failure is well documented at least since Gramsci's workers' councils in 1919 Turin. See, for an overview, Clegg & Dunkerly (1980, p.512).

20 Though M. Adler is one of the most innovative Marxist thinkers, nobody, to my knowledge, has acknowledged his original contribution to the analysis of the articulation between economic production and punishment. The most influential analysis has remained Rusche & Kirchheimer's. It has been critically assessed and expanded in different directions (Foucault, 1977; Jankovic, 1977; Melossi, 1978; Ignatieff, 1978; Melossi & Pavarini, 1981). In general, the functionalist and economicist biases in Rusche's analysis have been transcended by an emphasis on structural correspondences or homologies, which is particularly the case of Foucault and of Melossi & Pavarini. But, in my view these authors exaggerate such an emphasis by collapsing the mechanisms of social power of the workplace with those of the citizenplace. I will come back to Foucault later on in the text. As to Melossi & Pavarini, they try to combine Rusche & Kirchheimer with Pashukanis (1978) and derive the structural isomorphism between prisoners and workers from the logic of capital:

> If the punishment as deprivation of liberty is structured, then, on the model of 'exchange' (in terms of retribution by equivalent), its execution (read: penitentiary) is modelled on the hypothesis of manufacture, of the 'factory' (in terms of discipline and subordination (1981, p.186).

21 P.K. Edwards & H. Scullion have criticised Burawoy for focusing mainly on the creation of consent (1982:9). Based on broader empirical data they try to analyse how the control in the workplace relates both to consent and resistance.

22 High wages and 'work humanisation' have been the two most important factors of factory hegemony. Their strict dependence on the production cycle distinguishes them from the factors of the other forms of hegemony (family hegemony, state hegemony and world hegemony).

23 One of the most stimulating aspects of Burawoy's research is his concern with the comparative analysis of the labour process (U.S.A., Zambia, Hungary). His empirical research is particularly relevant to determine the impact of the worldplace upon the workplace in any given country.

24 As a matter of fact the same was true at the time of the householdplace and the workplace. The autonomy of these two structural places occurred with the capitalist development through the separation of production and consumption and the concomitant distinction between the public sphere and the private sphere (Dahl & Snare, 1978; Gamarnikow *et al.*, 1983).

25 In the sixteenth century textile workers in Milan worked under oath, sanctioned by the state, that they would not abandon the city. In 1682 Colbert sentenced to death the workers that abandoned France to work abroad (Adler, n.d., pp.72–3).

26 According to the functionalist sociology of the family, modernisation and industrialisation would bring more democracy to family relations (a more rational complementarity of male and female roles inside the family) (Parsons, 1959). This model was later to be challenged by women's studies: the participation of women in the labour force far from being an egalitarian trend has often contributed to the further subordination of women. However, with the expansion of the welfare state this subordination assumed a new form. It became more bureaucratic as a result of the increasing legalisation of family relations (state regulation of husband/wife and of parents/children relations; social security regulations; increasing resort to courts to solve family disputes) (e.g. Wilson, 1977; Barrett, 1980, p.226).

27 In this respect domestic law holds an intermediate position between production law and territorial law. It is both based on rights and interests. The rights in the domestic law are thus more unstable than rights in territorial law. Given the multiplex nature of relations inside the household, the exercise of rights is interwoven with (and limited by) the interests in the survival of the family as defined by the logic of affection maximising. This explains why the economic recession of the '70s and the changes it produced in the income pool of the family forced some newly acquired rights of the woman and the children to yield before the interests of 'mutual protection' and 'psychological equilibrium' inside the family.

28 A critique of Teubner can also be found in Macaulay (1983, p.104).

29 The following are some of the relations between juridical power and disciplinary power most commonly found in Foucault's work: juridical power is the wrong conception of power while disciplinary power is the right one; juridical power is the agent of disciplinary power; disciplinary power goes beyond juridical power; disciplinary power is less legal or exists where juridical power itself is less legal ("at

the extremities"); disciplinary power is colonised by juridical power; juridical power and disciplinary power are the two sides of the same general mechanism of power; they co-exist though they are incompatible; juridical power conceals and legitimates the domination generated by disciplinary power.

30 Foucault also criticises Marxists for defending a conception of zero-sum power (power in society is a fixed quantity; if one group has it the other does not) but in 1968 such an influential Marxist thinker as Poulantzas was already presenting a forceful critique of the zero-sum power conception (1978a, p.117) and in terms strikingly similar to those used by Foucault much later.

31 In a recent paper Handler justly emphasises that "domination arising out of the exigencies of the bureaucratic task finds a comfortable home in the ideologies of the working professions" (1983, p.62).

32 I use here the concept of *habitus* as elaborated by Bourdieu (1980, p.87).

References

Abel, R.(1979) Western courts in non-western settings: patterns of court use in colonial and neo-colonial Africa. In *The Imposition of Law* (Burman, S.B. & Harrel-Bond, B.E. Eds). New York: Academic Press.

Abel, R. (1982) The contradictions of informal justice. In *The Politics of Informal Justice* (Abel, R., Ed.) Vol **1**, p.267. New York: Academic Press.

Adler, M. (1922) *Die Staatsauffassung des Marxismus*. Vienna: Verlag der Wiener Volksbuchhandlung.

Adler, M. (n.d.) *Zuchthaus und Fabrik*, Leipzig: Ernst Oldenburg Verlag.

Bankowski, Z. & Mungham, G. (1976) *Images of Law*. London: Routledge and Kegan Paul.

Barrett, M. (1980) *Women's Oppression Today*. London: Verso Editions.

Billet, L. (1975) Political order and economic development: reflections on Adam Smith's *Wealth of Nations*. *Political Studies*, **35**, 430.

Bobbio, N. (1942) *La Consuetude Come Fatto Normativo*. Padova, Italy.

Bohannan, P. (1967) Introduction. In *Law and Warfare*. (Bohannan, P. Ed.). Garden City: Natural History Press.

Bourdieu, P. (1980) *Le Sens Pratique*. Paris: Éditions de Minuit.

Braverman, H. (1974) *Labor and Monopoly Capital*. New York: Monthly Review.

Brenner, R. (1977) The Origins of capitalist development: a critique of neo-smithian marxism. *New Left Review*, **104**, 25.

Burawoy, M. (1979) *Manufacturing Consent*. Chicago: University of Chicago Press.

Cain, M. & Kulcsar, K. (1982) Thinking disputes: an essay on the origins of the dispute industry. *Law and Society Review*, **16**, 3.

Carbonnier, J. (1979) *Sociologia Juridica*. Coimbra: Almedina.

Carson, W.G. (1979) The Conventionalization of Early Factory Crime. *International Journal of the Sociology of Law*, **7**, 37.

Clawson, D. (1980) *Bureaucracy and the Labor Process*. New York: Monthly Review Press.

Clegg, S. & Dunkerley, D. (1980) *Organization, Class and Control*. London: Routledge and Kegan Paul.

Coriat, B. *et al*. (1980) *Usines et Ouvriers Figures du Nouvel Order Productif*. Paris: Maspero.

Dahl, T. S. & Snare, A. (1978) The coercion of privacy. In *Women, Sexuality and Social Control* (Carol & Barry Smart Eds). London: Routledge and Kegan Paul.

Del Vecchio, G. (1957) *Persona, Estado y Derecho*. Madrid: Revista Occidente.

Dezalay, Y. (1985) Du fait au droit. Les juriditions disciplinaires comme institutionnalization de l'interaction entre l'ordre domestique et l'ordre juridique. Paper presented to the *Fourth European Conference of Critical Legal Studies*, Coimbra, Portugal.

Dicey, A.V. (1905) *Lectures in the Relation between Law and Public Opinion in England during the Nineteenth Century*. London: MacMillan.

Donzelot, J. (1977) *La Police des Familles*. Paris: Éditions de Minuit.

Edwards, P.K. & Scullion, H. (1982) *The Social Organization of Industrial Conflict*. Oxford: Basil Blackwell.

Edwards, R. (1979) *Contested Terrain*. New York: Basic Books.

Ehrlich, E. (1936) *Fundamental Principles of the Sociology of Law*. Cambridge: Harvard University Press.

Fitzpatrick, P. (1983) Law, plurality and underdevelopment. In *Legality, Ideology and the State* (Sugarman, D. Ed.) London: Academic Press.

Fitzpatrick, P. (1984) Law and societies. *Osgoode Hall Law Journal*, **22**, 115.

Foucault, M. (1976) *La Volonté de Savior*. Paris: Gallimard.

Foucault, M. (1977) *Discipline and Punish*. New York: Pantheon.

Foucault, M. (1980) *Power and Knowledge*. New York: Pantheon.

Galanter, M. (1981) Justice in many rooms: courts, private ordering and indigenous law. *Journal of Legal Pluralism*, **19**, 1.

Gamarnikow, E. *et al.* (Eds). (1983) *The Public and the Private*. London: Heinemann.

Gamble, A. (1982) *An Introduction To Modern Social and Political Thought*. London: MacMillan.

Gaudemar, J.-P. (1980) Le Troisième âge de l'usine? In *Usines et Ouvriers* (Coriat *et al*, Eds). Paris: Maspero.

Habermas, J. (1962) *Strukturwandel der Offentlichkeit*. Neuwied: Luchterhand.

Habermas, J. (1982) *Theorie des Kommunikativen Handelns*, 2 vols. Frankfurt: Suhrkamp.

Handler, J. (1983) *The discretionary decision: adversarial advocacy—reform or reconstruction?* Conference on Reflexive Law and the Regulatory Crisis, Madison.

Hartman, H. (1981) The Family as the locus of gender, class, and political struggle: the example of housework, *Signs*, **6**, **3**, 366.

Hay, D. *et al.* (1975) *Albion's Fatal Tree: Crime and Society in Eighteenth Century England*. New York: Pantheon.

Hayek, F. (1979) *Law, Legislation and Liberty*. Chicago: University of Chicago Press.

Hegel, G. (1981) *Grundlinien der Philosophie des Rechts oder Naturrecht und Staatswissenschaft im Grundrisse*. Berlin: Akademie Verlag.

Heydebrand, W. (1979) The technocratic administration of justice. In *Research in Law and Sociology A Research Annual*. (Spitzer, S. Ed.) Vol. **2**, 29ff.

Hirschman, A. (1977) *The Passions and the Interests*. Princeton: Princeton University Press.

Hobsbawm, E. (1975) *The Age of Capital 1848–1875*. London: Weidenfeld and Nicolson.

Hooker, M. (1975) *Legal Pluralism: An Introduction to Colonial and Neo-Colonial Laws*. Oxford: Clarendon Press.

Hunt, A. (1981) The politics of law and justice. *Politics and Power*, **4**, 3.

Ignatieff, M. (1978) *A Just Measure of Pain*. London: MacMillan.

Jänicke, M. (1980) Zur Theorie des Staatesversagens. In *Folgen reduzierten Wachstums für*

Politikfelder, Politische Vierteljahresschrift (Grottian, P. Ed.) Vol **11** (special issue), 132 ff.

Jankovic, I. (1977) Labor market and imprisonment *Crime and Social Justice*, fall–winter, p.17.

Luhman, N. (1972) *Reschtssoziologie*. Reinbek: Rowohlt.

Macaulay, S. (1983) Private government. *Disputes Processing Research Program Working Paper 6*. Wisconsin.

Marx, K. (1970) *Capital* Vol. **1**. New York: International Publishers.

Marx, K. (1973) *Grundrisse: Foundations of the Critique of Political Economy*. Harmondsworth: Penguin.

Mayo, E. (1933) *The Human Problems of an Industrial Civilization*. New York: MacMillan.

Meillassoux, C. (1975) *Femmes, Greniers et Capitaux*. Paris: Maspero.

Melossi, D. (1978). George Rusche and Otto Kirchheimer: Punishment and Social Justice. *Crime and Social Justice*, spring–summer, 73.

Melossi, D. & Pavarini, M. (1981) *The Prison and the Factory*. Totowa: Barnes and Noble.

Mill, J. (1921) *Principles of Political Economy*. London.

Moore, S. (1978) *Law as Process: An Anthropological Approach*. London: Routledge and Kegan Paul.

Nader, L. (Ed.) (1969) *Law and Culture and Society*. Chicago: Aldine.

Nonet, P. & Selznick, P. (1978) *Law and Society in Transition. Toward Responsive Law*. New York: Harper and Row.

Offe, C. (1984) *Contradictions of the Welfare State*. London: Hutchinson.

Parsons, T. (1959) The social structure of the family. In *The Family: Its Function and Destiny* (Anshen, R., Ed.) New York: Harper Row.

Pashukanis, E. (1978) *Law and Marxism. A General Theory*. London: Ink Links.

Poulantzas, N. (1978a) *Political Power and Social Classes*. London: Verso Editions.

Poulantzas, N. (1978b) *State Power and Socialism*. London: NLB.

Ramsay, H. (1977) Cycles of control: worker participation in sociological and historical perspective. *Sociology*, **11**, 481.

Renner, K. (1976) *The Institutions of Private Law and their Social Functions*. London: Routledge and Kegan Paul.

Rojas, F. (1984) *Nuevos Movimientos Populares. Nuevas Estrategias Estatales*. Centro de Investigacion y Education Popular (Bogotà), *Documento Ocasional*, **18**.

Rogers, B. (1981) *The Domestication of Women. Discrimination in Developing Countries*. London: Tavistock.

Rusche, G. & Kirchheimer, O. (1968) *Punishment and Social Structure*. New York: Russell and Russell.

Sabel, C. (1982) *Work and Politics*. Cambridge: Cambridge University Press.

Saffioti, H. (1977) Women, mode of production, and social formations. *Latin American Perspectives*, **12**, **13**, 27.

Samuels, W. (1979) The state law and economic organization. In *Research in Law and Sociology. A Research Annual* (Spitzer, S., Ed.) Vol. **2**, 65.

Santos, B. (1977) The law of the oppressed: the construction and reproduction of legality in Pasargada. *Law and Society Review*, **12**, 5.

Santos, B. (1980) Law and community: the changing nature of state power in late capitalism. *International Journal of Sociology of Law*, **8**, 379.

Santos, B. (1985) Estado e sociedade na semiperiferia do sistema mundial: O case

Portugues. *Analise Social*, (in press).

Selznick, P. (1969) *Law, Society and Industrial Justice*. New York: Russell Sage Foundation.

Smith, A. (1937) *An Inquiry Into the Nature and Causes of the Wealth of Nations*. New York: Modern Library.

Stein, L. von (1888) *Handbuch der Verwaltungslehre*. Stuttgart: J.C. Cotta.

Swart, K. (1949) *Sale of Offices in the Seventeenth Century*. The Hague: Nijhoff.

Taylor, A. (1911) *Principles of Scientific Management*. New York: Harper.

Taylor, A. (1972) *Laissez Faire and State Intervention in Nineteenth Century Britain*. London: MacMillan.

Teubner, G. (1983) Substantive and reflexive elements in modern law. *Law and Society Review*, **17**, 239.

Thompson, E.P. (1975) *Whigs and Hunters*. New York: Pantheon.

Trubek, D. (1983) Where the action is: critical legal studies and empiricism. *Disputes Processing Research Program Working Paper 10*, Wisconsin.

Unger, R. (1976) *Law in Modern Society*. New York: Free Press.

Vico, G. (1953) *Opere*. Milan: Riccardi.

Viner, J. (1927) Adam Smith and laissez faire. *The Journal of Political Economy*, **XXXV**, 198.

Voigt, R. (1980) *Verrechtlichung Analysen zu Funktion und Wirkung von Parlamentarisierung, Bürokratisierung und Justizialisierung sozialer politischer und ökonomischer Prozesse*. Königstein: Athenäum.

Wallerstein, I. (1980) The withering away of the states. *International Journal of Sociology of Law*, 369.

Weber, M. (1948) *From Max Weber. Essays in Sociology*. London: Routledge and Kegan Paul.

Wilson, E. (1977) *Women and the Welfare State*. London: Tavistock.

Women and National Development (1977). *Signs*, special issue, 3.

Wood, E. (1981) The separation of the economic and the political in capitalism. *New Left Review*, **127**, 66.

Wright, E. (1979) *Class Crisis and the State*. London: Verso Editions.

Part II
Legal Theories of State and Market

[4]

Constitutions and Commitment: The Evolution of Institutions Governing Public Choice in Seventeenth-Century England

DOUGLASS C. NORTH AND BARRY R. WEINGAST

The article studies the evolution of the constitutional arrangements in seventeenth-century England following the Glorious Revolution of 1688. It focuses on the relationship between institutions and the behavior of the government and interprets the institutional changes on the basis of the goals of the winners—secure property rights, protection of their wealth, and the elimination of confiscatory government. We argue that the new institutions allowed the government to commit credibly to upholding property rights. Their success was remarkable, as the evidence from capital markets shows.

This article focuses on the political factors underpinning economic growth and the development of markets—not simply the rules governing economic exchange, but also the institutions governing how these rules are enforced and how they may be changed. A critical political factor is the degree to which the regime or sovereign is committed to or bound by these rules. Rules the sovereign can readily revise differ significantly in their implications for performance from exactly the same rules when not subject to revision. The more likely it is that the sovereign will alter property rights for his or her own benefit, the lower the expected returns from investment and the lower in turn the incentive to invest. For economic growth to occur the sovereign or government must not merely establish the relevant set of rights, but must make a credible commitment to them.

The Journal of Economic History, Vol. XLIX, No. 4 (Dec. 1989). ISSN 0022-0507.

Douglass North is Luce Professor of Law and Liberty, Washington University, St. Louis, MO 63130. Barry Weingast is Senior Research Fellow, Hoover Institution, Stanford University, Stanford, CA 94305.

The authors gratefully acknowledge the helpful comments of Robert Bates, Gary Cox, Paul David, Aaron Director, John Ferejohn, Jack Goldstone, Max Hartwell, Derek Hirst, Leonard Hochberg, Paul Milgrom, Glenn Nichols, Roger Noll, Alvin Rabushka, Thomas Sargent, Kenneth Shepsle, Gordon Tullock, and David Weir. They also thank Elisabeth Case for her editorial assistance. Barry Weingast thanks the National Science Foundation (grant no SES-8617516) for partial support.

A ruler can establish such commitment in two ways. One is by setting a precedent of "responsible behavior," appearing to be committed to a set of rules that he or she will consistently enforce. The second is by being constrained to obey a set of rules that do not permit leeway for violating commitments. We have very seldom observed the former, in good part because the pressures and continual strain of fiscal necessity eventually led rulers to "irresponsible behavior" and the violation of agreements. The latter story is, however, the one we tell.

We attempt to explain the evolution of political institutions in seventeenth-century England, focusing on the fundamental institutions of representative government emerging out of the Glorious Revolution of 1688—a Parliament with a central role alongside the Crown and a judiciary independent of the Crown. In the early seventeenth century fiscal needs led to increased levels of "arbitrary" government, that is, to expropriation of wealth through redefinition of rights in the sovereign's favor. This led, ultimately, to civil war. Several failed experiments with alternative political institutions in turn ushered in the restoration of the monarchy in 1660. This too failed, resulting in the Glorious Revolution of 1688 and its fundamental redesign of the fiscal and governmental institutions.

To explain the changes following the Glorious Revolution we first characterize the problem that the designers of the new institutions sought to solve, namely, control over the exercise of arbitrary and confiscatory power by the Crown.[1] We then show how, given the means, motives, and behavior of the king during this century, the institutional changes altered the incentives of governmental actors in a manner desired by the winners of the Revolution. These changes reflected an explicit attempt to make credible the government's ability to honor its commitments. Explicit limits on the Crown's ability *unilaterally* to alter the terms of its agreements played a key role here, for after the Glorious Revolution the Crown had to obtain Parliamentary assent to changes in its agreements. As Parliament represented wealth holders, its increased role markedly reduced the king's ability to renege. Moreover, the institutional structure that evolved after 1688 did not provide incentives for Parliament to replace the Crown and itself engage in similar "irresponsible" behavior. As a consequence the new institutions produced a marked increase in the security of private rights.

As evidence in favor of our thesis, we study the remarkable changes in capital markets over this period. After the first few years of the Stuarts' reign, the Crown was not able systematically to raise funds. By

[1] Our discussion of the events prior to the Glorious Revolution (1603 to 1688) simply characterizes this period; it does not model or explain it. Moreover, since our history emphasizes the problems the winners (the Whigs) sought to solve, it necessarily contains strong elements of "Whig" history.

the second decade of the seventeenth century, under mounting fiscal pressure, the Crown resorted to a series of "forced loans," indicating that it could not raise funds at rates it was willing to pay. Following the Glorious Revolution, however, not only did the government become financially solvent, but it gained access to an unprecedented level of funds. In just nine years (from 1688 to 1697), government borrowing increased by more than an order of magnitude. This sharp change in the willingness of lenders to supply funds must reflect a substantial increase in the perceived commitment by the government to honor its agreements. The evidence shows that these expectations were borne out, and that this pattern extends well into the next century.

Since we focus on the evolution and impact of the political institutions, of necessity we slight the larger economic and religious context, even though in many specific instances these larger religious and economic issues were proximate sources of actions and policies that we describe. Indeed, no history of the seventeenth century is complete that does not describe both the growing markets and the evolving organizations that accompanied economic expansion as well as the persistent religious tensions, particularly between Catholic and Protestant. A more thorough study, one far too big for this essay, would attempt to integrate the change in opportunity costs of both the economic and *religious* actors as they intermingled with the immediate political issues on which we concentrate. But having said that, it is important to stress that our central thesis is a key part of the whole process by which an institutional framework evolved in England. We contend that while the English economy had been expanding and its markets growing, in order for economic development to continue the constraints described below had to be altered.

This essay proceeds as follows. Section I develops the importance of political institutions and the constitution and their relevance for the sections that follow. Sections II and III develop the narrative of the period, focusing respectively on England under the Stuarts and on the evolution of new institutions and secure rights following the Glorious Revolution. Section IV contains the central part of our analysis and reveals why these institutions made *credible* the government's commitment to honoring its agreements. Sections V and VI present our evidence from public and private capital markets.

I. THE ROLE OF POLITICAL INSTITUTIONS AND THE CONSTITUTION

The control of coercive power by the state for social ends has been a central dilemma throughout history. A critical role of the constitution and other political institutions is to place restrictions on the state or sovereign. These institutions in part determine whether the state produces rules and regulations that benefit a small elite and so provide little prospect for long-run growth, or whether it produces rules that foster long-term growth. Put simply, successful long-run economic performance requires appropriate incentives not only for economic actors but for political actors as well.

Because the state has a comparative advantage in coercion, what prevents it from using violence to extract all the surplus?[2] Clearly it is not always in the ruler's interests to use power arbitrarily or indiscriminately; by striking a bargain with constituents that provides them some security, the state can often increase its revenue. But this alone is insufficient to guarantee consistent behavior on the part of the ruler.

The literature on transactions costs and institutions emphasizes that while parties may have strong incentives to strike a bargain, their incentives after the fact are not always compatible with maintaining the agreement: compliance is always a potential problem. This literature also notes that when ex post problems are anticipated ex ante, parties will attempt to alter incentives, devising institutions or constitutions that promote compliance with bargains after the fact. Oliver Williamson says:

> Transactions that are subject to ex post opportunism will benefit if appropriate actions can be devised ex ante. Rather than reply to opportunism in kind, the wise [bargaining party] is one who seeks both to give and receive "credible commitments." Incentives may be realigned and/or superior governance structures within which to organize transactions may be devised.[3]

Problems of compliance can be reduced or eliminated when the institutions are carefully chosen so as to match the anticipated incentive problems. Under these circumstances, parties are more likely to enter into and maintain complex bargains that prevent abuse of political control by the state.

To succeed in this role, a constitution must arise from the bargaining context between the state and constituents such that its provisions carefully match the potential enforcement problems among the relevant parties. The constitution must be *self-enforcing* in the sense that the major parties to the bargain must have an incentive to abide by the bargain after it is made.[4]

[2] Throughout late medieval and early modern times, if rulers did not maintain a comparative advantage in coercion, they soon failed to be rulers. See William McNeill, *Pursuit of Power* (Chicago, 1983); Douglass North, *Structure and Change in Economic History* (New York, 1981); and Gordon Tullock, *Autocracy* (Dordrecht; 1987).

[3] Oliver Williamson, *Economic Institutions of Capitalism* (New York, 1985), pp. 48–49.

[4] Our formulation of the problem draws on the "new economics of organization." Application of this approach to political problems—and especially to the problem of providing institutions to enforce bargains over time—is just beginning. See, however, Barry R. Weingast and William Marshall, "The Industrial Organization of Congress; or Why Legislatures, Like Firms, Are Not Organized as Markets," *Journal of Political Economy*, 96 (Feb. 1988), pp. 132–63; and Terry Moe,

Consider a loan to a sovereign in which the ruler promises to return the principal along with interest at a specified date. What prevents the sovereign from simply ignoring the agreement and keeping the money? Reputation has long been noted as an important factor in limiting a sovereign's incentive to renege, and this approach has recently been formalized in the elegant models of modern game theory. The "long arm of the future" provides incentives to honor the loan agreement today so as to retain the opportunity for funds tomorrow. In many of the simple repeated games studied in the literature, this incentive alone is sufficient to prevent reneging.

Yet it is also well known that there are circumstances where this mechanism alone fails to prevent reneging.[5] In the context of current Third World debt, Jeremy Bullow and Kenneth Rogoff show that repeat play alone is insufficient to police reneging, and that more complex institutional arrangements are necessary. Similarly, in the medieval context, John Veitch has recently shown that medieval states had strong but not unambiguous incentives to develop reputations for honoring debt commitments, and that by and large they did so. Nonetheless, a series of major repudiations occurred when a second and typically more plentiful source of funds emerged. Edward I confiscated the wealth of the Jews in the late thirteenth century once the Italian merchants began operating on a larger scale; Phillip IV confiscated the wealth of the Templars under similar circumstances.

One important context in which repeat play alone is insufficient to police repudiation concerns variations in the sovereign's time preference or discount rate. States in early modern Europe were frequently at war. Since wars became increasingly expensive over the period, putting increasingly larger fiscal demands on the sovereign, the survival of the sovereign and regime was placed at risk. When survival was at stake, the sovereign would heavily discount the future, making the one-time gain of reneging more attractive relative to the future opportunities forgone. Indeed, there is a long history of reneging under the fiscal strain accompanying major wars.[6]

The insufficiency of repeat play and reputation to prevent reneging

---

"The New Economics of Organization," *American Journal of Political Science*, 28 (Aug. 1984), pp. 739–77.

[5] Paul R. Milgrom, Douglass C. North, and Barry R. Weingast, "The Role of Institutions in the Revival of Trade, Part I: The Medieval Law Merchant," Mimeo., Hoover Institution, Stanford University, 1989. Jeremy Bullow and Kenneth Rogoff, "A Constant Recontracting Model of Sovereign Debt," *Journal of Political Economy*, 97 (Feb. 1989), pp. 155–78; John M. Veitch, "Repudiations and Confiscations by the Medieval State" this JOURNAL, 46 (Mar. 1986), pp. 31–36.

[6] Joseph Schumpeter, "Fiscal Crises and the Tax State," in Richard A. Musgrave and Alan T. Peacock, eds., *Classics in the Theory of Public Finance* (London, 1962). John Hicks, *A Theory of Economic History* (Oxford, 1969). North, *Structure and Change*, and Veitch, "Repudiations and Confiscations." This is not to say that the sovereign will *never* honor commitments, only that he will not *always* do so.

provides for the role of political institutions. If the problem of variable discount rates is sufficiently important, individuals have an incentive to devise institutions to protect against reneging. It is important to observe that these institutions do not substitute for reputation-building and associated punishment strategies, but complement them.[7] Appropriately chosen institutions can improve the efficacy of the reputation mechanism by acting as a constraint in precisely those circumstances where reputation alone is insufficient to prevent reneging. The literature on the theory of the firm is replete with illustrations of how specific institutional features of the firm are necessary to mitigate an incentive problem that is insufficiently policed by reputation.[8]

This view provides an endogenous role for political institutions. Restrictions on the ex post behavior of the state improve the state's ability to maintain its part of bargains with constituents, for example, not to expropriate their wealth.[9] As we show below, this logic can be used to interpret the institutional changes at the time of the Glorious Revolution.

Our view also implies that the development of free markets must be accompanied by some credible restrictions on the state's ability to manipulate economic rules to the advantage of itself and its constituents. Successful economic performance, therefore, must be accompanied by institutions that limit economic intervention and allow private rights and markets to prevail in large segments of the economy. Put another way, because constitutional restrictions must be self-enforcing, they must serve to establish a credible commitment by the state to abide by them. Absolutist states which faced no such constraint, such as early modern Spain, created economic conditions that retarded long-run economic growth.

The ability of a government to commit to private rights and exchange is thus an essential condition for growth. It is also, as we shall see, a central issue in the constitutional debate in seventeenth-century England.

II. ENGLAND UNDER THE STUARTS: LIMITED CREDIBLE COMMITMENT TO RIGHTS

After the Crown passed from the Tudors to the Stuarts in 1603, revenue problems and their consequences become increasingly impor-

[7] Weingast and Marshall, "Industrial Organization of Congress"; Milgrom, North, and Weingast, "The Role of Institutions."

[8] Vertical integration is the standard example: because of potential transactions problems due to "asset specificity" or "appropriable quasi-rents," firms that internalize the problem via vertical integration outperform those which do not. See Williamson, *Economic Institutions*.

[9] In this sense our argument parallels that of James Buchanan and Geoffrey Brennan, who argue that the "recognition of the temporal dimensionality of choice provides one 'reason for rules'—rules that will impose binding constraints on choice options after the rules themselves have been established." James Buchanan and Geoffrey Brennan, *Reason of Rules* (Cambridge, 1981), p. 67.

TABLE 1
REVENUE SOURCES AND EXPENDITURE LEVELS, 1617

Revenue Source	Amount (£/year)
Crown Lands	£80,000
Customs and "new impositions"	190,000
Wards, and so forth (besides purveyance)	180,000
Total Revenue	450,000
Total Expenditures	486,000
Deficit	36,000

Source: David Hume, *The History of England* (Indianapolis, 1983), appendix to "The Reign of James I."

tant. At this time the king was expected to "live on his own," that is, to fund the government in the manner of an extended household. The execution of public laws and expenditures was not subject to a public budgetary process, and Parliament played only a small role in the decisions over expenditure and investment. The Crown therefore had considerable discretionary power over how and on what the money was spent. Parliament's main source of influence over policy resulted from its power to provide the Crown with tax revenue, typically for extraordinary purposes such as various wars. Parliament was also responsible for granting the Crown its revenue from other sources, such as customs, but in practice, the Stuarts, particularly Charles I, continued to collect the revenue without parliamentary consent.

Throughout the Stuart period revenue from traditional sources did not match expenditures. While figures for government expenditures during the Stuart period have not been collected as systematically as for the period following the Glorious Revolution, the following picture emerges.

At the beginning of the Stuarts' reign, Crown lands produced roughly half the annual revenue. To make up annual shortfalls, the Crown regularly resorted to sale of these lands.[10] Following the war with Spain in 1588, Elizabeth had sold 25 percent of the lands, raising £750,000. Still, James I inherited sizable debts from Elizabeth's war. Over his reign (1603–1624), another 25 percent of Crown lands were sold, and the remainder went during the reign of his son, Charles I (1625–1641). Sale of a major portion of a revenue-producing asset for annual expenses indicates the revenue problem was endemic. It also implies that over time the revenue problem had to get worse, for with every sale the expected future revenue declined. And, indeed, as Table 1 shows, for

[10] See, for example, Derek Hirst, *Authority and Conflict: England, 1603–1658* (Cambridge, MA, 1986), chap. 4, and Lawrence Stone, *The Crisis of the Aristocracy, 1558–1641* (Oxford, 1965).

the year 1617 total revenue did not match expenditures, leaving a deficit of £36,000 or of just under 10 percent of expenditures.

Under the Stuarts, therefore, the search for new sources of revenue became a major priority. An important new source which produced conflict between the Crown and Parliament was the raising of customs revenues through new "impositions." Indeed, in the 1630s such increases almost brought financial solvency, and with it the ability of the Crown to survive without calling Parliament.

Another method used by the Crown to raise revenue was to demand loans. The Crown did not, however, develop a systematic, regular relationship with moneyed interests, negotiating a series of loans in which it honored today's agreements because it wanted to avail itself of future loan opportunities. Indeed, just the opposite occurred. The Stuarts secured most of their loans under threat; hence they are known as "forced loans," of which more later. Repayment was highly unpredictable and never on the terms of the original agreement. In the forced loan of 1604/5 the Crown borrowed £111,891, nominally for one year; "although . . . ultimately repaid, £20,363 . . . was still due as late as December 1609."[11] The forced loan of 1617 (just under £100,000) was not repaid until 1628. The Crown behaved similarly on loans from 1611 and 1625. As time went on, such loans came to look more and more like taxes, but because these were nominally loans the Crown did not need parliamentary assent.[12]

The Crown's inability to honor its contractual agreements for borrowed funds is a visible indicator of its readiness to alter the rights of private parties in its own favor. Despite the significant incentive provided by the desire to raise funds in the future, the Crown followed its short-run interests, reneging on the terms to which it had agreed. As noted above, this type of behavior was not unique to England.

A second revenue-raising method was the sale of monopolies. While not the most important source of new revenue, it is particularly instructive because of its economic consequences.[13] In order to raise revenue in this manner, the Crown used patents in a new way. Originally designed to protect and promote the invention of new processes, patents came to be used to "reduce settled industries to monopolies under cover of technical improvements."[14] From a revenue standpoint, the best sources of new monopoly rights involved an

[11] Robert Ashton, *The Crown and the Money Market, 1603–1640* (Oxford, 1960), p. 35.

[12] Ashton, *Crown and the Money Market*, p. 36. Richard Cust, in his recent study of the 1626 forced loan, provides several instances of sanctions imposed on individuals refusing to provide funds: leading refusers were "either committed to prison or pressed in readiness for service abroad." Richard Cust, *The Forced Loans and English Politics* (Oxford, 1987), p. 3.

[13] Robert B. Ekelund, and Robert D. Tollison, *Mercantilism as a Rent-Seeking Society* (College Station, 1981).

[14] W. Price, *English Patents of Monopoly* (Boston, 1906). Examples include soap, tobacco, and starch.

economic activity that was profitable and whose participants were not part of the king's constituency. This led to a systematic search for and expropriation of quasi-rents in the economy. Moreover, as we will see in the next section, the Crown utilized a different system for enforcing these grants than that used for the older mercantilist controls, and one that was considerably more responsive to the Crown's interests. The system involved circumventing existing rights and the institutions designed to protect these rights.

Grants of monopoly clearly disrupted both existing economic interests in the targeted activity and those who depended on it (for example, suppliers and consumers). Monopoly grants thus acted as a tax that, since it expropriated the value of existing investment as well as future profits, was considerably greater at the margin than a 100 percent tax on profits. This risk lowered the rewards from all such new investments and hence discouraged their undertaking.

Beyond grants of monopoly, James, and especially Charles, used a variety of other, more subtle forms of expropriation of wealth. Because so many dimensions of public policy were involved, the political risk to citizens increased substantially over previous times. One important example was expansion of the peerage by the Crown, again in exchange for revenue.[15] While this expansion had broad social, cultural, and ideological implications, it also had significantly negative effects on existing peers. Expansion of the size of the House of Lords altered the value of an existing seat since it limited the ability of existing lords to protect themselves against the Crown.[16] Between the coronation of James I and the outbreak of the Civil War, the Stuarts' sale of peerages doubled the number of lay peers.

Governmental power was used in other ways to raise revenue. Employing the ancient power of purveyance, agents of the Crown seized various goods for "public purposes," paying prices well below market. Purveyance brought in an annual "unvoted" tax of £40,000 in the 1620s.[17] James also put hereditary titles up for sale: for example, offering to sell the title of baronet for £1,095 and promising that only a fixed number would be sold. This brought in £90,000 by 1614. But James soon reneged on this, lowering the price and selling more than the promised number. By 1622 the price had fallen to £220.[18] Through the

[15] F. W. Maitland, *Constitutional History of England* (Cambridge, 1908); Wallace Notestein, *The Winning of the Initiative by the House of Commons* (London, 1924); and Stone, *Crisis of the Aristocracy*.

[16] There were two separate reasons for this: the total number of voters was increasing, and the expansion added new members whose views systematically differed from those of existing nobles. The exchange that brought new nobles to the Lords undoubtedly entailed a commitment of support for the king.

[17] Hirst, *Authority and Conflict*, p. 103; and C. Hill, *Century of Revolution, 1603–1714* (2nd edn., New York, 1980), chap 4. See also John Kenyon, *Stuart England* (2nd edn., New York, 1985).

[18] Hirst, *Authority and Conflict*, pp. 113–14.

court of wards, the Crown managed the estates which had passed to minors. These were often openly run for the advantage of the Crown, not infrequently extracting the full value of the estate.[19] The Crown put "dispensations" up for sale, that is, the use of its powers to allow specific individuals to dispense with a specific law or restriction. "Sale" of this power was often used in conjunction with the enforcement or threat of enforcement of regulations that had not been enforced for years. At times the Crown simply seized the property of citizens. An especially egregious example occurred in 1640 when "the government seized £130,000 of bullion which private merchants had placed in the Tower for safety, causing numerous bankruptcies."[20]

This clash of interests between the king on the one hand and wealth holders and tax payers on the other was a major reason why the Crown failed to obtain grants from Parliament. In exchange for grants, Parliament demanded conditions and limits on the king's power that he was unwilling to accept. Parliamentary interests thereby exacerbated the problem they were attempting to eliminate. Withholding funds worsened the Crown's fiscal problems and intensified its search for alternative sources of revenue.

Institutional Basis of Stuart Policymaking

Both Parliament and the common law courts fought the Crown's use of monopolies and other changes in rights in its search for revenue. Parliament regularly presented the king with "grievances," lists of problems caused by the king that it wanted addressed.[21] Grievances were part of a larger bargaining process in which Parliament attempted, in exchange for revenue, to limit the Crown's power and its use of policymaking to expropriate wealth. Because of ever-present revenue problems, the Stuarts often called on Parliament for additional revenue. Parliamentary interests regularly demanded that in exchange for revenue the Crown respect traditional property rights and institutions: for example, that it cease declaring new monopolies. The Crown, in turn, was evidently unwilling to accept these restrictions and hence Parliament was often dissolved without having come to an agreement with the Crown.[22]

Attempts were also made to prevent the Crown's using the law to further its objectives. In 1624 Parliament passed the much-noted Statute

[19] Ibid., p. 103.

[20] C. Hill, *Century of Revolution*, p. 103.

[21] For details, see Notestein, *The Winning of the Initiative*.

[22] Part of the Crown's motivation appears to have been a desire to move toward the absolutism prevalent on the continent, notably in France and Spain. As Kenyon observes, at the onset of the seventeenth century, "any further adjustments [in the balance of power between Parliament and the Crown] were likely to be at the expense of Parliament" (Kenyon, *Stuart England*, p. 43). It almost succeeded. Hirst describes debates in Parliament in which the participants were explicitly concerned with this possibility (Hirst, *Authority and Conflict*, chap. 3).

of Monopolies prohibiting the use of patents to grant monopolies to existing businesses in exchange for revenue. In this manner it attempted to assert the traditional rights of secure property. In addition common law courts handed down the famous "Case of Monopolies" in 1601, making the Crown's use of monopolies illegal in common law. The Crown, however, was able to evade these restrictions. While these evasions often took forms of questionable legality, so long as the Crown did not depend on Parliament for revenue, it was able to use them in practice.

Understanding the subsequent institutional reaction to these royal policies requires that we study the institutional means by which the Crown ran the government. For our purposes three elements of the royal powers and institutions were central to the Crown's success. First, a major source of power for the Crown was the royal prerogative, by which the Crown issued proclamations or royal ordinances. By this means it could issue new rules; that is, it had quasi-legislative powers without recourse to Parliament. Crown rules were enforced, not through the common law court system, but through the prerogative courts and included the power to suspend laws and to dispense with laws for specific individuals.[23]

Second, the Star Chamber, combining legislative, executive, and judicial powers, played a key role. On issues concerning prerogative, the Star Chamber had come to have final say, and could in certain circumstances reverse judgments against the Crown.[24]

Finally, since the Crown was personally responsible for day-to-day government operations, it paid the judges, who served at its pleasure. Increasingly the Stuarts used their power over judges to influence their judgments. Judges—Chief Justices Coke (1616/17) and Crew (1627)—were openly fired for ruling against the Crown. Ultimately this tactic produced judges who by and large supported the Crown.[25]

The effect of these institutions was to combine in the Crown executive, legislative, and judicial powers, limiting external institutional checks. While royal proclamations did not have the same legal status as an act of Parliament, they were enforced directly through the common law courts. While these courts did not have to go along with the king—and often did not—ultimately he won through the higher court, the Star Chamber. Thus, while the common law was often against the

[23] Dispensations for individuals, like most powers under the Stuarts, were put up for sale (Maitland, *Constitutional History*, pt. IV).

[24] The Star Chamber, in which the most egregious examples of arbitrary power occurred, became a regular feature of Stuart England. See Maitland, *Constitutional History*, and Friedrich A. Hayek, *Constitution of Liberty* (Chicago, 1960), chap. 11.

[25] Coke's dismissal, "the first of a judge in over thirty years, ushered in a period of increasing royal pressure on the bench: in Charles's reign two other chief justices, Crew and Heath, and one chief baron of the exchequer court, Walter, were to follow Coke" (Hirst, *Authority and Conflict*, p. 121). See also Hayek's excellent and extensive discussion, in *Constitution of Liberty*, chap. 11.

king, the king could alter the jurisdiction of a dispute by issuing proclamations. The expanded use of the Star Chamber and the successful running of the government for substantial periods without Parliament limited the ability of traditional institutions to constrain the Crown. Effective possession of legislative and judicial powers also gave the Crown the ability to alter economic and political rights when it was convenient to do so. In comparison with the previous century, the rights that Parliament and other institutions were designed to protect were considerably less secure.

In response, a coalition formed against the Crown, seeking to preserve personal liberties, rights, and wealth. This raised the stakes of the political game to the various economic interests—in particular the value of opposing the king rose. Moreover, because the Crown attempted to extract from its own constituents a major portion of the advantages it had bestowed on them, the value of supporting the king declined. It is clear, however, that the opposition would have been unlikely to succeed, had the English Crown, like its French or Spanish counterpart, had a standing army with which to quell the initial uprising.

Civil War to Glorious Revolution

Eventually the opposition openly challenged the king, leading the country into civil war. But the ultimate opposition victory was not inevitable.

After seizing power, the opposition modified the institutions underpinning the Crown's most egregious behavior. Not surprisingly, the Star Chamber was abolished in 1641 by an act requiring that all cases involving property be tried at common law, thus adding another milestone along the route toward supremacy of the common law, so favorable to property rights. Restrictions against monopolies were now enforced. In an attempt to prevent the Crown from ruling for substantial periods without calling a Parliament, Parliament passed the Triennial legislation, which called for regular standing of the Parliament. The royal administrative apparatus was dismantled, and with it the royal ability to impose regulatory restrictions on the economy in conflict with the rights enforced by the common law courts.

Important changes reduced restrictions on labor mobility. Land tenure modifications simultaneously favored the development of private rights and markets and reduced the Crown's political hold over this once-important part of its constituency.[26] New and profitable opportunities resulted from lifting restrictions on land use and improving markets.

[26] See H. J. Perkins, "The Social Causes of the British Industrial Revolution," *Transactions of the Royal Historical Society*, 18 (1968). Hill, discussing the 1660 Act confirming the abolition of feudal tenures, notes that in the eighteenth century Blackstone called this Act a greater boon to property owners than the Magna Carta itself (*Century of Revolution*, p. 127).

After the Civil War a number of political innovations occurred, including the abolition of the monarchy and the House of Lords. Their failure led to pressure to bring back the king. With the Restoration of the monarchy in 1660, England was once again ruled by the Stuarts. It is critical for understanding the next series of events to notice a striking limitation of the institutional changes prior to the Restoration. While the details differ considerably, the next twenty-five years repeated the events of the earlier Stuarts' reign in one important respect. Political struggle with constituents resulted in the king's arbitrary encroachment. By far the most important instance of this—indeed, the one resulting in a nation united against the Crown—concerned the rechartering of local governments and political power. Rechartering came in reaction to the Whig-led "Exclusion Crisis"; it allowed the Crown to disenfranchise much of the opposition and thereby reduce impediments to its exercise of power. Of the 104 members of Parliament returned in the mid-1680s by the boroughs receiving new charters, only one Whig was elected. This converted "what had been a formidable, aggressive and highly organized opposition party into an impotent collection of a few individuals."[27]

Had the Crown succeeded in this political maneuver, there would be few checks on its powers, because it allowed the Crown to disenfranchise *any* opposition. But between 1686 and 1688, James II, having disenfranchised the Whig opposition, turned on his own supporters, causing his own constituents to join the opposition to remove him in the Glorious Revolution of 1688.

III. INSTITUTIONAL CHANGES FOLLOWING THE GLORIOUS REVOLUTION

At the same time it extended the Crown to William and Mary, Parliament restructured the society's political institutions in the Revolution Settlement. To understand the new institutions it is necessary to see clearly the problem the parliamentary interests sought to solve. The early Stuarts' use of the Star Chamber and the rechartering of the later Stuarts threatened the liberties and wealth of citizens, leaving them with little protection against Crown attempts to appropriate their wealth. But experience showed that simply removing the powers underpinning arbitrary behavior was insufficient to prevent abuse. Controlling Crown behavior required the solving of financial problems as well as appropriate constraints on the Crown. So the Glorious Revolution also ushered in a fiscal revolution.[28] The main features of the institutional revolution are as follows.

[27] Jones, *Revolution of 1688*, pp. 47, 50. As B. W. Hill observes, James's efforts to repack the constituencies "came near to success in every respect but one: they alarmed landed society, Tory as well as Whig." See B. W. Hill, *The Growth of Parliamentary Parties: 1689–1742* (Hamden, 1976).

[28] P. G. M. Dickson, *The Financial Revolution in England* (New York, 1967).

First and foremost, the Revolution initiated the era of parliamentary "supremacy." This settled for the near future the issue of sovereignty: it was now the "king in Parliament," not the king alone.[29] No longer would the Crown, arguing the "divine rights of kings," claim to be above the law. Parliamentary supremacy established a permanent role for Parliament in the on-going management of the government and hence placed a direct check on the Crown. The Crown no longer called or disbanded Parliament at its discretion alone.

Parliament also gained a central role in financial matters. Its exclusive authority to raise new taxes was firmly reestablished; at the same time the Crown's independent sources of revenue were also limited. For the Crown to achieve its own goals this meant it had to establish successful relations with Parliament. Shortly thereafter, Parliament gained the never-before-held right to audit how the government had expended its funds. Parliamentary veto over expenditures, combined with the right to monitor how the funds they had voted were spent, placed important constraints over the Crown.

Another important institutional change focused on the royal prerogative powers. These were substantially curtailed and subordinated to common law, and the prerogative courts (which allowed the Crown to enforce its proclamations) were abolished. At the same time the independence of the judiciary from the Crown was assured. Judges now served subject to good behavior (they could only be removed if convicted for a criminal offense or by action of both houses of Parliament) instead of at the king's pleasure. The supremacy of the common law courts, so favorable to private rights, was thereby assured.

Because the Stuarts had violated the personal liberties of their opponents (excessive bail, no writ of Habeas Corpus) as a means of raising the cost of opposition, reducing the arbitrary powers of the Crown resulted not only in more secure economic liberties and property rights, but in political liberties and rights as well. Political rights were seen as a key element of protection against arbitrary violations of economic rights.

Two final points are worth emphasizing. First, part of the glue that held these institutional changes together was the successful dethroning of Charles I and, later, James II. This established a credible threat to the Crown regarding future irresponsible behavior. The conditions which would "trigger" this threat were laid out in the Revolution Settlement, and shortly thereafter in the Declaration of Rights. Second, although parliamentary supremacy meant that Parliament dictated the form of the new political institutions, it did not assume the sole position of power within the government, as it did after the Civil War or in the nineteenth

[29] See, for example, Maitland, *Constitutional History*, pp. 298–301, or David Keir, *The Constitutional History of Modern Britain Since 1485* (London, 1966).

century. While substantial constraints were placed on the king, these did not reduce him to a figurehead.

IV. THE GLORIOUS REVOLUTION AND ENGLAND'S CREDIBLE COMMITMENT TO SECURE RIGHTS

The institutional innovations increased dramatically the control of wealth holders over the government. Since fiscal crises inevitably produced pressure on the Crown to break its agreements, eliminating unilateral control by the Crown over key decisions was a necessary component of the new institutions. As previously described, this occurred in two ways. First, by requiring Parliament's assent to major changes in policies (such as changing the terms of loans or taxes), the representatives of wealth holders could veto such moves unless they were also in their interest. This allowed action in times of crisis but eliminated the Crown's unilateral action. Second, several other ways for the Crown to renege on promises were eliminated, notably its ability to legislate unilaterally (through the prerogative), to by-pass Parliament (because it had an independent source of funds), or to fire judges who did not conform to Crown desires.

Two factors made the new arrangements self-enforcing. First, the credible threat of removal limited the Crown's ability to ignore the new arrangements. Second, in exchange for the greater say in government, parliamentary interests agreed to put the government on a sound financial footing, that is, they agreed to provide sufficient tax revenue. Not only did this remove a major motive underlying the exercise of arbitrary power, but for the new King William it meant he could launch a major war against France. The arrangement proved so satisfactory for the king that a host of precedents were set putting the new division of powers on a solid footing. As a consequence of these institutional changes, private rights became fundamentally more secure.[30]

Institutional and Political Constraints on Parliament

The triumph of Parliament raises the issue of why it would not then proceed to act just like the king? Its motives were no more lofty than those of the Crown. But the institutional outcome effectively deterred Parliament from similar behavior. Robert Ekelund and Robert Tollison provide the following general analysis:

> Higher costs due to uncertainty and growing private returns reduced industry demands for regulation and control in England. All this strengthened the emergent constitutional democracy, which created conditions making rent-seeking activity on the part of both

[30] Jones, on p. 6 of the *Revolution of 1688*, concludes: "None of its architects could have predicted its effectiveness in securing the liberties, religion, property and independence of the nation after so many previous attempts had failed."

monarch and merchants more costly. When the locus of power to rent-seeking shifted from the monarch to Parliament . . . the costs of supply of regulation through legislative enactment rose.[31]

They suggest that the natural diversity of views in a legislature raises the cost of supplying private benefits in the form of favorable regulation.

The framework of institutional evolution we have described complements their story. The embedding of economic and political freedoms in the law, the interests of principals (for example, merchants) in a greater measure of freedom, and the ideological considerations that swept England in the late seventeenth century combined to play a role in institutional change. The new constitutional settlement endowed several actors with veto power, and thus created the beginnings of a division or separation of powers.[32] Supplying private benefits at public expense now required the cooperation of the Crown, Parliament, and the courts. Only the Crown could propose an expenditure, but only Parliament could authorize and appropriate funds for the proposal, and it could do so solely for purposes proposed by the Crown. Erskin May summed up this procedure as, "The crown demands, the Commons grants, and the Lords assent to the grant." A balance of power between the Crown and Parliament significantly limited publicly supplied private benefits.[33]

Three other political factors help explain why the new era of parliamentary supremacy did not simply transfer power from the Crown to Parliament. In 1641 the centralized administrative apparatus which enforced royal attempts to alter rights and property was destroyed. The absence of such a structure prevented either the Crown or Parliament from similar encroachment. Because a new apparatus—even one that was initially quite limited—would allow its future expansion, many interests could be counted upon to oppose its initiation.

Second, the commercially minded ruling Whig coalition preferred limited government and especially limited political interference with the common law courts. Parliament was thus *politically* constrained from intervention in the courts. As R. Braun observes:

the Whig oligarchy was anxious to avoid encroachment upon the privacy of the business of those groups from which it drew its support. Not only the constitutional and institutional framework, but also the prevailing ideological basis of the [Whigs and their

[31] Ekelund and Tollison, *Mercantilism*, p. 149.

[32] We emphasize, however, that this division of powers was not a clear-cut system of checks and balances. Nor can it be considered a true separation of powers. The designers of the new institutions were far more worried about constraints on the Crown than on protecting the Crown from encroachments by Parliament. Thus in the latter half of the eighteenth century, the power of the Crown diminished, and with it the constraints (or checks) on Parliament. See A. F. Pollard, *The Evolution of Parliament* (London, 1926).

[33] Erskin May, *Parliamentary Practice* (17th edn., London, 1966; 1st edn., 1844). Further investigation of the procedures devised at this time is called for.

> constituents] prevented the central administrative apparatus of the British government from developing [a major regulatory and control function].[34]

Widespread regulation of markets by Parliament along the line of Colbert in France (or the Stuarts) would have led to a clash with the common law courts. Thus the political independence of the courts limited potential abuses by Parliament. Combined with the explicit institutional limits on Crown intervention, this assured the courts important and unchallenged authority in large areas of economic activity.

Third, the creation of a politically independent judiciary greatly expanded the government's ability credibly to promise to honor its agreements, that is, to bond itself. By limiting the ability of the government to renege on its agreements, the courts played a central role in assuring a commitment to secure rights. As we will see, this commitment substantially improved the government's ability to raise money through loans.

Thus the institutional and political changes accompanying the Glorious Revolution significantly raised the predictability of the government. By putting the government on a sound financial basis and regularizing taxation, it removed the random component of expropriation associated with royal attempts to garner revenue. Any interest group seeking private gain had now to get approval from both the Crown and the Parliament.

V. THE FISCAL REVOLUTION

To see the profound effects of the Glorious Revolution, we focus on one important element of public finance, government borrowing. Since capital markets are especially sensitive to the security of property rights, they provide a unique and highly visible indicator of the economic and political revolution that took place. Indeed, they are one of the few means for empirically evaluating the effects of the Glorious Revolution.

Prior to the Glorious Revolution, payments on loans were subject to manipulation by the Crown; rescheduling and delays in payments were common. As indicated in Table 2, money was raised through forced loans in 1604/5, 1611/2, 1617, and 1625. In each instance the Crown did not honor its terms. In the loan of 1617, for example, James I raised £100,000 in London at 10 percent for the period of one year. At the end of the year, although James paid the interest, he refused to repay the principal and demanded that the loan be renewed. No interest was paid over the next several years, and each year another renewal was

[34] R. Braun, "Taxation, Sociopolitical Structure, and State-Building: Great Britain and Brandenburg-Prussia," in Charles Tilly, ed., *Formation of Nation States in Western Europe* (Princeton, 1975).

TABLE 2
FORCED LOANS BY THE EARLY STUARTS, 1603–1625

Year	Amount	Rate (percent per year)	Repayment
1604/5	£111,891	10%	£20,362 unpaid as of Dec. 1609
1611/2	116,381	10	£112,000 unpaid as of Jul. 1616
1617[a]	96,466	10[b]	Unpaid until 1628
1625[c]	60,000	8	Unpaid until 1628

[a] Extension in 1624 secured by Crown lands.
[b] Unilaterally lowered by Charles I in 1624 to 8%.
[c] Secured by Crown lands.
Source: Robert Ashton, *The Crown and the Money Market, 1603–1640* (Oxford, 1960), chaps. 2 and 5.

"agreed" to. In 1624 Charles I lowered the interest rate to 8 percent; however, he did not pay any interest, nor did he repay the principal until 1628. Such behavior was hardly designed to gain the confidence of potential sources of loans. As Robert Ashton concludes, the "cavalier treatment which the Crown meted out to its creditors, and more especially to those most unwilling lenders who made more or less compulsory contributions through the medium of the Corporation of London" helps explain why London and the money interests supported the parliamentary cause.[35] Nor did the Stuarts attempt to develop a major international source of loans.[36]

Several financial innovations occurred under the late Stuarts, including some that were to play a key role in the "financial revolution" after 1688, for example, making notes "assignable," thus allowing them to be sold. The recent work of Glenn Nichols suggests that financial arrangements under the late Stuarts were far superior to those under the early Stuarts. Nonetheless, fiscal stress pressed the system to its limits, and led to a partial repudiation in the famous "stop the exchequer" in 1672. The debt in question, over a million pounds, shows that the late Stuarts—until that time, at least—could raise substantial sums.[37]

Institutional Innovations

A series of institutional innovations during the war with France (1689–1697) changed the way the government sought credit, facilitating the regularization of public finance. First, the government began as a

[35] Ashton, *Crown and the Money Market*, p. 113.

[36] Ashton reports only two such loans, the second of which (£58,400 in 1616) was still outstanding in 1636. Here too the Stuarts failed to develop a reputation for honoring agreements. By the 1630s the Crown was unable to borrow at all from either international sources or London.

[37] See Glenn O. Nichols, "English Government Borrowing Before the Financial Revolution," manuscript, Anderson College, 1988. For details about the stop of the exchequer, see Dickson, *Financial Revolution*. In exchange for its short-term notes, the Crown gave new long-term loans. Much of the interest from the latter was still unpaid at the time of the Glorious Revolution, however.

regular practice to earmark new taxes, authorized by statute for each new loan issue, to pay the interest on all new long-term loans. By earmarking taxes beforehand, parliamentary interests limited the king's discretion each year over whether to pay bondholders their interest.

Second, the first large, long-term loan (£1,000,000) secured by new taxes took place in 1693. By 1694, however, these funds were exhausted. When the government sought a new large loan, it invited the subscribers to incorporate as the Bank of England. The Bank was responsible for handling the loan accounts of the government and for assuring the continuity of promised distributions. Certain restrictions were also imposed: the Bank could not lend the Crown money or purchase any Crown lands without the explicit consent of Parliament. As Macaulay observed over a century ago, this created a strong instrument of the Whig party (and hence of commercial interests). Since loans to the Crown went through the Bank, "it must have instantly stopped payment if it had ceased to receive the interest on the sum which it had advanced to the government."[38] The government had thus created an additional, private constraint on its future behavior by making it difficult to utilize funds of a current loan if it failed to honor its previous obligations.

Two other changes are worth noting. In 1698 the government created a separate fund to make up deficiencies in the event that the revenue earmarked for specific loans was insufficient to cover the required distributions (as was the case for several loans). This explicitly removed the component of risk associated with each loan due to its ties to a specific tax.[39] Second, during this period the milling of coins began, reducing the debasement of the currency due to shaving of coins.

Government Loans, 1688–1740

Thus were the institutional foundations of modern capital markets laid in England. These institutional changes were more successful than their originators had hoped. The original subscription to the Bank of England, for instance, was expected to be slow and possibly unsuccessful. In actuality, one-third of the loan was subscribed on the first day and another third during the next two days. Ten days later the loan was fully subscribed.

To see the dramatic results of the fiscal revolution, we turn to the public finances during this period. Table 3 provides information on governmental expenditures and debt. On the eve of the Revolution governmental expenditures were about £1.8 million, reflecting a slow

[38] Lord Macaulay, *The History of England*, (London, 1914), vol. V, p. 2438.

[39] As David Ogg explains: "Thenceforth, the investor knew that, in lending money on a specified tax, he had parliamentary guarantee for the security of this investment, based not only on the particular fund, but on the whole of the national revenue." David Ogg, *England in the Reigns of James II and William III* (Oxford, 1955), p. 413. Regarding the second, see pp. 422–25.

TABLE 3
GROWTH OF GOVERNMENT DEBT, 1618–1740
(£ million)

Year	Governmental Expenditure[1]	Debt[2]	Prices[3] (1701 = 100)
Stuart England			
1618[4]	£0.5	£0.8	
mid-1630s[5]	1.0	1.0	
1680[6]	1.4		113
1688[6]	1.8	1.0[7]	99
Post Glorious Revolution			
1695	6.2	8.4	116
1697	7.9	16.7	122
1700	3.2	14.2	115
1710	9.8	21.4	122
1714	6.2	36.2	103
1720	6.0	54.0	102
1730	5.6	51.4	95
1740	6.2	47.4	100
1750	7.2	78.0	95

Note: Because these figures are obtained from a variety of sources, they are intended solely to provide an indication of underlying trends. Figures for expenditures and debt after the Glorious Revolution are most reliable.

Sources: 1. Government Expenditure, post-1688: B. R. Mitchell, *British Historical Statistics* (Cambridge, 1988), chap. 11, table 2.
2. Debt, post-1688: Mitchell, *British Historical Statistics*, chap. 11, table 7.
3. Prices: Mitchell, *British Historical Statistics*, chap. 14: 1680–97, table 1, part A, "consumer goods"; 1697–1750, part B, "consumer goods."
4. Government Expenditure and Debt, 1618: David Hume, *The History of England* (Indianapolis, 1983), "Appendix to the Reign of James I."
5. Government Expenditure and Debt, mid-1630s: Derek Hirst, *Authority and Conflict: England, 1603–1658* (Cambridge, MA, 1986), p. 174.
6. Government Expenditure, 1680 and 1688: C. D. Chandaman, *The English Public Revenue, 1660–1688* (Oxford, 1975), appendix 2, table 7, "Total Available for Ordinary Purposes."
7. Debt, 1688: H. Fisk, *English Public Finance* (New York, 1920), p. 93.

but steady increase over two decades.[40] Government debt was limited to about £1 million, or between 2 and 3 percent of GNP (estimated to be £41 million). Moreover, at a time when Holland was borrowing £5 million long term at 4 percent per year, the English Crown could only borrow small amounts at short term, paying between 6 and 30 percent per year.[41]

The Revolution radically altered this pattern. In 1697, just nine years later, governmental expenditures had grown fourfold, to £7.9 million. The immediate reason for the rise was the new war with France. But importantly, the government's ability to tap the resources of society

[40] C. D. Chandaman, *The English Public Revenue: 1660–88* (Oxford, 1975).

[41] For figures on government debt and GNP estimates, see B. R. Mitchell, *British Historical Statistics* (Cambridge, 1988). On interest rates, see Sidney Homer, *A History of Interest Rates* (New Brunswick, 1963), p. 149.

increased. This is evidenced by the increase in the size of government debt, which grew during the nine years of war from £1 million to nearly £17 million. This level of debt—approximately 40 percent of GNP—was previously unattainable. Moreover, the ability of the new government to finance a war at unprecedented levels played a critical role in defeating France. To put these figures in modern perspective, a trillion-dollar economy would have begun the period with $25 billion of debt, which in just nine years would grow to almost $400 billion.

Following the war, both government expenditures and the amount financed through debt were substantially higher than previous levels. By 1720 government debt was over fifty times the 1688 level and on the order of GNP. Financing wars by borrowing had another remarkable benefit. Previous instances of unexpected large wars were nearly always accompanied by large fiscal demands, the search for sources of revenue, and consequently unfavorable demands on wealth holders. Such demands were virtually eliminated by the new methods of finance. Another evidence of the new regime's increased predictability is indicated by the series of price changes. Despite sustained deficits resulting in the enormous increase in debt, government policy did not result in inflationary finance.[42]

At the same time that the scope of governmental borrowing increased, however, the market rate charged the government fell. Its initial long-term loans in the early 1690s were at 14 percent (see Table 4). By the end of the 1690s the rate was about half, between 6 and 8 percent. The rate continued to fall over the next two decades so that, by the 1730s, interest rates were 3 percent.

These numbers are impressive in two ways. First, the amount of wealth now available for use by others increased tremendously. Second, at the same time as governmental borrowing increased, the interest rate fell. Sharp increases in demand accompanied by decline in rates indicate that the overall risk associated with governmental behavior decreased considerably despite the enormous increase in the size of the debt. As the society gained experience with its new institutions,

[42] Prices rose a little over 20 percent between 1690 and 1710 (and then fell again between 1710 and 1730). But the enormous increase in debt during this period suggests that the government did not attempt to meet its debt obligations through inflationary finance. The modern view of inflation suggests two further inferences (see, for example, Thomas Sargent, *Rational Expectations and Inflation* [New York, 1986]). Since inflation in part reflects expectations about future governmental finance of deficits, the lack of major increases in prices suggests that the market did not expect inflationary finance. Since this pattern was maintained for several decades, it indicates that these expectations were "confirmed" in the sense that new information about current governmental behavior did not change expectations. Robert Barro provides evidence that budget deficits had almost no effect on prices from 1700 until the Napoleonic campaigns. Robert Barro, "Government Spending, Interest Rates, Prices, and Budget Deficits in the UK, 1701–1918," *Journal of Monetary Economics*, 20 (Sept. 1987), pp. 221–48.

TABLE 4
GOVERNMENT LONG-TERM BORROWING: INTEREST RATES, 1693–1739
(selected loans)

Date[a]	Amount	Interest	How Funded
Jan 1693	£723,394	14.0%	Additional excise
Mar 1694	1,000,000	14.0	Duties on imports
Mar 1694	1,200,000	8.0	Additional customs and duties
Apr 1697	1,400,000	6.3	Excise and duties
Jul 1698	2,000,000	8.0	Additional excise duties
Mar 1707	1,155,000	6.25	Surplus from funds of five loans from 1690s; duties
Jul 1721	500,000	5.0	Hereditary revenue of Crown
Mar 1728	1,750,000	4.0	Coal duties
May 1731	800,000	3.0	Duties
Jun 1739	300,000	3.0	Sinking fund

[a] Date of royal assent to loan act.
Source: P. G. M. Dickson, *The Financial Revolution in England* (New York, 1967), tables 2, 3, and 22.

particularly their predictability and commitment to secure rights, expectations over future actions began to reflect the new order.

These changing expectations were directly reflected in the capital market response. The new institutional underpinnings of public finance provided a clear and dramatic credible commitment that the government would honor its promises and maintain the existing pattern of rights. While underlying economic conditions were surely an important component of the large increase in debt, they alone can not explain the *suddenness* with which the debt increased, nor its magnitude. Even though the later Stuarts were more financially successful than their predecessors, nothing that came before the Glorious Revolution suggests the dramatic change in capital markets that it unleashed.

VI. IMPLICATIONS FOR PRIVATE CAPITAL MARKETS

Our thesis is that the credible commitment by the government to honor its financial agreements was part of a larger commitment to secure private rights. The latter was clearly a major factor for the institutional changes at the time of the Glorious Revolution. Data on general economic activity are sparse, so we cannot perform a major test of our thesis, but we can provide some support. As evidence we turn to the development of private capital markets and the necessary evolution of the financial foundation of long-run economic success.

While it is clear that the institutions underlying private capital markets go back at least several centuries, it is widely agreed among economic historians that private capital markets date from the early eighteenth century.[43] The rise of banks and an increasingly differentiated set of securities, providing a relatively secure means of saving, brought individual savings into the financial system. Ashton reports that this "meant that men were less concerned than their fathers . . . to keep quantities of coin, bullion, and plate locked up in safes or buried in their orchards and gardens."[44]

The institutions leading to the growth of a stable market for public debt provided a large and positive externality for the parallel development of a market for private debt. Shortly after its formation for intermediating public debt, the Bank of England began private operations. Numerous other banks also began operations at this time. This development provided the institutional structure for pooling the savings of many individuals and for intermediation between borrowers and lenders. A wide range of securities and negotiable instruments emerged in the early eighteenth century and these were used to finance a large range of activities.[45]

Phyllis Deane summarizes the development of private capital markets alongside that for public capital:

> The secondary effects of the Bank's financial transactions on behalf of the government stemmed from the new financial instruments which were thus created . . . and because [the instruments] issued by a credit-worthy borrower are themselves readily saleable, the effect was further to lubricate the channels linking savings and investment by creating a large stock of negotiable paper assets which new savers could buy. Similarly, the deposits from private sources could also be used as a basis for further credit to the private sector.[46]

As a consequence, private capital markets flourished.

Several sources of evidence support our claims. First, research on interest rates for various forms of private credit reveals that these roughly parallel rates on public credit.[47] Falling private rates increased the range of projects and enterprises that were economically feasible, thus promoting the accumulation of capital. As L. S. Pressnell concludes, the "accumulation of capital in the 18th century, which the

[43] This section summarizes the conclusions of the literature on the early eighteenth century. See, for example, T. S. Ashton, *An Economic History of England* (London, 1955); John Clapham, *The Bank of England* (New York, 1945); Phyllis Deane, *The First Industrial Revolution* (2nd edn., Cambridge, 1979); Dickson, *Financial Revolution*; Peter Mathias, *The First Industrial Nation* (2nd edn., London, 1983); and E. Powell, *The Evolution of the Money Market: 1385–1915* (London, 1966).

[44] Ashton, *Economic History*, p. 178.

[45] "The essence of the financial revolution of the early 18th century was the development of a wide range of securities in which new mercantile and financial companies—the chartered trading companies, the partnership banks, the insurance companies, etc.—could flexibly and safely invest and disinvest" (Deane, *Industrial Revolution*, p. 185).

[46] Ibid., pp. 184–85.

[47] Clapham, *Bank of England*; L. S. Pressnell, "The Rate of Interest in the 18th Century," in L. S. Pressnell, ed., *Studies in the Industrial Revolution* (London, 1960), p. 181; and Homer, *A History of Interest Rates*.

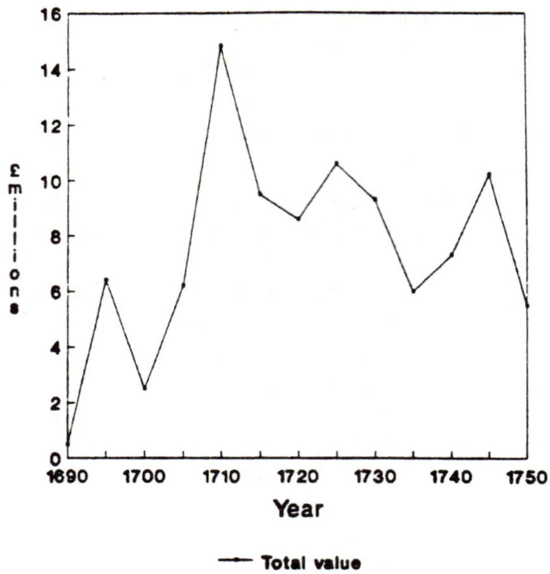

FIGURE 1

GROWTH OF THE STOCK MARKET: 1690–1750

Source: P. G. M. Dickson, *The Financial Revolution in England* (London, 1967), Appendix C.

declining trend of interest rates . . . clearly indicates, appears in this light as a major social and economic achievement."[48] Unfortunately the data from the first half of the eighteenth century, in contrast to those from the second half, are sketchy, and for the period prior to the Glorious Revolution, almost nonexistent.

Second, large-scale trading in private securities dates from this period.[49] Figure 1 shows the growth of one component of the market, short-dated securities. In the early 1690s the volume of these securities averaged £300,000 per year. Ten years later, volume averaged £3,400,000 per year, and by the early 1710s, £11,000,000 per year. While growth trailed off after the collapse of the South Sea Bubble, the market from 1715 to 1750 was far larger than that prior to the Revolution.

Third, the period saw the growth and development of banks. The Bank of England was followed shortly by numerous other banks in London. By the 1720s these numbered about 25. By 1750 there were 30; by 1770, 50; and by 1800, 70. While banks in areas outside London began to appear in large numbers only after 1750, Ashton argues that

[48] Pressnell, "Rate of Interest," p. 181.

[49] As Dickson notes, "The development of a market in securities in London in the period 1688–1756 was one of the more important aspects of the Financial Revolution." Dickson, *Financial Revolution*, p. 457.

TABLE 5
THE BANK OF ENGLAND'S NOTES AND DRAWING ACCOUNTS, 1698–1750
(£ thousands)

Year	Notes in Circulation	Drawing Accounts
1698	£1,340	£100
1720	2,900	1,300
1730	4,700	2,200
1740	4,400	2,900
1750	4,600	1,900

Note: Figures for 1720–1750 are averages for the five-year period beginning with the year listed.
Source: John Clapham, *The Bank of England: A History* (New York, 1945), vol. 1: *1694–1797*.

many of these areas were integrated into a national capital market much earlier.[50] "Inland bills and promissory notes played a considerable part in the trade of all parts of England and Wales. But nowhere had their use extended so far as in the north-west. The ubiquity of the bill was probably the reason why in this area formal banking made its appearance relatively late."[51]

The final set of evidence centers on the Bank of England's private activities in three areas. (1) Discounted bills. Systematic data on the Bank's discounting operations apparently do not survive. Nonetheless, sporadic reports are available and indicate a considerable growth of activity during the first few decades of the Bank's operations. For 1699 data reveal the following volume of notes discounted: 13–31 June, £8,534; 27 June–4 July, £14,000. By 1730 the *median* day's volume was over £10,000, and by 1760 days over £100,000 were common.[52] (2) Notes in circulation. During the eighteenth century the Bank's notes became a major medium of exchange, first in London, and then throughout England.[53] In the first two years of the Bank's operations the volume of notes grew to about £760,000 (see Table 5). By 1720 they numbered £2,900,000, and they were above £4,500,000 by 1730 and for the next few

[50] See Charles P. Kindleberger, *Financial History of Western Europe* (London, 1984), p. 74; and Mathias, *Industrialized Nation*. The earliest provincial bank cited by Mathias was in Bristol (1716), and there were not more than a dozen in 1750. By 1784, however, there were 120, and by 1800, 370 (Mathias, p. 151).

[51] Ashton, *Economic History*, p. 185. Ashton's claim is also supported by the study of credit instruments other than those provided by banks. B. L. Anderson, discussing the rise of inland bills, notes that their legal status was markedly improved in the first years of the eighteenth century. "This recognition of the bill as a transferable means of payment was a decisive turning point in the development of the English credit system. . . . [The] English practice made it an instrument of credit in a system of accommodation paper that was highly responsive to the community's demand for money." B. L. Anderson, "Money and the Structure of Credit in the 18th Century," *Business History*, 85 (No. 1, 1970), p. 90.

[52] Clapham, *Bank of England*, p. 126.

[53] While other banks issued notes, by far the largest source for most of the period we are studying are those of the Bank of England. Throughout this period, these notes were convertible to gold. See D. M. Joslin, "London Private Bankers, 1720–1785," in E. M. Carus-Wilson, ed., *Essays in Economic History*, vol. 2, pp. 340–59.

decades. (3) Drawing accounts. This early form of demand deposit seems to have become systematized about twenty years after the Bank's founding.[54] As shown in Table 5, drawing accounts were quite modest in the late 1690s. By 1720 they numbered more than a million pounds, growing to over two million by 1730. To summarize, the Bank expanded operations over several types of private credit. By 1720, a little over 25 years after the Bank's establishment, these sums reached substantial levels, showing the steady growth in financial services for private economic activity.

Thus it appears that the growth of private capital markets paralleled that of public capital markets. This development mobilized the savings of large numbers of individuals and, by mid-century, provided financial services in an integrated, national market. These funds appear to have financed a large variety of business activities and played a necessary role in the economic expansion throughout this century.[55] While these activities have not been studied in detail as they have for the period following 1750, 1688 appears to be a more abrupt break with the past than 1750. Returning to our main thesis, this growth indicates that the attempts to maintain secure private rights were largely successful. Although the evidence cannot be used to discern the precise level of security, it shows that it was substantial. A more systematic test awaits future research on these markets.

CONCLUSION

In this essay we have provided a brief account of the successful evolution of institutional forms that permitted economic growth to take place in early modern England. It is clear from this discussion of a century of civil war and revolution, however, that these institutional innovations did not arise naturally. Rather they were forced, often violently, upon the Crown. The Crown, however, nearly won the struggle. Had a standing army existed in England, it would have been under the control of the Crown, and the political and economic future of England would very likely have been different, potentially more in keeping with that of France and Spain.

We have shown how the political institutions governing society can be considered endogenously. Fiscal constraints and a revenue-seeking Crown, problems exacerbated by an uncooperative Parliament, created

[54] The only year before 1720 reported by Clapham is 1698.

[55] An additional piece of evidence concerns investment in transportation infrastructure, which also increased at this time. By 1724 there were over 1,160 miles of river open to navigation, double that of a century earlier. See Ashton, *Economic History*, p. 73; Mathias, *Industrial Nation*, p. 100. While the "canal age" is usually dated at mid-century, it "did not spring to life in 1750" but was the "conclusion of a mounting momentum of effort"; Mathias, *Industrial Nation*, p. 100. Both Ashton and Mathias noted that there were two big booms in improving rivers during this period, one at the turn of the century and one between 1718 and 1720.

a situation of insecure rights in which the wealth and welfare of individual citizens were at risk. Prior to the Glorious Revolution, institutions such as the Star Chamber enabled the Crown to alter rights in its favor in a manner that parliamentary interests were hard pressed to resist.

Given their means and motives, the triumph of parliamentary interests in the Glorious Revolution led to five significant institutional changes. First, it removed the underlying source of the expediency, an archaic fiscal system and its attendant fiscal crises. Second, by limiting the Crown's legislative and judicial powers, it limited the Crown's ability to alter rules after the fact without parliamentary consent. Third, parliamentary interests reasserted their dominance of taxation issues, removing the ability of the Crown to alter tax levels unilaterally. Fourth, they assured their own role in allocating funds and monitoring their expenditure. The Crown now had to deal with the Parliament on an equal footing—indeed, the latter clearly had the advantage with its now credible threat of dethroning a sovereign who stepped too far out of line. Fifth, by creating a balance between Parliament and the monarchy—rather than eliminating the latter as occurred after the Civil War—parliamentary interests insured limits on their own tendencies toward arbitrary actions. In combination, these changes greatly enhanced the predictability of governmental decisions.

What established the government's commitment to honoring its agreements—notably the promise not to appropriate wealth or repudiate debt—was that the wealth holders gained a say in each of these decisions through their representatives in Parliament. This meant that only if such changes were in their own interests would they be made. Increasing the number of veto players implied that a larger set of constituencies could protect themselves against political assault, thus markedly reducing the circumstances under which opportunistic behavior by the government could take place.

In the story we have told, the emergence of political and civil liberties was inextricably linked with economic freedom. Opportunistic behavior on the part of the Crown was often accompanied by abuse of the opposition's political rights. The Crown had jailed people without charge or for lengthy periods prior to trial, and had required excessive bail to raise the costs of opposition. Hence protection of political liberties emerged as a component of the political protection of economic rights.

The principal lesson of our article is that the fundamental institutions of representative government—an explicit set of multiple veto points along with the primacy of the common law courts over economic affairs—are intimately related to the struggle for control over governmental power. The success of the propertied and commercially minded interests led to institutions that simultaneously mitigated the motive underlying the Crown's drive to find new sources of revenue and also greatly constrained the behavior of the government (now the "king in Parliament" rather than the king alone). Though these institutional innovations failed to anticipate the decline of the power of the Crown and ascendancy of Parliament in the latter half of the eighteenth century, the system successfully balanced power for well over sixty years. In comparison with the previous century or with the absolutist governments of the continent, England's institutional commitment to secure rights was far stronger. Evidence from capital markets provides a striking indication of this.

Recent research that has significantly upgraded France's economic performance before the French Revolution has led to an overhauling of traditional interpretations of British as well as French economic history.[56] If England and France were almost at parity in economic performance, the clear implication is that institutions per se—and in particular, the institutional changes we have described—were not so revolutionary after all. Similarly, the elaborate bureaucratic structure inherited from Louis XIV was not such a hindrance to economic growth. But that conclusion ignores the consequences that followed. It is clear that the institutional changes of the Glorious Revolution permitted the drive toward British hegemony and dominance of the world. England could not have beaten France without its financial revolution; and the funds made available by the growth in debt from 1688 to 1697 were surely a necessary condition for England's success in this war with France as well as the next one (1703–1714), from which England emerged the major power in the world.[57]

France, like England, had an ongoing fiscal crisis; and Louis XIV did come to terms with his constituents to gain more revenue early in his reign. But his success was temporary, not rooted in fundamental institutional change, and it was outdistanced by the magnitude of the English success. France's economy lived on borrowed time, and ultimately the unresolved institutional contradictions resulted in bankruptcy and revolution.[58]

The comparison of growth rates alone is therefore insufficient to judge economic parity. While in 1690 France was the major European power, it declined in power and stature relative to England over the next century. More wars followed those at the turn of the eighteenth century,

[56] See, for example, F. Crouzet, "England and France in the Eighteenth Century," in Max Hartwell, ed., *Causes of the Industrial Revolution in England* (London, 1967).

[57] Dickson, *Financial Revolution*.

[58] See David Bien, "Offices, Corps, and a System of State Credit: The Uses of Privilege under the Ancient Regime," in K. Baker, ed., *The French Revolution and the Creation of Modern Political Culture* (New York, 1987), vol. 1, pp. 89–114; Philip Hoffman, "Taxes, Fiscal Crises, and Representative Institutions: The Case of Early Modern France," manuscript, California Institute of Technology, 1988; and Hilton Root and Daniel Ingberman,"Tying the King's Hands," manuscript, University of Pennsylvania, 1987.

so that in 1765—at the end of the Seven Years War, in which France suffered a humiliating defeat—it had lost its New World colonies (Canada and Louisiana) and was in financial peril from which it did not recover until after the revolution. The contrast between the two economies in mid-century is striking: in 1765 France was on the verge of bankruptcy while England was on the verge of the Industrial Revolution.[59]

It is always tempting to claim too much. Would Britain really have followed the path of continental countries if the Stuarts had won? Would there have been a first Industrial Revolution in England? One could tell a plausible counterfactual story that put more weight on the fundamental strength of English property rights and the common law that had evolved from the Magna Carta and which would have circumscribed royal behavior and ultimately forced "responsible government." One could point to the robust economy (particularly at the local level) that existed in seventeenth-century England despite the uncertainties we have described. There exists neither a definitive theory of economic growth which would define for us the necessary and sufficient conditions nor the evidence to reconstruct the necessary counterfactual story. But we are convinced from the widespread contemporary Third World and historical evidence that *one* necessary condition for the creation of modern economies dependent on specialization and division of labor (and hence impersonal exchange) is the ability to engage in secure contracting across time and space. That entails low transaction costs per exchange. The creation of impersonal capital markets is the single most important piece of evidence that such a necessary condition has been fulfilled. And we have told a story of how these institutions *did* come about in England.

As evidence against the counterfactual thesis, we again point to the financial revolution. A change of this magnitude in such a short period clearly hinged on the underlying constitutional reorganization. Because the financial revolution played a critical role in England's long-run success, the implication is that even if other forces would ultimately have led England to success under the Stuarts, they would have done so more slowly and probably less decisively.

We have thus shown how institutions played a necessary role in making possible economic growth and political freedom. Furthermore,

[59] Jeffrey Williamson's recent, if controversial, work provides further support for this thesis. It suggests that British growth rates rose substantially once the long series of wars with France, ending with the Napoleonic campaign, were over. If during this period England's growth rates were not substantially larger than France's, its ability to spend more on war without bringing financial peril meant at most lower domestic consumption and investment, and hence came at the expense of growth. France's near bankruptcy shows that, in comparison, it was living on borrowed time. See Jeffrey G. Williamson, "Why Was British Growth so Slow During the Industrial Revolution?" this JOURNAL, 64 (Sept. 1983), pp. 687–712.

it appears from our survey of seventeenth-century England, from the historical performance of other economies, and from performance records of current Third World economies, that the circumstances fostering secure rights and hence economic growth are relatively rare and deserve further exploration.

[5]

CONSTITUTIONS, PROPERTY AND REGULATION

P. P. CRAIG*

THE present article has three distinctive, albeit connected, aims. The first is simply to tell a story which has been largely forgotten. This story concerns the regulation of private property in circumstances where the holder thereof has monopolistic power or something close thereto. As will be seen, the common law developed a regime for controlling various aspects of such proprietary power, and did so for reasons of principle which are of continuing significance today.

The second, connected objective of the article is to show how the presence of a written constitution can raise the "stakes" within a particular area. Attempts at the regulation of private property in the United States were met by arguments that such regulation was unconstitutional. The battle over the constitutionality of the regulation was waged for more than 50 years, and the case law from the United Kingdom, alluded to above, was of seminal importance in many of the cases decided by the American courts in those years.

The final aim of the present article is to consider how far the "lost" United Kingdom authorities may be of relevance in the modern day. The privatisation of previously nationalised industries has led to the creation of a number of corporations which have monopoly power in varying degrees. How far the common law may have a role to play in controlling such concentrations of power, will be considered in the course of the ensuing analysis.

(1) THE UNITED KINGDOM CONTRIBUTION

The problem of controlling large aggregations of private property, which can allow the holders thereof to wield a species of public power, is not a new one. Both common law and statutory rules have existed for some considerable time in this area, placing restrictions upon the creation of new monopoly power through the medium of the royal grant of a patent.[1] The efficacy of such controls, however, was limited.[2] Of greater relevance for present purposes were the efforts of the courts to regulate the manner of trading of those who had such monopoly power, and the justifications afforded for such controls. It is this line of authority which, as will be seen, was of cru-

* Reader in Law, University of Oxford and Fellow of Worcester College.

[1] *Darcy* v. *Allen* (1602) 11 Co.Rep. 84.

[2] Letwin, *Law and Economic Policy in America: The Evolution of the Sherman Antitrust Act* (1965), pp. 27–29.

cial importance in the development of the United States case law in this area.

Allnutt v. *Inglis* is the seminal English authority.[3] The issue was whether the London Dock Company, which by licence from Parliament possessed a monopoly to receive certain wines, could lawfully exclude from the docks a cargo owner who had refused to pay their schedule of charges. Lord Ellenborough reasoned as follows. While a man could fix his own price for the use of his own property, he could not do so where the public have a right to resort to the premises and to make use of them. Where a person had the benefit of a monopoly, this entailed a correlative responsibility with the consequence that he could charge no more than a reasonable price for the service offered. The monopoly itself could be either "legal" or "factual"; it could result from the grant of an exclusive licence from Parliament, or it could exist because, on the facts, the provider of the service controlled the entirety of the space available for the warehousing of the goods. The statute which required that the goods be warehoused in the company's premises was not passed solely for the benefit of the company, but also for the benefit of the public and trade; the latter two purposes would be defeated if the dock company were at liberty to charge any price which they chose.

Similar reasoning is evident in other areas where monopoly power existed. In *Corporation of Stamford* v. *Pawlett*[4] the corporation had the right to hold two fairs each year. It customarily received a "toll" of 2d on the sale of certain items at the fair. The defendant refused to pay the toll. The court held that where the word toll was found in a charter, it should be taken to mean reasonable toll. It was not open to the King to allow a corporation to charge an unreasonable toll, and any such excess charge could be recovered in a legal action. The principle underlying such cases is the same as that expounded above: the grantee of rights to a market or fair becomes the holder of an exclusive privilege. The grant was not merely for his own benefit, but for the benefit of the public and trade: it could be defeated if any price whatsoever could be charged.[5]

The origin of the propositions in the cases considered above is to be found in the writings of Hale, rescued by Hargrave, and presented as a *Collection of Tracts Relative to the Law of England* in 1787. The principal tract was a treatise written by Lord Hale in three parts. It is the second of these, entitled *De Portibus Maris*, which is of particular relevance. Hale argued that three types of right meet in every port:

---

[3] (1810) 12 East 527. See also *Bolt* v. *Stennett* (1800) 8 T.R. 606.

[4] (1830) 1 C. & J. 57, 400.

[5] See also *Gard* v. *Callard* (1817) 6 M. & S. 69; *Wright* v. *Bruister* (1832) 4 B. & Ald. 116; *Att.-Gen.* v. *Horner* (1912) 107 L.T. 547; *Duke of Newcastle* v. *Worksop Urban District Council* [1902] 2 Ch. 145, 161; *Nyali* v. *Att.-Gen.* [1956] 1 Q.B. 1, 13–14; [1957] A.C. 253, 265–266, 273.

the *jus privatum*, the *jus publicum* and the *jus regium*. The *jus privatum* represented an interest in the form of a franchise which a subject could acquire by, for example, a charter. This would entitle him to charge certain tolls for the unloading and storage of merchandise. However, superimposed upon the *jus privatum* was a *jus publicum*, which was held, *inter alia*, by the users of the port facilities, and which imposed an obligation to the effect that the tolls should not be excessive.[6] Thus, if a wharf is erected by a person solely for his own advantage then he can make the most of his own, and charge whatever he can induce the customers to pay. Where there is only one facility which can be used, either because there is only one facility licensed by the Crown, or because, factually, there is no other such facility available, then the facility will be "affected with a public interest." A *jus publicum* operates, with the consequence that the tolls charged must be reasonable.

If direct support for the case law comes from Hale, indirect support is to be found in the closely related area of common callings. There is abundant authority for the proposition that those who exercise a common calling can charge only a reasonable price for their services.[7] The history of common callings is complex and cannot be fully explored here. Suffice it to say for present purposes that the origin of the term common calling was simply a service that was available to the public generally, a "holding out." There could therefore be common carriers, common innkeepers, and common millers. Those who exercised a common calling had a duty to serve at a reasonable price. Historically, this obligation appears to have evolved due to economic and social conditions. In times of social hardship, such as the period following the Black Death, it might be possible for a tradesman to exact "any price he pleased."[8] The obligation to serve at reasonable prices was intended to counteract this potential for abuse of market power. As the law developed, the types of industry which retained the label "common" tended to be those which possessed a monopoly character, such as railways and public utilities.

The relative paucity of direct case law on Hale's point may be partly due to the fact that Blackstone did not take up Hale's observations in this regard. A more realistic, or practical, explanation is probably to be found in the emerging framework within which utilities functioned in the nineteenth century, which obviated at least some of the need for direct, common law regulation of price. Many administrative functions were performed neither by central or local

[6] McAllister, "Lord Hale and Business Affected with a Public Interest" (1929–30) 43 Harv.L.R. 759.

[7] *Harris* v. *Packwood* (1810) 3 Taunt 263; *Peek* v. *North Staffs Ry.* (1862) 11 H.L.C. 473; *Great Western Ry.* v. *Sutton* (1869) L.R. 4 H.L. 226, 237–8.

[8] Arterburn, "The Origin and First Test of Public Callings" (1926–27) 75 Univ. of Penn.L.Rev. 411, 421.

government, but by corporations who were given special statutory authority in so far as this was necessary to enable them to carry out their tasks. The provision of most utilities, such as gas, water, lighting, railways and roads, was carried on by these means, even after the reform of the municipal corporations. It was in the nature of the activities performed by these bodies that they normally possessed a large degree of market power, albeit within a limited geographical area. The rates to be charged for the services had to be regulated. A common technique was for direct departmental supervision of the "tariff" which the statutory undertaking proposed to charge. The relevant trustees would forward to the Board of Trade a detailed list of prices which they intended to levy, specifying, for example, the rates for a certain wagon over a certain distance. The Board of Trade would have to approve such charges before they could be lawfully levied. Direct departmental supervision of price was therefore quite common in areas where market power existed, and this obviated the need for direct judicial control in such areas.[9] In other areas, boards were used to perform the same regulatory price control function.[10]

It is, however, the *constitutional* implications of Hale's observations which are most pertinent to the present inquiry. These are not framed explicitly as part of a constitutional discourse as such; nor does the reasoning in the later common law jurisprudence specifically address the topic in these terms. The reasoning is nonetheless of constitutional significance, as the developments within the United States case law will demonstrate. This can be appreciated as a matter of first principle even before the United States developments are addressed.

A legal system has to decide how to treat property rights. It has to determine what rights, immunities, powers and duties flow from the notion of property; and it has to decide what degree of protection to accord to property thus defined. It is common to afford property rights some measure of protection in the list of rights recognised by a written constitution. How much protection may well be contentious, but some measure is commonly found, if only to prevent the state from expropriating such rights without limit or without compensation. In determining whether the state has infringed such constitutional protections, some view must be taken of what the rights, immunities, powers and duties of property holders actually are. If one regards one such attribute as the power to fix a price untramelled by anything save "natural" market forces, then state regulation of pricing would be, in some way, a deprivation of property without

[9] Craig, *Administrative Law* (2nd ed., 1989), pp. 160–161; Chester, *The English Administrative System 1780–1870* (1981), pp. 118–119.

[10] Parris, *Government and the Railways in Nineteenth Century Britain* (1965); Arthurs, "*Without the Law,*" *Administrative Justice and Legal Pluralism in Nineteenth Century England* (1985). See also Robson, *Justice and Administrative Law* (1928), Chap. 3.

compensation. This would be so whether the medium of price control was a court, a tribunal or a statute.

The significance of Hale's observations, and of the case law applying them, is to deny that property does possess this attribute, at least in certain circumstances. It is to recognise, in however basic a form, some idea of public property rights. This phrase must be treated with great care. It can clearly cover property which is, in a literal sense, owned by the state. The precise consequences of this, in terms of how the attributes of ownership are construed, is a subject worthy of full analysis in its own right. More relevant for present purposes is the fact that Hale provides the foundations for regarding certain aggregations of property which are held in nominally private hands as nonetheless subject to constraints in the way that they are used. To put the same point in a different way, the rights, duties, powers and immunities which comprise the concept of property in this instance may well be different from the paradigm of pure private property. He provides the foundation for a constitutional discourse within which it is open to us, both to protect property rights within a constitution, and at the same time to accept that specific regulatory schemes need not be constitutionally damned as an infringement of such rights. Now some may doubt whether price regulation is efficacious, necessary or desirable; others may disagree as to which industries should be subject to this form of regulation; and yet others may argue that when property is "affected with a public interest" this should lead to a considerable modification of the rights, etc., which constitute the concept of property. What should be emphasised for present purposes is that once some form of protection of property rights is enshrined within a constitutional order, whether explicitly within a written constitution, or by way of convention within an unwritten constitution, then the resolution of the above issue *either way* will be a matter of constitutional argument.

The absence of a written constitution in the United Kingdom has meant that the constitutional status of property rights, like that of many rights, is less clear than in the case of a written constitution. There is, however, material which relates directly to the constitutional significance of property. The seminal statute and case law on the prerogative, which established that this was a right to take and pay, prevented the monarch or the executive from expropriating property by royal whim or executive fiat.[11] The sovereignty of Parliament did ensure that a statute could mandate any end, including therefore the expropriation of private property. This formal power of Parliament to prescribe any goal which it chooses is nonetheless not

[11] Bill of Rights 1689; *Att.-Gen.* v. *De Keyser's Royal Hotel Ltd.* [1920] A.C. 508; *Burmah Oil Co.* v. *Lord Advocate* [1965] A.C. 75.

immune from moral and political censure. If a Parliament were to pursue such a course, there is little doubt that this would be regarded as a breach of constitutional convention.

(2) Developments in the United States

In order to understand the United States case law on this topic it is necessary to place it in context. The particular context from which this jurisprudence arose was the development of substantive due process within the latter part of the nineteenth century.

Early attempts to utilise the Fifth and Fourteenth amendments in order to strike at the substance or content of regulatory provisions enacted by state or federal government did not prove to be a noted success. In the *Slaughter-House* cases[12] the Supreme Court considered the argument that a Louisiana law which prohibited livestock yards and slaughter houses within New Orleans (subject to an exception for a particular company), was contrary to, *inter alia*, the Fourteenth amendment. The contention was rejected. In the course of its judgment, the court indicated strongly that the objective of the due process clause within the Fourteenth amendment[13] was not to guarantee the substantive fairness of the laws which had been passed, but only to ensure that procedural due process had been complied with when the laws were enacted.

The latter part of the nineteenth century witnessed a significant increase in industrialisation. It was this development which prompted many states to attempt to regulate the emerging business activities, more particularly when those business activities enjoyed a measure of monopoly power. The response of industry was to attack the regulatory initiatives with the object of having them declared unconstitutional. The protection afforded by the Fourteenth amendment became one of the prime weapons used by those who sought to have such legislation invalidated. This was the arena within which the Supreme Court was forced to fashion and develop a conception of public property rights in order to *prevent* such regulatory schemes from being declared unconstitutional.

Munn v. *Illinois*[14] is the seminal case within this development. The state of Illinois had passed a law which fixed the maximum charges which could be levied for the storage of grain in warehouses. It was argued that this was in breach of the Fourteenth amendment. Waite C.J. delivered the majority opinion of the court, upholding the validity of the statute. The reasoning is of particular interest because it draws directly on the jurisprudence of the English courts.

[12] 83 U.S. (16 Wall.) 36, 21 L.Ed. 394 (1873).

[13] ". . . nor shall any State deprive any person of life, liberty, or property, without due process of law . . ."

[14] 94 U.S. (4 Otto) 77, 24 L.Ed. 113 (1877).

Waite C.J. reasoned as follows. When individuals joined together to form a society, they necessarily parted with some rights and powers. These powers entitled the government to regulate the conduct of its citizens *inter se*, and also enabled the government to regulate the manner in which each person could use his property, provided that such regulation was for the public good. This was exemplified by the statutory and regulatory devices which existed in England to control ferries, common carriers, innkeepers, millers and the like. It was also exemplified by the earlier exercises of Congressional power to regulate by statute the prices of wharfage, hackney carriages, etc. Thus, down to the time of the Fourteenth amendment, no one had supposed that such regulatory devices necessarily deprived an owner of his property rights without due process of law.

Waite C.J. then probes more deeply into the principled basis which served to justify such regulation. The foundation for this had already been laid with the idea that the state is entitled to exercise such a power when this is necessary for the public good. This theme is then imbued with greater substance, and the substance is derived from the English jurists and judicial decisions.

The property right which the Constitution protects is, says the Chief Justice, a right which derives from the common law. However, at common law a property right which is affected with a public interest ceases "to be *juris privati* only." The reasoning of Hale is brought to bear. While a man can charge what he likes for his goods in ordinary circumstances, he cannot do so where the property is affected with a public interest. Thus, if there is a public wharf, which all who come to that port must use, or where there is no other wharf in that port, then the duties which can be charged must be reasonable. Waite C.J. reinforces this reasoning with that employed in the leading English authorities, *Allnutt*[15] and *Bolt*.[16]

The essence of the argument of principle is therefore as follows. The ambit of the property right which is protected by the Constitution must be determined, in part at least by determining the scope of that right at common law. Even at common law certain property rights were restricted in certain ways. The Illinois statute which was under attack merely substituted a form of statutory price regulation for that which had previously existed and been justified on common law principles.

The Chief Justice then proceeds to apply the principle to the facts of the case. The business of grain warehousing was effectively in the hands of nine corporations. These handled the great preponderance of warehousing for seven or eight other states. Moreover, the prices

[15] *Supra*, n. 3.
[16] *Supra*, n. 3.

to be charged were effectively fixed between the nine each year, which gave them a virtual monopoly.

> "Under such circumstances it is difficult to see why, if the common carrier, or the miller, or the ferryman, or the innkeeper, or the wharfinger, or the baker, or the cartman, or the hackney-coachman, pursues a public employment and exercises a 'sort of public office,' these plaintiffs in error do not. They stand . . . 'in the very gateway of commerce,' and take a toll from all who pass. Every bushel of grain for its passage 'pays a toll, which is a common charge,' and therefore, according to Lord Hale, every such warehouseman 'ought to be under public regulation, *viz.*, that he . . . take but a reasonable toll.' Certainly, if any business can be clothed 'with a public interest and cease to be *juris privati* only,' this has been."[17]

The reasoning of the majority provoked a spirited dissent by Field J., which was to be repeated in similar form in later cases. He argued that the principle propounded by Hale was confined to instances where some special privilege had been granted by the state to, for example, a turnpike authority, or to the operator of a wharf. It was this grant of privileged status which justified the imposition of conditions relating to the price at which the goods could be sold.[18] Whether this was in fact so will be considered at a later stage.

The ambit of the principle propounded by Hale, and the correctness of the reasoning in *Munn*, were both discussed in *Budd* v. *State of New York*.[19] The case once again concerned the constitutionality of a state statute, which was passed to control the prices for grain elevators in New York. It was argued that the statute was in breach of the Fourteenth amendment.

The Supreme Court upheld the decision of the lower court and adopted much of its reasoning. The principle expounded in *Munn* was not, and should not be, confined to instances where there was some legal monopoly flowing from the grant of a special privilege by the state. The ability to control the reasonableness of price, whether by common law or statute, extended beyond this narrow instance. Regulation of the prices which could be charged by common carriers indicated that this was so, because common law and statutory regulation had long existed in these areas, even though the industries in question did not derive their power from a legal monopoly or the existence of a special governmental privilege.

Brewer J. dissented[20] on much the same ground as Field J. in the earlier case. The existence of a factual monopoly did not warrant state interference with price. This was warranted only where a firm's power was dependent upon a special privilege having been given by

---

[17] 94 U.S. 77, 86.
[18] *Ibid.*, pp. 88–94.
[19] 143 U.S. 517 (1892). See also *Brass* v. *North Dakota* 153 U.S. 391 (1894).
[20] 143 U.S. 517, 540–52.

the state; or when the service which was rendered was a public service; or when the property was devoted to a public use. The uncertainties inherent in this formulation were to surface in a number of later cases.

While several later decisions applied the reasoning in *Munn* to reach the conclusion that legislation should be upheld,[21] other cases held that particular state enactments were in breach of the Fourteenth amendment. *Chas Wolff Packing Co.* v. *Court of Industrial Relations*[22] exemplifies this latter group of cases. A Kansas statute declared, *inter alia*, that the manufacture of food, clothing and fuel were industries affected by a public interest, and established an Industrial Court to adjudicate on the wages paid in such industries. The Wolff Packing Co. was taken before the court and told to raise its wages. It refused to do so and argued that the statute was in violation of the Fourteenth amendment.

Taft C.J. held that there were three types of case in which a business could be said to be affected by a public interest, which would then serve to legitimate state legislation to control price.[23] One type of case concerned businesses which were carried on under a public grant of privilege or franchise. Public utilities, common carriers and railways came within this category. Another category of case concerned industries which had traditionally been subject to regulation, such as inns, cabs and mills. A third type of case concerned industries, which though not public at their inception, have become such, and therefore were amenable to state regulation. Cases such as *Munn* and *Budd* were treated as examples of this third category.

The court decided on the facts that the case did not fit within any of the above three categories. A mere declaration in the legislation that an industry was affected with a public interest was not conclusive. While the court retained the power to determine the parameters of the third category, it was held that this meant more than that the public welfare was affected by the continuity of the business or the price at which the goods were sold. In order to clothe a business with a public interest, it was necessary for there to be a peculiarly close relationship between the public and those engaged in that business. Only then would this generate an affirmative obligation on those who took part in that industry to be reasonable in their dealings with the public.

Tyson v. *Banton* provides a further example of the Supreme Court placing limits on the application of the principle in *Munn*. New York State enacted a law which regulated the price at which theatre tickets could be offered for sale, with the object of preventing fraud and

[21] See, *e.g. Chicago, Burlington & Quincy Ry.* v. *Cutts* 94 U.S. 155 (1877); *Dow* v. *Beidelman* 125 U.S. 686 (1888); *Stafford* v. *Wallace* 258 U.S. 516 (1922).

[22] 262 U.S. 522 (1923).

[23] *Ibid.*, pp. 534–535.

exorbitant charges. It was contended that the statute was unconstitutional, a contention upheld by the court.[24]

Sutherland J. reasoned as follows. The right of an owner to sell his property at the price which he chooses is an attribute of his proprietary right which is protected by the Fourteenth amendment. Therefore a restriction of that right must be justified; otherwise it will be held to be unconstitutional. The decision in *Munn* provided a justification for such regulatory legislation, but the ambit of the principle was not entirely clear.

In order to come within that principle there must be evidence from which it can be concluded that the business has been devoted to a public use, and this use has, in effect, been devoted to the public. Those cases in which regulatory legislation was upheld were due to the special character of the business. In such cases the industry in question could be held to have such a definable and substantial relation to the public interest to justify the indulgence of a legal fiction, whereby there had been a grant by the owner to the public of an interest in the use of the product. The reasoning of Hale should be restricted to instances where the industry could be said to be clothed with a public interest, either because its existence was dependent upon an express grant of governmental privilege, or because a "constructive grant" to the public could be said to have occurred. The business of selling theatre tickets could not be said to be cloaked with a public interest in either of these senses, and therefore the statute was invalid.

The case provoked an interesting and powerful dissent by Justices Stone, Holmes, Brandeis and Sanford.[25] They controverted the starting assumptions relied on by the majority. The constitutional theory that prices could not, as a general rule, be regulated, rested on the assumption that the public interest and private rights were both adequately protected by the ordinary competitive process; therefore the price regulation was not justified; and therefore the legislation could be deemed a taking of property without due process. However, the common thematic link to all cases where regulatory statutes had been allowed was that the ordinary competitive process was restricted, so that buyers or sellers were placed at such a disadvantage in the bargaining process that serious economic consequences would ensue for the community. This could occur *either* because the industry was accorded monopolistic status by the governmental grant, *or* because it occupied a strategic position which enabled it to impose its will on those who bought or sold its products.

A similar clash between a majority and a dissenting opinion is evi-

[24] 273 U.S. 418 (1927).
[25] *Ibid.*, pp. 450–454.

dent in a case decided a year after *Tyson*, which is the decision of the Supreme Court in *Ribnik* v. *McBride*.[26] The majority condemned a New Jersey law which sought to regulate the prices which could be charged by employment agencies, as being in breach of the Fourteenth amendment. Sutherland J. followed the reasoning in *Chas Wolff* and *Tyson*, and found that the industry was not affected by a public interest so as to warrant the existence of the regulatory legislation which was under attack. Once again this was met by a powerful dissent by Stone, Brandeis and Holmes JJ. Prices could legitimately be regulated, so they argued, whenever there was a combination of circumstances which seriously curtailed the regulative forces of the competitive process. In such instances the legislature might seriously anticipate harmful consequences to the community as a whole, where either buyers or sellers were placed at a distinct disadvantage in the bargaining process. In the present case the group being protected were the unemployed, who were in a weak bargaining position, a fact vindicated by a number of public investigations which had shown that such agencies were peculiarly prone to excessive charging.[27]

It is readily apparent from the preceding discussion that the majority opinions in cases such as *Chas Wolff*, *Tyson* and *Ribnik*, were themselves imbued with the same spirit as the majority opinion in the famous, or infamous, case of *Lochner* v. *New York*.[28] In that decision the Supreme Court invalidated a law passed by the state of New York which limited the number of hours which a baker could work. The Supreme Court held that this was unconstitutional, being an arbitrary and unnecessary interference with the liberty to contract between employer and employee, which was a liberty protected by the Fourteenth amendment. The powerful dissent by Holmes J. is well known.[29] The court should not be imposing its own view as to the most appropriate economic policy, in preference to that espoused by the legislature. That was precisely what the majority were doing, and it was both bad constitutional law and also bad in terms of the allocation of power between the legislature and the courts. Echoes of the same ideas can be found in the dissenting judgments in *Tyson* and *Ribnik*.

It was the demise of the economic substantive due process doctrine of *Lochner* which was to herald the Supreme Court's movement away from the related decisions in *Chas Wolff*, *Tyson* and *Ribnik*. The development can be briefly summarised in the following manner. These decisions were based ultimately on the idea that any state control of, for example, pricing was prima facie an interference with an

---

[26] 277 U.S. 350 (1928).
[27] *Ibid.*, p. 360.
[28] 198 U.S. 45 (1905).
[29] *Ibid.*, pp. 74–76.

aspect of proprietary rights, which would be unconstitutional unless justified in some manner. The conclusion that it was unconstitutional was reached by drawing on the negative implications of *Munn*: unless the industry *could* be said to be affected with a public interest, there was no warrant for the regulatory legislation. A restrictive interpretation of the reasoning used in *Munn* then serves to ensure that no such public interest was found on the facts of the case.

The contrast between this approach and that espoused by the dissents in *Lochner*, *Tyson* and *Ribnik* was of great significance. Two related themes characterise these opinions. On the one hand, the court should not substitute its view as to the most appropriate economic policy for that of the legislature. On the other hand, the reasoning in *Munn* is placed in a broader perspective which serves to justify the legislation under attack. Industrial regulation is warranted not only in cases where there is some *de jure* monopoly resulting from the governmental grant of a privilege. Such cases are viewed as but part of a broader picture, the principal theme of which is that there has been some failure of the competitive process, with the result that buyers or sellers will be disadvantaged. The existence of a *de jure* monopoly is simply regarded as an obvious instance where this might occur.

Three decisions exemplify the Supreme Court's movement away from the majority opinions in *Lochner*, *Chas Wolff* and *Ribnik*, towards a view which is more consonant with the dissenting opinions in those cases. In *Nebbia* v. *New York*,[30] a statute which sought to fix prices for the sale of milk was attacked. The legislation had been enacted to protect sellers who were in a bad bargaining position. It was argued that the industry did not come within any of the categories adumbrated above in which regulation was justified.

Roberts J. conceded that the case did not readily fall within these established categories, but upheld the law nonetheless.[31] There was no closed category of businesses which were affected with a public interest. To come within this class it was not necessary that the business be the result of a franchise granted by the government, nor that it possessed a monopoly. The phrase "affected with a public interest" meant nothing more than that it was subject to the exercise of the police power; it connoted only that there were adequate reasons for subjecting the industry to some control for the public good. Provided that the challenged regulation was a reasonable exercise of governmental power, the court should decline to intervene. The judgment made it clear that the court should not lightly find a choice of economic policy to be unreasonable: "a state is free to adopt whatever

[30] 291 U.S. 502 (1934).
[31] *Ibid.*, pp. 531–533.

economic policy may reasonably be deemed to promote public welfare, and to enforce that policy by legislation adopted to its purpose."[32] This idea was reinforced by the statement that the courts did not have the authority to establish an economic policy, or to overrule the legislative choice of the appropriate policy.

The decision of the Supreme Court in *Nebbia* did not, however, completely end the judiciary's involvement with economic substantive due process. Decisions continued to be made which were more redolent of earlier reasoning.[33] Notwithstanding the atavistic strain within these cases, the Supreme Court did move away from the old substantive due process ideas. As Nowak, Rotunda and Young state,

> "The court packing controversy of 1937 precipitated the permanent change in the court's application of the substantive due process concept. The court's decisions of 1937 and the years immediately following revealed the justices' total disenchantment with substantive due process as a constitutional theory that could protect property interests from government regulation and control. These decisions disclosed not only that the court no longer believed that economic issues were of constitutional magnitude, but also that the justices were prepared to apply new and objective constitutional standards to test the constitutionality of economic legislation."[34]

This transition is exemplified by the decision in *West Coast Hotel* v. *Parrish*,[35] in which the constitutionality of a state law setting minimum wages for women was upheld. An earlier decision of the court which had struck down an identical law from a different state,[36] and which had used reasoning imbued with the same spirit at the majority opinion in *Lochner*, was not followed. The court in *Parrish* rejected the argument that the state regulation violated contract rights which were protected by the Fourteenth amendment.

> "What is this freedom? The Constitution does not speak in terms of freedom of contract. It speaks of liberty and prohibits the deprivation of liberty without due process of law. In prohibiting that deprivation the Constitution does not recognise an absolute and uncontrollable liberty . . . Regulation which is reasonable in relation to its subject and is adopted in the interests of the community is due process."[37]

The court's movement away from the "old" substantive due process was further emphasised by the decision in *United States* v. *Carolene Products Co.*[38] Stone J. drew a distinction between the appropriate level of scrutiny for general regulatory legislation, and

---

[32] *Ibid.*, p. 537.

[33] See, *e.g. Stewart Dry Goods Co.* v. *Lewis* 294 U.S. 550 (1935); *Morehead* v. *New York ex rel. Tipaldo* 298 U.S. 587 (1936). See also *U.S.* v. *Butler* 297 U.S. 1 (1936); *Carter* v. *Carter Coal Co.* 298 U.S. 238 (1936).

[34] *Constitutional Law* (3rd ed., 1986), p. 353.

[35] 300 U.S. 379 (1937).

[36] *Adkins* v. *Children's Hospital* 261 U.S. 525 (1923).

[37] 300 U.S. 379, 391 (1937).

[38] 304 U.S. 144 (1938).

the type of review which should apply to legislation which restricted more fundamental constitutional values. Where the former was in issue the test was whether any state of facts which were known, or could reasonably be assumed, supported the legislation which was being attacked.[39] Moreover, the existence of facts which could support the legislative judgment was to be presumed; regulatory legislation which affected ordinary commercial transactions should not be held to be unconstitutional unless it was of such a character as to preclude the assumption that it rested on a rational basis.[40]

Where the statute affected fundamental constitutional values, the latter of the two categories adumbrated above, there might well be a narrower scope for operation of the presumption of constitutionality. This would be so when the legislation appeared on its face to come within a specific prohibition of the Constitution. A more searching judicial inquiry might also be required in cases where prejudice existed against discrete and insular minorities, thereby limiting the ordinary political processes through which such minorities could be protected.[41]

Subsequent decisions confirmed that the court would normally uphold regulatory legislation.[42] Whether the legislature used the work of Adam Smith, Spencer or Lord Keynes as its economic text was not to be a cause of judicial concern.[43]

(3) The Modern Context

The developments considered in the previous sections are of interest in themselves, in so far as they exemplify the differing ways in which the regulation of monopoly power can be affected by the existence or absence of a written constitution. However, the authorities considered above are of more than mere historical interest, and may well be of relevance to the present day problems of controlling certain aggregations of monopoly power.

The more particular context in which this issue arises concerns the regulation of monopoly power consequent upon the privatisation programme which has been continuing in the 1980s. The reasons for this programme were eclectic, and included: the improvement of

---

[39] *Ibid.*, p. 154.

[40] *Ibid.*, p. 152.

[41] *Ibid.*, pp. 152–153, n. 4. The meaning of the famous "footnote 4" has been much discussed. See, *e.g.* Powell, "Carolene Products Revisited" (1982) 82 Col.L.Rev. 1087; Brilmayer, "*Carolene*, Conflicts and the Fate of the 'Inside-Outsider' " (1986) 134 U.Pa.L.Rev. 1291; Ackerman, "Beyond *Carolene Products*" (1985) 98 Harv.L.Rev. 713. For a process-based interpretation of the case see Ely, *Democracy and Distrust: A Theory of Judicial Review* (1980), pp. 73–75; and for criticism of this approach, Craig, *Public Law in the United Kingdom and the U.S.A.* (1990), pp. 106–113.

[42] See, *e.g. Williamson* v. *Lee Optical Co.* 348 U.S. 483 (1955); *City of New Orleans* v. *Dukes* 427 U.S. 297 (1976).

[43] *Ferguson* v. *Skrupa* 372 U.S. 726, 731–2 (1963).

efficiency; the widening of share ownership; the reduction of governmental involvement in industry; the alleviation of the public sector borrowing requirement; and the encouragement of share ownership.[44] The cogency of these reasons has itself been contested. For example, the argument that privatisation will enhance economic freedom has been criticised because it assumes that a private monopoly will be less threatening to such freedom than a statutory monopoly, and because it defines freedom in a limited way to mean solely the absence of government intervention in the market, thereby foreclosing the viability of a more active role for the state, which is designed to enhance liberty.[45] The contention that privatisation will enhance economic efficiency has also been questioned. The comparisons with the performance of the industries when they were nationalised is problematic since these industries were continually subject to the shifting demands of governmental policy.[46] Moreover, even if one accepts that a change of ownership rights can have an effect on incentives and on behaviour, and hence on efficiency, by sharpening corporate incentives to cut costs and to fix prices in line with costs, the realisation of these benefits will "depend crucially upon the framework of competition and regulation in which the privatised firm is to operate."[47]

The industries which have been privatised fall into two categories, those in which the privatised company possesses a significant degree of market power, and those in which it does not. Only the former are of relevance here, even though significant problems of a differing kind may be attendant in the latter kind of industry.[48] Telecommunications and gas provide two examples of industries in which the privatised concern was left with a significant residue of monopoly power. The general problems which have been created by the decision to leave these industries with such power, and to forgo any structural reorganisation of the areas in question, have been examined in depth elsewhere.[49] The present discussion will therefore be confined to some observations on the way in which we view property rights in this area.

First, it is unlikely that the courts would need to utilise the power to set a reasonable price in the context of the recently privatised industries, since the relevant legislation itself contains a pricing formula. Difficulties undoubtedly exist with the application of this test,

---

[44] Vickers and Yarrow, *Privatization, An Economic Analysis* (1988), pp. 157–160; Kay, Mayer and Thompson (eds.), *Privatization and Regulation—The U.K. Experience* (1986), Chaps. 3, 4.

[45] Kay, Mayer and Thompson, *supra*, n. 44, Chaps. 5, 6.

[46] Vickers and Yarrow, *supra*, n. 44, Chap. 2.

[47] *Ibid.*, p. 158.

[48] Graham and Prosser, *Privatizing Public Enterprises: Constitutions, the State, and Regulation in Comparative Perspective* (1991), Chap. 5.

[49] *Supra*, nn. 44 and 48.

but it is questionable whether the courts would wish to become embroiled in the complexities which would be entailed in such disputes.[50]

Secondly, the point of principle inherent in the early English authorities is nonetheless still of significance. It provides part at least of the foundation for thinking about public property rights, and the application of this concept in this area. The matter can be presented as follows.

The early case law established, as we have seen, that the possession of monopoly power, whether *de jure* in the form of a grant of a franchise, or *de facto*, placed constraints on the manner of its exercise. The property was affected with a public interest which served to limit the price which its holder could charge. If this constraint were not imposed, then two consequences would ensue. On the one hand, the purpose of the original statutory grant of power might be defeated, since this was designed, for example in *Allnutt*, to benefit the public and trade, and not just the donee of the power. On the other hand, *given* that this was so, if the donee of the power was not subject to such constraint, it would also mean that he had obtained the property rights too cheaply. If the donee could indeed charge any price for the service, then the value of the grant made to him was commensurately greater; the public purse would be "robbed" by not reaping the full value of such a property right. Thus in circumstances where the matter arose as a contest between a private individual and the holder of the monopoly power, the courts were willing to constrain the latter, thereby ensuring that the statutory purpose was fulfilled, *and* also that the public purse was not inadequately recompensed.

The recognition of public property rights within our jurisprudence is not confined to the type of case considered above. It is also evident in other areas. Thus the concept that a local authority owes a fiduciary duty to its ratepayers is founded, in part at least, on the idea that such an authority is using public money and should be accountable for its use.[51] The application of the concept in particular cases may well be open to criticism,[52] but this does not mean that the concept itself is misguided.

It is nonetheless the case that the British jurisprudence is far from being fully developed in this area. One of the principal criticisms of the privatisation process has been that the assets of the industries in question have been sold too cheaply for a variety of reasons. These include the government's desire that the sales of the companies should be seen to be a success, and that the method of sale was not

---

[50] *Supra*, n. 48, Chaps. 6, 7.
[51] See, *e.g. Bromley L.B.C.* v. *Greater London Council* [1983] 1 A.C. 768.
[52] Dignan, "Policy-Making, Local Authorities and the Courts: the G.L.C. Fares case" (1983) 99 L.Q.R. 605; Loughlin, *Local Government in the Modern State* (1986), Chap. 3.

best suited to attaining the optimum return for the assets which were sold.[53] It is clear that the undervaluation of state holdings is a misuse of public funds. It is also clear that the response of the legal system to situations in which the state "owns" something is more muted than it is to situations in which the state commands another to do something with property owned by the individual.[54] Legal principles can be devised for such instances, as the work of Graham and Prosser has shown. In France, the Conseil Constitutionnel has applied constitutional provisions to the sale of state assets, holding that it would be unconstitutional to sell such assets for less than their real market value.[55]

The absence of a written constitution in the United Kingdom, and the tendency to regard the commercial use which the state makes of its "own" property as a subjective decision for the government of the day, renders it unlikely that the same result would be reached in this country. This should not, however, be taken to mean that the common law is devoid of any notion of public property rights. As in many other areas of the common law, we find strands of authority which may have been developed at different times and which only appear to encapsulate a broader principle when woven together. The more lasting significance of the British authorities considered above may well therefore be that they form one such strand of authority, from which a richer notion of public property rights can be developed.

---

[53] See, *e.g.* Vickers and Yarrow, *supra*, n. 44, p. 121.

[54] Daintith, "Legal Analysis of Economic Policy" (1982) 9 Jnl. Law & Soc. 191.

[55] *Supra*, n. 48, Chap. 3.

[6]

PUBLIC SERVICE LAW: PRIVATIZATION'S UNEXPECTED OFFSPRING

TONY PROSSER*

I

INTRODUCTION

The United Kingdom was the pioneer, if not of privatization, of a large scale privatization program extending to the public utilities: And it remains in the forefront of attempts to introduce forms of the new public management using private sector techniques in public administration.[1] One might think that this means that the role of public law, and of distinctive notions of public service embodied in law, have disappeared in those areas where privatization has taken place. Indeed, this perceived decline in public service law is the characteristic criticism of the British experience by commentators in Continental Europe. The Conservative governments of the United Kingdom certainly intended to replace hierarchical administrative controls with a marketplace in which resort to the courts on public law matters would be unnecessary.[2]

In this article, however, I hope to suggest a paradox. The United Kingdom has experienced a new growth of public service law in relation to the privatized utilities. This has resulted in a convergence of the tradition of the United Kingdom and that of nations such as France and Italy, where public service has played a central role in public law, due in part to a unique rhetoric of public service in the Continental tradition. Indeed, it could be argued that the regulatory reform that accompanied privatization has made possible the development of a distinct discipline of public service law in the United Kingdom.[3] In this article, I define public service law as law designed to make basic public services

---

This article is also available at http://www.law.duke.edu/journals/63LCPProsser.

* John Millar Professor of Law, The University of Glasgow, Scotland, U.K.

1. For examples of the massive literature on this subject, see M.E. BEESLEY, PRIVATIZATION, REGULATION AND DEREGULATION (2d ed. 1997); COSMO GRAHAM & TONY PROSSER, PRIVATIZING PUBLIC ENTERPRISES (1991); Michael J. Goldsmith & Edward C. Page, *Farewell to the British State?*, *in* PUBLIC SECTOR REFORM 147 (Jan-Erik Lane ed., 1997).

2. For an insider's view, see C.D. FOSTER, PRIVATIZATION, PUBLIC OWNERSHIP AND THE REGULATION OF NATURAL MONOPOLY 258-420 (1992).

3. For further discussion of public service law, see PUBLIC SERVICES AND CITIZENSHIP IN EUROPEAN UNION LAW (Mark Freedland & Silvana Sciarra eds., 1998); H.W. MacLauchlan, *Public Service Law and the New Public Management*, *in* THE PROVINCE OF ADMINISTRATIVE LAW (Michael Taggart ed., 1997). The Continental literature is, of course, enormous. *See, e.g.*, CONSEIL D'ETAT, ÉTUDES ET DOCUMENTS NO. 46, RAPPORT PUBLIC 1994 (1995); RENAUD DENOIX DE SAINT MARC, LE SERVICE PUBLIC (1996).

available to all citizens without discrimination. This may require modification of the operation of markets and recognition of the need to compensate for substantive inequalities by providing services to the disadvantaged. Thus, public service law has both a descriptive and a normative dimension. It is descriptive in that it is concerned with goods and services provided by institutions between the market and the state, which may include public enterprises at arm's length from government. It is normative in the sense that it is based on egalitarian rights derived from citizenship rather than an ability to bid in the marketplace.[4] My discussion of the development of a discipline of public service law in the United Kingdom will be limited to the privatization of public utilities.

II

THE ABSENCE OF A TRADITION OF PUBLIC SERVICE IN THE UNITED KINGDOM

In marked contrast with their Continental neighbors, the British have traditionally been reluctant to enshrine requirements of public service in their system of law. During the nineteenth century, however, a relatively little-known body of common law developed to ensure access to monopoly services and to avoid discrimination in the way in which such access was provided.[5] The best-known of these cases concerned access to a dock monopoly,[6] but other examples included rights of access to ferries, bridges, and other early public utilities.[7] These cases may represent an early attempt to develop competition law in the interest of economic efficiency by minimizing market distortions created by monopoly power. Implications of this trend in the case law reached beyond competition law, however. And as Paul Craig has documented, the cases suggest the recognition of some form of public property rights triggered by the possibility of restrictions on public access to essential, but privately owned, services.[8]

These cases could have supported the establishment of principles concerned with rights of equal access to public services, like those that developed in France that are described below. Indeed, in the United States, cases such as *Allnutt v. Inglis* were influential in forming a basis for the constitutional acceptance of utility regulation.[9] In the United Kingdom, however, they were largely forgotten, especially after the nationalization of the public utilities, culminating in the statutes of the Labour Government in the late 1940s. Certain nationalization statutes included a number of provisions to protect users, such as the stat-

4. For a similar conception, see Mark Freedland, *Law, Public Services and Citizenship—New Domains, New Regimes*, *in* PUBLIC SERVICES AND CITIZENSHIP IN EUROPEAN LAW, *supra* note 3, at 1.

5. *See* Paul P. Craig, *Constitutions, Property and Regulation*, 1991 PUB. L. 538.

6. *See* Allnutt v. Inglis, 104 Eng. Rep. 206 (K.B. 1810).

7. *See* Magistrates of Kircaldy v. Greig, 8 D. 1247 (Scot. 1846).

8. *See* Craig, *supra* note 5, at 542.

9. The seminal case is *Munn v. Illinois*, 94 U.S. 113 (1876). For a more detailed account, see Craig, *supra* note 5, at 543-51.

utes that required supply to be made available according to demand, and prohibited undue discrimination against particular types of users.[10] These statutes thus reflected the concerns of the nineteenth-century cases. However, these provisions did not constitute any coherent pattern of consumer protection. Furthermore, they were vague and difficult to interpret, and could not form the basis for a corpus of public service law.[11] Instead, the citizen's recourse against decisions of the public utilities was to be political rather than legal.[12] This approach proved to be remarkably ineffective, and was certainly incapable of resisting attempts to make the nationalized industries behave like ordinary capitalist businesses in the later days of nationalization.[13] The nationalized industries became notorious for poor customer relations, notably the ineffectiveness of arrangements to protect vulnerable families from disconnection of essential services.[14] There was one major achievement under nationalization: the creation of an infrastructure to provide what is now termed "universal service" throughout the United Kingdom. There was no parallel development of legal doctrines of public service, however, such as those that emerged in France. Technological advances were seemingly not reflected in new legal conceptions of citizenship.

At the time of privatization, British policymakers certainly had no intention of embodying principles of public service in law; indeed, the British Government was determined to avoid legal controls as much as possible.[15] Some perceived law as a way to facilitate meddling by courts, as well to create an unnecessary recourse to legal rights where market solutions would be more appropriate.[16] It would be a serious mistake to view the privatization process as having ended the relevance of public service to the utilities, however. Somewhat reluctantly, the British Government established new regulators for each utility sector, initially with the aim of restraining monopoly until it could be replaced by competition.[17] Nevertheless, political compromises had to be made, and the legislation setting out the duties of ministers and of the new regulators in relation to the public utilities contained a number of different duties mixing economic and social rationales.[18] For example, in all cases, meeting all reason-

10. *See, e.g.*, T. Sharpe, *Undue Price Discrimination and Undue Preference: A Legal Perspective*, 2 CONSUMER POL'Y REV. 33 (1992).

11. *See* Terence Daintith, *The United Kingdom*, *in* PUBLIC AND PRIVATE ENTERPRISE IN MIXED ECONOMIES (Wolfgang Friedmann ed., 1974). For the flexibility of the duties in practice, see *South of Scotland Electricity Board v. British Oxygen Co.*, 3 All E.R. 199 (1956).

12. For an overview of the problems, see TONY PROSSER AND PUBLIC CONTROL 194-221 (1986).

13. *See id.* at 36-74.

14. *See id.*; *see also* NATIONAL ECON. DEV. OFFICE, A STUDY OF UK NATIONALISED INDUSTRIES (1976).

15. The seminal statement of this view of regulation is contained in the report commissioned from an academic who later became a regulator of the electricity industry; that report formed the basis for the price control system adopted for each utility. *See* STEPHEN LITTLECHILD, REGULATION OF BRITISH TELECOMMUNICATIONS PROFITABILITY (1984); FOSTER, *supra* note 2.

16. *See generally* LITTLECHILD, *supra* note 15.

17. *See id.*

18. *See generally* TONY PROSSER, LAW AND THE REGULATORS 5-24 (1997).

able consumer demands forms part of the legislative requirements, reflecting a duty to provide a form of universal service.[19] Legislators retained prohibitions on undue preference or undue discrimination from the nationalization statutes, and they included special duties requiring ministers and regulators to pay special regard to the interests of consumers, especially those in rural areas, pensioners, and the disabled.[20] These by no means formed a general or consistent body of public service law in themselves, but are nevertheless important in suggesting that the utilities are different from other enterprises and that requirements based on social solidarity—to use the Continental phrase—are not irrelevant even after privatization. These duties are now partially replaced by a new duty in the Utilities Act 2000, which will be discussed in more detail after a description of the establishment and practice of the regulatory authorities.

III

THE INSTITUTION OF REGULATORY AGENCIES AND SOCIAL REGULATION IN PRACTICE

New independent regulatory authorities were thus established for each of the privatized utilities (telecommunications, water, rail, gas, and electricity).[21] The British system, unlike others, vests legal powers for each sector directly in Directors-General rather than in commissions, though they are assisted by regulatory offices. The regulatory offices are the Office of Telecommunications, the Office of Water Services, the Office of the Rail Regulator. the Office of Gas Supply, and the Office of Electricity Regulation; the latter have merged into the Office of Gas and Electricity Markets, shortly to be renamed the Gas and Electricity Markets Authority.[22] Originally, these offices were to have limited importance, which would wither away with the growth of competition. Instead, the regulators have now become a permanent and influential presence.[23] The regulators' main tasks have been to reset price controls for monopoly areas of utility operation, and increasingly to act as specialist competition authorities for those areas in which competition has been introduced, notably in telecommunications and the supply of gas and electricity. This latter role increased in importance in March 2000, when the regulators acquired the power to implement the reformed U.K. competition law in their respective sectors.[24]

19. *See* Telecommunications Act, 1984, § 3(1)(a) (U.K.); Gas Act, 1986, § 4(1)(a) (U.K.); Electricity Act, 1989, § 3(1)(a) (U.K.); Water Industry Act, 1991, § 2(3)(a) (U.K.); Railways Act, 1993, § 4(1)(b) (U.K.).

20. *See, e.g.*, Telecommunications Act, 1984, §§ 3(1)(a), 3(2)(a) (U.K.).

21. Those for gas and electricity have now been merged, and one regulatory authority has been added for the postal service. For details of the original authorities, see PROSSER, *supra* note 18. The arrangements for the postal service were announced in DEPARTMENT OF TRADE AND INDUS., POST OFFICE REFORM: A WORLD CLASS SERVICE FOR THE 21ST CENTURY, 1999, Cmnd. 4340 and are implemented by the Postal Services Act, 2000, §§ 1-5 (U.K.).

22. *See* Utilities Act, 2000, §§ 1-8 (U.K.).

23. For the view of the regulators as essentially temporary controls on remaining areas of monopoly, see generally LITTLECHILD, *supra* note 15.

24. *See* Competition Act, 1998, § 54, & sched. 10 (U.K.).

The regulators, however, have also treated some types of social regulation designed to protect consumers as within their power. All regulatory agencies have established service standards, which encompass general quality of service indicators as well as provide rights of compensation for individual consumers.[25] Certain utilities have encountered particularized social regulatory developments. In telecommunications, for example, one of the fears at the time of privatization was that the number of public phone booths would be drastically reduced, especially in rural and low-income areas. To avoid this, complex provisions were included in British Telecom's license restricting the circumstances in which such phone booths could be closed.[26] The regulator also mounted a major campaign to ensure that the phones actually worked. Competition has been permitted also in the provision of public phone booth services. As a result of these developments, the number of phone booths increased considerably, from under 80,000 in 1987 to about 140,000 now, although a decline in their profitability due to the growth of mobile telephony is likely to lead to price increases.[27]

The second area of regulation with a strong social dimension is that of special tariffs for low users. A low-user tariff emerged from discussions between British Telecom and the regulator leading to the review of the Company's regulated tariffs in 1989.[28] Proponents of the tariff justified it as maximizing the value of the telephone network as a national resource by permitting as many people as possible to be connected to it.[29] Later versions of the scheme, however, were targeted more closely toward those who could not afford to pay.[30] During the mid-1990s, a major review of universal service in telecommunications was carried out, inspired partially by the emergence of universal service concerns at a European level.[31] The consultative paper produced by the British regulator stressed the fundamental role that telecommunications services play in society and that this role requires that all people, whatever their income or geographical location, must have access to basic telecommunications facilities.[32] Following the universal service review, a new tariff was introduced to provide a limited service at very low cost, and steps were taken to reduce the level of disconnections for non-payment by fifty percent.[33] A further review of universal

25. *See* the Competition and Service (Utilities) Act, 1992 (U.K.).

26. See OFFICE OF TELECOMMUNICATIONS, A BETTER DEAL FOR PAYPHONE USERS (1998) (visited Nov. 16, 2000) <http://www.oftel.gov.uk/consumer/payp298.htm>.

27. *See id.*

28. *See* OFFICE OF TELECOMMUNICATIONS, UNIVERSAL TELECOMMUNICATIONS SERVICES: PROPOSED ARRANGEMENTS FOR UNIVERSAL SERVICE IN THE UK FROM 1997 (1997) (visited Nov. 16, 2000) <http://www.oftel.gov.uk/consumer/uniserv2/chap1.htm>.

29. *See id.*

30. *See id.*

31. *See id.*

32. *See* OFFICE OF TELECOMMUNICATIONS, UNIVERSAL TELECOMMUNICATIONS SERVICES (1999) (visited Nov. 16, 2000) <http://www.oftel.gov.uk/consumer/uts799.htm>.

33. *See id.*

service was initiated in 1999.[34] Perhaps the most interesting question raised by this review is how universal service will develop in the new world of media convergence. The universal service review had included the provision of enhanced services for schools and public libraries, but this was pursued separately with the establishment of a task force to assess the needs of such institutions and to propose a voluntary scheme for such access. Such a scheme is now being implemented by the industry and the government with advice from the regulator.[35] However, the 1999 consultation on universal service includes the issue of whether universal service principles should be extended beyond basic voice telephony to include the provision of higher bandwidth to permit fast access to Internet and other advanced services.

In the gas and electricity industries, the major social concern has been the disconnection of supply. In gas, disconnection for failure to pay had been used widely before privatization; however, disconnections rose immediately after privatization from 35,626 to 60,778 in 1987.[36] Two years later, the regulator announced a modification of British Gas's license introducing new procedures aimed at limiting disconnections.[37] The new provisions effectively prevented disconnection unless the customer had first been offered a pre-payment meter as an alternative. The meter allows payment by pre-paid token before consumption and can be set so as to recover debt. The effect was to reduce disconnections radically, with a drop to under 20,000 by 1990 and again to 14,000 in 1995, although by 1998, they had risen again to almost 30,000.[38]

Similarly, in electricity disconnections were running at the rate of 70,000 per annum before privatization. Provisions in the Electricity Act of 1989 and in the licenses issued to electricity companies prevented disconnection where there is a serious dispute, and required the issue of a code of practice that largely precluded disconnection unless a prepayment meter had been offered as an alternative. As a result, disconnections dropped dramatically to below 20,000 in the year after privatization, and by 1995-96, only 674 domestic customers were disconnected for non-payment of bills, with a further fall to around 400 in 1998.[39] Despite the recent price increase for gas, this decline in disconnections has proceeded at a remarkable rate, even if a couple of qualifications must be noted. First, developments in metering technology played an important part in the decline; and second, the figures hide the extent of "self-disconnection" through inability to pay with a prepayment meter.[40] Further discussion on recent developments to limit the effects of fuel poverty is given below.

---

34. *See id.*

35. *See id.*

36. *See* OFFICE OF GAS AND ELECTRICITY MARKETS, SOCIAL ACTION PLAN: DISCUSSION PAPER (May 1999) (visited Nov. 17, 2000) <http://www.ofgem.gov.uk/docs/socialac.pdf>.

37. *See id.*

38. *See id.*

39. *See id.*

40. For more information on these issues, see OFFICE OF GAS AND ELECTRICITY MARKETS, SOCIAL ACTION PLAN, *supra* note 36.

Because the supply of gas and electricity is now competitive, a large number of new suppliers have entered the market. There were considerable fears about the effect of these developments on social obligations. The first concern related to the practice of "cream skimming." By definition, opening up the market signalled an end to universal tariffs (which never fully applied to the energy market in the United Kingdom anyway). The fear was that new entrants would offer service only to the most profitable customers, assumed to be the larger consumers, leaving the poor as an unprofitable remainder retained by the former monopoly supplier. Second, it was feared that the social obligations applying to the monopoly supplier would not apply to competitors.

In gas, a number of strategies have been employed to avoid these problems. All competing operators have to be licensed, and legislation forbids the granting of a license that is framed in such a way as to exclude premises likely to be occupied by persons who are chronically sick, disabled, of pensionable age, or who are likely to default in the payment of charges.[41] This prevents a new supplier from excluding poor inner-city areas from supply, for example. Licenses require that all domestic customers in the license area be supplied with gas without undue preference or undue discrimination in the processing of applications, thus retaining a type of universal service requirement.[42] A dominant supplier also is prohibited from undue preference or undue discrimination in charges: Price caps will continue to apply to the key British Gas tariffs, including the tariff for supply by pre-payment meter, until April 2001 when the market is expected to be fully competitive.[43] All social requirements in the licenses, such as the disconnection procedures and special obligations toward old or disabled persons, apply to all suppliers, not just to the former monopolist. So far, these provisions have been successful in avoiding the worst of the predicted problems. There is evidence that new suppliers are offering deals for all types of consumers, not just the most profitable ones; however, the lack of innovative arrangements for savings and for greater reductions in tariffs for prepayment meter customers has been criticised.[44] Provision was also made for a levy on gas suppliers should any particular supplier be forced to bear an unfair share of the burden of uneconomic customers; however, this provision has never been used.[45] Similar provisions have been introduced for the competitive electricity market,

41. *See* Gas Act, 1986, § 7A(8)(b) (U.K.), as amended by Gas Act, 1995 (U.K.).

42. *See* DEPARTMENT OF TRADE AND INDUS., GAS ACT 1995: DETERMINATION OF THE STANDARD CONDITIONS OF GAS SUPPLIERS' LICENSES cond. 2(3) (1996).

43. OFFICE OF GAS AND ELECTRICITY MARKETS, REVIEW OF BRITISH GAS TRADING'S PRICE REGULATION: FINAL PROPOSALS (Feb. 2000) (visited Nov. 29, 2000) <http://www.ofgem.gov.uk/docs/pcfeb.pdf>.

44. *See* NATIONAL AUDIT OFFICE, GIVING CUSTOMERS A CHOICE: THE INTRODUCTION OF COMPETITION INTO THE DOMESTIC GAS MARKET, HC 403, 1998-99.

45. *See* DEPARTMENT OF TRADE AND INDUS., *supra* note 42, cond. 6.

and price controls are being retained until 2002, although here, there is no provision for a levy to support high social costs.[46] Finally, the Utilities Act 2000 contains new powers permitting the Secretary of State to adjust charges for electricity and gas to help disadvantaged groups of customers, and these powers permit the provision of cross-subsidy in their favour, although this is to be used only as a last resort.[47]

The story in water and sewerage is in many ways similar, although there has been no discussion of the introduction of a competitive domestic market. Controversy has centered mainly around the issue of disconnections. The health implications of living without a water supply are, of course, particularly severe, not just for the disconnected consumer, but for other households that can be affected by disease. Again, there was a substantial rise in the number of disconnections after privatization; by 1991-92 more than 21,000 households were disconnected each year.[48] In 1992, the regulator issued guidelines to the companies requiring improved procedures before disconnection took place.[49] These procedures resulted in a gradual but substantial drop in the number of disconnections to 10,000 in 1994-95.[50] The introduction of prepayment meters as an alternative is more difficult to implement for water utilities, although a number of companies did employ budget payment units that allow use of a card for advance payment, followed by an emergency credit period of a week.[51] However, a court ruled that these budget payment units were unlawful because they amounted to disconnection without the statutory protections required by the legislation and licenses.[52] The legislature has recently passed the Water Industry Act of 1999, which prohibits disconnection of water and sewerage services from residences for non-payment of charges and also prohibits the use of budget payment units. The Act also requires charging schemes to be approved by the Director General of Water Services in accordance with regulations issued by the Secretary of State.[53] The regulations enable those in vulnerable groups such as those with three or more dependent children or suffering from specified medical conditions to pay an average charge rather than that based on their metered consumption.[54]

---

46. For similar criticisms of the extent of benefits for disadvantaged consumers in the electricity market, see NATIONAL ELEC. CONSUMERS COUNCIL, ASSISTING DISADVANTAGED CONSUMERS: PRACTICAL PROPOSALS (1999).

47. *See* Utilities Act, 2000, §§ 69, 98 (U.K.)

48. *See* JOHN ERNST, WHOSE UTILITY? THE SOCIAL IMPACT OF PUBLIC UTILITY PRIVATIZATION AND REGULATION IN BRITAIN 149 (1994).

49. *See* OFFICE OF WATER SERV., GUIDELINES ON DEBT AND DISCONNECTION (1992).

50. *See* ALICIA HERBERT & ELAINE KEMPSON, WATER DEBT AND DISCONNECTION 6 (1995).

51. *See id.* at 69-73.

52. *See* R v. Director General of Water Services *ex parte* Oldham MBC, 31 H.L.R. 224 (1998), Case Note, R v. Director General of Water Services ex p. Oldham MBC, 9 UTIL. L. REV. 123 (1998).

53. *See* Water Industry Act, 1999, §§ 1-5 (U.K.).

54. The Water Industry (Charges) (Vulnerable Groups) Regulations, S.I. 1999, No. 3441, as amended by the Water Industry (Charges)(Vulnerable Groups)(Amendment) Regulations, S.I. 2000, No. 519.

The protection of universal service in the case of railroads has taken a different path. For some time, even before privatization, the government had made separate payments to protect socially necessary but economically inefficient lines.[55] This practice continues today in the form of franchise payments made to the companies operating rail services.[56] Detailed provisions limit service closures and protect a minimum level of service.[57] Historically, the procedures governing passenger service closures have been under public control, and in the past, closure hearings have been prolonged and controversial.[58] When there are objections to a proposed station or line closure, a regional committee must hold a hearing to investigate whether the closure will cause hardship. The committee reports its findings to the regulator, who then determines whether the closure will cause hardship and decides whether it will take effect.[59] The decision may be appealed to the minister, although the Transport Bill before the Parliament at the time of writing proposes that the decision be that of the minister rather than that of the regulator in all cases.[60] No rail closures of any importance have taken place since privatization, because of their political unpopularity, although the future position of rail closures after franchises have been renewed is less certain.[61] The franchise agreements also incorporate minimum service requirements on lines protecting potentially unprofitable services such as late evening trains.[62]

I do not wish to suggest that these somewhat particularistic attempts to prevent the exploitation of more vulnerable consumers are necessarily satisfactory. As mentioned above, in the competitive energy markets, a number of sources have expressed concern that, although poor families have gained, they have gained less than the more prosperous.[63] The major change in this area, however, is from consumer protection depending on the goodwill of an industry (or on very ineffective political mechanisms) to rules enforceable by regulators, normally taking the form of license conditions under which enterprises operate or codes of practice required by license conditions. Indeed, under public ownership, the interests of government and the enterprise could often coincide at the expense of the consumer. For example, raising energy prices and requiring the proceeds to be paid to the government through repayment of debt or as a direct levy may be used as a form of highly regressive surrogate taxation without the

---

55. *See* Transport Act, 1968, §§ 38-40 (U.K.).

56. *See* Railways Act, 1993, §§ 23-31 (U.K.).

57. *See id.* §§ 37-50.

58. *See, e.g.*, PROSSER, *supra* note 12, at 165-68.

59. *See* Railways Act, 1993, § 43 (U.K.).

60. *See id.* § 44.

61. For a decision by the courts preventing evasion of these procedures, see *Highland Regional Council v. British Railways Board*, 1996 SLT 274 (1st Div.).

62. For a successful challenge to the first version of the requirements, see *R v. Director of Passenger Rail Franchising*, ex parte *Save Our Railways*, TIMES (London), Dec. 18, 1995 (C.A.).

63. *See, e.g.*, NATIONAL ELEC. CONSUMERS COUNCIL, *supra* note 46.

inconvenience of passing legislation.[64] Although at the time of privatization there was a similar identity of interests between the government (which wanted to sell shares successfully) and industries (which wanted to be privatized on favourable terms in the later operation of the regulated utilities), the role of the regulators has brought questions about the best arrangements for protecting disadvantaged consumers far more into the open. Indeed, privatization has removed the direct incentive of government as owner to maximize industry returns. The creation of a network of independent regulators has brought to the forefront the question of how extensively constraints should be imposed on profit-maximization by utility enterprises. These constraints have been imposed by law, normally in the form of provisions in the licenses of the utility enterprises, rather than by informal and secretive intervention. The creation of independent regulators was originally viewed as a way of increasing investor confidence by preventing arbitrary intervention by governments after privatization. Paradoxically, however, it has formed the most important basis for the creation of an emerging body of public service law.

IV

REGULATORY AGENCIES AND REGULATORY REFORM

Two conclusions should be apparent from the description of the process of privatization in the United Kingdom. First, the utility regulators have not limited themselves to economic regulation; at times, they act for social reasons. Second, there is no coherent pattern to this; the interventions have been somewhat pragmatic and have differed from utility to utility. One problem hampering their efforts has been the concern that social interventions by regulators are undemocratic. Some argue that the regulator should be restricted to applying economic criteria with the aim of maximizing efficiency. Social goals, by contrast, should be left to government which, unlike the regulators, has a democratic mandate.[65] This view was shared to a degree by some of the utility regulators. For example, the former Director of Gas Supply refused to support energy-saving measures by levying a charge on consumers because she considered that to be a matter for the government and for Parliament to decide.[66] Currently, however, measures are under consideration to create a clearer division of responsibilities through the current process of regulatory reform.

The Labour Government elected in 1997 has been more sympathetic to the potential need for social regulation than its predecessors: "Ensuring that the services provided by [the utilities] are available to all members of society, including the most vulnerable, on fair terms, is important to the Government's

---

64. For additional examples of this, see PROSSER, NATIONALIZED INDUSTRIES *supra* note 12, at 63-69.

65. *See* FOSTER, *supra* note 2, at 316-23.

66. *See* PROSSER, *supra* note 18, at 110-13.

wider objective of creating a fairer society."[67] The question of how to create a more orderly set of arrangements for public access to utilities was a central aim of the review of utility regulation carried out in 1998 which resulted in the Utilities Act 2000.[68] The review concluded that "the Government, not regulators, should determine the social objectives of regulation," and proposed a new approach under which the government will issue statutory guidance to regulators in each sector.[69] However, where new measures with significant financial implications are to be imposed, new primary legislation will be passed, rather than using regulatory guidance. For example, regarding the controversial question of energy efficiency levies on consumers, the government has stated that new standards of performance to deliver energy and carbon savings through the establishment of energy saving schemes funded by a levy "would fall into the category of measures which should be implemented through new specific legal provision rather than relying on guidance to the regulator."[70] The new Act indeed includes specific powers to set efficiency standards by government.[71]

In one respect the Utilities Act 2000 has been a major disappointment in that during Parliamentary proceedings, the government decided to limit its applicability to the energy utilities (electricity and gas); telecommunications and water will thus wait for possible reform of regulation some time in the future.[72] Nevertheless, some important changes relating to social regulation have been included. Thus the energy regulator will have a duty to heed guidance issued by the minister on social and environmental matters.[73]

Existing duties respecting the elderly, the disabled, and those in rural areas are retained, and new duties regarding the interests of low-income consumers and the chronically sick have been introduced.[74] In place of the somewhat inconsistent and opaque duties applying to each regulator under the original utility statues, the Act gives the new energy regulator a single new overriding duty.[75] This duty will require it

> to protect the interests of consumers, wherever possible and appropriate, through promoting effective competition. The interests of consumers should be interpreted to

67. *See* DEPARTMENT OF TRADE AND INDUS., A FAIR DEAL FOR CONSUMERS: THE RESPONSE TO CONSULTATION 1998.

68. *See* DEPARTMENT OF TRADE AND INDUS., A FAIR DEAL FOR CONSUMERS: MODERNISING THE FRAMEWORK FOR UTILITY REGULATION, 1998, Cmnd. 3898; the final proposals are in the DEPARTMENT OF TRADE AND INDUS., *supra* note 67.

69. DEPARTMENT OF TRADE AND INDUS., *supra* note 68, ¶¶ 2.13-18, 5.4; DEPARTMENT OF TRADE AND INDUS., *supra* note 67, ¶¶ 10-14, at 57-62.

70. DEPARTMENT OF THE ENV'T, TRANSPORT AND THE REGIONS, UK CLIMATE CHANGE PROGRAMME, 1998, ¶ 66.

71. *See* Utilities Act, 2000, §§ 70, 99 (U.K.).

72. *See* SECRETARY OF STATE FOR TRADE AND INDUSTRY, PARL. DEB., H.C. (5th ser.) cols. 555-60 (2000).

73. *See* Utilities Act, 2000, §§ 70, 99 (U.K.).

74. *See* Utilities Act, 2000, § 9 (U.K.) (adding a new § 4(AA)(3) to the Gas Act, 1986 (U.K.)), § 13 (adding a new § 3(A)(3) to the Electricity Act, 1989 (U.K.)); DEPARTMENT OF TRADE AND INDUS., *supra* note 67, ¶ 13;.

75. *See* Utilities Act, 2000, § 9 (adding a new § 4(AA)(1) to the Gas Act, 1986 (U.K.), § 13 (adding a new § 3(A)(1) to the Electricity Act, 1989 (U.K.)).

include prices and conditions of supply, continuity and availability of supply, quality of supply, and, where relevant, the range of services offered. In defining the interests of consumers, due weight should be given to their long-term and medium-term interests as well as to their immediate or short-term interests.[76]

Although the importance of competition is explicitly addressed, the other matters mentioned clearly permit the energy regulator to take social considerations into account; indeed, the duty to comply with social and environmental guidance from ministers requires this. The reforms also envisage the creation of a more effective and independent form of consumer representation in relation to the utilities. Based on past experience, this will provide a channel for the continual monitoring of industry performance in relation to social concerns.[77]

In addition to the legislative reform, the Government also asked the energy regulators to draw up an action plan to ensure that disadvantaged customers benefit from the advantages of opening up the gas and electricity markets to competition.[78] The plan confirmed that measures had already been taken to protect such consumers, and that in the case of gas, research had shown that the proportion of customers changing to new suppliers was, in general, evenly distributed across all social groups. As mentioned above, however, the National Audit Office and others have expressed some concern that disadvantaged consumers have not benefited as much as others.[79] A remaining issue was the higher charges paid by prepayment meter customers. Some steps had been taken to reduce these prepayment charges, and other alterations in the charging system emerged as possibilities to benefit such customers.[80] The first version of the action plan, however, did little more than to restate the existing arrangements to protect vulnerable consumers in the liberalized markets described above. After criticism, a revised draft was considerably more far-reaching, including proposals both for more detailed research and the strengthening of the obligations imposed on energy supply companies. For example, companies would be required to accept more frequent cash payments and to accept improved codes of practice on pre-payment meters, and to charge a binding maximum fee for the permitted surcharge payable by customers for the use of such meters. These reforms have now been implemented.[81]

The move toward legally enforceable public service requirements has culminated in the plan announced in the summer of 1999 for reform of the Post Office implemented by the Postal Services Act 2000.[82] A new regulatory com-

---

76. *See* DEPARTMENT OF TRADE AND INDUS., *supra* note 67, ¶ 16.

77. *Id.* ¶¶ 17-21; *see also* Utilities Act, 2000, § 2 (U.K.) & sched. 2.

78. *See* OFFICE OF ELECTRICITY REGULATION & OFFICE OF GAS SUPPLY, THE SOCIAL DIMENSION: ACTION PLAN 2 (1998).

79. *See* NATIONAL AUDIT OFFICE, *supra* note 44.

80. *See* OFFICE OF GAS AND ELECTRICITY MARKETS, SOCIAL ACTION PLAN: A FRAMEWORK DOCUMENT 21 (Oct. 1999) (visited Nov. 21, 2000) <http://www.ofgem.gov.uk/docs/social.pdf>.

81. *See id.;* OFFICE OF GAS AND ELECTRICITY MARKETS, SOCIAL ACTION PLAN (Mar. 2000) (visited Nov. 21, 2000) <http://www.ofgem.gov.uk/docs/sapmarch.pdf>; OFFICE OF GAS AND ELECTRICITY MARKETS, SOCIAL ACTION PLAN: ENHANCING SOCIAL OBLIGATIONS: A PROPOSALS DOCUMENT (visited Nov. 21, 2000) (Jan. 2000) <http://www.ofgem.gov.uk/docs/socjan.pdf>.

82. *See* DEPARTMENT OF TRADE AND INDUS., *supra* note 21.

mission has been created, and its primary duty is to maintain universal postal delivery service throughout the United Kingdom at a uniform tariff. This duty is enshrined and defined in law for the first time.[83] Minimum criteria will also be set for access to services, such as the protection of rural post offices, and progress toward those goals will be monitored by the new regulator.[84] Even before the passage of the Postal Services Act, the universal service obligation was initially set out in regulations implementing the European Community Postal Services Directive.[85] As this example suggests, the long tradition of public service law in other European Community countries, such as France, is beginning to have a profound effect on the United Kingdom through E.C. law, and I shall now describe the French tradition before dealing with E.C. law in more detail.

V

PUBLIC SERVICE IN FRANCE

So far, I have described the domestic British influences that have resulted in the development of a new public service law in relation to utility services. These influences have included the institution of regulators independent from government and private enterprise, the failure to limit the statutory duties of the regulators to economic matters, and a more sympathetic attitude from the new Labour Government to social regulation in general. In addition, other Member States in the European Union, most notably France, have a tradition of protecting public service that is radically different from that of the United Kingdom. In the past this tradition had minimal effect on the United Kingdom, where political rather than legal protections were seen as the most appropriate way of ensuring that public service goals were protected. However, the Continental model has now begun to have an important influence due to the United Kingdom's membership in the European Union and the effect of E.C. law. It is thus essential to examine the protection of public service in other Member States, and France provides by far the most developed example.[86]

In France, the concept of public service has its roots in the Constitution. The Preamble to the 1946 Constitution includes a provision to the effect that "[a]ll property and enterprises of which the running has, or acquires, the character of a national public service or a *de facto* monopoly are to become public property."[87] There has been some doubt about the meaning of this provision, and it has been interpreted broadly by the *Conseil Constitutionnel*.[88] Notably, it

83. *See* Postal Services Act, 2000, §§ 1-5 (U.K.).

84. *See* DEPARTMENT OF TRADE AND INDUS., *supra* note 21, chs. 4, 7.

85. *See* Postal Services Regulations, 1999, S.I. 2107.

86. For a more general discussion of public service in the European Union, see PUBLIC SERVICES AND CITIZENSHIP IN EUROPEAN UNION LAW, *supra* note 3.

87. LA CONSTITUTION DU 4 OCTOBRE 1958, preamble (Preamble to Constitution, 1946) (amended 1992) (Fr.).

88. Notably in the *Privatizations* decision, see Conseil constitutionnel (Cons. const.), June 25-26, 1986, C.C. 207, 1986, No. 86-207 DC (visited Nov. 16, 2000) <http://www.conseil-constitutionnel.fr/decision/1986 /86207dc.htm>.

does not apply to local public services such as water, which has for some time largely been supplied by private companies operating under concession.

The concept of *service public* is much more fully developed in French administrative law than in British law.[89] It can be summarized as follows: "In French public law, public service is an activity in the general interest, provided by a public or private actor and subject to a special legal regime requiring equality of treatment, adaptation to changing needs and security of supply, etc."[90] The principle of public service has been implemented in two ways: through public ownership and through the granting of public service concessions for private concerns. Indeed, concessions also have been used to set out a framework for the operation of public enterprises. In much of the rhetoric concerning public service, an intrinsic interdependence of three elements has been assumed: (1) public service defined in law; (2) public ownership; and (3) a public monopoly to enable the distinctive tasks of public service to be achieved. It is important to point out, however, that in legal terms at least, *service public* is not synonymous with public ownership, or even with the granting of monopoly rights. *Service public* may also be a means of incorporating certain social principles into the operation of private enterprises in the market place; this is likely to be its most important role in the future.[91] It is also important to note that *service public* is essentially non-economic and distributive in nature: "It is the essence of *service public*, as a means of consolidation of the social contract and of social solidarity, that it contributes to some types of redistribution and of transfers between social groups."[92]

What are the actual requirements of a regime of *service public*? The basic requirement is that of equality, ensuring equal access to services and equal treatment of consumers unless there is good reason not to do so. This may result in a rule prohibiting arbitrary pricing distinctions or restrictive access conditions. Other principles of equality include continuity of public service, which has most often concerned the extent of a right to strike on the part of public sector workers. Equality may also require security of supply, a key issue in energy liberalization. *Service public* also requires political neutrality in the provision of services. Echoing concerns in Anglo-Saxon utilities regulation, the participation of consumers in the administration, or at least in the regulation of services, as well as transparency of administration also have become part of the require-

---

89. For a comprehensive overview, see PUBLIC SERVICES AND CITIZENSHIP IN EUROPEAN UNION LAW, *supra* note 3. There is a vast and fast-growing French literature on the subject.

90. Marc Debène & Olivier Raymundie, *Sur Le Service Universel: Renouveau Du Service Public ou Nouvelle Mystification?* 52:3 AJDA 183, 186 (1996). My translation is a loose one in view of the difficulty in conveying the flavour of the concept in English.

91. *See* CONSEIL D'ETAT, *supra* note 3, at 26-29. The point has been re-emphasised in the decision of the Conseil constitutionnel concerning the partial privatization of France Télécom. *See* Cons. Const., July 23, 1996, R.J.C. 1996, No. 96-380DC (visited Nov. 16, 2000) <http: www.conseil-constitutionnel.fr/decision/1996/96380dc.htm>. The issue has also been addressed in the recent and influential report to the Prime Minister by an official Commission on Public Service. *See* DENOIX DE SAINT MARC, *supra* note 3, at 17, 43, 77-78.

92. *See* CONSEIL D'ETAT, *supra* note 3, at 53 (author's translation).

ments of a *service public* regime.[93] These basic requirements are central principles of French administrative law but are implemented and supplemented by extensive statutory and regulatory requirements.[94] Though it is outside the scope of this article, the concept of *service public* has also played a major role in the regulation of broadcasting in France, particularly its attempts to defend public service broadcasting within the European Union and in relation to the GATT cultural exception.[95]

VI

CONFLICTS WITHIN THE EUROPEAN UNION OVER THE NEW CONCEPT OF PUBLIC SERVICE

Because of the differing degrees of legal protection of public services in the Member States of the European Union, there have been fierce conflicts within the European Union as to the degree to which public utility markets should be opened to competition.[96] The U.K. model of liberalization is often presented as a threat to the values of public service, while France's model is seen in the Anglo-Saxon world as protecting inefficient state enterprises through a system of special privileges.

In fact, both models find support in E.C. law. Thus, Articles 81 and 82 of the Treaty establishing the European Community[97] set out the basic principles of competition law that are made applicable to public enterprises by Article 86(1).[98] The rapid process of liberalizing the telecommunications industry, the first example of utility liberalization, took place through a model of utilities detached from direct government control and working in competitive markets.[99] Universal service remains a value to be protected by specific interventions within the competitive marketplace, rather than by any overall regime of public service.[100] Similar assumptions can be found in the arrangements adopted for the liberalization of civil aviation and, subject to greater qualification, electricity

93. All these principles are analysed in detail in *id.*

94. For an illustration of the application of public service principles to the French postal service, see Case T-106/95, Fédération Française des Sociétés d'Assurances (FFSA) v. Commission of the European Communities, 1997 E.C.R. II-229.

95. *See* Philip Schlesinger, *From Cultural Defense to Political Culture: Media, Politics and Collective Identity in the European Union*, 19 MEDIA, CULTURE & SOC'Y 369 (1997).

96. *See, e.g.*, Services of General Interest in Europe, COM(96)443 final.

97. Formerly articles 85 and 86; TREATY ESTABLISHING THE EUROPEAN COMMUNITY, Feb. 7, 1992, O.J. (C 224) 1 (1992), [1992] 1 C.M.L.R. 573 (1992) [hereinafter E.C. TREATY].

98. Formerly article 90(1), E.C. TREATY.

99. For a good summary of the early stages of this process, see A. Hunt, *Regulation of Telecommunications: The Developing EU Regulatory Framework and its Impact on the United Kingdom*, 3 EUROPEAN PUB. LAW 93 (1997).

100. *See, e.g.*, Developing Universal Service For Telecommunications in a Competitive Environment, COM(93)159 final; European Parliament and Council Directive 98/10/EC on the Application of Open Network Provision to Voice Telephony and on Universal Service For Telecommunications in a Competitive Environment, 1998 O.J. (L 101) 1.4. For an outstanding critical discussion, see Wolf Sauter, *Universal Service Obligations and the Emergence of Citizens' Rights in European Telecommunications Liberalization*, in PUBLIC SERVICES AND CITIZENSHIP IN EUROPEAN UNION LAW, *supra* note 3, at 117.

and gas. With regard to the structures of enterprises to be adopted in the future, Article 295 of the Treaty[101] apparently preserves neutrality between different forms of property ownership—in other words, whether an enterprise is publicly or privately owned. However, there is no doubt that state aid policies have been a major contributing factor to privatization throughout the European Union, as they require that public enterprises be treated no differently from enterprises that are privately owned.[102] Thus, what is the point of keeping enterprises public if they cannot be subject to a different regime? While this point must be qualified for the utilities, the notion in other cases has been important in shaping policy on privatization. Moreover, jurisprudence from the European Court of Justice has restricted or ended certain special privileges of public utilities. For example, one decision limited the ability of British Telecom to act anti-competitively even before it became privatized.[103] The Commission's support for this model of utilities operating in a competitive marketplace with a residual role for universal service has led to sustained criticism from Continental Member States. These states claim that the Commission is "a liberalisation machine, ultra-liberal and dogmatic."[104] In other words, it is alleged that the Commission has ignored the broader conception of public service.

On the other hand, the French-based model of public service has also had an important place within E.C. law. Thus, Article 86(1), applying the competition principles to public enterprises, is immediately qualified by the following subarticle that provides a limited defense against their application in the case of "services of general economic interest," in order that their application does not obstruct the performance of the tasks entrusted to bodies providing such services.[105] The jurisprudence of the European Court of Justice also indicates an acceptance of the legitimate role of public service. For example, in the well-known case of *Corbeau,* the Court accepted that the normal principles of E.C. competition law could be limited to permit the conferring of exclusive rights on a state monopoly to the extent necessary to preserve a universal service through cross-subsidy.[106] Similarly, in the *Almelo* decision, the Court specified that the competition rules could be modified if necessary to ensure a continued supply of electricity on demand to all types of consumers on the basis of uniform tariffs and non-discriminatory conditions throughout the areas covered by their

101. Formerly Article 222.

102. *See* Commission of the European Communities, Fourteenth Report on Competition Policy (1985), point 198; Case C234/84, Belgium v. Commission of European Communities, 1986 E.C.R. 2263, [1988] 2 C.M.L.R. 331, ¶ 13 (1986). The largest and most controversial example has been that of state aid to *Crédit Lyonnais. See* Commission Decision 98/490/EC of 20 May 1998 Concerning Aid Granted By France to the Crédit Lyonnais Group, 1998 O.J. (L 221) 28.

103. *See* Case C41/83, Italy v. Commission of European Communities, 1985 E.C.R. 873, [1985] 2 C.M.L.R. 368 (1985).

104. *See* Karel Van Miert, L'Europe, Vecteur De La Libéralisation, Speech, Paris, France (Oct. 21, 1996).

105. Formerly article 90(1), E.C. TREATY.

106. *See* Case C-320/91, Regie des Postes v. Corbeau, 1993 E.C.R. I-2533, [1993] 4 C.M.L.R. 621 (1993).

authorizations.[107] In early 1997, the Court of First Instance rejected a challenge to the way in which the French postal service had been compensated for its public service obligations, confirming the discretion given to Member States in arranging such compensation. Furthermore, the court found that support permitted under Article 86(2) would not constitute unlawful state aid.[108]

During the period preceding the Amsterdam Inter-Governmental Conference, which determined important reforms to the treaties on which the European Union is based, the European Centre of Enterprises with Public Participation and other pressure groups campaigning on behalf of public enterprises led a vociferous campaign in favor of the amendment of the treaty in a way that would have seriously weakened the application of Article 86(1). The proposed amendment would permit the Member States to decide which activities would form part of "services of general economic interest." The French and Belgian governments also proposed treaty amendments to guarantee universal rights of access to such services.[109] The European Parliament passed a resolution stating that the "fundamental principles of public service, *i.e.* accessibility, universality, equality, continuity, quality, transparency and participation in the context of the single market and respecting the principle of subsidiarity, should be incorporated in the Treaty."[110] The Commission itself made much more limited proposals for the addition of "a contribution to the promotion of services of general interest" to the list of Community activities in the treaty.[111] There was considerable political division within the Conference between the Member States favoring such an amendment and those, including the United Kingdom, who believed that current treaty provisions ensured an adequate balance between competition policy and the needs of a public service. What was eventually agreed upon was a French-inspired amendment to add a new Article 16 to the treaty as follows:

> Without prejudice to Articles 77, 90 and 92, and given the place occupied by services of general economic interest in the shared values of the Union as well as their role in promoting social and territorial cohesion, the Community and the Member States, each within their respective powers and within the scope of application of this Treaty, shall take care that such services operate on the basis of principles and conditions which enable them to fulfil their missions.[112]

---

107. *See* Case C-393/92, Almelo v. Energiebedrijf Ijsselmij NV, 1994 E.C.R. I-1477; *see also* Case C-157/94, Commission of European Communities v. Netherlands, 1997 E.C.R. I-5699.

108. *See* Case T-106/95, Fédération Française des Sociétés d'Assurances (FFSA) v. Commission of the European Communities, 1997 E.C.R. II-229.

109. *See, e.g.*, CENTRE EUROPÉEN À PARTICIPATION PUBLIQUE, EUROPE, CONCURRENCE ET SERVICE PUBLIC (1995); European Centre of Enterprises with Public Participation (CEEP), Europe, Competition and Public Service (Apr. 17, 1996) (press release).

110. Resolution of the European Parliament on the Intergovernmental Conference, 1996 O.J. (C 96) 77.

111. Communication from the Commission—Services of General Interest in Europe, COM(96)443 final.

112. TREATY OF AMSTERDAM, AMENDING THE TREATY ON EUROPEAN UNION, Oct. 2, 1997, O.J. (C 340) 16 (1997).

A Declaration stated that these provisions should be implemented "with full respect for the jurisprudence of the Court of Justice, inter alia as regards the principles of equality of treatment, quality and continuity of such services."[113] Other amendments aim to protect public service broadcasting.[114] It has yet to be seen whether these amendments have more than symbolic importance, but even if their practical effect is limited, they represent a fuller recognition of the role of public service in the basic principles of European law. Indeed, it has been argued strongly that they go much further than the merely symbolic, and provide a new concept of public service to promote cohesion and shared values, which must be respected by Member States.[115]

The more important practical development has been the emergence of more detailed principles in particular areas of liberalization. As mentioned above, this trend has reached its most advanced stage in the telecommunications industry.[116] Here, the dominant Continental model was that of a monopoly public enterprise which would be expected to deliver public service objectives; in practice, however, even legal requirements of public service often were not fulfilled.[117] This model has been succeeded by full telecommunications liberalization as a result of community action. Built into this liberalization have been requirements of universal service that go considerably farther than earlier requirements in guaranteeing a basic minimum standard and other service standards which may develop beyond basic telephony. As one commentator has put it, "[t]he paradoxical result may well turn out to be that true universal service will for the first time be available throughout the European Union after liberalisation has been completed."[118]

The European dimension has also had an important influence on the U.K. telecommunications universal service measures discussed above. The impact of E.U. policies in the United Kingdom is becoming apparent in the area of postal services, where, as part of an internal market, Community law requires a defined universal service obligation, which sets criteria for defining the monopoly services necessary for maintaining universal service, and maintains prices that are affordable, geared to costs, and non-discriminatory. It also requires the setting and publication of service standards and the establishment of a national regulatory authority separate from the public postal operator.[119] These policies

---

113. *Id.* art. 2(8), Declaration on Article 7d of the Treaty Establishing the European Community. The numbering quoted refers to the old numbers of the Treaty Articles; the new equivalents to arts. 77, 90, and 92 are arts. 73, 86, and 87.

114. *See* TREATY OF AMSTERDAM, Protocol on the System of Public Service Broadcasting in the Member States, 1997 O.J. (C 340) 109.

115. Malcolm Ross, *Article 16 E.C. and Services of General Interest: From Derogation to Obligation?*, 25 EUR. L. REV. 22 (2000).

116. *See* Sauter, *supra* note 100, at 122-23, 133.

117. *See id.*

118. *Id.* at 142; *see also* Universal Service For Telecommunications in the Perspective of a Fully Liberalised Environment, COM(96)73.

119. *See* Directive 97/67/EC on Common Rules For the Development of the Internal Market of Community Postal Services and the Improvement of Quality of Service, 1998 O.J. (L 15) 14.

were indeed introduced into the United Kingdom as a result of E.C. obligations before the implementation of fuller postal reforms.

The relationship between the open-ended legal concept of public service and the more limited concept of universal service as an exception to a presumption in favor of competitive markets remains the subject of considerable debate, especially in France. The more limited concept of universal service has prevailed in the European Union.[120] It is possible, however, that the practical differences between the two are relatively small. Moreover, particularly in the field of telecommunications, Continental concerns preserving the public service tradition have influenced the evolution of E.C. law. These concerns, in turn, have provided reasons for moderating, on social grounds, the free play of market competition in the operation of the U.K. utilities. Nor has the traffic been only one way, for there have been examples of the Anglo-Saxon model influencing countries with a strong public service tradition. Apart from the extensive adoption of independent regulatory commissions,[121] more specific examples include France's adoption of a Charter of Public Services in 1992 in an attempt to spell out the requirements of public service in greater detail. This charter is analogous to the U.K. practice of using service standards.[122] Italy also adopted a law on the delivery of public services in 1994, which sets out fundamental principles of public service based on the French model. Those principles, however, will be implemented by service standards similar to British practice.[123]

VII

CONCLUSION

What has occurred in the United Kingdom is thus a move toward the development of a body of legal doctrine closer to the concept of public service enshrined in other European legal systems. I do not wish to argue that this is a direct result of privatization itself. Rather, it has been due largely to the creation of regulators independent of government and enterprise, thus making some legal framework to structure relations inevitable.[124]

It is, of course, not impossible that such a regime could exist while retaining public ownership. Indeed, in the United Kingdom, postal services, and in Scotland, water and sewerage, are subject to independent regulation while remain-

120. *See, e.g.*, P. Barbet and A. Gonzalez, *La Notion de Service Universel dans les Télécommunications*, LXIII REVUE INTERNATIONALE DE DROIT ECONOMIQUE 59 (1999); John Bell, *The Concept of Public Service Under Threat? An Illustration from Energy Law*, 5 EUROPEAN PUB. L. 189 (1999).

121. *See* Giandomenico Majone, *The Rise of Statutory Regulation in Europe*, *in* REGULATING EUROPE 47 (Giandomenico Majone ed., 1996).

122. *See* M. Bechtel et al., *Chronique de l'Administration*, 62 REVUE FRANÇAISE D'ADMINISTRATION PUBLIQUE 335, 337 (1992).

123. *See* Direttiva del Presidente del Consiglio de Ministri, Jan. 27, 1994, Gazzetta Ufficiale della Repubblica Italiana, n. 43 (Feb. 22, 1994).

124. This is the major difference from New Zealand, where such regulatory arrangements were not established.

ing under public ownership.[125] Indeed, it may be that publicly owned enterprise is necessary to establish the infrastructure for universal service, though not necessarily for its operation.

The second major influence has come about through Britain's membership in the European Union. Again, while pressing for the opening of utility markets to competition (though not always requiring privatization), the European Union has fostered the separation of regulation from operation of the enterprise, thereby making a legal framework necessary. Continental public service concerns have infiltrated this liberalization, requiring clearer legal definitions of limitations on the operation of the free market undertaken on distributive grounds.

In the United Kingdom, the new public service law is not mainly administered by the courts, but by the regulatory bodies themselves. This has advantages such as the avoidance of damaging litigation while retaining the courts as adjudicators in cases of real difficulty. It is clear that we are now seeing the beginning of the replacement of ineffective political controls over public enterprise by legal principles that include elements of social solidarity and rights of access to essential services.[126] Privatization in the United Kingdom has given birth to some unexpected offspring.

125. The example of the Post Office is discussed in detail *supra* notes 74-85 and accompanying text; *see* DEPARTMENT OF TRADE AND INDUS., *supra* note 21. For the new arrangements for water and sewerage services in Scotland, see the Water Industry Act, 1999, §§ 12-13, sched. 2.

126. This argument is made at greater length in Tony Prosser, *Theorising Utility Regulation,* 62 MODERN L. REV. 196 (1999).

[7]

The Proper Scope of Government Viewed from an Ordoliberal Perspective: The Example of Competition Policy

by

WERNHARD MÖSCHEL

The paper focuses on competition policy, which is at the center of ordoliberal thinking. Important characteristics are the emphasis on individual freedom, from which the goal of economic efficiency is merely derived; the strong role for the state in the preservation of the prerequisites of competition, combined with a reserve towards intervention by government in market prices; the rule of law rather than discretionary decisions; and the embedding in the economic order of a free and open society. Other views (impossibility of competition, uselessness of competition law, selective intervention) are contrasted in order to explain these characteristics. (JEL: B 25, K 21, L 40, L 50)

1 Introduction

Ordoliberalism stands for a doctrine of economic policy, one might even say of social philosophy; this doctrine has been defined by economists and some jurists like Walter Eucken, Franz Böhm, Alfred Müller-Armack, Leonhard Miksch, Wilhelm Röpke, Alexander Rüstow, and others.[1] Its significance is based less on the novelty of the elements or the overall perspective than on its decisive influence on the unfolding of the social market economy after World War II in the Federal Republic of Germany. That influence was introduced into politics particularly by Ludwig Erhard. He was first the Director of Economic Administration in the unified American–British zone of occupation and later Minister for Economic Affairs during the first fourteen years of the Federal Republic of Germany. The influence of ordoliberalism still persists. It can be found also in the founding treaties of the European Community and thereby in an international legal system with characteristics similar to a constitution.

With regard to the proper scope of government, these ordoliberals have developed scarcely any analytical and deductive theory (see FISCHER [1993], NÖRR [1994, 139–158], and WILLGERODT [1998]). They have preferred rather an inductive approach. For that reason I shall focus on a concrete example, which is at the

[1] Surveys are given in BLUM [1969], WULFF [1976], and FIKENTSCHER [1983].

Journal of Institutional and Theoretical Economics
JITE 157 (2001), 3–13 © 2001 Mohr Siebeck – ISSN 0932-4569

center of ordoliberal thinking: competition policy. The proper scope of government, in that method, is designed more as result, as conclusion, than as an abstract premise.

Leaving aside some nuances and distinctions of detail, I would like to point out four elements: (a) competition policy primarily oriented to the goal of securing individual freedom of action, from which the goal of economic efficiency is merely derived; (b) a strong role for the state in the preservation of the prerequisites of the competitive system, but a distinct reserve towards intervention by government in free-market prices; (c) the shaping of competition policy into a rule of law rather than a mechanism of discretionary decisions; (d) the embedding of competition policy in the economic order of a free and open society, this order being also the framework for other parts of the legal system, such as company law, labour law, and workers' participation.

2 *Goal of Competition: Freedom or Efficiency*

The actual goal of the competition policy of ordoliberalism lies in the protection of individual economic freedom of action as a value in itself, through the restraint of undue economic power. Franz Böhm once illuminated this idea by the aphoristic formula, "the one who has power has no right to be free and the one who wants to be free should have no power" (BÖHM [1955, 4217] and MESTMÄCKER [1980]). Economic efficiency as a generic term for growth, for the encouragement and development of technical progress, and for allocative efficiency is but an indirect and derived goal. It results generally from the realisation of individual freedom of action in a market system (nondilemma thesis). This has to be emphasised, because of some misunderstanding. The scholars of ordoliberalism have also used economic models for the description of their ideas, for instance, the model of perfect competition as it was developed in the traditional theory of competition.[2] Such models, however, served only for the description of general effects of a market system, illustrating them in what might be called a chemically pure form. That did not imply, however, that those partly unreal premises were to be integrated as goals into practical competition policy. Any attempts to disprove or ridicule the ordoliberal concepts of competition as unrealistic miss this point.

It might be helpful at this point to consider some of the other views on market behaviour and how they differ from the ordoliberal concepts of competition. These other views fall into three categories: (i) the impossibility of competition, (ii) the uselessness of competition law, and (iii) selective intervention in competition (MÖSCHEL [1977], [1983, 50–53]).

---

[2] Walter Eucken's term "complete competition" is not synonymous with perfect or pure competition. What counts for him is the absence of coercive power (see SCHMIDTCHEN [1984, 60], LENEL [1975, 62f. and 71–75], and WILLGERODT [1975]).

2.1 *Impossibility of Competition*

There have been three main developments in economic theory that spell out the difficulties of achieving a perfectly competitive market. First, there is the concept of monopolistic or imperfect competition developed by Edward Chamberlin and Joan Robinson, which reached the peak of its popularity in the 1930s. From this market model, the general necessity of government intervention is deduced. Arthur BURNS [1936], for example, spoke of the decline of competition and gave this title to his famous book. Second, there is John K. Galbraith's doctrine of the technological and innovative superiority of modern industrial structures (GALBRAITH [1974]). In his view this superiority is realised by large-scale industrial enterprise that is not subject to the restraint of competition. This economic power, being a necessary result of the system, is supposed to be controlled by the formation of a countervailing market power through, if necessary, direct parliamentary intervention. Finally, there is the Marxist theory of the inevitable development of competitive capitalism into monopoly capitalism, to which politics, the state, and the legal system are in any event subject.

The competition policy of ordoliberalism rejects such approaches as ultimately faulty in analysis and rashly passive in policy.

2.2 *Uselessness of Competition Law*

The doctrine is related to laissez-faire concepts. Most influential here are the several strands of thought of the so-called Chicago school,[3] which emphasise the eroding and self-healing powers of competition itself. First of all, this doctrine attacks the governmental restraints of trade that escape the direct influence of the competitive process because of their mandatory character. The basic premise of such an approach is the long-term perspective. It does not, unlike the Marxist approach, deny in the last analysis the feasibility of a rule of law, but rather the idea of law as an attempt to correct reality.

This differs from the ordoliberal point of view in its fundamental values. Ordoliberal policy does not rely exclusively on the long-term process of self-healing of the overall society, but protects the individual's economic freedom of action as a value in itself against any impairment of excessive economic power. Eberhard Günther, the first president of the German Federal Cartel Authority, put his criticism of the laissez-faire doctrine in the following way (GÜNTHER [1968, 38]):

> "The hope of the dependent and weak, of all people who have experienced for themselves the potential of economic power, would be gone, as well as the demand for legal protection of a humane economic order which checks that power and the arrogance of the powerful. This demand would be ridiculed [under laissez-faire] as a charade or plain absurdity, as an economic order with an idealistic halo, or as the tying of prosaic economic processes to eternal values."

---

[3] See BORK [1978], POSNER [1979], and a critical survey in FOX [1981].

A little more briefly, Walter ADAMS [1976, 13] expressed the same idea: "The freedom of the sheep to coexist with the wolf is meaningless in the absence of a shepherd."

The central objection from the laissez-faire side, that any antitrust law ultimately does more harm than good, is rejected from an ordoliberal point of view as not proven. There remains the question of how to frame any particular law. The problem is not *a priori* insoluble.

2.3 Doctrines of Selective Intervention

The ordoliberal view of competition also differs from the widespread doctrines of selective intervention (MÖSCHEL [1984]). One of these admits of exceptions to the competitive order for the achievement of previously defined, supraindividual goals. Usually, these are determined by a governmental authority. As examples, one may take the goal of: (a) equilibrium in foreign trade (export cartels); (b) structural policy (agreed production restraints in structural crises, orderly marketing); (c) full-employment policy (permission for mergers to preserve jobs); (d) currency policy (interest-rate cartels); and so forth. These policies do not envisage competition as a process of economic coordination on the basis of freedom of action. Rather, such policies represent a kind of governmental management technique for the achievement of concrete goals. This differs clearly from the ordoliberal concept of competition.

The problem is somewhat different if competition is encouraged in order to achieve the results that free competition is expected to produce. Such a test of performance could still be considered as an inverse analysis of causality. The ordoliberal competition policy deems that to be irreconcilable with a legal and economic system based on the freedom of contract and competition. The reason for this lies in a contradiction: freedom is eliminated if the content of decisions is determined in advance. Friedrich August von Hayek's famous formula of competition as an exploratory process represents the same viewpoint. Therefore, criteria of competition policy that attribute a normative significance to the prerequisites of free competition, in the sense of sufficient freedom of action, are preferable to those that deem the performance to be more essential (MESTMÄCKER [1963]). Additionally, the limitations inherent in the application of law have to be observed, if competition policy is to be submitted to a standard within the rule of law.

3 Philosophical Basis of the Ordoliberal Competition Concept

The actual basis of ordoliberal competition is deduced, in the author's opinion, from an appreciation of law and justice based on contract ("equity" as used by economists). This is contrary to the various concepts of utilitarianism.

In this respect, the ordoliberal competition policy is obviously related to the intellectual tradition of idealist German philosophy, particularly that of Immanuel

Kant, which had been strongly influenced by classical English moral philosophy (DWORKIN [1980a], [1980b]). Modern currents in American antitrust law that lean directly upon wealth maximisation (as in Richard Posner's constrained utilitarianism or Oliver Williamson's trade-off and transaction-cost approach, as well as property-rights doctrines as far as these can be traced to the Kaldor-Hicks criterion),[4] are obviously incompatible with the ordoliberal system of values. Ordoliberalism treats individuals as ends in themselves and not as the means of another's welfare. Soulless economic determinism – this strange reproach has been levelled in the name of Catholic social doctrine (VON NELL-BREUNING [1975, 465]) – is far removed from this concept of value, which is to be found, as the title of Wilhelm RÖPKE's [1958] book indicates, beyond supply and demand. Such a competition policy focuses on the legitimisation of economic freedom in order to prevent this freedom from destroying its own prerequisites. A law against restraints of competition, from this point of view, effects limits that are inherent in private law and can be considered, under a systematic analysis, as a continuation of private law by other means. Such a private-law system, however, is not devoid of purpose and substance (contrary to a few legal traditions), nor is it a mere social technique; it is part of a normative order that is based on the equality of rights and on personal liberty. It is obvious that this is also related to a specific view of the role the state has to play. Franz Böhm created for this idea the term "*Privatrechtsgesellschaft*" (private-law society).[5]

4 *Role of the State*

The preceding discussion has already made the point that the ordoliberal approach to competition policy is connected with a specific understanding of the role of the state. Within the ordoliberal school, Franz BÖHM [1950] and his pupil Ernst-Joachim MESTMÄCKER [1973] examined this question most thoroughly. It goes beyond the superficial observation that ordoliberal competition policy calls for a strong state (unlike the laissez-faire approaches) and that the state is to guarantee that all parties obey the rules of the game. In a legal sense, that means merely a partial order; in a political sense, it means an exception to general economic policy. Behind this is a well-developed theory of *economic constitutionality.* The meaning of this term, which was coined by Franz Böhm and which many misunderstand, is not directed at whether a concrete, historical constitution, for example, the constitution of the Federal Republic of Germany, safeguards a particular economic system constitutionally and accordingly hinders the ordinary legislator from intervening – an economic constitution in a formal sense. It is concerned, rather, with whether structural parallels exist between the political constitution, on

[4] See the critical survey in MÖSCHEL [1984].

[5] BÖHM [1966], formalised in the context of value and price by GRASS AND STÜTZEL [1983, 343–350].

the one hand, and free trade, on the other. These parallels should be seen as legal problems requiring solution. The common point should be regarded as being the problem of power. Just as it is the first task of a political constitution to tie governmental power to the law, so it is the first task of an economic constitution to solve the problem of private economic power. What matters is that legal principles, as they have been developed in constitutional law with respect to the exercise of governmental power, must now be developed with respect to the acquisition and exercise of private economic power in a manner that remains consistent with the economic system (MESTMÄCKER [1975, 414]):

> "Holders of economic power jeopardize the economic legitimization of free trade if they make use of the competence of individual planning in order to eliminate the price system; they destroy the basis of private autonomy if they replace freely negotiated contracts with a unilateral act of will; they tamper with the freedom of trade if they coerce by means of open impairment, or drive out of the market, consumers, employees, or suppliers who do not give in to the predefined market strategy; finally, they jeopardize political liberties and the independence of the government since economic power has a tendency to be converted into political power."

The ordoliberal response to this problem is not to increase the power of the state, which would be capable of misunderstanding the economic liberties of its citizens as merely a category of waiver, as something prelegal or pregovernmental. Nor would the ordoliberals treat the problem as within the competence of society, the strongest groups of which might succeed in defining their specific interests as the common good and promoting them through the government. The point is rather to protect the liberty of action of the individual as well as of the government. Thus, the proposed response suggests a substantive separation of powers in the state's relations with society and within society itself. This is accomplished according to the principle of functional differentiation (MESTMÄCKER [1973, 191]). The law is its most important device.

From this point of view a competition policy that is framed in rules of law appears to be, first, a distribution of competence between society and the state, and second, at the same time a method of solving conflicts that might arise between citizens in using their individual liberties of action. Competition law is comparable with conflict between laws in that competition law also embodies rules that apply when laws are used by private decision-makers. As far as action by government is concerned, countermeasures by enterprises can most easily be resisted by an effective regulation of competition. Take, for example, macroeconomic measures by government (say, acting through a central bank) to combat inflation: the more enterprises groan under the yoke of competition, the less they can evade such measures (MÖSCHEL [1983, 2 and 8f.]). Conversely, government policy that gives priority to the way in which transactions between individuals are governed complies with the logic of an economic system. The countless individual, market-integrated plans are only subject to the wishes of the individuals concerned. Government policy should protect the process of reaching an individual decision rather than alter the results (MESTMÄCKER [1975, 416], MÖSCHEL [1977, 348], [1983, 53f.]). The scepticism towards performance criteria is confirmed once more in the shaping of antitrust law.

5 Rule of Law versus Discretionary Decisions

The preceding discussion can be related to a further characteristic of ordoliberal competition policy, namely that it relies on a rule of law which, in contrast to political ad hoc decisions, has continuity. This derives from the historical experience that protection of competition is impeded if it is determined by political decisions; merger control in France or Great Britain is an example of this. This view has been generally accepted within the Law Against Restraints of Competition (MÖSCHEL [1983, 183–186 and 576–582]).

More important is a second dimension, which clearly distinguishes ordoliberal competition policy from the views, for instance, of Friedrich August von Hayek. He considered the extent of arbitrariness in regulation and intervention to be far too great and was very sceptical of the practice of American antitrust law. He did not believe, however, that his idea of the rule of law as an abstract general framework for exploratory processes that arise out of free interactions could be realised in competition policy (HAYEK [1971, 336ff.]). He therefore largely abandoned rules in the area of competition. Ordoliberal competition policy is aware of the same problem, but does not give up.[6] It is realised that certain behaviour can stifle competition. The economist Corwin D. EDWARDS [1949, 8] expressed it this way:

> "Although the maintenance of competition will not guarantee that the economy will work well, impairment of competition by monopolistic restrictions, public or private, increases the chance that it will work badly."

In this context, there may be only second-best solutions. Ordoliberal competition policy trustingly considers the application of the law to be a process of exploration in itself. It might succeed in putting general legislative clauses into concrete terms in the long run. It is undisputed that a system of control by law has its price (MÖSCHEL [1977, 49f.]). From the universe of all pertinent economic factors, rules of law can only isolate such factors as can be judged in an abstract or general way and can be established in a particular case. They are necessarily rough rules of thumb. Effects that cannot be foreseen by those to whom the rule is addressed cannot be appropriate for rules of conduct. What is amenable to the proceedings of cartel agencies and especially of courts has to be taken into account. "A complete survey of our economic organization and a choice between rival philosophies"[7] is

---

[6] On the example of predatory pricing see MÖSCHEL [1979] and MESTMÄCKER [1984, 159–230].

[7] The Supreme Court of the United States established a *per se* rule against price cartels. See United States *v.* Trenton Potteries, 273 US 392, 397/98 (1927), United States *v.* Topco Associates, Inc. 405 US 596, 611 (1972).

certainly not required. Thus arises the particular academic task related to competition policy, which is to put academic insights and suggestions into such formulas as can be cast into binding law.

6 Competition Policy and the General Economic System

The last characteristic of ordoliberal competition policy is its belief that competition policy is not isolated but rather part of the framework of a general economic system. This point is best made clear by the distinction between formative and regulative principles, as formulated by Walter Eucken for his "Policy for a Competition Order" (EUCKEN [1968, 254–304]). They are introduced now by way of example. I do not want to discuss them in regard to content – only the way of thinking, the methodological approach, is to be clarified. He regards the following principles as formative: (*a*) *Primacy of monetary policy:* The currency should be kept stable and isolated from political influence. Eucken, therefore, preferred a commodity reserve currency rather similar to the Graham Plan of 1937. (*b*) *Open market:* Market access should be freed from governmental restrictions of all kinds – access restrictions, patent systems, protective duties – as well as private restrictions. The last-named come within competition law. (*c*) *Private property:* This is a condition of a competition order, in the sense both of a liberal and of an economically efficient order of conduct. It links the capacity to take decisions and responsibility. On the other hand, competition is considered to be a condition for preventing private property in producer goods from creating "feudal" spheres of influence. (*d*) *Freedom of contract:* This guarantees freedom of competition. It is not treated in a formal sense, however, but rather in a material one, which relates to the prerequisite of its functioning. Contracts that restrain trade do not realise but abuse freedom of contract and constitute endogenous perversions. (*e*) *Synchronisation of control and liability:* Eucken considered this to be both a postulate of equity and a prerequisite for the functioning of an efficient competitive system. He referred to the problem of controlled enterprises, the problem of limited companies, and the problem of limitation of liability in standard contracts. On the question of public companies that are controlled *de facto* by the management, he logically insisted on stringent personal responsibility of the management. (*f*) *Constancy of economic policy:* Continuity of governmental action is one of the most important prerequisites to enable the individual to take an economic decision, such as whether to invest, so that he can be held responsible for his decision.

To these principles, Eucken added four further ones, which he called *regulative principles.* Under the heading of the "monopoly problem," he discussed chiefly cases which could be called "natural monopolies." He favoured a special form of control, which he thought should be administered by an independent agency (the monopoly agency) and which would be orientated towards criteria analogous to competition. The second principle he called "incomes policy." In contrast to, for example, von Hayek, he approved of income redistribution by means of progressive taxation. Under the heading "economic calculation," he discussed the internalisation of external costs, including, *inter alia,* environmental protection. Finally, he investigated the anomalous reaction in the labour market, which had already been described by the mercantilists. He did not consider this to be a real problem in a functioning competitive order, but as a necessary evil to be ascribed to the fixing of minimum wages.[8]

More important than this not very systematic or well-balanced list of principles is the method of approach. It offers a theoretical reference system from which criteria can be deduced for judging numerous economically important problems under the heading of conformity, neutrality, or impairment. An academic discussion of the system's prerequisites becomes feasible when points of view are put forward that are supposed to be justified only ideologically or can be decided on political grounds only. The discussion of worker participation may be one example. Franz BÖHM ([1951], [1967], and [1971]) made the most important contribution from an ordoliberal point of view in this area. EUCKEN [1968, 320] put it briefly:

> "If the individual firm's business planning is impaired by worker participation, then the functioning of the order as a whole is jeopardized."

This reference to the system as a whole is the decisive point.

Theorists of ordoliberal thinking were in many cases practical, experienced, and reliable men. The image of idealistic dreamers does not fit them; they were, rather, strict realists. In the narrow field of competition policy they wrote an altogether successful chapter – at least in a historical and comparative perspective. Their innermost intention probably was what is engraved on the entrance to the American Supreme Court: Equal Justice Under Law. The ancient Greeks called this *isonomia* (HAYEK [1953] and BÖHM [1957, 174]). Demosthenes once said that *isonomia* is the loveliest word in the Greek language. As a gifted speaker, he probably knew what he was talking about.

References

ADAMS, W. [1976], "Antitrust, Laissez-Faire, and Economic Power," pp. 11–17 in: F. Neumark, K. C. Thalheim, and H. Hölzer (eds.), *Wettbewerb, Konzentration und wirtschaftliche Macht*, Festschrift für Helmut Arndt, Duncker & Humblot: Berlin.

BLUM, R. [1969], *Soziale Marktwirtschaft: Wirtschaftspolitik zwischen Neoliberalismus und Ordoliberalismus*, J. C. B. Mohr (Paul Siebeck): Tübingen.

BÖHM, F. [1950], "Die Idee des Ordo im Denken Walter Euckens," *Ordo*, 3, 15–64.

-- [1951], "Das wirtschaftliche Mitbestimmungsrecht der Arbeiter im Betrieb," *Ordo*, 4, 21–250, reprinted in: E.-J. Mestmäcker (ed.), 1980, *Freiheit und Ordnung in der Marktwirtschaft*, Nomos: Baden-Baden.

---

[8] EUCKEN [1968, 321ff.] accepted trade unions as a factor of order in the labour markets in so far as they respected limits set by the market forces.

-- [1955], *Stenographische Berichte des 2. Deutschen Bundestages*, 76. Sitzung Bonn, March 24, 1955, Hans Heger: Bonn.

-- [1957], "Die Forschungs- und Lehrgemeinschaft zwischen Juristen und Volkswirten an der Universität Freiburg in den dreißiger und vierziger Jahren des 20. Jahrhunderts (Das Recht der Ordnung der Wirtschaft)," pp. 95–113 in: H. J. Wolff (ed.), *Aus der Geschichte der Rechts- und Staatswissenschaften in Freiburg im Breisgau*, Eberhard-Albert-Verlag: Freiburg.

-- [1966], "Privatrechtsgesellschaft und Marktwirtschaft," *Ordo*, 17, 75–151, reprinted in: E.-J. Mestmäcker (ed.), 1980, *Freiheit und Ordnung in der Marktwirtschaft*, Nomos: Baden-Baden, pp. 105–168.

-- [1967], "Der Zusammenhang zwischen Eigentum, Arbeitskraft und dem Betreiben eines Unternehmens," pp. 11–45 in: K. H. Biedenkopf, H. Coing, and E.-J. Mestmäcker (eds.), *Das Unternehmen in der Rechtsordnung*, Festgabe für H. Kronstein aus Anlaß seines 70. Geburtstages am 12. September 1967, C. F. Müller: Karlsruhe.

-- [1971], "Mitbestimmung als Gleichberechtigung von Kapital und Arbeit oder als Vertragsanspruch der Arbeitnehmer aus dem Arbeitsverhältnis," pp. 543–565 in: F. Böhm and G. Briefs (eds.), *Mitbestimmung – Ordnungselement oder politischer Kompromiß*, Seewald: Stuttgart.

BORK, R. H. [1978], *The Antitrust Paradox: A Policy at War with Itself*, Basic Books: New York.

BURNS, A. R. [1936], *The Decline of Competition*, McGraw–Hill: New York.

DWORKIN, R. M. [1980a], "Is Wealth a Value?" *Journal of Legal Studies*, 9, 191–226.

-- [1980b], "Why Efficiency?" *Hofstra Law Review*, 8, 563–590.

EDWARDS, C. D. [1949], *Maintaining Competition*, McGraw–Hill: New York, Toronto, London.

EUCKEN, W. [1968], *Grundsätze der Wirtschaftspolitik*, 4. Auflage, J. C. B. Mohr (Paul Siebeck): Tübingen.

FIKENTSCHER, W. [1983], *Wirtschaftsrecht*, Vol. II, C. H. Beck: München.

GRASS, R.-D., AND W. STÜTZEL [1983], *Volkswirtschaftslehre*, Vahlen: München.

FISCHER, T. [1993], *Staat, Recht und Verfassung im Denken von Walter Eucken: Zu den staats- und rechtstheoretischen Grundlagen einer wirtschaftsordnungspolitischen Konzeption*, P. Lang: Frankfurt.

FOX, E. M. [1981], "The Modernization of Antitrust: A New Equilibrium," *Cornell Law Review*, 66, 1140–1192.

GALBRAITH, J. K. [1974], *Wirtschaft für Staat und Gesellschaft*, Dromer–Knaur: München, Zürich.

GÜNTHER, E. [1968], "Zehn Jahre Gesetz gegen Wettbewerbsbeschränkungen: Rückblick und Ausblick," p. 35 in: Studienvereinigung Kartellrecht e.V. (eds.), *Zehn Jahre Gesetz gegen Wettbewerbsbeschränkungen*, III. Forum Bonn, Carl Heymanns Verlag: Köln–Berlin–Bonn–München.

HAYEK, F. A. von [1953], "Entstehung und Verfall des Rechtsstaatsideals," pp. 33–65 in: A. Hunold (ed.), *Wirtschaft ohne Wunder*, Eugen Rentsch: Zürich.

-- [1971], *Die Verfassung der Freiheit*, J. C. B. Mohr (Paul Siebeck): Tübingen.

LENEL, H. O. [1975], "Walter Euckens ordnungspolitische Konzeption, die wirtschaftspolitische Lehre in der Bundesrepublik und die Wettbewerbstheorie heute," *Ordo*, 26, 22–78.

MESTMÄCKER, E. J. [1963], "Probleme des Bestmöglichen in der Wirtschaftspolitik," pp. 656–661 in: E. von Beckerath and H. Giersch (eds.), *Probleme der normativen Ökonomik und der wirtschaftspolitischen Beratung*, Schriften des Vereins für Socialpolitik, New Series, 29, Duncker & Humblot: Berlin, reprinted by E. J. Mestmäcker, 1978, *Recht und ökonomisches Gesetz*, Nomos: Baden-Baden.

-- [1973], "Macht–Recht–Wirtschaftsverfassung," pp. 183–200 in: H. K. Schneider and C. Watrin (eds.), *Macht und ökonomisches Gesetz*, Schriften des Vereins für Socialpolitik, Vol. 71/I, Duncker & Humblot: Berlin.

-- [1975], "Wirtschaftsordnung und Staatsverfassung," pp. 383–419 in: H. Sauermann und E. J. Mestmäcker (eds.), *Wirtschaftsordnung und Staatsverfassung: Festschrift für Franz Böhm zum 80. Geburtstag*, J. C. B. Mohr (Paul Siebeck): Tübingen.

-- [1980], "Competition Policy and Antitrust: Some Comparative Observations," *Zeitschrift für die gesamte Staatswissenschaft*, 136, 387–390.

-- [1984], *Der verwaltete Wettbewerb: Eine vergleichende Untersuchung über den Schutz von Freiheit und Lauterkeit im Wettbewerbsrecht*, J. C. B. Mohr (Paul Siebeck): Tübingen.

MÖSCHEL, W. [1977], *Wettbewerb im Schnittfeld von Rechtswissenschaft und Nationalökonomie, in Tradition und Fortschritt im Recht: Festschrift zum 500jährigen Bestehen der Tübinger Juristenfakultät*, J. C. B. Mohr (Paul Siebeck): Tübingen.

-- [1979], "Die Idee der rule of law und das Kartellrecht heute: Am Beispiel der gezielten Kampfpreisunterbietung," *Ordo*, 30, 298–311.

-- [1983], *Recht der Wettbewerbsbeschränkungen*, Carl Heymanns Verlag: Köln–Berlin–Bonn–München.

-- [1984], "Antitrust and Economic Analysis of Law," *Zeitschrift für die gesamte Staatswissenschaft*, 140, 158–161.

NÖRR, K. W. [1994], *Die Leiden des Privatrechts*, J. C. B. Mohr (Paul Siebeck): Tübingen.

POSNER, R. A. [1979], "The Chicago School of Antitrust Analysis," *University of Pennsylvania Review*, 127, 925–948.

RÖPKE, W. [1958], *Jenseits von Angebot und Nachfrage*, Eugen Rentsch: Zürich-Stuttgart.

SCHMIDTCHEN, D. [1984], "German 'Ordnungspolitik' as Institutional Choice," *Zeitschrift für die gesamte Staatswissenschaft*, 140, 22–78.

VON NELL-BREUNING, O. [1975], "Können Neoliberalismus und katholische Soziallehre sich verständigen?" pp. 459–470 in: H. Sauermann and E.-J. Mestmäcker (eds.), *Wirtschaftsordnung und Staatsverfassung: Festschrift für Franz Böhm zum 80. Geburtstag*, J. C. B. Mohr (Paul Siebeck): Tübingen.

WILLGERODT, H. [1975], "Fehlurteile über vielzahligen Wettbewerb," *Ordo*, 26, 97–130.

-- [1998], "Die Liberalen und ihr Staat – Gesellschaftspolitik zwischen Laissez-faire und Diktatur," *Ordo*, 49, 43–78.

WULFF, M. [1976], *Die neoliberale Wirtschaftsordnung: Versuch einer dynamischen Analyse der Konzeption und der Realität*, J. C. B. Mohr (Paul Siebeck), Tübingen.

Wernhard Möschel
Lehrstuhl für Bürgerliches Recht,
Handels- und Wirtschaftsrecht
Universität Tübingen
Wilhelmstr. 7
72074 Tübingen
Germany
E-mail: wernhard.moeschel@uni-tuebingen.de

Part III
Regulatory Rules

[8]

"Which Arrow?": Rule Type and Regulatory Policy

J. M. Black

Lecturer in Law, London School of Economics[1]

The decisions involved in rule making have been described by one regulator as finding answers to the question: "which arrow is to be taken from the quiver?"[2]. What type of rule, in other words, should be adopted? The issue of rule type is not one which appears on its face to be a matter which should be of great concern in the formation of rules. *What* the rule should say is clearly a policy decision; *how* it should say it does not immediately appear to be significant. However, as the quote indicates, the choice of rule *type* may be a particular regulatory policy in itself. It raises three main questions: what different types of rules may be used; what targets are being aimed at; and is the process as strategic as the quote suggests? This article seeks to address these questions through an analysis of rule making by financial services regulators. Its concern is to understand the nature of the rule making process and the reasons rule makers adopt different types of rules.

Rule making has not been a central focus of attention for those concerned with the operation of regulatory agencies or bureaucracies. The rise and rise of delegated legislation has been documented,[3] and concerns about the control of the process and the legal status of the rules raised,[4] but there have been few extensive studies of the way in which agencies exercise their rule making powers once delegated to them. The focus of those studies which have been done has generally been on overall policy

[1] I would like to thank Dr Rob Baldwin, Professor Denis Galligan, Dr Doreen McBarnet and Dr Chris McCrudden for comments on earlier drafts of this article. Responsibility for the views and errors contained remains my own.

[2] A. M. Whittaker, "Legal Technique in City Regulation" (1990) 43 C.L.P. 35, p.48. (Mr Whittaker is an officer at SIB).

[3] See, for example, G. Ganz, *Quasi-Legislation* (1987).

[4] J. Beatson, "Legislative Control of Administrative Rule Making: Lessons from the British Experience" (1979) 12 *Cornell Int'l LJ* 199; M. Asimov, "Delegated Legislation in the US and UK" (1983) 3 OJLS 253; R. Baldwin and J. Houghton, "Circular Arguments: The Status and Legitimacy of Administrative Rules" [1986] P.L. 239.

formation and implementation,[5] although more recent studies have indicated that the choice of rule type may be of significance.[6]

Fundamental reasons for the choice of rule type are suggested by the work on rules and discretion. While again the focus of this work has not been rules or rule type, in highlighting the advantages and disadvantages of rules and discretion it illustrates why the choice of rule type matters. Further, the association of rules or standards with different forms of bureaucratic rationality, substantive and formal, suggests that in forming rules rule makers are constantly addressing the tensions which exist between them.

However, neither the empirical studies nor the theoretical debate provides a comprehensive framework in which rule making can be analysed. In order to begin to develop such a framework, the article argues for a dimensional analysis of rules which can be applied to any rule system. Rules should be seen not as monoliths, but as comprising separate facets or dimensions. This understanding of rules can then be used in the analysis of rule making decisions in order to illustrate and understand what different types of rules may be adopted and why. The article identifies three main objectives which financial services rule makers have aimed to achieve in adopting rules of particular types: a balance between flexibility and certainty; a change in the perceptions of the regulation held by the regulated and the wider community; and the exercise of control over the regulated and other regulators. The article shows that the process of rule making contains both strategic and non-strategic elements. While it exhibits some elements of rationality, it is not a wholly rational process. Moreover, even if the decision is to an extent strategic, constraints operate on it, arising both from the inherent nature and limitations of rules and from factors external to the rule: the political, legal and regulatory context. Finally, rules cannot be seen as discrete decisions. Rules are bargained over, and they are built.

The first part of the article thus proposes a dimensional analysis of rules which can be applied to any rule system. The second part discusses the few existing studies on rule making and points to a need to move beyond their concerns and approaches to begin to develop a theoretical framework for the analysis of rule making. This is developed and applied in the third part of the article in which the rule making process of financial services rule makers is analysed, focusing principally on the change from detailed rules to a three tiered rule system of Principles, Core Rules and Third Tier rules. Finally the article examines the stra-

[5] J. C. McCrudden, "Codes in a Cold Climate: Administrative Rule Making by the Commission for Racial Equality" (1988) 51 M.L.R. 409; R. Baldwin, "Health and Safety at Work: Consensus and Self Regulation" and I. Ramsay. "The Office of Fair Trading: Policing the Consumer Marketplace", both in R. Baldwin and J. C. McCrudden, *Regulation and Public Law*, (1987).

[6] R. Baldwin, "Why Rules Don't Work" (1990) 53 M.L.R. 321 and D. McBarnet and C. Whelan, "The Elusive Spirit of the Law: Formalism and the Struggle for Legal Control" (1991) 54 M.L.R. 848.

tegic and non-strategic aspects of the rule making process and the constraints which operate on it.

Types of rules

Rules are often seen as relatively precise formulations: "a legal precept attaching a definite legal consequence to a definite detailed state of fact".[7] As such they are contrasted with standards, which are seen as less precise, requiring some judgment in their application.[8] The definition of a rule that will be used here is one which is more general: "a general norm mandating or guiding conduct or action in a given type of situation".[9] Within this general category rules may vary in their type, but not simply in the manner which the usual rules/standards distinction suggests. A dimensional analysis which recognises the different aspects of rules illustrates more clearly the range of rule types which may exist. Rules have four dimensions, and may vary in each of these[10]: substance (what the rule says); character (whether it is permissive or mandatory: may or shall); status (its legal force and the sanction attaching to it) and structure. The last is the most complex, and has four aspects; the scope or inclusiveness of the rule; precision or vagueness (the degree to which behaviour under the rule is prescribed); simplicity or complexity (the degree to which the rule may be easily applied to concrete situations) and clarity or opacity (the degree to which the rule contains words with well-defined and universally accepted meanings).[11] Rule type is a function of only three of the dimensions: character, status/sanction and structure.

These dimensions are descriptive rather than normative. Further, with the exception of the clarity of the rule, they are objective. Clarity is subjective: it is dependent upon the readers' ability to understand what the rule requires. So a requirement of "reasonableness" may be clear in a particular community, as a consensus exists as to what conduct would be seen as reasonable. If no such consensus exists, then the rule is opa-

[7] R. Pound, *Jurisprudence* (1959) vol 1, p.124. For a similar definition see J. L. Jowell, *Law and Bureaucracy* (1975) p.135.

[8] See, for example, Jowell (1975), p.137, H. Hart and A. Sachs, *The Legal Process*, (1958) p.157 and D. Kennedy, "Form and Substance in Private Law Adjudication" (1976) 89 *Harvard LR* 1685.

[9] W. Twining and D. Meirs, *How to do things with Rules* (1991), p.131.

[10] For other dimensional approaches to rules see C. S. Diver, "The Optimal Precision of Administrative Rules" (1983) 93 *Yale LJ* 65, who identifies three: transparency, accessibility and congruence. (The first two are embodied here in the dimension of structure, the last is a normative assessment: how far does the rule achieve its objectives); and R. Baldwin, (1990), *op. cit.* who identifies five: specificity, inclusiveness, accessibility (embodied here in the dimension of structure), status and force, and prescription or sanction.

[11] For a fuller discussion of these dimensions, see J. M. Black, "Regulators as Rule Makers: The Formation of the Conduct of Business Rules under the Financial Services Act 1986", unpublished D. Phil thesis, Oxford University, 1994 and *Regulators as Rule Makers* (forthcoming).

que.[12] The interrelationship of these dimensions is complex. As will be seen below, the rule's substance may affect its structure, as may its status or the sanction attaching to it. A rule may be precise and simple: *e.g.* "Send information within fourteen days", but the greater the degree of precision the greater the likelihood that the rule will become more complex: *e.g.* "send information on costs and expenses, surrender values, projected returns and cancellation provisions within fourteen days". This will increase further if "costs and expenses" are separately defined and prescribed. Rules may be precise, complex and clear: clarity is a function of the manner in which the individual requirements are defined. So, for example, a rule which states that licences may be granted to persons fulfilling a list of conditions is complex, and it is clear if those conditions are well understood. However if they are not,—being defined in terms of reasonableness, for example, or requiring a person to be "fit and proper"—, then the rule is both complex and opaque. Similarly, the status of the rule or sanction attaching to it may vary: precise, complex rules may be of the status of guidance or they may have legal force. Breach of that rule may lead to disciplinary action, or to a civil action or prosecution.

Rule making by regulators

Rule making is an aspect of policy making and rules have been described as the " 'skin' of a living policy".[13] The choice of rule type, this would suggest, is part of a regulatory policy. But why would rule makers pay attention to the type of rule which they formulate? What difference does it make if a rule provides that "sufficient information must be given" rather than: "the following information must be given", followed by a long list of precise requirements? Why does it matter whether the rule is only a guidance, or the sanction is disciplinary (*i.e.* imposed by the regulator with no court involvement)?

Why rule makers make the rules they do has not been the subject of extensive research. There has been considerable development in the last decade or so in studies on the use of discretion,[14] the enforcement of rules,[15] and the reactions of the regulated to particular types of rules, or "creative compliance".[16] This work looks essentially at *responses* to

[12] See further L. L. Fuller, *The Morality of Law* (1969), p.64 and drawn on by Jowell (1975), p.167.

[13] C. S. Diver, "Regulatory Precision", in K. Hawkins and J. A. Thomas, *Making Regulatory Policy* (1989), p.199.

[14] See particularly K. Hawkins, *Environment and Enforcement* (1984), "Discretion in Making Legal Decisions" (1986) 43 *Washington and Lee LR* 1161, and K. Hawkins (ed), *The Use of Discretion* (1992); D. J. Galligan, *Discretionary Powers* (1986) and R. Baldwin and K. Hawkins, "Discretionary Justice, Davis Reconsidered" [1984] P.L. 570.

[15] See K. Hawkins (1984), G. M. Richardson *et al.*, *Policing Pollution: A Study of Regulation and Enforcement* (1983) and B. Hutter, *The Reasonable Arm of the Law* (1988).

[16] The use and manipulation by the regulated of specific rules to circumvent or undermine the purpose of regulation using an emphasis on legal form and literalism: see McBarnet and Whelan (1991).

rules. It is concerned with the reactions of different actors to rules: officials within organisations charged with the implementation or enforcement of a particular policy, or those actors outside the organisation whose behaviour the rules are meant to regulate. Rules are considered, but incidentally. The existence of the rule is taken as given. The interest and focus of this work is on what happens next: how is that rule applied; to what extent does it constrain the exercise of discretion; to what extent is its implementation or application affected by other considerations, and what form do those considerations take? The work on discretion and enforcement, particularly, questions the assumptions which are made in the rules/discretion debate, criticising the monolithic conceptions of discretion which are employed, the decision making processes which it assumes, and the assumption that the debate makes about the effectiveness of rules in confining discretion. It is not concerned with why the rule provides what it does, adopts a particular structure or has a certain sanction attaching to it.

One of the implications of the relatively limited focus on rules is that despite the advances in the understanding of the nature and use of discretion, there has been little advance in understanding why regulatory agencies make the rules that they do.[17] There are two exceptions. The first is the work by law and economics writers which is concerned with the "optimal precision" of rules.[18] "Optimality" is assessed according to an efficiency criterion in which four categories of costs and benefits are weighed: the rate of compliance, the over and under-inclusiveness of the rule, the costs of rule making and the costs of applying the rule.[19] Rules which are precise are seen as more costly to draft, but less costly to enforce. They are also seen as providing greater predictability, and so encouraging compliance, by increasing the probabilities as perceived by the person subject to the rule that non-compliance is punishable, and compliance is not. These assumptions lead to certain specific recommendations of optimal rule type. Diver, for example, argues that where the rule is directed at an audience which is large, diverse and remote, or where incentives for non-compliance are otherwise high,—for example

[17] Even in the U.S. where rule making by regulatory agencies has long been a focus of attention, this question has not been addressed. Rules have either been posited in opposition to adjudication or discretion in a debate on the relative merits of each or as to the models of justice or administration which they assume. Alternatively, the problems of rule making have been discussed in the particular context of U.S. statutory, judicial and executive constraints, which are prompting concerns at an "ossification" of the process. On the need for less formal methods of rule making, see M. Asimov, "Nonlegislative Rulemaking and Regulatory Reform" (1985) 34 *Duke LJ* 381, C. H. Koch and B. Martin, "FTC Rulemaking through Negotiation" (1983) 61 *N Carolina L.R.* 275. For recent discussions of the issues see "Symposium on Rulemaking" (1992) 41 *Duke L.J.*

[18] I. Ehrlich and R. Posner, "An Economic Analysis of Legal Rulemaking" (1974) 3 J.L.S. 257; R. A. Posner, *An Economic Analysis of Law* (1986), ch. 20; C. S. Diver (1983) and (1989), J. S. Johnston, "Uncertainty, Chaos and the Torts Process: An Economic Analysis of Legal Form" (1991) 76 *Cornell L.R.* 341, and in the use of rules in the context of private ordering of transactions, see W. H. Hirsch, "Reducing Law's Uncertainty and Complexity" (1974) U.C.L.A. L.R. 1233.

[19] Diver (1983), pp.73–4.

where compliance with the rule requires a person to forgo considerable benefits, or where non-compliance is difficult to detect,—then more detailed rules should be used.[20]

The second exception is the few studies which have been done on rule formation, which have been concerned to examine empirically the formation of rules and have not sought to apply the law and economics writers' predictions or suggestions. Nor have they all been concerned with the issue of rule type. They indicate the impact the structure of the rule making process has on rule formation as a whole,[21] and the extent to which the perceived legitimacy of the rules or the issuing body affects the content of the rule.[22] They do also indicate, however, that the question of what type of rule to use can be a significant issue of regulatory policy.[23] Normative assessments have been made as to the nature of rules that should be produced. Rules have been criticised on the basis that they are insufficiently precise, and so do not aid enforcement.[24] Baldwin, for example, argues that rule makers should adopt a compliance-oriented approach to rule making, taking into account the enforcement strategies which will have to be used to achieve compliance.[25] In the area of health and safety Baldwin found that on the whole enforcers prefer more specific rules.[26] However, rule makers prefer across the board regulation in the interests of uniformity and consistency. The fact that rule makers have adopted the rule types they have is attributed by Baldwin to their different preferences, and failures in the rule making process arising from organisational and political constraints and the nature of the process itself. However, while precise rules may aid enforcers,[27] work in the area of tax and accountancy indicates that they have other drawbacks.[28] It further shows that regulators do pay considerable attention to compliance, if not to enforcement, when forming rules, but that the rules which they perceive to be necessary are not those which in fact Diver would recommend. McBarnet and Whelan look at the dynamic interplay between regulated and regulator in the formation of rules. The regulated adopt a strategy which they term "creative compliance": the use and manipulation of rules as a combi-

[20] Diver (1989), pp.233–5.

[21] McCrudden (1988); Baldwin (1990).

[22] McCrudden (1988).

[23] Baldwin (1987), McBarnet and Whelan (1991).

[24] Baldwin (1990); Hawkins and Thomas also argue that vague and imprecise rules impede the enforcement process, failing to recognise the limited ability of both officials and the regulated to cope with uncertainty: K. Hawkins and J. Thomas, "Rule Making and Discretion: Implications for Designing Regulatory Policy" in K. Hawkins and J. M. Thomas (eds), *Making Regulatory Policy* (1989).

[25] Baldwin (1990).

[26] Whilst most enforcement strategies operated independently of the rules, enforcers did indicate that preferences for rule type varied with the enforcement strategy adopted, the type of employer and the nature of the risk: Baldwin (1990).

[27] Although enforcement officials studied by Hutter were more equivocal as to their preferred type of rule, Hutter (1988).

[28] McBarnet and Whelan (1991).

nation of specific rules and an emphasis on legal form and literalism to circumvent or undermine the purpose of regulation.[29] The regulatory response has been to reinstate control by adoption of anti-formalistic approaches which are more flexible, open-textured and policy-orientated. This includes an emphasis on purpose, avoiding use of statute and courts, using professions to formulate guidance and regulation of standards of practice, reflecting the substance of transactions and relationships and implementing spirit rather than letter of the rule.[30] The strategy is undermined by the regulated's continual demand for certainty, which leads to the formation of regulatory guidance and precedents, and so to the re-introduction of formalism. They thus posit cycles of formalism in which detailed rules are replaced by purposive ones, which in turn are replaced by detailed requirements, facilitating creative compliance behaviour.

Formalism and anti-formalism; rules and discretion: finding the "right balance"
These theoretical and empirical studies indicate that the choice of rule type matters, either because it can affect enforcement, or because it affects the compliance behaviour of the regulated. However, if we are to understand why rule makers choose to make different types of rules we need to understand at a more fundamental level the nature of the consequences arising from that choice. We can then begin to develop a framework for understanding the rule making decision, seeing whether rule makers pay attention to these consequences, and why.

The debates concerning the nature of rules and discretion and the types of rationalities which are exhibited by administrators at any particular time are instructive as they indicate some of the reasons why the adoption of different types of rules is significant. The pattern identified by McBarnet and Whelan of cycles of formalism echoes the writings of sociological theorists concerned with identifying and explaining the changes in the form that law has taken in society.[31] The use of purpose orientated rules or precise detailed stipulations is associated, drawing on Weber, with different forms of rationality.[32] Formal rationality, or decision according to the literal letter of the rule, is contrasted with substantive rationality, where decisions are made according to the substantive goals of the policy. However, as Galligan notes, a tension exists between the two forms,[33] and "Weber's ideal types serve as focal points around which those [decision making] strategies are centred, with each exerting a pull and influence on that process, so that in practice decision making is likely to be a complex mixture of the two."[34]

One of the implications of this tension is that one of the central issues

[29] *ibid.*, p.849.
[30] *ibid.*, p.851 and p.854.
[31] See, for example, R. Pound, *Introduction to the Philosophy of Law* (1954), P. S. Atiyah, *From Principles to Pragmatism* (1978).
[32] M. Weber, *Economy and Society*, G. Roch and C. Wittich (eds) (1968).
[33] Galligan (1986), pp.68–72.
[34] *ibid.*, p.71. See also R. Cotterrell, *The Sociology of Law: An Introduction* (1984), p.319.

in the exercise of discretion is to discover configurations of these rationalities which are the most suitable to achieve certain goals, whilst respecting other values.[35] The resolution of the competing demands of certainty and flexibility, uniformity and individualisation, is seen to be the combination of different types of rules (or in the language of this literature, rules and standards) to achieve the "right balance" of discretion at any one time.[36]

The issue of the "right balance" arises from the perceived advantages and disadvantages of rules and discretion, in which the advantages of one tend to be the disadvantages of the other.[37] The issue has been seen as one best assessed in the context of individualised decision making.[38] However, rule makers may try to achieve that balance through the use of rule type. In choosing the type of rule to use, or arrow to fire, the rule maker may thus be trying to resolve the tensions between rules and discretion, or formal and substantive rationality. The dimensional analysis of rules posited above is particularly valuable in illustrating how this may be achieved. In the rules/discretion debate a simplistic model of rules tends to be used, in which rules are contrasted with standards, but beyond an intimation that one is more precise than the other, no further analysis is done. The dimensional analysis of rules set out above indicates that "formalism", or rigidity within a system of rules, may be a function of a number of the dimensions: the legal status of the rule, its structure and its character. A detailed rule is given "flexibility" if it is purely recommendatory, or its breach leads to only a discretionary sanction. Moreover, rules which are detailed and precise may prompt a formalistic approach to their interpretation and application. Those which are more purposive and require judgment in their application facilitate a purposive approach, or substantive rationality. Finally, the structure of the rule affects the amount of discretion the person subject to the rule has: rules which are less specific and more vague confer greater discretion on the interpreter of the rule as to how the rule should be applied than rules which are clear and precise.

While suggesting that rule makers are in their choice of rule type responding to the tensions between different types of rationalities takes us further towards an answer, it is not complete. We need to ask how this is manifested. Is it reflected in a desire simply to balance flexibility and uniformity, or are rule makers trying to affect the interpretation (formalistic or purposive) which is given to the rule? We still need to know why the rule maker wanted to strike that paricular balance in that particular case. Is it simply a question of overriding preference: do rule makers always prefer a certain type of rule, as Baldwin's study suggests? Is the choice of rule type a particular tactical choice, for example to counter the "creative compliance" behaviour of the regulated, or is the

[35] Galligan (1986), p.71.
[36] See Galligan (1986), chap. 4.
[37] For a summary of the arguments see Jowell (1975).
[38] Galligan (1986), p.166.

process less strategic? Is the rule maker unconstrained in that choice? Finally, given that the different rationalities involve competing notions of justice and accountability, can the tensions between them in fact be resolved? We will turn now to examine the rule making decisions of financial services regulators to see what types of rules they have used, and the extent to which the choice of rule type has been a conscious and strategic decision.

Rule making by financial services regulators

Rule making has been a continual exercise in financial services regulation.[39] The Financial Services Act 1986 established a system of regulation for all those conducting investment business.[40] It requires all persons carrying on investment business to be either authorised or exempt.[41] Authorisation may be obtained through membership of one of the recognised regulatory bodies.[42] There are essentially three levels of regulators: the executive, on which rule making and enforcement powers were initially conferred, the Securities and Investments Board or SIB, to which those powers were delegated,[43] and the self-regulatory organisations, or SROs.[44] SIB and the SROs are private companies limited by guarantee, established solely for the purposes of regulating investment firms. SIB exercises statutory powers; the SROs operate on the basis of contract. There are currently five SROs, each of which has been authorised by SIB to regulate a different area of the market, and each has its own disciplinary and membership processes and its own rule book.[45]

SIB has a range of rule making powers, most of which were conferred in amendments made to the 1986 Act. SIB has the power to issue principles, designated (or core) rules and codes of practice which apply to its

[39] For details see Black (1994) and forthcoming.

[40] "Investment" and "investment business" are widely defined in Schedule 1 of the Act. For early proposals on the nature of the regulation see L. C. B. Gower, *Review of Investor Protection: A Discussion Document* (London, 1982), *Review of Investor Protection, Report, Part I*, Cmnd. 9125 (London, 1984) and *Report, Part II* (London, 1985). See also the White Paper: DTI, *Financial Services in the UK: A New Framework for Investor Protection*, Cmnd. 9432 (London, 1985).

[41] S.3 FSA (unless otherwise indicated, all section numbers refer to the Financial Services Act 1986).

[42] Authorisation may be obtained through membership of the self-regulatory organisations (s.7), the recognised professional bodies (s.15), or directly from SIB (s.25, s.114). Automatic authorisation is conferred on insurance companies authorised under the Insurance Companies Act 1982 (s.22) and friendly societies registered under the Friendly Societies Act 1974 (s.23), and on persons authorised to carry on investment business in an E.C. member state (s.31).

[43] Under s.114, Financial Services Act 1986 (Delegation) Order 1987.

[44] SIB is also responsible for recognising professional bodies, clearing houses and investment exchanges.

[45] These are the Securities and Futures Authority (SFA), the Investment Management Regulatory Organisation (IMRO), the Life Assurance and Unit Trust Organisation (Lautro) and the Financial Intermediaries' Managers' and Brokers' Association (Fimbra) and the Personal Investor Authority PIA). Lautro and Fimbra are due to cease operating in 1995, their members transferring to PIA. For the background to the formation of PIA see *Retail Regulation Review: Report of a study by Sir Kenneth Clucas on a new SRO for the Retail Sector*, SIB, March 1992.

own and SRO members.[46] Its rules have to conform to broad statutory criteria, which require that they make proper provision, for example, for disclosure, require firms to act with due skill, care and diligence and promote high standards of integrity and fair dealing.[47] The power of the SROs to make rules arises from their constitutions, and not from the legislation. Each SRO had to have a complete rulebook in place before it could be authorised, however, and SRO rules, like SIB rules, are subject to scrutiny by the Director General of Fair Trading to ensure that they do not restrict or distort competition to a significant extent. SRO rules are otherwise required to provide an "adequate" level of investor protection.[48] The sanctions for breaches of the rules of SIB and the SROs vary, but not, as one would imagine, with their legal source. Breach of the Principles is subject to discretionary disciplinary action by the person's regulator.[49] Breach of the Core Rules and SRO rules is subject to both disciplinary action and to civil actions on the part of a private investor.[50]

The rule making process involves the formation of policy proposals, which may or may not be accompanied by draft rules, which are published for consultation and sent to all those who hold a copy of the rules.[51] Responses are then reviewed internally, and in the case of significant changes to the rules further proposals are made. Once the rules are formed, the OFT reviews them to assess their effects on competition, and then reports to the Treasury. The Treasury may then require SIB and the SROs to amend the rules if they affect competition to a significant extent.[52]

While rule making has been continual, two main phases can be identified: the formation of the initial rule books in 1987–8 and the change to the New Settlement in 1990–1, which was enabled by the 1989 statutory amendments. SIB has used the powers to issue 10 Principles and 40 Core (designated) Rules.[53] The New Settlement, as the new rule system was termed, represented a striking change in the type of rules used by SIB. It was a move from detailed, specific rules to vaguer, more purpose-oriented rules, with little change in their substance.[54] The SROs' rules,

[46] S.47A and B, inserted by s.192 CA 1989, s.63A and B, inserted by s.194 CA 1989, and s.63C, inserted by s.195 CA 1989.

[47] Schedule 8.

[48] Schedule 2, para 3(1), amended by s.203(1) Companies Act 1989.

[49] S.47A(3), inserted by s.193(1) CA 1989, and s.63A, inserted by s.194 CA 1989.

[50] S.62A, inserted by s.193(1) CA 1989. This right of action was initially given to all investors, and subsequently restricted to private investors only.

[51] SIB is under a statutory duty to consult, Schedule 9, para. 12. The SROs consult with their members and representative bodies.

[52] Ss.119–123.

[53] SIB, *Statements of Principle*, March 1990; *Core Conduct of Business Rules*, January 1991. The Core Rules were designated to apply to members of SFA in December 1991 (SIB, *Core Conduct of Business Rules, Commencement for Members of SFA*, CP 55, December 1991) and to IMRO in August 1991 (SIB, *Core Conduct of Business Rules, Commencement for Members of IMRO*, CP 54, August 1991).

[54] The main deregulatory element was the restriction in the application of some of the rules to private investors.

or third tier rules, are more detailed, expanding or clarifying the Core Rules, and stipulating their application to the market area which they regulate.

Which arrow? The choice of rule type

The rule system as a whole, therefore, is made up of rules which vary in their precision, which have different sanctions attaching to them, and which apply to different areas of the market. Why has such a complex combination of rule types been used? Analysis of the rule making decisions indicates that the process involves a complex interaction of both strategic and non-strategic behaviour. Rule making has in part involved conscious policy decisions as to the choice of rule type. However, as we will see below, there are limits to the rationality of the process. Three principal aims have been pursued through the choice of rule type: to provide both certainty and flexibility, to induce compliance and to affect the degree of control exercised. Analysis of the reasons for the pursuit of these aims reveals the nature and interaction of deeper objectives which go far beyond the substantive objectives of investor protection and market efficiency that one might expect.

Certainty and flexibility

The rule making decisions of the financial services regulators indicate that they are concerned to use rule type to address the tensions between formal and substantive rationality by addressing the most immediate tension between certainty and flexiblity. The demands of the regulated in relation to rule type are consistent in their inconsistency. The continual demand in responses to the consultative papers has been that the rules should be sufficiently certain to enable firms to know what is expected of them, but sufficiently flexible to allow business practices to develop. The initial rules of SIB and the SROs were criticised as being too complicated, too detailed, too long, and too difficult to understand. Their length, detail and complexity meant that their application was at once both uncertain and inflexible.

The initial impetus for Principles arose from the conviction of the second chairman of SIB, amongst others, that the underlying rationale of the individual rules was not clear. SIB thus drafted a replacement rule book which contained nearly one hundred Principles. Although at this stage the idea of a three tier rule system had not been formulated, and the Principles were later adapted to meet a further objective, discussed below, the aim to combine the benefits of different types of rules within one rule system remained. The Principles are relatively imprecise and vague; they are purposive, and so provide greater flexibility in their application. The SROs' rules are far more detailed, so providing greater certainty and predictability as to the rule's application in a particular instance. The Principles override these rules, so that issues of application and interpretation are to be resolved in the light of their provisions. The combination of rules of different structure, detailed and general, is thus aimed at aiding the regulated by providing both certainty and flexibility. The Principles also aid the rule maker in that they reduce the pressures for precision which arise out of a fear of creating gaps in the rules. One SRO official in interview described the Principles as a "safety net", relieving the pressure for the SRO to ensure that all situations were covered in the SRO rules.

Not only the structure but the sanction attaching to the rule can be used in an attempt to resolve the tension between certainty and flexibility. The use of detailed provisions, for example, has been given flexibility by changing their status from rules to guidance. The use of guidance is a direct result of the contradictory demands of certainty and flexibility. As one official explained: "there is a tension in the desires of members—they want vague, general rules like the Principles and detest the detailed rule books, but they also want certainty and detailed information of what is expected of them. Guidance is an attempt to resolve this tension." Guidance thus indicates what type of conduct will be accepted as compliance, but removes the irritant of prescription.[55]

Changing the sanction can also mean that rules which have a structure which is less precise and detailed can be used on their own, not necessarily in combination with detailed rules, and still provide certainty. Here we see the nature of the interaction of the different rule dimensions. In the financial services context, the restriction in the application and availability of the right of civil action for breach of the rules[56] had the greatest impact on rule structure, and enabled the refinement from the one hundred principles to ten. Many of the demands for certainty which were prevalent when the initial rules were being formed arose from the provision of this right of action to all investors. In the uncertain climate of the time there was a strong fear on the part of the regulated of extensive litigation between professionals. As the chairman of SIB explained,

> "[Section 62] had a serious adverse effect on the SIB rulebook. The problem was that it focused the attention of practitioners, and more particularly their lawyers, on amending the rules, not to improve them generally, but simply to minimize the possibility of claims. This led to long and complicated provisions, attempting to draw fine distinctions to provide safe harbours for legitimate industry practice, while maintaining the essence of the original objective of the rule."[57]

SIB did not initially propose changing the sanction attaching to the Prin-

[55] However, although the status of guidance reduces the level of detailed conduct prescribed by rules, in the realities of day to day business operation it is likely that the difference between conduct which is prescribed and that which is recommended is merely semantic.

[56] The right of action provided to all investors for the breach of any SIB or SRO rule in s.62 FSA 1986 was amended to make the right available to private investors only, and the Principles were exempted from its scope: s.193(1) CA 1989.

[57] D. Walker, "Financial Services: The Principles Initiative", (1989) BJIBFL 51.

ciples,[58] but their structure was not considered by the SROs and regulated to be acceptable unless the Principles were subject to discretionary disciplinary action only.[59] Why should the change of sanction matter? Why were opaque rules perceived to be too uncertain and so unacceptable unless there was no possibility of court action for their breach? The conviction was strong, but the reasoning for it was unarticulated. The reasons for the perceptions become clear however if we consider how uncertainty can arise. Uncertainty can arise from opaque rules, as those subject to the rule cannot be sure that all others, including enforcers, will interpret the rule in the same way. However, as was noted earlier, opacity is a subjective dimension: whether or not the rule is clear depends on the ability of the reader to understand what the rule requires in a particular circumstance. Opaque terms, such as a requirement to "exercise due care", may have a particular meaning in a particular community. The requirement is thus clear to that community, although not to persons who are outside it. Further, those who are not part of that community may not share this interpretation. If outsiders are to be involved in interpreting and enforcing the rule, therefore, the community cannot rely on its own consensus as to the meaning of the rule being adopted. Certainty is thus reduced, and has to be regained through detailed rules. The system must therefore be closed off from outside involvement in rule interpretation and application for opaque rules to be capable of providing certainty. One of the simplest ways to effect this closure is through the rule's sanction: to state that breach will give rise to disciplinary action by regulators (insiders) only.[60] To apply this analysis to the financial services context, excluding the right of action from those most likely to use it (professional investors), and from the most opaque rules (the Principles), effectively closed the regulatory system, eliminating the courts (outsiders) as potential interpreters of the rules.[61] This closure of the system, effected by the change in the sanction attaching to the rule, thus attempted to ensure that opaque rules would receive a common interpretation, so increasing certainty in their operation.

Changing perceptions; inducing compliance

Attempting to resolve the tensions between certainty and flexibility has involved the use of the rule's sanction and the combination within one rule system of rules of different structure. Rule structure has also been used to induce compliance, and rules which are relatively simple, vague opaque, in other words more purposive in their effect, have been intro-

[58] *ibid.*, p.53.

[59] See, for example, an article by IMRO's then chief executive, John Morgan, "The Difference between Rules and Principles", F.T. March 29, 1989.

[60] The use of sanction in this way is akin to the use of an ouster clause in ousting the jurisdiction of the courts.

[61] Although the potential for judicial review remains.

duced. The clearest manifestation of this approach was the initial formation and refinement of the Principles. The aim of the Principles was not simply to act in combination with more detailed rules in an attempt to resolve the tensions discussed above, but to play a more informing and influencing role in enabling and inducing compliance with the rules.

Compliance inducement has been prompted by a set of motivations far more complex than the formal/substantive rationality debate would indicate. In part it is a fairly "hard nosed" concern with regulatory effectiveness. The formation of the Principles indicates that this had two aspects. The first was an attempt to ensure complete coverage of the rules:—"to remove the unmeritorious technical defence of a lacuna in the rules".—[62] The second was an attempt to emphasise that mere observance of the literal meaning of the rule, while flouting its purpose, would not be accepted as compliance. That compliance should be "with the spirit and not just the letter" was frequently stressed in the period prior to the change in rule structure.[63] The adoption of more opaque rules, of disciplinary status only (see above), was in large part aimed at pre-empting or foiling the "creative compliance" behaviour of the regulated.

The strategy was also more subtle: the change in structure and status of the rules manifested in the Principles was addressed not simply and directly at "creative compliance" behaviour but at what that behaviour symptomised. "Creative compliance" symptomised a loss of regulatory goodwill, a break down in relations between the regulated and regulator, relations which the system had been meant to foster. It was feared that the mass of detailed rules was alienating the regulated and as a result undermining the legitimacy of the regulation. The change was not simply a response to sectoral demands, however: in changing the rule type, the regulators aimed to change the perceptions the regulated had of the regulation in an attempt to alter their internal attitude towards it. The greater the acceptance of the regulation, the greater compliance would be.

The nature and strength of this reason for the adoption of the Principles can be more clearly assessed by looking briefly at the background to the regulation. Prior to the Financial Services Act most areas of the market had not been regulated. The rhetoric which surrounded the Act's formation was that the regulation would combine the advantages of the sensitivity and flexibility of self regulation with the sanctions of a statutory scheme. The regulation which appeared in the form of the initial rules was not what had been expected. The Bank of England in particular felt that the regulation was harming business, and did not

[62] SIB, *Conduct of Business Rules: A New Approach*, November 1988, Commentary, para. 10.

[63] See for example, *A New Approach*, Commentary, para. 10; D. Walker, quoted in the *Economist* July 30, 1988; M. Blair (chief legal officer at SIB), (1989) BJIBFL, and A. M. Whittaker (legal officer at SIB), "Financial Services, Developing the Regulatory Structure", (1989) BJIFBL 5.

have the acceptance of the regulated, or more specifically, the City.[64] The fear of alienation, manifested in non-compliance or creative compliance, thus led to a strategy of co-optation. Co-optation was not attempted simply through involving the regulated in the rule making process,[65] although this was done, but by changing the type of rules used.

The attempts to change the internal attitude to the regulation were expressed through the idea of a "regulatory contract", an idea adopted by the last two chairmen of SIB. Regulation, according to SIB's second chairman, Sir David Walker, represented a contract between the regulator and regulated, in which the regulator agreed not to interfere in the detailed operation of the regulated, but in return expected compliance which went beyond mere obedience to the letter of the law.[66] In other words, if you, the regulated, act properly, we, the regulators, will not need to be so specific.

The notion of a "regulatory contract" was accompanied by an emphasis on a particular interpretation of self-regulation as "regulation of the self".[67] In other words, each person and each firm should act as its own internal monitor, mentally assessing behaviour against the basic principles of the regulation. There was a fear that the regulation was seen by firms as a matter for compliance officers only, no one else knowing, or caring, what the regulation provided. However, detailed rules are difficult to absorb as they are hard to assimilate. Ten Principles, on the other hand, would be easily memorable and so be able to act as internal benchmarks against which conduct could be assessed. They would enable chief executives to understand the basic tenets of the regulation, and to create a climate of compliance within the firm. They would thus improve compliance in a complex area by lifting the issue into the boardroom and reminding the chief executive that there were basic principles that should govern the conduct of his business. Literal compliance with the rules was not to be a substitute for management integrity: the Principles would help chief executives to see the moral wood for the technical trees. Moreover, it was stressed that they required no more than good business practice, which if followed would increase confidence in the firms and markets, so aiding business. Regulation, in other words, was good for you.

Exercising control

The third aim sought through the use of rule type has been the exercise of different degrees of control. The addressees of this strategy have not

[64] See R. Leigh Pemberton, "The Markets, the City and the Economy" (1988) BEQB 59, and *Financial Times* February 27, 1988, February 29, 1988 and May 5, 1988.

[65] For suggestions that participation in regulation may be a strategy of co-optation, see Baldwin and McCrudden (1987), p.6.

[66] This was recently re-iterated by SIB's current chairman, Andrew Large: *Financial Services Regulation: Making the System Work*, SIB, May 1993, para. 6.5.

[67] This phrase was frequently used by officials when asked in interview what they thought "self regulation" meant.

only been the regulated, however, but the regulators. Rules of different structure afford different amounts of discretion to those being regulated by them. The sense in which discretion is being used here is that advocated by Galligan and Hawkins: there is no clear dividing line between rules and discretion; rather the two are inextricably interwoven. Discretion in this sense is interstitial: it is "the space . . . between legal rules in which legal actors may exercise choice."[68] The rule may vary the amount of discretion which that legal actor has.[69]

Studies of discretion have indicated that how that discretion is used, and indeed the extent to which that discretion is constrained by the rule system as a whole, cannot be determined by an analysis of the rule alone. In applying the rule, enforcers and officials are subject to a range of extraneous factors, with the result that they may be both more and less constrained than the rule would indicate. The regulated may manipulate them; their compliance may be determined by a complex cost/benefit calculation. Moreover, detailed rules in one area may simply displace discretion to another.[70]

However, rule makers have used detailed rules in an attempt to control behaviour by reducing the amount of discretion that the person has as to how to act. The question which is being asked is essentially, to what extent can the rule makers trust the regulated to behave as they want them to. The issue here is not that the regulated are too clever and will manipulate detailed rules to serve their own ends (as it is in creative compliance). Rather it is that in the absence of detailed rules the regulator feels that there will be insufficient compliance: the regulated will simply not act according to the standards of behaviour that the regulator requires unless that behaviour is specified. Contrary to the implications of the creative compliance literature, therefore, the regulator does not want to use a more substantive approach. Rather it is felt that this approach cannot be used. Rule makers cannot afford to confer that discretion as they do not trust how it will be used. This confidence in such rules may be misplaced,[71] but this does not alter the fact that that confidence exists, or at least that such rules are seen as marginally more effective than other types.

Rule makers therefore consider the extent to which they feel they can rely on the person applying the rule to act to further the rule's purpose: detailed rules are, to an extent, a sign of distrust. The regulators have explicitly referred to this aspect of rules. The current chairman of SIB, Andrew Large, emphasised recently that the more SIB felt able to rely on rising standards of competence and business ethics of the regulated,

[68] K. Hawkins, "The Use of Legal Discretion: Perspectives from Law and Social Science", in K. Hawkins (ed.) (1992), p.11.

[69] See further *ibid.*, p.36.

[70] Baldwin and Hawkins (1984), p.582.

[71] Empirical studies indicate that the ability of rules to control actions of officials is severely limited: Galligan (1986), Hawkins (1993), and Baldwin and Hawkins (1984).

the less prescriptive the rules might be able to become.[72] The type of rule used can thus vary with the person to whom the rule is primarily addressed. Where regulators feel they can rely on the object of the rule, then a rule which requires the regulated to exercise judgment will be used to replace detailed rules.[73]

While the objects of the decision have in these cases been the regulated community, the use of detailed rules in an attempt to exert control has also been evident in relations between all levels of regulators. The highly detailed nature of SIB's initial rule book is attributed by SIB largely to the requirements of the DTI. The DTI's approval of the rules was necessary before the statutory powers could be transferred to SIB. Once they have been transferred, the Secretary of State has no power to order their amendment unless they are significantly anti-competitive. The DTI was in part responding to pressures from the regulated in requiring detailed rules (see above). However it was also uncertain as to how SIB would use its rule making powers once they were transferred. The imposition of detailed rules can be seen in part as an attempt to control that use, even though subsequent amendments would be out of their control.

Conversely, the introduction of the vaguer, more opaque Principles and core rules was at one level a deliberate conferral by SIB of a greater degree of discretion on the SROs. One of the main criticisms of the initial SIB rules had been that they did not leave SROs room to write their own. A move to vaguer, more purposive rules was thus a way of affording SROs that room for manoeuvre. SIB stressed that it would be "standing back" from third tier rule making,[74] recognising that the previous rule system had involved an "unsustainably intrusive role" for SIB.[75]

However, the greater discretion conferred by the change in rule structure was in part negated by the change in the application of the rules and the sanctions attaching to them. Under the 1989 amendments the Principles and designated rules (core rules) of SIB applied directly to all members of SROs. The application of these rules to members of the SROs enabled SIB to assert control over the central provisions of the SROs' rule books. Previously, SROs had to follow SIB's rules simply because of the requirement that their rules provide equivalent protection; now SROs are effectively bound by SIB's rules because their members are. SIB's rules are now more clearly legislative in nature, and centralising in their effect.

Whilst the objectives sought via the Principles were largely a change in the perceptions of the regulation with the aim of inducing greater compliance from the regulated, those sought by the core rules relate to

[72] Large Report (1993), para. 6.5.

[73] For examples, see further Black. *op. cit.*, chaps. 6 and 7.

[74] SIB, *Regulation of the Conduct of Investment Business, A Proposal*, August 1989, paras. 21 and 24.

[75] SIB, *Achieving and Judging Adequacy*, CP 39, April 1990.

the relations between the regulators themselves. The stated aim of the Core Rules was to set what was referred to as the "common core" or "harmonising backbone" of the regulation,[76] ensuring consistency between SROs' rule books, and so meeting the criticisms of divergence and inconsistency between the SROs' rule books which had prevailed.[77] However, the reasons behind their introduction lie more deeply, in the institutional structure of the regulation. The New Settlement, and particularly the existence of the Core Rules, makes little sense unless one understands the extent and nature of the pressures which the institutional structure exerts.

The regulatory structure is essentially federal and exhibits consequent tensions between the role of the centre and the autonomy of the outlying bodies. It is the result of the compromises made between differing views of what the role of the regulation, and hence its structure, should be. As the Act was being formed, market efficiency claims pushed simultaneously for self-regulation, which it was felt offered sensitivity and flexibility, and for oversight lest self-regulation degenerated into cartels and restrictive practices. Investor protection claims pushed for public interest regulation with tough enforcement (central statutory body) and awareness of market practices to ensure abuses were addressed (practitioner regulation).[78] The result was a network of agencies whose relative roles were ill-defined.

This structural ambiguity became a source of severe friction between the two tiers of regulators, SIB and the SROs.[79] Many of the criticisms of the initial SIB rules were essentially directed at the role the rules oriented SIB was playing in the regulation. It was felt by many in the City, the SROs and the Bank of England that the 1987 rules represented an over-centralisation of the regulation and the Governor of the Bank of England publicly stated that the "practitioners' contribution had been overshadowed".[80] SROs also publicly urged SIB to adopt a less intrusive role, threatening that self-regulation would otherwise come to an early end.[81]

Rule type was thus used to define the nature of that relationship: less specific and detailed rules would confer greater discretion on the SROs, but at the same time changes in the application of SIB's rules and their extension to the members of SROs would ensure greater control and

[76] See SIB, *Regulation of Conduct of Business, A Proposal*, August 1989; *Achieving and Judging Adequacy*, April 1990; *The Proposed Core Rules*, CP 42, October 1990.

[77] The functional organisation of the regulation means that one film could belong to more than one SRO. Divergencies in provisions were thus highlighted, and served to increase the complexity of the regulation for the regulated firm.

[78] For elaboration see, for example, Gower's *Discussion Document* and *Report, Part I*, R. Leigh Pemberton, "Changing Boundaries in Financial Services", (1984) BEQB 40, "The UK Approach to Financial Regulation", (1986) BEQB 48 , and the 1985 White Paper.

[79] For a contemporary statement as to its view of the respective roles of SIB and the SROs and the aims behind the New Settlement see SIB, *A Forward Look*, October 1989.

[80] R. Leigh Pemberton, "The Markets, the City and the Economy" (1988) BEQB 59.

[81] See, for example, a speech by the then chief executive of IMRO, John Morgan, to the National Association of Pension Funds, quoted in FT February 27, 1988.

uniformity in the rules of the SROs, which were now more clearly subsidiary regulators.

Summary
Rule type has thus been used to achieve three main aims of resolving the tension between certainty and flexibility, inducing compliance and affecting the degree of control exercised. The dimensional analysis of rules enables us to see how different dimensions have been used to achieve these aims. These dimensions interact: changes in the sanction may confer flexibility on detailed rules, as in the formation of guidance, or certainty on opaque rules through closure of the system, as in the formation of the Principles. It is notable however that detailed rules have remained a central aspect of the rules to which firms are subject. There have been no cycles of formalism as there has never really been a move away from formalism. Vague or purposive rules have been used not to replace detail but to complement it.

The analysis indicates not simply the "first order" reasons, or aims of the rules, but the deeper, underlying reasons why these aims were pursued at all. These include a desire to improve the effectiveness of the rules in terms of comprehension, accurate application and compliance with them, an attempt to secure acceptance of the regulation, and to educate the regulated in the underlying principles of the regulation. The object of the rules has not simply been the regulated. The introduction of the New Settlement, particularly the Core Rules, represents an attempt to resolve the tensions between the role of SIB and that of the SROs which arose from the ambiguities of the institutional structure through the adoption of a particular type of rule. The policy behind them was one of simultaneously conferring discretion, through changing the rule structure, and centralisation through changing the application of the rule. As the relationship between the institutions changes, this affects the rules. This dynamic continues to be important as is illustrated in the current policy of "de-designation", in which particular core rules are no longer applied to the members of particular SROs.

Constraints on rule making

The attention paid to the types of rules which should be formed, manifested particularly in the New Settlement, indicates that rule making and choice of rule type has been to a significant extent a self-conscious and tactical exercise. Rule type has of itself been an important part of regulatory policy. However we must be wary of falsely representing both the "choice" open to the rule maker and the rationality of the process itself. Not all rule types are suitable for all purposes: trade-offs have to be made as the rule maker has to decide which to pursue. The rule making process is not one of complete comprehensive rationality. The rule is the culmination of a series of decisions of a process of amendment and reformulation as priorities alter or regulatory strategies, initially hazy and ill-formed, become increasingly defined. Finally, rule makers do not function in a polital vacuum: politicians, consumer groups, the regulated and the media all criticise and make demands for the type of regulation which they think should be instituted, which demands are often competing. This is not a surprising occurrence. What is significant is the extent to which the choice of rule type is affected by them.

Which target? Tradeoffs in the choice of rule type

What emerges from an analysis of rule making by financial services regulators is that not all types of rule are suited to all purposes, and that the nature of rules imposes limitations on their effective use. The adoption of particular regulatory techniques may mean that only rules of a certain structure can be used. Conduct regulation—the requirement to act in a particular way, usually to exercise judgment—is a technique relied upon quite heavily by the regulators. It is a less onerous form of regulation than structural regulation (which structures the market in a particular way), permitting the person to carry on the business he or she would normally conduct, but requiring the exercise of higher standards of behaviour in so doing.[82] Firms are required to exercise standards of fair dealing, to give the best advice, or to recommend suitable products. The rule maker is essentially requiring the adviser to exercise judgment, relying on the adviser to exercise it well. The reliance may be misplaced, however. The suitability rule is one of the most widely breached rules in the regulatory system and the current concern over the sale of personal pensions stems from non-compliance with it. The regulators' answer, however, is not in a formalistic approach in which the rules are made more detailed. This is not because of the potential for creative compliance, but because of the inherent nature and limitations of rules themselves. The rule maker cannot formulate a more detailed rule: the circumstances of its application are too wide and varied and abstractions and generalisations cannot be made. However, neither can the rule maker create good judgment where none exists. The rule maker has reached the limits of rules as a regulatory instrument and has to rely on other forms of regulation to achieve the purpose: training and competence tests.

A rule such as the suitability rule thus relies on the skill of the regulated, and poses problems for enforcement. As noted earlier, enforcement studies indicate a preference among enforcement officials for detailed rules. Not only may detailed rules be incompatible with the regulatory technique chosen, however. As in the example above they may compromise the standard of behaviour attained. An example is the rule which requires brokers to deal at the best price available.[83] To aid

[82] An example of structural regulation was the old Stock Exchange rule that a person either had to sell shares for their own account (jobbers) or act as agents for another (brokers). When this was removed, so that brokers could also deal for their own account, it was replaced with conduct regulation, which imposed duties to deal at the best price etc.

[83] Core Rule 22.

enforcement the rule stipulated that this price is that shown on the automatic quotation screen at the time of the transaction. However very few deals are done at this price: most are done at better prices. Enforcement considerations therefore lead to a lower standard of behaviour being stipulated than that which the operators in the market expect to receive. Aiming the rule at enforcement thus compromises the achievement of high standards of conduct. It also has a deeper impact in that it affects the attitude the regulated have to the regulation to its relevance, and to the understanding they think the regulators have of the business which they are regulating.[84]

The context of rule making

Rules represent not one decision, but a series of decisions, each building on or modifying the last. Changes or developments may be prompted by changes in the market which occur while the rule is being formed, and will usually result in a lengthening of the rule to accommodate and provide for such changes. The reasons for increased length and precision may also be due to the need, as perceived by the rule makers, to accommodate the demands of those to be subject to the rule: rules are bargained over. The reasons for the complex and precise structure of the initial rules, for example, arose directly from the constant need to accomodate the demands of the regulated for certainty, or exclusion. As one official explained, a rule would initially consist of a provision which was quite wide in scope and fairly imprecise. Successive sub-clauses would then be added to accommodate the demands for precision, or to provide exclusions from the rules. It is a process which becomes self-perpetuating. Once exclusions start to be provided within the rule, its generality is undermined. This can reduce the flexibility available in its application. It can also reduce its certainty, as it becomes unclear whether, where specific exclusions are provided, everything not excluded must be included, or whether further exclusions may be implied. Finally, increasing the level of specificity and precision can paradoxically create more "gaps" in the rules, which more detailed rules are used to fill.[85]

The process of rule making may also close off options. Rules cannot be seen as discrete decisions, made in isolation from other decisions on other rules in the rule system. When the rule making process is analysed from a holistic perspective, rather than simply looking at the formation of individual rules in isolation,[86] it becomes clear that decisions made as

[84] SFA's guidance now provides that in determining whether the firm has taken reasonable care to ascertain the best price available SFA will have regard to the conventions of the market: SFA rule 5–39.

[85] See, for example, the debates over disclosure rules in retail regulation discussed in Black (1994), chapter 7: SIB, *Life Assurance and Unit Trust Disclosure*, CP 23, May 1989, *Life Assurance and Unit Trust Disclosure*, CP 27, August 1989, *Retail Regulation Review: Discussion Paper 3, Disclosure*, October 1991, and *Retail Regulation Review: Disclosure, Polarisation and Standards of Advice* CP 60, March 1992.

[86] For the need to do this in relation to individualised decisions, see Hawkins (1993), pp.27–35.

to the overall nature of the rule system affect and/or constrain the decisions made with respect to individual rules. This may determine the structure of the rule, or the sanction attaching to it, particularly where there is a hierarchical rule system. The choice of rule type is then constrained, and determined by the tier in which the rule should be, and not necessarily by what rule type is best suited to the particular substantive aim of the rule.

The knowledge and approach of the regulators themselves limits the rationality of the process and affects the type of rule formulated. The detailed structure of the initial rules, as we have seen, was due in part both to the DTI and to the provision of the right to civil action for their breach. It was also due to the lack of information and experience which everyone, regulated and rule maker, had of financial services regulation and uncertainty as to the new shape of the financial services markets. Regulation prior to the Act has been described as "primitive",[87] and most aspects of the markets were being regulated for the first time.[88] The rule makers on the whole were civil servants and parliamentary draftsmen with little experience of financial services. The regulated were preoccupied with how the regulation would apply to their particular areas of business operation and were not in a position to review the rule books as a whole.

This inexperience was exacerbated by the speed with which the rules had to be made. There was no time for regulators to learn from experience in drafting their initial rules, nor was there even time to review the rules once drafting had finished to assess their overall coherence. The deregulation of the Stock Exchange, or Big Bang, had already occurred and the City was undergoing fundamental structural changes — changes which were giving rise to profound conflicts of interest in the way business was conducted.[89] The rules thus had to be formulated at considerable speed, and the regulators admit that the rules which emerged were essentially a first draft and in need of considerable revision.

Finally, rule making has been affected by the perceptions of politicians, the regulated and the media concerning the role regulation is meant to be playing in the market area in which it operates. In seeking legitimacy, the regulators seek to gain acceptance of these different constituencies, whose demands are not uniform. They affect the choice of rule type, however, as different types of rules are perceived as involving particular regulatory approaches, and as having different levels of efficacy. These assumptions have already been illustrated in the expectations surrounding the use of the Principles: the consequence of the more general rule would be to alter the perceptions of the regulation, increase its acceptability, and increase compliance. Detailed rules, on the other hand, are associated with greater control, and so have been

[87] L.C.B. Gower, " 'Big Bang' and City Regulation", (1988) 51 MLR 1, p.6.

[88] For details see Gower, *Discussion Document*, chap. 3.

[89] For a summary of the nature of these conflicts, see the Law Commission, *Fiduciary Duties and Regulatory Rules*, CP No.124 (1992), para. 2.4.12.

equated in the rhetoric surrounding the regulation with tough regulation, with upholding investor protection.

The association of rule type with regulatory approach means that as the political climate varies in the demands it makes for the intensity of the regulation, so pressures for different types of rules are exerted. These vary with different groups: politicans, the regulated, the media; over time, with different constituencies making different demands in different periods; and between markets. The initial demand of the Government was for tough regulation. This then changed to requiring a more flexible regulatory approach. Detailed rules are perceived as necessary in market areas where private, individual investors are involved, where the objective of investor protection is seen to be of greater concern. However, in the wholesale market, where mainly professional investors are involved, investor protection concerns are outweighed by concerns for market efficiency, prompted by fears that "over-regulation" will drive business from London. More substantive, purposive regulation which gives greater flexibility is thus demanded. Sir Kenneth Berrill, SIB's first chairman, identified the dilemma thus: "in working out the rules, we need constantly to strike the balance between on the one hand stringent safeguards for investor protection and on the other market operation and development, including scope for flexibility and innovation."[90]

Detailed rules have also been associated with effective regulation. In forming its initial rules SIB argued that detailed rules were necessary to ensure high standards of behaviour, given the competitive environment and actors who varied considerably in their competence and honesty.[91] In introducing the Principles, therefore, the regulators were concerned to convince those who were worried about regulatory laxity that the Principles would be meaningful, and enforceable. As one official stated, "one of the aims was to sell the idea that rules did not have to be as specific as the old rule book to be effective." Paradoxically, the Principles are now used by SIB to defend itself against charges of over-regulation.[92]

Conclusion

The choice of rule type has been a significant part of the policy decisions made by financial services regulators. The determination of which type of rule to use has been a complex decision, in which rules have been used to induce compliance, affect the degree of control exerted and resolve the tension between certainty and flexibility. Underlying this use of rules have been deeper objectives which go beyond the substantive goals

[90] L.S.Gaz., February 12, 1986.

[91] SIB, *The SIB Rulebook: An Overview*, October 1987, para. 10.

[92] See, for example, the response of Mr Andrew Large to the Treasury and Civil Service Select Committee, Financial Services Regulation, Minutes of Evidence, 1992/3, H.C. Paper no.733–i, para. 39.

that one would expect of investor protection, market efficiency and international competitiveness. Rules have been used in an attempt to gain legitimacy for the regulation and to gain the acceptance of the regulatory and political community. Rules have been used as signals, to influence conduct, alter perceptions and communicate expectations. Rule type has been in a reflexive relationship with the function of the rule making body. It has defined, and been defined by, the position of that agency in the institutional structure.

There are trade-offs to be made in exercising the choice, and constraints which operate upon it. Other decisions made in relation to different rules limit the extent to which a choice is available: even if rule makers can choose which arrow to take from the quiver, they may not be able to determine what the quiver holds. Finally, the process is not wholly rational. There have been non-strategic reasons for the choice of rule type: lack of time, lack of knowledge, pressures for certainty and the self-perpetuating nature of detailed rules have led particularly to an increase in detail and complexity.

The reasoning of financial services regulators in the exercise of their rule making function is clearly limited at some levels to its particular context. However, this study identifies a number of uses of rule type which may be applicable in other contexts. Addressing issues of formalism and substantive rationality, of compliance and control, need not be context-specific; underlying aims to secure acceptance and legitimacy are also likely to be of general concern. Further studies on rule making are needed to determine whether these issues are of concern to other regulators, how they are addressed, and indeed whether rule type is itself a significant part of the rule making decisions of regulators operating in other fields. As rules abound and their effectiveness varies greatly, understanding the reasons why they were made is the first step in developing suggestions as to how they should be made.

[9]

DISCRETIONARY JUSTICE: DAVIS RECONSIDERED

ROBERT BALDWIN* AND KEITH HAWKINS†

I. DAVIS'S APPROACH TO DISCRETION

KENNETH Culp Davis's book *Discretionary Justice*[1] was first published in 1969 and stands as a landmark in administrative law.[2] Lawyers were told in the book to stop concentrating on those activities that were already governed by precise rules and to study instead the use and control of discretionary powers. It was in confining, structuring and checking "unnecessary" bureaucratic discretions (principally by administrative rule-making) that Davis saw the greatest opportunity to increase justice to individuals. Fifteen years later, it is clear that Davis has profoundly altered the way in which scholars regard administrative law, and, more importantly, that his influence on government has been enormous. Thus, for instance, parole and sentencing decisions have been radically revised and structured in a majority of American states,[3] and the Supreme Court has required federal agencies to engage in rulemaking.[4]

So persuasive has *Discretionary Justice* been, however, that it is important to re-examine Davis's thesis, to suggest some of its limitations, and to argue against unduly legalistic interpretations of his work. We are therefore concerned in this article to explore Davis's conceptions of administrative decision-making and justice, and to argue that, by setting Davis's work in a broader context, it may usefully be amended.

First, though, three sentences from Davis's own conclusions should be offered to summarise his position[5]:

---

* Lecturer in Law, Brunel University.

† Senior Research Fellow, Centre for Socio-Legal Studies and Fellow of Wolfson College, Oxford. For their help with this paper, we are grateful to colleagues at the Centre for Socio-Legal Studies, Oxford, and also to Christopher McCrudden, Rajeev Dhavaan and Harold Pepinsky. We also wish to thank Professor Kenneth Culp Davis who was kind enough to comment on an early draft. Readers may take for granted that not all of the above persons agree with the arguments presented here.

1 See, Kenneth Culp Davis, *Discretionary Justice: A Preliminary Inquiry* (1969). Hereafter page numbers refer to this volume.

2 See *e.g.* J. Skelly Wright, "Beyond Discretionary Justice" (1972) 81 Yale L.J. 575, 590. For early British reviews, see S. A. de Smith (1970) 33 M.L.R. 594, B. A. Hepple [1969] C.L.J. 313, and also A. W. Bradley, "Research and Reform in Administrative Law" (1974) 13 J.S.P.T.L. 35.

3 See, *e.g.* Gottfredson, Wilkins and Hoffman, *Guidelines for Parole and Sentencing* (1978). Davis's work is explicitly acknowledged at the outset in the report on *Courts* by the U.S. National Advisory Commission on Criminal Justice Standards and Goals (1973).

4 See *Morton* v. *Ruiz,* 415 U.S. 199 (1974); and K. C. Davis, *Administrative Law Treatise,* (1979), Vol. 2, pp.128–52.

5 See Davis (1969), pp.215–233.

"The strongest need and the greatest promise for improving the quality of justice to individual parties in the entire legal and governmental system are in the areas where decisions necessarily depend more upon discretion than upon rules and principles and where formal hearings and judicial review are mostly irrelevant."[6]

"The proper goal is to eliminate unnecessary discretionary power, not to eliminate all discretionary power."[7]

"The hope lies, I think, not in better statutory standards, but in earlier and more elaborate administrative rule-making and in better structuring and checking of discretionary power."[8]

Thus, although Davis's proposals concentrate on the limitations that should be placed on discretionary power, he does freely concede the need for discretion in a government of laws and men. Indeed, he criticises the "extravagant version of the rule of law" that has no place for discretion.[9] He states that there *is* a place in modern government for discretion. He aims, as we have seen, not to eliminate all discretion or indeed to maximise control over it, but says at the start of his inquiry as well as at the end:

"The answer is, in broad terms, that we should eliminate much unnecessary discretionary power and that we should do much more than we have been doing to confine, to structure and to check necessary discretionary power. The goal is not the maximum degree of confining, structuring and checking; the goal is to find the optimum degree for each power in each set of circumstances."[10]

In spite of such statements, however, it is easy for the reader to put down Davis's book with the broad impression that discretion is a potentially dangerous phenomenon constantly needing to be shackled. Thus, he argues that 90 per cent. of injustice in administration flows from discretionary activity and that

"In a government of men and of laws, the portion that is a government of men, like a malignant cancer, often tends to stifle the portion that is a government of laws."[11]

Despite Davis's assertions about the indispensability of discretion for the individualisation of justice, the use of such language also reflects a view of discretion as a corrupting force, a nasty growth, that constantly erodes the basis of "justice." This impression is encouraged at other points in the book:

"Our governmental and legal systems are saturated with excessive discretionary power which needs to be confined, structured and checked."[12]

---

[6] p.216 (emphasis in original).
[7] p.217.
[8] p.219.
[9] p.28–44.
[10] pp.3–4.
[11] p.25.
[12] p.27.

> " . . . the problem about discretion at all governmental levels in the United States is almost entirely that of excessive discretionary power and is seldom that of inadequate discretionary power."[13]
>
> "Almost all administrators do less structuring through rules than they can and should do."[14]

In accordance with this view, Davis's central concern is "what can be done that is not now done to minimise injustice from exercise of discretionary power."[15] As Judge Henry Friendly put it: "Discretionary justice thus begins to look suspiciously like non-discretionary justice."[16]

We should pause at this point and note what Davis means by the terms "discretion" and "justice" for these concepts impose limitations on his thesis. Of the former, he says: "A public officer has discretion whenever the effective limits on his power leave him free to make a choice among possible courses of action or inaction."[17] This is a concept of similar breadth to Jowell's "the room for decisional manoeuvre possessed by a decision maker."[18] The advantage of such breadth is that it allows Davis to make broad prescriptions on such matters as structuring and checking. The disadvantage is that it underemphasises variations in the nature and context of discretionary powers: between, for example, the discretion to make a policy or rule and the discretion to apply or vary the policy; between an individual's discretion and an organisation's; between discretions that are wholly constrained by law and those that are defined by a mixture of controls.

Other commentators, of course, have analysed discretion in different ways. Dworkin's[19] weak/strong distinction is probably the best known contribution to thinking about the matter from a jurisprudential point of view. The literature of social administration is also helpful.[20] Thus, David Bull[21] has both distinguished "officer discretion" from "agency discretion" and argued that there are at least three different activities with respect to which the term "discretion" is used: interpreting rigid rules; taking decisions in areas where it is deemed inappropriate to have such rules; and using the freedom to depart, in exceptional circumstances, from these rules.[22]

---

[13] p.54.

[14] p.103.

[15] p.3.

[16] H. J. Friendly, "Judicial Control of Administrative Action" (1970) 23 J.Leg.Ed. 63, 65.

[17] p.4.

[18] J. L. Jowell, "The Legal Control of Administrative Discretion" [1973] P.L 179.

[19] R. Dworkin, *Taking Rights Seriously* (1977).

[20] See, *e.g.* R.M. Titmuss, "Welfare 'Rights' Law and Discretion" (1971) 42 P.Q 42; Michael Hill, "Some Implications of Legal Approaches to Welfare Rights" (1974) 4 *British Journal of Social Work* 187; and David Bull, "The Anti-Discretion Movement in Britain: Fact or Phantom?" [1980] J.S.W.L. 65.

[21] *Loc. cit.*, p.67.

[22] For another analysis of the varieties of Discretion and rationality, see J. Mashaw, *Bureaucratic Justice* (1983), pp.72–3.

Failure to distinguish between these various types of discretion leads to difficulties. Bull, himself, is concerned about the confusion of two issues: the extent to which Parliament should leave to agencies or officials a discretion to cover exceptional circumstances and whether checks can be imposed on the *inevitable* power of officers at the point of delivery of a service to make judgments on eligibility (in the case of welfare benefits). Some, Gilbert Smith for instance,[23] have gone further and warned that *a priori* definitions of discretion unhelpfully ride roughshod over differences in application and use, that attention to a particular context of an activity is preferable and that "there is a danger that 'discretion' simply becomes a residual category for unexplained variance."

Indeed, the elusiveness of the concept of discretion is more apparent on attempting to distinguish it from related notions such as power, choice or authority. Dworkin makes this argument[24] in stating that the concept of discretion is at home only in one sort of context: when someone makes decisions subject to standards set by another authority. The quality of the discretion thus varies according to the nature of the "doughnut" of authority that surrounds it. In some cases, as Dworkin reminds us, "the official may have discretion from one stand-point though not from another."[25]

There is, indeed, an element of circularity about this doughnut, one that Bankowski and Nelken[26] explain well: discretion is really about power but because it appears to be connected with rules (in the "delegated power" notion of discretion), it tends to be viewed as a problem of legality or as the lack of a rule-bound solution. In fact, as we shall see in looking at the notion of "decision," life is rarely so uncomplicated. It is by no means always possible to isolate a precise delegation or decision point. As a result, the notion of "discretionary decision" spends much of the time out of its depth.

These points can be taken *vis-à-vis* Davis. Much of the difficulty with *Discretionary Justice* arises from the need to develop varying approaches to the control of different varieties and contexts of discretion. Davis would no doubt sympathise with this view, but his readers should be wary of the difficulties concealed by a concept of discretion that, though defined, is essentially unexplored and ask whether Davis employs throughout his book a concept that is

[23] Gilbert Smith, "Discretionary Decision-making in Social Work" in M. Adler and S. Asquith (eds.), *Discretion and Welfare* (1981) (hereafter Adler and Asquith), pp.60–61.

[24] See Dworkin, *op. cit.* p.31; and T. McGlew and A. Robertson, "Social Change and the Shifting Boundaries of Discretion in Medicine" in Adler and Asquith, p.201.

[25] Dworkin, *op. cit.* p.31.

[26] Z. Bankowski and D. Nelken, "Discretion as a Social Problem" in Adler and Asquith, pp.249–251.

consistent in form or unproblematic. The discussion in the rest of this paper indicates that it may be neither.

As for justice, we might, like Bradley,[27] ask why justice is chosen as the yardstick for all governmental activity. Davis, moreover, is not concerned directly with *social* justice or with policy-making, but states:

> ". . . this essay is concerned primarily with a portion of discretionary power and with a portion of justice—with that portion of discretionary power which pertains to justice, and with that portion of justice which pertains to individual parties."[28]

He, of course, acknowledges the close relationship of discretionary justice and policy-making but his concern with individualistic justice slants his account and restricts its wider applicability. He concentrates on decisions that are made by individuals rather than by organisations or groups, and decisions that affect private citizens and not, say, sectors of the population. His conception of decision is also individualistic in the sense that he is concerned with the exercise of discretion in the handling or disposal of *cases* and does not address the ways in which choices are made about *policy*. Policy, after all, may be regarded as speaking to the handling of classes of case or as decisions about how to decide. Thus, there emerges a concept of administrative justice that diminishes policy considerations and makes it easy both to focus attention on those demands typically made of administrators by lawyers (fairness, openness, predictability, etc.) and to minimise the importance in public decision-making of such factors as efficiency, adaptability, the accessibility of remedies and the furtherance of public rather than private interests.

A concept of administrative justice which does not pay full regard to policy matters is too limited because it overlooks the substantial recourse to administrative discretion exercised by organisational actors and by legislatures in, for example, wide and diverse areas of social and economic regulation. In recognition of the complexities of the regulatory task and the difficulties of framing legal rules which will speak to the subtleties and uncertainties of individual regulatory problems, legislatures prefer administrative officials to employ policy-making discretion to translate broad legal aspirations into routinely workable practices. To the extent that Davis's conception of discretionary behaviour is premissed upon case discretion (rather than policy discretion as well), it is unnecessarily restricted. Other commentators also regard an administrative law preoccupied with individual as opposed to

[27] Bradley, *loc. cit.* p.37.

[28] pp.5–6.

policy or collective issues as seriously flawed.[29] Thus, Patrick McAuslan has critically contrasted post-war movements in administrative law with developments in the administrative processes of collective consumption:

> "[Administrative law] has, even where collective agencies of grievance-handling have been created, concentrated overwhelmingly on refining, elaborating, extending and discussing remedies for individuals against the administration. The [administrative processes of collective consumption] have developed a multitude of agencies, processes and systems for deciding upon policies and allocating resources between the different programmes of collective consumption where the law is facilitative rather than regulatory . . ."[30]

Davis does state that controls over discretion may be taken too far, but, given his view that discretionary power is in most cases too extensive, he regularly argues as if one may automatically improve any scheme of administration simply by increasing the confining, structuring and checking of power. Such is his approach that, especially in Chapter 4 of *Discretionary Justice,* his argument almost boils down to a simple plea for greater openness in government: "Openness is the natural enemy of arbitrariness," he writes,[31] "and a natural ally in the fight against injustice." Indeed, in another place[32] Davis has reduced his whole position to the 12-word slogan: "As far as feasible—open standards, open findings, open reasons, open precedents." On the face of it, this proposition is persuasive and attractive. But it is too simple.

At this point we should be clear that *procedural* justice and *substantive* justice raise very different issues for those who would control discretion. Procedural justice is relatively unproblematic and there is an immediate attractiveness in calls for open and fair procedures. (We readily agree, for example, with Davis's adverse criticisms of the Federal Parole Board procedures of the 1960s.) To call for the structuring of discretion on substantive matters is, however, to go much further. This raises such questions as whether it is possible to lay down in advance the matters to be taken into account in making a decision or whether rule-makers can outline the relative weights to be given to such matters. What certainly cannot be assumed is that increased openness or structuring will necessarily increase substantive justice. Davis states that the Parole

[29] See, *e.g.* D. J. Galligan, "The Nature and Function of Policies Within Discretionary Power" [1976] P.L. 332.

[30] P. McAuslan, "Administrative Law, Collective Consumption and Judicial Policy" (1983) 46 M.L.R. 1, 7. See also the distinction between "*gesellschaft*" law (atomic individualism and private interests) and "bureaucratic-administrative" law (emphasis on legal regulation rather than adjudication between individuals) discussed in Adler and Asquith, pp.19–21 and A. E. Tay and E. Kamenka, "Beyond Bourgeois Individualism" in E. Kamenka and R. S. Neale (eds.), *Feudalism, Capitalism and Beyond* (1975).

[31] p.98.

[32] K. C. Davis, "Discretionary Justice" (1970) 23 J.Leg.Ed. 56, 60.

Board "can easily enhance the quality of justice it administers" by increases in openness.[33] This may be true in a procedural sense but does not follow as a matter of substantive justice.

What should not be forgotten are the trade-offs between procedural and substantive concerns, between, say, openness and the efficiency with which statutory objectives are achieved.[34] It is Davis's opinion that to subject discretion to open rules, policy statements, and so on will push matters in the direction of "justice,"[35] but, as Albert J. Reiss Jr. has pointed out, [36] Davis does not consider the opposite use of rules and how, in certain circumstances, bureaucracies use structuring to circumvent the interests of individuals. Nor does Davis show how "injustice" occurs because discretion is unstructured, or how (or the conditions under which) structuring in fact leads to less "arbitrary" conduct by officials.

Indeed, the unfortunate fact is that, in certain circumstances, attempts to regulate with rules may lead to *more,* not less, of the mischief to be avoided with increased use of discretionary powers. Thus, the Criminal Justice (Scotland) Act 1980 attempted to regularise the practice of "helping with police inquiries" (the process in which it is unclear whether persons being held for questioning by the police are arrested or not). It did so by creating a new statutory police power to detain on suspicion for six hours and by combining this with administrative rules on detention procedures. Scottish Office research, however, has indicated that, far from regularising police practices, this legislation has encouraged extra-legal detention: officers have been by-passing formalities and recording procedures by threatening to resort to those very formalities, and they have been doing so in an irregular manner.[37] The wider lesson is that, since any enforcement power may be renegotiated in this way, the potential of structuring as a method of regularising bureaucratic action may easily be exaggerated. Another example of the point that more rules lead to considerable difficulties (and a nice irony, given Davis's admiration of the detailed drafting of the Federal tax legislation) is provided in Susan Long's analysis of the enforcement of American tax laws. She

---

[33] p.133.

[34] For a balancing of "transparency, congruence and simplicity" in rules as well as an argument for an efficiency criterion for rule precision, see Colin S. Diver, "The Optimal Precision of Administrative Rules" (1983) 93 Yale L.J, 65, and Diver, "Regulatory Precision" in K. O. Hawkins and J. M. Thomas (eds.), *Regulatory Policy-making* (forthcoming, 1985).

[35] pp.226–227.

[36] Book Review of *Discretionary Justice* (1970) 68 Mich.L.R. 794.

[37] See G. R. Baldwin, "Police Discretion and Law Reform: the Police and Criminal Evidence Bill 1983" Division of Criminological and Legal Psychology of the Psychological Society, 1984. *Issues in Legal Psychology,* No.7: "Legislation for Policy today" (forthcoming, 1985).

discovered that the very complexity of the legislation did not decrease but increased the agency's effective discretion:

> "Complexity, and the uncertainty it spawns, has been a double-edged sword for the IRS [Internal Revenue Service]. On the one hand, it has enhanced many of the agency's powers. Indeed, historically the IRS has sought to exploit this uncertainty 'to protect the government's revenues'—using it as a license to decide cases in whatever way serves the government's interest at the time. . . . The law's complexity, however, cuts in another direction. While increasing tax violations, it makes IRS's burden in providing criminal intent (rather than simple civil errors) more difficult."[38]

Long quotes the United States Commissioner on Federal Paperwork as reporting that a college-level reading ability is required to understand the instructions for the simplest tax form:

> "Varying fact patterns present in individual tax situations make determining the 'correct' tax a matter of judgment on which opinions differ even among experts. . . . Complexity itself adds to the potential for tax violations. Today, except for relatively simple returns taking the standard deduction, it is difficult to speak of a 'correct' return."[39]

So it is not even clear whether structuring by rule-making will reduce discretion at all. Reiss has pointed out[40] that there are many circumstances in which a discretionary decision may be "announced as a rule." Thus, administrators who can choose *which* rule to apply or who can make a new rule on the spot can hardly be taken to be strictly constrained by existing rules. Indeed, Davis concedes that "A rule does not necessarily eliminate discretion."[41] Unless, then, there is a rule to cover all decisions, the only course is for Davis to advocate the pursuit of "the right mix of rule and discretion"[42] in relation to each individual action. He makes general pleas, and suggests ways to curb discretion, but he gives little help in describing how the "optimum" levels of control over discretion may be recognised or arrived at. Nevertheless, he sees the key to the problem of discretion as resting with the promulgation of administrative rules and states:

> "The general objective should be to go as far as is feasible in making rules that will confine and guide discretion in individual cases."[43]

He adds a footnote, however:

> "Unfortunately, how far is feasible, is a question that must be determined for each discretionary power in each particular context."[44]

---

[38] S. B. Long, "Social Control in the Civil Law: The Case of Income Tax Enforcement" in H. L. Ross (ed.), *Law and Deviance* (1981), pp.206–207.

[39] *Ibid.* at p.205.

[40] A. J. Reiss Jr., "Research in Administrative Discretion" (1970) 23 J.Leg.Ed. 69.

[41] K. C. Davis, "An Approach to Legal Control of the Police" (1974) 52 Texas L.R. 703, 706.

[42] *Ibid.*

[43] p.221.

[44] p.221, note 15.

The real issue, then, is contained in the footnote, in the word "feasible," and here is the problem. Davis states that "absolute discretion is not always an evil,"[45] that untrammelled discretion may in some instances even be good but that restrictions on discretion may be useful if used at the optimal level. Davis's reader may feel at this point like a patient who is offered medicine by a doctor with a warning: it may cure him if used correctly but too much or too little may be fatal—that it all depends on the individual. The patient may protest that the doctor's advice is useless unless medical science can help with the real problem—of judging the right dosage.

Unfortunately, the problem is not merely one of choosing the right point on a sliding scale (the controls on discretion operate differently according to the context) and it is necessary to resist the temptation to solve all issues of justice (or accountability or whatever) by inventing a new rule. Here, the danger is to fall into the assumption that justice can be broken down into rules of infinite inclusiveness. Practical notions of justice, not to say the dictates of effective enforcement, far from demanding a mechanical equality of treatment, require that rules are applied with a degree of discretion that caters for individuals and particular circumstances. As Dennis Galligan has said:

> "To individuate is to recognise that, except in rare cases, decisions are not made in splendid isolation from each other but in a context of continuity where criteria and categories are generalised to influence and even determine the outcome of the particular decision, while allowing for proper account of its unique characteristics."[46]

More recently, Daniel Gifford[47] has gone further than Davis in an attempt to offer guidance on how to determine the optimum allocation of rules, standards and discretionary power in regulatory agencies. His analysis, as we shall see, exposes some of the limitations of Davis's own assumptions. Gifford argues that regulatory issues may be represented in a six cell matrix in which the horizontal scale represents the degree to which relevant facts or factors recur in decisions and the vertical scale measures the degree of importance (in terms of regulatory goals) of each case. We end up with the following types of issue: (1) important ones, which involve factors that do not recur; (2) significant cases with recurring patterns in which sporadically occurring elements intrude; (3) significant cases where the relevant factual considerations are

[45] p.152.

[46] Galligan, *loc. cit.* On the "Professional Treatment" model of justice with its recognition of incompleteness of facts, singularity of individual contexts and intuitive nature of judgments, see Mashaw, *op. cit.* Chap. 2.

[47] "Discretionary Decision-making in the Regulatory Agencies: A Conceptual Framework" in Hawkins and Thomas, *op. cit.*; see also Diver, *loc. cit.*

repetitious; (4) cases with recurring patterns whose individual disposition has little effect on the attainment of regulatory goals; (5) cases of little importance with sporadic elements intruding; and (6) non-recurring issues of little significance.

What is wrong with the Davis and Friendly[48] theses, says Gifford, is their idea that the needed narrowing of discretion will come from rules, standards and precedents which will gradually emerge as the agency acquires more information about its tasks and that the needed information will come, in part, from the repetition of the decisional process itself. Gifford argues that the underlying assumption of such approaches is that factual considerations recur. Davis and Friendly concentrate on issues in cells 3 and 4 but largely fail to deal with the other four kinds of decision. This is the reason why Davis's notion of agency decision-making differs from that of, say, Sharfman,[49] historian of the Interstate Commerce Commission, who emphasises not standards or rules in decisions but the non-repetitious caseload of the agency and its ad hoc or "managerial" mode of decision-making. According to Gifford, both the ability to develop standards or rules and their worth in future regulatory activity will be a function of the number of times the issue would be likely to arise and the degree to which the resolution of the issue would aid in disposing of those cases.

To summarise the first part of our argument, it is not enough to assume that "structuring" by standards or rules is always either practicable or helpful or that discretion can be fixed on a purely quantitative scale. What is needed, in Gifford's terms, is both a match between issue-types and procedures for resolution and an opening out of the decision-making process by exposure of all relevant factors taken into account, whether they be standards, principles, political considerations or whatever the context or "frame"[50] within which discretionary decisions are made—what Gifford has termed "decisional referents."[51]

If Davis is to be accused of not going as far as Gifford, he might reply that his was only a "preliminary inquiry" and that judgments concerning the "optimum" levels of control over discretion can only follow the study of many proposals "in each of the thousands of specific contexts of particular discretionary powers."[52] If, however, attention is focused unduly on legal and rational as

[48] H. J. Friendly, *The Federal Administrative Agencies: The Need for Better Definition of Standards* (1962).

[49] I. L. Sharfman, *The Interstate Commerce Commission* (1931).

[50] See K. O. Hawkins, "Thinking About Legal Decision-Making" in J. Shapland (ed.), *Issues in Criminological and Legal Psychology*, Vol. 4 (1983).

[51] D. J. Gifford, "Decisions, Decisional Referents and Administrative Justice" (1972) 37 Law & Contemp.Prob. 3.

[52] p.232.

opposed to other values, then a solid basis for such studies is not offered. Our position is that a proper appraisal of discretionary justice must recognise the part played in decision-making by moral, political, organisational, and economic values, in addition to legal ones. It is, thus, in order to reassert the significance of non-legal values that we take a different view of discretion. Davis was principally concerned to show how discretionary power could be eliminated or controlled. We consider some of those reasons why attempts to reduce discretion or to increase controls over it may not necessarily be the desirable or feasible course of action. In Part II we take a closer look at the nature of a legal decision itself and in Part III consider arguments for a broader view of discretion. The object of doing this is to go beyond exhortations that discretionary judgments be limited "optimally" towards isolation of some of those factors that determine the levels and kinds of control that may be deemed appropriate to certain kinds and applications of discretion. We look at the evidence that to *increase* discretionary power by removing confines, structures and checks—to provide for stronger rather than weaker discretion in Dworkin's sense[53]—may not necessarily be undesirable. We also stress the political values involved in various choices which must be made. Davis advocates the setting of optimum levels of control as if "justice" (like "law") is an obvious, taken-for-granted matter, almost a value-free, non-political factor, one enjoyed equally by all parties. We shall argue that, whatever level of confining, structuring or checking is chosen, this position inevitably involves the asumption of a political stance.

II. The Nature of Legal Decision-making

Lawyers and legal scholars have often fallen into the trap of employing a limited conception of decision-making that does violence to the inherent complexity of decisions which are made in a wide variety of legal settings. One result of this is a tendency to see a "decision" at a particular point in the legal process as an isolated matter, as something logically separable from what surrounds it in the processing of cases. this conception in turn tends to lead to a particular view about the control of discretionary powers. Decisions, in short, are seen as simple, discrete and unproblematic as opposed to complex, subtle and woven into a broader process. (Indeed, decisions may well appear to be simple and discrete because the structure of the legal process often requires them to be that way and because decision-makers have an interest in making them appear as such.)

[53] See R. Dworkin, *op. cit.* pp.31–34. For a sustained account of the strengths and weaknesses of legal control over discretions, see J. L. Jowell. "The Legal Control of Administrative Discretion" [1973] P.L. 178 (hereafter "Jowell").

Take the example of parole decision-making (which was the target, in the work of the Federal Parole Board, for some of Davis's most interesting (and withering) criticism). The "decision" of a parole board is typically treated in the literature within a rationalist paradigm as a choice by an individual or panel which is based on "factors" or "criteria."[54] In quantitative analyses of such decision behaviour, these "factors" or "criteria" are derived from observed input to the decision-maker(s) which is then related to observed output (the decision made). This mechanistic analysis reflects a mechanistic image of decision-making in which there is little conception of it as a continuing process, as a subtle and shifting affair which is a matter of seemingly endless human interpretative work. Such an approach pays too little attention to the problematic nature of the information on which the decision is presumably based, to the interpretative work involved in defining issues as relevant and also to the ways in which cases proceed through the organisational handling system with its own sequence of administrative decisions. "Facts of the case" are thus treated as representing some taken-for-granted reality rather than as the products of complex legal and organisational processes in which reality is socially constructed and recontructed. "Decisions" in such cases involve, in practice, choices between different versions or interpretations of reality. Meaning is given to the "facts" of the case by the moral or ideological stance of the decision-maker and a whole series of frameworks within which any legal decision-maker works: symbolic, socio-political, economic and organisational. Individual differences in interpretation and in decision are then usually resolved by negotiation so that something representing a decision of the board is produced.

One result of a rationalist conception of the decision as a discrete entity is that quantitative research or unsystematic observation of decision outcomes tends to produce evidence of seeming disparities, *e.g.* in sentencing decisions about apparently similar cases. This lends weight to the view that much discretionary behaviour tends to be "arbitrary" or "capricious" (one of the implicit themes of *Discretionary Justice*). However, we need to question ourselves carefully as to how we recognise "disparity." It is important to emphasise here that we are not alleging that disparity does not occur. Indeed, it is a simple matter experimentally to show the extent to which individuals, given exactly the same information about a case, will often respond by making strikingly

[54] See, *e.g.* R. O. Dawson, *Sentencing: The Decision as to Type, Length and Conditions of Sentence* (1966); and D. M. Gottfredson, L. T. Wilkins and P. B. Hoffman, *op. cit.* For a different view, see K. O. Hawkins, "Assessing Evil: Decision Behaviour and Parole Board Justice" (1983) 23 B.J.Crim. 101.

different decisions.[55] What we do urge, however, is a more sensitive understanding of the nuances of natural decision processes so as to understand more fully how outcomes are arrived at and what they represent, and also a greater resistance to the temptation *automatically* to brand apparent variation in discretionary outcomes as an evil. To regard the decision problem from the decision-maker's point of view, with the same information available to that decision-maker, will in many cases reveal a patterned, rational process at work, even in those kinds of decision (like parole or sentencing judgments) readily characterised by lawyers as exercises of largely "unfettered" discretion. In short, it is the narrow legalistic conception of "decision" upon which many accusations of capriciousness are founded and it is this narrow conception that implies that one answer to the "problem" of discretion lies in structuring.

A second consequence of regarding legal decisions as discrete in character is the belief that discretionary power, which exists at a particular point in the legal or administrative process, can effectively be controlled by attention at that one point alone. In fact, discretion so permeates a legal bureaucracy or the linked stages in the civil and criminal justice systems that such simple controls are rarely feasible. To structure or confine discretion at one point in a system without attention to the way that discretionary behaviour is often shaped in response to, or in anticipation of, the behaviour of others leads to the phenomenon of *displacement.* Squeeze in one place and, like tooth-paste, discretion will emerge at another. For example, sentencing and parole practice in the state of California was radically overhauled in the mid-1970s partly in response to substantial concern about the way in which discretionary power was being employed by the Adult Authority (the state's administrative sentencing and parole board).[56] Critics were concerned with the seeming disparities in decisions made about apparently similar cases, about the uncertainties created in a system in which discretionary decisions to fix terms of imprisonment were not announced in advance of the service of those terms, and generally about the apparent arbitrariness of the Adult Authority's practices. In short, their views were the stuff of which Davis would approve. The response was to obliterate all post-conviction

[55] See, *e.g.* P. T. Takagi, "Evaluation Systems and Adaptations in a Formal Organisation: A Case Study of a Parole Agency" unpublished Ph.D. dissertation, Stanford University (1967).

[56] We recognise that other matters also had a part to play in the change of sentencing and paroling policy in this state and others, though this does not alter the point we wish to make here. The illustration is drawn from an unpublished paper by Keith Hawkins, "On fixing time: Reflections on Recent American Attempts to Control Discretion in Sentencing and Parole." which was presented to the Howard League Seminar Series on "The future of Parole" at the London School of Economics in October 1980.

discretion to fix or change prison terms (except for remission for good behaviour during imprisonment). The suspicion of discretionary decision-making was also sufficiently strong for the legislature to reject a sentencing model based on judicial discretion. Instead, the legislature, in the words of the California Penal Code, declared "that the elimination of disparity and the provision of uniformity of sentences can best be achieved by determinate sentences *fixed by statute* in proportion to the seriousness of the offense as determined by the Legislature" (our emphasis).

The result of this striking change was not, however, to eliminate discretion in sentencing, but simply to displace it. The evidence suggests that pre-trial bargaining between prosecutors and defendants over charge or plea has continued unabated. Since, in imprisonable cases, conviction for a particular offence is now automatically—in the absence of judicial or administrative discretion—tied to a precise term of years, this means that real authority to fix actual sentences of imprisonment has been transferred to prosecutors who are unaccountable officials getting their work done by bargaining in private—using their discretion, that is, in ways which Davis would almost certainly condemn. Thus, even where confining or structuring is in Davis's terms "feasible," it may actually accomplish far less than some would have us believe, and may, indeed, have adverse consequences.

A broader idea of the nature of a "decision" is important for further reasons. First, many kinds of decision are largely uninformed by legal rules because legislatures are unable or unwilling to contemplate the complexities of particular case decisions. They are often quite happy to restrict themselves to vague statements and broad objectives, leaving questions of action in routine cases to the discretion of administrative officials. For example, the Water Act 1973, requires the Regional Water Authorities to take action "necessary or expedient . . . for the purpose of conserving, redistributing or otherwise augmenting water resources" and "securing proper use of water resources" (s.10), and generally speaks of "the restoration and maintenance of the wholesomeness of rivers" and "the enhancement and preservation of amenity" (s.1).[57]

In any case, the influence of rules on decisions is unclear. What decision-makers may articulate as "criteria" or "principles" may amount to no more than justifications for judgments already reached on other grounds. Furthermore, we should also contemplate the possibility that the rationality of decision-makers has been

[57] See further K. O. Hawkins, *Environment and Enforcement: Regulation and the Social Definition of Pollution* (1984).

exaggerated and that many kinds of legal decision in practice are made without being logically thought through.

A second point is that what is regarded as a "decision" actually consists of two very different components. We typically regard a legal decision as concerning action, *e.g.* arrest, sentence or settlement. More subtle, however, are the prior decisions to be made in defining the "facts" or matters deemed relevant to the decision. "Facts" in legal cases are by no means self-evident, but have to be matters for interpretation by decision-makers. Some of the central concepts in legal decisions, such as "crime" or "record," "culpability" or "compliance", often involve considerable interpretative work by a decision-maker, because the exercise of discretion involves a search for meaning. Furthermore, choices must be made about definitional issues or choices about which pieces of information are to be treated seriously. To claim that a rule is being followed is to take for granted the interpretative work surrounding fact-finding and, indeed, the judgments made about the rule itself, its nature and relevance.[58] Davis tends to apply his remedies at the *formal* locus of discretionary authority, whereas in fact many decision-makers (like parole board members) may be doing little more than ratifying decisions already made for them by those who supply "information" and assessments. Information suppliers can thus in certain circumstances consciously achieve desired decision outcomes. For example, it can be shown that different decisions tend to be made in response to a single value shift in a sentence appearing in a report, even though the words employed do not change. A probation officer who reports that "He has been getting drunk recently, but has continued to work well" will achieve fewer decisions to revoke parole than one who writes: "He has continued to work well, but has been getting drunk recently."[59]

Thirdly, it is important to bear in mind that there are variations in the number and kinds of decision-maker. Some are apparently individuals, such as policemen or judges. We say "apparently" because effective decision-making authority in legal systems does not usually rest in one place but is more often diffused among those who provide information, evaluation or opinion. Thus, there can be few cases in which an individual makes a decision alone, without a supply of material or knowledge which comprises a

[58] See, *e.g.* R. M. Emerson, "Holistic Effects in Social Control Decision-Making" (1983) 17 Law and Society Rev. 425.

[59] See further, J. O. Robison *et al.*, "By the Standard of His Rehabilitation: Information, Decision and Outcome in Terminations from Parole: the Implementation of Penal Code Section 2943," Research Report No. 39, Department of Corrections, State of California (1971); K. O. Hawkins, "Thinking About Legal Decision-making," *loc. cit.*; and "Assessing Evil: Decision Behaviour and Parole Board Justice," *loc. cit.*

"case." Policemen may act alone in making decisions about the arrest of an individual, but a judge in the courtroom must rely on a lengthy often formal process conducted largely by others before making a decision, say, about the sentencing of a convicted offender. Many legal decisions, however, are made by panels or groups of individuals—for example, tribunals, appeal courts, juries and parole boards. In those settings there is not only a flow of information to the individuals concerned but the possibility of a variety of interactional effects between them in the process of reaching a decision. Since the law often requires a binary choice to be made as to the culmination of the discretionary process (guilty/not guilty, paroled/not paroled, and so on), interaction of this kind assumes central importance where individuals do come to different conclusions about the proper decision. A negotiating process commonly results in one outcome that purports to be—and is treated as—a collective view. There is also, of course, a further category of mixed decisions where the outcome is neither the product of an individual's nor a panel's judgment but is routinely the result of negotiations between a number of individuals or groups of individuals representing different parties or interests. Thus, decisions about charging in criminal cases emerge from interaction between police and prosecuting authorities.

Defining "justice," then, is difficult enough when discretion is assumed to be discrete in character and to reside in particular individuals at finite points in the legal process. In reality, however, we have argued that matters are far more complex. Thus, when decisions emerge from a process, there may, at each formal discretionary point, be quite different value systems operating, and concerning which a separate notion of justice is to be formulated. For instance, the broad concerns of police discretion are not the same as those of sentencing or paroling discretion, and the preoccupations of inspectors in a regulatory agency, who typically regard themselves as "at the sharp end," may be quite distinct from those of their supervisors at head office who may be more concerned with matters of broad agency policy, organisational image, or self-preservation.[60]

A final issue is the kind of decision produced as a result of the exercise of discretion. We have already suggested that many of the key legal decisions have binary outcomes. Although the world is not a simple place, the law likes to address social problems with the rigours of binary logic: one is "married" or not; a member of a "family" or not; "unemployed" or not (even though in reality

[60] Hawkins, *op. cit.* (1984); K. Young, "Discretion as an Implementation Process" in Adler and Asquith.

people might find it difficult to use such uncompromising descriptions). Complex issues are thus rendered into binary form, because law is in the business of solving problems. This causes difficulties that go beyond those involved in a single interpretative process. There are some kinds of decision that wholly defy neat categorisation. Thus, American parole boards often make deferred decisions as a bargaining ploy in marginal cases—they decide to release but not for six months.[61] Is this, in binary terms, a decision to "release" or to "deny"? In fact, it is not so much a "decision" made as a bargain struck: the release provisionally agreed upon may be revoked if an undertaking (for example, about improved conduct in prison) is not fulfilled.

III. Discretion Reconsidered

What does all this tell us about discretionary justice? It helps to see Davis's advocacy of structuring, confining and checking from a different perspective. Davis's thesis, it should be clear now, is cast in a rationalist paradigm and rests on a narrow view of discretionary behaviour—as simple, unproblematic, and mechanistic. The broader view, derived from a naturalist paradigm, which pays attention to the complexity of the decision-making process, shows that there may be less to the idea of structuring than meets the eye. Controlling a particular "decision" cannot necessarily be assumed to have a revolutionary impact on the wider decision-making process—and any impact it does have may be unanticipated or undesirable, or both. That a revised view of discretionary power is required becomes more clear on considering a number of particularly difficult problems that are encountered in attempting to confine, structure and check discretions.

1. Access to justice, rights and efficiency

To create rights for individuals and to legislate for openness may not in practice be to protect or improve the status of those individuals. To judicialise the procedures for allocating welfare benefits, to grant rights protected by law and to provide for legal representation at all instances of welfare decision-making may not be in the interests of the recipient if it means that to gain any benefit he or she has to go through the process of hiring and instructing lawyers and has to endure the vast increase in decision-making time consequent on judicialisation of procedures.[62] To

[61] K. O. Hawkins, "Some Consequences of a Parole System for Prison Management," in D. J. West (ed.), *The Future of Parole* (1972).

[62] See R. M. Titmuss, "Welfare 'Rights' Law and Discretion" (1971) 42 P.Q. 113; Jowell; *cf.* Charles Reich, "Individual Rights and Social Welfare: The Emerging Legal Issues" (1965) 74 Yale L.J. 1245.

introduce lawyers and rights may not only fail to eradicate discretion but may prejudice the very people the system is supposed to benefit. On this point, Davis himself is clear[63] that the way to improve welfare administration is not to increase emphasis on rights in adjudication but to improve the informal procedures that precede and substitute for adjudication.

The real point, however, is that administrative formalisations of procedure and the creation of further protections can no more be assumed to render a state of affairs just than can resort to "lawyers' law." Titmuss pointed to the defects of "legalism" defined as "an insistence on legal rules based on precedent and responsive only very slowly to rapidly changing human needs and circumstances."[64] It cannot, however, be taken for granted that all administrative rules will prove more responsive to such needs. "Justice" is a multi-dimensional phenomenon. Concern for *procedural* justice may run counter to the underlying concern for substantive justice. A procedure may be made more open to the point of inefficiency (*e.g.* arguing about shares in a fruit crop while it rots); procedural concessions may be used to disguise worsened substantive rights[65] (a fair hearing may be worth far less to a welfare claimant than an increase in benefit); or rights may be given that are either unenforceable or short-circuited by bureaucrats. In Mashaw's terms, the problem is to resolve the tensions that exist between different perspectives of bureaucratic justice. Thus, he outlines three justice models for a disability programme under the headings "Bureaucratic Rationality," "Professional Treatment" and "Moral Judgment."[66] Each model differs in its emphasis upon goals, and synthesising such divergent models is more complex than choosing the optimal point on a single continuum between minimum and maximum discretion.

There are other difficulties left unresolved by Davis. At no point, as we have noted, does he describe the *circumstances* in which rule-making will or will not be more "just" to individuals than unstructured discretion or adjudication. It is easy for critics of the "extravagant version" of the rule of law to state that in, say, welfare cases, adjudicative methods and judicialisation may disadvantage claimants, but it is similarly arguable that, without proper regulation of rule-making procedures, these procedures may be used as unjustly as adjudication—for example to allow low-level staff to administer complex issues in a scheme whose objective is

[63] p.186.
[64] Titmuss, *loc. cit.*, p.124.
[65] See Adler and Asquith, pp.16–18 and 169–170.
[66] Mashaw, *op. cit.*, Chap. 2.

bureaucratic convenience,[67] or to exclude the ill-organised individual from rule-making in favour of larger and more powerful groups.[68] Thus, Jeffrey Jowell[69] points out that administrators under certain conditions use rules as "shields" that allow decisions to be routinised, reasons for any finding to be readily produced, and decision-makers to be both insulated from political pressures and lent authority for any particular exercise of power.

It may, in some instances, be better for an administrative body to resist the temptation to make rules and to concentrate instead on the adjudicative process. Thus, where decisions are taken in a rapidly changing economic sphere, to purport to decide on the basis of outdated rules may help no one. Similarly, in certain areas the extreme tendency to indulge in over-inclusive rule-making and the dangers of this (for example, of discrediting the agency and of encouraging rule avoidance by enforcers) may render the enterprise pointless. Policy-making by trial-type adjudication has a number of advantages over rule-making.[70] It is open and flexible; it deals with particulars; it gives opportunities to examine hypothetical instances, and it makes the discussion of alternatives available to those affected by any policy. Again, it cannot be assumed that a discretion limited by rules or standards is necessarily better than one that is less confined but more often exercised and reviewed.

A second point concerns the notion of justice again. Just as a variety concepts of justice may apply to the same bureaucracy, there may be found within any group of parties affected by a decision-maker some very different conceptions of "justice." Thus, for example, when considering the decisions of a body that distributes air transport licences, a large and long-established airline may think that a just system is one that is judicialised, rational, based on published rules, supportive of the status quo and amenable to low-risk planning. A more aggressive operator who benefits from some chaos and who wishes to expand markets rapidly may have a very different notion of a just regime—as fast-reacting, and not necessarily based on slowly-developed and published rules but open to innovation and the rewarding of enterprise. To argue consistently in favour of rule-making and adherence to those rules is therefore to express a particular political position.

Davis rightly urges that discretions (and the feasibility of limiting them) should be dealt with in their particular contexts, but we

[67] See T. Prosser, "The Politics of Discretion: Aspects of Discretionary Power in the Supplementary Benefits Scheme" in Adler and Asquith, pp.165–166.

[68] See B. A. Hepple, book review of *Discretionary Justice* [1969] C.L.J. 313.

[69] Jowell, *op. cit.* pp.190–191.

[70] See D. L. Shapiro, "The Choice of Rule-making or Adjudication in the Development of Agency Policy" (1965) 78 Harv.L.R. 921.

would add that those contexts should not be viewed narrowly as a result of restrictive conceptions of "decision" or "justice." The economic, political, administrative and social effects of different methods of controlling discretion may vary enormously. Crucial factors in assessing the feasibility of controlling discretion include the kinds of decision to be made (social, economic, technical, etc.), the sorts of client dealt with, and the gravity of consequence of each decision. Compare, for instance, the different kinds of decision involved in supplementary benefits and civil aviation licensing. In the case of the former, there are large numbers of decisions on matters of only moderate economic importance (though not to those involved) that affect persons lacking extensive resources or expertise. In aviation licensing, relatively few decisions are taken but these may be of considerable economic consequence and affect a limited group of parties who are well-equipped to argue their case. To structure discretion in the one instance may serve as a device for the rapid processing of cases at the cost of individualisation, while in another area, such as aviation or broadcasting licensing, structuring may have the very different effect of allowing powerful economic interests to have more say in policy-making and greater opportunity to co-ordinate their planning with the regulatory strategies in force. Depending on status and organisation, then, structuring and other forms of control of discretion make decision-making more or less responsive to the interests of affected parties.

Instead, therefore, of extolling the virtues of controlling discretion in the interests of "justice," the questions before administrative lawyers should be redrafted on a wider basis. The first issues in looking at any discretionary power should be political ones: what values should be advanced? What sort of accountability should be sought here? What are the appropriate concepts of justice and how can tensions between them be resolved? What degree of inefficiency should be suffered for the sake of perceptions of fairness or openness? What are the practical limitations of these remedies or rights in such a context? What can be accomplished by legal as opposed to administrative and other systems of control?[71]

2. *Expertise and judgment*

Davis's concern with individualised justice rather than policy-making raises questions about the ability of his argument to deal with the accelerating fusion in modern government of policy-making and adjudication. Increasingly, agencies are being set up in

[71] On the difference between the strategic and functional limits of law, see Jowell, *op. cit.* esp. Chap 5.

Britain to exercise an expert, professional or technical judgment, to make policy, to decide issues between parties and so to relieve central government of difficult problems. Thus, in the last 20 years, Britain has seen the birth of a number of multi-powered regulatory agencies such as the Independent Broadcasting Authority, the Civil Aviation Authority, the Gaming Board, the Equal Opportunities Commission, the Commission for Racial Equality and the Office of Fair Trading.

These bodies respond to the need in modern government for judgments to be made on matters that involve, *inter alia*, general political policy, as well as economic, technical and social issues, and this has to be done in rule-making as well as in adjudication. Thus, agencies decide whether an airline's traffic forecasts seem over-optimistic or whether a television company will be able to attract personnel of the promised calibre. Such exercises of judgment demand that an agency is left an area of discretion within which its decisions are given weight. As Reiss has pointed out, Davis is happy dealing with rule-following bureaucrats but is less concerned with the problems of technocratic or professional decision-makers:

> "Bureaucracies are built on rules and on the notion that decisions must be made according to those rules and with relatively little choice in applying them. Professional decision-making is based on quite the opposite model—the necessity to exercise judgment when confronted with the individual case."[72]

To this extent, Davis's approach is attuned to the "transmission-belt" model of administration in which statutory objectives are applied to particular facts in unproblematic fashion, but, as Richard Stewart has pointed out,[73] this model is of diminishing utility in systems of government that delegate ever-broader powers to peripheral bodies.

Roberto Unger[74] lends support to this view, arguing that the movement from the liberal to the welfare state has a marked effect on the role of law. Government assumes managerial responsibilities in areas where the complexity and variability of factors are too great to allow recourse to general rules. There is a rapid rise in the use of open-ended standards in legislation, administration and adjudication. This is accompanied by a turn from *formalistic* styles of reasoning (in which all legal choices can be deduced sufficiently from rules) to *purposive* reasoning in which the decision about how to apply a rule depends on a judgment (by an administrator or

[72] Reiss, Book Review of *Discretionary Justice* (1970) 69 Mich.L. R. 792.

[73] R. B. Stewart, "The Reformation of American Administrative Law" (1975) 88 Harv.L.R. 1067.

[74] R. M. Unger, *Law in Modern Society* (1976).

judicial agent) as to how the purposes ascribed to a rule may most effectively be achieved. A formal notion of justice, says Unger, is persuasive in the realm of exchanges between individuals but is less so when dealing with issues of government and distribution. Davis calls rule-making procedure "one of the greatest inventions of modern government,"[75] but the very nature of post-liberal government may limit the potential of such procedures.

3. Polycentricity and the justiciable

Closely related to this argument is the point that there are certain areas of activity that are ill-suited to regulation in accordance with pre-formulated rules, principles and standards (whether adjudication is involved or not). This may be for the reasons noted above—because special expertise is required—or for two other main reasons: the nature of the matter to be decided upon or the practicalities of enforcement.

Looking at the nature of the issues to be decided, it has often been argued that some issues are "polycentric"[76] rather than amenable to binary answers. In polycentric issues, many factors interact so as to shift the grounds of decision-making from beneath the lawyer's feet. In these cases, rational justification offers a less solid foundation for decisions than balanced judgment or assessment of values. To attempt to restrict the makers of such decisions by means of rules, principles, standards or procedural demands would be to employ the wrong tools, indeed almost to make a category mistake (*e.g.* a rule that after each match the team spirit should accept a drink).[77] We agree with Davis's urging that agencies should open out their procedures so far as is feasible, but the picture he constructs is misleading if applied in this context. He portrays a situation in which bureaucrats constantly resist structuring and by so doing keep it below an "optimal" ceiling. The implication is that it is in nearly all cases impossible to press controls beyond that optimal point—the bureaucrats will be too efficient in their resistance.

This model—a tug-of-war—misleads first because it is by no means difficult even to exceed the "optimal point": after all many United States agencies are criticised for their over-inclusive structuring via rule-making.[78] (It is perhaps indicative of the sort of rule-bound world that Davis envisages that he refers to the 4,000 pages of double-column fine print that constitute the Federal Tax

[75] p.65.

[76] M. Polanyi, *The Logic of Liberty* (1951); P. Weiler, "Two Models of Judicial Decision-making" (1968) 46 Can. Bar Rev. 406; L. Fuller, *The Morality of Law* (1964), p.83; Jowell, pp.213–214.

[77] See G. Ryle, *The Concept of Mind* (1970), p.18.

[78] See, *e.g.* E. Bardach and R. A. Kagan, *Going by the Book* (1982).

Regulations as "an especially admirable body of law."[79]) Davis states that the "cancer" of discretion tends to prevail over rules but to assume this would be to belittle those strong bureaucratic influences that foster the multiplication of rules. Eugene Bardach and Robert A. Kagan[80] have recently focused attention not on the propensity of bureaucrats to under-structure but on their tendency to regulate excessively (by filling in the "holes" in regulatory schemes) with over-indulgent rule-making.

4. Enforcement and discretionary power

A broad distinction can be made between two kinds of reason for limiting the extent of legal regulation in an area of decision-making. Thus, Jeffrey Jowell distinguishes the *strategic* issue of "whether legal techniques will prove effective means to achieve certain ends" from the *functional* one of whether it is possible to submit a task to legal control.[81] The strategic issues deal with practicalities (*e.g.* can the actions of the constable on the beat be governed by rules?): functional questions deal with more formal matters (can rules be devised to govern the activity at all?).

Some of the problems of enforcing a set of rules, principles or standards may be regarded as strategic matters. There are many circumstances that militate in favour of a large degree of discretionary power and against maximising Davis-style controls. One problem is controlling the enforcers. The example of the Scottish criminal justice legislation given in Part I indicates that both legal and administrative rules may simply be ignored or by-passed by enforcement officials who see them as impediments to "getting the job done."[82] In such circumstances, it is necessary to resort to alternatives to the sort of controls advocated by Davis.

Another problem is how to enforce successfully. In the case of agencies given the function of enforcing a body of law in a specialist area, the attainment of broad social objectives is often sought in a setting that either lacks effective legal sanction, does not allow the application of such sanctions, or does not allow the employment of one set of legal rules across the board. Whereas it might be argued that (in terms of substantive fairness) all supplementary benefit claimants should be treated similarly, practical and political circumstances would make such notions of fairness far more difficult to apply in some other regulatory fields, for example, when dealing with water or air pollution. If fixed

---

[79] p.43; see also our discussion in the text at note 37.

[80] Bardach and Kagan, *op. cit.*

[81] Jowell, *op. cit.* p.133.

[82] For police enforcement and a discussion of working, inhibitory and presentational rules, see the Policy Studies Institute Report, *Police and People in London* (1983), Vol. IV.

standards were set and enforced on factories without discretionary intervention (*i.e.* according to the "transmission-belt" model of administration),[83] larger factories might comply but a number of smaller operators might well go out of business. A public outcry against oppressive regulation would doubtless ensue and the agency would be discredited (as happened with the Occupational Safety and Health Administration in the United States). Other considerations, such as limitations on resources and time, also rule out non-discretionary enforcement. In practice, as researchers have found,[84] regulators at field or street level have to go about their business by negotiation and bluff. Such are the sanctions in pollution matters that there is a further point: automatic resort to law (even if there were the resources of time, staff and money to make it possible), risks demonstrating on a large scale the inadequacies of many penalties, exposing the law to ridicule and making further enforcement yet more difficult. In these circumstances, in short, a large measure of discretion is preferable to the exercise of rigidly controlled power for a number of reasons:

(*a*) certain enforcement activity involves a large core element of discretion that is unavoidable (*e.g.* environmental enforcement, policing);
(*b*) sanctions may be weak and their application excessively costly;
(*c*) achievement of public-interest ends may more efficiently be obtained by discretionary power (more, that is, may be achieved at less political expense);
(*d*) those affected by a discretionary power might be no better protected were a change made to strictly defined powers; and
(*e*) rigidly controlled discretions might overload the capacity of other parts of the legal system to handle the consequences.

For these reasons, we have reservations about some of the arguments recently made by one author who does offer guidance on optimal levels of discretion. Colin S. Diver is concerned with the "optimal precision" of rules and with the payoffs between what he deems the qualities of transparency, congruence and simplicity in rules. He develops an efficiency criterion for selecting the optimal precision of a regulation, but in doing so says, for example:

> "Increasing a rule's verbal clarity should reduce the cost incurred by both the regulated population and the government, of applying a policy to specific circumstances."
>
> "A major affirmative argument for regulatory precision is to promote voluntary compliance by the rule's addressees."[85]

---

[83] Stewart, *loc. cit.*
[84] See Hawkins, *op. cit.* (1984) and H. L. Ross and J. M. Thomas, "Blue Collar Bureaucrats and the Law in Action: Housing Code Regulation in Three Cities," unpublished paper (1981).
[85] Diver, *loc. cit.*

It is by no means clear from British experience, however, in such areas as the regulation of pollution, that a system of precise commands strictly enforced with prosecutions would be any more effective in securing compliance than negotiations based on (and indeed the result of) more vague rules. It is even less clear that precision plus enforcement would turn out to be more cost-effective. Precision in fact may lead to increased use of prosecution, but also ironically to a more costly and ineffective system of enforcement.[86]

Here once again we see the limitations of dealing with discretion without considering the degree of political (or other) accountability that is appropriate. A high level of discretion may be controlled in a way that owes little to Davis's methods. Thus, it is arguable that controlling police stops and searches may be far more efficiently accomplished by making the force accountable to local communities than by structuring that discretion with detailed rules that few officers will remember and fewer will use as working guides. To look to the rules and not to accountability is unjustifiably to give priority to one particular type of control mechanism—a view resulting from the notion of discretion as the hole in the doughnut of rules.

Rule-making by enforcement officials may, moreover, be highly contentious in constitutional terms. Davis puts the issue thus: "But can enforcement policies be determined through rule-making if substantial reformulation of enacted law results? For instance, if a statute flatly provides that gambling is a crime, can the police formally, through rules, provide that church bingo games and social poker games are not a crime?"[87] His answer is "Yes": if it is a choice between "secret ad hoc policies" through ad hoc decisions and open policies adopted through rule-making, then the latter are preferable.[88] Davis says it is "confused thinking" to prefer secret ad hoc policies on the basis of respecting enacted law, but there is a real danger here of allowing enforcement officials to prevail over the law for the sake of being "realistic." No one would quibble with the adoption of policies that do not fetter discretions that are conferred and defined by statute, but openly to allow such fettering, whether for resource or policy reasons, is to set up law-makers quite outside the democratic process. Furthermore, in a federal or localised system, it opens up the possibility of divergent laws and practices in different areas of the country. To refuse legislative

[86] See P. W. J. Bartrip and P. T. Fenn, "The Evolution of Regulatory Style in the Nineteenth Century British Factory Inspectorate" (1983) 10 J. Law and Soc. 201; P. W. J. Bartrip and P. T. Fenn, "The Administration of Safety: The Enforcement Policy of the Early Factory Inspectorate, 1844–1864" (1980) 58 Pub. Admin. 87.

[87] p.93.

[88] See, on this point, K. C. Davis, *Police Discretion* (1975), Chaps. 3–5.

power to officials is to accept that a disparity exists between the word of the law and the realities of enforcement; it is to uphold the legitimacy of the legislative process, but it is also to impose considerable limitations on the use of structuring devices.

5. Confining, structuring and checking: when spoiled for choice

Since different procedures such as rule-making and adjudication have various merits and disadvantages,[89] there are choices to be made between the various forms of control that may be exerted over discretionary power. It would be wrong to assume that all controls over discretion "shoal" like mackerel—running in parallel and changing direction in miraculous simultaneity. In the case of an agency, it would be easy to propose, for example:

(i) increases in the precision of its statutory objectives;
(ii) increases in ministerial and democratic controls over the agency;
(iii) it should publish statements of policy, rules of practice, hypothetical guidance, etc.;
(iv) it should judicialise its procedures;
(v) it should open out its rule-making, findings, reasons and precedents; and
(vi) it should open out and control its informal procedures.

To advocate the concurrent implementation of the above six proposals would be to misunderstand the way that administrators work. Some of the above strategies are largely incompatible (*e.g.* judicialising procedures and increasing ministerial control), so it cannot be assumed that the more of the six that are implemented the more just or efficient the regime created will be. As we have already noted, there is no point in creating specialist bodies only to fetter their powers to exercise judgment with detailed rules.

There is no given hierarchy of methods of structuring discretion. When there exist choices between statutory objectives, formal provisions for ministerial guidance, self-administered policy statements and formally issued rules, what dictates the appropriateness of one method or the other is, as Davis acknowledges, the particular circumstances of the field of decision-making—whether, for instance, flexibility is required or more durable guidance. These circumstances are complex, however, and a concern for political accountability makes it difficult to opt for a particular technique of control on the basis merely of the "size" of discretion. Thus, the *inclusiveness* of rules is liable to increase when moving from statutory objectives to ministerial guidance to agency-issued rules, but the degree of political *accountability* involved is liable to

[89] See Shapiro, *loc. cit.;* and G. O. Robinson, "The Making of Administrative Policy: Another Look at Rule-making and Adjudication and Administrative Procedures Reform" (1970) 118 U.Pa.L.R. 485.

diminish. In one sense, control over discretionary power increases (*i.e.* in detail); in another it decreases. The choice, therefore, is between packages made up of sometimes contradictory parts, and it would be misleading to argue as if one simply measured the quantity of a homogeneous entity called discretion and then assessed its desirability.

At another level, there are more difficulties. The appropriateness of different devices to limit discretion may depend on an assessment of a body's status and functions. Thus, whether to structure licensing decisions by means of detailed rules may depend on whether an agency is seen as being essentially engaged in policing and enforcing standards or distributing largesse or operating an industry or regulating private management (indeed, there is almost inevitably some divergence of view about the broad purposes of regulatory activity). Where there is such uncertainty or disagreement within particular organisations and governments, the choice of suitable methods of controlling discretion becomes even more problematic.

The argument can be taken further. In some instances, there are reasons for using one device for the control of discretion rather than another and, by so doing, *increasing* discretionary power. One interpretation of Davis's writing (not necessarily his own) is that checking is a way to cut down discretionary activity to add to confining and structuring. Another view, however, is that the checking device may be used as an *alternative* to confining and structuring. One study of such practices was described in 1967[90] when Gabrielle Ganz examined the operation of the Control of Offices and Industrial Development Act 1965, the Industrial Development Act 1966 and the Local Employment Act 1960. There the decision had been taken to confer discretionary powers instead of mandatory duties on the Government. In the case of the 1960 Act, there were none of the safeguards of openness, fairness, and impartiality that had been recommended by the Franks Report; there was no right to a hearing; reasons were not given for decisions, nor was there any right to appeal. Informal processes, internal reviews, parliamentary checks and "treating each case on its merits" were emphasised rather than judicialisation or openness. There had been "a retreat from law in this area,"[91] but Miss Ganz concluded:

> "The working of this machinery shows that the interests of the individual may be as effectively protected by a purely administrative process as by legal rules. Just as the private individual may respond better to persuasion than force, so the official may act more humanely

[90] G. Ganz, "The Control of Industry by Administrative Process" [1967] P.L. 93.

[91] *Ibid.* at p.104.

when he is operating an informal negotiating machinery than when he has to satisfy formal rules."[92]

To make this point is not to say anything incompatible with Davis's views on checking: it is to caution against structuring as a method of first resort and to warn that the choice of whether to check or structure is more than an issue of quantifying something called "discretion." After all, how an official exercises a discretion may be far more important than how much discretion is possessed.[93]

Similarly, there is a temptation, to be resisted, to treat judicial review as another control over discretion that can be added beneficially to any mixture of such controls. For his part, Davis's inclination is to clear away any obstacles to judicial review.[94] The implication again is that there is nothing to fear in openness, judicialisation and review:

> "The worst that can happen from opening the judicial doors in a doubtful case will be that a court will decide on the merits."[95]

To "open the doors" to the courts is portrayed as a fairly marginal change that brings worthwhile benefits to individuals; but there are a number of reasons why facilitating judicial review on substantive issues might considerably (and adversely) affect the way that the administration works. (Arguments that the courts should be ready to interfere to protect procedural safeguards are less contentious since this avoids second-guessing on the merits.) The following possible effects come to mind readily but are insufficiently dealt with by Davis:

(i) Judicial review makes the courts rather than the agencies the ultimate arbiters of policy. It puts non-experts in charge of those who have been asked to exercise special judgment and it increases the hand of lawyers as opposed to experts in deciding specialist issues which are translated into legal terms. The hearings process may differ so radically from the administrative decision-making process as to produce wildly divergent results and to introduce inconsistency to a decision-making process by interfering on a case-by-case basis.[96]

(ii) It makes the agency decision a staging post to the courts, it encourages defensive decision-making by regulatory bodies, and it threatens to demoralise agency staff.

---

92 *Ibid.* at p.105.

93 P. Nonet, *Administrative Justice: Advocacy and Change in a Government Agency* (1969), quoted in Bradley, *loc. cit.* p.37.

94 Davis, *loc. cit.* pp.157–161, 207–214.

95 p.230.

96 See Mashaw, *op. cit.* pp.190 and 202, who would abolish judicial review in favour of internal bureaucratic law in the case of social security administration.

(iii) It slows down decision-making and increases costs.
(iv) It increases private rather than public control of regulation since private parties in the main dictate the bases of challenge of the public interest agency. Fairness to particular individuals may, as a result, prevail over general considerations of public interest.

6. The public interest and political choices

It follows from the last section that one ground for advocating more rather than less discretion may be the political choice to be taken between public and private interests. A factor in such a choice will be the degree of autonomy that people are prepared to allocate to bureaucrats. Davis's clear concern is to improve the hand of private sector lawyers who wish to further the interests of their clients at undisclosed cost to the pursuit of the public interest: he is backing the *gesellschaft* rather than the bureaucratic-administrative model of law again.[97] The evil genies here turn out to be government lawyers:

> "Our system is the result of long-term, rudderless drift, and the main wind that has blown has been the constant ingenuity of government lawyers to win their cases. Private lawyers, even the ablest, have often been outwitted by the extreme of specialization in the technical defenses by the government lawyers . . ."[98]

In political terms, then, Davis's concern is that government officials have proved too effective in pursuing their objectives (perhaps bureaucratic ones rather than public interest ones) where these are at variance with certain private interests. His argument assumes that to allow private lawyers more ready recourse to the judiciary will inevitably improve "justice." What is really advocated is a shift in authority away from largely public regulatory interests to those of private concerns together with a similar shift of decision-making power away from administrators and government towards the judiciary.[99]

IV. Conclusion: The Appropriate Control of Discretion

We have focused on three main aspects of Davis's approach to discretion: his conception of discretionary justice; his legalistic ideals; and his limited help in judging when the optimum level of control over discretion is reached. In his "preliminary inquiry,"

[97] See the references cited at note 30, *supra*.
[98] pp.159–160.
[99] One might contrast Davis's advocacy of greater freedom for private parties to approach courts with the House of Lords' recent espousing of procedural protections for public bodies in applications for judicial review: see *O'Reilly* v. *Mackman* [1983] A.C. 120 (esp. Lord Diplock).

Davis argued that advances in administrative law could be made in the following way:

> "Not only must almost every proposal be examined in each of thousands of specific contexts of particular discretionary powers, but the first necessary step has to be to bring together for the first time a tremendous amount of information about the discretionary functions now performed within our federal, state, and local governments . . . The need for more descriptive and critical studies of the realities about the administration of government programs seems to me urgent."[1]

We strongly agree, and urge that, if Davis's outstanding contribution is to be built on, discretionary behaviour should be dealt with not as an unproblematic matter but as part of complex social, organisational and political processes. Treatments of discretion tend to err in at least two ways: by looking at particular powers without consideration of their essential nature or their broader context, or by being mere exhortations that are premissed upon assumptions about the homogeneity of discretion. In order to improve any understanding of the potential of various controls over discretion, attempts must be made to see the strengths and weaknesses of various control devices and to predict both the interaction between them and their implications for the operation of other parts of the administrative process. Efforts should be made to isolate those features which in social and political life affect what can be done to control discretion and which bear on the choices to be made in setting up different control systems. Lawyers, for their part, can contribute by resisting the assumption that any move to limit discretion is of necessity a good in itself.

[1] pp.232–233. For an extensive listing of discretionary powers, see the Law Reform Commission of Canada's Catalogue of Discretionary Powers in the *Revised Statutes of Canada* (1970).

[10]

The Politics of Legalism: Rules versus Standards in Nursing-Home Regulation

JOHN BRAITHWAITE AND VALERIE BRAITHWAITE

Australian National University

PRECISE RULES give more explicit guidance than vague standards. It would seem to follow that regulators will enforce precise rules more reliably than vague standards. This article demonstrates empirically that this is not necessarily so. It also induces from data on nursing home regulation the beginnings of a theory of a reliability paradox. We show how pursuit of reliability for a part of the law can increase the unreliability of a whole body of law. Reliability is used here with the standard scientific meaning of the extent to which measures give consistent results, as contrasted with validity, which means the extent to which measures assess the 'true' position. A 12-inch ruler that in truth is 13 inches long gives reliable (consistent) but invalid (untrue) measurement.

Our aim is to contribute to the rules-versus-standards debate in law, to regulatory policy analysis and to debates about reliability in science. A rule is taken to be a legal norm of the form, in circumstance X, do Y or not-Y. A standard, in contrast, enjoins the pursuit or achievement of a value, a goal or outcome, without specifying the action(s) required to do so. The divide is not a neat one, the world being full of rules about standards and standards about rules. Nevertheless, some bodies of law are more dominated by standards and others more by rules.

Social & Legal Studies (SAGE, London, Thousand Oaks, CA and New Delhi), Vol. 4 (1995), 307–341

THE RELIABILITY PARADOX OF REGULATORY INSPECTION

The sociolegal literature on rules versus standards is itself paradoxical. On the one hand, there is a literature claiming to show that American law is more standards-oriented, British law more oriented to rules. The most important contribution to this literature, Atiyah and Summers' (1987) *Form and Substance in Anglo-American Law*, makes the more general claim that American law is more substantive, British law more formal (see also Krotoszynski, 1990). On the other hand, the comparative literature on regulatory enforcement concludes that enforcement in other nations is less formal than in the United States (see generally, Bardach and Kagan, 1982; Braithwaite, 1987), including Britain (Day and Klein, 1987; Hawkins, 1984; Vogel, 1986), Sweden (Kelman, 1981), Australia (Grabosky and Braithwaite, 1986) and Japan (Badaracco, 1985; Haley, 1988; Upham, 1987; Vogel, 1979). Data collected for the present study of nursing-home regulation fit both stories in terms of the British–American comparison, in that British nursing-home regulation operates with more precise and formal rules than the more substantive, standard-like American nursing-home regulations, while British regulatory practice is more discretionary, more oriented to securing improvement in the quality of care and less interested than in the USA with collecting evidence for litigation concerning non-compliance with rules. While American law is more substantive and less formal than British law, British nursing-home regulatory practice is less formal than is American practice.

It may be that these opposite tendencies are indeed both true and have their origins in the same historical variable: the greater distrust of the state in America, compared to Europe and Asia (see Kagan, 1991; Vogel, 1986). Distrust of the legislature by the courts and by litigants energized by the more vigorous American separation of powers (an institutionalization of distrust) is one factor that may have resulted in the creation of a more substantive jurisprudence by American courts. Distrust of the executive by interest groups (litigants) and the courts has led them to pursue the limitation of administrative discretion, driving regulators to more formal regulatory enforcement. In other words, courts and interest groups in America operationalize institutionalized distrust of the state by going substantive with statutory interpretation and by driving the executive to go formal with application of the law. Courts and interest groups play the separation of powers to seize power from the legislature by judicial discretion in the interpretation of statutes, just as they seize power from the executive by limiting its discretion.

While this is a way of reconciling two literatures on the greater formality of British jurisprudence and the greater formality of American regulatory enforcement, in this article we deal with a different comparison. We find that both Australian nursing-home law and Australian nursing-home regulatory practice are less formal than in the USA, which may express a higher degree of trust among the legislature, the executive, the industry and advocacy groups – tripartite consensus building. This has meant in this arena (since 1987 reforms) that private interests rarely used courts or lobbied parliamentarians for more formal laws to achieve their objectives (Braithwaite, 1994).

The cross-national comparison illuminates themes from the American Critical Legal Studies (CLS) literature on rules versus standards, particularly the work of Duncan Kennedy (1976) and Mark Kelman (1987). Kennedy and Kelman see a reliance on standards as premised 'on the hope of moral dialogue and ultimate consensus, since the standards will remain contentless unless such moral dialogue succeeds in overcoming the skeptical sense that one person's conception of what is just is nothing more than either a whimsical taste or a rhetorical cover for a self-serving program' (Kelman, 1987: 62; see also Michelman, 1986). Our case study shows this hope being more or less realized in Australia at least for one little domain of regulation for a very short period of history.[1] The point that Kelman and Kennedy make is that rules do not depend on communities seeking consensus; standards do.[2] Kelman and Kennedy contend that the rule mentality is therefore a liberal individualist one, a contention disputed by Pierre Schlag (1985; see also Radin, 1989: 806 and n. 88; Rose, 1987: 606–10; Sullivan, 1992).

From another ideological perspective, we would put it that a rule-orientation in law conduces to liberal individualism, whereas a standard-orientation can both conduce to and depend on a degree of republican community. Rather, if it does not depend on a degree of republican community among those concerned with a particular issue, like nursing-home regulation, a standards-orientation will conduce to unchecked domination. Meidinger (1987) reports the existence of 'regulatory communities' even in the USA.

In the rules-versus-standards debate, CLS scholars pick up themes from American Legal Realists, who were fond of showing how the presumed precision of rules enabled imprecision. One reason they pointed to was that courts usually confront a choice of which of a number of precise yet contradictory rules they choose to invoke in a particular situation: 'each rule was in fact radically undercut by its fratricidal twin' (Kelman, 1987: 48; see Schlag, 1985: 409). Moreover, both realists and critical scholars indicate that often when the nominal rule is formally clear and consistent, the real operative rule for invoking it is opaque and inconsistent. The speed limit is 60, but the operating rules are that anything up to 65 or so will be ignored or let off with a warning (unless contempt is shown to the police officer or the officer wants to detain a person to check out compliance with some other rule). Hence the law and society injunction: study the law in action rather than the law in books. If your concern is consistency, you are bound to be misled unless you study consistency of the law in action. Our present study seeks some clarification of the rules-versus-standards debate by examining law in action. It shows empirically what CLS scholars assert when they say 'the text cannot define its context' (Schlag, 1985: 410):

> If we concede that the sector of the social world cordoned off by directive can be affected by the external world, then the only way in which a directive can be certain is if it is sufficiently flexible to accommodate the effects of the external world.

This refutes the view that 'the choice between formulating or interpreting a legal directive as a rule or as a standard is a choice between . . . certainty or flexibility, uniformity or individualization' (Schlag, 1985: 399). Rather, there are contexts where standards are both more certain and more flexible, more uniform and more individualized than rules. Nursing home regulation we find here to be one such context. It will be shown to be a context where plural dialogue framed by few standards (rather than many rules) is better.

Consistency of compliance assessments has come to assume pre-eminent importance in policy-making within regulatory bureaucracies. This is especially true of political debates about nursing-home reform and regulation in Western democracies. It is our contention that this central regulatory preoccupation with consistency is misplaced and that reliability is not the most important desideratum of a set of standards for inspecting nursing homes or any other industry. We propose a paradox in which reliability is more likely to be achieved when reliability is not the central objective of public policy. When we make other objectives our central concern – such as designing standards which best foster a regulatory dialogue about how a nursing home can improve quality of life outcomes – an indirect effect may be that better reliability of ratings is achieved. We advance this paradox by considering recent reforms in Australia and then comparing them to the state of American nursing-home inspection.

NURSING-HOME REFORM IN AUSTRALIA

Following a series of nursing-home scandals, consumer activism and two parliamentary enquiries (McLeay Report, 1982; Giles Report, 1985), the Australian government launched a package of nursing-home reforms in 1987. The first element of the package was a new set of 31 outcome-oriented standards negotiated through the active collaboration of federal and state governments, industry and professional, union and consumer groups. The consensus standards that attracted the assent of all these groups were so broad that they were attacked as 'motherhood statements' by many who were not immediately engaged in their negotiation. We agreed with these critics at the time. Moreover, while the standards were marketed as 'Outcome Standards for Australian Nursing Homes', many of them (listed in Table 1) did not look like outcomes to us. Since then, we learned that degree of outcome-orientation is primarily a matter of regulatory process design rather than standard-wording (Braithwaite et al., 1990: 135–41), a point to which we return.

Another fundamental concern we had about the new Australian standards was that they just could not be reliable. They were broad, subjective, lacking in detailed protocols,[3] and the process by which they were to be rated was absolutely unattentive to sampling issues. Moreover, the process was resident-centred when we knew that a high proportion of residents would be confused and unreliable informants. Compounding these problems was a shift toward the inclusion of many 'soft' social and resident rights standards, in contrast to the previous exclusive focus on 'harder' structural or health-care inputs, that could be checked with a ruler, a thermometer or by confirming a doctor's signature. It was inconceivable to us that standards concerned with the resident's right to 'privacy and dignity' or a 'homelike environment' could be rated reliably. We certainly thought these standards were a 'good thing' because they would stimulate a dialogue that was sorely needed. But we harboured the deepest of doubts that they could be legally enforceable, doubts shared at the time also by the government's lawyers, industry's legal advisers, and the consumer movement.

In 1987, when we started an international comparative study of nursing-home regulation in Australia, the USA, Britain and Japan, we were rather embarrassed by the Australian standards. We would say to American regulators: 'We know they are only a start and we have a lot of work to do to flesh out the kinds of guidelines and protocols that you have built up over the years.' They in turn would look aghast at how broad, vague, undefined and unenforceable these quaint Antipodean standards were. Since that time, our research findings provided quite strong grounds for believing that the broad, unrefined Australian standards are not just more reliable than US standards but more reliable by a wide margin. Furthermore, observations of 59 nursing-home inspections in Australia and 44 in the USA between 1988 and 1993 suggest that the reason Australian ratings are more reliable is precisely because they are more (a) broad, (b) subjective, (c) undefined with regard to protocols, (d) resident-centred and (e) devoid of random sampling.

THE AUSTRALIAN RELIABILITY STUDY

Inter-rater reliability studies are extremely rare in the literature on regulatory inspectorates. In fact, the nursing-home inspection data from the USA and Australia that we discuss in this article are almost the only reliability data of which we are aware on any type of regulatory inspectorate in any country.[4] There are two reasons for the rarity of such research. First, government agencies are normally fearful of studies which might show that their judgements about compliance with the law are arbitrary and capricious. Such data might be used by defence lawyers to destroy the legal foundations of the regulatory regime. Second, such studies are difficult to do – expensive, logistically a nightmare, and intrusive for the organizations being inspected. Funding agencies, governments and regulated organizations are all therefore resistant to regulatory reliability research.

Elsewhere (Braithwaite et al., 1991: 12) we discuss how these sources of resistance were overcome in this study. An essential step toward overcoming industry resistance was the need to avoid compounding the disruption of a government inspection with a reliability inspection immediately before or after. We did this by placing a single reliability rater in the nursing home at the same time as the government inspection team. The government inspection team of two or three inspectors spends an average of 6.5 hours inspecting the facility. Australian facilities tend to be much smaller than US facilities, the median number of beds being 38. Because the reliability raters had to do the job alone, they generally arrived before the team and left after them, occasionally having to come back for a second day.[5] The single reliability raters could compensate for the need to do the work of two and sometimes three others in five additional ways, beyond spending more time in the facility: (1) they did not need to stop to explain problems to facility staff and management; (2) they did not need to take extensive notes for use in an official report; (3) they did not need to collect the evidence to document a finding in the event of enforcement action; (4) they did not need to stop to compare notes with other team members; and (5) they also had the advantage of being more senior, experienced nurses. We were able, therefore, to sell the study to nursing homes on the grounds that the only extra disruption they would confront was having one additional inspector in their home for the duration of the normal standards monitoring visit, and perhaps a little longer.

Methodologically, there are both advantages and disadvantages to this approach. A disadvantage is that guidelines had to be enforced to prevent the team and the independent rater from communicating with each other in any way about standards during the visit. This we believe was successfully negotiated (Braithwaite et al., 1991). An advantage is avoiding the problem of sequential visits whereby the nursing home has the opportunity of rectifying problems identified by the visit of the first team before the second team arrives.

SAMPLE

Details on the selection of the two independent raters, the 30 inspection teams from New South Wales and Victoria, and the sampling frame for the nursing homes are provided elsewhere (Braithwaite et al., 1991: 13–15). Only one nursing home refused to cooperate in a quota sample of 50 nursing homes with quotas for (a) number of beds in the home, (b) non-profit-for-profit status, (c) state and (d) composition of the inspection team. The sampling for the reliability study had to be quota sampling because the inspectors at the time were in the midst of working through the stratified random sample of homes that we had selected for our wider evaluation (Braithwaite et al., 1990). Within the discretion allowed by their quotas, independent raters were instructed to be especially on guard against a bias toward 'easy' nursing homes. They were told: 'If you have to err, err on the side of homes which are more likely to be problem homes, because these will be the homes which give you more opportunities to disagree with the team.' As it turned out, independent raters did err quite significantly on the side of homes with more problems. While the average number of 'met' ratings for all homes was 23, the average number of 'met' ratings for homes in the reliability study was 18.

RESULTS

Agreement between the independent rater and the government inspection team was measured at three points in time. After the team completed its visit, the team met (usually the next day) to discuss as a team the positives and negatives observed on each standard and to agree on initial ratings. Soon after, they would meet with the independent rater to compare their (blind) initial ratings. The percent of agreement between these initial (totally independent) ratings are provided in the first column of Table 1. The standards are rated into three categories – 'met', 'action required' and 'urgent action required'.[6] On Standard 1.1, 84 percent agreement means that for 84 percent of the nursing homes, the team and the independent rater gave the home exactly the same rating on this 3-point scale. Once both sides had been apprised of each other's ratings, they were asked to discuss why they had reached different conclusions on certain standards. During this discussion, one side would sometimes persuade the other that they were wrong. On occasion, the combining of their information caused both sides to conclude that they had been wrong. This generated the 'after conferring' ratings, the measure of agreement in the second column of Table 1. After the team had been back to the nursing home for a further visit to advise the nursing home of their ratings (giving the nursing home an opportunity to provide further information that might rebut them), the team passed this information on to the independent rater. Both sides then had the opportunity to change their ratings again in light of the feedback from the nursing home. These final ratings were the basis for calculating agreement in the third column of Table 1. At each stage, the reasons for disagreement and changes of heart were recorded. Data on the reasons for disagreement on different standards are elaborated elsewhere (Braithwaite et al., 1991: 18–30). Broadly, disagreements based on the collection of different information were equal in number to disagreements based on different interpretations of the standards.

A high level of overall agreement was recorded for all standards. Not surprisingly, this level of agreement increased slightly after conferring. Receipt of negotiation feedback from the nursing home made only a minor difference – on some standards increasing agreement slightly, on others reducing it slightly. There are some surprising results in Table 1. For example, the 'homelike environment' standard (4.1), which no one we know would have predicted to be reliable, was rated quite consistently – with 88 percent blind agreement rising to 94 percent after conferring. Similarly, it was assumed that reliability was implausible on the 'soft' social and residents' rights standards. Yet soft standards such as 5.1, 'The dignity of residents is respected by nursing home staff,' were rated with impressive reliability.

The first suspicion one should harbour about the exceptionally high agreement in Table 1 stems from an assumption that in a majority of cases both teams and independent raters give nursing homes met ratings. As a statistical artifact, it follows therefore that met-met agreement will be very common. For example, if the probability of getting 'a met' is 0.9, the likelihood of getting two mets on purely statistical grounds from two independent assessors is going to be 0.9×0.9, that is, 0.81. Conversely, if the probability were lower for a met, that is 0.5, the likelihood of two mets is much lower (0.25). Two considerations render this explanation for high reliabilities implausible. First, with the Australian standards, 12 of the 31 had proportions of mets under 50 percent. In the US system, the distribution tends to be more extreme (met ratings often over 90 percent). Second, with the Australian data, independent raters are not more likely to agree with teams on 'met' ratings than they are on 'action required' and 'urgent action required' ratings. It is simply not true that our high reliabilities

TABLE I

Overall Agreement between the Team and the Independent Rater[a] and the Kappa Coefficient[b] (n = 50)

Standard	*Initially* (%)		*After Conferring* (%)		*After Negotiation* (%)	
1.1 Residents are enabled to receive appropriate medical care by a medical practitioner of their choice when needed.	84	(0.76)	90	(0.85)	92	(0.88)
1.2 Residents are enabled and encouraged to make informed choices about their individual care plans.	90	(0.81)	92	(0.85)	90	(0.81)
1.3 All residents are as free from pain as possible.	90	(0.61)	94	(0.75)	94	(0.70)
1.4 All residents are adequately nourished and adequately hydrated.	90	(0.86)	92	(0.87)	94	(0.90)
1.5 Residents are enabled to maintain continence.	78	(0.56)	86	(0.73)	86	(0.73)
1.6 Residents are enabled to maintain and, if possible, improve their mobility and dexterity.	90	(0.81)	96	(0.92)	96	(0.92)
1.7 Residents have clean healthy skin consistent with their age and general health.	98	(0.91)	98	(0.91)	98	(0.90)
1.8 Residents are enabled to maintain oral and dental health.	96	(0.91)	96	(0.91)	96	(0.91)
1.9 Sensory losses are identified and corrected so that residents are able to communicate effectively.	84	(0.66)	86	(0.71)	88	(0.74)
2.1 Residents are enabled and encouraged to have visitors of their choice and to maintain personal contacts.	90	(0.77)	94	(0.86)	96	(0.90)
2.2 Residents are enabled and encouraged to maintain control of their financial affairs.	94	(0.86)	94	(0.86)	96	(0.90)
2.3 Residents have maximum freedom of movement within and from the nursing home, restricted only for safety reasons.	94	(0.85)	98	(0.95)	94	(0.75)
2.4 Provision is made for residents with different religious, personal and cultural customs.	94	(0.84)	98	(0.94)	96	(0.88)
2.5 Residents are enabled and encouraged to maintain their responsibilities and obligations as citizens.	90	(0.62)	94	(0.77)	98	(0.90)
3.1 The nursing home has policies which have been developed in consultation with residents and which, regarding their daily activities, – provide an appropriate balance between residents' rights and effective management of the nursing home, – and are interpreted flexibly taking into account individual resident needs.	88	(0.75)	92	(0.84)	92	(0.83)
3.2 Residents and their representatives are enabled to comment or complain about conditions in the nursing home.	84	(0.71)	94	(0.89)	90	(0.81)
4.1 Management of the nursing home is attempting to create and maintain a homelike environment.	88	(0.77)	94	(0.89)	94	(0.89)
4.2 The nursing home has policies which enable residents to feel secure in their accommodation.	86	(0.73)	90	(0.81)	92	(0.84)
5.1 The dignity of residents is respected by nursing home staff.	92	(0.88)	98	(0.97)	98	(0.97)
5.2 Private property is not taken, lent or given to other people without the owner's permission.	96	(0.94)	98	(0.94)	98	(0.97)
5.3 Residents are enabled to undertake personal activities, including bathing, toileting and dressing in private.	88	(0.82)	94	(0.91)	94	(0.91)

Standard	Initially (%)		After Conferring (%)		After Negotiation (%)	
5.4 The nursing home is free from undue noise.	94	(0.87)	96	(0.91)	92	(0.82)
5.5 Information about residents is treated confidentially.	90	(0.80)	96	(0.92)	96	(0.92)
5.6 Nursing-home practices support the residents' right to die with dignity.	96	(0.86)	98	(0.94)	98	(0.93)
6.1 Residents are enabled to participate in a wide range of activities appropriate to their interests and capacities.	92	(0.84)	94	(0.88)	94	(0.88)
7.1 The resident's right to participate in activities which may involve a degree of risk is respected.	94	(0.85)	96	(0.90)	94	(0.82)
7.2 Nursing-home design, equipment and practices contribute to a safe environment for residents, staff and visitors.	82	(0.71)	92	(0.87)	90	(0.84)
7.3 Residents, visitors and staff are protected from infection and infestation.	92	(0.87)	98	(0.97)	96	(0.94)
7.4 Residents and staff are protected from the hazards of fire and natural disasters.	94	(0.91)	94	(0.91)	96	(0.94)
7.5 The security of buildings, contents and people within the nursing home is safeguarded.	98	(0.96)	98	(0.96)	98	(0.96)
7.6 Physical and other forms of restraint are used correctly and appropriately.	92	(0.87)	92	(0.87)	90	(0.83)

[a] Overall agreement means the team and the independent rater gave exactly the same rating. These were for ratings made using the new format of met, action required and urgent action required. The percent agreement was identical under the old format (met, met in part, not met) with the exceptions of Standard 5.6: 94 96 96; and Standard 7.2: 84 90 88.

[b] The kappa coefficients are in parentheses next to the percent figures of overall agreements.

reflect ease of agreement when the standard is met compared with difficulty in reaching agreement when it is not met (agreement for all standards by rating categories is presented in Braithwaite et al., 1991: 19–22).

Based on factor analytic work, we elsewhere argue that it is psychometrically defensible to add scores on the 31 standards to obtain a total compliance score (Braithwaite et al., 1990, 1992), something that would probably not be defensible on American Medicaid survey results. Overall, the inter-rater reliability coefficient for the blind ratings of the total compliance score is 0.93, increasing to 0.96 after conferring and remaining at 0.96 after negotiation with the nursing home. These reliability coefficients show no major variation by raters, state, size of home, level of disability of residents or ownership status. While these data show impressive intrastate reliability within the two largest Australian states, they do not demonstrate interstate reliability. That is, while two inspectors trained in the same state give the same ratings, they may both give different ratings from an inspection in a different state. Indeed, our qualitative fieldwork inclines us to agree with critics who say there are serious problems of interstate reliability.

The weakness of this reliability study is that the reliability rater is an individual rather than another team. Our expectation, however, was that reliance on an individual as the reliability rater would reduce rather than increase reliability. We expected that the reliability rater would fail to pick up information that the team picked up by virtue of having at least one extra set of eyes and ears. We tried to compensate for this by allowing the reliability rater to stay in the nursing home longer than the team did and by using reliability raters who, in our opinion, were more experienced and acute observers than the average team member, but we never expected that this would fully allow the reliability rater to overcome the information-gathering deficit. This interpretation of why reliance on a single rater would reduce rather than increase reliability was borne out by the results of the study. At the conferring and negotiation stages, there were more cases of the reliability rater agreeing that she had made an erroneous rating by missing vital information than there were cases of teams agreeing that they had made erroneous ratings by failing to pick up some vital piece of information.

In addition to this reliability work, we also report some encouraging validation studies on the standards (Braithwaite et al., 1991; Braithwaite et al., 1992). Of particular interest here is that we asked 410 directors of nursing[7] to give their own nursing homes ratings on the 31 standards soon after an inspection team had visited their nursing home. The average agreement of directors of nursing with team ratings across the 31 standards was 92 percent, the lowest being 84 percent on homelike environment ratings (4.1). Directors of nursing naturally gave themselves higher ratings than did the teams, but the correlation between their total compliance scores and scores given by teams was 0.88. The consensus of industry understanding on the meaning of these standards that permits such a result is based on 93 percent of directors of nursing in Australia having attended a course on the standards. This process also led to an extraordinarily high level of belief in the 'clarity', 'desirability' and 'practicality' of the standards by directors of nursing and proprietors (Braithwaite et al., 1990, 1991, 1992). The worst result for any of the standards on these three criteria was on Standard 2.2, 'Residents are enabled and encouraged to maintain control of their financial affairs,' for which 24 percent of directors of nursing had doubts about the standard's practicality.

American Reliability Studies

How then do these Australian reliability results compare with the results of American reliability work? The first major empirical study of nursing home inspection was the Wisconsin Quality Assurance Project. That project piloted its own quality of care measure which was independent of the state regulatory process (Gustafson et al., 1980). Based on just 11 criteria, it was a much simpler measure than that used by Wisconsin state inspectors. Five two-person teams of nursing-home professionals visited nine nursing homes, giving 45 data points for the calculation of reliabilities. An average reliability coefficient on this simple measure of quality of care of 0.78 was obtained. This measure was also validated against a global 0–100 assessment of the quality of care of each home ($r = 0.76$), the global assessment itself having been found to be reliable (Gustafson, 1977). This pilot therefore demonstrated that two-person teams could rate the quality of care in nursing homes with reasonable reliability. Unfortunately, when the two measures of quality of care were correlated with the number of deficiencies cited by the last government inspectors to visit the nursing home, the correlations were not statistically significant at the 0.05 level. This early study thus gives us the first clear clue to the direction in which we are led by our results: Reliable ratings of the quality of care in nursing homes are possible when professional raters use a limited number of criteria; *but* when raters use the large number of specific American regulations as their criteria, reliability is lost. This was the pilot study on the Wisconsin quality of care instrument.

In the final study, 12 homes were visited by 3 teams (36 data points). The reliability and validation of the simple quality of care instrument improved slightly compared to the pilot, but a very low association of this simple instrument with the number of citations issued by government inspectors of 0.12 was found on another sample of 65 homes (Gustafson et al., 1982). So we get the same general picture as in the pilot – reliable rating of a simple quality of care measure combined with a poor relationship of this reliable measure with compliance ratings from government inspections.

Another particularly discouraging finding of the Wisconsin project is summarized in the final report:

> The final important result in problem identification came from a comparison of problems identified by federal validation teams versus the QAP and traditional processes. There were no differences in methods in terms of the number of conditions found out of compliance. However, there were substantial differences between state and federal teams at the standard and element level. (Gustafson et al., 1982: 5)

This sounds discouraging but it was actually something of an understatement. It is true that 'There were no differences . . . in the number of conditions found out of compliance.' Neither the state inspectors nor the federal validation inspectors found any 'conditions' out of compliance, so there was perfect agreement! Condition-level was the most serious level of non-compliance rating and was rarely given. A freedom of information request to the funding agency, the United States Department of Health and Human Services, by Dr John Gardiner revealed that at the next level of seriousness of citation – the standard level – the state inspectors had cited three standards as out of compliance for the 20 homes in the study, while the federal validation team cited 28. Total deficiencies cited at the standard and element levels (the latter being the lowest level of seriousness) for the 20 nursing homes were 437. There was agreement on only 8 percent of these between the state and federal validation teams. For 92 percent of these deficiencies, one team was citing something that the other team had not cited.

One reason for these disturbing differences could be that the federal validation surveys (inspections) were done on average 30.5 days after the state survey. However, the internal memorandum secured by Dr Gardiner's freedom-of-information request pointed out: 'While changes at the facility between surveys do cause differences in findings, most facility changes are corrective actions which would reduce the deficiencies between the first (State) and second (Federal) surveys.' In fact, deficiencies rose sharply between the first set of inspections and the second. Moreover, the memorandum pointed out: 'The majority of deficiencies found on the second (Federal) survey existed, and should have been identified during the first (State) survey.'

Another major University of Wisconsin study was published in 1985 on data from New York, Massachusetts and Wisconsin (Zimmerman et al., 1985). While the number of data points for the reliability coefficients was only 13 (two teams visiting 13 homes in New York and Massachusetts), the results were much better. This time, with the teams in the nursing homes at the same time and in different states, 58 percent of deficiencies cited were cited by both teams. An impressive 84 percent of deficiencies detected by state teams were also detected by independent teams, though there was a much larger number of deficiencies detected by independent teams which were not detected by state teams.

Both teams returned to these nursing homes four months later to assess whether the deficiencies on which the two teams agreed had been corrected. The state teams judged 96 percent to be corrected and the independent teams 71 percent. In this study multiple regressions using the Wisconsin quality of care indicator found only weak validation of the number of deficiencies detected by inspectors ($p < 0.1$), but much stronger validation of the total severity of deficiencies detected ($p < 0.05$).

The third American reliability study of the ratings of compliance with nursing-home regulations was based on double inspections of 21 Tennessee homes (Spector et al., 1987). There was a one-day interval between visits to the nursing home. Both teams were inspectors from the Tennessee Department of Health and Environment. Both teams were large (averaging 8.7 for the (official) first team and 5.5 for the second validation team); and both had unusual breadth of disciplinary coverage – always including nurses, a generalist, a social worker, physiotherapist and pharmacist. The official team also included a dietician, sanitarian and fire inspector.

Only 25 percent of the regulations cited by the official team were also cited by the validation team (Spector et al., 1987: 119–23). Again, one might have expected that the second team would have found less because the nursing home would have acted to correct the deficiencies detected by the first team. The second team, however, found twice as many deficiencies as the first.[8] These studies highlight the reliability paradox. How can the US system which involves many more inspector-hours in the nursing home, larger multidisciplinary teams and more sophisticated protocols on more precisely specified standards produce such low reliability, while the Australian system produces such high reliability?

While all the studies we are comparing from both sides of the Pacific have considerable deficiencies, the tenor of the findings are so diametrically opposed that it is hard to make sense of them in terms of method error.[9] This is especially so since we believe that the very extensive fieldwork we have undertaken since 1987 (see Braithwaite et al., 1993: Appendix A, 'Data and Methods'), including observing nursing-home inspectors doing their work during 103 inspections in the two countries, makes sense of our counterintuitive findings. To this interpretive work we now turn.

WHY ARE AUSTRALIAN STANDARDS MORE RELIABLE?

We advance five answers to the question of why Australian nursing-home standards are more reliable than US standards: It is because they are (1) broad; (2) undefined with regard to protocols; (3) subjective; (4) resident-centred; and (5) devoid of random sampling. Put even more provocatively, we will show why the very desiderata revered within the received scientific wisdom of American gerontology are responsible for the unreliability of nursing-home inspection. The tendency of the gerontological consultants who advise US governments on nursing-home inspection policies is to cast blame at the competence of nursing-home inspectors. Our experience is that American nursing-home inspectors seem of better-than-average competence compared to business regulatory inspectors from many fields that we have observed in Australia and other parts of the world. What our investigation calls into question is the competence of the scientific analysis that has been offered of the American process.

1. THE EFFECT OF BROADNESS OF STANDARDS ON RELIABILITY

The Australian standards in the words of one consumer advocate are 'wishy-washy and blunt'. Their breadth and vagueness certainly makes them appear an implausible regulatory instrument. Consequently, there is pressure under the surface in Australia for standards that look more scientifically and legally respectable. Before we succumb to such pressures, it is well to contemplate how those pressures have been played out in the USA during the past 25 years.

Historically, what has happened in the United States is that key political players in the nursing-home regulatory game came to be critical of broad, vaguely defined standards. The industry has been at the forefront of this criticism; when nursing home X gets a not met rating on a broad standard on which nursing home Y in similar circumstances gets a met rating, home X screams about inconsistency. It complains to its industry association about the vagueness of the standard leading to 'subjective' and 'unfair' judgements by inspectors. The industry association representing these member grievances pleads for the standard to be 'tightened up'. Consumer groups also agree that the standards should be made more specific, but for different reasons. They are concerned that vague standards are unenforceable. Legislators have been responsive to these pleas because they feel frustrated that inspectors are not cleaning up the industry the way they had hoped; their analysis fits nicely with that of the industry and consumer groups. These standards, the legislators conclude, are so vague that they give the inspectors too much discretion to subvert the legislative mandate. This indeed is also the analysis of many top regulatory bureaucrats in the federal government. They are frustrated at the failure of the states to deliver federal hopes. Part of the blame they lay at the door of standards so vague as to allow wide discretion for inaction. Finally, the technocrats – the behavioural and medical scientists and the lawyers – despair at vague standards. The scientists believe in tight protocols to ensure that the same things are being assessed in exactly the same way using precisely defined criteria. The lawyers believe, like the consumer advocates, that vague standards are difficult to enforce in the courts and, like the industry associations, they believe that vague standards result in abuse of discretion.

Hence, if there is one thing that all of the influential players of the American regulatory game have agreed upon it is that broad standards which are not tightly specified must be narrowed. The consequence has been an historical process of all these constituencies succeeding in having one broad standard broken down into two narrower standards; then later each of those two standards being subdivided into three standards.

By 1986 the logical conclusion to this process was reached to the point where there were over 500 federal standards ('Tag numbers'). Outcome-oriented reforms in 1986 reduced these to 357, but this was short-lived respite with the 1987 Omnibus Budget Reconciliation Act (OBRA) reforms[10] adding a large number of new and tighter standards. Moreover, in some states, the number of state standards exceeds the federal standards by a factor of two or three. In most states, federal and state standards are surveyed simultaneously. The upshot is that most of the people who inspect US nursing homes are checking compliance with over a thousand regulations – a stark contrast with the 31 Australian standards. How do they cope with such a daunting task? The answer is that they do not. Some of the standards are completely forgotten, not suppressed by any malevolent or captured political motive, just plain forgotten. Such standards are never cited in the states where they are forgotten. Then there are those that become familiar by some accident of enforcement history that gave prominence to a particular standard in a particular state. Referring to state regulations, one midwestern inspector said: 'We use 10 percent of them repeatedly. You get into the habit of citing the same ones. Even though possibly you could use others [for the same offence]. Most are never used.'

The professional background of the inspection-team members is one important criterion that selects which standards will be attended to. Administrator: 'If you've got a nurse, it will be nursing deficiencies in the survey report; if a pharmacist, you'll get pharmacy deficiencies; a sanitarian, sanitary deficiencies; a lawyer, patient rights, etc.' We observed a Medicaid survey team to rate all dietary standards in a facility 'met' for the reason that the dietary problems looked so serious. How can that make sense? The team felt that the dietary problems were so bad that they could not check them all out properly and get all the other standards checked in the time-frame required by the Health Care Financing Administration (HCFA) to complete the survey; so they 'deferred' the dietary problem for two weeks until a dietician could be booked for a specialist survey. When we went out with the dietician two weeks later on this survey, sure enough, a great number of the dietary standards rated met in the survey report submitted to the federal government were rated 'not met'.

The point of these examples is that when surveyors have an impossible number of standards to check, arbitrary factors will cause particular standards to be checked in some homes but neglected in others, causing endemic unreliability. At its best, the American process works in the following way. The inspectors meet together at the conclusion to their information-gathering, as they do at certain intermediate points during the inspection, to share the problems they have found. When a number of negative findings are judged to constitute a pattern of non-compliance of a particular type, a search begins for a 'Tag number' which can be written up as not met. Once all the problems have been agreed and Tag numbers found to write not mets for them, the team leader ticks met for all the remaining standards. As she does so, she does not read them or think about them and she certainly does not check with her colleagues that someone has collected the information necessary to reach that met rating. Usually she will not discuss with her colleagues the possibility that the same pattern of conduct that caused one standard to be rated not met should also cause several other standards to be out of compliance (for example, an inappropriate use of restraint may cause standards concerned with restraint, following physician's orders, resident choice, mobility and freedom of movement to all be out of compliance).[11] In other words she makes one valid not met rating and several invalid met ratings as a result of this strategy. This we said was the American process at its best. At its worst, the team partitions responsibility for the standards, each writing up their own standards with little input from the other team members.

What is the relevant contrast with the Australian process in this regard? It is not easy for Australian teams to keep 31 standards in their heads even though none of them has mandated protocols. Yet they can make a fist of it. More critically, after their visit the team can (and generally does) sit down to discuss, standard by standard, the evidence collected by all team members relevant to each one. This dialogue is formalized by the team agreeing on a list of positives and negatives to be written beside each standard. Sometimes they will find that they have not collected the data necessary to reach a reliable rating on the standard. They must then take steps to collect the extra information. There is no escape from this because the team is required to sit down with the management of the nursing home, to summarize the positives and negatives on each standard and to give reasons for their final ratings. Again the American 'exit conference' is different in that it reports only exceptions. Nothing is said about standards that have been ticked met. It would be difficult to do so since the team has neither debated compliance with them nor assured themselves that they have collected the data relevant to them. The crucial difference is that Australian teams actually do deliberate on all their standards and collect the evidence that they judge sufficient to support that deliberation.

It is not the fault of American inspectors that they do not do this – the number of standards and protocols with which they must live makes this quite impossible. The end result of demands for more specific standards with more clearly defined protocols that cover all the things judged to be important for nursing homes is an inspection package that is structurally unreliable. The pursuit of the reliability of parts causes the unreliability of the whole.

If American inspectors give up on keeping all these standards in their heads, what is their cognitive coping strategy? It seems to us that they have a gestalt of the prohibitions codified in the regulations – for example, that good infection control is required; that privacy must be protected; that good nursing practice should be followed. It is likely that professional training informs these gestalts more than the law does. They then decide whether a citation ought to be written by deciding whether it offends against one of these gestalts. Then they search for the appropriate regulation under which to cite it. 'What will we call it? How about 1220 A? What about 1220 B? Why don't we use both of them?'

After explaining to a number of surveyors this interpretation, based on our observation of how they coped, they agreed that this was basically how they did it. When we pointed out that the most troubling implication of this process from the point of view of reliability was that depending on how hard they searched through the standards, they might find one or two or three deficiencies to write out, one of them said, tellingly: 'Or they might find none at all and have to mush it in.' Decisions about how hard to search for multiple citations for essentially the same problem are driven by a 'professional judgment' of 'how serious overall their problems have been' or 'how hard they've been trying.' 'You can write it out under [X] and create a repeat violation because they got a deficiency on [X] last time. Or you can write it out under [Y] so its just an element, which has no real consequences. Or you can put it out under both [X] and [Y], putting out a whole standard.'[12]

Hence, hand-in-hand with a paradox of reliability is a paradox of discretion. More and more specific standards are written by lawmakers in the misplaced belief that this narrows the discretion of inspectors. The opposite is the truth: the larger the smorgasbord of standards, the greater the discretion of regulators to pick and choose an enforcement cocktail tailored to meet their own objective. A proliferation of more specific laws is a resource to expand discretion, not a limitation upon it (Baldwin and Hawkins, 1984).

The beauty of a small number of broad standards is therefore that one can design a regulatory process to ensure that the ticking of a met rating means that a proper process of information-gathering and team deliberation has occurred on that standard. One accountability check in Australia is that whenever enforcement action is appealed, the team's worksheets listing all of the positives and negatives they found under each of the 31 standards must be tabled before the Standards Review Panel. Until 1990, teams were required to write a report for the nursing home with a statement in support of the rating for each of the 31 standards. This proved an impossible burden with reports often running over 50 typed pages. As a result, from 1990, the report gives a statement in support of the compliance ratings of standards grouped under seven objectives. This makes for 10-page reports which are more consumer-friendly.

In summary, the smaller the number of standards, the better the prospects of ensuring that (a) the most vital information for assessing the total quality of life and quality of care of residents is pursued; (b) lying behind each rating is a collective deliberative process on what that particular rating should be; (c) there is effective public accountability to audit that (a) and (b) actually occur; and (d) inspectors have the capacity to stand back to document the wider patterns in the problems they have identified, to see the wood for the trees. These indeed are just some of the ways that 'loose laws' can make for better public policy (Goodin, 1982: 59–72).

2. THE EFFECT OF PROTOCOLS ON RELIABILITY

The same argument against the proliferation of standards can be extended to the proliferation of protocols for rating standards. The misplaced faith of the legislator for narrowing broad discretion results in the enactment of more specific laws. The misplaced faith of the consultants from the scientific establishment of gerontology results in protocols to narrow discretion. When there are the number of protocols that are supposedly followed in the American process, all the inspector can do is fill out the forms mandated for certain protocols and essentially fudge the other protocols that cannot be checked. Realizing that this is the way the game is played, advocates of protocols for certain standards that they regard as especially important lobby the federal government to mandate auditable protocol forms that the state inspectors must fill out. While this improves the attention given to the lobbyist's cherished regulation, it further worsens the structural malaise of the process.

The commendable shift to resident interviews in the OBRA reforms to the survey process introduced in October 1990 has already fallen prey to the disease of the proliferation of protocols. Our observations during the early months of the new process illustrated the unintended consequences. Interviewers started at the beginning of the schedule for the resident interviews only to find that either they ran out of time or the resident became exhausted before they had got very far through the schedule. Thus, items placed early in the schedule were done according to protocol, and later items were fudged or ignored. For this and other reasons we will come to soon, we therefore agree with the exasperated surveyor who said to us: 'Our own questions are better than the nonsense on the OBRA forms.' When we raised this and other examples of OBRA protocols being selectively and partially followed, one state survey manager replied: 'We'll streamline it. In time we'll do it our way rather than follow the HCFA protocol.' The trouble is of course that every state has no choice but to streamline, and each state streamlines in its own way. Streamlining error is the inevitable consequence of overly ambitious pursuit of reliability through the proliferation of protocols.

Protocols can work well in the context of a social science evaluation, but fail in practice because in the evaluation study the protocol does not have to compete for limited time with 30 other protocols. There are, however, other reasons why a protocol that succeeds in the evaluation study fails in inspection practice. An evaluation might show that a protocol of putting a tick in a box for the name of every resident that participates in each activity can be done reliably. Moreover, scores from following the protocol are validated against more sophisticated detailed assessments of the effectiveness of activities programmes. Unfortunately, however, what was valid at the evaluation stage quickly becomes invalid at the implementation stage.

Administrators are quick learners in the business of getting good survey results. If ticks in activities boxes are what count, droves of sleeping residents will be wheeled into activities programmes to get the numbers up. Never mind that the quality of the activities programme will be compromised by the clutter of sleeping residents; it's beating the protocol that counts. This is why nursing-home administrators love protocols: 'Give us the rules and we'll play the game.' Imprecision, undefined evidence-gathering procedures, make it harder for the efficient administrator to beat the system. In Australia, because there are no defined protocols for inspectors, nursing-home management has no choice but to focus on the outcomes for which the inspectors are searching. This makes their life more painful and uncertain. When protocols are defined, the administrators showed us how they create a documentation system, a paper trail that matches the protocols the inspectors follow: 'You can achieve paper compliance without real compliance. You can fool most inspectors on most standards with paper compliance.'

The source of unreliability then becomes the rare inspector who looks behind the paper trail to the quality of care that is actually being given. Validity then becomes the major source of unreliability!

American evaluators have been systematically blind to these possibilities. When they fail to find reliability after innovations to 'tighten up' the standards and protocols, they call for more of the same. They conclude that the tightening and refinement did not go far enough. Consider, for example, the evaluation of the state of New York's methodologically sophisticated and pace-setting Sentinel Health Events (Office of Health Systems Management, 1985). The Sentinel Health Events were not legal standards but outcome measures designed to be at the heart of the innovative New York regulatory system. When this study obtained poor reliabilities for nursing-home ratings using the Sentinel Health Events, the evaluators concluded:

> It is important to note that although the Stage I and Stage II reliabilities were disappointing, it is expected that the old system in New York State of PaCS (the system to be implemented nationally in April 1986) would have even less reliability. This is because the new system in New York has far more structure than either the old system or PaCS. (Office of Health Systems Management, 1985: 105)

The assumption that more structure is better was particularly obstinate in light of the reasons for unreliability that were diagnosed in the New York study. The first and 'extremely prevalent' reason found was that 'some surveyors (incorrectly) extended protocol requirements by noting a quality issue when no such quality issue is defined in the Protocol' (Office of Health Systems Management, 1985: 39). An illustration of an 'incorrect' deviation from protocol arose when one surveyor who was supposed to assess improvement of a decubitus ulcer on the basis of 'chart review' found inadequate care and deterioration by *observing* care being given:

> The protocol states that only a chart review is necessary for this protocol, so the first cause for difference of opinion was a result of one surveyor doing more than he/she was instructed to do. (Office of Health Systems Management, 1985: 36)

This clearly illustrates the pathology of punishing surveyors for looking beyond the trees specified in their protocols to the wood. The orthodoxy of science is to disapprove of the nurse who used her/his initiative to follow her/his suspicion by digging deeper and to approve the nurse who reached the wrong conclusion because she/he followed the protocol. The orthodoxy of science is naïve here. It is naïve to believe that nurses, who are socialized to care about the patients they encounter, who are trained to use their initiative as professionals to get to the bottom of problems, can be turned into uncaring, mindless automatons who simply stick to the protocols.

Given that many nurses will be caring enough and have the initiative to follow the evidentiary trail toward conclusions of poor quality care, we think it best to design inspection systems which both assume and encourage this, rather than systems that attempt to control it. We think that when a resident is being seriously neglected, two different nurses, with free rein to follow whatever evidentiary trail they pick up, are both more likely to detect the neglect than are two nurses who we ask to be automatons by following a standard protocol. This is particularly so with the many idiosyncratic types of neglect that the designers of the protocol never foresaw. As one Australian inspector pointed out: 'There are a hundred different reasons for residents to be incontinent.' The advantage of wide procedural discretion over tight definition of protocols in generating valid ratings seem to us especially profound when we are considering team inspections. This is because when one team member fails to latch on to an evidentiary trail that will lead to a not met rating the other team member may succeed in latching on to it, or one may discover the missing link in an evidentiary chain pieced together by the other. With our own reliability data, after all, the main source of disagreement was the single independent rater failing to pick up information that the team had detected (and vice versa to a lesser extent).

Inspectors boxed in by a proliferation of protocols cope in another way that makes it difficult for them to see the wood for the trees: *task-specialization*. One surveyor takes responsibility for filling out the forms required from record interviews and another completes the reviews of resident records. We observed very little reading by one surveyor of the protocols filled out by another. In the busy work of getting the huge number of survey forms completed, the process of following up problems identified in a resident interview by tracking down residents' records (and vice versa) is profoundly compromised. This is not to say such follow-through does not occur in the USA; it is just to say that it occurs more freely in the more free-wheeling Australian process. Protocols kill initiative under a pile of paper. With nursing-home staff and nursing-home inspectors alike, excessive demands for task-orientation distract attention from the outcomes that matter. The result is the creation of nursing-home bureaucracies and regulatory bureaucracies that miss the big picture.

This pathology of protocols is just a specific illustration of the more general problem of formalized regulation forgetting that 'policy problems can be solved only by taking account of numerous interdependent and highly variable factors which oblige decision-makers to manage a kind of cybernetic process involving tentative probe, feedback, adjustment, and reconciliation' (Schuck, 1979: 29). The pursuit of precision, either by protocols or by the proliferation of ever-narrower rules, causes an unreliability that is a symptom of a deeper and many-sided malaise of regulatory failure. This is especially depressing since the pursuit of precision usually fails in its own terms – it fails to deliver precision. There might be 30 or 40 US regulations for every one in Australia, but the American standards still seem vague. In the language game of regulation, the problem of one vague concept is solved by splitting into three vague concepts or by defining protocols with other vague concepts. An alternative we suggest to the perpetual struggle to get the words right is to concentrate more on getting the processes of dialogue right. Certainly there is merit in keeping the words simple. This is a necessary precondition to accomplishing processes of dialogue that will deliver reliable judgements on those simple words.

3. *THE EFFECT OF SUBJECTIVITY OF STANDARDS ON RELIABILITY*

When we spoke to senior regulatory bureaucrats in the United States and to social scientists who had been involved in the development and evaluation of nursing home surveys, a common type of comment was: 'There are some things that the process cannot do reliably. So you don't do them. Examples are: "Are the staff pleasant? Is the room tastefully decorated?"' The thought occurred to us that if the Hyatt Hotel group adopted the view that decor and staff pleasantness were matters for which it could not set reliable standards (and therefore should not bother with), it would soon be bankrupt. In business, a head office effectively enforces all manner of 'soft' standards on franchisees by adopting a qualitative approach to evaluation of performance. In these cases, dialogue informs an evaluation that is made against the yardstick of 'What is it, subjectively, that consumers want?' Admittedly, some of these subjective assessments are easy and some are hard. You don't have to talk to many consumers to realize that they don't like vermin running around their hotel room or their nursing home. But to judge reactions as to how warm and non-institutional is the decor or what they think of their continental breakfast, you really need to work hard at talking to consumers. Surely one reason that American nursing homes are so cold, institutional, and unattentive to decor compared for example to English nursing homes is precisely the attitude that such things are so subjective as to be beyond control.

The reliability of the 'homelike environment' standard (4.1 in Table 1) in Australia shows that this American posture is in error. A properly subjective approach on a standard such as this involves talking to residents about whether they feel free to put up personal mementos in an area they define as their private space, whether there are spaces in the facility that they feel are inviting and homelike for chatting with friends, whether they feel there are inviting garden areas they can use. This subjectivity often comes under attack in Australia. For example, managers of nursing-home chains complain to us that they have provided exactly the same food to two nursing homes; the team in one home gives them a 'met' rating for the food and in the other home they get an 'action required' rating. There is absolutely no inconsistency here if the residents at the two homes have different subjective views about the food. Two teams will never agree on what is nice food, but we have found that they can agree, with high reliability, on whether the residents in a nursing home generally like the food they are getting. Reliability is accomplished by rejecting objectivity in favour of subjectivity.

The impetus to reform subjectivity in standards through objective criteria and protocols is dangerous because quality of life, which is what nursing-home care should be about, is ultimately an irreducibly subjective matter. The paradox of objectivity is that its pursuit undercuts a desideratum on which the industry, politicians, consumer groups and gerontologists (if not the lawyers) generally agree. This is that the regulatory process should be more outcome-oriented. The trouble is that inputs (the temperature of the food as it leaves the serving line; the size of the room) are generally more 'objective' than outcomes (satisfaction of residents with the food and the comfort of the room). Objectivity disempowers residents and empowers nursing-home managements who know how to get objective inputs in a row for inspection day – reams of documentation of the temperatures on food lines. Subjectivity, in contrast, means that residents are empowered because it is no longer the documents under the control of management that matter; it is what they as residents think and want that counts.

Even the vision of outcomes which enjoys most support within the American gerontological establishment is an 'objective' conception – counting the number of residents with decubitus ulcers or the number of restrained residents (Institute of Medicine, 1986; Office of Health Systems Management, 1985; Phillips, 1987). Collecting such objective outcome information is something we applaud. However, it must be pointed out that it is a process that does little to shift power over the definition of regulatory problems out of the hands of management into the hands of consumers. Administrators can handle a regulatory process that counts decubitus ulcers or restraints. They can keep control of their own evaluation because they know what the score is objectively before the inspector walks through the door. Consequently, they are ready with a defensive documentary record to prove that the residents with the bedsores were all turned two-hourly, that there are physicians' orders, psychiatric assessments to justify the restraints they want to keep and the like (Wiener and Kayser-Jones, 1989). Hence, while the outcome of the number of restrained residents can be measured very reliably and while this is an extremely valuable thing to do, it does not solve the problem of reliably assessing a law that requires proper use of restraints (such as Standard 7.6 in Table 1). Reliable assessment of a legal standard requires investigative common sense, determination and the imagination to uncover leads and follow them. The protocol-following automatons lauded by the objective-outcomes movement will be incapable of doing this job reliably. Their protocols would not allow them reliably to find that over 90 percent of the American nursing homes we have seen fail to meet the Australian restraint Standard 7.6. Instead, they mostly conclude that American homes where half the residents are tied up or chemically restrained meet the US standards, and where they find non-compliance, they find it unreliably.

4. THE EFFECT OF BEING RESIDENT-CENTRED ON RELIABILITY

Being resident-centred means two things for us: first, it means relying on residents as a source of information for rating standards and, second, it means participation in a regulatory dialogue where quality of life outcomes for residents are the ultimate criteria of regulatory evaluation. Critics regard this as an orientation that is a prescription for unreliability because most residents are so sick or confused that what is a subjectively good outcome for them is unknowable in most particular cases. Moreover, for the same reason, they are incapable of being meaningfully interviewed. Our research team deals with both these objections elsewhere at greater length (Braithwaite and Makkai, 1993). Briefly, we should at least say here that most resident outcomes that are the focus of debate within any sensible regulatory system will be uncontrovertially bad. We know that getting burnt in a fire, getting pills prescribed for someone else, or getting a decubitus ulcer are outcomes that residents are keen to avoid without having to ask them. Second, we use our fieldwork data to argue elsewhere that skilled inspectors know how to find those residents in a nursing home who will be outstanding informants on those issues that do require subjective feedback from residents and they also know how to get some useful information even from residents who spend most of their life extremely confused (Braithwaite and Makkai, 1993). The critics argue that it is harder, or even impossible, for a nursing home with many extremely high disability or demented residents to comply with standards under the more resident-centred process that we have in Australia. Our data do not show this to be the case (Braithwaite and Makkai, 1993).

In practical terms, the Australian nursing-home regulatory process is more resident-centred than any we know. Yet we have seen that this resident-centred process seems to have high reliability. It is true, as the critics point out, that Australian inspectors are often misled by confused residents. However, we also found it true that these errors are almost invariably corrected long before they affect final ratings. In our reliability study, inspectors being misled by confused residents did not even register as a reason for disagreements, though one side picking up useful information from residents that the other side missed was one of the more important reasons for disagreements (Braithwaite et al., 1991). Moreover, with our study of reasons for 889 disagreements between inspectors and directors of nursing on ratings, in only 3 percent of disagreements was one of the reasons given for disagreement that the director of nursing felt that the team had relied on misinformation from residents (Braithwaite et al., 1990: 73).

These data show that interpretive errors in a subjective, resident-centred process can be and are corrected through a process of dialogue. First, dialogue with residents and their carers is important. Second, with nursing-home staff and within the team, there is dialogue about whether the seven quality of life objectives of the Australian standards are being secured: health care, social independence, freedom of choice, homelike environment, privacy and dignity, variety of experience and safety. Consistency does not easily fall out of such processes of dialogue; it comes painfully and with a lot of backtracking and moving in circles as new inconsistencies are discovered along the way.

Ultimately, however, consistency will be greater to the extent that the *only* debate is about resident outcomes. When the debate is theoretically only about whether an input required in a rule is delivered, in practice the outcomes that motivated the rulemakers' specification of the input will unpredictably intrude into regulatory judgements. This is inevitable because sensible people do not like to enforce the law when its enforcement will defeat the very purposes for which the law was enacted. Because business regulatory laws (such as those that regulate health care) deal with such complex, changing and individually variable problems, mismatch between legally mandated input and desired outcome is exceedingly common.

Let us illustrate with a comparatively simple example. We observed a Chicago sanitarian point out during an exit conference following an inspection that it is against the regulations to have a male and a female in adjoining rooms sharing the same toilet. The sanitarian concedes that in this particular case neither resident is capable of using the toilet and that moving either of them would be upsetting to them. He says that he is going to turn a blind eye to the rule for the sake of the residents, but he warns management that someone else from the department could come along and cite them for this. In other words, he is pointing out that because there is such a mismatch between rule and outcome, he is giving an unreliable ruling. With Australian inspectors confronting such a predicament, there will be no such unreliability. Since what is the best outcome for the residents is clear and since inspectors are instructed only to be concerned about outcomes, dialogue should quickly lead to a reliable result.

Our claim is that dialogue about resident-centred outcomes conduces to more reliability than recourse to authoritative interpretations of the meaning of words in rules. A word like privacy is certainly a very slippery word, as is health or pain as a matter of fact. In a resident-centred process when the question arises 'But is this really an invasion of privacy?', the answer is discovered through a process of dialogue about what are the senses of privacy that are important to this particular resident. Dissension is more likely when the question is to be resolved by pitting one inspector's conception of what privacy means against another's; consensus is more likely when the professional responsibility of both is to focus on the practical sense of privacy that is subjectively important to that resident in that situation. There will always be inconsistency in trans-situational 'objective' judgements of whether privacy has been invaded. Resident-centred contextual dialogue about privacy outcomes, in contrast, can often reach reliable conclusions.

It follows that progress with increasing reliability is less likely to come from handing down more sharply defined authoritative interpretations of what privacy is, more likely to come from improving processes of dialogue. Dialogue occurs at many levels, all of which allow scope for improvement. Inspectors can improve their dialogue with residents by learning how to deal with resident intimidation, how to capture the moments of clarity of thought that normally confused residents experience, how to communicate non-verbally with residents when verbal communication is poor, how to use third parties (roommates, relatives) to draw out uncommunicative residents, how to mobilize translation support with non-English speaking residents. Moreover, group discussions with residents (e.g. with Residents' Councils), something on which American inspectors are much more advanced than those in Australia, can draw out some people who will not be drawn one on one.

Inspectors can improve their dialogue with each other by scheduling interim discussions during the course of an inspection, learning how to be active listeners, learning how to break deadlocks by framing the sticking points on which more subjective information from residents is needed. They can also learn when it is wise to draw on the wider experience of a supervisor or to get the perspective of nursing-home staff on an issue. They can learn how to select crucial conflicts over consistency to be put on the agenda for regular meetings of all inspectors. Training courses can be improved by making them more genuinely dialogic – showing videotapes of real regulatory encounters and asking trainees to debate the appropriate compliance rating, for example. Attempts have been made to improve dialogue at most of these levels in both the USA and Australia, but with highly variable commitment and success.

Focusing reform energy on processes of dialogue rather than on rules recognizes something that the community of scholars who work on regulation and policing have begun to realize. This is that it is simply not true that police officers make decisions mostly by reference to rules (Shearing and Ericson, 1991). They do not, should not and could not do so. Police culture, Shearing and Ericson (1991) point out, is not a book of rules, but a storybook. Police learn how to handle difficult situations by hearing stories about how competent officers handled similar situations or by themselves experiencing and retelling such stories:

> Stories constitute a consciousness, a sensibility, a way of being out of which action will flow without recourse to specific instructions. Unlike rules, stories do not address action directly but rather constitute a sensibility out of which action flows. (Shearing, personal communication, 1993)

Stories instruct the participants in a regulatory culture how to 'read', via a 'poetic apprehension', the layers of meaning in a situation. Shearing and Ericson (1991) show how this poetic apprehension is communicated through analogous reasoning – like advising young officers to avoid provocation in difficult situations by 'acting as if you were on holidays'. Nursing-home inspectors communicate a resident-centred sensibility, for example, with the analogous reason: 'Is this a home that you could be happy for your mother or grandmother to live in?' Reliable ratings will be maximally possible with a regulatory culture that accomplishes a common set of sensibilities through processes of dialogue.

Hence, a hotel chain can get staff pleasantness and decor to a state that appeals to consumers, but it will not accomplish this with a set of decor rules. Rather, it seeks to cultivate the right sort of sensibilities in its management and quality assurance staff with stories, concrete examples and analogies. Staff civility and pleasant decor then follow from these sensibilities.

The importance of legal standards is more in setting the framework and focus for storytelling, less as words that utter explicit guidance. To be good at framework-setting and focusing dialogue, standards must be simple and few in number. Like good poetry, they must engage us by being replete with silences, leaving us to make of them what we can: 'For in leaving to us the talk of making sense of what is before us, this silence forces our continuous and attentive engagement with the poem itself' (White, 1984: 27).

5. *THE EFFECT OF RANDOM SAMPLING ON RELIABILITY*

Yet another way in which the paradox of reliability came about in the past was on the question of the random sampling of residents. The behavioural and medical scientists who were influential in shaping the American process as it emerged in the 1980s believed that randomness was important to valid and reliable ratings. The old-fashioned inspection practice of allowing inspectors to concentrate their evidence-gathering on residents of their choice was viewed as unscientific. Many key players in the industry association were also vigorous advocates of random sampling, but for different and perhaps more sophisticated reasons. Some regulators alleged that these industry players supported random sampling because it would inhibit inspectors from following their noses to the residents who were getting the worst deal out of the nursing home. The lawyers had a hand in this shift as well. Up until October 1990, when the USA abandoned random sampling of residents for nursing-home inspections, standard training practice would confront the American inspector with the scenario of a company lawyer challenging their findings by questioning their competence in the statistical theory which would warrant the judgement that a 'pattern' of non-compliance existed.

Our observations of the random-sampling process revealed endemic cheating by inspectors. They would cheat for both principled and unprincipled reasons. When on the initial tour of the nursing home, the inspector met a resident who complained of mistreatment or who manifested signs of neglectful care, the inspector would sometimes cheat by putting that resident into the random sample even though she/he was not randomly selected. On one occasion, an inspector from another part of the state asked the team to put a friend of hers who was suffering from a decubitus ulcer in the sample. On another occasion, a complainant was fudged into the sample to protect her – so that the problem would appear to have been discovered by the team. In another multistorey nursing home, where care seemed to vary by floor, the team decided to 'improve' on the standard sampling protocol by stratifying the sample by floor. These were all examples of principled cheating.

Examples of unprincipled cheating included the following. The team member met on the tour a resident who was a friend she enjoyed talking to. After a 20-minute chat with her over lunch, she realized that she had already collected half the information she needed from this resident. So she slipped her into the random sample. In another type of fudging repeatedly observed, the inspector would find a resident with multiple problems – restraint, catheter, decubitus ulcer and others. Because the sampling protocol demands a number of residents with each of these types of special problem, this resident became 'a good one to do'. Slipping such a resident into the sample reduced the total number of residents investigated. We say these latter examples are of unprincipled cheating, but the teams did not view it this way. We have already made the point that systematic data collection to rate hundreds of regulations is impossible; the cheating, they contended, made an impossible job a little more possible.

Even when the cheating was clearly principled rather than designed to cut corners, surveyors were under no illusion that it was cheating that required concealment:

Surveyor: 'There are ways of bending these things [the sample]. That doesn't cause us any problem.'
JB: 'How do you mean?'
Surveyor: 'Well you can just number the list of patients where you are selecting every fifth one: 1,2,3,4,6,5.'

It is a sad commentary on the unreflexive empiricism of the behavioural sciences that so many books are written on the statistics of sampling, while no one does empirical studies of random sampling in practice. Our own observations are of a wide gulf between science in the books and science in action, even with surveyors with considerably more education and training in sampling protocols than the average opinion survey interviewer, for example.

The reasons for the gulf in this domain are multiple, but include: (a) laziness; (b) job survival; (c) the view that they have more serious professional obligations than to the numbers games of scientists; and (d) the view that they have a more sophisticated or rounded practitioner's view of randomness than the theoreticians. The last of these is the most interesting: surveyors who stratify by floor or who put into the sample someone they bump into on the tour have a social construction of randomness which they will defend as superior to the protocol they have been given. This then is just a special case of the naïvety of assuming that because protocols exist, they will be followed; because something works in a pilot, it will work in day-to-day practice. Behavioural scientists are empirically neglectful of behaviour in science. One lesson of observing nursing-home inspections is that trained professionals expect and extract working conditions where they exercise professional judgement: they simply refuse to succumb to demands that they follow instructions like machines. Inspection procedures should never be based on the hope that this will not happen; they should be designed on the expectation that it will.

Hence, random sampling in nursing-home inspection in the USA up to 1990 tended to fail in one of two ways. In some cases the team cheated by slipping bad cases into the sample, thereby defeating randomness. In other cases, they refrained from cheating when they saw bad cases; they settled for the randomly selected case and let the bad case slip by that might have been their best chance of getting to the deepest problems in the facility. As argued earlier, our own view is that inspectors are most likely to find problems of non-compliance reliably when their initiative in following evidentiary leads is cultivated instead of controlled.

The final reason why random sampling reduces reliability in regulatory inspections is that it is extraordinarily time-consuming. It distracts a great deal of time from the more important work of gathering evidence on all the standards (or in the US case, at least a larger fraction of the standards). We would observe one team member on the first day of a pre-1990 US inspection do little more than participate in the initial tour and gather all the information on residents and their categories of care in order to select the sample, selecting it with the correct number in each category (variably according to the number of qualified residents in the home), and recording the selected sample to prove that the sampling protocol had been followed. On one occasion, we observed four nurses debate for 37 minutes whether, for sampling purposes, group therapy counted in the 'physical therapy' category. A call to the supervisor was eventually needed to resolve the dispute. All this effort for the dubious statistical virtue of randomly selecting 16 residents from a population of 80! The USA made a sound scientific decision when it abandoned random sampling in October 1990.

DISCUSSION

The first point we should make toward a conclusion is that our hypothesis that the US nursing-home inspection process is much less reliable than the Australian process may simply not be true. None of the quantitative studies has large samples, and all have design flaws. They do, nevertheless, amount to superior information on the reliability of nursing-home inspection than we have on any other area of business regulatory inspection we know. We would be surprised if our hypothesis were wrong, however, not only because of the dramatically different results of the quantitative reliability studies but because of the convergent conclusion from our extensive qualitative fieldwork.

It could be argued that even if our empirical claim about the comparative reliability of nursing-home inspection were right, this is simply a statistical artefact. When an American inspector finds a problem that should be cited, there are 499 different ways he/she can cite it under the wrong standard (if there are 500 standards). When an Australian decides to give a not met rating, there are only 30 ways he/she can get it wrong (with 31 standards). Of course this is an overstatement because clearly there is little risk of fire-safety citations being written under a quality of food standard. Nevertheless, the basic point remains that more standards means more ways classification errors can occur.

To point this out, however, is not to erect a defence of the American standards. It is no comfort to nursing-home operators who feel they have been treated inconsistently to tell them that they unfortunately have been victims of a statistical artefact. If inspectors give the wrong ratings because of the many standards under which they might write non-compliance, then this is a bad feature of the design of a system with too many standards. It is the design features of this system that cause the unreliability. At the outset to this article, we said that reliability is not the only, or even the most important, criterion for evaluating a regulatory process. For one thing, reliability is not validity. A common assertion about nursing homes from industry participants in all the countries we visited for this research is that competent people can assess validity rather easily: 'When I go into a home, I can look around and fairly quickly tell if it is a well-run nursing home or a nursing home with problems. If I can do it, they [surveyors] can because they go to different homes all the time' (Pennsylvanian administrator). This kind of assertion does not sit well with American researchers who find low reliability in the ratings of US inspection teams. It may be, however, that both the genius and the limitation of the Australian process is that it engages with the nursing home only at that rather broad level of the quality of care and life, and it is at this broad level that reliability can be achieved, as in this oft-repeated wisdom of the industry.

Once the team follows protocols that cause it to dig deeper, reliability may become problematic. In failing to dig deep, the process may in some senses be reliable but not valid. Consider Standard 2.2, 'Residents are enabled and encouraged to maintain control of their financial affairs.' This is assessed by a team member asking the person responsible for managing resident accounts (and for liaison with guardians or relatives who manage accounts) to explain the nursing home's system for ensuring that the standard is met. Documentary evidence of these systems will then be sighted. In addition, the team will ask residents and visitors if they are experiencing any problems in maintaining resident control of their financial affairs. What we have found is that different raters who only dig this deep in their investigations of this matter will come up with the same ratings. However, if one of the teams were to dig deeper and conduct a full-scale financial audit of all of the residents' accounts, it might find instances of residents being deceived and defrauded by the nursing home. By one team digging deeper, interteam reliability would have been shattered, but this team would be making a more valid rating. What we may have with Australian standards monitoring is a process that reliably reveals those sorts of problems that can be revealed by shallow digging.

Overall, we doubt that the American process digs deeper than the Australian process does, because Australian facilities that are identified as 'homes of concern' at the initial visit usually get many more follow-up visits than do American homes with comparable problems. However, there is no doubt that at the initial visit stage, there are several important ways in which the American process digs deeper. An example is the US requirement for a systematic survey of errors in the administration of medications. US inspections often uncover quite frightening 'med-pass error rates' of 10 percent and more. Australian standards monitoring visits reliably fail to uncover such problems. American inspectors observe treatments being given to a sample of residents. Mostly these are observations of the treatment of decubitus ulcers. This deeper digging in the American process uncovers many problems that remain reliably submerged in the Australian process – Class III ulcers that are documented and treated as Class II or poor infection-control practice in the treatment of bedsores. The biggest difference is with the deeper digging that American inspectors do in checking the documentation of resident care, though, unlike the other domains of deeper digging we have discussed, we doubt that this is reason for superiority in the US process (Braithwaite, 1994). Moreover, we do not believe that the lower reliability of the US process is caused by its successes in collecting greater amounts of information than the initial Australian visit. On the contrary, the greater unreliability of the American process is caused by the fact that most of its hundreds of ratings are made on the basis of no information or at least no deliberation of any information.

In summary, we think it is fair to describe the initial Australian visit as reliably uncovering problems that can be exposed by shallow digging and reliably failing to uncover problems that can only be exposed by digging deeper. Moreover, it would improve the validity of the Australian process to adopt certain elements of the American process, such as the systematic observation of treatments. This is not to deny our more fundamental assertion that the best way to find the deepest problems is to follow leads rather than follow protocols. A police department that relies exclusively on the most sophisticated regimen of random patrol will not solve murders.

CONCLUSION

The classic work on the optimal precision of regulatory standards has been that of Colin Diver (1980, 1989). Diver identifies three problems with regulatory standards – vagueness, overinclusiveness and complexity. Vague rules leave citizens to guess at their meaning in particular circumstances. Overinclusive rules command actions that are not beneficial (or are harmful). Overinclusive rules accomplish a poor fit between outcomes desired by policymakers and the requirements demanded by literal adherence to the rules. A complex set of rules is long, full of contradictions between one part of the rules and another, and dogged by verbal intricacy.

Diver (1989) advances three qualities of well-drafted legal rules – transparency, congruence and simplicity – to deal respectively with the three problems of vagueness, overinclusiveness and complexity. Clearly, the 31 Australian standards in Table 1 satisfy the criterion of simplicity. Congruence between desired outcomes and legal requirements, we have seen, is accomplished by shifting to a radical outcome-orientation wherein if resident outcomes cannot be shown to be put at risk by an action, then that action involves no violation. The problem of vagueness, however, is not dealt with by making the rules transparent. Different citizens cannot look at the Australian standards as if through a transparent window and see the same image. Transparency is accomplished at the next stage of the process. Vagueness about meaning is clarified by empowering the beneficiaries of the rules to define the meanings of the standard that are important to them in a particular situation. Because there is no way of solving the problem of vagueness at the level of the wording of rules without also rendering the rules overinclusive and complex,[13] the solution is to leave the words vague but to specify the interpretive evidence that is privileged and to require a regulatory dialogue about this evidence. Laws that fail the transparency test as disembodied law can be the starting point for a process that solves the vagueness problem through mandating which subjectivity is privileged (and mandating dialogue focused on that subjectivity). The law fails the vagueness test, but the package of law–outcome–subjectivity–dialogue passes it. That is, two people just applying the law are likely to reach different conclusions about the same evidence; two people who use the law to guide outcome-oriented dialogue are likely to reach the same legal conclusion in a specific context. Dialogic accountability within the process, especially when this includes a requirement for consultation with residents and staff about the ratings given to their nursing home, prevents vague wording from being translated into unbridled discretion for inspectors, and therefore unreliability.

Like any solution, of course, there are limits to it. There will arise interpretations of 'freedom', subjectively defined by residents, that will be disallowed by inspectors as beyond the range of acceptable definitions of freedom or impossible to satisfy in a nursing home context. Freedom to assault other residents is a case in point, but this still allows wide scope for a disparate variety of constructions of freedom that are tolerated in a liberal democracy, even if they are abhorrent to the inspectors. For example, one Australian resident invoked the standards to insist on his freedom to use the services of a prostitute; this conception of freedom was respected.

Whatever its limitations, the Australian policy is an attempt to break radically with the past in an approach to averting overinclusiveness and complexity, while using dialogue and empowerment to render vague wording outcome-accountable. This puts an alternative to an American nursing-home industry that pleads for simplicity in the law at the same time as it drives the law to greater complexity through persistent complaints about inconsistency. It puts an alternative to consumer advocates who call for more outcome-oriented and resident-centred regulation, but who scream unaccountability and unenforcibility as soon as vague wording appears in regulations. It puts an alternative to regulators who want consistency by some means other than back-breaking protocols that actually worsen reliability. It challenges the clarity of thinking in American governmental reports that pretend mutually contradictory critiques such as the following can be reconciled without radical regulatory transformation: 'There are too many regulations'; 'The regulations are too vague'; and 'The regulations are too picky, detailed' (Illinois Legislative Investigating Commission, 1984: 20–1).

The transformations we advocate involve: (a) opting for standards that are simple and few in number (in preference to many specific rules); (b) structuring the regulatory process to be resident-centred and outcome-oriented; and (c) trusting dialogue (not just top-down 'training') among people who have been persuaded to care about those outcomes. These are our conditions for regulatory context that renders text reliable.

These conclusions can be read as part of a more general questioning of the claim that precision and the elimination of discretion though detailed regulatory law is a path to either greater consistency or equity (Hawkins, 1992). Precision tends to 'permit by implication conduct that the rule was intended to forbid' (Posner, 1977: 425). Detailed laws can provide a set of signposts to navigate around for those with the resources to employ a good legal navigator (Schoer, 1993). While our focus here has been restricted to the effects of precision on consistency, precision-driven inconsistency can be theorized as a strategic resource of the powerful, particularly of repeat players who have an interest in playing for rules as well as for outcomes (thereby opening up a pattern of loopholes that suit the big players). As Max Weber (1954) showed: '[T]he more formal and complex the body of law becomes, the more it will operate in favour of formal rational bureaucratic groups such as corporations' (Sutton and Wild, 1978: 195). Marching under the banner of consistency, business can co-opt lawyers, social scientists, legislators and consumer advocates to the delivery of strategically inconsistent regulation of limited potency.

NOTES

This project has enjoyed the funding support of the Australian Department of Health, Housing and Community Services, the Australian Research Council, the American Bar Foundation and the Australian National University. The authors are indebted to the support of their colleagues on the Nursing Home Regulation in Action Project, David Ermann, Diane Gibson, Miriam Landau and Toni Makkai. Valerie Braithwaite benefited from a visiting appointment at the Buehler Center on Aging, Northwestern University, during the US field work. Thanks to Paul Finn and James Morauta for comments on this article.

1. At another point, Kelman (1987: 44) puts the hope that has been realized here another way: 'Rules are bad because they inevitably have gaps and conflicts and are thus less mechanically applicable than they might appear. . . . The open invocation of an apparently vague standard, though, may be reasonably predictable in practice because even relatively detailed tacit community norms so converge that application of vague policy sentiments to cases poses little danger of disagreement.' It would be overstating our results to say that we found little disagreement, though one might say these data show 'a surprisingly low level of disagreement'.
2. '[C]onversation and explanation of one's conduct are avoided . . . a rule's a rule, don't complain to me' (Kelman, 1987: 63).
3. There is a 20-page set of Standards Monitoring Guidelines (Department of Community Services and Health, 1988). But these instruct inspectors only in 'key issues' and some of the things to 'look for' under each standard.
4. A British study was conducted of the reliability of two standard protocols for the inspection of residential care homes (Gibbs and Sinclair, 1991). Residential care homes are for residents who require less extensive care than those in nursing homes, though in practice the extensiveness of care between the two types of institution overlaps considerably. Gibbs and Sinclair's (1991) results from 48 homes fall between the US and Australian results reported in this article. A global reliability coefficient of 0.38 increased to 0.67 when the instrument was culled to include only high reliability items. This was a test-retest reliability with four weeks between inspections.
5. Part of the study was to check whether unreliability was caused by the reliability rater, in part, being in the facility at different times from the official team. This turned out to be a very minor source of unreliability (Braithwaite et al., 1991).
6. The definitions of these three categories are:
   Met The team considers that residents are experiencing the quality of life and care

described in the standard. This does not necessarily mean there is not room for improvement or that the home could not operate more efficiently.
Action Required Either the standard is fully met for the majority of residents and the other residents are not experiencing neglect, abuse, denial of rights or any other significant detriment or substantially met for all residents and the home is taking action to address those minor concerns identified.
Urgent Action Required For one or more residents there is an identified abuse, neglect, denial of rights *and/or* other significant detriment.

7. The Australian director of nursing is the chief executive of the nursing home, combining the functions of administrator and director of nurses in the American system.
8. Another aspect of the same project was to compare the effect of this new survey process (PaCS) with the then existing process on deficiencies cited. Both processes were rating identical standards. However, the new PaCS process, which became the official US process from 1986 to 1990, was slightly more resident-centred than the old process was (though nowhere near as resident-centred as the Australian process). This test was conducted on a larger sample of 51 nursing homes, with the second team entering the home within a day or two of the first departing. PaCS teams cited 50 percent more deficiencies than did the teams surveying the same standards under the less resident-centred process (Spector and Drugovich, 1989).
9. One might hypothesize, for example, that American nursing homes being larger make reliability more difficult. But within our Australian study, the reliabilities are much the same for large and small homes. Large Australian homes are rated much more reliably than those in the Wisconsin study that produced the best US result.
10. This was a major reform to nursing home regulatory law. The new survey process based on the reform came into effect in October 1990. Omnibus Budget Reconciliation Act of 1987, Pub. L. No. 100–203, Paras 4203–4213.
11. A limited amount of such cross-referencing, however, may be done by a 'quality assurance' officer back at head office.
12. This was a 1989 inspection which predated abolition of the distinction among 'elements', 'standards' and 'conditions of participation' in Medicaid.
13. Rorty would say there is no way of solving it at all: 'words take their meaning from other words rather than by virtue of their representative character, and the corollary that vocabularies acquire their privileges from the men who use them rather than from their transparency to the real' (Rorty, 1979: 368; see also Wittgenstein, 1972: 29–39).

References

Atiyah, P. S. and Robert S. Summers (1987) *Form and Substance in Anglo-American Law*. Oxford: Clarendon Press.

Badaracco, Joseph L. (1985) *Loading the Dice: A Five Country Study of Vinyl Chloride Regulation*. Boston, MA: Harvard Business School Press.

Baldwin, Robert and Keith Hawkins (1984) 'Discretionary Justice: Davis Reconsidered', *Public law*: 570–89.

Bardach, Eugene and Robert A. Kagan (1982) *Going by the Book: The Problem of Regulatory Unreasonableness*. Philadelphia, PA: Temple University Press.

Braithwaite, John (1987) 'Negotiation versus Litigation: Industry Regulation in Great Britain and the United States', *American Bar Foundation Research Journal* 2: 559–74.

Braithwaite, John (1994) 'The Nursing Home Industry', pp. 11–54 in A. Reiss and M.

Tonry (eds), *Organizational Crime: Crime and Justice: A Review of Research Volume V*. Chicago, IL: University of Chicago Press.

Braithwaite, John, Valerie Braithwaite, Diane Gibson and Toni Makkai (1992) 'Progress in Assessing the Quality of Australian Nursing Home Care', *Australian Journal of Public Health* 16(1): 89–97.

Braithwaite, John, Toni Makkai, Valerie Braithwaite and Diane Gibson (1993) *Raising the Standard: Resident-Centred Nursing Home Regulations in Australia*. Canberra: Australian Government Publishing Service.

Braithwaite, John, Toni Makkai, Valerie Braithwaite, Diane Gibson and David Ermann (1990) *The Contribution of the Standards Monitoring Process to the Quality of Nursing Home Life*. Canberra: Department of Community Services and Health.

Braithwaite, John and Toni Makkai (1993) 'Can Resident-Centred Inspection of Nursing Homes Work with Very Sick Residents?', *Health Policy* 24: 19–33.

Braithwaite, Valerie, John Braithwaite, Diane Gibson, Miriam Landau and Toni Makkai (1991) *The Reliability and Validity of Nursing Home Standards*. Canberra: Department of Health, Housing and Community Services.

Day, Patricia and Rudolf Klein (1987) 'The Regulation of Nursing Homes: A Comparative Perspective', *Milbank Quarterly* 65: 303–47.

Department of Community Services and Health (1988) *Nursing Home Standards Monitoring Guidelines*. Canberra: Department of Community Services and Health.

Diver, Colin S. (1980) 'A Theory of Regulatory Enforcement', *Public Policy* 28: 257–99.

Diver, Colin S. (1989) 'Regulatory Precision', pp. 199–232 in K. Hawkins and J. M. Thomas (eds), *Making Regulatory Policy*. Pittsburgh, PA: University of Pittsburgh Press.

Gibbs, Ian and Ian Sinclair (1991) 'A Checklist Approach to the Inspection of Old People's Homes', Report to the Department of Health. York Department of Social Policy and Social Work, University of York.

Giles Report: Senate Select Committee on Private Hospitals and Nursing Homes (1985) *Private Nursing Homes in Australia: Their Conduct, Administration and Ownership*. Canberra: Australian Government Publishing Service.

Goodin, Robert E. (1982) *Political Theory and Public Policy*. Chicago, IL: University of Chicago Press.

Grabosky, Peter and John Braithwaite (1986) *Of Manners Gentle: Enforcement Strategies of Australian Business Regulatory Agencies*. Melbourne: Oxford University Press.

Gustafson, David H. (Project Manager) (1977) *Monitoring Quality of Nursing Home Care: Final Report*. Madison, WI: Department of Health and Social Services.

Gustafson, David H., Charles J. Fiss, Judy C. Fryback, Peggy A. Smelser and May E. Hiles (1980) 'Measuring the Quality of Care in Nursing Homes: A Pilot Study in Wisconsin', *Public Health Reports* 95(4): 336–43.

Gustafson, David H., Robert Peterson, Sandra Casper, Ann Macco, Richard Van Koningsveld and Edward Kopetsky (1982) *The Impact of the Wisconsin Quality Assurance Project: A Field Evaluation*. Madison, WI: University of Wisconsin.

Haley, John O. (ed.) (1988) *Law and Society in Contemporary Japan: American Perspectives*. Dubuque, IA: Kendall Hunt.

Hawkins, Keith (1984) *Environment and Enforcement: Regulation and the Social Definition of Pollution*. Oxford: Clarendon Press.

Hawkins, Keith (ed.) (1992) *The Uses of Discretion*. Oxford: Clarendon Press.

Illinois Legislative Investigating Commission (1984) *Regulation and Funding of Illinois Nursing Homes*. Springfield, IL: Illinois General Assembly.

Institute of Medicine (1986) *Improving the Quality of Care in Nursing Homes*. Washington, DC: National Academy Press.

Kagan, R. A. (1991) 'Adversarial Legalism and American Government', *Journal of Policy Analysis and Management* 10(3): 369–406.

Kelman, Mark (1987) *A Guide to Critical Legal Studies*. Cambridge, MA: Harvard University Press.

Kelman, S. (1981) *Regulating America: Regulating Sweden: A Comparative Study of Occupational Safety and Health Policy*. Cambridge, MA: MIT Press.

Kennedy, Duncan (1976) 'Form and Substance in Private Law Adjudication', *Harvard Law Review* 89: 1685–778.

Krotoszynski, R. J. (1990) 'Autonomy, Community, and Traditions of Liberty – The Contrast of British and American Privacy Law', *Duke Law Journal* 6: 1398–454.

McLeay Report: The House of Representatives Standing Committee on Expenditure (1982) *In a Home or at Home: Accommodation and Home Care for the Aged*. Canberra: Parliament of the Commonwealth of Australia, October.

Meidinger, Errol (1987) 'Regulatory Culture: A Theoretical Outline', *Law and Policy* 9: 355.

Michelman, Frank I. (1986) 'The Supreme Court, 1985 Term – Foreword: Traces of Self-Government', *Harvard Law Review* 100: 4–77.

Office of Health Systems Management (1985) *Evaluation of the New York State Residential Health Care Facility Quality Assurance System*. Standards and Surveillance, Division of Health Care, Office of Health Systems Management. Albany, NY: New York State Department of Health.

Phillips, Colleen (1987) *Developing Outcome Norms to Monitor Quality of Care in Rhode Island Nursing Homes*. Providence, RI: Rhode Island Department of Health.

Posner, Richard (1977) *Economic Analysis of Law*. Boston, MA: Little, Brown.

Radin, Margaret Jane (1989) 'Reconsidering the Rule of Law', *Boston University Law Review* 69: 781.

Rorty, Richard (1979) *Philosophy and the Mirror of Nature*. Princeton, NJ: Princeton University Press.

Rose, Carol M. (1987) 'Crystals and Mud in Property Law', *Stanford Law Review* 40: 577–610.

Schlag, Pierre (1985) 'Rules and Standards', *UCLA Law Review* 33: 379–430.

Schoer, Ray (1993) 'Self-Regulation and the Australian Stock Exchange', in P. Grabosky and J. Braithwaite (eds), *Business Regulation and Australia's Future*. Canberra: Australian Institute of Criminology.

Schuck, Peter H. (1979) 'Litigation, Bargaining and Regulation', *Regulation* 3: 26–34.

Shearing, Clifford D. and Richard V. Ericson (1991) 'Towards a Figurative Conception of Action', *British Journal of Sociology* 42: 481–506.

Spector, William D. and Margaret L. Drugovich (1989) 'Reforming Nursing Home Quality Regulation: Impact on Cited Deficiencies and Nursing Home Outcomes', *Medical Care* 27: 789–801.

Spector, William D., Adrianna H. Takada, Margaret L. Durgovich, Linda L. Laliberte and Richard Tucker (1987) *PaCS Evaluation: Final Report*. Baltimore, MD: Health Care Financing Bureau.

Sutton, Adam and Ron Wild (1978) 'Corporate Crime and Social Structure', in P. Wilson and J. Braithwaite (eds), *Two Faces of Deviance*. Brisbane: University of Queensland Press.

Sullivan, Kathleen, M. (1992) 'The Justices of Rules and Standards – Foreword', *Harvard Law Review* 106(1): 24–123.

Upham, Frank K. (1987) *Law and Social Change in Postwar Japan*. Cambridge, MA: Harvard University Press.

Vogel, David (1986) *National Styles of Regulation: Environment Policy in Great Britain and the United States*. Ithaca, NY: Cornell University Press.

Vogel, Ezra F. (1979) *Japan as No. 1: Lessons for America*. Cambridge, MA: Harvard University Press.

Weber, Max (1954) *On Law in Economics and Society*. New York: Clarion.

White, James Boyd (1984) *When Words Lose Their Meaning: Constitutions and Reconstitutions of Language, Character and Community*. Chicago, IL: University of Chicago Press.

Wiener, Carolyn L. and Jeanie Kayser-Jones (1989) 'Defensive Work in Nursing Homes – Accountability Gone Amok', *Social Science and Medicine* 28(1): 37–44.

Wittgenstein, Ludwig (1972) *Philosophical Investigations*, trans. G. E. M. Anscombe. Oxford: Blackwell.

Zimmerman, David, J. Robert Egan, David Gustafson, Charles Metcalf and Felicity Skidmore (1985) *Evaluation of the Three State Demonstrations in Nursing Home Quality Assurance Procedures*. Baltimore, MD: Health Care Financing Bureau, September.

[11]

Talking about Regulation

Julia Black

Law Department, London School of Economics

This article[1] is concerned with conversations; conversations which occur between the regulated and the regulator about rules, their interpretation and appropriate application or waiver in the individual regulatee's circumstances. Such conversations occur in the grey world of regulatory operation and implementation, where law plays a key structuring role but where its operation is a matter of continual interpretation, adjustment, and discussion. The locations for such conversations may vary within the regulatory process and indeed within the regulatory body, but whatever their location they concern the meaning and application of rules. They may be manifested in guidance, waivers, no-action or comfort letters, non-sanctioning of breaches, or the formation of requirements tailored to the individual regulatee's circumstances; they may occur at a fairly high level in the regulatory organisation, or at the relatively low-level and hidden world of enforcement; they may be an implicit part of the regulatory process, or explicitly incorporated into the regulatory structure through the adoption of particular techniques of regulation and rule making.

There are different ways in which such conversations can be conceptualised and explained, conceptualisations and explanations which have normative overtones. Conversations ameliorate the limits of rules; they meet the perennial problem of how to resolve the tension between certainty and flexibility; they allow for more general rules to be written which serve as better, because more comprehensible, guides to behaviour, whilst allowing for adjustment to individual circumstances: a form of "acoustic separation" of law. Conversations have the postmodern credentials of flexibility, communication, responsiveness, and enable individual regulatees to participate in the decision as to the rule's application in their case.

But we can also anticipate problems with such conversations; conversations cannot be so easily seen as a necessarily welcome feature of regulation. They raise issues of consistent, fair and objective treatment, of access, participation

[1] This paper has benefited from discussions which I have had at various times with colleagues, particularly Rob Baldwin, Damian Chalmers, Judith Freedman and Colin Scott, and from the comments on the article's entirety from Rob Baldwin and Tim Cross. My thanks go to them all; the usual responsibilities remain my own.

and accountability. The question which this article thus explores is what is the place, both normatively and descriptively, of bilateral conversations in a generalised system of regulation? The article looks first at instances of conversations in the regulatory process, then at the reasons and justifications for them and the problems which they raise, before considering ways in which conversations could be structured to address some of these issues. It suggests that conversations between regulator and regulated in some form are probably an inevitable feature of regulation. However, it argues that simply "having a chat" is not necessarily enough: conversations, if they are both to provide the advantages which they have the potential to offer, and to meet the concerns which inevitably they raise, have to be both nurtured and carefully structured. Only then can conversations provide the responsiveness and flexibility which may be needed, whilst ensuring adequate safeguards of due process and preserving the integrity of the regulatory function.

Four elements, it is suggested, are central to the effective operation and acceptability of regulatory conversations: commitment, access, authority, and trust and accountability. As the extensive work on discretion and bureaucratic decision making indicates, however, designing structures to ensure particular modes of behaviour is not a straightforward task. So in adjusting the institutional and organisational context in which conversations occur we need to be sensitive to the limitations of such a structuring process. Ways need to be found to use and accommodate conversations whilst not shifting them outside those structures or silencing them completely.

Forms of conversation

The conversations being referred to are communications and discussions between a regulatory official or officials and a regulated individual or firm as to the application of a generally applicable rule in their particular case. Rules in this sense include primary, secondary and tertiary rules,[2] and so may be embodied in, *inter alia*, statute, regulatory rules, circulars, guidance, licenses or franchise agreements. Conversations are not synonymous with regulation, rather they are a feature of the day to day operation of a regulatory system and the interaction between regulator and regulatee concerning the meaning and application of rules. Conversations may involve guidance or rulings on the rule's application, its elaboration, either by the firm or the regulator, or its effective modification or waiver. No clear cut distinction is thus being envisaged between rule formation and rule application: conversations may involve the development of previously written rules in such a way that a rule is effectively revised; rule application may thus lead to rule re-formulation. What is not included in the idea of a "conversation" however is the broader policy formation process and the initial construction of the regulatory framework. Rather, attention is placed on those conversations which occur within the regulatory framework once it has been set.

[2] The classification adopted is Baldwin's: R. Baldwin, *Rules and Government* (1995).

Conversations may occur at a number of different points within the regulatory process and with officials in different parts of the regulatory organisation. They may be centralised or decentralised. Conversations may be part of the inevitable course of the regulatory process, and may or may not have explicit sanction within the regulatory system. Alternatively (or in addition), they may be a consciously adopted regulatory strategy; the regulator may issue only very broad rules, anticipating that it will then engage in a process of negotiation, a conversation, with individual regulatees as to how those broad rules will apply to those circumstances, including perhaps the approval of rules written by the firm or individual to guide its own behaviour in compliance with the generally applicable norm.

Generalisations as to their nature can only take us so far. To illustrate the phenomenon, it is worth exploring some examples of different types or occasions of conversations. Three broad occasions for conversations are considered here: the process of rule application, that of supervised rule-formation, and that of monitoring and enforcement.[3]

Rule application: guidance and waivers

Guidance given to individual regulatees as to the meaning or application of the rule may be given informally or as a result of a formal process. It may or may not have legal status, and it may or may not lead to further action, such as the granting of a waiver or no-action letter. Three different systems of regulation, which are not of the archetypal "command and control" model, in which guidance and/or waivers play a central role are takeovers, tax collection and E.C. competition law.

Takeovers

The regulation of takeovers and mergers relies heavily on guidance, and indeed the conversational approach is one of its principal modes of operation. The Take-over Panel is a non-statutory body which regulates the conduct of takeovers and mergers of all public companies in the British Isles.[4] Its code consists of 10 general principles and 38 rules, elaborated by sub-rules and notes, rules on substantial acquisition of shares and various disclosure forms. These are supplemented from time to time by statements of practice or policy issued by the Panel.[5] The operation of the Panel is notable in that its authority is almost universally accepted, and its conduct largely praised.[6] The day to day

[3] These categorisations are adopted for convenience of exposition only; they are not necessarily analytically distinct: rule application is clearly involved, for example, in monitoring and enforcement.

[4] It also applies to private companies if their equity share capital has been listed on the London Stock Exchange or other exchange at any time in the last ten years or they have filed a prospectus for the issue of shares in that time, or if dealings in their equity share capital have been advertised in a newspaper for a continuous period of six months or more in the last 10 years.

[5] For texts of these and comments thereon see Weinberg and Blank, *Takeovers and Mergers* (1989, updated); see also G. Stedman, *Takeovers* (1993).

[6] There are exceptions: probably the greatest challenge to the Panel's authority was in the St Piran case in 1981. Its conduct in the recent bid by CalEnergy for Northern Electric has also been criticised: see reports in the *FT*, *The Times* and *The Independent*, December 28, 1996.

work of the Panel is done by its executive, staffed by a combination of permanent members and those on secondment from a range of legal and financial City institutions. The principal functions of the executive are providing advice and guidance on compliance, giving rulings on interpretations of the Code, and monitoring compliance.[7] The Introduction to the Code stipulates that where there is any doubt at all as to whether a proposed course of conduct is in accordance with the Code, advisers to the parties should consult the executive in advance.

It is indeed common practice for the Panel, in the form of the executive, to be closely involved in takeover proceedings. The advice and rulings of the executive are frequently sought, and significantly, the executive will give rulings on hypothetical situations.[8] The key to the Panel's operation is its flexibility and the speed of its responses: advice or rulings are sought or given mainly over the telephone, the executive requiring only two hours at most, and rulings are given within 24 hours. If the executive wishes to consult the other parties before giving a ruling, it usually does so by telephone. Staff meet daily to take decisions on matters of importance and to review decisions taken to try to ensure consistency. Guidance and rulings of the executive are authoritative; if the parties want to appeal against them they can do so to the Panel within one month, or sooner if the executive so stipulates. Alternatively, the executive can itself refer a matter to the Panel if it is a particularly difficult, unusual or important point. Both referrals and appeals are in fact rare, with the Panel seldom overruling the executive.[9] Both processes are speedy, and it usually only takes three to four days to convene the Panel.[10] Appeals are private and are conducted on an informal basis with no formal rules of evidence. Parties give written submissions prior to the hearing, including the executive and shareholders (subject to some restrictions to prevent vexatious or frivolous submissions).[11] The parties may call witnesses as they wish, but no party can be represented by counsel. The Panel operates in complete confidence: rulings are not published, and even Panel decisions on appeal remain confidential unless the issue is particularly important or controversial. In all events, the transcript of the appeal hearing is not disclosed unless all parties agree.

The operation of the Panel provides an example of a system of regulation which relies on quite a sophisticated form of conversation. The Panel is the final interpreter of its own rules, giving it the authority to provide a flexible

[7] Its statement of operations which prefaces each Annual Report emphasises that the major function of the Executive is to provide guidance, and strongly encourages early consultations with it.

[8] In 1993–1994 it had detailed consultations in 81 takeovers in which documents were sent to shareholders, 340 other consultations and 750 queries which involved such hypothetical situations: Takeover Panel, *Annual Report 1993–1994*. In 1994–1995, the figures were 108 takeovers and 201 consultations respectively, with no figures given for hypothetical enquiries: Takeover Panel, *Annual Report 1994–1995*.

[9] In the period March 31, 1989–March 31, 1996 there were only 25 appeals to the Panel, 3 of which were upheld (figures compiled from the Takeover Panel's Annual Reports 1990–1996).

[10] For a discussion see Weinberg and Blank, *op. cit.* n. 5, paras 3–512—3–513. The process can be far quicker: in the recent CalEnergy bid for Northern Electric, the panel heard two appeals against rulings of the executive and another hearing seeking a further appeal in one week: see T. Burt, "Under the rapid fire of a bid battle", *The Times* December 28, 1996.

[11] Although shareholders cannot appear in person at the hearing.

system of regulation[12]; its rulings are binding; the procedure is speedy, and third parties have some limited rights of participation. This form of conversation provides an interesting comparison to that of the Inland Revenue's practice of giving advice with respect to the application of tax legislation.

Inland Revenue

The Revenue gives guidance and advice of a range of different degrees of formality, ranging from the generalised, published guidance on legislation, down to informal communications between accountants and local tax inspectors. At the more formal level, the Revenue issues generalised guidance on legislation in the form of Statements of Practice (I.R. 131), Extra-Statutory Concessions (I.R. 1) and the Tax Bulletin, and the Revenue has also started publishing its internal guidance manuals which are used by officials giving advice.[13] There are some specific legislative provisions which allow for consents or notifications (clearances) in respect of specific anti-avoidance and other provisions to be given prior to the transaction, which are binding on the Revenue,[14] and the taxpayer may appeal against an adverse ruling on specific legislative clearances to the Special Commissioners, and then to the High Court. At a less formal level, the Revenue also advises individuals on the tax implications of transactions both before and after they have occurred, but their advice comes in a range of legal and administrative forms and with different degrees of bindingness. The broad parameters and operation of the system are set out in the Inland Revenue's *Code of Practice on Information and Advice*,[15] which states the conditions in which, and issues with respect to which, advice on the application of tax legislation will be given.

Broadly, advice will be given on the application of legislation, double tax treaties, statements of practice, and "other areas concerning matters of major public interest in developments in an industry or in the financial sector".[16] Specifically the Code provides that advice will not be given where it would assist with tax planning or would amount to advice on transactions designed to avoid or reduce tax, and the applicant is required to give full disclosure of the facts of the transaction and the statutory provisions on which advice is sought. Advice given prior to a transaction is not formally binding on either the Revenue or the taxpayer; there is therefore no system of appeal against adverse rulings. Rather, the circumstances in which the Revenue is bound are set by

[12] Its interpretations of its own rules are subject to judicial review, but following *Datafin*, these interpretations will be assessed on the basis of the reasonableness of the interpretation rather than its correctness: *R. v. Panel on Take-overs and Mergers, ex p. Datafin* [1987] 1 All E.R. 564.

[13] See *Simon's Tax Intelligence*, 1994–1997.

[14] These include Treasury special consents under the Income and Corporation Taxes Act 1988, s.765 (mainly used for non-E.U. corporate finance transactions); notification under ICTA, s.707 (obtaining tax advantage from transactions in securities); capital gains tax clearances with respect to share for share transfers and reconstructions under, principally, s.138 of the Taxation of Chargeable Gains Act 1992; and issues relating to transfers of insurance business under s.444A(8) of the ICTA 1988. See further R. Fraser, "Pre-Transaction Rulings", *Tax Journal*, February 15, 1996, p. 14.

[15] Inland Revenue, *Code of Practice 10*, 1995.

[16] *ibid.*, 5.

the doctrine of legitimate expectations,[17] but the taxpayer may complete his or her tax return in accordance with his or her own interpretation of the statute. Moreover, the taxpayer does not have to mention which interpretation of the statute, the taxpayer's or the Revenue's, has been adopted in the return.

The Revenue does however operate a non-statutory system of giving binding rulings on the application of tax legislation to particular transactions *after* the transactions have occurred (but before the tax return has been filed).[18] The rulings are issued by the person's local tax office, and are not published.[19] The Revenue is bound by a ruling given in favour of the taxpayer as long as the applicant complied with all the conditions of the ruling.[20] However, if the ruling is adverse for the taxpayer, the latter can still complete his or her return on the basis of his or her own interpretation of the statute, and has a right of appeal to the Special Commissioners if the Revenue disagrees with that interpretation. No penalty will arise as long as the treatment adopted was reasonably arguable.[21]

With respect to giving advice or rulings, therefore, the conversation between the Revenue and the taxpayer is of a quite different nature from that which occurs between the parties to a takeover and the Panel. The Revenue is not presumed to be the final authority in interpreting the tax legislation, and it is open to the taxpayer to adopt a different interpretation from that of the Revenue, and indeed not to tell the Revenue which has been adopted. The Revenue will not give rulings which are formally binding on the tax effect of transactions prior to their occurring (although the Revenue may treat such rulings as binding in practice[22]), and unlike the Panel, will not give advice on hypothetical situations. Notably, the Revenue has a strong concern that in giving advice or rulings it should not assist individuals to reduce their tax burden, so depriving the Revenue of income. Indeed this concern was one of the primary motivating factors in the Revenue's refusal last year to introduce a system of pre-transaction rulings.[23] Whilst informal advice is therefore available, and often freely so, conversations are significantly restricted in nature, and those which formally bind the parties only occur in very limited circumstances.

E.C. Competition Law

Conversations may also take the form of waivers, granting of exceptions, or no action or comfort letters. The difference between the two forms is essentially

[17] *R. v. IRC, ex p. Preston*; *R. v. IRC, ex p. MFK Underwriting* [1990] 1 W.L.R. 1545; *R. v. IRC, ex p. Matrix Securities* [1994] S.T.C. 272; *R. v. IRC, ex p. Unilever plc* [1996] S.T.C. 681.

[18] The system is set out in Inland Revenue, *Post-Transaction Rulings, A Consultative Document*, (Inland Revenue, 1994), which has been implemented (see I.R. Press Release, September 26, 1996). On the issue of rulings generally see D. Sandler, *A Request for Rulings* (Institute of Taxation, 1994); W. Chan, "Binding Rulings" (1997) 18 *Fiscal Studies* 189.

[19] *Post Transaction Rulings*, para. 31.

[20] *ibid.*, para. 15.

[21] *ibid.*, para. 30.

[22] I thank Judith Freedman for this point.

[23] The proposals were set out in Inland Revenue, *Pre-Transaction Rulings, A Consultative Document* (I.R., 1995). The decision not to proceed was announced in a Revenue Press Release (September 26, 1996), contained in *Simon's Tax Intelligence* 1996, at 1574.

that in the case of guidance, the conversation is as to the precise application of the rule; in the case of waivers, the rule prima facie applies, but the individual is exempted from its application in particular circumstances. As with guidance or rulings, waivers may be more or less central to the operation of the regulatory process. They raise slightly different issues, however, and indeed at first glance whilst a system of guidance seems a necessary concomitant to any system of regulation, a regulatory regime which relies principally on the giving of individualised exemptions seems slightly odd. An example of a system in which waivers play a central role, however, is E.C. competition law, where the application for waivers is one of the principal vehicles for the operation and development of competition policy.

Article 85 of the Treaty of Rome prohibits restrictive practices and cartels; Article 85(3) of the Treaty permits the granting of exceptions to this general prohibition, primary responsibility for which is given to the Commission.[24] Parties apply to the Commission to see whether it considers any aspects of agreements to which they are party, or aspects of their business conduct fall within Articles 85 and 86.[25] The Commission may grant a negative clearance, that is a certification that facts in its possession provide no grounds for intervention under Articles 85 or 86,[26] or an individual exemption, in which it declares that the prohibition in Article 85(1) is inapplicable to the agreement in question; the exemption is granted for a fixed period and may be subject to conditions.[27]

The formal procedures provided in the regulation for granting such clearances are quite involved. Prior to granting a negative clearance, the Commission is required to publish in the *Official Journal* a summary of the relevant application and invite all interested third parties to submit observations within a specified time, which must not be less than a month.[28] The final

[24] Reg. 17, passed under Art. 87, gives the Commission the power to take decisions ordering the termination of agreements, granting exemptions under Art. 85(3) and imposing fines and periodic penalty payments. Reg. 17 deprived national authorities of their power under Art. 88 to decide on the application of Art. 85 in particular cases, thus effectively conferring on the Commission a monopoly of decision making power, subject to review by the ECJ under Art. 173. See generally, D. Wyatt and A. Dashwood, *European Community Law* (1993, 3rd ed.), Chaps 13–16; Whish, *Competition Law*; Butterworth's *Competition Law* (1989, updated).

[25] With certain specified exceptions largely superseded by the block exemptions (Wyatt and Dashwood, *op. cit.*, n. 24, p. 474). The incentive to notify comes from the provision in Reg. 17, Art. 4(1) which states that the person or undertaking cannot be subject to an exemption unless it has notified the Commission, even if it fulfils the substantive conditions for exemption. The date of notification determines how far the grant of exemption may be retrospective: if the agreement was entered into after Reg. 17 came into force, then the exemption is only effective from the date of notification; prior to that it is void. Once they have notified, firms are immune from fines. The immunity is temporary and contingent however. If the Commission finds that in fact the agreement is not exempt, it may impose fines.

[26] As Art. 85(3) which permits the granting of exemptions is not applicable to national courts, any exemptions issued by the Commission, including negative clearances, are probably not binding on national courts.

[27] Reg. 17, Art. 8. In addition, if the applicant is seeking a determination on the application of a block exemption regulation it may notify the Commission of an agreement, and the Commission has a period, usually six months, to express its opposition; if it does not do so, the agreement is brought within the exemption. See generally, Wyatt and Dashwood, *op. cit.*, n. 24, pp. 426–436.

[28] Reg. 17, Art. 19(3).

decision must also be published.[29] The applicant has access to all documents relied on in constructing the Commission's case, and a right to be informed of the facts and considerations on which the decision is to be made. Applicants and those whose interests are likely to be adversely affected by the decision are entitled to a hearing,[30] although they cannot question the Commission. The hearing is presided over by a Hearing Officer, appointed to emphasise the objectivity of the hearing, who reports to the Commission with his views, which are not disclosed to the parties.[31] The procedure for issuing an individual exemption is slightly less involved: a notice must again be published in the *Official Journal* prior to adopting the decision, and the decision must be published.[32] If it is proposing to impose an onerous condition the Commission must notify parties and give them the opportunity of making representations.

The formal proceedings are in practice used in only a small minority of cases.[33] Due to their time consuming nature and in order to meet the demand for exemptions which it receives, the Commission has resorted to less formal processes for handling cases in the form of comfort letters and negotiated settlements. Comfort letters have been described by the ECJ as merely "administrative letters".[34] They are signed by an official in D.G. IV, usually a Director, and cannot be invoked against third parties.[35] They may be used to state that Article 85 is not applicable, or that there are grounds for exemption under Article 85(3), and signal that the file will be closed, but that it may be reopened if material factual or legal circumstances change. Initially, no public notification of the issuance of a comfort letter was given. Following judicial consideration of the issue, the Commission stated that to increase their legal value, they would be accompanied by prior and subsequent publication of a notice in the *Official Journal*, to give interested parties an opportunity to comment.[36] However, notification is in practice rarely given: in 1992, for example in only eight of 176 cases closed by comfort letter was a notice published.[37] Further, in addition to issuing comfort letters, the Commission also simply reaches a settlement with the applicants. Again this is not binding

[29] Reg. 17, Art. 21(1).

[30] Reg. 17, Art. 19.

[31] Created in 1982 after concerns relating to the objectivity of proceedings: European Commission, 11th Report on Competition Policy, points 26 and 27. The role is set out in 12th Report on Competition Policy, point 36 and 23rd Report on Competition Policy, point 205.

[32] Exemption may be revoked where there has been a material change in the facts, where obligation attaching to grant has been breached, where decision was based on incorrect information or induced by deceit or where exemption was abused by the parties (revocation may be retroactive in the last 3 cases).

[33] In 1992, only 20 out of 1064 cases led to a formal decision: European Commission, 22nd Report on Competition Policy, point 126.

[34] Perfumes cases: Joined Cases 253/78 and 1–3/79, *Procureur de la Republique v. Giry and Guerlain* [1980] E.C.R. 2327; [1981] 2 C.M.L.R. 94; Case 99/79, *Lancome v. Etos* [1980] E.C.R. 2511; [1981] 2 C.M.L.R. 164; Case 31/80, *L'Oreal v. De Nieuwe AMCK* [1980] E.C.R. 3775; [1981] 2 C.M.L.R. 235.

[35] Perfumes cases; *IBM v. Commission* [1981] E.C.R. 2639; [1981] 3 C.M.L.R. 635.

[36] 11th Report on Competition Policy, point 15; 12th Report, point 30.

[37] 22nd Report on Competition Policy, point 126. The figures in 1993 were 7 out of 749 (23rd Report, point 208).

on third parties, and settlements are not accompanied by any form of publication or notice. Settlements are by far the most frequent method of dealing with applications: in 1992, for example, over half of applications were dealt with in this way.[38]

Supervised rule formation

In the examples given above, the conversation which is occurring is as to the application of rules which have been formulated by the regulator or are embodied in some form of primary legislation. Other forms of conversation are possible. Firms could, for example, formulate their own rules under the supervision of, and in negotiation with, a regulatory body.[39] The conversation here would be not just about the application of a general rule in a particular instance, but the application of a general set of rules to a particular firm, and ways in which the firm could formulate a rule system of a greater degree of specificity which would be tailored to its own operations, whilst achieving the general social objectives enshrined in the more general rules. This system of firm-written rules may take a range of forms: the regulatory body could formulate very simple, general rules, and the firm write their own more detailed rules under those; or the regulatory body could formulate a set of "default" rules which will apply to firms unless they choose to adopt their own, again, in negotiation with, and subject to, the approval of the agency.[40]

Examples of regulatory systems which involve the use of self-written rules include aspects of U.S. environmental regulation, of health and safety regulation in mines in the U.S. and Australia,[41] and nursing homes in Australia.[42] The technique is also mandated by regulators in certain areas of banking and

[38] Indeed, on the application form, the applicant has to indicate whether or not it would be prepared to accept a comfort letter. With respect to structural co-operative joint ventures, the Commission has formally stated that it will deal with individual applications by way of comfort letter unless the parties specifically indicate that they require formal clearance: 22nd Report on Competition Policy, point 121.

[39] This is a form of regulation advocated by Ayres and Braithwaite, and forms part of their model of "enforced self regulation". The other part focuses on compliance and enforcement processes. The firm is primarily responsible for their enforcement and for monitoring its own compliance; the rules can however be enforced by the regulatory body. The model is set out in a range of places: see primarily I. Ayres and J. Braithwaite, *Responsive Regulation: Transcending the Deregulation Debate* (1992).

[40] *ibid.*, pp. 108–109. Ayres and Braithwaite draw a parallel between this model and that of company law. Company statutes set out a standard form set of articles which firms may or may not adopt, analysed in the economic literature as a standard form contract: J. Easterbrook and D. Fischel, "The Corporate Contract" (1989) 89 *Colum. L.R.* 1416. The analogy is true to the extent that certain aspects of the corporate governance structure are mandated and thus cannot be contracted around (though according to what criteria is unclear: see further B. Cheffins, *Company Law: Theory, Structure and Operation* (1997) at 227–264), but it falls down in that company members are otherwise free to choose the form of their relationship; there is no regulatory body with which they have to negotiate or whose approval they have to seek. The freedom of private actors to choose their regulatory regime is thus curtailed far more in the enforced self-regulation model. Whether this is an advantage or disadvantage of course depends on one's view of the appropriate role of the state.

[41] Ayres and Braithwaite, *op. cit.*, n. 40 at pp. 116–118; see further J. Braithwaite, *To Punish or Persuade: Enforcement of Coal Mine Safety* (1985).

[42] J. Braithwaite *et. al.*, *The Contribution of the Standards Making Process to the Quality of Nursing Home Life: A Preliminary Report* (1990).

securities business. The international regulator of banking, the Basle Committee, has recently stated that firms will be able to use their own internally formed models to calculate the extent of their market risk, which will then be used to set capital requirements.[43] The models have to conform to broad regulator-set parameters, but can otherwise take the form that the firm chooses. The Securities and Futures Authority already operates a similar system with respect to aspects of options trading.[44] A slightly different system, which does not involve the regulator assessing the firm's risk evaluation model but rather involves the bank pre-committing itself to a certain level of portfolio loss, has been advocated by economists at the Federal Reserve Bank in the U.S.[45] The pre-committed amount sets the bank's minimum capital requirement. If the bank exceeds its own estimates of its portfolio trading loss, it faces a regulatory penalty. The technique is not confined to prudential supervision. In the retail area of financial regulation, the Personal Investment Authority is also discussing the introduction of firm-written rules for some areas of the regulation—for example training or record keeping.[46]

Monitoring and enforcement

In the examples given above, conversations have concerned the elaboration of and guidance on the application of rules in particular cases, the waiver of those rules, and approval of and reliance on firm-written rules. They have been both centralised and decentralised, and occurred at different levels within the regulatory organisation. The final example of conversations to be considered are those which occur during the process of routine monitoring and enforcement. These tend by their nature to be decentralised and relatively low-level. They may involve the same elaboration, adjustment or waiver of the rule, or the same guidance as to its meaning, as that which is involved in the process of guidance or waivers discussed above. The principal differences are that the conversation is not necessarily initiated by the regulatee, but occurs in respect of application of the rule, and in situations where it has been breached. The issue may thus not be so much whether the rule applies, but what should happen in the case of its breach.

That such conversations occur as part of the enforcement process has been well observed by a number of empirical studies of the enforcement of social,

[43] Basle Committee on Banking Supervision, *An Internal Model-Based Approach to Capital Market Risk Requirements* (1995); *id, Overview of the Amendments to the Capital Accord to Incorporate Market Risks* (1996).

[44] SFA Board Notice 254. The details are set out in SFA, "The Model Review Process", available from the SFA Risk Assessment Group.

[45] P. H. Kupiec and J. M. O'Brien, *Recent Developments in Bank Capital Regulation of Market Risks* (Federal Reserve Board, Finance and Economics Discussion Paper 95–51, 1995); *id., Bank Capital and Value at Risk* (FMG Special Paper No. 90, LSE, 1996).

[46] PIA, *Evolution Project*, (PIA, 1996); PIA, *PIA's Evolution Project: The Next Steps* C.P. 23 (PIA, 1997).

particularly environmental and health and safety, regulation.[47] These studies show the enforcement process to be one of negotiation, often involving bargaining (waiver of one rule breach in return for compliance with another), bluff (as to the legal requirements, the range of penalties at the agency's disposal), and the assertion and presentation of the legal authority of the agency. Whether the enforcement process consists of a conversation (what is usually styled the "compliance" model of enforcement—in other words one of conciliation, education and negotiation), or whether it is adversarial (the "deterrence" model) is shaped by a number of factors.[48] These include the nature of the breach (one-off or persistent) and judgments as to its seriousness (the extent to which it is in excess of limits set by the rule, for example, or the nature of its consequences), assessments made of the nature of the regulatees (whether they are well or ill-intentioned, well or ill-informed, and whether the breach was careless, negligent or malicious), and the social and moral legitimacy of the regulation being enforced. To anticipate in part the following discussion, the presence of such conversations is often seen by enforcers to be a necessary part of the regulatory process, particularly given the moral ambivalence surrounding breach of regulatory rules[49]. It is also hailed by some as a sign of "responsive" regulation,[50] the absence of such conversations giving rise to what Bardach and Kagan have notoriously characterised as regulatory unreasonableness.[51]

The reasons for conversations

In the examples noted above, conversations, in the form of guidance, waivers, rulings, or approval of the firm's own rules or the regulator's responses in cases of breach, form a central part of the regulation, and indeed may be adopted as a deliberate part of regulatory strategy. The reasons for this vary in part with the nature of the conversation. The granting of rulings, waivers or comfort letters, for example, provide advantages both for the regulator and the regulated. The regulated can address uncertainty in the rule's application by seeking an assurance that if it takes a particular course of action, the regulator will not proceed against it, or can seek an exception from the rule or its waiver in particular instances.[52] From the regulator's point of view, this strategy enables tailoring of the regulation to fit particular circumstances, which the agency

[47] See for example, K. Hawkins, *Environment and Enforcement. Regulation and the Social Definition of Pollution* (1984); G. Richardson, A. Ogus and P. Burrows, *Policing Pollution: A Study of Regulation and Enforcement* (1983); R. Baldwin, "Why Rules Don't Work" (1990) 53 M.L.R. 321; D. Vogel, *National Styles of Regulation: Environmental Policy in Great Britain and the United States* (1986); E. Bardach and R. Kagan, *Going by the Book: The Problem of Regulatory Unreasonableness* (1982); R. Kagan and J. Scholz, "The Criminology of the Corporation and Regulatory Enforcement Strategies" in K. Hawkins and J. Thomas (eds), *Enforcing Regulation* (1989); R. Kagan, "Understanding Regulatory Enforcement" (1989) 11 *Law and Policy* 89.

[48] See further B. Hutter, *Compliance* (1997).

[49] Hawkins, *op. cit.*, n. 47.

[50] P. Selznick, *The Moral Commonwealth: Social Theory and the Promise of Community* (1993), p. 470.

[51] Bardach and Kagan, *op. cit.*, n. 47.

[52] Even if these are not formally binding, they may bind the agency under the doctrine of legitimate expectations.

may want to ensure for a range of reasons. These may be concerns of regulatory equity (for example, if the application of the rule in particular circumstances would not further its purpose and nor would the waiver undermine the policy goal of the rule). Alternatively, waivers or exemptions may prevent or reduce hostility to the regulation and alienation of regulatees, and may simply be an attempt to provide regulation which suits the circumstances of the regulatee in the hope of saving time and resources later in attempting to ensure enforcement.

A slightly different set of advantages may accompany conversations which occur during a process of supervised rule formation. Such a process has the potential to avoid the problems of regulator written rules and, depending on its design, of "command and control" regulation. Rules could adjust more quickly to changing business environments, as the regulator could simply require firms to write rules to meet new situations rather than having to engage in a lengthy rule making process itself. The regulator could tap the knowledge and expertise of firms in designing regulation. Regulation would thus permit innovation and cover a greater range of corporate activity than regulator-formed rules[53]. Companies would be more committed to the rules they have written. Overall costs of regulation would be reduced: the regulator would not have to bear the costs of rule formation and the firm does not have to undergo the costs and confusion of having two rule books—the regulator's and its own in-house rules. Further, by giving to the firm the opportunity to design regulation, it could avoid what may be termed the "rationality clash" which is seen by some as the underlying cause of regulatory failure.[54] Regulators may use the technique in such a way as to ensure that the tailored rules structure the regulated's incentives to improve compliance, fine tuning requirements as becomes necessary (as in the examples of prudential regulation given above).

Conversations which occur during the enforcement process are also frequently accompanied by their own set of rationales and advantages. The enforcement process is often as much about promoting a willingness to comply as it is about ensuring exact compliance with a particular rule. The reasons for the adoption of a compliance approach may relate to the resource constraints, both temporal and financial, of the agency, but they are likely to be more complex.[55] A compliance approach tends to be adopted where there is an on-going relationship between regulator and regulated, and particularly where the individuals involved know one another or share a common background or outlook.[56] It is usually adopted to prevent the alienation of the regulated since the more "bullying" approach of sanctioning every breach can stimulate oppo-

[53] See Ayres and Braithwaite, *op. cit.* n. 39, pp. 112–113.

[54] G. Teubner, "After Legal Instrumentalism? Strategic Models of Post Regulatory Law" in G. Teubner (ed.), *Dilemmas of Law in the Welfare State* (Berlin, 1985); *id.*, "Regulatory Law: Chronicle of a Death Foretold" [1992] *Social and Legal Studies* 451.

[55] Hawkins for example found that resource constraints played no part in the lack of prosecutions of regional water authorities: Hawkins, *op. cit.*, n. 47, p. 192.

[56] K. Hawkins, "Compliance Strategy, Prosecution Policy and Aunt Sally, A Comment on Pearce and Tombs" (1990) 30 *B.J. Crim* 444; see also D. Black, *The Behaviour of Law* (1976).

sition to the regulation by the regulated, prompting non-co-operation in investigations and the compliance process.[57] More significantly, the greater the feeling of alienation, the less are firms likely to implement the necessary measures to ensure on-going compliance with the regulation in the periods between inspections, and perhaps the more likely they are to engage in minimal or creative compliance strategies.[58] A compliance approach can thus be used in an attempt to stimulate compliance. The adoption of a compliance approach may thus have significant strategic advantages. It may also be adopted as a matter of necessity, and, as noted, because of the moral ambivalence surrounding the issue of regulatory rule breaches.[59]

There are more fundamental reasons for conversations in regulation, however, which suggest that conversations are an inevitable feature of regulation, even if they are not formally mandated or do not form part of the central strategy of regulation. Conversations provide a means of addressing one of the central problems which pervade any system of regulation, whatever its design: the limitations of rules.

The problems of using rules are familiar. The inability of rules to control behaviour is well documented,[60] as is their manipulation by those pursuing strategies of creative compliance.[61] These problems have their roots in deeper ground, notably the inherent properties of rules themselves. Rules are anticipatory, generalised abstractions which when endowed with legal status provide authoritative reasons for action. Each one of these elements, anticipatory, generalised, authoritative, is the source of difficulty. Limitations of foresight, and the inherent nature of generalisations, mean that rules will inevitably be either under- or over-inclusive in relation to their purpose, failing to include situations which they should, or including situations they should not.[62] At the same time, the need for interpretation in their application means that they are also indeterminate, due to the inherent indeterminacy of language and the subjective and contingent nature of the interpretation of the fact situations to which rules are to be applied. Their status as authoritative communications, often with sanctions for their breach attached, however, means that rules act as limits on their own application and are thus imperfect tools of decision making. In Schauer's words "[r]ules doom decision making to mediocrity by mandating the inaccessibility of excellence".[63] Further, their status throws into sharp relief the problem of rules' indeterminacy: the possibility for sanction for the rule's breach means that it becomes important

[57] Bardach and Kagan analyse the impact of this "regulatory unreasonableness": Bardach and Kagan, *op. cit.*, n. 47.

[58] Hawkins, *op. cit.*, n. 56; Kagan and Scholz, *op. cit.*, n. 47; Bardach and Kagan, *op. cit.*, n. 47.

[59] Hawkins, *op. cit.*, n. 47; Kagan and Scholz, *op. cit.*, n. 47; Braithwaite, *op. cit.*, n. 41.

[60] For a recent cataloguing of their advantages and disadvantages see C. Sunstein, "Problems with Rules" (1995) 83 *Calif L.R.* 954.

[61] D. McBarnet and C. Whelan, "The Elusive Spirit of the Law: Formalism and the Struggle for Legal Control" (1991) 54 M.L.R. 848.

[62] See I. Ehrlich and R. A. Posner, "An Economic Analysis of Legal Rulemaking" (1974) *J. Legal Studies* 257; F. Schauer, *Playing by the Rules* (1991), Ch. 2; *id.* "Formalism" (1988) 97 *Yale L.J.* 509 at 539; D.J. Galligan, *Discretionary Powers* (1986), pp. 69–70.

[63] Schauer, *op. cit.*, n. 62 (1988) at 539.

to know whether a particular action is one covered by and in compliance with the rule or not.

These problems of using rules in an attempt to control or guide behaviour pervade regulation and transcend the current debate on alternative regulatory techniques: the death of command and control regulation does not mean the death of rules. Competition, corporation, contract and tax law are not renowned for their rulelessness or simplicity. Ways of using rules or overcoming their limitations have thus been an increasing matter of consideration. A number of writers have identified various dimensions to rules, and ways of using these different dimensions for different purposes or in different contexts have been suggested.[64] Focus has also been placed on the interpretive aspect of rule use, on the need to foster an understanding between the rule maker and the rule's addressees as to the rule's meaning and intended application through the development of interpretive communities.[65]

A conversational use of rules is a further way in which some of the problems of rules, notably those of interpretation, inclusiveness and entrenchment, can be overcome. As noted above, part of the problem of rules is that they are legally binding statements or reasons for action. As they are anticipatory and generalised, they may over- or under-include; but their entrenchment means that they cannot easily be adjusted, hence the charge of the "inflexibility" of rules. The contrast is sometimes drawn with conversations.[66] Conversations allow for adaptability. In conversation, the problems of generalisations and to an extent of open texture can be, and are, resolved by latitude in interpretation and understanding on the part of those participating in the conversation, and by the possibility of further elaboration or definition of generalisations made and statements uttered. For example, I may state that the weather is always miserable in February, but it is open to me then immediately to qualify that by saying there may be days in February in which the sun shines; or accept that in Australia the weather in February is in fact very pleasant. Conversation uses generalisations, and can tolerate them simply because it has the capacity for retraction, modification, qualification, clarification and embellishment. It is when this process cannot or does not occur that the over- or under-inclusiveness of generalisations poses a problem.

Conversations not only allow for adjustment, they also aid interpretation. As has been well observed, rules do not apply themselves; they need to be interpreted. Interpretation is however a contested exercise. There is no inherent, fixed meaning to rules or to language; the meaning, and hence the application, of a rule is not an objective fact but is contingent on the interpretive community reading the rule.[67] The contingency of the application of the rule on the interpretation it receives suggests a particular vulnerability of

[64] C. S. Diver, "The Optimal precision of Administrative Rules" (1983) 93 *Yale L.J.* 65; Baldwin, *op. cit.*, n. 2; J. Black, "Which Arrow? Rule Type and Regulatory Policy" (1995) P.L. 27; *id. Rules and Regulators* (1997).

[65] Black, *op. cit.*, n. 64 (1997), Chap. 1.

[66] See Schauer, *op. cit.*, n. 62 (1991), pp. 38–42, and B. Bix, *Law, Language and Legal Determinacy* (1994), pp. 19, 184.

[67] See further Black, *op. cit.*, n. 64 for discussion.

rules. Rules may receive a number of interpretations and thus be applied in a number of ways. Conversations which involve elaboration of the rule's meaning allow the problem of interpretation to be addressed. They can thus meet the need for certainty in the rule's operation, a need which itself stems from the legal status of rules, and the concomitant rule of law concerns that rules should be able to guide behaviour and allow individuals to plan their lives.[68]

Justifying conversations: conversations and responsiveness

So conversations provide practical solutions for both regulators and regulatees, and meet the problems posed by the inherent limits of rules, providing a resolution to the tension between certainty and flexibility. They may further be justified on the basis that they provide a means by which the place of the individual in a generalised system of regulation is recognised. There is a well-observed tension between different models of bureaucratic behaviour, models which have both descriptive and normative dimensions. The first, that of bureaucratic administration or formal rationality, is that which draws on Weber's model of formal/legal rationality. Rules are comprehensive, and applied consistently according to their terms by bureaucrats who are unmoved by broader ethical, social or political considerations and unmotivated by bias. The second, that of administrative justice, in contrast, emphasises the purposes of the regulation and the circumstances of the individual. It requires, *inter alia*, adjustment of the rules to suit the individual's circumstance, and has a substantive not a formal notion of equal treatment.

The tension between the two models has engendered significant debate. There is also a third, which effectively denies the dichotomy between form and purpose, rule and discretion, and that is reflexive or "postbureaucratic" rationality.[69] Flexibility and responsiveness are its hallmarks. As Selznick states:

> Communication is less firmly channeled [sic]; authority is more diffuse; consultation and participation are more strongly encouraged. The system is open and fluid in many ways .... A postmodern spirit of openness, adaptation, participation, and problem-solving prevails. The idea of top-down, authoritarian administration is rejected.[70]

Having a conversation does not necessarily mean that the regulation is simply for that reason taking the model of "responsiveness"; that model has itself additional requirements. To quote Selznick once more:

[68] F. Hayek, *Law, Legislation and Liberty* (1961); J. Raz, "The Rule of Law and its Virtue" in *The Authority of Law* (1979); *id.*, *Ethics in the Public Domain* (1994), Chap. 17. For a recent discussion see P. Craig, "Formal and Substantive Conceptions of the Rule of Law: An Analytical Framework" [1997] P.L. 467.

[69] See G. Teubner, "Substantive and Reflexive Elements in Modern Law" (1983) 17 *Law & Soc. Rev.* 239.

[70] Selznick, *op. cit.*, n. 50, pp. 286–287.

> [We must distinguish] responsiveness from opportunistic adaptation or capitulation to pressure. A responsive institution maintains its integrity while acknowledging the legitimacy of an appropriate range of claims and interests. Mere openness is not enough, however. A spirit of consultation must prevail and authority be subject to criticism and reconstruction, while the institution's basic commitments, and its capacity to function, are preserved and protected.[71]

A conversational approach has the potential to develop into a model of administration which has the responsiveness or reflexivity which this form of rationality advocates. Moreover, its central element, communication, resonates favourably with the essentially participatory models of decision making which reflexive rationality envisages.[72]

Further, a conversational approach may itself uphold principles of fair treatment and due process. As Galligan suggests, the achievement of social goals is mediated through the fair treatment of persons, which in turn recognises that people have rights about the way they are treated by government.[73] Engaging in conversations about the meaning and application of rules is thus an important way in which the place of the individual in the bureaucratic process is recognised; conversations are the human face of bureaucratic regulation.

Problems with conversations

The experience of many of those regulatory systems which operate a conversational approach at some level suggests however that conversations are not necessarily an unproblematic phenomenon whose presence in the regulatory system can be given an unreserved welcome. It may be that conversations facilitate the use of particular rule types which may in some circumstances be desirable, it may be that they are the human face of bureaucracy; but it is argued here that it is necessary if they are to meet these concerns that they occur within the context of certain procedural and other requirements.

The danger of conversations is in part that they have the potential to confer on the regulation a schizophrenic character so that it publicly represents one thing whilst in practice operating quite differently.[74] It is not simply this bifurcation which is problematic, however: the principal sources of difficulty are the conditions in which and degree to which this difference occurs, and further the extent to which the decisions as to the rule's application are being

[71] *ibid.*; p. 463.

[72] R. Mayntz, "The Conditions of Effective Public Policy: A New Challenge for Policy Analysis" (1983) 11 *Policy and Politics* 123; Teubner, *op. cit.*, nn. 54, 69.

[73] D. J. Galligan, *Due Process and Fair Procedures* (1997).

[74] Some would argue that such a duality can be justified: see M. Dan-Cohen, "Decision Rules and conduct Rules: On Acoustic Separation in Criminal Law" (1984) 97 *Harvard L.R.* 625. Dan-Cohen roots his analysis back to Bentham's distinction between laws which create offences and laws which command punishment to be administered when an offence has been committed. On Bentham's analysis see further J. Bentham, *An Introduction to the Principles of Morals and Legislation, Concluding Note*, esp. paras 6 and 8; *id.*, *Of Laws in General*, Chap. 14, both in J. H. Burns and H. L. A. Hart (eds), *The Collected Works of Jeremy Bentham* (1970). Dan-Cohen's analysis may be subjected to criticism on a number of grounds, which cannot be entered into here. See, for example Sunstein, *op. cit.*, n. 60.

determined by a body which is not recognised as legitimate to make those decisions. It is when an exceptions process, for example, effectively becomes a vehicle for policy change, that objections may arise.[75] Or where it is the regulator who is alone determining the nature and terms of the bifurcation, for unless an idea of legal pluralism is accepted[76] the regulator lacks the legitimacy which the court is afforded to determine the meaning and application of the rule in particular instances. The practice may lay the agency open to the charges of capture, inconsistency and inequity, of emptying the law of any meaningful content, and of undermining the regulation and, more particularly, its public interest or social objectives.[77] This is particularly so if the adjustment of the rule is largely invisible to those observing the agency, or even to others within the regulatory system.

A conversational approach in itself, therefore, whilst it may be flexible and responsive, does give rise to, and indeed is in turn affected by, issues of participation, transparency, the standing of participants in the conversation, and the nature of distribution of authority and decision making for the conduct of the conversation. At one level, these issues can be seen as examples of the familiar trade off between efficiency and due process.[78] But the way in which this trade off is in practice achieved often satisfies no-one. In the context of E.U. competition law, for example, although the procedural protections accompanying the formal process for granting exemptions allow for greater third party participation, that process is very rarely used as it makes such significant demands on time and resources. The informal process which has thus developed is much quicker, but participation of interested third parties is restricted if not eliminated; publicisation of the actual application of the law in individual circumstances is limited or non-existent; the ability of others to know what the law is in practice is subsequently impeded, giving rise to legal uncertainty, and it becomes difficult, if not impossible, to monitor the agency's activity. The practice of dealing with cases by settlement or by comfort letter has been criticised on the following bases: the lack of legal certainty[79]; the lack of consistency as to when formal or informal decisions are made, and as

[75] For an example see P. H. Schuck, "When the Exception Becomes the Rule: Regulatory Equity and the Formation of Agency Policy through an Exceptions Process" (1984) *Duke L.J.* 163. Schuck attributes this use of a waiver strategy to achieve a policy change to a desire on the part of the agency to avoid the requirements of the Administrative Procedure Act 1946 which would operate if the policy were embodied in a rule change.

[76] On resistance to such a notion in English public law see H. Arthurs, "Reforming Administrative Law: A Slightly Dicey Business" (1979) 17 *Osgoode Hall L.R.* 1, and *Page v. Hull University Visitor* [1993] 1 All E.R. 97.

[77] Inserting the terms "public interest" here is not so much to subscribe to a particular theory of regulatory genesis, but to emphasise that it is only if we accept that regulation has at least in part some public interested objectives that worrying about its effective implementation and operation makes sense. If regulation is simply there to provide benefits for certain sectional, private interests, then why engage in a debate as to how best it may attain those ends?

[78] See Baldwin, *op. cit.*, n. 2 above, pp. 33–58.

[79] They are not binding on third parties (*IBM v. Commission* [1981] E.C.R. 2639). The Commission is presumably bound under the doctrine of legitimate expectations. However due to the particular features of Art. 85, the letters/settlements are not binding on national courts, at least presumably in so far as they grant exemptions (national courts cannot implement Art. 85(3), which grants exemptions). See further Wyatt and Dashwood, *op. cit.*, n. 24, pp. 480–481 for a discussion.

between informal decisions; the lack of transparency of the practice; and the lack of involvement of a hearing officer or equivalent to ensure the objectivity of the process.[80] The experience of the Commission thus shows all too clearly that whilst administrative and business realities may demand the sacrifice of due process and accountability values in return for the speedy resolution of decisions, that sacrifice is a cause of discontent amongst that same business community and their legal advisors.

These concerns may be exacerbated when the conversation occurs at the level of enforcement officers. Systems designed to increase participation and openness may more easily operate at the initial stage of rule formation rather than the subsequent stages of rule application and enforcement. Ensuring that others can participate in the conversation at these subsequent stages in the process could make significant demands on the time of both regulator and regulated, render the process unwieldy, and perhaps affect the willingness of either the regulator or regulated to participate in the conversation at all.[81] Adoption of this type of conversational approach thus may mean that even if the rule formation process is one of negotiation between, or otherwise involved the participation of, a wide range of interests, those interests may be effectively excluded from the implementation of that rule in the enforcement process. Participation at one stage in the regulatory process namely rule formation, is negated at another. Partly on this basis, the practice of adopting a compliance approach in enforcement has attracted significant criticism on the grounds that it is an unauthorised and pragmatic condoning of breaches of the rules, constituting effectively an illegitimate alteration of the regulation in favour of the regulatee, undermining its central policy aims.[82]

The issues which arise are not simply due to the pressures of time or other bureaucratic constraints. Conversations also depend for their successful operation on matters which cannot simply be achieved by improved organisational or procedural design: matters of trust and legitimacy. The operation of such a strategy as firm-written rules or the operation of an extensive system of guidance or waivers in which regulation is tailored to fit the particular regulatee, for example, depend significantly on the degree to which the regulator is prepared to trust the regulatees to formulate rules which will meet the overall social goals without the regulator dictating the requirements of those rules. These strategies, and those of compliance approaches to enforcement, also depend on the degree to which the public is prepared to trust both firm and regulator to construct a system of regulation which will in fact achieve those goals.

These concerns are fundamentally linked to that of legitimacy: to what extent is such bi-lateral rule making accepted, and by whom? Different

[80] See generally I. von Bael, "The Antitrust Settlement Practice of the E.C. Commission" (1986) 23 C.M.L.R. 61; D. Waelbroeck, "New Forms of Settlement of Antitrust Cases and Procedural Safeguards: Is Regulation 17 Falling into Abeyance?" [1986] E.C.L.R. 268.

[81] On the prerequisites for successful negotiation, see P. Harter, "Negotiating Regulation" (1982) 71 *Georgetown L.J. 1.*

[82] F. Pearce and S. Tombs, "Ideology, Hegemony and Empiricism: Compliance Theories of Regulation" (1990) 30 *B.J. Crim* 423.

regulatory communities or constituencies may have different criteria of legitimacy.[83] Indeed, it may be that conversations, in undermining the uniformity of the rule by its individualised adjustment, illustrate what may be described as the "legitimacy paradox" of regulators: regulators' legitimacy comes in large part from their ostensible pursuit of public interest regulatory goals, no matter how vague, ill defined or contradictory they may be. Conversations involving, for example, waivers or a compliance approach to enforcement may be necessary to maintain the legitimacy and acceptability of the regulation to one community, the regulatees. However, they may be seen by others as an illegitimate approach to adopt, and further as evidence of collusion between regulator and regulatee, of capture or too cosy relationships. What therefore may be necessary to maintain the regulators' legitimacy for one audience may be contrary to that which is necessary to maintain it for another.

These concerns are also critically linked to the expectations which surround the role (and rule) of law. Many of the criticisms which attend the conduct of conversations stem directly from the role which is played by law within that conversation. The significance of law in the expectations surrounding conversations does not stem from the fact that legal rules are "hard edged" in some way.[84] Nor is it, as some legal-linguistic theorists have suggested,[85] that they are entrenched and not susceptible to constant change, alteration and retraction (at least at the level of the formal, public statement of the rule), in the way that generalisations and statements which form part of the course of conversation can be modified and altered as the conversation adopts different courses or paths. It is rather the host of other values and considerations which come with the definition of a norm as "legal", and moreover, of a process as "public". The use of law inevitably imports a set of values with which the regulatory system has to conform: "rule of law" values that law should be certain, general, open, stable and prospective. Moreover, the governmental nature of the bodies operating the regulatory system imports a further familiar set of values: of due process, transparency, openness and participation.[86] Thus although law does not play the determinative role which classic formulations of the legal paradigm ascribe to it (that what the rule says is what the world does), the values which are embodied in the liberal legal paradigm do influence the expectations actors have of the manner in which law, or those administering it, should operate.

These values are not simply the plaints of unreconstructed public lawyers. As noted in the examples above, they are shared by other participants and observers of the regulatory system, and can have a direct bearing on the conduct of the conversation. It is interesting to note, for example, that in the

[83] For an idea of "legitimacy communities" see R. Barker, *Political Legitimacy and the State* (1990).

[84] See for example the analogy drawn by Feldman between the "wall" of law and the "rushing stream" of non-legal norms: M. Feldman, "The Social Limits to Discretion" in K. Hawkins (ed.), *Uses of Discretion* (1992), p. 183.

[85] See for example Bix, *op. cit.*, n. 66; Schauer, *op. cit.*, n. 62.

[86] These values may be imported irrespective of the state's involvement: Habermas, for example, sees participation as necessary for the legitimacy of law, irrespective of public involvement: J. Habermas, *Of Facts and Norms* (transl. 1996).

debate surrounding the operation of E.C. competition regulation the issue of the legal status of comfort letters has been directly linked to that of due process: the greater the participation and openness of the exemption process, the greater could be the legal status and bindingness of such letters.

The inevitability of conversations indicates that these issues have to be addressed if regulation is to retain a degree of effectiveness and acceptability both to regulatees and to society as a whole. Moreover, conversations should not be seen simply as regrettable but unavoidable features of regulation. As noted above, they carry with them considerable benefits of flexibility, responsiveness, tailoring; facilitating, or indeed manifesting alternative forms of regulatory technique, forms which are attuned to the structure, operation and incentives of individual regulatees. How then can the institutional structure which surrounds such conversations be adjusted to enhance their legitimacy and effectiveness?

Structuring conversations

Questions of effectiveness and of acceptability and legitimacy are both contested and inextricably bound together. It may not be possible to measure a system's effectiveness independently of the acceptability of the process or result to different communities. Indeed, the degree of its effectiveness may contribute to the extent to which it is regarded as legitimate. Conversely, unless the system is regarded as legitimate by those who participate in it or observe it, then to an extent its effectiveness is of little value. Without exploring further here the complexity of the relationship, it is suggested that the criteria against which a conversation should be assessed are those of Selznick's model of responsive regulation, *viz*. that in the conversation both regulator and regulated should maintain the integrity of the regulation and its commitment to its goals (however vague or contradictory they may be), while acknowledging the claims and interests of an appropriate range of persons.[87] To this end, it is suggested that four elements are central to the effective operation and acceptability of regulatory conversations.[88] These are commitment of its principal participants, regulator and regulatee, to a meaningful discourse; the nature of the opportunities of others to access the conversation; the distribution of power and authority between the different conversants; and the trust and accountability which exist between the participants and which surrounds the regulatory system.

Commitment

To consider first the issue of commitment. For dialogue to be successful, the conversants have to be committed to the process. It may be that certain

[87] Selznick, *op. cit.*, n. 50, p. 463.

[88] The specification of these four conditions is not intended to deny the need for principles of due process, non-discrimination or other basic civil, political or social rights: rather the intention is to focus on those elements which are central to the ways in which conversations in particular can be structured so as to achieve the aims identified, a structure which both depends on, and is in some instances a further specification of, those principles.

preconditions are necessary for that commitment to be present, both for the regulator and the regulatee. On the part of the regulatee, although it may seem that engaging in a conversation with the regulator as to the exact application or possible waiver of a rule may be advantageous in conferring certainty, there may for a number of reasons be a reluctance on the part of those being regulated to participate. Indeed, seeking such exemptions or advice, and thus initiating the conversation as to the application of the rules, may itself be a complex decision, and the firm may conclude that certainty comes at too high a price. The firm may be reluctant to give the disclosures which are necessary, particularly if the process for applying for a waiver, guidance or ruling is formal, and if details of the application and/or decision are published.[89] Further, in applying to the regulator for advice or an exemption, the regulated runs the risk not only of receiving adverse advice or being refused, but also of alerting the regulator to the transaction or to the firm's operation more generally, where, in the absence of the application, the regulator might have continued in ignorance of the practice. Or regulatees may fear that seeking advice on the application of a rule would signal to the regulator that the firm was incompetent, applying the rules improperly or not at all. They may be right: PIA's proposed approach to enforcement, for example, includes frequent calls from compliance officers as one of its "danger signs" in assessing the compliance profile of the individual firm.[90] Work on compliance officers suggests that regulatees may thus require some relationship of trust to exist between themselves and the regulator before they feel confident that a request for advice will not trigger alarm bells in the regulator's enforcement office.[91]

On the part of the regulator, conversations are a way of addressing the information asymmetries which inevitably exist between regulator and regulatee concerning the latter's operation. There are several ways in which regulators could encourage conversations which would address these asymmetries. For example, they could prompt firms to seek advice or exemptions by making application for exemptions compulsory (as under E.C. competition law).[92] Another strategy is the approach adopted by the Panel, which is to permit applications for advice to be made on a hypothetical or anonymous basis. Both approaches encourage the regulatee to instigate communication with the regulator, providing the regulator with a flow of information

[89] On the reluctance of firms to notify the Commission of arrangements that may infringe Art. 81, despite the danger of invalidity due to failure to notify, see I. Forrester and C. Norall, "the Laicization of Community Law: Self Help and the Rule of Reason: How Competition Law is and could be Applied" (1984) 21 C.M.L.R. 11–51; on the reluctance of banks to have their individual capital requirements published, see C. Hadjiemmanuil, *Banking Regulation and the Bank of England* (1996); on the reluctance of firms to have their applications for tax rulings published, see W. Chan, "A Useful Hybrid?" *Tax Journal*, June 2, 1997, p. 9.

[90] *PIA Evolution Project: The Next Steps*, para. 172.

[91] See M. Weait, *The Role of the Compliance Officer in Firms Carrying on Investment Business in the City of London*, (unpublished D. Phil thesis, Oxford University, 1995), pp. 77–79; 158–160.

[92] If the parties have not notified the Commission under Art. 85(2) they are subject to fines even if the agreement is not in breach of the competition rules, although even this may still not have the desired effect: see Forrester and Norall, *op. cit.*, n. 89.

as to the rule's application. This may indicate problems such as over- or under-inclusion, which the regulator may then address through amending the rule or seeking its amendment. Further, with respect to exemptions, the agency is put on notice about the transaction and therefore has the opportunity to control more effectively the giving of exemptions, rather than leaving it to the monitoring or investigation processes.

However, whilst undoubtedly the process of the regulated seeking advice or exemptions could be advantageous for the regulator, there may nonetheless be reluctance to participate. This, for example, is the position of the Inland Revenue. Indeed the Revenue finds itself in a position almost of a conflict of interest which inhibits its conduct as a conversational partner. On the one hand it wants to provide certainty to taxpayers, on the other its principal duty is to collect taxes, and indeed to maximise the revenue which can be lawfully collected. The Revenue has been set a target of obtaining an additional £2 billion over the next three years, and under the "Spend to Save" initiative, the Revenue will be deploying 2,000 more staff over that period to counter tax avoidance and evasion.[93] The Revenue's concern that any advice given could facilitate tax avoidance makes it a very ambivalent conversational partner, and whilst it may willingly engage in conversations on an informal basis, it is prepared to enter those which lead to binding rules only in particularly defined circumstances. Indeed the approach which is required under the "Spend to Save" initiative is implicitly one of regulatory unreasonableness and not one of responsiveness, flexibility and dialogue.[94]

Commitment is not only a question of attitude; it also depends on the harsh factors of resources. Concern over the resource implications of adopting a central strategy of advice or rulings was a significant factor in the Revenue's decision not to proceed with a system of pre-transaction rulings, for example. Again the Revenue was particularly concerned not to prejudice its tax enforcement activity, and did not want resources to be switched from enforcement to advice, an issue of particular resonance in the area of tax as enforcement is a high yield, low cost activity, the results of which (more money for the Exchequer) are highly visible and tangible. Unlike many regulators, the Revenue can to some extent measure the scale of its success.

Adopting a technique of firm-written rules may also be highly resource intensive. Approval of firm-written rules essentially requires the regulator's role

[93] Moves which have prompted fears that the Revenue will use its considerable powers of investigation to pursue what are in reality cases of tax avoidance (which is legal) as opposed to tax evasion (which is not). See, for example, T. Murray and C. Glasson, "Beyond the Pale", *Tax Journal*, January 30, 1997, p. 10.

[94] Moving to this more adversarial style of operation after long adopting a more co-operative approach may bring the IRC other problems. It was such a change in approach which led to the judicial review in *R. v. IRC, ex p. Unilever* [1996] S.T.C. 681. A cooperative arrangement between Unilever and the tax office had existed for 20 years, whereby Unilever claimed relief for tax losses simply by deducting losses from profits and not submitting returns showing losses separately until beyond the maximum time limit of 2 years after the accounting period to which they related had elapsed. The Inland Revenue then without warning objected to the returns on the grounds that they had been made out of time, and therefore relief for loss could not be obtained (a sum amounting to £95.5m.). The court held that the practice had given rise to a legitimate expectation on Unilever's part, and that the Revenue's demand was unfair and an abuse of power.

to move from that of regulator to that of consultant. Given the level of commitment of regulatory resources necessary to assess the different rules which firms formulate or to negotiate the individualised application of a rule, it may be necessary that the agency be well resourced and/or that the regulatees be relatively few in number for the agency to be able to engage fully in the negotiation and approval exercise. Such an approach also requires the regulatees to be well-resourced, or at least willing to commit the resources they have to such a project. Firms are subject to a whole web of regulation in the course of their operations. If all the discrete elements of this regulatory web adopted this model, it could be potentially costly for the firm (although very good for the lawyers who would probably be employed to write the rules).[95]

The costs may, therefore, be high, and it is no answer, contrary to what Ayres and Braithwaite suggest,[96] that these can be reduced by, for example, making the process of approval routine and carried out by low level officials acting in accordance with internal guidelines. Resources here interact with attitude in determining the commitment of parties to the conversation. This form of conversation can only work effectively if the agency engages in the process, and really does treat each individual set of rules individually, and not in accordance with internally set general guidelines applied either by rote or out of a concern—which may or may not in turn be generated by the agency's search for legitimacy in the wider public—to exercise as much control as possible over the regulated firms. The importance of the agency's approach to the regulation is highlighted by the experience of an analogous regime in financial services regulation in the U.K. The Financial Services Act 1986 initially provided that the rules of the subsidiary self-regulatory organisations (SROs) were to be "equivalent" to those of the Securities and Investments Board (SIB). This provision was interpreted very narrowly by SIB, which in effect required that the SROs' rules be the same as SIB's. It was only a change in regulatory approach at SIB which led to greater freedom on the part of the SROs in forming their rulebooks.[97] Further, without such commitment, the process of approval will become routinised and the self-written rules will only be approved if they accord with the agency's internal guidelines, which may or may not be published. Again, the experience of the administration of unit trust regulation prior to the Financial Services Act 1986 provides some evidence of this. Under the Prevention of Frauds (Investment) Act 1958 all unit trusts had to be approved by the Department of Trade. The system was criticised trenchantly by Gower in his report: it could take months to approve a trust

[95] Even if this approach were adopted by only some of that web, the willingness to commit resources to writing rules would probably depend on how central the regulation is to the firm's operations. In very hazardous industries, for example mining, oil refining, chemicals, health and safety regulation is central, and so firms may be willing to commit resources to writing supervised rules; investment firms, in contrast, may not be. For them, securities regulation is central to their operations. They are more likely to invest resources in writing rules for compliance with that rather than with health and safety regulation, which is more incidental to their day to day operation.

[96] *op. cit.*, n. 39 at p. 121.

[97] Although accompanied by an amendment in the statutory wording from "equivalent" to "adequate", the amendment was largely of semantic significance, signalling rather than requiring a change in regulatory approach. See Black, *op. cit.*, n. 64 (1997), Chap. 3.

deed; there was no published body of law which indicated when approval would be granted; and the regulation was administered by low level officials who were ignorant of the area, which had led to ossification.[98] The danger with such an approach is that the pressures of bureaucratisation mean that the commitment necessary to ensure the benefits of individual tailoring will be lost.

Access

The second element is access to the conversation, who participates in it. We have seen that it can be the closed nature of conversations, the fact that they are bi-lateral and that third parties are excluded, which can be at once their most necessary and their most contentious aspect. Conversations pose the risk, noted above, that participation in one forum of the regulatory process, policy and initial rule formation, is negated at another, that of rule application. As the experience of E.C. competition law suggests, however, too elaborate procedures run the danger of rendering the process ineffective. Moreover, the regulated's desire to maintain the privacy and confidentiality of its operations may mean that opening the process up to others has the effect that the conversation ceases, or simply moves to a more private forum.

There is thus a tension between the need and desire for privacy and confidentiality on the part of the individual and the wish for openness and transparency on the part of others, both regulatees and the wider public. In resolving this tension, it is suggested that there is a need to distinguish different forms and occasions of access and participation. Participation is easier to achieve when the general policy and the rules embodying it are being determined, and indeed those who advocate a participative approach tend to concentrate on just this stage of policy or rule formation.[99] Participation can also be a feature of the *post hoc* accountability of the regulators, with broader interests being involved in monitoring regulators and reporting processes including information on the operation of the process.

Participation in the conversation itself, however, is harder to achieve, and indeed it is questionable whether it is always justified. Direct participation is perhaps only necessary where the third party's position will be directly affected by any agreement which is reached between the regulator and individual regulatee. Requiring it in other instances, given the regulatee's desire for privacy, is likely simply to shift the conversation to another forum, or end it altogether. Pragmatic considerations need not be the only justification for restricting third party access to the conversation concerning the rule's application. This approach, it is suggested, would moreover be consonant with a notion of fair treatment which Galligan posits, in that it balances the need to ensure the achievement of the general social goals of the regulation with a recognition of the position of the individual where that individual's position is central to the application of the rules.[1]

[98] L. C. B. Gower, *Review of Investor Protection: Discussion Document* (HMSO, 1982), paras 3.06 and 8.

[99] See for example Teubner, *op. cit.* nn. 54, 69; Mayntz, *op. cit.*, n. 72.

[1] Galligan, *op. cit.*, n. 73, esp. pp. 52–96.

Authority

Participation is linked to the third element, that of authority. The distribution of authority within the regulatory system to determine the interpretation of rules is critical to the operation of a conversational approach, and to the respective standing of participants in the conversation. The effectiveness of the conversational approach is primarily contingent on who has the authority, *de facto* or *de lege*, to determine the interpretation and application of the rule in the individual circumstance. An obvious example is that of giving guidance: guidance is of greater use to the regulated firm if it knows that it can rely on it. This requires two things: first, that the regulator cannot backtrack, but is bound by its interpretation, and second, that it cannot be overridden, that it is the final arbiter of the rule.

However, the issue of authority to determine the rule's application is also central to the legitimacy of the conversational process. The question of where that authority should lie thus has a number of aspects. There are clearly the issues of speed and certainty; the fewer the number of bodies who are involved in interpreting the rules, the less complicated and lengthy any appeals process, the more the regulated can rely on the regulator's decision. Further, if the immediate regulator does not have the authority to interpret the rules, but this authority resides with another body, then unless this final body participates in the initial conversation, possibilities are opened up of strategic play by the regulated to force the immediate regulator to agree with it rather than have the matter referred on.[2]

The locus of authority, and in particular keeping authority to determine the meaning of rules within the regulatory system, which may entail excluding courts from an appeal process, also has other, less obvious implications. These are that it may permit the development of an interpretive community, that is a shared body of understandings as to the meaning and application of rules within the regulated community. The arguments for such a development thus stem not from the usual assertions of regulatory expertise, often used as a legitimating basis for giving the regulator authority to make final determinations,[3] but from the potential for tacit understandings as to the rules' operation and therefore greater certainty to be engendered, with subsequent implications for the type of rules which could be adopted.[4]

Authority to determine the application of rules tends however to come only with certain pre-conditions attached, although what these are can vary with the particular context in which the regulator operates. Primarily, the regulated have to be prepared to accept that final authority for the interpretation of rules lies within the regulatory system, subject of course to judicial review.[5] This

[2] Dangers for example recognised by Lord Donaldson M.R. in *Datafin* in determining the court's approach to review of the Panel's decisions: *R. v. Panel on Take-overs and Mergers, ex p. Datafin* [1987] 1 All E.R. 564.

[3] R. B. Stewart, "The Reformation of American Administrative Law" (1975) 88 *Harvard L.R.* 1669; Baldwin, *op. cit.*, n. 2, above.

[4] See further, Black, *op. cit.*, n. 64 (1997), Chap. 1.

[5] On the exercise of that review power with respect to regulatory rules, see further J. Black, "Reviewing Regulatory Rules and Rule Making Processes" in J. Black, P. Muchlinski and P. Walker (eds), *Commercial Regulation and Judicial Review* (forthcoming, 1998).

acceptance cannot be taken for granted: in considering whether it should move to a system of broad rules supplemented by individualised guidance or firm-written rules, for example, PIA ask explicitly whether firms would be prepared to accept that the regulator's view should prevail where there is a conflict of judgment between PIA and the firm on its application.[6]

Central to the question of acceptability and legitimacy is the question of whether the final arbiter should be independent and objective, so fulfilling the classic rule of law requirements, or whether it is acceptable or indeed desirable for that arbiter explicitly to pursue policy objectives. In the case of the Inland Revenue, for example, it has been argued that given the Revenue's obligation to maximise tax revenue collected there is a danger that the legislation will not be correctly applied[7]; some have therefore argued that a system of pre-transaction rulings should be operated by a body independent of the Revenue.[8] The case for an independent agency to administer E.C. competition policy is also hotly debated, where the issue is whether an independent agency will adopt a purer and more single minded pursuit of competition policy than the Commission.[9] What participants in both debates share is a concern that whoever has the authority to apply the rules should do so consistently and objectively and not arbitrarily; where they differ is as to the type of institutional and organisational structure which will best ensure this.

The location of this authority affects not only the conduct of the conversation and the relationship between the conversants, but the issue of effective third party participation. A good example of the effect of the distribution of authority on the conduct of a conversation is that of telecommunications regulation. The regulator does not have the power to impose a particular alteration or application of the licence issued to network operators, but needs the consent of the regulated.[10] If consent is not forthcoming, the matter is referred to the MMC, to whose rulings the regulator has then to have regard. The provisions of the licence are not simply relevant to the licence holder, however. Because of the particular history of the regulation, the licence of one firm, British Telecom (B.T.), is effectively the instrument for regulating the rest of the telecommunications sector. The regulatory structure established on B.T.'s privatisation was designed for a duopoly, B.T. and Mercury Communications (MCL). Changes in technology mean that telecommunications is no longer a natural monopoly, and other entrants have come into the market. Changes to the regulatory regime,

[6] PIA, *PIA's Evolution Project: The Next Steps*, para. 178.

[7] Indeed it is this danger which Galligan highlights as being the problematic aspect of conversations in the context of due process: Galligan, *op. cit.*, n. 73, pp. 283–284.

[8] R. Fraser, "Pre-Transaction Rulings, Part 2" *Tax Journal*, February 22, 1996, p. 18. The same concerns as to lack of impartiality and objectivity surround the discussion on the introduction of a general anti-avoidance provision: see for example the responses to the Chancellor's suggestion in the Budget Speech of introducing such a clause in the *F.T.* July 3, 1997.

[9] See, for example, C-D. Ehlermann, "Reflections on a European Cartel Office" (1995) 32 C.M.L.R. 471–486; K. Van Miert, "The Proposal for a European Competition Agency" (1996) 2:2 *Competition Policy Newsletter* 1.

[10] As indeed is the case in the regulation of water, electricity, gas, and certain parts of environmental regulation.

however, can only occur through modifications of B.T.'s licence, changes to which B.T.'s consent is statutorily required.[11] Although such a bi-lateral, consensual arrangement may be appropriate in a contractual situation, in a regulatory environment such as this it is less acceptable as it gives one regulatee, the licensed operator, a significant amount of power to determine the nature of the general regulatory regime, and indeed of key aspects of the industry itself.[12] Questions thus arise as to the ability of others who may be affected by the terms of the licence provision to participate in such negotiations. However, despite recent attempts by Oftel to open up the process of consulation and negotiation over the conditions of, in particular, B.T.'s licence,[13] in requiring B.T.'s consent to any change the regulatory structure places limits on the impact that the views generated by such a participative process can have on the final decision. As Scott comments, given the scope which the regulation allows for bilateral bargaining between the regulator and B.T., and the effective veto which B.T. has, it is tempting to ask whether such a transparent and participative process provides simply a veneer of openness over a system which is structurally closed.[14] The B.T. example also illustrates very clearly how different elements of the institutional structure in which the conversation occurs may operate in tension, restricting the opportunities for other elements to be recognised.

Trust and accountability

Authority, commitment and participation are thus central to the conduct of conversations. The final element which is essential for their effective conduct and acceptability is that of trust and accountability. The two are inextricably linked, as it is only through accountability that the regulator can build a reputation for fairness and pursuit of regulatory goals, a reputation which will in turn engender trust in its actions on the part of the regulated and the wider public. Indeed, trust is important at a number of levels. Firms have to trust the

[11] If B.T. does not consent, the DGT may refer the matter to the MMC (s.15(1) T.A., although the Secretary of State may veto a referral (s.15(3) T.A.)). The MMC then decides whether the existing licence is in the public interest; if they find it is not, the DGT has a discretion to amend it without the operator's consent.

[12] Judicial failure to recognise the regulatory nature of the licence agreement is evident in the case of *Mercury Communications Ltd v. DGT* [1996] 1 W.L.R. 48. See further A. McHarg, "Regulation: a private law function?" [1995] P.L. 551; J. Black, "Constitutionalising Self Regulation" (1996) 59 M.L.R. 24.

[13] In his response to the National Audit Office's review, the Director General of Telecommunications stated: " . . . it is particularly important in telecoms where there is increasing competition in different segments of the market and where regulatory decisions can have different effects on different players. OFTEL needs to have a clear picture of how possible changes in the regulatory regime will affect all the different players in the industry—both in the short and the long term. It is vital, therefore, that proposals for change are fully aired and discussed with all the stakeholders in the industry." Report by the Comptroller and Auditor General, *The Work of the Directors General of Telecommunications, Gas Supply, Water Services and Electricity Suppy,* (1995–96) H.C. 645, Response of the Director General of Telecommunications, Overview, para. 7. See further, T. Prosser, *Law and the Regulators* (1997), Chap. 3.

[14] C. Scott, "Re-regulating Interconnection and Deregulating Prices—The U.K. Experience", paper presented to the Communications Research Forum, Melbourne, October 1996, p. 15. See also C. Scott, "Regulators discretion and licence modification: the *Scottish Power* case" [1997] P.L. 400.

regulator to treat them fairly and consistently under the rules; the regulator has to trust the firm to speak honestly; the public has to trust the regulator not to discriminate or act arbitrarily, and not to deviate from or otherwise prejudice the social goals (however ambiguous and conflicting) which the regulation is meant to achieve. The less open and transparent the regulatory system, the more, in other words, it relies on private conversations between regulator and individual regulatees, the more that trust is needed, and the less it may be forthcoming. Systems of regulation, such as that of banking supervision, which rely heavily on bi-lateral conversations between regulator and individual regulated firms to determine the exact form that regulation should take in their instance, are thus extremely vulnerable to suspicion and mistrust.[15]

Trust can be developed essentially by regulators establishing a reputation for fair and consistent treatment, and their resistance to capture.[16] Such a reputation can be engendered through a willingness to be accountable; to provide qualitative information as to the broad content and nature of the conversations which it has. These could include post hoc reports as to the extent and nature of guidance, rulings or waivers given; the publication of firms' rules which have been approved, for example, and statements of enforcement practice. Consistency of treatment can be ensured through internal reporting systems and centralised monitoring and recording of enforcement practices, guidance, rulings or waivers, and qualitative assessment and comparison of firm written rules. In focusing on trust, therefore, what is emphasised is the need for regulation to be responsive not just to wider interests in its formation and to the regulated in its operation, but to the claims of society as a whole in the integrity of its function.

Conclusion

Conversations about rules are both a necessary and inevitable part of the regulatory process, almost regardless of the form that that process takes. The examples drawn on here illustrate that whether it adopts the classic "command and control" model, or whether it is enabling, facilitative, and incentive-based, whether it occurs in a self regulatory, statutory or E.U. context, regulation inevitably involves rules. Given the nature of rules, regulation will inevitably involve conversations about those rules. Further, focusing on those conversations highlights the dynamic aspect of the regulatory process, and denies a linear conception of that process, whereby rules are made and then enforced, invoking instead a continuous process of rule adjustment and individualisation, rooted in communication and discussion.

Such conversations are not only inevitable, they are also desirable: they "oil the wheels" of the regulatory process; their absence is the hallmark of

[15] With respect to the Bank of England, see for example Hadjiemmanuil, *op. cit.* n. 89, pp. 141–143; B. Quinn, *Rules v. Discretion: The Case of Banking Supervision in the Light of the Debate on Monetary Policy*, Financial Markets Group Special Paper No. 85 (LSE/FMG, 1996).

[16] For a discussion of the role of the regulator's reputation in financial regulation see C. Goodhart et al., *Financial Regulation: Why, How and Where Now?*, Monograph for the Central Bank Governor's Meeting, June 6, 1997 (FMG, LSE, 1997).

regulatory unreasonableness; they may permit flexibility, adaptability and responsiveness; and they recognise the position of the individual in a generalised system of regulation. They are nevertheless surrounded by concerns as to their operation and legitimacy, concerns which come not simply from public lawyers, but from those who operate in and observe the regulatory system. Moreover, they may not achieve the ideals of responsiveness: a regulatory system may appear to involve conversational elements, but the conversants may be rather ambivalent communicators. Consideration of conversations has, therefore, to take into account the commitment to the process of those involved, as well as the broader question of their legitimacy. This in turn raises issues of authority, participation, trust and accountability, issues in which the tensions between privacy and transparency, the pursuit of social goals and the recognition of individual needs have to be resolved. These issues are central to the legitimacy and ultimate effectiveness of the conversational process. Moreover, because the process has echoes of communication theory and models of procedural regulation, the questions it raises also resonate there: of rights of access and standing within the process; of the operational limits on the process, the numbers that can be involved, the stages in the regulatory process at which that involvement is most likely and most feasible; and of the dangers of undermining the open and participative process which characterised the initial formation of the regulatory policy and rules by the later, less visible dialogues which occur between regulator and regulated.

In resolving these issues, there is a need to structure the distribution of authority and the forms and occasions of participation and accountability in such a way that they do not operate in conflict either with each other or with the willingness and commitment of regulator and regulated alike to the conversation. In part, then, the call is for a need to recognise that, as Lacey states, "the insights about the complexity of administrative processes should feed back into social and political reflection on what kinds of administrative processes we want to set up and how to overcome difficulties in realising the social goals of our institutions."[17] It is also, however, necessary to remember exactly why those administrative processes are so complex, and to recognise that in that complexity lie the limits to what prescription of administrative processes can achieve. As has been stressed throughout, conversations are both an inevitable and, in certain circumstances, a desirable part of the regulatory process. Ways therefore need to be found to structure, use and accommodate them whilst not shifting them to another, more private, forum or silencing them altogether.

[17] N. Lacey, "The Jurisprudence of Discretion" in Hawkins (ed.), *op. cit.*, n. 84, p. 384.

Part IV
Organizations and Institutional Variety

[12]

Separated Powers and Positive Political Theory: The Tug of War Over Administrative Agencies

JONATHAN R. MACEY*

Perhaps the most intriguing thing about the United States Constitution is the way that its basic principles keep recreating themselves in new and unexpected contexts. Quite recently, for example, the complex matrix of checks and balances under the constitutional separation of powers embodied in Articles I, II, and III has found new support in the work of scholars espousing positive political theory (PPT).

PPT shows why a robust system of checks and balances is particularly important in the modern administrative state. On the one hand, modern government could not function if Congress were prohibited from delegating large chunks of authority to administrative agencies. On the other hand, these delegations, coupled with Congress's remarkable sophistication at designing internal rules of organization to control agency behavior, puts added pressure on the courts and the executive to fulfill their roles in the constitutional scheme without undermining the ability of the state to operate.

PPT does not solve the venerable question of how the nonlegislative branches can fulfill their obligation to check and balance Congress without intruding on the constitutional authority of the legislature to make law. PPT does, however, reveal with remarkable clarity how this problem has reconstituted itself in the modern administrative state.

A recurring theme in the literature on PPT is how Congress can arrange its own structure and internal rules in order to control the actions of the administrative agencies to which they have delegated authority.[1] The goal of Congress is to ensure that administrative agencies generate outcomes that are

---

* J. DuPratt White Professor Of Law, Cornell Law School.

I am grateful for comments and guidance from William Eskridge, Cynthia Farina, Geoffrey Miller, Andrew Rutten, Edward Schwartz, Kenneth A. Shepsle, Pablo Spiller, Cass Sunstein, and Barry Weingast, as well as from participants in the Law and Government Workshop at the University of Chicago. I wish to thank Robert C. Torch of the Cornell Law School class of 1993 for valuable research assistance.

1. *See, e.g.*, Murray J. Horn and Kenneth A. Shepsle, *Commentary on "Administrative Arrangements and the Political Control of Agencies": Administrative Process and Organizational Form as Legislative Responses to Agency Costs*, 75 VA. L. REV. 499, 499 (1989) (employing "assumption of intelligent foresight" to conclude that elected politicians in creating agencies devise initial enactments which will protect against the influences of bureaucrats and subsequent political coalitions); Matthew D. McCubbins, Roger G. Noll & Barry R. Weingast, *Structure and Process, Politics and Policy: Administrative Arrangements and the Political Control of Agencies*, 75 VA. L. REV. 431, 481 (1989) [hereinafter McNollgast, *Structure and Process*] (legislatively imposed procedural constraints play a critical role in controlling bureaucratic agents); Matthew D. McCubbins, Roger G. Noll & Barry R. Weingast, *Administrative Procedures as Instruments of Political Control*, 3 J.L. ECON. &

consistent with the original understanding that existed between Congress and the various interest groups that were parties to the initial political compromise. The problem facing Congress can be described as bureaucratic drift, which refers to changes in administrative agency policies that lead to outcomes inconsistent with the original expectations of the legislation's intended beneficiaries.

Perhaps the most obvious example of Congress's efforts to retain political control over administrative agencies, and thereby control bureaucratic drift, is the legislative veto. The legislative veto allows Congress to delegate rulemaking authority to an agency, but retain the right to invalidate agency action.

Other more subtle mechanisms for controlling bureaucratic drift exist. In particular, Matthew McCubbins, Roger Noll, and Barry Weingast (McNollgast) have observed that Congress has established complex systems of rewards, sanctions, and ex post monitoring to control agency behavior.[2]

A wide variety of rules of administrative law, including the prohibitions on *ex parte* contact, the legislatively mandated standards for judicial review, the assignment of burdens of proof in challenges to agency decisions, the allocation of discretionary budgetary funds, and the delay built into the administrative process, all contribute to the creation of a political environment that causes agency decisions to mirror the political equilibrium at the time of the original enactment and can be explained as efforts to control bureaucratic drift.[3] Similarly, Congress can utilize what Matthew McCubbins and Thomas Schwartz refer to as "fire alarms," which are formal and informal mechanisms by which the targeted beneficiaries of legislation can notify politicians when an agency generates outcomes that deviate from the interests of the beneficiaries, thereby triggering formal investigations and other legislative responses.[4]

In an important critique on the PPT literature concerning bureaucratic drift, Murray Horn and Kenneth Shepsle argue that the strategies described by positive political theorists to control bureaucratic drift create a second

---

ORGANIZATION 243, 273-74 (1987) (elected politicians should use administrative procedures in addition to or instead of monitoring and sanctions to achieve bureaucratic compliance).

2. *See* McNollgast, *Structure and Process, supra* note 1, at 434 (congressional investigations into the performance of an agency may take place through annual budgetary process, the reauthorization of an agency's programs, and watchdog agencies such as the Office of Management and Budget and the General Accounting Office).

3. *See* McNollgast, *Structure and Process, supra* note 1, at 440-44 (discussing provisions of the Administrative Procedure Act, 5 U.S.C. §§ 553(b)-(c), 556-557 (1982), and other legislative measures as efforts to subject agencies continually to the types of political pressures in existence at the time of enactment).

4. Mathew McCubbins & Thomas Schwartz, *Congressional Oversight Overlooked: Police Patrols Versus Fire Alarms,* 28 AM. J. POL. SCI. 165 (1984).

sort of drift: legislative drift.[5] Legislative drift results where the preferences of politicians evolve over time, creating a legislative environment inconsistent with the preferences of the original political coalition. The tension between bureaucratic drift and legislative drift observed by Horn and Shepsle arises because the strategies for monitoring and enforcing legislative deals described by positive political theorists such as McNollgast require the deployment of legislative staff or legislative authority by subsequent legislatures to monitor agency personnel. Increasing legislative authority over an agency reduces the potential for bureaucratic drift. As legislative authority over an agency grows, however, the agency becomes more vulnerable to the changing preferences of subsequent legislators.

In a recent paper, I attempted to extend the literature on congressional control of agency behavior by arguing that the politicians who create administrative agencies can constrain the behavior of bureaucrats not only by establishing the procedural and substantive rules under which the administrative agencies operate, but also through the original organizational design of the agency itself.[6] Unlike the congressional monitoring and enforcement mechanisms described above, the structural designs I discussed do not involve the trade-off between bureaucratic drift and legislative drift described by Horn and Shepsle.

In particular, I argued that Congress's ability to design and structure an agency will "hardwire" the agency to generate decisions that reflect the original understanding of the enacting coalition.[7] Congress can set the jurisdictional parameters of an agency, thereby determining which interest groups will have access to the agency, and on what terms. In addition, Congress can affect the relative abilities of various interests to influence future legislative actions and control *ex ante* the outcomes generated by an administrative agency by controlling which industries and interests will be reflected in the agency's staffing decisions, by determining how "independent" the agency will be from Congress, and by strengthening certain interest groups relative to others.[8]

---

5. Horn & Shepsle, *supra* note 1, at 503-04 (arrangements that legislators craft to control bureaucratic drift necessarily allow future coalitions to intervene in agency implementation, but the involvement of future coalitions creates legislative drift).

6. Jonathan R. Macey, *Organizational Design and Political Control of Administrative Agencies*, 92 J.L. ECON. & ORGANIZATION (forthcoming Feb. 1992) (manuscript on file with *The Georgetown Law Journal)* [hereinafter Macey, *Organizational Design*].

7. *Id.* (manuscript at 48) (Congress in structuring agencies creates institutional mechanisms that will produce outcomes consistent with the political equilibrium existing at the time of initial delegation).

8. *Id.* (manuscript at 34, 39, 47-48) (congressional decisions as to whether an agency will exist independently or within the executive branch, whether an agency regulates a single industry or multiple industries, and whether an agency will have broad or limited discretion all influence what interest groups will be able to influence an agency and the extent to which they may do so).

The scholarship described above has focused extensively on the relationship between agencies and Congress; yet Congress's ability to control administrative agencies will be affected by the other branches of government. The role of these other branches in constraining or facilitating congressional control of agency decisions has not been considered. That is the goal of this article.

Consistent with the basic principle that the separation of powers is designed to raise the decision costs of government,[9] I will describe the effects of judicial review of agency decisions and the effects of executive branch involvement in agency decisions, and will show that the involvement of these other branches seriously undermines Congress's efforts to design procedural, substantive, and structural rules to control agency behavior. In particular, despite generally granting great deference to agencies, the courts systematically act to broaden the array of interests with access to the administrative rulemaking process. But even the executive, whose actions are more politically motivated than the judiciary's, serves a salutary role in my analysis by reducing the benefits that legislators obtain from passing interest group oriented legislation, thereby raising the costs of rent-seeking. Viewing agency enactment legislation as a "deal" between interest groups and lawmakers, it is obvious that the value the interest group places on the legislation will increase symmetrically with the "deal's" durability. However, interference with the power of Congress to control administrative agencies impedes the ability of politicians to make credible commitments to interest groups. This in turn lowers the price politicians can demand for providing legislation to favored groups by reducing the willingness of such groups to pay for new laws.

In Part I of this article, I argue that judicial inquiry into administrative agency decisions reflects a delicate judicial balancing act designed to promote public-regarding legislation. The balancing act reflects a deep ambivalence on the part of judges about the nature of administrative law and about how to develop jurisprudential standards for administrative agencies that will serve the public interest.

In the Part II of the article, I argue that the executive branch also has responded to Congress's efforts to control administrative agencies through

9. Jonathan R. Macey, *Transaction Costs and the Normative Elements of the Public Choice Model: An Application to Constitutional Theory,* 74 VA. L. REV. 471, 494-95 (1988) (separation of powers increases the cost to interest groups of achieving a legislative goal by lowering the probability of success); Jonathan R. Macey, *Promoting Public-Regarding Legislation Through Statutory Interpretation: An Interest Group Model,* 86 COLUM. L. REV. 223, 225 (1986) [hereinafter Macey, *Promoting Public-Regarding Legislation*] (separation of powers requires the various branches of government to share power, thereby increasing the decision costs of government) (citing Peter H. Aranson et al., *A Theory of Legislative Delegation,* 68 CORNELL L. REV. 1, 2-3 (1982); Cass R. Sunstein, *Interest Groups in American Public Law,* 38 STAN. L. REV. 29, 44 (1985)).

rules of structure, substance, and procedure. The President's increasingly bold efforts to influence the outcomes of the administrative rulemaking process come in direct response to Congress's increasing sophistication at developing techniques to control bureaucratic behavior. Thus, consistent with the very idea of the system of checks and balances that comprises the separation of powers, the executive and Congress are involved in a healthy, ongoing tug of war over control of administrative agencies. This struggle results in delegations to agencies that are more public-regarding, and, in agency rulemaking, less subject to capture by special interests than would be the case if the process were dominated only by one branch.

I. THE JUDICIAL RESPONSE TO THE ADMINISTRATIVE STATE: A PERSPECTIVE FROM POSITIVE POLITICAL THEORY

The problem facing courts is both subtle and complex. On the one hand, it would seem clear that courts should scrutinize agency deliberations with great care, granting little, if any, deference and generally hindering agency efforts to promulgate rules. This is because administrative agencies, like legislatures, are subject to substantial interest group influence. In order to prevent agency capture by special interest groups, the judiciary should subject agency action to rationality review and rigorous means-ends analysis.[10]

On the other hand, close judicial scrutiny of agency decisions may facilitate rather than impede interest group activities. Building a modicum of delay into the process of administrative agency rulemaking benefits poorly organized groups by providing them with the time necessary both to learn about proposed actions by administrative agencies and to galvanize into an effective political coalition to respond to those proposals. Courts have imposed a variety of requirements on the process of administrative rulemaking that result in the imposition of this modicum of delay.[11] For example, the judicially imposed requirement of notice and comment periods, the requirement that agencies provide interested parties with the right to participate in an elaborate paper hearing process that generates a documentary record, and the requirement that agencies articulate the basis and purpose of their deci-

---

10. Macey, *Promoting Public-Regarding Legislation, supra* note 9, at 263-64 (because judges are immune from the political pressures that influence agency officials, rationality review and means-ends analysis of agency action by the judiciary can prevent agency capture).

11. Professor Richard Pierce has been the leading administrative law scholar to catalogue the delays that have followed judicial invalidations of administrative agency decisions. *See* Richard J. Pierce, Jr., *The Unintended Effects of Judicial Review of Agency Rules: How Federal Courts Have Contributed to the Electricity Crisis of the 1990s,* 43 ADMIN. L. REV. 7 (1991) (describing how a series of federal courts of appeals decisions has constrained the Federal Energy Regulatory Commission's (FERC) power to implement changes in regulatory policy); Richard J. Pierce, Jr., *Unruly Judicial Review of Rulemaking,* NAT. RESOURCES & ENV'T, Fall 1990, at 23 (judicial reversals of FERC rules have discouraged the FERC from engaging in systematic policymaking).

sions[12] all create the sort of delay that can help to even the playing field between relatively diffuse, poorly organized groups, and highly organized, well-financed special interests.

By contrast, however, the extraordinary delay that results from constant reversals of agency decisions can benefit highly organized groups relative to poorly organized groups because the comparative advantage of the highly organized groups lies in their ability to retain their cohesiveness over a long period of time. Thus, while a delay in agency rulemaking from two days to two months probably serves the public interest by permitting a more diverse set of interests to become involved in the process, an extension of the rulemaking process from two months to two (or ten) years probably is contrary to the public interest because it has the opposite effect.

Consistent with a public-interest oriented view of the judiciary, courts have erected a complex legal infrastructure to govern agency rulemaking that incorporates some, but not too much, delay into the regulatory process. In interpreting the Administrative Procedure Act (APA),[13] courts "have built on the opportunity for comment and 'concise general statement' requirements of § 553 to transform notice and comment procedures into a far more elaborate 'paper hearing' process that generates a documentary record and an elaborate agency opinion as the basis for 'hard look' judicial review."[14] Thus, the overall portrait of administrative law that emerges is deference, coupled with delay. Professor Susan Rose-Ackerman has trenchantly summarized the consequences of this legal infrastructure:

> [I]f an agency acts in a rushed and careless manner, its efforts may not be upheld by the courts. The most important example of this was the attempt early in the Reagan administration to repeal the passive restraint standard for automobiles without a careful analysis of alternatives. The Supreme Court turned back this effort with even the most conservative members of the Court supporting the basic requirement that obviously relevant options be considered. Countering this decision, however, were two other Supreme Court cases giving agencies discretion to overrule a previous administra-

---

12. The Administrative Procedure Act (APA) imposes the basic requirements of notice and opportunity for public comment. 5 U.S.C. § 553 (1988). These requirements have been used by the courts to ensure that rulemaking will include participation by interested parties and be based on a careful and detailed record. *See* Motor Vehicle Mfrs. Ass'n v. State Farm Mut. Auto Ins. Co., 463 U.S. 29, 34, 56-57 (1983) (National Highway Traffic Safety Administration "failed to present an adequate basis or explanation" for rescinding requirement that cars be equipped with passive restraints, and therefore arbitrary and capricious standard not met); Macey, *Organizational Design, supra* note 6 (manuscript at 35-36).

13. 5 U.S.C. §§ 551-559, 701-706 (1988).

14. STEPHEN G. BREYER & RICHARD B. STEWART, ADMINISTRATIVE LAW AND REGULATORY POLICY 597 (2d ed. 1985). *See* United States v. Nova Scotia Food Products Corp., 568 F.2d 240 (2d Cir. 1977) (remanding as inadequate FDA rules regarding methods of preventing botulism in whitefish because agency had ignored comments that its rules would render such fish commercially unsaleable).

> tion's interpretation of a statute and upholding an agency's power to determine its own enforcement agenda. Nevertheless, the lesson of these cases, taken together, seems to be that regulatory reform efforts within agencies can only succeed if officials articulate a principled justification based on an understanding of the facts. . . . [G]enuine reform requires expertise and commitment.[15]

Thus, while courts generally defer to administrative agencies' decisions, courts have acted in a variety of subtle but effective ways to drive a wedge between Congress and administrative agencies, thereby fulfilling their role in the constitutional scheme of raising the decision costs of government so as to make law more public-regarding. The purpose of this Part of the article is to describe the complex processes by which the federal courts accomplish this result. In Part I.A I examine the substance of judicial review of agency decisionmaking. I argue that, regardless of the standard of deference articulated by the courts, the courts are willing to overturn decisions and interpretations by administrative agencies even where such decisions and interpretations are within the scope of the agency's presumed expertise. Courts are particularly likely to take this initiative where an administrative agency's decision violates a court's intuitions about what is fundamentally fair or "reasonable."[16] Courts' willingness to examine the decisions of administrative agencies under a reasonableness standard forces such decisions into the public spotlight and pushes agency rulemaking in a more public-regarding direction.

In Part I.B I examine the rules that the judiciary has created to determine whether interest groups have standing to challenge an agency's decisions. I show that, in addition to examining the substance and process of agency rulemaking under a reasonableness standard, courts have gone to great lengths to tailor the rules of standing to aid those groups that have been excluded from the initial legislative deal that generated the administrative agency in question. Exclusion from an initial legislative compromise puts the groups so excluded at a tremendous disadvantage in subsequent rulemaking.[17] Courts respond to the exclusion of a group by Congress by adjusting their traditional rules of standing to provide these disenfranchised groups with some measure of review.

Thus, I contend that the entire body of law concerning whether interest

15. Susan Rose-Ackerman, *Defending the State: A Skeptical Look at "Regulatory Reform" in the Eighties,* 61 U. COLO. L. REV. 517, 525-26 (1990) (footnotes omitted).

16. *Cf.* Chevron U.S.A. Inc. v. Natural Resources Defense Council, Inc., 467 U.S. 837, 843-44 (1984) (judiciary must give effect to the intent of Congress in evaluating an agency's construction of a statute; in absence of clear legislative intent, court will defer to reasonable statutory interpretation by agency).

17. Macey, *Organizational Design, supra* note 6 (manuscript at 29) ("The initial jurisdictional design of an agency will determine which interest groups will have ready access to the agency . . . .").

groups have standing to challenge decisions by administrative agencies can best be explained as an effort by the courts to protect groups that lost at the time of the initial deal between the interest groups and the Congress that designed the agency. Courts tend to grant standing to those groups that were excluded from the original deal; they tend to deny standing to those groups that were included in the original deal.

Courts are able to determine which groups were excluded from a deal by looking at the jurisdictional structure of the agency whose actions are being challenged. Interest groups that are repeat players before an agency are likely to be favored by an agency over groups that seldom interact with the agency. Single interest group agencies are likely to favor the interest groups they regulate over other groups. Courts' unwillingness to tolerate this favoritism raises the costs to interest groups of lobbying Congress to create administrative agencies that are structured to permit easy capture by those same groups. In this way, the Court's rules on standing move the law in a public-regarding direction.

Finally, in Part I.C I discuss the legislative veto, which is Congress's most blatant attempt to control the bureaucratic drift of an administrative agency. The Supreme Court's declaration that the legislative veto is unconstitutional provides the most direct evidence that the independent judiciary is sensitive to the threat posed by administrative agencies to the separation of powers and the system of checks and balances. The Court's decisions in *INS v. Chadha*[18] and *Metropolitan Washington Airport Authority v. Citizens for the Abatement of Aircraft Noise, Inc.*[19] provide strong support for the thesis that the judiciary does not want Congress to be too successful in its efforts to control administrative agencies. Rather, the Court consistently has acted to raise the costs of administrative delegations so that such delegations do not become too attractive to special interests.

A. JUDICIAL ABDICATION TO ADMINISTRATIVE AGENCIES: *CHEVRON*

Any analysis of the role of the federal courts in undermining legislative "hardwiring" of administrative agencies must begin with consideration of *Chevron U.S.A. Inc. v. Natural Resources Defense Council, Inc.*[20]

This case involved a challenge to the Environmental Protection Agency's (EPA) "bubble" policy, which implemented a new method of measuring dis-

---

18. 462 U.S. 919, 945-59 (1984) (legislative veto provision in Immigration and Naturalization Act found unconstitutional because it defeated the separation of powers as embodied in the Presentment Clauses and bicameralism requirement of the Constitution).

19. 111 S. Ct. 2298, 2301 (1991) (holding unconstitutional an act of Congress making creation of a board of review composed of members of Congress with veto power over agency decisions a condition to transfer of airport operating control to agency).

20. 467 U.S. 837 (1984).

charges of industrial pollution under the Clean Air Act.[21] Under the EPA's new policy, the agency could define the statutory term "stationary source" to mean an entire manufacturing plant.[22] Prior to this reinterpretation, the EPA had treated the term "stationary source" to mean any polluting device within a plant.[23] The new definition reduced the costs of complying with the Clean Air Act for manufacturers in certain states.

The issue in *Chevron* was whether the EPA's new definition of the term "stationary source" violated the Clean Air Act. The Supreme Court, exhibiting its traditional deference to what it regards as "reasonable" agency determinations, upheld the EPA's construction of the relevant statutory language. The Court noted that "considerable weight should be accorded to an executive department's construction of a statutory scheme it is entrusted to administer."[24] The Court held that so long as Congress has not directly addressed the issue before the agency and has not foreclosed the agency's interpretation, then the agency's construction of the statute should be upheld unless it is unreasonable or otherwise impermissible.[25]

Chevron has been described as a case of monumental importance.[26] In an important recent article, Professor Cass Sunstein characterized *Chevron* as "one of the very few defining cases in the last twenty years of American public law,"[27] and asserted that "[i]n its allocation of governmental authority and in its production of outcomes in the real world, the importance of the case far exceeds that of the Supreme Court's more celebrated constitutional rulings on the subject of separation of powers in the 1980s, probably even if all of these are taken together."[28]

Clearly, the case is troubling for those who view the proper role of the judiciary as increasing rather than decreasing the costs to interest groups of implementing special interest oriented legislation. As Justice Scalia has observed, the decision appears to be "a striking abdication of judicial responsibility" and "quite incompatible with Marshall's aphorism that, '[i]t is

21. *Id.* at 839-40 (construing regulations promulgated to implement permit requirements under the Clean Air Act Amendments of 1977, Pub. L. No. 95-95, 91 Stat. 685 (codified as amended at 42 U.S.C. §§ 7401-7626) (1988)).

22. *Id.* at 840.

23. *Id.* at 857.

24. *Id.* at 844 (footnote omitted).

25. *Id.* at 843-45.

26. Antonin Scalia, *Judicial Deference to Administrative Interpretations of Law,* 1989 DUKE L.J. 511, 512 (describing *Chevron* as the most important case in administrative law since Vermont Yankee Nuclear Power Corp. v. Natural Resources Defense Council, Inc., 435 U.S. 519 (1978) (agencies not required to engage in rulemaking procedures beyond those imposed by the APA or other statute)).

27. Cass R. Sunstein, *Law and Administration After* Chevron, 90 COLUM. L. REV. 2071, 2075 (1990).

28. *Id.* (footnote omitted).

emphatically the province and duty of the judicial department to say what the law is.' "[29]

But, as noted above, existing rules of administrative law that are designed to promote participation in the process of making administrative law would be undermined if judicial second-guessing of agency rulemaking allowed the administrative process to drag on for too long. To permit "appropriate political participation in the administrative process,"[30] that process must offer potential participants some reasonable prospects for closure. Otherwise, relatively diffuse, poorly organized or poorly funded groups will be at a great disadvantage relative to groups that are better organized.

In a previous article I described how Congress can organize administrative agencies so as to reduce the agency costs associated with congressional delegations to such agencies.[31] To the extent that such delegations represent special interest oriented legislation, close judicial scrutiny of these delegations is in the public interest. To put the issue simply, to the extent that regulatory capture of executive agencies is a concern, robust judicial involvement in the decisionmaking process of agencies is an effective antidote. Complete judicial abdication to agencies would not serve the public interest.

On the other hand, the standard of judicial deference reflected in *Chevron* may be consistent with the public interest because it helps to limit the delays often associated with judicial review of agency rulemaking. An extremely broad reading of *Chevron* would create enormous possibilities for judicial abdication of agency decisions. This would reflect an extremely naive view of the administrative state: one in which courts view not only Congress, but also administrative agencies, as somehow sacrosanct, and one in which any interference by courts into the lawmaking process is antimajoritarian and therefore suspect.

In this respect, the result in *Chevron* is similar in force and effect to the result in *Vermont Yankee Nuclear Power Corp. v. Natural Resources Defense Council, Inc.*[32] In *Vermont Yankee,* the Court held that, while lower federal courts may review agency rules for arbitrariness and may remand for failure to provide sufficient explanation of their rules,[33] agencies are not required to engage in rulemaking procedures beyond those imposed by the APA or other

---

29. Scalia, *supra* note 26, at 513-14 (citing Marbury v. Madison, 5 U.S. (1 Cranch) 137, 177 (1803)).

30. Scalia, *supra* note 26, at 517.

31. Macey, *Organizational Design, supra* note 6 (manuscript at 28-47) (describing how Congress may "hardwire" an agency to ensure that it continues to serve the preferences of the political compromise that leads to the initial delegation to the agency, thereby making the cost of such delegation low).

32. 435 U.S. 519 (1978).

33. *Id.* at 535 & n.14. *See also* 5 U.S.C. § 706(2)(A) (1988) (scope of judicial review of agency action).

relevant statutes.[34] Thus, the Court has established a time-bounded framework for agency action. The agency must move slowly enough to allow weak groups a chance to mobilize, but not so slowly that such groups will be unable to maintain an effective political coalition.

The result in *Chevron* should not be interpreted as reflecting the wholesale abdication by judges of their constitutional authority to decide what the law is. First, as the Court in *Chevron* itself made clear, courts may draw upon "traditional tools of [statutory] construction" when evaluating the interpretations of statutes formulated by administrative agencies.[35] In particular, courts will decline to defer to administrative agencies when their interpretation of a statute contradicts the plain meaning of the law, the overall structure of a statutory scheme, the relevant legislative history, or even the underlying purposes of the statute.[36]

As Professor Sunstein has observed, whenever a "court has a firm conviction that the agency interpretation violates the statute, that interpretation must fail. This is so even if a reasonable person might accept the agency's view."[37] In other words, while the first part of the two-part test articulated in *Chevron* requires courts to defer to an administrative agency's construction of a statute unless that construction thwarts Congress's will, courts are not reluctant to find that an agency has in fact thwarted Congress's will.[38] This illustrates that "the mere fact of a plausible agency view is insufficient for deference."[39]

Thus, even after *Chevron,* courts have considerable latitude in evaluating the decisions and interpretations of administrative agencies. In particular, where Congress has passed a piece of special interest legislation and couched it in public interest terms in order to reduce the political costs associated with the enactment, courts are likely to find that an attempt by an administrative agency to interpret the statute in the way most favorable to a particular interest group contravenes Congress's intentions. For example, Congress

---

34. *Vermont Yankee,* 435 U.S. at 548, 558.

35. *Chevron,* 467 U.S. at 843 n.9.

36. *See, e.g.,* Dole v. United Steelworkers of Am., 494 U.S. 26 (1990) (overturning Secretary of Labor's interpretation of the Paper Reduction Act as inconsistent with the object of the Act); Board of Governors v. Dimension Fin. Corp., 474 U.S. 361 (1986) (overturning Federal Reserve Board's attempt to regulate NOW accounts and commercial loan substitutes as violative of the plain meaning of the underlying statute because such accounts and loans were outside the statutory grant of jurisdiction).

37. Sunstein, *supra* note 27, at 2092.

38. *See* INS v. Cardoza-Fonseca, 480 U.S. 421 (1987) (rejecting INS's interpretation of the statutory phrase "well-founded fear" on the grounds that statutory text and legislative history suggested an alternative meaning of this phrase); *id.* at 452-55 (Scalia, J., concurring) (since statutory text is clear, there is no justification for a discussion of whether deference to the administrative agency is warranted).

39. Sunstein, *supra* note 27, at 2092 (footnote omitted).

may pass a statute that is shrouded in public interest rhetoric, knowing full well that the enabling legislation creates an institutional dynamic within the relevant administrative agency that makes it more probable than not that certain interest groups will prevail in the interpretive process that gives life to the underlying statutory enactment. But it is this public interest rhetoric that will motivate the judicial inquiry into the statute, and will cause courts applying the *Chevron* principle to nullify agency decisions.

Often the decisions promulgated by an agency will be a better reflection of Congress's will than Congress's own articulation of its intentions due to the public interest rhetoric that accompanies an initial statutory enactment. Such public interest rhetoric may belie an underlying naked preference for a special interest group. This rhetoric may be ignored by the agency, but it will not be ignored by the courts. Ironically, courts will view the agency's construction as invalid on the principle that Congress retains the ultimate power to make law. Because courts take Congress at its word when it declares that a statute was enacted to serve the public interest, courts often will thwart the will of Congress by invalidating an agency order that is inconsistent with Congress's formally articulated public interest justification for a delegation to an agency.

In addition to the courts' persistent willingness in the wake of *Chevron* to find an agency's interpretation to be inconsistent with Congress's unambiguous intentions, under the second prong of *Chevron,* courts may decline to defer to agency decisions that are "unreasonable."[40] While the term "reasonable" suggests that courts will give agencies "considerable latitude," the reasonableness requirement imposes a meaningful constraint on Congress's ability to enact wealth transfers costlessly:

> The reasonableness inquiry should probably be seen as similar to the inquiry into whether the agency's decision is "arbitrary" or "capricious" within the meaning of the APA. That inquiry requires the agency to give a detailed explanation of its decision by reference to factors that are relevant under the governing statute.[41]

The requirement that agencies make detailed explanations of their decisions has two consequences. First, it undermines the ability of Congress to use agency resources to stifle poorly organized interests' efforts to monitor and control the behavior of administrative agencies. Second, the requirement that agencies make detailed explanations of their actions lowers the costs to poorly organized groups of finding out about what agencies are doing. Absent such a requirement, only highly organized, well-funded groups would have access to the administrative process. Thus, even if courts do not often

40. *See supra* notes 16, 21-25, and accompanying text.
41. Sunstein, *supra* note 27, at 2105 (footnotes omitted).

find that administrative agencies have acted unreasonably, the requirement that agencies give a detailed explanation of their actions makes it more difficult for Congress to hide special interest legislation by promulgating statutes that involve vague delegations to administrative agencies. Further, requiring agencies to make detailed explanations makes it difficult for Congress to structure an agency so that it is likely to be captured by powerful special interests.

Indeed, if one were to identify a manifestation of judicial unwillingness to review administrative agency action, it would not be *Chevron*: it would be *Heckler v. Chaney*.[42] *Chaney* involved an attempt by death row inmates to cause the Food and Drug Administration to bring suit to stop the states' use of lethal drug injections in human executions on the grounds that such injections violated the Food, Drug, and Cosmetics Act.[43] The Supreme Court declined to intervene on the grounds that an agency's refusal to initiate an enforcement proceeding is presumptively unreviewable.[44] The Court reasoned that an agency's limited resources force it to make judgments about its agenda and priorities.[45] Thus, an administrative agency may bring an enforcement action against one party despite the fact that the agency's enforcement strategy does not implicate similarly situated competitors.[46]

Quite clearly, the courts' unwillingness to second-guess agency inaction enhances agency discretion. The costs to Congress of implementing wealth transfers through administrative agencies would be much greater if courts routinely substituted their own views on how agency resources should be allocated for those of the agencies themselves. However, even in the arena of agency inaction it is possible to underestimate the role of the courts in setting agency agendas. Courts are willing to intercede in nonenforcement decisions where such decisions result from a misapplication of substantive law rather than from an exercise of managerial discretion.[47] Similarly, where Congress sets clear guidelines governing an agency's enforcement discretion, courts will review nonenforcement.[48] Thus, in *Dunlop v. Bachowski*,[49] the Court

42. 470 U.S. 821, 837-38 (1985) (an agency's decision not to take enforcement action is not reviewable by the courts, but rather is an issue for Congress).

43. *Id.* at 823.

44. *Id.* at 838 (an agency's refusal to take enforcement action falls within the APA's exception to reviewability provided by § 701(a)(2) because it is action "committed to agency discretion") (quoting 5 U.S.C. § 701(a)(2) (1988)).

45. *Id.* at 831 (in deciding how to use its resources, agency must "balanc[e] a number of factors which are peculiarly within its expertise").

46. Moog Indus., Inc. v. FTC, 355 U.S. 411, 413-14 (1958) (in absence of a "patent abuse of discretion," Court could not hold Federal Trade Commission's cease and desist orders against particular firms in abeyance pending the entry of similar orders against similarly situated firms).

47. *Chaney*, 470 U.S. at 832-33 (presumption of unreviewability of agency inaction is rebutted when substantive statute provides guidelines for agency's exercise of enforcement powers).

48. *Id.* at 833 ("Congress may limit an agency's exercise of enforcement power if it wishes, either

upheld review of the Secretary of Labor's decision to decline to challenge a union election when the underlying statute had ordered the Secretary to bring suit where there was probable cause to believe there was a violation of the Labor-Management Reporting and Disclosure Act.[50]

As the preceding discussion suggests, while courts generally defer to decisions and interpretations of administrative agencies, the judiciary has not abdicated its authority to overturn agency initiatives. Where an agency's decision or interpretation of a statute violates a canon of statutory construction,[51] or where the agency's interpretation is inconsistent with the public interest patina of the original statute,[52] or where a court deems the agency's action "unreasonable,"[53] the agency's decisions will be accorded no deference.

Finally, and most importantly, the deferential standard of *Chevron* must be interpreted in the context of the entire infrastructure of administrative law. In particular, the judiciary's insistence that administrative agencies afford interested persons the opportunity to participate even in informal rulemaking, and the transformation of notice and comment procedures into forums for granting hearings to outside groups greatly enhance the participatory nature of the administrative rulemaking process. Taken together, the judiciary has created a legal environment in which the process of administrative rulemaking contains mechanisms to ensure that the rulemaking process proceeds slowly enough for poorly organized interest groups to galvanize into effective political coalitions when the need arises, but does not become so fossilized that such groups are unable to maintain their cohesiveness.

B. JUDICIAL "RE-ENFRANCHISEMENT" OF CERTAIN DISENFRANCHISED GROUPS

Courts' sensitivity to the concerns of individuals and interest groups that were "structurally disenfranchised" by the creation of a particular agency has hampered congressional efforts to control administrative agencies through agency structure and design. As used here, the term "structurally disenfranchised" describes the situation of some interest groups after Congress creates an administrative agency. Those groups that were the winners in the struggle that culminated in the original enactment find themselves

---

by setting substantive priorities, or by otherwise circumscribing an agency's power to discriminate among issues or cases it will pursue.").

49. 421 U.S. 560 (1975).

50. *Id.* at 567 & n.7 (agreeing with court of appeals that because statute required action under some circumstances, the decision not to act was subject to judicial review).

51. *See supra* notes 36-38, 47-50 and accompanying text.

52. *See supra* notes 37, 41-42 and accompanying text.

53. *See supra* notes 40-41 and accompanying text.

structurally enfranchised by the agency in a number of ways: (1) bureaucrats in the agency are drawn from the ranks of these groups;[54] (2) competition between the agency and other agencies for bureaucratic turf causes the agency to champion the interests of the groups it regulates over the interests of groups it does not regulate;[55] (3) Congress will authorize or command the agency to expend resources to reduce the costs of monitoring the agency's future performance;[56] and (4) Congress will further structure the agency's rulemaking process so as to tilt the odds in favor of certain groups and away from others.[57]

But courts have been extremely sensitive to the concerns of groups that have been disenfranchised by an initial legislative enactment. This sensitivity has manifested itself in two ways. First, courts have declined to give the usual deference they accord to administrative agencies' interpretations when a disenfranchised interest group challenges a regulatory enactment. Second, courts have molded the rules of standing so as to allow these disenfranchised groups access to the courts, even when their interests are not within the group Congress ostensibly was regulating in the original legislation.

1. Broadening an Agency's Horizons

Courts' willingness to abandon their traditional deference to administrative agencies when such agencies are being inattentive to the interests of groups structurally disenfranchised in the initial legislative enactment seriously compromises Congress's ability to use agency structure and design to influence future agency action. *Citizens to Preserve Overton Park, Inc. v. Volpe*[58] is a powerful illustration of the phenomenon of judicial re-enfranchisement.

In *Overton Park,* the Secretary of Transportation approved the use of federal funds to finance the construction of a six-lane, high speed expressway through the middle of a 342-acre city park near the center of Memphis, Ten-

---

54. *See* Macey, *Organizational Design, supra* note 6 (manuscript at 37-39) (need for bureaucrats to be "experts" generally leads to regulators being selected from industry to be regulated; in addition, factors such as compensation and term of office can be set to favor certain industry participants).

55. *Id.* (manuscript at 40) (an industry generally opposes efforts by agencies other than its traditional regulator to exert authority over it, thereby causing the industry and its regulator to champion one another's cause).

56. *Id.* (manuscript at 35) (enabling legislation can raise or lower the costs of monitoring agency action).

57. *Id.* (manuscript at 48) ("The initial agency structure and design will also determine the nature of the agency's rulemaking process, thereby enabling poorly and meagerly financed groups to overcome their inability to monitor the day-to-day decisions of an agency and to maintain an effective political coalition after the initial compromise has been struck.").

58. 401 U.S. 402 (1971).

nessee.[59] The Court refused to defer to the Secretary's decision, and remanded the case for review to determine whether the Secretary of Transportation violated the Department of Transportation Act and the Federal-Aid Highway Act by granting federal funds for highway projects through public parks when a feasible and prudent alternative route existed.[60]

Thus, *Overton Park*, along with similar opinions involving other regulatory agencies, can be best characterized as an example of "venturesome statutory construction" designed to force agencies to give weight to interests and concerns that they would not otherwise have considered.[61] As Professor Richard Stewart has observed, the courts' protection of disenfranchised interests is not confined to the environmental area: a number of decisions reviewing the EPA's implementation of the Clean Air Act "reflect judicial disquiet with the EPA's disregard of the economic and other social costs in carrying out its environmental protection mission."[62]

Professor Stewart recognizes that the special substantive and procedural restrictions imposed on certain administrative agencies do not appear to have been imposed on agencies selected at random. Rather, agencies such as the Nuclear Regulatory Commission, the Federal Power Commission, the Civil Aeronautics Board, and the Highway Transportation Department were singled out for particularly strict judicial scrutiny.[63] Professor Stewart attributes this special attention to the fact that these agencies "pursue missions that threaten environmental quality, or [are] agencies with environmental responsibilities whose dedication to environmental quality is suspect."[64] In other words, where an agency has authority over issues that affect the environment, but is structured in such a way that environmental interests are underrepresented, courts will be particularly sensitive to the environmental aspects of the agency's rules. Thus, courts use their authority to review administrative agencies' rulemaking to re-enfranchise disenfranchised environmental groups.

This judicial re-enfranchisement is not limited to the environmental area.

---

59. *Id.* at 406.

60. *Id.* at 411, 420 (plain language of both Department of Transportation Act and Federal-Aid Highway Act provides "clear and specific directives to Secretary, allowing judicial review of Secretary's actions"). Because the Secretary of Transportation made no formal findings, the Court could not determine whether the Secretary's decision satisfied the statutory standards. *Id.* at 420. On remand, the court would consider the entire administration record available to the Secretary at the time of the decision, as well as any testimony from administration officials it chose to require. *Id.*

61. Richard B. Stewart, *The Development of Administrative and Quasi-Constitutional Law in Judicial Review of Environmental Decisionmaking: Lessons From the Clean Air Act*, 62 IOWA L. REV. 713, 718 (1977) (observing that judges have been enthusiastic in construing statutes as conferring narrow agency authority in order to protect various environmental interests).

62. *Id.* at 720.

63. *Id.* at 719-20.

64. *Id.* at 719.

Professor Stewart observes that, contemporaneous with the decisions involving heightened protection for environmental quality

> are analogous ones imposing similar constraints on agencies in order to protect a variety of nonenvironmental interests, such as those of television viewers, airline passengers, consumers of food, Indians, corporate shareholders, patients being treated with prescription drugs, the poor, classical music lovers, and the handicapped. The common theme that underlies all of these decisions is a developing judicial perception of agency bias or indifference towards the interests in question and a determination to promote more adequate consideration of these interests by administrators. These parallel developments suggest . . . a more general judicial concern to protect interests that are underrepresented in the administrative process or vulnerable to agency bias rather than a special solicitude for environmental values.[65]

The observation that "reviewing courts have attempted to curb agency bias and promote a more balanced agency consideration of all of the interests affected by its decisions"[66] is strong support for the more general argument that courts do, in fact, serve as a check on the proclivity of the more politicized branches to trade legislation for political support. The courts use their ability to review agency action as a means of curbing administrative agency bias toward the group or groups that were structurally enfranchised in the original legislative enactment.

2. Enfranchisement Through Liberal Rules of Standing

Another mechanism by which judges enfranchise groups whose interests are antithetical to the interests likely to dominate a particular agency is by granting disenfranchised groups access to the courts to challenge agency rulings. As Professor Richard Pierce has observed:

> Standing to obtain judicial review of agency action is a critical determinant of a party's ability to participate effectively in the agency's decisionmaking process. Agencies' administrators recognize that they must respond to arguments made by parties that can challenge policy decisions in court, but they can ignore with relative impunity arguments made by parties that lack that power.[67]

---

65. *Id.* at 720.

66. *Id.* at 763.

67. Richard J. Pierce, Jr., *The Role of the Judiciary in Implementing An Agency Theory of Government*, 64 N.Y.U. L. REV. 1239, 1283-84 (1989). The arguments about standing presented here differ in certain important respects from Professor Pierce's excellent treatment of the standing issue. Professor Pierce argues for a generally more expansive law of standing. *Id.* at 1284-85 (restricting administrative law standing will allow agencies to systematically favor special interests). I argue that existing doctrine already reflects a fairly expansive approach to the issue. In particular, I argue that the Court has been sensitive to disenfranchised groups when deciding standing cases, and is especially likely to grant standing to such groups. Finally, Professor Pierce views the law of stand-

In this respect, what is notable about the rules of standing fashioned by the Supreme Court is that the Court has allowed narrow special interest groups to challenge the outcomes generated by an administrative agency when that special interest group has been structurally disenfranchised from the decisionmaking process within the agency whose decision is being challenged.

Investment Company Institute v. Camp[68] is a striking example of the judiciary's willingness to enlarge the law of standing to enfranchise special interest groups that have been structurally excluded from the process of administrative lawmaking. In *Camp,* the Court struck down a regulation issued by the Comptroller of the Currency that permitted commercial banks to operate certain types of mutual funds.[69] The Court invalidated the regulations on the grounds that they violated sections of the Glass-Steagall Act, which separates commercial banking from investment banking and securities dealing.[70] The mutual fund under review called for customers to tender between $10,000 and $500,000 to a commercial bank along with an authorization making the bank the customers' managing agent.[71] In exchange for the money and the authorization, the customers recovered "units of participation" reflecting the customers' proportional interest in the fund's assets.[72] Customers were free to transfer and redeem these units of participation.[73]

The Comptroller of the Currency is a single-interest-group regulatory agency. That interest group is comprised of national banks, which have received the undivided loyalty of the Comptroller in their efforts to enter the business of dealing in securities.[74] As I have pointed out elsewhere, the Court's repeated invalidation of the Comptroller's decisions illustrates the judiciary's ability to place "severe obstacles on the efficacy and longevity of special interest legislation."[75] The Court's willingness to strike down deci-

---

ing as a morass. *Id.* at 1275-76 (rules on standing lack doctrinal uniformity). I think my theory that the Court has developed an interest-group-sensitive standing doctrine brings simplicity and coherence to what appears to Professor Pierce and others to be a doctrinal morass. However, I share Professor Pierce's view that appropriate rules of standing can impede special interest groups from gaining control of the regulatory process. *Id.* at 1283 (proper rules on standing respond to problems in administrative agencies' decisionmaking caused by conflicting interests and factionalism.

68. 401 U.S. 617 (1971).

69. *Id.* at 639 (regulation allowing banks limited entry to mutual fund investment business violates liberal terms of Glass-Steagall Act).

70. *Id.* at 623-39 (construing the Banking Act of 1933 (Glass-Steagall), Pub. L. No. 66, 48 Stat. 162 (codified as amended in scattered sections of 12 U.S.C.)).

71. *Id.* at 622.

72. *Id.*

73. *Id.*

74. Jonathan R. Macey, *The Political Science of Regulating Bank Risk,* 49 OHIO ST. L. REV. 1277, 1284-85 (1989) (Comptroller's willingness to allow commercial banks to engage in behavior conflicting with the purposes of the Glass-Steagall Act demonstrates that the Comptroller has been "captured" by national banks).

75. Jonathan R. Macey, *Special Interest Groups Legislation and the Judicial Function: The Di-*

sions by the Comptroller strongly supports the proposition that the Court has not abandoned its constitutional role as a check on the power of the more political branches of government.

In addition to the substantive result reached in *Camp,* the fact that the Investment Company Institute was granted standing[76] is, in and of itself, rather remarkable. This plaintiff was not just a narrow special interest group, but rather a professional trade association representing investment companies.[77] The Investment Company Institute was not bringing suit to vindicate some generalized notion of the good. Instead, the group was seeking to prevent entry into the industry by a new and possibly more efficient competitor. In other words, the interests of the trade association seem directly contrary to the public interest, which usually rests on the side of increased competition in the mutual fund business.

The Court's decision to grant standing in *Camp* relied on the analytic framework articulated in another case involving the Comptroller, *Association of Data Processing Service Organizations, Inc. v. Camp.*[78] In that case, the Court permitted a trade group of data processors to sue to prevent the Comptroller from authorizing banks to enter the business of providing data processing services to retailers and other banks.[79] The Court's two-part test gives standing to interest groups challenging the actions of administrative agencies so long as: (1) the group would suffer harm, economic or otherwise, as a result of the agency's ruling; and (2) the interest is "arguably within the zone of interests to be protected or regulated by the statute or constitutional guarantee in question."[80]

In still another case involving the Comptroller, *Clarke v. Securities Industry Association,*[81] the Court found standing to permit the interest group representing the securities industry to challenge the Comptroller's decision allowing commercial banks to enter the discount brokerage business.[82] Here the Court noted that the zone of interests test was "not meant to be espe-

lemma of Glass-Steagall, 33 EMORY L.J. 1, 40 (1984) (judicial treatment of agency action under the Glass-Steagall Act demonstrates that an independent judiciary, not being a "beneficiary of the bargain between the legislature and the interest group" has no incentive to enforce the bargain other than as it is reflected in the words of the statute).

76. *Camp,* 401 U.S. at 620-21.

77. *Id.* at 618.

78. 397 U.S. 150 (1970).

79. *Id.* at 153-55 (data processors had standing to challenge regulation because they faced the possible injury of reduced profits due to new competition and because Bank Service Corporation Act was intended to protect competitors).

80. *Id.* at 152-53.

81. 479 U.S. 388 (1977).

82. *Id.* at 403 (interest group had standing to challenge regulation where its alleged injury implicated policies of the National Bank Act and where it is reasonably inferred that Congress expected and intended to rely on such challenges as a check on agency disregard of the law).

cially demanding," but rather to prevent standing only when "the plaintiff's interests are so marginally related to or inconsistent with the purposes implicit in the statute that it cannot reasonably be assumed that Congress intended to permit the suit."[83]

Interestingly, the Court's willingness to grant standing to interest groups has not been transformed into a more general inclination to afford standing in cases where the structural bias does not exist. In particular, well-known cases such as *Simon v. Eastern Kentucky Welfare Rights Organization*[84] and *Allen v. Wright*[85] deny standing to seemingly deserving plaintiffs who wish to challenge Internal Revenue Service (IRS) rulings that clearly cause them harm. In *Simon,* the Court denied standing to a welfare organization and several indigent individuals who wanted to challenge an IRS ruling reducing the amount of indigent care that hospitals must provide in order to retain their tax-exempt status.[86] In *Allen v. Wright,* the Court denied standing to the parents of black children who attended public schools and who wanted to sue the IRS to force it to adopt adequate standards and procedures for denying tax-exempt status to racially discriminatory private schools.[87]

Similarly, where the interest group challenging an agency's action has not been disenfranchised, but rather enjoys regular and repeated access to the agency's decisionmaking apparatus, standing will be denied even though the group is dissatisfied by the agency's decision. Thus, in *Air Courier Conference of America v. American Postal Workers Union,*[88] the Court denied standing to unions representing postal employees who were challenging a Postal Service rule suspending the Service's statutory monopoly in the international remailing market.[89] In the *Postal Workers* case the Court ruled that, despite a number of provisions in the Postal Reorganization Act[90] improving the pay and working conditions of postal employees, such postal employees were not

83. *Id.* at 399.

84. 426 U.S. 26 (1976).

85. 468 U.S. 737 (1984).

86. 426 U.S. at 40-43 (while *Camp* weakened the requirement of injury, requirement still must be satisfied; welfare organizations lacked standing because no injury to themselves as organization, and indigent individuals lacked standing because injury at hands of hospital not clearly traceable to tax regulations).

87. 468 U.S. at 755, 758-59 (parent group challenging lack of effective standards to deny tax exempt status to racially discriminatory private schools lacked standing because it could not ground "injury" in mere government violation of the law, abstract stigmatic injury, or diminished access to desegregated education where causal link to injury not shown).

88. 111 S. Ct. 913 (1991).

89. *Id.* at 918, 921 (while possible adverse effect on postal worker employment constituted injury in fact, unions failed to show that employment of postal workers fell within zone of interests protected by the Private Express Statutes creating the postal service monopoly).

90. Postal Reorganization Act of 1970, Pub. L. No. 91-375, 84 Stat. 719 (1970); Pub. L. No. 91-448, 84 Stat. 921 (1970) (codified in scattered sections of 39 U.S.C.).

within the zone of interests the postal monopoly was designed to protect.[91]

The unions representing the postal workers were intimately involved in the elaborate political compromise that led to the 1970 Postal Reorganization Act, which reenacted the Private Express Statutes that create the post office's statutory monopoly.[92] As a result, these unions had never been disenfranchised from the political process that led to the rule suspending the Postal Service's statutory monopoly in international remailing; thus, they hardly needed to be re-enfranchised by the Court.

A major, perhaps decisive, difference between the cases denying standing and cases granting standing to aggrieved groups is the nature of the administrative agencies involved in the underlying decisions. Standing is granted where the agency involved is likely to be structurally biased against the plaintiff-groups;[93] the Court denies standing where the relevant regulatory agency is not structurally biased against the plaintiff-group.[94] The IRS, unlike the Comptroller of the Currency, is not a single-interest-group regulatory agency. The plaintiff-taxpayers in *Simon* and *Allen v. Wright* were not disenfranchised by the legislation creating the IRS in the way that the plaintiffs in *Clarke* were disenfranchised by the legislation that established the Comptroller of the Currency. That legislation led to the capture of the Comptroller's office by national banks, and to the systematic exclusion of other interests from the rulemaking process within the Comptroller's office. By contrast, the plaintiffs in *Simon* and *Allen v. Wright* were not disenfranchised *ab initio* relative to other groups.

One might argue that the Court's liberal rules of standing are contrary to the public interest because they impede the ability of the Comptroller to help consumers by allowing banks to enter into a number of highly concentrated industries, particularly investment banking. Such entry would serve the pub-

---

91. 111 S. Ct. at 920-21 (to construe Postal Reorganization Statute as relevant statute in zone of interests analysis when violation of Private Express Statutes is crux of challenge would render zone of interests test meaningless).

92. *Id.* at 916 ("[A] 'key impetus' and 'principal purpose' of the PRA [Postal Reorganization Act] was 'to implement various labor reforms that would improve pay, working conditions and labor-management relations for postal employees.' ") (citing lower court findings).

93. *See supra* notes 67-83 and accompanying text; *see also* United States v. Students Challenging Regulatory Agency Procedures, 412 U.S. 669 (1973). This case involved a challenge by law students to the Interstate Commerce Commission's approval of a freight rate that, in the view of the students, would be environmentally unsound because it would discourage the use of recycled materials. *Id.* at 676. The students argued that they should be granted standing to sue because the rate increase would lead to more litter and to degradation of natural resources, and thus impair the students' ability to enjoy forests, parks, and natural resources. *Id.* at 678. While the Court recognized that this was an "attenuated line of causation," the students nonetheless were permitted to go forward with their suit. *Id.* at 679, 686-89 (Court followed *Camp* analysis to conclude that because student group alleged "specific and perceptible harm" from alleged violation of National Environmental Policy Act, group had standing, although Court did not address "zone of interests" issue).

94. *See supra* notes 84-92 and accompanying text.

lic interest not only by leading to lower prices for investment banking services, but also by making the capital formation and allocation process more competitive, creating a generally more efficient economy. However, Congress, not the courts, is the source of the initial industry cartelization. Courts' willingness to undermine these initial legislative deals by making it more difficult for interest groups to control the process of lawmaking by the administrative agencies they have captured means that Congress will likely enact fewer special interest oriented statutes.

Thus, the rules of standing, like the general procedural and substantive rules discussed in the previous section, reflect a judicial concern with interests that are systematically unrepresented in an agency's initial structure and design. The willingness of courts to intercede on behalf of such structurally disenfranchised groups indicates that the independent judiciary serves as an important constraint on wealth transfers to special interest groups. The courts' response promotes public-regarding legislation and complicates Congress's ability both to design and structure administrative agencies so as to enfranchise those groups that dominated the initial process of legislative enactment and to disenfranchise those groups that lost when Congress passed the relevant legislation.

A prominent scholar of administrative law recently observed that those "who have studied the Supreme Court's opinions on standing overwhelmingly concur with Kenneth Davis's characterization: standing law suffers from 'inconsistency, unreliability, and inordinate complexity.' "[95] While this may be true in the abstract, the Supreme Court's rules of standing are rational and coherent when viewed as a judicial response to the problem of special interest group capture of administrative agencies. In a nutshell, the Court tends to grant standing to special interests that were systematically excluded from legislative compromises if those compromises produced broad delegations to agencies easily captured by the interests that were part of the initial deal. In this way the Court impedes Congress's ability to influence agency behavior through structure and design.

C. THE JUDICIAL RESPONSE TO THE LEGISLATIVE VETO

The Supreme Court's response to congressional efforts to implement a legislative veto is perhaps the most obvious example of the Court's practice of impeding Congress' efforts to control administrative agency discretion. The legislative veto simply is a statutory provision that gives Congress (or some subpart of Congress)[96] the authority to nullify the action of an administrative

95. Pierce, *supra* note 67, at 1275 (quoting 4 KENNETH C. DAVIS, ADMINISTRATIVE LAW TREATISE § 24:1, at 208 (2d ed. 1983) (footnote omitted)).

96. The subpart may be one house, or just a committee of one house or the other.

agency. Creation of a legislative veto has typically followed a broad grant of discretion to an agency. For example, Congress delegated to the Federal Trade Commission (FTC) the authority to promulgate rules to regulate certain industry trade practices and to stop business practices it determines to be "unfair," but retained the authority to nullify the FTC's rules through legislative veto.[97]

Congress used the legislative veto with increasing frequency from its inception in 1932[98] until the Supreme Court's decision in *INS v. Chadha,*[99] which held the legislative veto to be unconstitutional.[100] In *Chadha,* the Court was confronted with Section 244(c)(2) of the Immigration and Nationality Act,[101] which reserved for either house of Congress the power to veto by resolution decisions of the Immigration and Nationalization Service and Attorney General to suspend deportation proceedings against aliens overstaying their visas.[102] When Congress overturned a decision by the Attorney General to decline to deport Chadha, both Chadha and the Immigration and Naturalization Service (INS) sued to declare Section 244(c)(2) unconstitutional as contrary to the bicameral requirement of the separation of powers doctrine[103] and violative of the Presentment Clauses.[104] The Supreme Court affirmed the court of appeals decision that Congress's retention of the legislative veto was unconstitutional.[105] The Court noted that after previously employing an inefficient private bill procedure for making decisions on allowing deportable aliens to remain in the United States, "Congress made a deliberate

---

97. *See* Federal Trade Commission Improvement (Magnuson-Moss Warranty) Act, Pub. L. No. 93-637, § 202(a), 88 Stat. 2183, 2193 (1975) (current version at 15 U.S.C. § 57(a) (1988) (amended to include legislative veto in Federal Trade Commission Improvements Act of 1980, Pub. L. No. 96-252, § 21, 94 Stat. 374, 393-96 (lapsed by statute 1982)).

98. The first legislative veto was enacted when Congress gave President Hoover the power to reorganize executive departments. Stephen Breyer, *The Legislative Veto After Chadha,* 72 GEO. L.J. 785, 786 (1984).

99. 462 U.S. 919 (1983).

100. *Id.* at 959 (legislative veto in Immigration and Nationality Act destroys "carefully crafted restraints" in Constitution meant to protect against arbitrary government action, and is therefore unconstitutional). Justice White, in his dissenting opinion in *Chadha* listed 56 statutes that contained legislative veto clauses, and noted that 200 laws containing a legislative veto had been enacted in the 50 years prior to *Chadha.* Justice White noted that 56 statutes containing a legislative veto were enacted between 1932 and 1939, 19 during the 1940s, 34 during the 1950s, 49 during the 1960s, and 89 in the first half of the 1970s. *Chadha,* 462 U.S. at 944-45, 976 n.12 (White J., dissenting) (quoting James Abourezk, *The Congressional Veto: A Contemporary Response to Executive Encroachment on Legislative Prerogatives,* 52 IND. L.J. 323, 324 (1977)). Judge Stephen Breyer has observed that "[s]ince 1932, veto clauses have proliferated like water-lilies on a pond (or algae on a swimming pool, depending on one's point of view." Breyer, *supra* note 98, at 786.

101. Act of Oct. 24, 1962, Pub. L. No. 87-885, 76 Stat. 1247, 1248 (codified at 8 U.S.C.A. § 1254(c)(2) (West 1970)) (repealed 1986).

102. *Chadha,* 462 U.S. at 928.

103. U.S. CONST. art. I, § 1 & § 7, cl. 2.

104. *Id.* § 7, cls. 2, 3.

105. *Chadha,* 462 U.S. at 959.

choice to delegate to the Executive Branch, and specifically to the Attorney General, the authority" to make such decisions.[106] Congress could alter this earlier delegation of authority "in only one way; bicameral passage followed by presentment to the President. Congress must abide by its delegation of authority until that delegation is legislatively altered or revoked."[107]

More recently in *Metropolitan Washington Airport Authority v. Citizens for the Abatement of Aircraft Noise,*[108] the Court addressed Congress's attempt to transfer operational control of Dulles and Washington National airports to the Metropolitan Washington Airport Authority (MWAA) from the Department of Transportation. The MWAA is an organization created by compact between the District of Columbia and the State of Virginia.[109] Congress conditioned its transfer of operational authority over these airports upon the creation of a Board of Review which would have authority to veto any decisions made by the MWAA.[110] This Board of Review was to be composed of nine congressmen "acting in their individual capacities" as users of these two airports.[111] The Court struck down this attempt at giving veto power to congressional interests,[112] thereby impeding Congress's ability to control agency decisionmaking ex post. The Court made it clear that Congress's power to make law is bounded by the separation of powers: Congress cannot exercise executive power, and it can only exercise legislative power in conformity with Article I's bicamerality and presentment requirements.[113] *Airport Authority* and *Chadha* provide good examples of how the courts thwart congressional efforts to retain control over administrative agencies. The legislative veto cases, like the standing cases, democratize the administrative process by strengthening poorly organized interest groups relative to well-organized ones.

Defenders of the legislative veto argue that the veto permits the broad delegations of congressional authority necessary to modern regulatory decisionmaking without abandoning the political accountability of Congress.[114]

---

106. *Id.* at 954.

107. *Id.* at 954-55.

108. 111 S. Ct. 2298 (1991).

109. *Id.* at 2301.

110. *Id.*

111. *Id.* at 2303 (proposed bills altered to provide that Board of Review members act in individual capacity after opinion from Department of Justice informed Congress that veto by Board of Review composed of Congressmen *qua* Congressmen would constitute legislative action subject to Constitutional requirements of bicameralism and presentment).

112. *Id.* at 2312.

113. *Id.* at 2311 (Congress may neither invest itself with executive or judicial power nor exercise its legislative power in violation of the carefully crafted requirements of Article I of the Constitution).

114. Breyer, *supra* note 98, at 787-88 (legislative veto over regulatory actions effectuates needed compromise between political accountability and complex decisionmaking in administrative state).

This argument is flawed for a number of reasons. First, it assumes that Congress is accountable (presumably to the people) in some way when it utilizes the legislative veto to nullify the decision of an agency. In fact, the legislative veto is utilized by Congress to favor individuals or narrow interest groups. By definition, the subject of a particular legislative enactment is extremely narrow. It will commonly be a particular administrative act that has reached the attention of Congress, but rarely will be of such moment that it catches the attention of the popular press or the public. Consequently, the congressional veto inevitably will be the focus of interest group struggle, rather than public-spirited political debate. Thus, the legislative veto is not about congressional accountability to the people; it is about congressional accountability to special interest groups.

Second, the power to veto the actions of administrative agencies may be given to a single house of Congress, or even to a single committee within Congress, rather than to both houses acting together. There is no reason to believe that these committees are any more politically accountable to the general public than the agencies themselves.[115]

Finally, and perhaps most importantly, the political accountability argument in favor of the legislative veto criticizes the Supreme Court's decision in *Chadha* as formalistic, lacking in appreciation for "the purposes, the effects, [and] the practical virtues of the legislative veto."[116] But this approach to *Chadha* fails to acknowledge that the Court's "simple reliance on the logic and letter of the Constitution"[117] does not mean that the outcome cannot be defended on instrumentalist grounds. Indeed, the Court's seemingly formal emphasis on the Constitution's "single, finely wrought and exhaustively considered procedure" as specified in Article I[118] is remarkably well-tailored to confront and respond to the fundamental obstacles to political accountability that Kenneth Arrow and others have advanced.[119]

---

115. *See* Barry R. Weingast & William J. Marshall, *The Industrial Organization of Congress; or Why Legislatures, Like Firms, Are Not Organized as Markets*, 96 J. POL. ECON. 132, 143-48 (1988) (explaining how the committee system in Congress helps solve the nonsimultaneity of performance that exists between politicians and interest groups).

116. Breyer, *supra* note 98, at 790 (arguing that the Court's decision in *Chadha* is formalistic rather than functional).

117. *Id.* (recognizing *Chadha*'s lack of concern with the "wisdom or utility" of a legislative veto).

118. *Chadha*, 462 U.S. at 951.

119. Under Arrow's Theorem, majority voting will lead to cycling results and therefore prevent consistent and coherent public policy. *See* William T. Mayton, *The Possibilities of Collective Choice: Arrow's Theorem, Article I, and the Delegation of Legislative Power to Administrative Agencies*, 1986 DUKE L.J. 948, 950-51 (describing Arrow's application of Cordorcet's paradox to methods of collective choice). This failure to produce the community preference defeats political accountability. Mayton argues that the requirement of Article I counters the forces predicted by Arrow's Theorem to allow rational policymaking, a result of the " 'order and stability' that the framers prized." *Id.* at 956.

In particular,

> [o]nce legislation is proposed, because of the bicameral nature of the Congress, approval by what is, in effect, a supermajority of the legislators is required to pass the statute. Thus, to some extent article I establishes a decisional process that, by forestalling cyclical majorities, can yield coherent and consistent legislative choices."[120]

Moreover, by creating an independent federal judiciary and a federal executive with authority to veto acts of Congress, the Constitution creates a system in which "each of the three branches of government must appeal to different constituencies for political support, thereby further reducing the power of interest groups to affect political outcomes."[121]

Apologists for the legislative veto fail, then, to appreciate that the lawmaking process is only "politically accountable" when the requirements of Article I are met. Otherwise, the system of checks and balances is unable to operate, as in the case of the legislative veto. The consequence of failing to comply with the letter of Article I is that the high degree of consensus necessary for passing a statute will be lacking and the probability that the process will be tainted by special interests will be high. By strictly enforcing Article I, the Court in *Chadha* impedes Congress's efforts to lower the decision costs of government, making it easier for special interests to control the political process. Thus, the outcome in *Chadha* ultimately will produce more political accountability, not less. In this way, the Court's opinion reflects the principles that informed the very structure of the Constitution.

Without the legislative veto, special interest legislation will be less attractive to powerful special interest groups. To see why this is so, it is useful to return to Professor Shepsle's distinction between bureaucratic drift and legislative drift.[122] Indeed, nowhere is Professor Shepsle's argument about the tension between bureaucratic drift and congressional drift more powerfully displayed than in the context of the legislative veto.

The interest groups most desirous of obtaining a legislative veto proviso as part of a special interest group compromise will be those groups *least* concerned about legislative drift relative to bureaucratic drift. Indeed, only those groups confident of their ability to control future legislatures will place a value on obtaining a legislative veto as part of a legislative package. Powerful, well-organized special interests, confident of their ability to maintain an effective, well-financed political coalition, will place a high premium on a legislative veto because such groups will expect to be able to control future

---

120. Jonathan R. Macey, *Transactions Costs and the Normative Elements of the Public Choice Model: An Application to Constitutional Theory*, 74 VA. L. REV. 511-12 (1988) (footnotes omitted) (citing Mayton, *supra* note 119, at 956).

121. *Id.* at 510.

122. See *supra* note 5 and accompanying text (describing bureaucratic drift and legislative drift).

Congresses or congressional committees. By contrast, poorly organized, poorly financed groups, who are able to galvanize into an effective political coalition in order to advance their interests in one piece of legislation, will be unable to exert a sufficiently sustained political influence over time to derive much value from the legislative veto. Similarly, these poorly organized groups probably will be unable even to monitor an agency's decisionmaking process closely enough to know whether to advocate the utilization of the veto in a specific instance. Thus the Court's decision in the legislative veto cases pushes the lawmaking process in a more public-regarding direction by advantaging poorly organized groups relative to well-organized interests, and by ensuring that legislative acts are not taken without achieving a high degree of consensus.

Because invalidating the legislative veto raises the costs to Congress of enacting statutes containing broad delegations of authority to administrative agencies, one of two possibilities will occur when Congress considers broad delegations after *Chadha*. In some instances, Congress may determine that the benefits of passing a particular statute are not worth the drawbacks. Alternatively, and probably more often, the additional costs on Congress imposed by *Chadha* will not result in Congress declining to pass a law, but rather in Congress delegating power to an agency unqualified by the possibility of legislative veto. In the latter case, weak groups will benefit relative to strong groups, because strong groups are better able both to monitor agencies and control Congress than weak groups. Without the ability to monitor agencies and Congress, the legislative veto is of little or no value to special interests.

II. THE ROLE OF THE EXECUTIVE

The President's influence over administrative agencies further confounds Congress's ability to control such agencies ex post. Indeed, even if we assume (counterfactually) that Congress somehow can perfectly control both bureaucratic drift and legislative drift, the presence of the executive, like the presence of the independent judiciary, impedes Congress's ability to control agencies, and thereby raises the costs to special interest groups of obtaining broad-based delegations from Congress.

Presidential involvement in the regulatory process comes in direct response to congressional involvement in that process. In the post-World War II period, a relatively stable political equilibrium has emerged in which the Presidency is controlled by the Republican party, while the Congress is controlled by the Democratic party. Inevitably, the policy differences between Congress and the President have manifested themselves in the struggle for influence and control over the administrative state. In light of these policy differences, the executive's ability to influence administrative agencies raises the costs to Congress of enacting laws that include broad delegations of authority to agencies. Consistent with the theory of checks and balances inherent in the separation of powers, Congress will not engage in a broad delegation to an agency unless there is a high degree of consensus with the President with respect to policy. The necessity for a broad consensus lowers the probability that narrowly focused special interest groups will dominate the delegation process, because such groups will have to capture the executive branch as well as both houses of Congress to accomplish their goals.

Thus, a large part of the story of the modern administrative state is the story of the struggle between Congress and the President for control and influence of administrative agencies. Indeed, some commentators would take issue with McNollgast's basic assumption that Congress is the key policy actor with respect to administrative agencies.[123] Defenders of close congressional control of administrative agencies identify three sources of executive interference with congressional control: the appointments power, the Office of Management and Budget, and executive control over agency money and staff.[124]

A. THE APPOINTMENTS POWER

The executive's influence over agency policy stems from the presidential appointments power.[125] Critics of the way this power recently has been used cite such appointments as James Edwards to Secretary of Energy and Ann Burford to Director of the Environmental Protection Agency as examples of the executive appointing people who intended to dismantle the agencies they were entrusted to administer.[126] Three comments are in order. First, there is no evidence that any of these people succeeded, or even came close to succeeding, in their alleged attempt to destroy the agency they administered. Second, as my colleague Cynthia Farina trenchantly has observed, the appointments power of the President is a "deeply considered and much debated attempt to balance executive and legislative involvement in the selection pro-

---

123. *See, e.g.,* CLINTON ROSSITER, THE AMERICAN PRESIDENCY 26-28 (2d ed. 1960) ("[W]e may therefore consider [the President] to be the Chief Legislator.").

124. Congressman Edward Markey, Remarks at Program Presented by the Section of Administrative Law and Regulatory Practice, American Bar Association (Oct. 14, 1988), *in* 41 ADMIN. L. REV. 491, 494 (1989) (Office of Management and Budget, control over money and staff, and appointments power were three "weapons" used by executive in "deregulatory war" in 1980s).

125. *Id.* at 494 (executive possesses power to appoint to agencies people who share executive's policy goal).

126. *Id.* at 494-95 (Secretary of Energy John Edwards admitted that he was given the job of dismantling the Department of Energy; applicant for Director of the Environmental Protection Agency was asked by its OMB budget director whether he would be willing to bring the agency "to its knees").

cess."[127] The power of appointments was vested in the President by the framers because the Federalists thought that the legislature would abuse the power even more than the President, and not because the President was considered to be a particularly reliable repository for this authority.[128] Indeed, from a balance of powers perspective, the question is not whether the President is abusing his constitutional power to make appointments, but whether an alternative institutional arrangement (such as vesting the appointments power in Congress) would be superior. There is no reason to believe it would.

Finally, if the appointments power vests too much power in the President, the fault lies with Congress, which has acquiesced in this usurpation of authority, rather than with the President, who simply is playing the political game as best he can and utilizing his appointments power along the way. After all, the power to withhold consent from appointments suggested by the President has the potential to make "the Senate a powerful (if not quite equal) partner with the President in choosing top administrators."[129] Moreover, besides the obvious palliative of taking a more active role in confirmation hearings, the Senate could respond even more forcefully to any perceived usurpation of authority. For example, the Senate or a subcommittee of the Senate formally could recommend to the President specific people it deems appropriate to fill particular vacancies, and then demand that the President provide reasons for refusing to nominate somebody on the list.[130] Alternatively, the Senate could condition funding for projects considered particularly important by the President upon the satisfactory performance of regulatory agencies' duties. Any balance of powers problem that may exist due to executive usurpation of congressional authority through the appointments process is due at least as much to the Senate's quiescence as to the executive's imperialism.

B. THE MYTH OF THE OMB "STRANGLEHOLD"

The same point can be made in response to the argument that the Office of Management and Budget (OMB) has further solidified the President's grip on the process of administrative rulemaking. Administrative agencies must

---

127. Cynthia R. Farina, *Statutory Interpretation and the Balance of Power in the Administrative State*, 89 COLUM. L. REV. 452, 504 (1989) (footnote omitted).

128. GORDON S. WOOD, THE CREATION OF THE AMERICAN REPUBLIC, 1776-1787, 435, 452, 551-52 (1969) (vesting appointment power in legislature would create faction and corruption and threaten the successful operation of the separation of powers).

129. Farina, *supra* note 127, at 504.

130. John W. Selfridge, *Senate Can Do More on Court Nominations*, N.Y. TIMES, July 7, 1991, § 4, at 10. When Oliver Wendell Holmes retired from the Supreme Court in 1932, the Senate recommended specific successors to the President in the interest of maintaining balance on the Supreme Court. *Id.*

obtain OMB clearance for proposed legislation, as well as for legislative testimony, through the OMB Office of Information and Regulatory Affairs.[131] Critics have charged that the powers given to OMB are "a powerful conduit for injecting the President's views directly into the rule-making process."[132] However, as with the appointments power, the executive acting through OMB has only as much power as Congress is willing to allow. Congress has required Senate confirmation of the appointment of the director of the Office of Information and Regulatory Affairs,[133] and in doing so has undermined the President's ability to usurp regulatory authority from agencies by using OMB as a filter for proposed legislation. The Senate's recent stubborn unwillingness to confirm a nominee to that position is clear evidence that, like the President, the Senate can play hardball to restore the balance of power when it so desires.

C. THE POWER OF THE PURSE

It is difficult to credit the contention that the executive can control agency behavior through its ability to deny agencies the money and staff they need to carry out their statutorily assigned functions. There are no credible examples of this having taken place, even at the height of the so-called "Reagan Revolution." Congressman Edward J. Markey (D-Mass.) has cited the refusal of OMB to allow the Federal Savings and Loan Insurance Corporation (FSLIC) to hire additional bank examiners in 1981 as evidence of executive use of the power of the purse to control an agency.[134] However, Congress could have used its appropriations power[135] to increase funding to the FSLIC in response to the growing severity of the savings and loan crisis. The truth is that Congress, not the executive, was the primary beneficiary of the delay in recognizing the savings and loan disaster. Individual Senators, including the "Keating Five" and congressmen such as Speaker Jim Wright, reaped huge political bonanzas—and paid a huge political price—for their participation in the scandals that caused the savings and loan debacle.[136] It seems

131. 31 U.S.C. § 501 (1988); 44 U.S.C. § 3503(b) (1988).

132. Farina, *supra* note 127, at 506.

133. 44 U.S.C. § 3503(b).

134. Markey, *supra* note 124, at 495-96 (OMB refusal to grant more bank examiners to the FSLIC in a timely manner represented "blind pursuit of deregulation" in face of "pressing need for governmental intervention" occasioned by the savings and loan crisis).

135. U.S. CONST. art. I, §§ 7, 8.

136. Jonathan R. Macey & Elizabeth H. Garrett, *Market Discipline by Depositors: A Summary of the Theoretical and Empirical Arguments,* 5 YALE J. ON REG. 215, 221 (1988) (describing efforts of Speaker of the House Jim Wright to "pressure regulatory agencies to forbear from closing insolvent savings and loan associations in his home state of Texas"); Jonathan R. Macey, *While Politicians Fiddle Banking Crises Explode,* L.A. TIMES, Sept. 23, 1990, at M4 (describing efforts by 'Keating Five' Senators to prevent federal regulators from closing down insolvent thrift institutions).

that the problem here is not too much interference by the executive in the affairs of an agency, but too little.

The second example Congressman Markey gives of executive control of administrative agencies through its control over the purse involves the Securities and Exchange Commission (SEC).[137] Congressman Markey claims that in order to retard the war on insider trading, "throughout the 1980s the SEC was consistently given less employees by the administration than in its budget request—hundreds of employees less."[138] This account of the activities of the SEC in the 1980s is entirely counterfactual. First, the issue of insider trading actually moved to the top of the SEC's agenda in the 1980s.[139] Immediately after taking office in 1980, John Shad, whom President Reagan appointed as Chairman of the SEC, gave several speeches announcing the SEC's tough new policy on insider trading. At one point he declared that the Commission would "come down [on insider trading] with hobnail boots."[140] Indeed, during the 1980s the SEC's enforcement effort against insider trading increased exponentially, giving rise to several notorious scandals throughout that decade.[141] The SEC's budget requests typically were granted during this period, and the budget consistently grew during a time of general fiscal belt-tightening.[142] Thus, while Congress and the President were both applauding the SEC's efforts to combat insider trading, the SEC responded rationally by moving the fight against insider trading to the top of its regulatory agenda.

It is Congress, not the executive, that is in charge of appropriations. Budgetary appropriations to administrative agencies can only be a source of great congressional authority, not presidential authority.[143] As Professor Harold Bruff has observed, Congress's "[y]early budgetary hearings in both houses provide an opportunity for the appropriations committees to review agency performance, and to affect future policy either by changing appropri-

---

137. Markey, *supra* note 124, at 496 (SEC given insufficient number of employees to keep up with growth of Wall Street so that fewer than half of all insider trading complaints were investigated).

138. *Id.* at 496.

139. David D. Haddock & Jonathan R. Macey, *Regulation on Demand: A Private Interest Model, with an Application to Insider Trading Regulation,* 30 J.L. & ECON. 311, 332 (1987).

140. Kenneth A. Noble, *S.E.C. Chief Plans Insider Trading Curb,* N.Y. TIMES, Oct. 26, 1981, at D1.

141. Haddock & Macey, *supra* note 139, at 333 (between January 1982 and August 1986, the SEC increased its rate of enforcement by 600%).

142. *See* Jonathan R. Macey, *From Judicial Solutions to Political Solutions: The New, New Direction of the Rules Against Insider Trading,* 39 ALA. L. REV. 355, 380 (1988) (the SEC's success in procuring such budget increases was partially a result of its own efforts to keep the law as vague as possible to maximize the demand for its services as an administrative agency).

143. Harold H. Bruff, *Presidential Power and Administrative Rulemaking,* 88 YALE L.J. 451, 457-58 (1979) (budgetary appropriations are explicit constitutional powers available to Congress to influence agency action).

ation levels or by expressing pleasure or displeasure with past actions."[144] The fact that Congress does not use its power effectively only reinforces the point that any perceived tilt in the constitutional balance of powers toward the executive branch is a result of congressional acquiescence as much as presidential usurpation.

It seems clear that it is more difficult for the executive branch, which is politically accountable to a national constituency, to be captured by narrow special interests than it is for a specialized administrative agency to be captured by such interests. Similarly, it is even more difficult for Congress, which is accountable to a vast number of overlapping constituencies, to be captured by special interests than it is for an agency. A fortiori, it is more difficult for special interests to capture an agency *and* Congress *and* the executive, than to capture any one of these entities alone. To the extent that the separation of powers requires the agreement of all three, then interest group capture becomes even more costly.

CONCLUSION

This article starts with the basic premise of positive political theory that Congress utilizes a variety of sophisticated techniques to control the behavior of the bureaucrats in administrative agencies (i.e., to control what Professor Shepsle has described as bureaucratic drift). In particular, Congress's ability to fashion complex procedural rules, rigid substantive rules, and basic organizational and structural rules establishes a regulatory infrastructure likely to produce regulatory outcomes that mirror the preferences of the parties to the legislative compromise that produced the original legislation. The purpose of this article has been to examine the impact of the Supreme Court and the President on Congress's efforts to control bureaucratic drift.

What this article illustrates is that, unfortunately for Congress and for special interest groups, the initial establishment of an administrative agency's organizational structure and jurisdictional parameters is not conclusive. The independent judiciary, which is not a party either to the original interest group deals that lead to the establishment of administrative agencies or to the structural enfranchisement of certain groups and the structural disenfranchisement of others, has no incentive to enforce such deals. Similarly, the President, who often is politically accountable to the public for the outcomes generated by administrative agencies, will want to pull the agency in a direction compatible with his own views of the public interest.

I also have responded to critics of the executive branch who charge that

---

144. *Id.* at 458 (footnote omitted). *See* 2 STAFF OF SENATE COMM. ON GOV'T OPERATIONS, 95TH CONG., 1ST SESS., STUDY ON FEDERAL REGULATION 18-43 (Comm. Print 1977) (describing techniques and processes used by the Appropriations Committee to oversee government agencies).

the balance of power between the President and the executive has shifted too much in favor of the President. As noted above, the struggle between the two political branches is a healthy one, and fully consistent with the framers' notion of a healthy balance of power. The executive's increased efforts to control the federal bureaucracy in recent years is both a consequence of the increasing power of that bureaucracy and a reaction to Congress's increasing sophistication in developing its own strategies for control of the administrative state.

Thus, consistent with the basic idea imbedded in the separation of powers that the independent judiciary and the executive serve as an important constraint on legislative excess and political dealmaking, both the courts and the executive branch have developed a number of devices for mitigating Congress's ability to disenfranchise certain groups. In particular, the courts' liberal rules of standing for structurally disenfranchised interest groups, coupled with the courts' general unwillingness to defer to administrative agencies that have been inattentive to disenfranchised groups, demonstrate that Congress's attempts at agency "hardwiring" through structure and design will not always be successful.

[13]

QUANTIFYING REGULATORY PENALTIES: AUSTRALIAN COMPETITION LAW PENALTIES IN PERSPECTIVE

KAREN YEUNG*

[Despite the shortcomings of the monetary penalty as a form of punishment for corporate offenders, it is widely used in regulatory law and is likely to continue to be a feature of regulatory design. But how should the quantum of regulatory penalties be determined? In order to answer this question, this article critiques and contrasts two theories of punishment which have been expounded in relation to traditional crimes: deterrence theory (which claims that the purpose of punishment is to deter would-be offenders from committing crimes) and desert theory (which claims that the primary purpose of punishment is to communicate social blame or censure for the commission of crimes). Although commercial regulation is primarily concerned to deter undesirable behaviour, rather than to express moral condemnation of that behaviour, it is nevertheless suggested that a fair and effective regulatory penalty regime should combine the essential features of both models. Penalties should be set at a level which is sufficiently high to deter future contraventions of the law, provided that any given penalty award is not unfairly disproportionate to the seriousness of the offence. The final part of the paper reviews the approach taken by Australian courts in quantifying penalties for contraventions of Australian competition law in light of the suggested analytical framework.]

CONTENTS

I Introduction 441
II Theories of Penalty Setting 444
  A General Theories of Punishment 444
  B The Deterrence Approach 445
    1 Penalties as Prices for Violations 446
    2 The Injury to Others Model ('Optimal Deterrence') 447
    3 The Unlawful Gain Model ('Absolute Deterrence') 448
    4 Enforcement Costs, Detection Rates, Risk Neutrality and Legal Error 449
  C The Desert Theory of Penalty Setting 451
  D Deterrence and Desert Models Compared 452
    1 The Deterrence Model 452
    2 The Desert Model 455
    3 Differences in Philosophical Foundation 456
  E Regulatory Penalties: Which Model? 457
    1 Regulatory Offences, Moral Condemnation and Strict Liability .. 458
    2 A Hybrid Solution 460
III Competition Law Penalties and the Australian Experience 463
  A The Australian Regulatory Framework 464

* Fellow in Law, Linnells' Lecturer in Commercial Law, St Anne's College, The University of Oxford. This article is based on a research report prepared by the author when acting as a consultant to the Australian Competition and Consumer Commission and is published with the kind permission of the Commission. The views expressed do not in any way represent the views of the Commission and are entirely those of the author. I am indebted to Frances Hanks, Timothy Endicott, Dan Prentice, Terry O'Shaughnessy and Liora Lazarus for their helpful comments on earlier drafts. Any errors remain my own.

1 The Deterrence Model 464
2 The Desert Model 467
B Australian Competition Law Penalties 468
1 Penalty Setting, 'Deterrence', 'Punishment' and 'Morality' 470
IV Conclusion 474

I INTRODUCTION

In *ACCC v Pioneer Concrete (Qld) Pty Ltd*,[1] three companies were ordered by the Federal Court to pay penalties of A$6.6 million each for fixing the price of pre-mixed concrete in Queensland. In addition, five of the companies' senior employees were penalised A$50,000 each, and one employee was penalised A$100,000 for knowing involvement in the price fix.[2] The penalties ordered by the Court are the highest on record for contraventions of the prohibitions contained in Part IV of the *Trade Practices Act 1974* (Cth) ('*TPA*'), which forms the basis of Australian competition law. The size of the penalty awards, and a number of subsequent penalty awards of considerable magnitude, have caused public disquiet.[3] Some commentators, particularly those from the industry arena, have decried the levying of exorbitant penalties, while others claim that heavy financial penalties are essential in order to ensure that competition regulation is effective in protecting the welfare of consumers by maintaining the integrity of the competitive process.[4] Indeed, the current Chairman of the Australian Competition and Consumer Commission ('ACCC'), Australia's public competition and consumer law regulator, has suggested that even heavy financial penalties may be insufficient to deter unlawful anti-competitive practices, and has therefore suggested that further consideration should be given to the introduction of criminal sanctions for breach of Part IV of the Act.[5] The purpose of this paper is to consider how regulatory penalties should be quantified and, in particular, how penalties for contravening competition law should be quantified.

Although this analysis focuses on penalties for competition law violations, it is equally applicable to other areas of the law where financial penalties are payable for regulatory offences. As the twentieth century draws to a close, economic and social activity within industrialised societies is more heavily regulated than it has ever been since the onset of industrialisation.[6] The widespread adoption of policies of 'deregulation' by governments of many Western industrialised economies since the 1970s may have reduced the extent of direct state interven-

[1] [1996] ATPR ¶41-457.

[2] Ibid 41,583.

[3] See, eg, *TPC v TNT Australia Pty Ltd* [1995] ATPR ¶41-375; *ACCC v Australian Safeway Stores Pty Ltd* [1997] ATPR ¶41-562; *ACCC v NW Frozen Foods Pty Ltd* [1996] ATPR ¶41-515; *ACCC v J McPhee & Son (Australia) Pty Ltd* [1998] ATPR ¶41-628.

[4] R Featherston, 'Negotiated Penalties — Trick or Treat?' (Paper Presented at the Trade Practices Workshop, Business Law Section, Law Council of Australia, Fremantle, 1995). Cf Stephen Corones, 'Collusive Tendering — Are the Penalties a Deterrent?' (1996) 17 *Proctor* 16.

[5] See the comments of Professor Allan Fels referred to in Corones, above n 4, 16.

[6] Anthony Ogus, *Regulation: Legal Form and Economic Theory* (1994) ch 2.

tion in social and economic activity, but not its entire withdrawal.[7] State regulation continues to apply to a diverse spectrum of economic and social activities, ranging from health and safety, consumer protection, environmental pollution and the use of reproductive technology, through to financial services, public utilities and so-called 'essential facilities'. Although the institutional design of regulatory regimes can vary considerably in the level of state intervention involved and in their reliance on either, or both, positive incentives to encourage the desired behaviour ('carrots') or through the imposition of sanctions for undesirable behaviour ('sticks'), there is no doubt that the use of sanctions to deter undesirable behaviour (sometimes referred to as 'command-and-control' regulation) is likely to continue to be an enduring feature of regulatory design. The effectiveness of regulation in bringing about the desired form of behaviour by the regulated parties depends crucially, however, on both the level of penalty for non-compliance and the willingness of regulators to impose penalties for non-compliance with the law. This paper is concerned with the first of these issues: how should the quantum of regulatory penalties be determined?[8]

In order to answer this question, the first part of this examination draws upon theories of punishment expounded in the criminal sentencing context which have sought to explain not only why the law is justified in punishing those who commit crimes, but also why the quantum of punishment should be fixed at a particular level. Two alternative theoretical approaches are examined, each resting on entirely different philosophical foundations: the 'deterrence' approach as expounded by advocates of the economic analysis of law, which seeks to 'price' unlawful conduct in order to minimise social costs arising from unlawful conduct; and the 'desert' approach, which takes the view that those who break the law 'justly deserve' punishment, and therefore, the sanctions for violating the law should be commensurate with the nature of the wrongfulness of the sanctioned

7 See generally Cosmo Graham and Tony Prosser, *Privatizing Public Enterprises: Constitutions, the State and Regulation in Comparative Perspective* (1991).

8 The use of the monetary penalty as a sanction for corporate offenders has been criticised by a number of academic commentators as ineffective. For example, it has been argued that monetary penalties: do not pinch directly on the managerial nerves of corporate governance; do not necessarily result in corporate offenders taking internal disciplinary action against the individuals responsible; provide inadequate incentives for the corporation to revise its internal controls so as to guard against repeat offences; convey the impression that offences are purchasable commodities and tend to under-emphasise the socially undesirable nature of corporate offences; may have adverse spillover effects (externalities) on shareholders, workers, consumers and other third parties; are prone to evasion through the use of corporate group structures; and the penalty levels required to reflect the seriousness of the offence, or to effect deterrence against further offences, may exceed the capacity of the corporation to pay (the 'deterrence and retribution trap'): see, eg, John Coffee Jr, '"No Soul to Damn, No Body to Kick": An Unscandalized Inquiry into the Problem of Corporate Punishment' (1981) 17 *Michigan Law Review* 386; Brent Fisse and John Braithwaite, 'Sanctions Against Corporations: Dissolving the Monopoly of Fines' in Roman Tomasic (ed), *Business Regulation in Australia* (1984) 129, 130–3; Brent Fisse and John Braithwaite, *Corporations, Crime and Accountability* (1993); Australian Law Reform Commission ('ALRC'), *Compliance with the* Trade Practices Act 1974, Report No 68 (1994); ALRC, *Sentencing: Penalties*, Discussion Paper No 30 (1987). Despite these shortcomings, the monetary penalty occupies an important position within regulatory enforcement and is likely to continue to do so for the foreseeable future. On the use of the monetary sanction in US regulatory enforcement, see Colin Diver, 'The Assessment and Mitigation of Civil Money Penalties by Federal Administrative Agencies' (1979) 79 *Columbia Law Review* 1435.

conduct. In other words, while the deterrence theory regards punishment as the 'price' of unlawful conduct, the desert theory regards punishment as communicating state censure and disapprobation of the offender.[9] It is argued here that neither model can be regarded as superior to the other. Both suffer from intractable problems, but are nevertheless capable of generating reasonable, practical outcomes — an effective penalty regime should be assessed both by its ability to deter undesirable conduct, while also ensuring that the penalties imposed in any individual case are fair and just. Thus, a regulatory penalty regime should be a hybrid, reflecting components of both models, rather than adhering to either model in its 'pure' form.

The second part of this analysis then attempts to illustrate how these theoretical approaches to penalty setting apply to the quantification of penalties for breach of competition law. The aim of competition regulation is to facilitate competitive markets based on the view that competition will lead to the efficient allocation of resources in society, thereby benefiting consumers. The Australian approach to quantifying competition law penalties is then examined in light of the Australian regulatory framework for competition regulation and the principles developed by the Australian Federal Court in order to identify whether these principles conform to either theoretical model. An examination of the case law reveals disagreement between individual judges concerning whether the proper aim of penalty setting for Australian competition law violations is 'deterrence' or 'punishment'. This tension is largely attributable to whether the deterrence or desert model is the preferred theoretical basis for penalty setting. Although individual judges have attempted to articulate the theoretical basis for their decisions, it appears that they are not adhering exclusively to one or other of the two models, but are in fact adopting a combination of both models in a manner which largely conforms to the hybrid model advocated here.[10]

Because the analytical approach taken in this paper is not specific to competition regulation, but can be applied to any form of economic and social regulation which relies upon the use of legal sanctions for non-compliance, it is important to clarify what is meant by the term 'regulatory law'. Although the term 'regulation' can be used to refer to any form of behavioural control, a narrower definition is used here. Regulation refers to state intervention in economic and social activity, aimed at directing or encouraging behaviour valued by the community, so as to facilitate the pursuit of collectivist goals which might not otherwise be realised, and which constitutes a form of 'public law' in the sense that it is generally for the state (or its agents) to enforce the obligations which cannot be overreached by

[9] See below Part II(C).

[10] However, this examination makes no empirical assessment of the extent to which the actual quantum of penalties imposed for contraventions properly fulfil the courts' stated goals or whether the actual penalties which have hitherto been imposed are too high or too low. A recent empirical analysis of penalties for price fixing under the *TPA* indicated that the approach taken by courts largely conforms with economic reasoning, with the exception of the courts' treatment of small business offenders: David Round, John Siegfried and Anna Baillie, 'Collusive Markets in Australia: An Assessment of their Economic Characteristics and Judicial Penalties' (1996) 24 *Australian Business Law Review* 292.

private agreement between the parties concerned.[11] Thus, traditional areas of the criminal law do not fall within the domain of regulatory law because criminal activities are not 'valued by the community'. What distinguishes regulatory offences from traditional crimes is that regulatory offences do not generally attract the same degree of moral condemnation typically associated with traditional crimes.[12] Regulated conduct is prohibited not primarily because of its moral improbity, but because it undermines the collectivist goals which the regulatory scheme seeks to facilitate.[13] Likewise, the area of law typically encompassed within the private law of obligations, such as laws relating to contract, property and tort, fall outside the realm of regulatory law because they are concerned to empower individuals and groups to pursue their own welfare goals in a market system of organisation, subject only to basic restraints, rather than a system of public law to implement collectivist goals. By contrast 'regulatory law', when used in the present context, denotes the law which implements the collectivist system which has a directive function — citizens are compelled by a superior authority, the state, to behave in particular ways with the threat of penal sanctions if they do not comply.[14]

II THEORIES OF PENALTY SETTING

A *General Theories of Punishment*

In order to examine the theoretical basis for determining the quantum of penalties for violating the law (whether regulatory law or otherwise), it is first useful to examine, in general terms, the theoretical basis for punishing those who break the law ('the offender'), because any attempt to answer the question 'how much should we punish?' is in part determined by the separate but related question, 'why do we punish?'.[15] Although this paper is concerned with regulatory offences which, unlike traditional criminal offences, carry little or no connotations of moral improbity, both criminal and regulatory offences involve the application of the coercive power of the state to visit some form of 'hard treatment' on the

[11] Ogus, above n 6, 1–5.

[12] Andrew Ashworth, *Principles of Criminal Law* (1995) 50–1; Genevra Richardson, Anthony Ogus and Paul Burrows (eds), *Policing Pollution* (1983) 17; H L A Hart, *Punishment and Responsibility* (1968) 236. For further discussion, see below Part II(E).

[13] Hart, *Punishment and Responsibility*, above n 12, 235–6.

[14] The definition of regulation is largely drawn from that of Ogus: Ogus, above n 6, 2. Ogus does not, however, include competition regulation within the scope of his examination of regulatory law, because competition law is intended to reinforce rather than overreach the market system: see Ogus, above n 6, 30. However, within his analysis, Ogus nevertheless includes the regulation of natural monopolies, externalities and information deficits, which are all forms of market failure justifying the need for regulation. Anti-competitive commercial practices which are the subject of competition regulation are also instances of market failure which justify the need for regulation. Competition law is concerned to achieve the collectivist goal of efficient resource allocation, which would not otherwise be achieved in the absence of legal regulation, and thus displays the hallmarks of regulatory law.

[15] Hart, *Punishment and Responsibility*, above n 12, 14. See also H L A Hart, *Law, Liberty and Morality* (1963) 37.

offender.[16] Accordingly, the various theories which have been advocated in order to justify the imposition of punishment for criminal offences are directly relevant to the justification of punishment for regulatory offences.

In the criminal law context, five possible theoretical justifications for punishment have been identified: deterrence (which seeks to deter people from committing crimes); rehabilitation (which seeks to achieve rehabilitation of the offender); incapacitation (which seeks to incapacitate offenders so as to render them incapable of reoffending for substantial periods of time); desert (which seeks to ensure that offenders receive their 'just deserts' for crime committed); and restoration or reparation (which is concerned that victims of crime receive justice).[17] Three of these theories are prima facie unsuited to penalty setting in the context of regulatory law: rehabilitation seems to have little application to economic and social regulation where corporations are the primary offenders;[18] incapacitation is usually confined to particular groups, such as 'dangerous' offenders and career criminals and thus has little application to economic and social regulation; and restoration is the primary function of private actions to enforce regulatory law, rather than the basis for determining the quantum of punishment payable to the state in proceedings commenced by a public regulator.[19] This leaves the competing theories of deterrence and desert as possible theoretical bases for determining the quantum of penalties for regulatory offences.

B *The Deterrence Approach*

Deterrence as a justification for the punishment of crime is based on the notion that punishment is warranted by reference to its crime prevention consequences.[20] The deterrence approach to punishment has historically been associated with classical utilitarian philosophy, famously advocated by the English jurist and philosopher Jeremy Bentham in the nineteenth century, based on utilitarian goals of deterring future unlawful behaviour.[21] According to Bentham, punishment was justified primarily in order to prevent others from committing the same offence,

16 Cf Joel Feinberg, 'The Expressive Function of Punishment' (1965) 49 *The Monist* 397.

17 Andrew Ashworth, *Sentencing and Criminal Justice* (1992) ch 3. Although these theories are concerned with the justification of punishment generally, the appropriate severity of punishment is, in part, determined by the general justification for punishment: Hart, *Punishment and Responsibility*, above n 12, 14.

18 Jack Bilmes and John Woodbury, 'Deterrence and Justice: Setting Civil Penalties in the Federal Trade Commission' (1991) 14 *Research in Law and Economics* 191, 195. However, consider also Brent Fisse, 'Rethinking Criminal Responsibility in a Corporate Society: An Accountability Model' in Peter Grabosky and John Braithwaite (eds), *Business Regulation and Australia's Future* (1993) 255 and Celia Wells, *Corporations and Criminal Responsibility* (1993) 21.

19 Restorative theories of punishment are not solely or necessarily concerned that victims of crime should receive financial compensation. Restorative theories also encompass the perception that crime involves a conflict between the offender and victim which requires resolution — in which the victim is given rights to participate in the process of dispute resolution: Andrew von Hirsch and Andrew Ashworth, 'Restorative Justice' in Andrew von Hirsch and Andrew Ashworth (eds), *Principled Sentencing* (1998) 300–11.

20 Ibid 395.

21 Jeremy Bentham, 'The Principles of Penal Law' in John Bowring (ed), *The Works of Jeremy Bentham* (1838–43) 396.

the disutility visited on the offender being outweighed by the utility to society arising from the deterrent effect of punishment, thereby preventing future crime.

A modern variant of the utilitarian theory of deterrence is advocated by proponents of the economic analysis of law.[22] An economic approach to sentencing is primarily concerned to minimise the social costs caused by crime. Because crime imposes costs on society both directly (in the damage wrought by criminal conduct) and indirectly (in the costs incurred by society in apprehending, convicting and punishing offenders), the aim of the law should be to set punishment at a level which deters crime to the level at which the total costs to society are minimised. Although not all advocates of the deterrence theory of punishment necessarily support the economic theory of crime deterrence, it is focused upon in this paper because it provides specific guidance for determining the quantum of punishment and therefore provides a theoretical basis for the quantification of regulatory penalties.

1 *Penalties as Prices for Violations*

The economic variant of the deterrence approach to penalty setting (the 'deterrence model') regards conduct which violates the law as a commodity which may be effectively 'purchased' by requiring the offender to pay a penalty for breaking the law. The deterrence model depends crucially on the assumption that individuals and firms are rational actors who act in the pursuit of self-interest in order to maximise their individual welfare. In other words, it assumes that, when deciding whether to engage in a particular activity, each actor first calculates whether the estimated benefits *to the actor* of that activity will exceed the estimated costs to the actor of engaging in that activity. If so, then the actor will engage in the activity. Thus, if the estimated benefits of violating the law outweigh the estimated costs of engaging in unlawful behaviour, then the actor will rationally decide to break the law.[23]

Because conduct which violates the law may cause harm to others, thereby imposing costs on society, violating the law is to be discouraged. The imposition of penalties for violation of the law has the effect of increasing the estimated cost of violation. Penalties thus create financial incentives which deter firms and individuals from engaging in unlawful conduct.[24] A penalty is simply the 'price' of violating the law.

The fundamental aim of the deterrence model is the pursuit of economic efficiency. Economics is concerned with allocating society's resources efficiently, based on the view that by so doing, the overall welfare of society is maximised. The essential decision-making criteria in economics is based on a simple cost-benefit analysis: if the benefits *to society* of a particular activity outweigh the costs to society, then the activity is efficient and should be encouraged because it enhances the overall welfare of society. If this analytical approach is applied to

22 The pioneering work is by Gary Becker, 'Crime and Punishment: An Economic Approach' (1968) 76 *Journal of Political Economy* 169. See generally Robert Cooter and Thomas Ulen, *Law and Economics* (2nd ed, 1997); Richard Posner, *Economic Analysis of Law* (2nd ed, 1977).

23 Cooter and Ulen, above n 22, 389–94.

24 Ibid 391; Posner, *Economic Analysis of Law*, above n 22.

penalty setting, then the correct quantum of penalty is that which will deter unlawful conduct to an 'efficient' level.

Assuming that detecting and penalising violators is costless, then the efficient level of unlawful conduct occurs where the net costs to society arising from the unlawful conduct are minimised.[25] If the unlawful conduct in question has no beneficial effects on society while imposing costs on society, or if the costs of the unlawful conduct always outweigh its benefits, then the efficient level of unlawful conduct is zero.[26] Therefore, the aim of penalty setting should be 'absolute deterrence' of the unlawful conduct in question. On the other hand, if the unlawful conduct, although costly to society, also confers some benefits on society, then the aim is to set the quantum of penalties at a level which ensures that unlawful conduct which imposes a net cost on society is deterred but conduct which results in a net benefit to society is not deterred. Therefore, the aim of penalty setting in such cases should be 'optimal' rather than 'absolute' deterrence. These two possible interpretations of the effects of unlawful conduct reflect the two different policy prescriptions or variants of the deterrence model: the 'unlawful gain' model and the 'injury to others' model.

2 *The Injury to Others Model ('Optimal Deterrence')*

The 'injury to others' variant of the deterrence model of penalty setting aims to achieve 'optimal' deterrence of unlawful conduct. Optimal deterrence seeks to deter only inefficient violations of the law, while efficient violations of the law should not be deterred. This variant of the deterrence model assumes that conduct which violates the law may have some beneficial effects which may potentially outweigh its costs.[27] If the net gain to society arising from the unlawful conduct in any given instance exceeds the harm to society caused by that conduct, then the conduct is welfare-enhancing and should not be deterred. For example, a factory's production operations may pollute a nearby river in breach of environmental laws, thereby causing harm to others. However, the factory's production is also beneficial to society, because it generates profit for the factory owner and may provide consumers with goods which would not otherwise be available. If that benefit exceeds the harm so caused, then the factory should not be deterred from operating, albeit in a manner which pollutes the river. It is important to note that the benefits accruing to the offender as a result of the unlawful conduct can legitimately be characterised as a gain to society as a whole — the mere fact that the gains are generated as a result of unlawful conduct is immaterial.[28]

In order to achieve its objective of optimal deterrence, the penalty for violating the law should be set at a level which equals the total cost of the harm to others

25 Becker, above n 22; Posner, *Economic Analysis of Law*, above n 22; Cooter and Ulen, above n 22, 395–400.

26 Becker, above n 22; Kenneth Dau-Schmidt, 'An Economic Analysis of the Criminal Law as a Preference-Shaping Policy' [1990] *Duke Law Journal* 1, 11–13.

27 Becker, above n 22.

28 The standard view among economists is that, even in the realm of traditional crimes, the criminal's unlawful benefit should be factored into a determination of the optimal quantum of punishment: Cooter and Ulen, above n 22, 396.

caused by the unlawful conduct. When an actor's activity imposes costs on others which are not borne by the actor, these costs are known as 'externalities'.[29] Legal regulation is required in order to ensure that these externalities are attributed to the actor. By setting the penalty level to reflect the injury caused to others, the imposition of a penalty causes the actor to 'internalise' the cost of the harms to others caused by the actor's conduct. In other words, requiring the actor to pay a penalty for violating the law ensures that the actor bears the full cost of its unlawful action.

Because the unlawful activity may generate social benefits, the injury to others variant of the deterrence model is concerned to avoid the problem of 'over-deterrence' which arises if penalties are set at an excessively high level. Over-deterrence should be avoided because it results in the deterrence of unlawful behaviour which may be welfare-enhancing. Accordingly, it follows that the gain made by the violator and the ability of the violator to pay the penalty so levied are not relevant to the calculation of penalties. Taking account of the gain made by the violator in calculating the appropriate penalty would lead to over-deterrence, by deterring unlawful conduct which may generate a net gain to society. Taking account of the violator's ability to pay would have the effect of over-deterring larger, more profitable firms, while under-deterring smaller, less profitable firms.[30]

3 *The Unlawful Gain Model ('Absolute Deterrence')*

The 'unlawful gain' variant of the deterrence model also seeks to deter firms and individuals from violating the law because of the harmful effects of such conduct. The unlawful gain model differs crucially from the 'injury to others' model, however, in that it aims to achieve 'absolute' deterrence of unlawful conduct, not merely 'optimal' deterrence. The aim of absolute deterrence follows from the premise that the unlawful conduct is either utterly without any redeeming social benefits, or the social benefits are always outweighed by the costs of unlawful conduct, and thus the total social costs are minimised by completely eliminating unlawful conduct.[31]

In order to achieve its objective of absolute deterrence, the penalty for violating the law should be set at a level which is at least equal to the net gain to the offender arising from the unlawful conduct.[32] By effectively disgorging the violator's ill-gotten gain, this eliminates any incentive to violate the law. If the actor knows that there is no opportunity to gain from unlawful behaviour, then the rational actor will refrain from violating the law.

29 Ogus, above n 6, 33–5; Robert Officer and Philip Williams, 'The Public Benefit Test in an Authorisation Decision' in Philip Williams and Megan Richardson (eds), *The Law and the Market* (1995) 157, 159.

30 Bilmes and Woodbury, above n 18, 202–3; Becker, above n 22.

31 Dau-Schmidt, above n 26, 11–13.

32 See also Bentham's first rule: the value of the punishment must not be less in any case than what is sufficient to outweigh that of the profit of the offence: J H Burns and H L A Hart (eds), *Jeremy Bentham: An Introduction to the Principles of Morals and Legislation* (1970) 166.

Because the unlawful gain variant of the economic model is based on the premise that the unlawful conduct in question always imposes a net cost on society, this model does not contemplate the possibility of over-deterrence arising from excessively high penalty levels.[33] The crucial determinant for setting the appropriate penalty level is the gain arising from the offender's unlawful conduct. Accordingly, the harm to others caused by the unlawful conduct is irrelevant — even if the harm to others exceeds the gain to the offender, it is sufficient if the penalty is set at a level equal to the offender's gain, for in so doing it eliminates any incentive to violate the law, thereby deterring all violations of the law. It also follows that the gain to the offender represents the *minimum* penalty level: a penalty which exceeds the gain to the offender is consistent with the unlawful gain model because it eliminates the incentive of potential offenders to act unlawfully.

4 *Enforcement Costs, Detection Rates, Risk Neutrality and Legal Error*

The two variants of the deterrence model described above have assumed that the probability of detecting a violation of the law and levying a fine on the offender is 100 percent. It has also been assumed that there are no costs involved in enforcing the law. In other words, it is assumed that all violations of the law are detected without costs being incurred in the detection process. However, neither assumption is realistic. Accordingly, the deterrence model must be adjusted in order to take into account of the cost of enforcing the law ('enforcement costs') and the probability of detection.[34]

If the assumption of zero enforcement costs is relaxed, then the cost of enforcing the law must be factored into the determination of the optimal enforcement strategy required by the deterrence model. In relation to the 'injury to others' variant of the model, this is achieved by adding the enforcement costs to the penalty calculated under the assumption of zero enforcement costs, thus ensuring that those contemplating violating the law 'internalise' the enforcement costs involved in detecting and penalising the violation.[35] In relation to the 'unlawful gain' variant of the deterrence model, the existence of enforcement costs may affect the enforcement strategy adopted by the enforcer, rather than the quantum of penalty. Although the unlawful gain variant of the deterrence model should be applied to conduct which is always welfare-reducing so that it should be deterred absolutely, if the cost of harm caused by the conduct is less than the enforcement costs incurred in eliminating the conduct, then no enforcement action should be taken.

In addition, it is impossible in practice for all violations of the law to be detected and pursued, particularly given the limited resources available to enforcement agencies. In deciding whether or not to comply with the law, rational actors calculate whether the expected benefits of violating the law exceed the expected

33 Robert Cooter, 'Prices and Sanctions' (1984) 84 *Columbia Law Review* 1523, 1532–3; Warren Schwartz, 'An Overview of the Economics of Antitrust Enforcement' (1980) 68 *Georgetown Law Journal* 1075, 1079–80.

34 Cooter and Ulen, above n 22, 399–404.

35 Ibid.

costs. Because the assessment is made *ex ante*, based on *expected* rather than the actual costs and benefits, the relevant costs to the actor of violating the law are based on the *expected* penalty from violation. Where the probability of detection for violating the law is less than 100 percent, this has the effect of lowering the actor's expected costs of violating the law. It is therefore necessary to adjust the penalty according to the probability of detection. For example, if the optimum penalty assuming a 100 percent probability of detection is $1000, and if the probability of detection is 50 percent, the penalty must be increased to $2000 ($1000 ÷ 0.5). It follows that the same level of deterrence can be achieved by escalating the penalty level in response to a decline in the probability of detection.[36]

The preceding analysis has also assumed that offenders are risk neutral. However, if potential offenders are risk averse, they will be deterred by lower penalties, and thus the optimal penalty required to achieve the requisite level of deterrence should be reduced accordingly. Correlatively, if potential offenders are risk taking, they will need to face higher penalties before they will be deterred from violating the law, and thus the optimal penalty should be increased by the relevant risk aversion factor.[37]

Finally, the deterrence model of penalty setting assumes that legal error is avoided. In other words, the model assumes that legal rules are perfectly formulated and applied by courts so that all relevant conduct that inflicts harm on others is detected and penalised but that no benign conduct is penalised. However, some legal error is inevitable in practice, because legal decisions are inevitably based on incomplete information.[38] Thus, some conduct may be penalised although it may in fact be benign. Likewise, some conduct may escape penalty although it is in fact harmful. The possibility of legal error means that firms may substitute away from marginal conduct which is at risk of contravening the law if faced with the threat of penalties for contravention.[39] Legal error therefore results in the misallocation of resources and thus imposes costs on society. Moreover, the higher the penalty levels, the greater the costs arising from legal error as firms increasingly substitute away from marginal but benign activities.[40]

36 Richard Posner, *Antitrust Law: An Economic Perspective* (1976) 223–4; Becker, above n 22. For a more detailed discussion of the multiplier principle, see Richard Crasswell, 'Deterrence and Damages: The Multiplier Principle and its Alternatives' (1999) 97 *Michigan Law Review* (forthcoming).

37 Cooter and Ulen, above n 22; Becker, above n 22.

38 Cooter and Ulen, above n 22.

39 Richard Posner, 'An Economic Theory of the Criminal Law' (1985) 85 *Columbia Law Review* 1193.

40 Cooter and Ulen, above n 22, 286–7; Michael Block and Joseph Sidak, 'The Cost of Antitrust Deterrence: Why Not Hang a Price Fixer Now and Then?' (1980) 68 *Georgetown Law Journal* 1131.

C *The Desert Theory of Penalty Setting*

The desert theory of punishment differs radically from the deterrence theory due to its fundamentally different philosophical foundations. Desert theorists regard punishment for criminal conduct as a form of retributive justice. The essential concern of desert theory is that the offender should receive his or her 'just deserts' for violating the law.[41] There are several different approaches within desert theory which seek to explain why the law is justified in punishing those who commit crimes. For example, Moore argues that there is a fundamental intuitive connection between crime and punishment: we are justified in punishing because, and only because, offenders deserve it.[42] Andrew von Hirsch, one of the principal proponents of desert theory, relies on the communicative feature of punishment to explain why society is justified in punishing those who commit crimes and to argue that punishment primarily expresses blame or censure, thus conveying disapprobation of the offender and concurrently acknowledging to victims and potential victims that they have been wronged by criminal conduct.[43]

The principle of 'just deserts' not only provides the moral justification for punishment, but also provides the theoretical basis for determining the quantum of punishment. Desert theorists argue that the quantum of punishment must be determined by the principle of proportionality. The proportionality principle requires that the severity of the punishment must be commensurate with the seriousness of the offence.[44] According to von Hirsch, the requirement of proportionality provides the central role in determining the quantum of punishment because the severity of punishment communicates the degree of blame attributed to the crime. Hence, punishments should be ordered according to the degree of blameworthiness of the conduct — the more serious the conduct, the

41 Andrew von Hirsch and Andrew Ashworth, 'Desert' in Andrew von Hirsch and Andrew Ashworth (eds), *Principled Sentencing* (1998) 141–9.

42 Michael Moore, 'The Moral Worth of Retribution' in Andrew von Hirsch and Andrew Ashworth (eds), *Principled Sentencing* (1998) 150. Classic retributive theory, chiefly associated with Kant, regards criminal responsibility not only as necessary, but also as a sufficient condition for punishment, which society is therefore obliged to impose:

> Even if a civil society resolved to dissolve itself with the consent of all its members — as might be supposed in the case of a people inhabiting an island resolving to separate and scatter themselves throughout the whole world — the last murderer lying in prison ought to be executed before the resolution was carried out. This ought to be done in order that everyone might realize the desert of his deeds[.]

Immanuel Kant, *The Philosophy of Law* (Hastie trans, 1887) 194–8, cited by Paul Weiler, 'The Reform of Punishment' in Canadian Law Reform Commission, *Studies on Sentencing* (1976) 140.

43 von Hirsch and Ashworth, *Principled Sentencing*, above n 19. von Hirsch also regards punishment as serving a secondary purpose of deterring others from crime. Penal 'hard treatment' provides an additional (modest) prudential supplement to the law's moral voice by creating a disincentive to at least some of those who are insufficiently motivated by the moral tone of censure.

44 Andrew von Hirsch, *Censure and Sanctions* (1993). In contrast, Feinberg argues that the proportionality principle requires that the seriousness of the crime should be proportionate to the public condemnation expressed by punishment, rather than the degree of 'hard treatment' imposed on the offender: Feinberg, above n 16.

more severe the punishment.[45] Other desert theorists claim, however, that the principle of proportionality merely provides a limiting, rather than defining, principle to determine the quantum or severity of punishment. For example, Morris argues that proportionality is a limiting principle which allows the quantum of punishment to be based on other grounds provided that the quantum falls within the outer limits of proportionality: punishment must not be too severe so as to be oppressive, nor too lenient so as unduly to depreciate the seriousness of the offence committed. Although individual commentators have put forward several variants of the desert theory, for the purposes of this paper it will suffice to accept the core notion that punishment is a form of retributive justice which demands that the severity of the punishment should be commensurate with the seriousness of the offence.

Because the quantum of penalty must be proportionate to the seriousness of the offence, it is necessary to provide criteria which enable the 'seriousness' of offences to be determined. Desert theorists identify two key components to the concept of seriousness: harm and culpability.[46] Harm refers to the extent of the injury caused by the violation of the law. The greater the harm caused, the greater the appropriate penalty. Culpability refers to factors of intent, motive and the circumstances that bear on the degree of the actor's blameworthiness.[47] It follows that violations of the law which are deliberate and calculated should be penalised more heavily than those which are committed carelessly or in ignorance of the law.

D *Deterrence and Desert Models Compared*

Although the two theoretical models described are primarily concerned with determining the severity of punishment for traditional criminal offences, they are general in nature and can be applied to any area of the law where financial penalties are payable for unlawful conduct. In this section, the strengths and shortcomings of each model are briefly compared and contrasted.

1 *The Deterrence Model*

The most significant strength of the deterrence model is that it is theoretically capable of generating a specific quantum of penalty. Because the model is based on a series of theoretically quantifiable variables, it provides a non-arbitrary, principled and systematic approach to the practical problem of penalty setting. Accordingly, both variants of the deterrence model can encourage consistency in penalty setting and may reduce the appearance of arbitrariness.

Bilmes and Woodbury claim that the deterrence model is particularly valuable in acknowledging the need to factor the probability of detection into the calcula-

[45] Andrew von Hirsch, 'Doing Justice: The Principle of Commensurate Deserts' in Hyman Gross and Andrew von Hirsch (eds), *Sentencing* (1981) 243.

[46] Ibid; Hart, *Punishment and Responsibility*, above n 12.

[47] Andrew von Hirsch and Kathleen Hanrahan, *The Question of Parole: Retention, Reform or Abolition?* (1979) 16.

tion of penalty.[48] If violations of the law are difficult to detect, this justifies increasing the penalty. Factoring the probability of detection into the penalty setting equation does not, however, inexorably lead to the acceptance of the deterrence model of penalty setting. For example, it could plausibly be argued that the probability of detection is related to the 'seriousness' of the violation, which is a factor relevant to determining the penalty level under the desert model. Thus, the more covert the behaviour involved (and, therefore, the smaller the probability of detection), the greater the seriousness of the contravention, thereby justifying an escalation in the level of the penalty. Alternatively, the probability of detection could be used as a criterion for determining the allocation of enforcement resources, while utilising the desert model for penalty setting.[49]

Despite its appeal, the deterrence model suffers from several significant shortcomings, both in practice and in principle. Firstly, it is a behavioural model grounded on the crucial assumption of rationality. This assumption — that those who violate the law do so on the basis of an *ex ante* calculation that the expected benefits of violating the law outweigh the expected costs — may not accurately reflect reality.[50] In the criminal context, empirical studies have failed to provide reliable findings about the relative deterrent effects of various types and levels of penalty for various offences.[51] That said, the assumption of rationality may be more readily accommodated within the area of economic and social regulation which primarily concerns commercial behaviour by profit maximising firms rather than individuals.[52] But even in the regulatory context, empirical studies suggest that corporations are not solely driven by self-seeking individuals who are concerned exclusively with profit maximisation, and may be also motivated by non-financial concerns including a concern for social responsibility and respect for the rule of law.[53]

Secondly, while the deterrence model provides a theoretically coherent and complete basis for penalty setting, applying the model to real world circumstances generates intractable problems in practice. Quantifying variables such as loss, gain and probability of detection with any degree of precision may be impossible to achieve at reasonable cost. Indeed, precise objective calculation may be impossible — for example, calculating the extent of the harm arising

48 Bilmes and Woodbury, above n 18, 202.

49 Ibid 208.

50 Ibid 205.

51 Ashworth, *Sentencing and Criminal Justice*, above n 17, 60–1; Deryck Beyleveld, 'Deterrence Research as a Basis for Deterrence Policies' (1979) 18 *Howard Journal of Criminal Justice* 135.

52 Ashworth, *Sentencing and Criminal Justice*, above n 17, 60; Abraham Goldstein, 'White-Collar Crime and Civil Sanctions' (1992) 101 *Yale Law Journal* 1895, 1898; Fisse and Braithwaite, 'Sanctions Against Corporations', above n 8.

53 Ian Ayres and John Braithwaite, *Responsive Regulation: Transcending the Deregulation Debate* (1992) 19–23; John Martin, 'Making the Giant Competitive Rather than Crushing — Industry Perspectives on Regulation Enforcement' in Peter Grabosky and John Braithwaite (eds), *Business Regulation and Australia's Future* (1993) 169. Note however, that the focus on the firm as economic actor compounds the rationality problem, because the firm is controlled by directors, whose objectives and motivations may not be wholly aligned with that of the firm. The relationship between company shareholders and managers generates a classic principal–agent problem. But arguably, the rationale is consistent — shareholders can incur greater monitoring costs as the penalty level rises: Bilmes and Woodbury, above n 18, 203; Fisse, above n 18, 255.

from a violation may inevitably require some subjective assessment of harms that cannot be precisely quantified. As a result of such estimation problems, the penalties thereby calculated may in practice be no less arbitrary than penalties assessed under a less scientific model.[54]

Finally, the deterrence model is largely amoral. As a consequentialist model, its concern is solely with preventing future contraventions of the law. Notions of fairness and morality have no role to play. Accordingly, the deterrence model is prone to generating counter-intuitive results and outcomes which appear to be at odds with fairness and justice. For example:

1 The deterrence model posits that there is a direct and interchangeable relationship between the probability of detection and the size or severity of the penalty. Thus, if an actor is risk neutral, the same level of compliance can be achieved by varying the size of the penalty in response to a variation in the probability of detection. However, if this approach is applied to achieve a desired outcome it can result in the calculation of penalties which society would regard as excessively harsh and oppressive. For example, assume that one aim of the law is to eliminate street litter, and that if all instances of street littering were detected, absolute deterrence would be achieved if a penalty of $10 applied to the offence of littering. However, if in fact because the risk of detection for littering were tiny (say, 0.001 percent), then according to the deterrence model a $1 million penalty ($10 ÷ 0.001 percent) would be required in order to ensure that littering is sufficiently deterred. Imposing penalties of such extreme magnitudes may be both unrealistic and oppressive.[55]

2 According to the injury-based (optimal deterrence) penalty model, repeat violations by the same offender suggest that penalties should be lower for that offender, because a finding of violation raises the probability of detection. In so doing, the injury-based penalty model ignores the social meaning of repeat violations. Lowering the penalty levels for repeat offences is directly contrary to the approach taken by the desert model, which imposes higher penalties for repeat offences on the basis that the offender's culpability increases with repeat offences.[56]

3 According to the benefit-based (absolute deterrence) penalty model, the loss caused to others arising from the violation is irrelevant to the calculation of penalty. The crucial variable is the gain made by the offender. It follows that even if the violation inflicts massive harm to others but confers only a small

54 Bilmes and Woodbury, above n 18, 208.

55 This point is powerfully put by Sir Ian McKay, 'Penalties, Remedies and Court Processes under the *Commerce Act 1986*: A Commentary on the Ministry of Commerce Discussion Document' (Paper presented at the Ninth Annual Workshop of the Competition Law and Policy Institute of New Zealand, Wellington, 1998). See also Hart, *Punishment and Responsibility*, above n 12, 25. Even economists acknowledge that threatening competition law violators with draconian sanctions may not be optimal due to the inevitability of legal error: Block and Sidak, above n 40.

56 This problem is avoided by the unlawful gain variant of the economic model, because it aims to achieve absolute deterrence. Thus, while under-deterrence is possible, over-deterrence is not. Note however, that the relevance of prior convictions has been the subject of debate between desert theorists: see Andrew von Hirsch, 'Desert and Previous Convictions' in Andrew von Hirsch and Andrew Ashworth (eds), *Principled Sentencing* (1998) 191.

benefit on the offender, the penalty should be correspondingly small. It may appear therefore that the violator has 'gotten off lightly', particularly by those injured by the unlawful conduct.[57]

4 At a more abstract level, one criticism of the deterrence theory of punishment is that it could justify the punishment of an innocent person if that were certain to deter several others, without any respect for the rights of the innocent person.[58] Individuals are regarded merely as numbers to be aggregated in the overall calculation of social costs. The deterrence model shows no respect for the moral worth and autonomy of each individual.[59]

The above examples provide powerful illustrations of various ways in which the deterrence model can generate results which are unfair and unjust. The deterrence model purports to predict and deter future behaviour, rationality is assumed, and considerations of fairness are ignored.

2 *The Desert Model*

While the primary weakness of the deterrence model is arguably its capacity for generating counter-intuitive results which are unfair, this constitutes the greatest strength of the desert approach to penalty setting. Because the aim of the desert model is to ensure that a 'just' penalty is imposed on the offender, the penalty level is designed to reflect social values of fairness.[60] Thus, repeat violations will lead to an escalation in penalty levels, so as to express moral outrage at the offender's apparent wilful disregard of the law.

Furthermore, the more open-ended nature of the desert model's inquiry into factors which bear upon the seriousness of the violation can potentially accommodate consideration of many of the variables which form the basis of the deterrence model. The notion of harm, which is one of the two components upon which the concept of seriousness is founded, is strongly linked to the injury-based variant of the deterrence model. Thus, where a violation of the law imposes large losses on others, this will increase the perceived seriousness of the violation and hence the level of penalty. Similarly, where the offender's conduct is covert and deliberately concealed, thus lowering the probability of detection, the perceived culpability of the offender is increased and an escalation of the penalty is justified. While the desert model allows these variables to be factored into the

57 This can be avoided by increasing the penalty to reflect the greater of the loss to others or gain to the offender — because the absolute deterrence model prescribes a minimum penalty and knows no concept of over-deterrence.

58 Ashworth, *Sentencing and Criminal Justice*, above n 17, 61; Andrew von Hirsch and Andrew Ashworth, 'Deterrence' in Andrew von Hirsch and Andrew Ashworth (eds), *Principled Sentencing* (1998) 47; Alan Goldman, 'Deterrence Theory: Its Moral Problems' in Andrew von Hirsch and Andrew Ashworth (eds), *Principled Sentencing* (1998) 80.

59 von Hirsch and Ashworth, 'Deterrence', above n 58; cf Nigel Walker, 'Deterrence' in Nigel Walker (ed), *Punishment, Danger and Stigma* (1980).

60 von Hirsch, *Censure and Sanctions*, above n 44, 104–5; Max Neiman, 'The Virtues of Heavy-Handedness in Government' (1980) 2 *Law and Policy Quarterly* 11. In contrast, Walker argues that the moral basis for penal censure is obscure unless the censure can be shown to have social utility, and fails to explain why the offender 'ought to be punished': Nigel Walker, 'Modern Retributivism' in Hyman Gross and Ros Harrison (eds), *Jurisprudence: Cambridge Essays* (1992).

penalty assessment process in the manner advocated by the deterrence model, it does not require such precise quantification of the relevant variables.

While the primary strength of the deterrence model is its ability to generate (at least in theory) a precise penalty figure, it is this quality which constitutes the principal weakness of the desert approach to penalty-setting. The desert approach is not theoretically capable of assigning a particular penalty to a particular offence.[61] The desert model is premised on the notion that offences can be ranked according to the degree of seriousness. This generates two difficulties, arising from the two dimensions of proportionality. Firstly, it assumes that a ranking of the relative seriousness of offences is possible (ordinal proportionality), when in practice this may be a controversial and complex task.[62] Secondly, even if it were possible to devise an accurate and acceptable ranking of offences on the basis of relative seriousness which thus enables the relative magnitude of the penalty to be determined, this cannot generate the absolute magnitude of the penalty (cardinal proportionality).[63]

The lack of precision inherent in the desert model also provides considerable scope for inconsistency and the appearance of arbitrariness in setting penalty levels. Concerns about inconsistency in penalty setting and sentencing generally have led to a variety of attempts by law and policy-makers to develop a more structured approach to sentencing.[64] While the desert model strives to set penalties at a fair and just level, inconsistency in the overall approach to penalty setting can potentially undermine this objective.

3 *Differences in Philosophical Foundation*

The different strengths and weakness of the two models are a product of their fundamentally different philosophical foundations.[65] The deterrence model assumes that people and firms are rational actors who make decisions according to a scientific cost-benefit calculus. Morality and popular conceptions of a 'just society' have no role to play. The deterrence model's vision of society is one in which scarce resources are efficiently allocated — all consumers needs and

61 Bilmes and Woodbury, above n 18, 198; Ashworth, *Sentencing and Criminal Justice*, above n 17, 66–7.

62 See, eg, ALRC, *Sentencing of Federal Offenders*, Discussion Paper No 15 (1980); ALRC, *Sentencing: Penalties*, above n 8. In the trade practices context, the ALRC stated that it did not accept that all contraventions of the *TPA* are equally serious and proposed that a maximum pecuniary penalty be determined in relation to each provision of the *TPA* where a breach is punishable, and that the determination be based on a considered analysis of the typical relative gravity of a contravention of each relevant provision: ALRC, *Compliance with the* Trade Practices Act 1974 *(Cth)*, Discussion Paper No 56 (1993) Proposal 6.10.

63 It could be argued that, according to the desert approach, the penalty should be at least as large as the offender's gain, according to the moral principle that no-one should profit from a wrong: see Bilmes and Woodbury, above n 18, 199.

64 ALRC, *Sentencing of Federal Offenders*, above n 62; ALRC, *Sentencing: Penalties*, above n 8; *Federal Sentencing Guidelines 1998* (USA).

65 The different values which underlie the two models are borne out in the decisions of the Australian Federal Court when attempting to set out principles which should guide the Court when setting penalties for violations of Australian competition law. Some judges have claimed that the purpose of penalty setting is deterrence and claimed that 'morality' has no role to play, whilst other judges have claimed that 'punishment' may be a legitimate aim in setting penalties for competition law violations: see below Part III.

wants, as indicated by their willingness to pay, are satisfied at the lowest possible cost. Within the deterrence model, penalties have no intrinsic value — they are simply signalling devices, indicating to potential offenders the likely cost of violating the law. The message conveyed by the imposition of a penalty as perceived by the deterrence model is, 'your conduct is costly, and you must therefore pay'. It says nothing about the wrongfulness of the conduct. It is a consequentialist, forward-looking model — penalties serve no purpose other than to indicate to potential offenders the likely cost of committing an offence.

By contrast, the desert model is overtly moral. The proportionality principle, upon which the desert model is founded, reflects the moral premise that 'the punishment must fit the crime'. Unlike the deterrence model, the desert model focuses not on the costs of the unlawful conduct, but on its wrongfulness. Punishing wrongful conduct is regarded as a necessary requirement of a just society.[66] The message thereby conveyed by the imposition of a penalty is 'your conduct is wrongful, and you must therefore be punished'. It is primarily a backward looking model — penalties serve to censure or blame offenders for their wrongful conduct.[67]

The two models clash directly in one important respect. According to the deterrence model, if the probability of detection is less than 100 percent, then the quantum of penalty must be increased by dividing the penalty calculated (under the assumption that detection is 100 percent certain) by the probability of detection. Thus, the smaller the probability of detection, the greater the magnitude of the penalty. By inflating the penalty level in this manner, the deterrence model conflicts directly with the proportionality principle on which the desert model is founded. A penalty so magnified would be regarded by the desert model as *ex hypothesi* disproportionate to the extent of the offender's wrongdoing. Because wrongfulness encapsulates the harm caused by the offender's unlawful conduct, then a penalty which significantly departs from the size of the harm caused would fail to meet the proportionality criteria.[68]

E *Regulatory Penalties: Which Model?*

As the preceding discussion illustrates, both models suffer from intractable problems but nevertheless possess characteristic strengths and can provide coherent guidance when attempting to resolve the practical problem of setting penalties. Neither model can clearly be regarded as superior to the other. Given the stark differences in philosophy and approach taken by the two models, which model is best suited to determining the quantum of penalties for violations of regulatory law?

66 Hart, *Punishment and Responsibility*, above n 12, 222–3.

67 Neiman, above n 60, 21.

68 Richard Posner, 'Retribution and Related Concepts of Punishment' (1980) 9 *Journal of Law and Economics* 71.

1 *Regulatory Offences, Moral Condemnation and Strict Liability*

The above theoretical models arose from attempts by legal theorists and philosophers to explain the justification and severity of punishment for traditional criminal offences.[69] There is, however, a perceived distinction which has been made by some judges between *mala in se*, conduct which is 'wrongful in itself' and which is thus treated as 'criminal' in societies with very different social and economic values, and *mala prohibita*, conduct which cannot be so characterised and which is the subject of specific proscription.[70] The paradigm of criminal responsibility involves the notion of individual wrongdoing, generally with a degree of awareness of the act or its consequences.[71] By contrast, the defining characteristic of laws which are aimed at regulating economic and social activity is that the breach of such laws does not commonly attract the same degree of moral condemnation which accompanies the commission of traditional crimes.[72] Regulatory law is primarily concerned to facilitate the achievement of collectivist goals by discouraging behavior which is considered to be inimical to those goals and thus detrimental to collective welfare. The punishment of regulatory offences is a practical means of controlling an activity, without necessarily implying the element of social condemnation which is characteristic of traditional crimes.[73]

Some commentators argue, however, that it is possible to attach moral opprobrium to regulatory offences, claiming that traditional crimes arouse moral disgust partly because they have been labeled criminal for so long.[74] Richardson, Ogus and Burrows attempt to find a middle-ground by arguing that an element of blame can be attached to many regulatory offences in so far as the commission of an offence amounts to a failure by the offender to take reasonable care in carrying out the regulated activity.[75] Others have distinguished regulatory laws which seek to protect economic interests, from regulatory laws which are concerned to promote other social interests (such as public health, industrial safety and environmental hygiene).[76] Kadish argues that the stigma of moral reprehensibility is not naturally associated with regulatory law which is primarily concerned to protect economic interests (such as competition law, securities regulation, export controls and the like), but does not make the same claim in relation to regulatory laws which seek to protect non-economic interests.[77]

69 von Hirsch and Ashworth, *Principled Sentencing*, above n 19.

70 Ogus, above n 6, 79; Hart, *Punishment and Responsibility*, above n 12, 236; *Sherras v De Rutzen* [1895] 1 QB 918, 922 (Wright J).

71 Richardson, Ogus and Burrows, above n 12, 56.

72 Ibid 17; Ashworth, *Principles of Criminal Law*, above n 12, 1; Hart, *Punishment and Responsibility*, above n 12, 236. Cf Wells, above n 18, 7–8.

73 Ashworth, *Principles of Criminal Law*, above n 12, 1. Feinberg argues that penal sanctions for such regulatory offences do not constitute 'punishment', although the imposition of such sanctions visits 'hard treatment' on the offender because they do not convey reprobative symbolism, which he regards as the essence of punishment: Feinberg, above n 16.

74 Vilheim Aubert, 'White-Collar Crime and Social Structure' (1952) 58 *American Journal of Sociology* 263; Wells, above n 18, 26.

75 Richardson, Ogus and Burrows, above n 12, 18.

76 Sanford Kadish, 'Some Observations on the Use of Criminal Sanctions in Enforcing Economic Regulations' (1963) 30 *University of Chicago Law Review* 423.

77 Ibid 425–6.

Nonetheless, it cannot be denied that considerably less moral stigma attaches to the commission of regulatory offences when contrasted with traditional crimes, at least in relation to regulatory offences which are aimed at safeguarding collective economic interests or where the consequences of a regulatory offence are minor in their effects (such as car parking infringements and so forth). The lack of significant moral condemnation attaching to the commission of regulatory offences has implications for the theories of punishment outlined above. In particular, it presents desert theorists with a serious dilemma. If punishment is warranted because a just society is required to censure offenders for their blameworthy conduct, then it follows that punishment is not justified in the absence of any wrongdoing associated with the commission of a regulatory offence.[78] The dilemma is less acute where a regulatory offence is committed deliberately in wilful defiance of the law, for it is possible to argue that the deliberate flouting of the law provides an independently adequate ground for condemnation.[79] Deterrence theorists, on the other hand, face no such dilemma. Because the purpose of punishment is to prevent future harm and thereby safeguard collective interests, the punishment of regulatory offences is justified in order to deter others from such conduct.[80]

The dilemma faced by desert theorists is compounded by the fact that many regulatory offences are strict liability offences.[81] While criminal offences typically depend on proof of some form of mens rea, be it intent, knowledge or recklessness, in order to establish the commission of an offence, regulatory violations often discard mens rea so that a regulatory offence may be committed without the need to establish any mental element on the part of the offender. In other words, liability is visited on the offender for breach of regulatory law without proof of the offender's culpability or subjective wickedness. The imposition of strict liability means that even the actor who takes all due care to avoid committing the offence, but nevertheless accidentally engages in the proscribed conduct, acts unlawfully and may therefore be punished.[82] For the desert theorist, the absence of any need to establish the offender's culpability strongly suggests that punishment of the offender cannot be justified because it has not been shown that the offender is morally blameworthy. It has been argued,

78 Ibid 445; Ashworth, *Principles of Criminal Law*, above n 12, 50; Richardson, Ogus and Burrows, above n 12, 17. Feinberg argues that the imposition of sanction without moral culpability does not generate any dilemma because sanctions for regulatory offences do not constitute 'punishment'. This is because the essence of punishment is its reprobative symbolism, which is not attached to regulatory sanctions. However, he concedes that where the penalties are 'severe' then the argument loses cogency and cannot justify regarding the safeguards of culpability requirements and due process requirements as irrelevant: Feinberg, above n 16.

79 Kadish, above n 76, 445. Cf Sir John Smith, *Smith & Hogan Criminal Law* (8th ed, 1996) 109.

80 For this reason, Hart has observed that many modern retributivists concede that there 'is a vast area of the criminal law where what is forbidden or enjoined by the law is so remote from the familiar requirements of morality', that punishment is to be justified and measured mainly by utilitarian consequences: Hart, *Punishment and Responsibility*, above n 12, 236. See also Richardson, Ogus and Burrows, above n 12, 17.

81 Richardson, Ogus and Burrows, above n 12, 16, 57. On the growth of strict liability offences, see Leonard Leigh, *Strict and Vicarious Liability* (1982) 14–16.

82 Ashworth, *Principles of Criminal Law*, above n 12, 160.

however, that the moral problems posed by strict liability offences are outweighed by the cost savings and practical expediency of dispensing with the requirement of proof of fault, particularly where the penalties are relatively small and the liberty of the individual is seldom at stake.[83]

The use of strict liability for regulatory offences may also have implications for deterrence theorists. Although it has generally been argued that strict liability strengthens the deterrent effect of the law by encouraging extreme care to be taken when carrying out the regulated activity, the deterrence impact of strict liability is unclear. It may be that strict liability reduces the incentive to take care, because liability may arise if the proscribed conduct occurs, however careful the actor may have been.[84] Kadish argues that the dilution of the requirement of culpability and the consequent proliferation of convictions without grounds for condemnation tends in the long run to impair the effectiveness of punitive sanctions both in the area of economic regulation and traditional crimes.[85]

2 *A Hybrid Solution*

Because regulatory law's central concern is to modify behaviour by reference to its perceived undesirable effects on collective welfare, rather than to express moral condemnation of the offence, the theoretical justification for punishment of those who violate regulatory law appears to rest firmly on the deterrence theory of punishment. Does it therefore follow that, because the justification for punishment of regulatory offences rests primarily on deterrence rather than desert, the *quantum* of penalty for violation should be determined in accordance with the economic variant of deterrence theory?

If one subscribes to the view that a system of punishment should adhere to only one value, then this question must be answered in the affirmative.[86] However, as H L A Hart has powerfully argued, 'any morally tolerable account' of punishment 'must exhibit it as a compromise between distinct and partly conflicting principles.'[87] Although the question of 'why punish?' is related to the question 'how much to punish?', they are nevertheless separate and independent questions.[88] Put differently, an important distinction must be made between questions of liability, in respect of which notions of fairness and morality arguably have little or no role to play in the regulatory context, and questions of sanction, which inevitably implicate the social and moral order.[89] It is therefore perfectly consistent to

83 Richardson, Ogus and Burrows, above n 12, 17. Ashworth has pointed out the fallacy of this argument, however, on the basis that an assessment of fault is required (at least in relation to serious offences) in order for a court to pass sentence on a proper basis: Ashworth, *Principles of Criminal Law*, above n 12, 51, 163.

84 Richardson, Ogus and Burrows, above n 12, 16–17.

85 Kadish, above n 76, 444.

86 The relevant variant of the deterrence model would then depend on whether the regulated conduct has the potential to be net welfare-enhancing (so that the 'injury to others' variant of the model should apply) or is always net welfare-reducing (so that the 'unlawful gain' variant of the model should apply).

87 Hart, *Punishment and Responsibility*, above n 12, 1.

88 Ibid 3.

89 In *TPC v CSR Ltd* [1991] ATPR ¶41-076, the leading authority for the setting of Australian competition law penalties, French J fell into the trap of conflating the question of liability with

accept that the only justification for a system of punishment of regulatory offences is to deter future harms, but also to accept that the quantum of punishment for such offences should take issues other than deterrence into consideration.[90]

Accordingly, although the justification for punishing regulatory offences rests on deterrence, it does not necessarily follow that penalties for regulatory offences must be quantified in accordance with the deterrence theory of punishment, let alone the economic variant of deterrence theory. Not only can a system of state punishment seek to implement a plurality of values without falling into logical incoherence, but it is positively desirable that it should do so, thereby reflecting the multiplicity of societal goals which may legitimately be pursued by the state in punishing those who break the law. State punishment for regulatory offences should therefore encapsulate the essential concerns of *both* the deterrence and desert theories of punishment. Assuming that the state is justified in regulating the proscribed activity by the imposition of penal sanctions, it is important that the severity of those sanctions should be sufficient to deter potential offenders from engaging in the proscribed conduct, otherwise the regulatory scheme is unlikely to be effective. The deterrence justification for regulatory offences suggests that the quantum of regulatory penalties should, in the first instance, be set at a level that is sufficiently high to deter the offender and others from contravening the law.

On the other hand, a system of punishment must not overlook the requirements of fairness in seeking to secure effective regulation.[91] The mere fact that there is little or no moral condemnation attached to the commission of a regulatory offence, nor a need to prove culpability by the offender to establish liability, does not necessarily imply that moral considerations and issues of culpability are irrelevant to the penalties levied thereunder.[92] Although conceptions of fairness and morality do not play a central justification for regulatory law, wholly ignoring considerations of fairness in penalising regulatory offenders would be objectionable in principle.[93] The fact remains that penalties for regulatory offences are, after all, a form of legal punishment. As such, penalties impose burdens on citizens which are backed by the coercive power of the state and thus possess an intrinsic moral dimension.[94] Penalties have significant consequences,

the question of sanction. Thus he erroneously concluded that, because issues of morality are not relevant to the former question, they are not relevant to the latter question. See below Part III.

90 Hart, *Law, Liberty and Morality*, above n 15, 90.

91 Lucia Zedner, 'Reparation and Retribution: Are They Reconcilable?' (1994) 57 *Modern Law Review* 228, 243.

92 The ALRC identified four different functions which a remedial court order for contravention of the *TPA* is designed to serve, which included 'deterrence and, as a secondary or incidental outcome, retribution': ALRC, *Compliance with the* Trade Practices Act 1974, above n 8, 29.

93 Hadden refers to the British Law Commission's study of strict liability for health and safety offences under the *Factories Act* (UK) which indicates that the presence of culpability was an important factor which enforcement officials took into account in exercising their discretion to prosecute: Tom Hadden, 'Strict Liability and the Enforcement of Regulatory Legislation' [1970] *Criminal Law Review* 496.

94 John Brigham and Don Brown, 'Distinguishing Penalties and Incentives' (1980) 2 *Law & Policy Quarterly* 5.

both for the citizen on whom they are levied and for the society in which they operate. When a penalty is imposed for violating the law, it communicates the message 'you broke the law, you must be penalised'.[95] Because penalties for violation of the law involve the imposition of 'hard treatment' on citizens by the state, it is essential in any liberal democratic society that the limits on the scope of punishment are properly circumscribed.[96] Democratic societies recognise the moral worth and autonomy of citizens and cannot therefore justify visiting disproportionately harsh punishment on those who break the law.[97] While the quantum of regulatory penalties should in the first instance be guided by the goal of deterrence, the proportionality principle is an important delimitation on the intrusive powers of the state.[98] Accordingly, exclusive reliance should not be placed on the deterrence model as the basis for determining penalty levels because this could theoretically permit the imposition of draconian, or unfairly lenient, sanctions on an individual offender.

Ignoring considerations of fairness would not only be unacceptable as a matter of principle, but would also be unwise as a matter of practice. As the preceding section demonstrates, the application of the deterrence model of penalty setting may generate unfair results. If a penalty scheme departs too greatly from moral consensus, this can (particularly over time) undermine the perceived legitimacy of the regulatory regime within which penalties operate.[99] Not only does this bring the law into disrepute, but may eventually undermine the legitimacy of the regulatory system.[100] Without the confidence and support of the regulated parties, and the society in which they operate, the regulatory system will inevitably fail to achieve its objectives.[101] The stigmatising power of punishment for unlawful conduct is one of society's most powerful tools for encouraging compliance with the law.[102] A penalty scheme must not be too out of step with intuitive conceptions of fairness and justice lest it fail to inculcate in those who violate the law a sense of the wrongfulness of their conduct.

95 Feinberg, above n 16.

96 'Two things are morally wrong: (1) to condemn a faultless man while inflicting pain or deprivation on him however slight (unjust punishment); and (2) to inflict unnecessary and severe suffering on a faultless man even in the absence of condemnation (unjust civil penalty)': ibid.

97 Hart, *Punishment and Responsibility*, above n 12, 25; Francis Allen, 'The Decline of the Rehabilitative Ideal' in Andrew von Hirsch and Andrew Ashworth (eds), *Principled Sentencing* (1998) 14, 17.

98 This invocation of the proportionality principle differs slightly from the proportionality principle arising from the 'just deserts' model of punishment, because its primary concern is to avoid the use of oppressive or unfair state power against the citizen, rather than to ensure that the degree of censure or blame attributed to those who violate the law is commensurate with the seriousness of the violation: Hart, *Punishment and Responsibility*, above n 12, 181–2.

99 Ibid 25.

100 McKay, above n 55.

101 Peter Grabosky, Clifford Shearing and John Braithwaite, 'Introduction' in Peter Grabosky and John Braithwaite (eds), *Business Regulation and Australia's Future* (1993) 1, 6; Brigham and Brown, above n 94, 6.

102 John Coffee Jr, 'Does "Unlawful" Mean "Criminal"?: Reflections on the Disappearing Tort/Crime Distinction in American Law' (1991) 71 *Boston University Law Review* 193.

In summary, the deterrence justification for regulatory offences suggests that the quantum of regulatory penalties should, in the first instance, be set at a level that is sufficiently high to deter the offender and others from contravening the law. But, in any given case, if the goal of general deterrence requires the imposition of a penalty of a magnitude that would be disproportionate to the seriousness of the offence, then the goal of deterrence (be it 'absolute' or 'optimal', depending on whether or not the unlawful conduct is potentially welfare-enhancing) must give way to the moral principle that the 'punishment must fit the crime'. In other words, the proportionality principle should circumscribe the outer limits of the range of acceptable penalties. Within that range, the deterrence model can be used to determine a particular quantum of penalty.[103] An effective penalty regime for regulatory offences should be based on a hybrid of the two models, so that the quantum of punishment reflects the goal of deterrence provided that it is not unfairly disproportionate to the seriousness of the offence.

III Competition Law Penalties and the Australian Experience

The final section of this paper seeks to illustrate the application of the theoretical models examined above by focusing on penalties for violation of competition law, focusing in particular on the Australian experience of competition regulation. Laws aimed at regulating competition provide a prime example of regulatory law: the purpose of competition law is to eliminate certain restrictive commercial practices, not because such practices are worthy of moral condemnation, but because they lead to the inefficient allocation of resources by impairing the competitive process and thus diminish the overall welfare of society. It is particularly valuable to examine how Australian law has approached the task of penalty setting for competition law violations because a significant volume of case law has developed in relation to the penalty-setting process and because of recent controversy concerning the very substantial penalties which have been imposed on some offenders.[104]

103 The use of the desert principle to locate the outer limits of penal sanctions has been advocated by several criminal law theorists: Frances Allen, *The Decline of the Rehabilitative Ideal* (1981); von Hirsch, 'Doing Justice', above n 45; cf von Hirsch, *Censure and Sanctions*, above n 44, ch 6. The proposed solution is a compromise one, and may be criticised by purists on that basis. However, I share the view of Judge Frank Easterbook who stated that,

> there is no first best solution to the enforcement of anti-trust laws. If one existed in theory, it probably could not be achieved in the face of very expensive litigation. Fancy rules are costly to administer and they breed error. Only second-best solutions are available. This is my excuse for offering marginal adjustments in existing rules rather than some thoroughgoing revamp.

Frank Easterbrook, 'Allocating Antitrust Decisionmaking Tasks' (1987) 76 *Georgetown Law Journal* 305, 353.

104 The use of negotiation between the regulator and the suspect firms and individuals has also been controversial: see Jeremy Thorpe, 'Determining the Appropriate Role for Charge Bargaining in Part IV of the *Trade Practices Act*' (1996) 4 *Competition and Consumer Law Journal* 69.

A *The Australian Regulatory Framework*

Australian competition law is largely embodied in a series of statutory prohibitions contained in Part IV of the *TPA*. The Australian regulatory framework is based on a dual adjudication system: it is for courts to determine whether the Part IV prohibitions have been contravened and to impose pecuniary civil penalties on offenders, but it is for the ACCC as an independent administrative authority to determine whether conduct which would otherwise contravene the Act confers a net public benefit to the community and should therefore be granted legal immunity from the prohibitions.[105] The ACCC cannot grant such legal immunity unless the conduct has first been notified to the ACCC or the parties have applied to the ACCC for authorisation of the proposed conduct.[106] Thus, the legislative prohibitions contained in Part IV of the Act are not absolute. Immunity from the prohibitions is available in relation to net welfare-enhancing conduct (with the exception of monopolisation under s 46) via the authorisation and notification process.

Before attempting to identify which model best explains the approach taken by Australian courts when setting competition law penalties, it is useful first to consider how the deterrence and desert models could be expected to apply in the competition law context.

1 *The Deterrence Model*

If the deterrence model is applied to competition law violations, should the aim of penalty setting be 'optimal' or 'absolute' deterrence? As previously noted, if the practices sought to be prohibited may in some circumstances be welfare-enhancing, then economic theory suggests that the 'injury to others' variant of the model should be applied so as not to deter welfare-enhancing violations. Apart from price fixing and bid-rigging agreements between competitors, which are universally condemned as economically inefficient, not all horizontal restraints (ie, where competition is restricted by co-ordination between firms which operate at the same level in the supply chain) are unequivocally anti-competitive and inefficient.[107] The same is true of vertical restraints (ie, where a restraint is imposed by one firm on another operating at a different level in the supply chain). A vertical restraint implemented by a firm with market power may be inefficient and thus welfare reducing, but the same type of restriction by a firm lacking market power may be benign, and may well have net pro-competitive effects.[108] Thus an evaluation of the market power of the firms engaged in the

105 Maureen Brunt, 'The Australian Antitrust Law after 20 Years — A Stocktake' in David Round (ed), *Review of Industrial Organisation* (1994) 483.

106 *TPA* s 93.

107 Presley Warner and Michael Trebilcock, 'Rethinking Price-Fixing Law' (1993) 38 *McGill Law Journal* 679; Frank Easterbrook, 'Detrebling Antitrust Damages' (1985) 28 *Journal of Law & Economics* 445.

108 For an analysis of vertical restraints, see F M Scherer and David Ross, *Industrial Market Structure and Economic Performance* (1990) 541–69.

restrictive practice in the particular case may be required before the restraint can be condemned as inefficient.[109]

There is a considerable body of literature (largely written in the US) which is concerned with identifying the optimal basis for determining the penalty level for 'antitrust' (ie, competition law) violations so as to provide a measure of the appropriate level of damages which should be payable in a private antitrust suit against an offender. A theme that appears throughout the economic literature is a concern to avoid 'over-deterrence' which follows from the belief that welfare-enhancing violations of the law should not be deterred.[110] Posner cites by way of example a market-power enhancing merger which imposes costs of $1 million on society but confers benefits, as a result of the lower costs of the merged entity arising from economies of scale and scope, of $2 million. Posner argues that if the purpose of antitrust law is to promote efficiency, such a merger should be permitted but if the penalty is set substantially above the social cost of the violation then the merger will be deterred.[111] Thus, it is widely assumed by such theorists that some anti-competitive practices which violate the law may have net welfare-enhancing effects.[112]

If this strand of economic reasoning is adopted,[113] then it follows that competition law penalties should aim to achieve optimal deterrence, rather than absolute

109 This distinction may be reflected in the way in which substantive rules are constructed. For example, horizontal price fixing is illegal per se (ie, on proof that the price fixing conduct occurred) while exclusive dealing is only unlawful if it has the purpose or likely effect of substantially lessening competition in a market: *TPA* ss 45, 45A, 47. See Richard Posner and Isaac Ehrlich, 'An Economic Analysis of Legal Rulemaking' (1974) 3 *Journal of Legal Studies* 257.

110 Easterbrook, 'Detrebling Antitrust Damages', above n 107, 449–50.

111 Posner, *Antitrust Law*, above n 36, 222.

112 William Landes, 'Optimal Sanctions for Antitrust Violations' (1983) 50 *University of Chicago Law Review* 652, 653; Posner, *Antitrust Law*, above n 36; Easterbrook, 'Detrebling Antitrust Damages', above n 107; Kenneth Elzinga and William Breit, 'Private Antitrust Enforcement: The New Learning' (1985) 28 *Journal of Law and Economics* 405. The underlying reason why some economists claim that anti-competitive conduct may, in certain circumstances, be efficient and thus welfare-enhancing occurs because efficiency is not a unitary concept. Efficiency has three possible dimensions: allocative efficiency, productive efficiency and dynamic efficiency: see *Re 7 Eleven Stores Pty Ltd* [1994] ATPR ¶41-357, 42,677 ('*Re 7 Eleven*'). Allocative efficiency arises when economic resources are allocated between different goods and services in precisely the quantity which consumers wish (their desires being expressed by the price they are prepared to pay on the market). Productive efficiency occurs when goods and services are produced at the lowest cost possible using current technology. Dynamic efficiency refers to the capacity of the market to adapt to change and incorporate new processes and products. There may be circumstances in which a reduction in allocative efficiency resulting from anti-competitive action may be outweighed by the gain in productive or dynamic efficiency accompanying such action.

113 Some economists take the view that monopoly pricing can never be welfare enhancing. For example, Schwartz is unconvinced that the exercise of monopoly power could result in cost savings to the monopolist and thus generate social benefits, basing his view on the standard deadweight loss argument against monopoly: Schwartz, above n 33, 1081–2. On this view, it follows that competition law penalties should aim to ensure absolute deterrence, and thus the unlawful gain model for penalty setting is to be preferred. Yet Schwartz then goes on to argue that a loss-based penalty measure is to be preferred because a gain-based remedy will not fully reflect the harm to society caused by the monopolist's conduct, and thus fails to achieve the objective of efficiently allocating enforcement resources to minimise the harm associated with monopoly. However, he concedes that if a loss-based remedy is adopted, there is a possibility that the gain to the violator may exceed the loss to others and therefore fail to deter monopoly conduct, but he claims that this will rarely occur in practice: Schwartz, above n 33, 1083. In other words, although Schwartz favours absolute deterrence of monopoly conduct, he nonethe-

deterrence. The 'injury to others' variant of the deterrence model is therefore the preferred basis for penalty setting.[114] An exception to this approach should be made in cases of blatant horizontal price fixing and bid-rigging in respect of which penalties should be set so as to achieve absolute deterrence, thus utilising the 'unlawful gain' model, based on universal acceptance that such conduct is inefficient and confers no redeeming benefits on society.[115]

The goal of 'optimal' rather than 'absolute' deterrence appears to underpin the Australian institutional framework for regulating competition because restrictive practices which would otherwise breach the statutory prohibitions may be immune from penalty if the practice is notified to, or authorised by, the ACCC. It does not, however, follow that the courts should adopt the injury-to-others model (which aims to achieve optimal deterrence) as the basis for quantifying penalties for contraventions of the *TPA*. The institutional mechanism for ensuring that net welfare-enhancing anti-competitive practices are not deterred is via the authorisation and notification process. The task of evaluating whether the public benefits from proposed anti-competitive conduct does not rest with the courts, but with the ACCC as an independent competition regulator.[116] The task of courts when applying the legislative prohibitions is confined to considering only the effect or likely effect of the relevant conduct on competition; it does not extend to examining any other effects (whether welfare-enhancing or otherwise).[117]

Accordingly, it is necessary to ensure that penalties are structured so that firms proposing to engage in allegedly welfare-enhancing anti-competitive conduct face appropriate incentives to notify or to seek authorisation from the ACCC, thereby enabling the alleged social benefits to be evaluated and weighed against any potentially harmful anti-competitive effects. Therefore the penalties should be set so as to ensure that violations of the prohibitions are deterred absolutely,

less supports the injury to others model for calculating penalties rather than the unlawful gain model. Schwartz seems to conflate two distinct ideas: i) the quantum of penalty; and ii) the allocation of enforcement resources. He implicitly assumes that the allocation of enforcement resources will logically be determined by penalty size. But this is not an inevitable or necessary link.

114 Posner favours the injury to others variant of the deterrence model, recognising that monopoly pricing may yield cost savings for the monopolist, so that if such cost savings exceed the deadweight loss to society which is caused by monopoly pricing, it is inappropriate to deter the conduct because it is net welfare-enhancing. The New Zealand Ministry of Commerce, however, rejects Posner's reasoning without providing any adequate justification for so doing, simply stating that '[g]iven that this is a contentious argument and that the size of the deadweight loss is usually small compared with the monopoly profit, for the purposes of this document we have adopted the illegal gain rather than the "total harm" approach': New Zealand Ministry of Commerce, *Penalties, Remedies and Court Processes under The* Commerce Act 1986*: A Discussion Document* (1998) 9.

115 The adoption of two different penalty standards could generate some counter-intuitive results. If the gain to the violator in a price fixing case is very small, but the loss inflicted is very large, according to the absolute deterrence standard, the penalty should be that of the small gain. By contrast, if in a rule of reason case, the same dimensions of gain and loss arise, then according to the optimal deterrence model the penalty should be the large loss. From an outsider's perspective, the result seems inequitable. But, this could be adjusted to allow for the greater loss-based penalty to be awarded in the price fixing case because the absolute deterrence model knows no concept of over-deterrence. It would therefore be possible to set penalties for price fixing at whichever is greater of the loss to others or the gain to the violators.

116 Officer and Williams, above n 29, 157.

117 For a discussion of the Australian institutional approach, see Brunt, above n 105, 510–12.

thus encouraging firms to seek authorisation of anti-competitive practices which provide net social benefits. Anti-competitive conduct which is welfare-enhancing should not be deterred, because authorisation can be sought and granted if net public benefit is established.

The only conduct which cannot be authorised is misuse of market power which is prohibited by s 46 of the *TPA*.[118] In order to establish a breach of s 46, the applicant must establish that the respondent: a) had a substantial degree of power in a market; b) has taken advantage of that power; c) for a proscribed purpose. If the conduct in question can be explained on grounds of productive efficiency then the respondent has not 'taken advantage' of its market power.[119] Thus the substantive prohibition contained in s 46 is structured with a built-in safeguard in order to ensure that conduct which is productively efficient and thus net welfare-enhancing is not caught by the prohibition. Assuming that legal error is avoided in applying s 46 so that only welfare-reducing conduct is prohibited,[120] then conduct which contravenes s 46 should be prohibited absolutely and penalties for breach should be assessed in accordance with the 'unlawful gain' model so as to secure absolute deterrence.[121] If this view is adopted, then penalties for contravening Australian competition law should be set according to the unlawful-gain variant of the economic model, rather than the injury to others variant.

2 *The Desert Model*

If the desert model is applied to competition law penalties, it is necessary to establish both: 1) the seriousness of competition law violations relative to other violations of the law which are punishable by monetary penalty and the relative seriousness of specific competition law violations relative to each other (thereby establishing a scale of ordinal proportionality); and 2) the magnitude of the penalty scale itself, which involves specifying the monetary amount which fairly reflects society's disapproval of the unlawful conduct (thereby establishing a scale of cardinal proportionality). Once ordinal and cardinal proportionality scales have been established, the quantum of penalty for any given violation of the prohibitions can be determined by reference to the seriousness of the violation.

118 However, conduct which is authorised or notified in relation to conduct prohibited by *TPA* ss 45, 45B, 47 and 50 is immune from contravening s 46: *TPA* s 46(6).

119 *Queensland Wire Industries Pty Ltd v The Broken Hill Proprietary Company Ltd* (1989) 167 CLR 177; Frances Hanks and Philip Williams, 'Implications of the Decision of the High Court in *Queensland Wire*' (1990) 17 *Melbourne University Law Review* 437, 444–6.

120 It is conceded that the assumption of zero legal error is unrealistic in practice: see above n 38 and accompanying text. Conduct which does not satisfy the 'take advantage' test and thus does not breach s 46 of the Act is not necessarily welfare-enhancing.

121 Economists might criticise the Australian institutional scheme on the basis that requiring the public competition regulator to scrutinise *ex ante* all conduct alleged to be welfare-enhancing (assuming that an authorisation application is made) is more costly than a regime in which courts evaluate whether particular anti-competitive conduct is welfare-enhancing if challenged in litigation. The latter regime underlies the approach taken to misuse of monopoly power in s 46 of the Act — it places the onus on individual firms to assess for themselves whether their conduct is likely to be efficiency-enhancing: Warner and Trebilcock, above n 107. But such a criticism is empirical in nature, and it is by no means certain that an alternative institutional regime would be less costly in total than the existing regime.

It is immediately apparent, however, that the establishment of a penalty scale which ranks the severity of competition law violations relative to other violations of the law is a complex task which is practically impossible to achieve with any scientific precision. Nonetheless, in theory it may be possible to rank the seriousness of competition law violations relative to other types of commercial conduct which is subject to regulation and punishable by monetary sanction — such as laws relating to insider trading, disclosure of corporate information, financial services regulation and so forth, by reference to the potential harm caused by such practices valued in monetary terms. The relative culpability of offenders as indicated by the offender's actual mental state, such as the deliberateness of the offence and knowledge of the illegality may also provide some assistance in ranking the 'seriousness' of specific violations of the law.

However, establishing the magnitude of the penalty scale in financial terms so as to reflect the extent of society's disapproval cannot be achieved in any principled, non-arbitrary way. There is no quantum of penalty which suggests itself as uniquely appropriate for competition law violations.[122] Australian competition law sets the statutory maxima for penalties at A$10 million for corporations and A$500,000 for individuals, but these penalty ceilings cannot be explained other than as the legislature's intuitive perception of the suitable magnitude of penalties.[123]

Assuming that reasonable solutions can be found to overcome the difficulties inherent in establishing a scale of proportionality, then a penalty scheme which is based on the just desert model could rest on the proportionality principle in order to determine the quantum of penalties, with the 'seriousness' of violations determined by the extent of the harm caused by the violation and the culpability of the offender. Hence the greater the loss caused by the violation, the greater the quantum of penalty. Similarly, an 'innocent' breach of the law would be penalised less severely than a breach arising from deliberate action taken by the offender in knowing violation of the law.

B *Australian Competition Law Penalties*

The final section of this paper attempts to identify which model best explains the quantum of Australian competition law penalties. While the responsibility for initiating and conducting civil enforcement proceedings in order to recover

122 von Hirsch, *Censure and Sanctions*, above n 44, 19.

123 Under European Community competition law, the negligent or intentional infringement of the prohibitions contained in arts 85(1) and 86 of the *Treaty Establishing the European Economic Community as Amended by Subsequent Treaties*, opened for signature 25 March 1957, 298 UNTS 3 (entered into force 1 January 1958) range from ECU 1000 to ECU 1 million or up to 10 percent of the turnover in the preceding business year of each of the undertakings participating in the infringement: Council Regulation No 17/62, OJ L13, 21 February 1962. Under US antitrust law, breach of the *Sherman Antitrust Act of 1890*, 15 USC ss 1–7 (1993) is punishable by fines of up to US$10 million (for corporations) and US$350,000 (for individuals). In the US, the setting of fines for antitrust offences is subject to the guidelines laid down in the *Federal Sentencing Guidelines 1998* (USA) pt R.

penalties from suspected offenders lies with the ACCC,[124] it is the Federal Court of Australia which decides whether a breach of the Act has occurred and, if so, the quantum of penalty to be imposed.[125] Statutory guidance is provided to the Federal Court in determining the level of penalty for a breach of Part IV in s 76(1) of the Act which confers on the court a very wide discretion to determine the quantum of penalty but sets out a list of relevant matters which the court must take into account when exercising that discretion. For this purpose, relevant matters include, but are not limited to:

- the nature and extent of the act or omission;
- any loss or damage suffered as a result of the act or omission;
- the circumstances in which the act or omission took place; and
- whether the person has previously been found by the court in previous proceedings under the *TPA* to have engaged in any similar conduct.[126]

The statutory criteria do not, of themselves, appear strongly to reflect either of the theoretical models for penalty setting described above. However, it could be argued that these criteria fit more comfortably with the desert model of penalty setting, for all the stated criteria are matters which pertain to the 'seriousness' of the unlawful conduct. On the other hand, the listed criteria could be broadly interpreted as providing a basis for inclusion of the specific quantifiable variables which are utilised by the deterrence model. The statutory criteria are not exhaustive, however, and the court's ultimate task is to determine a penalty 'as it determines to be appropriate having regard to all relevant matters'. Accordingly, it is necessary to look more closely at the case law to identify how the Federal Court has approached the task of penalty setting under s 76 in order to identify the theoretical basis upon which the Court has proceeded.[127]

There have been a significant number of decisions in which the courts have considered the operation of s 76. The leading authority concerning penalty setting for contraventions of Part IV of the *TPA* is the judgment of French J in

[124] The *TPA* expressly stipulates that penalties imposed for breach of Part IV of the *TPA* are not criminal in nature. Hence the rules of civil rather than criminal procedure apply in the conduct of penalty proceedings: *TPA* s 78.

[125] In recent years, however, the quantum of penalty has largely been determined by negotiation between the ACCC and the respondent, subject to the court's approval: Thorpe, above n 104.

[126] The ALRC sought public submissions on whether the *TPA* should provide guidelines for courts imposing a penalty for contravention of the Act and what the content of those guidelines should be. In its final report, the ALRC noted that many of the submissions opposed the proposal on the ground that it would intrude too much on judicial discretion and was unnecessary. The ALRC concluded that detailed guidelines such as the *Federal Sentencing Guidelines* (USA) were unnecessarily complicated and inflexible. However, it favoured some guidance and proposed that three additional factors should be required to be taken into account by courts in assessing penalties: (if the contravener is a corporation) whether a revision of the contravener's compliance controls is necessary and the extent to which defective internal controls have been revised in light of the lessons learned from the circumstances in which the contravention occurred; how much, if any, profit was made as a result of the contravention; and whether the contravener continued the relevant conduct notwithstanding a written request from the ACCC to discontinue it: ALRC, *Compliance with the* Trade Practices Act 1974 (1993), above n 62, Proposal 6.9; ALRC, *Compliance with the* Trade Practices Act 1974 (1987), above n 8, 124.

[127] See generally Arie Frieberg, 'Monetary Penalties Under the *TPA*' (1983) 11 *Australian Business Law Review* 4.

TPC v CSR Ltd.[128] In particular, French J elaborated on the criteria which are relevant to a determination of the appropriate level of penalty,[129] stating that:

> The assessment of a penalty of appropriate deterrent value will have regard to a number of factors which have been canvassed in the cases. These include the following:
>
> 1 The nature and extent of the contravening conduct.
>
> 2 The amount of loss or damage caused.[130]
>
> 3 The circumstances in which the conduct took place.
>
> 4 The size of the contravening company.[131]
>
> 5 The degree of power it has, as evidenced by its market share and ease of entry into the market.
>
> 6 The deliberateness of the contravention and the period over which it extended.[132]
>
> 7 Whether the contravention arose out of the conduct of senior management or at a lower level.[133]
>
> 8 Whether the company has a corporate culture conducive to compliance with the Act, as evidenced by educational programs and disciplinary or other corrective measures in response to an acknowledged contravention.
>
> 9 Whether the company has shown a disposition to cooperate with the authorities responsible for the enforcement of the Act in relation to the contravention.[134]
>
> The first three factors are all expressly mentioned in s 76. They can be regarded as measures of the scope and impact of the conduct and it is conducive to deterrence that the greater the significance of these elements, the heavier the penalty should be.[135]

1 *Penalty Setting, 'Deterrence', 'Punishment' and 'Morality'*

French J also made a number of strong statements of principle concerning the determination of penalties under Part IV of the Act which, at first blush, suggest

128 [1991] ATPR ¶41-076 ('*CSR*').

129 The factors considered by courts to be relevant to a determination of penalties for price fixing agreements have been analysed in detail by economists Round, Siegfried and Baillie, above n 10, 300–1.

130 In particular, courts may consider the economic impact of the contravening conduct on the market — a greater effect warranting a heavier penalty. Cf *TPC v Allied Mills Pty Ltd* (1981) 37 ALR 256 with *TPC v Malleys Ltd* [1979] ATPR ¶40-118.

131 Courts have taken the view that the larger the corporation involved in the contravention, the larger the appropriate penalty, on the basis that what would deter a small company might have little effect on a very large one: *TPC v Carlton and United Breweries Ltd* [1990] ATPR ¶41-037; *TPC v TNT Australia Pty Ltd* [1995] ATPR ¶41-375, 40,168 ('*TPC v TNT*').

132 Systematic, deliberate defiance of the law is considered to warrant heavier penalties: *TPC v TNT* [1995] ATPR ¶41-375.

133 The higher the level of management responsible for participation in the contravention, the more serious the infringement and the higher the level of penalty: ibid 40,167.

134 Cooperation with enforcement authorities has been regarded as a mitigating factor which justifies a reduction in penalty: ibid 40,169–70.

135 *CSR* [1991] ATPR ¶41-076, 52,152–3.

that the deterrence model informs the Court's approach to penalty setting. In his view, the sole purpose of such penalties is to deter future contraventions of the Act. Morality has no role to play.

> Punishment for breaches of the criminal law traditionally involves three elements: deterrence, both general and individual, retribution and rehabilitation. Neither retribution nor rehabilitation, within the sense of the Old and New Testament moralities that imbue much of our criminal law, have any part to play in economic regulation of the kind contemplated by Pt IV. Nor, if it be necessary to say so, is there any compensatory element in the penalty fixing process ... The principal, and I think probably the only, object of the penalties imposed by s 76 is to attempt to put a price on contravention that is sufficiently high to deter repetition by the contravenor and by others who might be tempted to contravene the Act.[136]

The view that punishment has no role to play in the determination of penalties under s 76 was recently endorsed by the majority of the Full Federal Court in *NW Frozen Foods Pty Ltd v ACCC*.[137] The majority rejected the approach taken by Heerey J in comparing the culpability of the appellant with that of another corporation in an earlier price fixing case in which sizeable penalties were imposed. By so doing, Heerey J had, in the Full Court's opinion, engaged in an exercise of punishment which was not the purpose of penalties imposed under s 76.[138]

By claiming that the only object of penalties imposed by s 76 is to 'price' contraventions so as to deter future contraventions by the offender (ie, specific deterrence) and other potential offenders (ie, general deterrence), French J appears to provide powerful endorsement of the deterrence model as the theoretical basis for penalty setting for breach of Part IV, although he does not make clear which variant of the deterrence model is to be applied. The express rejection of morality and punishment as having any relevance to the determination of penalties also appears to reject outright the desert model as the basis for penalty setting. Despite these statements, an examination of the general body of case law, the specific criteria enumerated by French J as relevant to penalty setting, and the reasoning adopted by French J in the *CSR* case itself, indicates that the court in fact pays more lip-service than adherence to the deterrence model of penalty setting and in practice adheres more closely to the principles underlying the desert model of penalty setting.

Although French J has stated that notions of morality and punishment have no role to play in the setting of penalties under s 76, the issue is by no means settled. In *NW Frozen Foods*, Carr J expressly stated that 'the cases decided to date on the question of the assessment of pecuniary penalties have not ruled out or excluded punishment as one of the purposes of s 76 of the *Trade Practices Act*', and deliberately left the issue open.[139] This comment was referred to in

136 Ibid 52,152.
137 (1996) 71 FCR 285 ('*NW Frozen Foods*').
138 Ibid 296–7.
139 Ibid 299.

ACCC v Australian Safeway Stores[140] by Goldberg J who stated that, apart from the above-cited statement of French J in *CSR*, he was 'unable to find any positive statement in any of the cases that the purpose of the imposition of penalties by s 76 "is not punishment".'[141] Goldberg J considered the matter to be significant, because 'in an appropriate case where there has been a flagrant and wilful contravention [a court] might take the view that a severe penalty was warranted, having regard to the deliberateness and wilfulness of the contravention.[142] In other words, the culpability of the offender may be relevant to determining the quantum of penalty. Similarly, Heerey J in *ACCC v J McPhee & Son (Australia) Pty Ltd*[143] stated that he did not necessarily agree with the statements of French J in *CSR* cited above. While Heerey J acknowledged that contravention of Part IV provisions are not criminal offences and that deterrence remains a primary objective of the imposition of penalties,

> nevertheless s 76 imports into the penalty fixing process concepts of moral responsibility long known to the criminal law. In other words, the sources of the substantive provisions of Pt IV are doubtless economic policy and theory, but the penalties for contraventions are to be applied in a moral universe.[144]

A closer examination of the comments made by French J in *CSR* reveals that he conflated the substantive rules for determining whether a contravention of the *TPA* has occurred with the principles to be applied in determining the level of penalty for contravention. Put differently, he confused the question of breach with the question of penalty.[145] These are separate and independent questions. There are two strands of reasoning which led French J to his conclusion that morality has no role to play in penalty setting. First, because the purpose of the *TPA* is directed to regulating competition, the statutory provisions are regulatory rather than penal in nature. Secondly, the High Court in *Queensland Wire Industries v Broken Hill Proprietary Ltd* expressly rejected the view that morality was relevant when determining whether s 46 of the *TPA* (misuse of market power) has been contravened.[146] According to French J, it therefore followed that morality was irrelevant to setting penalties for contraventions of the *TPA*. But both strands of reasoning are concerned with the issue of breach: the first goes to the subject matter of the *TPA*, and the second to the substantive rules which

140 [1997] ATPR ¶41-562, 43,810.

141 Ibid 43,811. The disagreement between individual Federal Court judges concerning whether the goal of penalty setting pursuant to s 76 of the *TPA* is limited to 'deterrence' or also includes 'punishment' seems to suggest that the courts are assuming deterrence to mean 'absolute' rather than 'optimal' deterrence. On this view, absolute deterrence arises from setting the quantum of penalty at the level at which the offender would be indifferent to committing the offence or not thereby eliminating any incentive to offend. A penalty which sought to inflict 'punishment', on the other hand, would be a sum of money which would make the offender prefer not to have committed the offence.

142 Ibid 43,811.

143 [1998] ATPR ¶41-628.

144 Ibid 40,891.

145 This error is referred to by Goldberg J in *ACCC v Australian Safeway Stores Pty Ltd* [1997] ATPR ¶41-562, 43,811.

146 (1989) 167 CLR 177, 194 (Deane J). See also *TPC v Commodore Business Machines Pty Ltd* [1989] ATPR ¶40-976, 50,672; *TPC v TNT* [1995] ATPR ¶41-375.

define unlawful behaviour. While French J correctly stated that morality has no place in determining whether a *breach* of the *TPA* has occurred, it does not necessarily follow that morality has no place in determining the appropriate *penalty* which should apply in respect of a breach.[147] Indeed, it is argued that ignoring moral considerations in setting penalties for breach of Part IV would be undesirable and unwise, lest the regulatory regime lose the respect and support of the regulated parties.

Furthermore, on a closer examination of the nine factors cited by French J as relevant to a determination of penalty setting, six are concerned with matters of culpability and cannot be easily reconciled with the deterrence theory of penalty setting nor regarded as devoid of moral content. For example, the deliberateness of the contravention is irrelevant to the deterrence model. Indeed, the injury to others variant of the deterrence model is grounded on the notion that deliberate contraventions of the law are desirable and should occur if their net effect is welfare-enhancing. Because the deterrence model assumes that each actor is rational, all contraventions are assumed to be deliberate. By contrast, the deliberateness of a contravention lies at the core of the concept of culpability, which is fundamental to a determination of the penalties levied in accordance with the desert model. Similarly, the adoption of a compliance program and culture by the offender has no bearing on the calculation of penalties under the deterrence model. If the law is violated, then the offender must pay. All other things being equal, an offender who provides evidence of a culture of compliance should be penalised to the same extent as the offender who sets out deliberately to contravene the law.[148]

Furthermore, the comments of Smithers J in *TPC v Stihl Chain Saws (Aust) Pty Ltd*[149] were quoted by French J with approval, thus implicitly acknowledging that morality and fairness have a legitimate role in determining penalties under s 76:

> The penalty should constitute a real punishment proportionate to the deliberation with which the defendant contravened the provisions of the Act. It should be sufficiently high to have a deterrent quality, and it should be kept in mind that the Act operates in a commercial environment where deterrence of those minded to contravene its provisions is not likely to be achieved by penalties which are not realistic. It should reflect the will of Parliament that the commercial standards laid down in the Act must be observed, but not be so high as to be oppressive.[150]

Accordingly, the Federal Court's overall approach to determining the quantum of penalties under s 76 appears to be guided by a combination of the principles upon

147 See above Part II(E).

148 The other criteria which appear to have no apparent relevance to the economic model are: the nature and extent of the contravening conduct, the circumstances in which the conduct took place, whether the contravention arose out of the conduct of senior management or at a lower level, and whether the company has shown a disposition to cooperate with the authorities responsible for the enforcement of the Act in relation to a contravention. However, note that in Round's study, economists could simply assign economic value to judicial criteria as proxies for economically relevant variables: Round, Siegfried and Baillie, above n 10.

149 [1978] ATPR ¶41-091.

150 *CSR* [1991] ATPR ¶41-076, 52,152.

which the deterrence model and the desert model are founded. In the first instance, the Court claims to be guided by the principle of deterrence, which it defines as requiring penalties to be set sufficiently high so as to deter both the individual offender and those contemplating contraventions of the law in future. On the other hand, the Court has also referred to the importance of penalties being proportionate to the seriousness of the offence, thus indicating that the notion of 'just desert' which underlies the desert model should also guide the Court in determining the quantum of penalty. Some of the criteria which the Court has taken into account in penalty setting can be accommodated within the deterrence model, while other criteria appear to fit much more comfortably within the desert model.

Ultimately, the Court has correctly acknowledged that 'the fixing of the quantum of penalty is not an exact science. It is not done by the application of a formula, and, within a certain range, courts have always recognised that one precise figure cannot be incontestably said to be preferable to another'.[151] In general, the framework of principles which the court has developed to determine the appropriate quantum of penalty strike a reasonable balance between the need to ensure that penalties serve to deter future contraventions, and the need to inculcate into offenders the sense that unlawful conduct is unacceptable and will not be tolerated, while avoiding penalties which would be regarded by society as disproportionate and oppressive.

IV Conclusion

This paper has examined two theoretical models which can be applied to determine the quantum of penalties for regulatory offences: the 'deterrence' model and the 'desert' model. The deterrence model is based on economic efficiency and seeks to 'price' unlawful conduct at a level which will deter firms from engaging in such conduct so as to minimise the social cost of unlawful conduct. Two variants of the deterrence model can be identified. The 'injury to others' model, which aims to deter unlawful conduct to its optimal level, by deterring only unlawful conduct which is net welfare-reducing to society. Thus, the relevant quantum of penalty is measured by the cost of harm to others caused by the offender's wrongful conduct. On the other hand, the 'unlawful gain' model is concerned to achieve 'absolute' deterrence, in order completely to eliminate unlawful conduct, based on the assumption that such conduct is always net welfare-reducing. Thus, the relevant quantum of penalty is measured by the size of the offender's unlawful gain, for by disgorging the offender's ill-gotten gain, the incentive to violate the law is eliminated. By contrast, the 'desert' model regards punishment as a means of censuring offenders for wrongdoing and thus seeks to punish offenders in proportion to the wrongfulness of their unlawful conduct, which is reflected in the seriousness of the unlawful conduct as indicated by the offender's culpability and the extent of the harm thereby caused.

151 *TPC v TNT* [1995] ATPR ¶41-375, 40,165 (Burchett J).

Neither theoretical model is superior to the other. Both have certain strengths and weaknesses. The advantages of the deterrence model are its theoretical capacity to generate a specific quantum of penalty and its recognition of the need to take account of the probability of detection in calculating the penalty. On the other hand, the deterrence model assumes that firms and individuals are solely motivated by rational selfish welfare-maximisation, which may not accurately reflect reality, even in the commercial context. It also generates intractable problems in practice when attempting to quantify variables which are inherently incapable of precise quantification. Its main limitation, however, is its disregard for concepts of fairness and justice, so that penalties determined in accordance with the deterrence model may generate counter-intuitive outcomes which may undermine public confidence in the regulatory system. By contrast, the greatest strength of the desert model is its deliberate concern that penalty levels should be fair. However, its greatest weakness is its imprecision and inability to generate a precise quantum of penalty in any given situation, which can lead to inconsistency and arbitrariness in penalty setting.

Although it may be tempting to suggest that the deterrence model is preferable to the desert model as the basis for quantifying regulatory penalties because regulatory law is primarily concerned with achieving economic and social goals rather than expressing moral outrage at the proscribed conduct, this overlooks the important distinction between liability and penalty. While issues of fairness and morality may have little or no role to play in determining whether certain conduct is unlawful, such notions are inevitably implicated in the process of state penalisation of unlawful conduct. A penalty scheme must not be too out of step with societal notions of fairness and justice, lest it fail to inculcate those who violate the law with a sense of the wrongfulness of their conduct, and lead to an erosion of public confidence in the regulatory system. Accordingly, it is suggested that a fair and effective regulatory penalty regime should combine the essential features of both models: penalties should be set at a level which are sufficiently high to deter future contraventions of the law, provided that any given penalty award is not unfairly disproportionate to the seriousness of the offence.

A review of Australian competition law and the principles emerging from the case law in determining the level of competition law penalties are replete with incantations of the aim of deterrence and the irrelevance of morality, suggesting that the Federal Court adheres to the deterrence model in quantifying penalties. On closer examination however, it appears that both the desert and deterrence models inform the Court's approach to penalty setting, striking a reasonable balance between the need to deter future contraventions of the Act while avoiding oppressive or unfairly disproportionate penalties.

[14]

Compliance-oriented regulation should be understood as a holistic approach to regulatory design, implementation, monitoring, and enforcement in which the guiding principle is the achievement of regulatory outcomes. Compliance-oriented regulation is therefore distinctively concerned with the effects of public regulation in preexistent regulatory space where it must compete with private normative orderings. This article sets out the principles of compliance-oriented regulatory innovation together with evidence on their effectiveness. The widespread implementation of in-house corporate compliance systems in recent years means that compliance-oriented regulators need to be particularly concerned with nurturing compliance capacity among regulatees, fostering regulatory community through compliance professionalism, and developing standards for corporate compliance functions.

REINVENTING REGULATION WITHIN THE CORPORATION
Compliance-Oriented Regulatory Innovation

CHRISTINE PARKER
University of New South Wales

"Compliance"-oriented regulation is now recognized as a major strand of regulatory strategy and policy. Empirical studies have focused on individual tax, environmental, financial, and occupational health and safety officials' reliance on education, persuasion, and cooperation rather than deterrence to persuade businesses to preventively comply with regulatory goals (e.g., J. Braithwaite, 1985; Hawkins, 1984; Hutter, 1997). Regulatory

AUTHOR'S NOTE: *This article is partially based on a report prepared for the October 1998 meeting of the OECD Regulatory Reform Group, Paris, titled "Draft Paper on the State of Regulatory Compliance." This article was also presented at the London School of Economics Regulation seminar series in 1998, in which a number of helpful comments were received. The author wishes to acknowledge the research assistance of Charlotte Heindow and the helpful suggestions and comments of Julia Black, John Braithwaite, Cesar Cordova-Novion, Rex Deighton-Smith, Michael Power, Colin Scott, Lindsay Stirton, and the anonymous referees for* Administration & Society.

ADMINISTRATION & SOCIETY, Vol. 32 No. 5, November 2000 529-565 agencies are experimenting with programs that provide incentives for voluntary implementation of sophisticated compliance systems by business and sanctions for lack of a program (e.g., Feitshans, 1997). The global deregulatory movement is maturing in some countries into a regulatory reform movement that moves beyond the cost-benefit analysis of regulatory impact assessment to principles for "better regulation" (e.g., Better Regulation Taskforce, n.d.; see Organization for Economic Cooperation and Development [OECD], 1997a). In the United States, for example, the "re-inventing regulation" program (Geltman & Skroback, 1998; Nesterczuk, 1996) aims to control "regulatory inflation" by ensuring that the design of regulation and regulatory enforcement strategy meets its goals in an effective and efficient way that maximizes voluntary compliance by business from the beginning. Some governments have even produced comprehensive approaches to encouraging compliance-oriented regulation, and the OECD has produced a report on the issue (see Parker, 1999c).[1] These developments are all consistent with the broader style of the "new regulatory state," which uses enforced self-regulation and incentives for voluntary compliance to steer corporate conduct toward public goals without interfering too greatly with corporate autonomy and profit (Baldwin, 1997; J. Braithwaite, 2000; Grabosky, 1995; Manning, 1987; Parker, 1999a, 1999b).

The orientation of regulators and regulatory policy toward the goal of maximizing business compliance with regulatory objectives rather than seeking out and punishing noncompliance with specific rules is a pervasive topic of debate in regulatory scholarship. However, the different ways in which "compliance" is used in the literature provoke unnecessary confusion based on unclarified meaning. For example, in the debate between Pearce and Tombs (1990, 1991) and Hawkins (1990) in the pages of the *British Journal of Criminology*, there appears to have been controversy over whether Hawkins's descriptions of compliance-oriented regulatory inspection styles were intended to be taken as normative models and whether he was advocating that such strategies should be relied on as a sole enforcement strategy. In this article, I seek to clarify confusion by proposing a holistic understanding of compliance-oriented regulation as a basis for ongoing policy and scholarly debate. Mine is a "pragmatic" approach in the Deweyan sense in which empirically based knowledge is allowed to interact with normative theory (Selznick, 1992, p. 23). I use *empirical* evidence on the nature and success of regulatory innovations and implementation of in-house compliance systems to build a conception of how compliance-oriented regulation *ought* to be understood.

This article defines compliance-oriented regulation not as regulatory policy tied to a particular enforcement strategy but as (a) an outcome-based approach to total regulatory design (from initiation of regulation to enforcement) (b) in which the likely interaction of public regulation with preexisting "regulatory space" to produce compliance or noncompliance with regulatory objectives is a central consideration.

This article uses evidence on a variety of regulatory innovations to show that compliance-oriented regulatory policy must be a holistic process based on choosing strategies by reference to whether they will contribute to the outcome of compliance with regulatory goals. This approach sidesteps the usual distinction drawn between compliance- and deterrence-oriented regulatory regimes and emphasizes that compliance-oriented regulation is more than an issue of enforcement strategy. I also argue that it is through seeking to understand, manipulate, and work with the interaction between public regulation and preexisting regulatory space (see Hancher & Moran, 1989; Scott, 1998; Shearing, 1993) that compliance-oriented regulatory policy makers seek to maximize compliance with regulatory goals. A proper understanding of compliance-oriented regulation therefore involves not just an understanding of regulators' strategy but of market and management orderings, private compliance constituencies and gatekeepers, and internal organizational regulatory systems. In-house corporate compliance systems are currently an important place in which this interaction occurs. The final sections of this article therefore explain how regulatory innovations are encouraging the proliferation of corporate compliance systems and what factors are likely to help make corporate compliance systems effective at accomplishing desirable outcomes.

REGULATORY SPACE AND COMPLIANCE-ORIENTED REGULATION

REGULATORY SPACE

The definitive feature of compliance-oriented regulation is that it is regulation designed to solve a problem on the basis of evidence about what is likely to achieve the regulatory objective. This leads to the recognition that the outcome of pubic regulation is likely to be conditioned by preexisting and potential indigenous normative orderings in the target population including regulatees' capacity to comply, managerial and cultural orderings within organizations, self-regulatory capacities of industry associations, and gatekeeper roles played by third parties including professionals (e.g., auditors, lawyers, safety professionals), standards-setting organizations, insurance companies, rating agencies, and others. The distinctive characteristic of compliance-oriented regulation is that it recognizes that regulated entities already contain or exist within regulatory space (Hancher & Moran, 1989; Scott, 1998; Shearing, 1993). It takes seriously the interaction of public regulation with preexisting regulatory space.

Regulatory space is a metaphor that emphasizes that the state must always compete with other regulatory orderings for social control in any particular circumstance. It recognizes that wherever we look in society, all sorts of formal and informal social controls already exist—family norms, school rules, common business practices, corporate operating procedures, gang subcultures. Public agencies that seek to regulate members of society never issue their regulation onto a blank slate. Rather, it enters a social space in which all sorts of other orderings already "regulate" how people behave. As Shearing (1993) explains it,

> One way of thinking about this is to imagine regulation as taking place in a space in which different regulatory schemes operate simultaneously. The occupants of this space may change but it is never empty. If one set of regulatory influences diminishes this simply changes the relationship between occupants of this space. (p. 72)

This perspective fits in with a broader concern in political theory and policy studies with the role of the contemporary state vis à vis the market and civil society. Thus, a number of scholars have recognized that a unique concern of the contemporary state is to govern by "the devising of forms of regulation which permit and facilitate natural regulation" (Gordon, 1991, p. 19; see also Garland, 1997). The popular U.S. book *Reinventing Government* (Osborne & Gaebler, 1992) picked up this theme in the aphorism that the role of government should be to "steer" not "row." The idea was that government should leverage its resources by facilitating spontaneously occurring activity in markets and civil society to help accomplish public policy objectives. This approach to governance has had a direct impact on regulatory practice and theorizing. In the United States, for example, the "re-inventing regulation" program (Geltman & Skroback; 1998, Nesterczuk, 1996) aims to control regulatory inflation and ensure that the design of regulation and regulatory enforcement strategy meets its goals in an effective and efficient way that maximizes voluntary or natural compliance with policy objectives from the beginning.

A number of scholars predict that the "new" regulatory state (see J. Braithwaite, 2000; Parker, 1999a, 1999b) will turn from being predominantly concerned with compliance with technical rules to a concern with accomplishing substantive compliance with regulatory goals by whatever means is appropriate and feasible including enforced self-regulation, incentive-based regimes, harnessing markets, conferring private rights and liabilities, and relying on third-party accreditation to standards and insurance-based schemes (Baldwin, 1997; Grabosky, 1995; Manning, 1987; Sparrow, 1994). The objective will be to steer corporate conduct toward public policy objectives in the most effective and efficient way rather than fruitless expenditure of government and business resources on traditional styles of regulation that ignore the effects of indigenous regulatory orderings.

COMPLIANCE-ORIENTED REGULATION

In the literature on regulation, the "compliance" approach to regulation is often identified with the use of persuasive and collaborative strategies by regulators to win regulatee's cooperation. For example, Friedrichs (1995, p. 284) distinguishes *compliance*, which uses persuasion and cooperation, from *deterrence*, which involves prosecution and punishment. A body of empirical studies, particularly from Britain, has shown that in practice certain individual tax, environmental, financial, and occupational health and safety officials have often relied on education, persuasion, and cooperation rather than deterrence to persuade businesses to preventively comply with regulatory goals in certain circumstances (e.g., J. Braithwaite, 1985; Hawkins, 1984; Hutter, 1997). As a normative matter, arguments in favor of cooperative and persuasive strategies are based on the assumption that business firms will see that they need to develop a long-term relationship with regulators. The firm may therefore be persuaded to "forgo short-term temptations to cheat on an agency that cannot easily monitor its activities" through techniques such as "negotiating compliance requirements sensitive to the particular characteristics of the firm" and "avoiding unnecessary short-term confrontations" as long as the regulators' long-term goals are being achieved (Scholz, 1994, pp. 425-426). For example, Bardach and Kagan (1982), commentators on U.S. regulation, take the view in their influential *Going by the Book* that "good and bad apples are intermixed in the regulatory population" (p. 66) and that

> the preponderance of regulated enterprises usually are good apples; in these firms, the pressures of the market and the liability of law roughly coincide

> with regulatory goals; citizen complainants and internal corporate compliance staff use the threat of inspectors' visits to push for adherence to regulation; and a relatively small number of well-publicized severe punishments for regulatory noncompliance act as a sufficient deterrent. (p. 162)

Ayres and Braithwaite's (1992) theory of responsive regulation provides a robust game theoretic analysis of the conditions in which such cooperation is likely to succeed. As Scholz (1994) explains, in theory the strength of this strategy is that over time,

> the firm persuades more and more firms to cooperate. The agency can then focus more of its limited prosecutorial resources on the fewer and fewer bad firms, thereby increasing penalties and the incentives of firms to cooperate. Given greater incentives, the agency can insist on higher levels of performance by cooperative firms as the regulation becomes more accepted by the business community. (p. 442; but see Scholz, 1994, p. 443 for a discussion of the limits to this strategy)

Critics sometimes deride compliance-oriented regulatory policies on the grounds that companies will only do "the right thing" to the extent it is in their self-interest to do so. Pearce and Tombs (1990, 1997; Tombs; 1992), for example, argue that because all corporations have profit maximization as their main goal, they will always be "amoral calculators" who only ever comply with regulatory requirements when the penalties are heavy enough to ensure their calculations come up with the correct answer. Incentives for self-regulation, they argue, must therefore be backed up by punitive enough forms of regulation in the public sphere to make sure companies consistently do their sums right. Pearce and Tombs seem to see compliance-oriented regulation as relying solely on incentives for voluntary compliance or a persuasive, educative approach to inspections. But logically, compliance-oriented regulatory design must incorporate monitoring and enforcement of compliance; otherwise, regulators cannot meaningfully and discriminately apply incentives, persuasion, and cooperation to organizations that are complying or attempting in good faith to comply. It is impossible to argue with the logic of Pearce and Tombs's argument that strategies that seek to encourage voluntary compliance should be backed up by more punitive sanctions.

However, this is not a simple matter of abandoning the quest for compliance and switching to deterrent sanctions as soon as persuasion fails. Compliance-oriented regulation is not a matter of substituting persuasion and cooperation for inspections and penalties. It is a holistic approach toward regulation in which mixes of regulatory strategies appeal to the complexity and variety of motivations underlying compliance. The emphasis is on the substantive policy objectives of the regulation and whether the regulatory policy instruments chosen are capable of accomplishing those objectives, not on compliance with rules that may or may not be effective at achieving the desired result. Compliance-oriented regulation, therefore, is a total package in which all the factors of regulatory rule making, monitoring, and enforcement are designed to elicit a particular regulatory objective by defining and analyzing a problem, designing a regulatory solution tailored to the target population, and monitoring and enforcing its implementation. Indeed, the elements of compliance-oriented regulation can be expressed in the following seven principles that clearly incorporate monitoring and enforcement:

1. problem identification and analysis,
2. harness private capacity to secure compliance through alternatives to public regulation,
3. use process or outcome-based regulation where possible to maximize voluntary compliance,
4. rewards and incentives for high/voluntary compliance,
5. informed monitoring for noncompliance,
6. dialogue and restorative justice when voluntary compliance fails, and
7. tit-for-tat enforcement when restorative justice fails.

These principles are interwoven into the discussion that follows. In the following two subsections, I discuss two cornerstones of effective compliance-oriented regulatory innovation. The first is the data collection and analysis processes of problem identification, analysis, and monitoring that is essential to Stages 1 and 5 above. The second is the distinctive enforcement style of principles 6 and 7 of compliance-oriented regulation.

PROBLEM IDENTIFICATION, ANALYSIS, AND MONITORING

Compliance-oriented regulation aims at maximizing the "leverage" of government resources and activities by strengthening the factors working in favor of compliance and by weakening or eliminating those working against. This requires the ability to analyze the various factors that will determine whether regulatory policy instruments can achieve their ultimate objectives in the target population. Compliance considerations should be designed into policy making and regulation from the beginning. Compliance issues cannot just be part of an enforcement strategy tacked on the end. Ex ante compliance analysis ensures that policy makers and regulation drafters consider what policy objectives they actually want to achieve, whether it is feasible to achieve that, and if so the best way to do so. It seeks to avoid reflexive regulation making that accomplishes nothing. Once regulation is in place, ex post compliance analysis helps governments evaluate regulation and determine whether it should be maintained, repealed, or amended by asking whether it is doing the work it is supposed to be doing. If regulation is to be maintained, compliance analysis allows regulators to determine where resources such as information, advice, monitoring, and sanctions should be targeted to achieve the desired policy objectives.

Because regulatory agencies cannot enforce every rule or cover every problem, the use of information and risk analysis to focus on high-priority problems can make an impact on compliance. For example, one dramatic way in which innovative information management combined with risk assessment and prioritization was used to increase compliance outcomes was a U.S. Occupational Safety and Health Administration (OSHA) experiment initiated in 1993 in Maine. The Maine OSHA office used its databases to identify the 200 employers with the highest number of injuries in their area. Each was given work-site-specific injury and illness profiles and then given a choice: Either they could use OSHA's help to survey hazards and correct and implement work-site safety systems or else they would be targeted for more frequent traditional comprehensive inspections because of their risk prioritization. According to OSHA, total workers compensation claims dropped by 35% in those work sites during the program. A total of 182 employers identified 95,800 hazards and abated 55,200 of them (in comparison with the 36,780 that OSHA inspectors had discovered and cited in the previous 8 years at those sites). At least 320 work-site health and safety committees were established. Nearly 60% of employers reduced their injury and illness rates even as fines and inspections diminished (OSHA, 1998; Sparrow, 1996).[2]

Although compliance-oriented regulation requires knowledge of compliance trends so that governments and regulators can identify and prioritize problem areas and evaluate whether regulatory solutions have had the desired effect, most governments find it very difficult to collect aggregate and systematic data on compliance trends. Few governments and regulators have consistently collected compliance rates or assessed the effects of regulatory interventions on social phenomena over time (e.g., environmental results, health effects, decline in injury rates). Reliable data on compliance trends over time are very difficult to collect for a number of reasons. First, existing statistics on regulatory actions such as enforcement and inspections are an inadequate basis for drawing conclusions about compliance trends because compliance rates cannot be derived from a focused or biased inspection program, and almost all current enforcement and/or inspection programs are necessarily focused, biased, or not comprehensive for practical reasons. A second reason that it is difficult to collect reliable data on compliance rates is that regulatory inflation (growth in amount of regulation) and regulatory instability (changes in regulation) make it extremely difficult to draw conclusions about compliance trends over time. Actions or behaviors that were legal at one time become illegal at another so that the compliance goalpost is continuously moving. Perceptions that rates of compliance are decreasing may reflect the fact that the amount or unpredictability of regulation is increasing over time rather than that business is doing less to comply over time. It is possible that business compliance is increasing but that regulation is increasing or changing at an even greater rate, leaving a "compliance lag" that creates the impression (but not necessarily the reality) of less compliance. In other words, in a context of regulatory inflation, the overall rate of compliance can be falling even while the compliance "effort" by regulated enterprises is static or increasing. Third, governments and regulators also face a host of technical problems with measuring regulatory impacts or effects: Impact measures are problem specific and therefore difficult to aggregate into overall compliance trends. Causality is usually impossible to prove and disaggregate from the effects of other factors (such as general economic conditions). The difficulty of measuring things that did not happen makes it particularly difficult to measure the impacts of regulations that prohibit or are aimed at preventing undesirable events.

Just as compliance-oriented regulatory design begins with defining and analyzing the regulatory problem by reference to the external target population, so it must use monitoring to determine whether regulatory design is having its desired effect on the target population. One important way of matching monitoring to compliance-oriented regulatory design is to use the information collected about the regulatory problem to develop a risk-based approach to targeting inspections. Here, regulators are beginning to decide when and where to do inspections by analysis of data on where risks of noncompliance are likely to be highest. Because not all regulated entities can be monitored or inspected all the time, a rational system for deciding which to target when can make a significant difference to compliance. Regulatees can be tiered according to size (number of employees; operating revenues, assets, market share) or other factors (degree of risk, ability to comply, geographic location, level of government funding).

For example, there is evidence that tiering monitoring activities according to size has had significant effects in improving tax compliance. In Uruguay, Bolivia, and Sri Lanka, the percentage of stop-filers among the approximately 1,000 largest taxpayers dropped from 10% to 1% with the establishment of large-taxpayer units during the period from 1987 to 1991. In Argentina, the Two Thousand Taxpayer System or DOS-MIL was established in 1991 to monitor the 900 largest taxpayers in the Buenos Aires metropolitan area. During the period 1990 to 1994, VAT collection rose from 2.1% of GDP to 6.3% of GDP (Silvani & Baer, 1997). A number of British financial regulators have developed quite sophisticated models for tiering regulatory and inspection requirements for financial institutions according to assessments of risk. For example, the Investment Management Regulatory Organisation (IMRO) (a frontline regulator formerly recognized by the Financial Services Authority in England and now superseded by a new regulatory regime) successfully piloted the relative risk assessment model to determine the degree of risk to investors that a firm may generate. The assessment is based on the inherent risks of the products sold or managed by the firm, the capital base of the firm, the experience and ability of the management and staff of the firm, and the attitude of the firm toward investor interest and compliance issues including the standard of the firm's compliance system. Firms were rated on a 3-point scale solely for IMRO use and their rating used to determine how frequently IMRO inspectors would visit firms and how closely they monitored their activities (Fry, 1997, p. 350-351; IMRO, 1997).

COMPLIANCE-ORIENTED REGULATORY ENFORCEMENT

In an unusually rigorous study, Burby and Paterson (1993) compared cooperative enforcement with sanction-oriented enforcement for improving compliance with North Carolina State environmental regulation. Their research shows how deeply interwoven regulatory design and choice of enforcement strategy are in their ultimate effects on compliance. Their study found that

> while deterrence of violations through monitoring and inspections stimulates compliance with both specification and performance standards, building commitment and capacity to obey the law through a cooperative approach to enforcement has much more impact on the degree of compliance attained for performance standards than for specification standards. (p. 754)[3]

In their study, compliance-oriented regulatory design in the form of performance standards was more effectively enforced by cooperative strategies that were in turn backed up by potential application of deterrent sanctions than by the application of deterrent sanctions alone. Where regulatory design was more traditional—specification rules—traditional deterrent enforcement alone was no less effective than adding cooperative enforcement. How then can monitoring and enforcement be designed to be compliance oriented?

Compliance-oriented regulation is aimed at providing incentives and encouragement to voluntary compliance and nurturing the ability for private actors to secure compliance through self-regulation, internal management systems, and market mechanisms where possible rather than automatically using punishment for breaches of the rules as the first regulatory tool (see discussion below). When organizations do fail to comply in the first instance, a compliance-oriented regulatory approach would attempt to restore or nurture compliance rather than reverting immediately to a purely punishment-oriented approach. In criminal process, "restorative justice" requires an offender to confront his or her responsibility for wrongdoing by facing his or her victim/s and together resolving how to put the wrong right (for example, by paying restitution or doing community service). Restorative justice gives the offender a chance to be restored back into full citizenship in the community on remedying the wrong. The aim is not only to provide a better remedy for the victim than imprisonment or a fine would provide but also to help transform the offender into a more law-abiding person in the future. This is often achieved by enlisting the support of members of both the victim's and offender's families and communities to support victim and offender in the restorative process (Cragg, 1992; Galaway & Hudson, 1990; Marshall, 1985; Messmer & Otto, 1992; Van Ness, 1986).

Although the evidence on the effectiveness and fairness of restorative justice for individual offenders is still being evaluated, there is good evidence that restorative justice is an effective approach to corporate law breaking (J. Braithwaite, 1999). One study found that in the United Kingdom, the mines with the best safety records are those that thoroughly include everyone concerned (workers, management) after accidents and near accidents to reach consensual agreement on what must be done to prevent recurrence of the accident or near accident and discuss safety results with workers even when there was no near accident (J. Braithwaite, 1985, p. 67). Another example of the success of restorative justice processes in regulating safety is the self-regulatory Institute of Nuclear Power Operators (INPO), which was set up after the Three Mile Island accident to develop standards, conduct inspections, and investigate accidents. Safety has increased significantly since Three Mile Island across a number of indicators including data that show that scrams (automatic emergency shutdowns) per unit have declined in the United States from seven per unit in 1980 to one in 1993 (Rees, 1994). One of the restorative regulatory mechanisms that has contributed to this success is meetings in which senior nuclear officials from all companies meet together, and three vice presidents give a detailed explanation of a recent accident at their utility and what went wrong:

> More than a detailed explanation of an accident, it also involves "baring your soul and telling all to your peers (people that you know) that you screwed up," explains an INPO official. "You know, I'm not a Catholic, but it's probably like going to confession. In the end you'll feel better, but when you're there it's pretty difficult." . . . Within an ongoing relationship sustained by close ties (whether a family or occupational community), wrongdoing arouses the disapproval of a significant other (whether a parent or professional peer), thus invoking a sense of remorse and repentance in the wrongdoer, which leads to reacceptance (reintegration) by the significant other. Wrongdoing, shame and reintegration—that distilled to its essence, is the family [restorative] model of social control. (Rees, 1994, pp. 106-107)

Makkai and Braithwaite's (1994b) cross-country evaluation of nursing home regulation and inspections has also found significant evidence for the effectiveness of restorative justice mechanisms in controlling organizational wrongdoing. For example, in one part of the study, one dimension of the level of restorative justice used in the postinspection conference held to discuss the inspection findings in 242 Australian nursing home inspections was measured. The levels of compliance found in that inspection and in the next inspection 18 to 24 months later were then compared. Where the inspection team had used restorative justice (i.e., it clearly disapproved breaches of the rules but also terminated disapproval by pointing to something positive or offering praise for moving to fix that which was disapproved), noncompliance was reduced by 39% between the first and second visits. Where inspection teams used purely negative and punitive approaches and did not also offer praise and forgiveness, noncompliance increased by 39%. Where inspection teams were purely tolerant and understanding but did not make clear their disapproval for breaches of the rule, noncompliance either increased or stayed the same.

Like Burby and Paterson's (1993) study that showed how performance-oriented regulatory design, cooperative enforcement strategies, and deterrent sanctions are interwoven, this study shows how a truly compliance-oriented approach combines cooperation, persuasion, and education with strong monitoring and enforcement. Makkai and Braithwaite (1994b) concluded that

> the most stigmatizing inspectors manage to effect significant reductions in the compliance of the nursing homes they inspect. At the same time, tolerant and understanding inspectors who believe in saying nice things at all times are almost equally ineffective because these tolerant, understanding

> inspectors fail to express disapproval when the standards set down in the law are not met. The effective inspectors are those who believe in strong expressions of disapproval combined with strong commitments to burying the hatchet once such robust encounters are over, to terminating disapproval with approval once things are fixed, to tempering disapproval for poor performance on one standard with approval for good performance on other standards, to avoiding humiliation by communicating disapproval of poor performance within a framework of respect for the performer.[4] (p. 379)

Restorative justice must also be backed up by the possibility of more punitive sanctions. Indeed, the evidence shows that persuasive and compliance-oriented enforcement methods are more likely to work where they are backed up by the possibility of more severe methods (J. Braithwaite, 1985; Burby & Paterson, 1993). The idea is that regulators should engage tit for tat in restorative or persuasive enforcement strategies depending on the responses of the regulated entity. A regulator can start with persuasive or restorative strategies and then move to more punitive strategies if voluntary compliance fails. If the application of punitive sanctions succeeds in bringing about compliance, then the regulator can revert to a trusting demeanor. If it does not bring about compliance, then the regulator must invoke harsher sanctions. The wider the range of strategies (from restorative to punitive) available to the regulator, the more successful tit-for-tat enforcement is likely to be.

This principle has been demonstrated theoretically and empirically in Ayres and Braithwaite's (1992) pyramid of enforcement strategies. The pyramid is a schematic representation of the idea that instead of using their most drastic regulatory strategies first, regulators should trade on the goodwill of those they are regulating, encouraging them to comply voluntarily, using more drastic regulatory measures only when that fails and reverting to a trusting demeanor when these strategies achieve their goal: "Compliance is optimised by regulation that is contingently cooperative, tough and forgiving" (p. 51). In this model, prioritizing restorative, compliance-oriented means of regulation in time ensures that cooperative, voluntary measures are used more frequently without compromising the possibility of using harsher measures where necessary.

COMPLIANCE-ORIENTED REGULATORY DESIGN

Compliance-oriented regulation begins with rigorous identification and analysis of the facts of the problem to be regulated and faces noncompliance with enforcement mechanisms aimed at nurturing and restoring compliance. In between these phases, Stages 2, 3, and 4 above describe the principles of compliance-oriented regulatory design. Compliance-oriented regulation seeks to take account of the fact that state regulation is not the only player in regulatory space by seeking to coopt or even create private regulatory institutions and to push responsibility for achieving regulatory objectives onto nonstate actors through (Stage 2) harnessing private capacity to secure compliance with regulatory goals, (Stage 3) using process and outcome-based regulation to encourage compliance, and (Stage 4) using rewards and incentives for high/voluntary compliance.

HARNESS PRIVATE CAPACITY TO SECURE COMPLIANCE WITH REGULATORY GOALS

The first principle of compliance-oriented regulatory design is to attempt to harness private capacity to secure compliance with regulatory goals through (a) codes of conduct and self-regulation, (b) voluntary agreements between government and industry, (c) industry standards and internal management systems, and (d) economic instruments and market mechanisms (see Grabosky, 1995). This approach recognizes that compliance with regulatory goals is more likely to be achieved if regulatory design works with preexistent regulatory systems or is able to foster the development of such systems.

The most basic self-regulatory schemes involve voluntary compliance with a code of conduct that includes some dispute resolution arrangement. There is little systematic evidence on the effectiveness of self-regulatory schemes, although many individual schemes have been shown to have failed (e.g., Jeffcott & Yanz, 1998; Pearce & Tombs, 1990). The British Office of Fair Trading (OFT) (1998) has recently reevaluated its scheme for encouraging voluntary codes of conduct on the basis that "successive monitoring exercises revealed patchy levels of compliance and fairly widespread ignorance or apathy among traders and the public alike" (p. 13). However, there is evidence that some self-regulatory schemes have been effective at improving regulatory goals: One is the Chemical Industry Association's Responsible Care scheme, which started with the Canadian Chemical Producers' Association and now operates in 41 countries and reaches around 88% of the global chemical industry (OECD, 1997b, pp. 13-20). Since 1987, the U.S. chemical industry claims to have used Responsible Care to reduce releases of toxic chemicals to the environment by 49%, reduced disposal in deep wells by 46%, and reduced off-site transfer for treatment and disposal by 56% (Gunningham, 1998).

It seems likely that self-regulatory schemes work best when there is strong governmental and community interest in checking that they are working well coupled with the potential threat of regulation, as in the Responsible Care scheme, and where self-regulatory design includes a fair and efficient dispute resolution system involving an external or independent ombuds office.

The use of voluntary agreements with individual companies or industry associations gives government a greater capacity to be involved in consultation, participation, and partnership with private bodies than self-regulation does. Globally, voluntary agreements are being extensively used to avoid the need for restrictive regulation and legislation in controlling greenhouse gas emissions. In this area, voluntary agreements are an attractive means of discharging international obligations to reduce emissions without imposing politically unpalatable regulation or carbon taxes. In Norway, for example, 325 companies are participating in such programs in 12 trade groups covering 80% of energy used in industry (Jutsen, 1995). Despite Australia's recent recalcitrance over greenhouse gas emissions targets in the international arena, in 1995-1996 the threat of a carbon tax under a previous government was real enough for industry associations to initiate the idea of the Greenhouse Challenge Program. More than 100 members, including approximately 80% of enterprises in the electricity business, are now implementing plans to reduce greenhouse gas emissions that will be audited by government. Their combined commitments would enable year 2000 emissions from these companies to stabilize at or below 1995 levels, which means a reduction of 16% from the "no action" level. The first annual reports that have been received confirm that this target is on track to be achieved (Greenhouse Challenge Office, 1997). Voluntary agreements seem to work well when there is potential for government and industry to agree on what needs to be done, and it is basically in industry interest to comply if government offers some quid pro quo for doing so, such as technical advice and assistance in the case of the Australian Greenhouse Challenge Program.

Third, governments can enlist the support of internal corporate management to achieve regulatory goals (safer workplaces, less pollution, consumer understanding of products, etc.) in a way that is consistent with their own individual business goals through encouraging the adoption of industry standards and internal management systems that embody regulatory goals. For example, the OFT (1998) has recently raised the possibility of replacing its endorsement of certain industry codes of conduct with industry standards for fair practice. The European Commission is also encouraging companies to improve environmental outcomes by voluntary participation in an eco-audit scheme via an eco-audit logo and accreditation of environmental auditors, standards for environmental management systems, and environmental statements published by companies (Aalders, 1993). A number of studies, particularly in the environmental area, have purported to show that the implementation of environmental management systems can produce outcomes that are good for the environment and good for business (e.g., Elliott, 1998, p. 128; McInerney & White, 1995; Schmidheiny, 1992; but cf. Beder, 1997, p. 130). However, the evidence suggests that implementation of internal management standards that ensure compliance with regulatory goals is likely to be patchy and weak (see Table 1 and discussion below) unless government backs them up with some sanction or incentive for implementation.

For example, since 1988 the Netherlands government has been attempting to stimulate the development and adoption of Internal Company Environmental Management systems (ICEMs), which would include internal monitoring, environmental reporting, and auditing. By 1995, only 35 companies had implemented ICEM on the basis of BS 7750 (the standard designed by the British Standards Institute) as determined by recognized and validated auditing bureaus. The government's target had been 10,000 by 1995. However, there has been some success in linking ICEM implementation with environmental permits. Companies with ICEMs of a high enough standard are entitled to obtain a more flexible environmental permit that allows them a greater degree of self-regulation and more lenient enforcement policies. An evaluation of 16 companies that had either established a link between their ICEM and their environmental permit under the Environmental Management Act of 1993 or were in the process of doing so found that in 10 of the 16 companies the link proved to be a success. The others failed because the firm asked for more flexibility than allowed or because the government eventually opted for a stricter permit (Aalders, 1993; Aalders & Wilthagen, 1997).

A fourth way in which governments can harness private capacities to achieve regulatory goals is through market incentives such as the application of taxes, charges, subsidies, user pricing, or refund schemes to internalize externalities; or through limiting the ability of organizations to engage in an undesirable activity and making the right to do it tradable in the marketplace through tradable permits. There has been little experience to gauge the success of economic instruments in increasing achievement of regulatory goals, and measurements of their success remain difficult and controversial (Crandall, Rueter, & Steger, 1996; Levin, 1985). Where

TABLE 1

Summary of Studies on Implementation of Corporate Compliance Programs

Author and Year	*Country*	*Sample*	*Response Rate*	*Findings*
Ward/Price Waterhouse (1997)	United States	5,000 companies	262	86% had a formal compliance policy; 9% were developing a policy; 5% had no policy. The top eight areas covered by compliance programs were the following: ethics, conflicts of interest, and gifts (86%); employment/labor law (75%); antitrust, trade regulation, and procurement (68%); environmental, health, and safety (65%); lobbying, government relations, and political contributions (60%); securities law (55%); intellectual property (52%); international business practices (46%).
Weinberger (1990)	United States	27 Missouri-based top 1,000 U.S. companies	74%	70% had implemented formal policy re insider trading
V. Braithwaite (1993)	Australia	All companies reporting to Affirmative Action Agency	100%	86% issued affirmative action policy to all staff; 70% set objectives for affirmative action progress for year ending 1990.

(Continued)

TABLE 1 Continued

Author and Year	*Country*	*Sample*	*Response Rate*	*Findings*
Still (1997)	Australia	Top 75 financial institutions reporting to Affirmative Action Agency	100%	87% of management actively promotes workplace free of sexual harassment; 81% formal procedures in place to deal with complaints of sexual harassment.
Shwartz (1998)	Canada	Not reported	Not reported	65% had explicit compliance standards and procedures in place; 63% had produced publications that communicated these standards and procedures to staff and management; 58% had assigned responsibility to high-level personnel to oversee compliance; 54% periodically reviewed or audited compliance program; 47% monitored systems to detect misconduct; 44% used training programs to communicate standards and procedures to staff; 41% had mechanisms to enforce compliance procedures; 38% had systems whereby employees could report misconduct without fear of retribution.
Andersen (1996)	Norway	100 top corporate managers	100%	31% strongly engaged in environmental, health, and safety (EHS) work; 37% medium to strongly engaged in EHS work; 32% not interested in implementing EHS actions; 29% companies with sales up to 10 million NOK had no knowledge of requirement for EHS system; 6% companies with sales of more than 100 million NOK had no knowledge of requirement for EHS system.

they have been used, they have been very complex, and their success remains dependent on government monitoring and enforcement of compliance with permit conditions.

PROCESS AND OUTCOME-BASED REGULATION

Where it is not possible to harness private alternatives to public regulation, compliance-oriented regulation maximizes the possibility for voluntary compliance in the design of government-mandated rules. One way in which voluntary compliance might be increased is through using regulation to mandate the policy goal itself via broad outcome standards instead of prescribing technical rules or procedures that might be expected to result in the achievement of the goal. By focusing on results (outcomes) rather than on the means for achieving them (inputs), standards permit each regulated entity greater freedom of action to find the lowest cost or best means of complying for itself and can therefore increase compliance and innovation. The disadvantages of such an approach are that there may be uncertainty regarding what constitutes acceptable compliance, it may favor larger firms with a greater capacity to innovate over smaller firms, and it may be difficult for regulators to monitor and enforce compliance with broader standards.

There is some evidence that broad outcome-based standards are actually easier to apply, monitor, and enforce than many specific rules, especially if they have been developed in a process of dialogue and consultation between regulator and regulatee. For example, U.S. nursing homes must meet more than 500 federal standards in addition to a multitude of state standards to demonstrate they reach an appropriate level of care. By contrast, in Australia there are only 31 broad outcome-oriented standards for nursing homes that were settled consensually between industry and major stakeholders. A myriad of U.S. rules about treatments, dressings, and recording of pain problems in care plans are replaced by a single "freedom from pain" standard. Braithwaite and Braithwaite's (1995) research on the implementation of the two sets of rules showed that it is the broad Australian standards that are more reliably rated by inspector teams than the narrow and specific U.S. rules. Australian inspection teams can discuss all the standards with each other, ensure that they have collected evidence on positives and negatives for each nursing home relevant to compliance with each standard, and discuss both positives and negatives of each standard with the nursing home staff. They can also use the outcome-based standards to talk to residents and staff about how quality of care could be improved, and, as a result, agreed action plans to restore residents' rights to quality of care were overwhelmingly implemented. Braithwaite and Braithwaite concluded that the quality of care and compliance with the law had improved in Australia with the introduction of the 31 outcome standards. In contrast, U.S. inspection teams can only tag several standards that have not been met to raise problems. As a result, they concentrate on discussing the unmet standards.

Some innovative regulatory regimes require firms to introduce a management system aimed at achieving a desired regulatory outcome without setting any specific rules for what firms are required to do. This can produce behavior designed to prevent problems before they occur and place firms in more direct control of firm-specific hazard reduction rather than one-size-fits-all solutions worked out by government agencies. For example, process regulations are often based on requiring organizations to take a systematic approach to identifying, controlling, and minimizing risks. For example, there is a movement in both occupational health and safety and food regulation toward requiring firms to engage in their own process of hazard identification, risk assessment, and risk control to achieve safety outcomes. "HACCP" principles are being recognized internationally as a way of minimizing food adulteration risks (OECD, 1997b, pp. 41-51).

The advantages of process regulations include that they give firms the opportunity to incorporate regulatory goals into other business goals and operating procedures, and their flexibility may make controversial regulation more politically palatable. For example, Australia's affirmative action regime fits in with business goals of good human resource management rather than imposing particular targets for equal employment. In 1986, the Australian Affirmative Action (Equal Employment Opportunity for Women) Act of 1986 (Cth) was passed mandating all companies with more than 100 employees to develop an equal employment opportunity (EEO) policy, set objectives, monitor them, and submit a report on their progress to the federal Affirmative Action Agency each year. An evaluation of compliance with the Affirmative Action Act found that 96% of those businesses registered with the Affirmative Action Agency had submitted a report to the agency as required by the act (V. Braithwaite, 1993). Commitment to the business goal of human resources management correlated highly with both procedural compliance with the eight steps and the more substantive compliance measure of reported implementation of practices that actually accommodated women in the workplace. This suggests that regulatory design can increase the potential for compliance by fitting in with management goals (V. Braithwaite, 1993). Other research has shown that women's managerial representation has increased at a significantly higher rate in firms covered by the legislation than in those that are not and that affirmative action programs in general have steadily improved since the regime was introduced (Affirmative Action Agency, 1998, p. 22).

However, broad outcome-based standards are not always the most effective form of regulation. For example, international regulators of intentional oil pollution at sea found that setting an outcome standard (that no less than a certain amount of oil could be discharged) was a complete failure in compliance terms. Instead, what worked was an international regime that mandated a certain type of technology for the design of ship ballasts that made intentional oil pollution much more difficult (Mitchell, 1994, p. 171ff). Although regulators are often criticized for mandating a particular technology rather than allowing business to reach the same outcome by whatever means suits them, in this case monitoring implementation of the technology was much easier than monitoring oil pollution at sea. Ship builders and classification societies accepted the new regime and acted as third-party enforcers, or gatekeepers, by not building and not insuring ships without the mandated technology (segregated ballast tanks). Thus, the regulatory regime created obstacles to noncompliance in the first place using deterrence as a backup and relied on nonstate actors, on whom the operators are dependent and who have no economic interest in avoiding the costs of regulation, to monitor compliance. These processes were reinforced by also requiring flag states or classification societies nominated by them to inspect tankers for required equipment during construction or retrofitting plus regular inspections afterward, a system that piggybacked on the existing inspection system used by classification societies.

REWARDS AND INCENTIVES FOR HIGH/VOLUNTARY COMPLIANCE

The third principle of compliance-oriented regulatory design is to formulate rules and, particularly, monitoring and enforcement regimes to encourage compliance by providing incentives or rewards for high voluntary compliance and compliance innovations. Rewards for particularly high compliance can include a reduced burden of routine inspections, penalty discounts for minor incidents of noncompliance that do occur, simplified licenses and permits, permission to use a label or mark certifying a high level of compliance, and indemnities for voluntary disclosure and correction of nonfraudulent noncompliance. Rewards and incentives for a generally high compliance performance can recognize the good-faith efforts of enterprises that usually comply but occasionally inadvertently breach regulation. For example, providing a penalty reduction when noncompliance does occur, or an indemnity if the enterprise reports and corrects the violation, avoids a situation in which the regulator must take "unreasonable" enforcement action against a basically compliant enterprise.

Appropriate government and public recognition can encourage well-intentioned enterprises to become "compliance leaders." This provides models for other enterprises to follow and can pull up overall compliance performance in a market sector through dynamics of market leadership. In particular, rewards for "compliance leaders" who meet certain standards can help meet desired policy outcomes voluntarily (for example, an improvement in air quality via greater emissions reduction) without having to use unreasonable coercion with all regulated entities. Governments can also use rewards and incentives to encourage a small group of compliance leaders to enter experimental programs for new regulatory approaches (such as moving from rule-based to standard- or process-based regulation). In this way, the enterprises receive rewards for high compliance with policy objectives under the experimental regime, and governments learn from them how to practically reform existing regulatory approaches and what is feasible to expect of business. Many of the compliance innovations described in this article were first introduced to a small group of enterprises in this way. However, rewards and incentives are suitable mainly only for enterprises that are compliance leaders. They are therefore not an adequate regulatory strategy on their own because compliance laggards and enterprises that act in bad faith will still require traditional enforcement and punitive sanctions. In most situations, when using rewards and incentives, regulators must also be careful that the requirements enterprises must meet to qualify for rewards be kept relevant and move up as overall compliance performance in an industry sector moves up.

One well-established example of how rewards and incentives can improve socially desirable outcome is OSHA's Voluntary Protection Program (VPP). Under this program, OSHA recognizes outstanding achievement by companies that successfully integrate a comprehensive safety and health program into their total management system. The program was adopted by OSHA in 1982 and now covers about 214,000 employees at

370 sites throughout the United States. Applicants to VPP must demonstrate in writing that their occupational safety and health compliance program includes management commitment and employee involvement, work-site-based job hazard analysis including baseline surveys of working conditions throughout the facility, hazard prevention and control, and safety and health training. The process also requires follow-up using annual program evaluations, verified by OSHA on-site every 1 to 5 years. Employers with exceptional programs receive special recognition including the lowest priority for enforcement inspections, the highest priority for assistance, appropriate regulatory relief, and penalty reductions of up to 100%. For other firms, a sliding scale of incentives is offered. In 1991, of the 178 companies in the program, 9 sites had no injuries at all. Overall, VPP sites' injury incidence rates were 55% below expected average for similar industries. Thirty-one had no lost workday injuries, and overall the companies were 51% below expected lost workday injuries in similar industries. Many sites boasted production improvements, reduced absenteeism, and lower workers' compensation costs (Feitshans, 1997).

Another way that regulatory design can provide incentives for high voluntary compliance is by providing that the existence of an effective compliance system will provide companies or individuals with a reduction of penalty if they are found to have breached the law. The most significant development of this kind is the U.S. *Federal Sentencing Guidelines* for organizations (see Gruner, 1994). These guidelines were promulgated by the U.S. Sentencing Commission (USSC) (a judicial agency) and went into effect in absence of congressional action. Companies with good compliance programs (defined by certain elements in the guidelines) are given decreased fines when they commit an offense. Those that do not have a compliance program in place are placed on probation and required to implement one. This has spread to many other regulators who are now willing to not prosecute at all if an enterprise can show it has a program in place that meets the USSC guidelines. The guidelines have had a significant impact on the implementation of compliance policies among U.S. companies generally (irrespective of whether they have had any contact with a regulator): Surveys have found that up to 20% of companies surveyed introduced an internal system for ensuring regulatory compliance for the first time because of the guidelines and up to 45% added vigor to their internal compliance system because of the guidelines (Harvard Law Review, 1996, p. 1787; Price Waterhouse, 1997).

IN-HOUSE COMPLIANCE SYSTEMS AND REGULATORY INNOVATION

IN-HOUSE COMPLIANCE SYSTEMS

Compliance-oriented regulation is aimed as much at reinventing regulation within private regulatory space, such as corporations, as at reforming external regulatory agencies. Compliance-oriented regulatory strategies attempt to penetrate right inside businesses to transform and harness management systems, operational processes, and organizational cultures to regulatory goals. Each of the compliance-oriented regulatory innovations described above will tend to encourage the proliferation of in-house corporate compliance systems as a means of companies taking responsibility for in-house self-regulation to meet regulated outcome standards, implement codes of conduct and management standards, respond to rewards and incentives, or fulfill undertakings to implement a compliance assurance system after a breach has occurred. Internal corporate compliance systems, then, will be one of the important formal functions where the interaction between external regulation and internal management systems occurs. Because of its monopoly on legitimate coercion (i.e., legal and regulatory sanctions), the state can have a great impact in the regulatory space inside companies. But the precise nature of the impact is not controllable because of the complex ways in which state regulation interacts with preexisting orderings. To understand compliance-oriented regulation, it is important to look not just at strategies used by external regulators but at the internal workings of the company, the ethics and professionalism of internal compliance constituencies, and the way they interact with management as well as external regulators.

Organizational actors are already voluntarily implementing compliance programs as a response to perceived risks of legal liability, major ethical breaches, and other adverse publicity outcomes. For example, in the United States, a 1996 Price Waterhouse survey of corporate compliance practices in 262 large companies found that 86% had a formal compliance policy, 9% were developing a policy, and only 5% had no policy (Ward, 1997). In Canada, a 1998 KPMG survey of corporate compliance practices found that 65% of Canada's largest companies had explicit compliance standards and procedures in place. A total of 63% had produced publications that communicated these standards and procedures to staff and management, and 58% had assigned responsibility to high-level personnel to oversee compliance (Schwartz, 1998). Table 1 summarizes the quantitative evidence available on the implementation of corporate compliance programs. The evidence suggests that corporate compliance programs are strongest in the areas of environmental, occupational health and safety, and financial services regulation (see, e.g., Aalders & Wilthagen, 1997, p. 421; Andersen, 1996; Genn, 1993). EEO and affirmative action compliance policies are also widely implemented but to a lesser extent. The evidence also shows that corporate compliance systems are much more likely to be implemented by large enterprises than small and medium-sized enterprises (SMEs).

The implementation of corporate compliance programs does not of itself necessarily represent an increase in compliance or in optimal regulatory outcomes. Indeed, it is possible that corporate compliance systems are a response to unnecessarily complex laws and high risks of private liability and bad publicity. But on the whole, the growth in adoption of corporate compliance programs illustrates a widespread acceptance among big business of the need to be seen to be responsive to, and ensure compliance with, reasonable regulatory requirements and social pressures. From the regulator's point of view, at least three factors will affect the success of these regulatory interactions within the organization: regulators' ability to nurture compliance capacity in business, the emergence of compliance professionals to act as mediators between regulators and organizations, and the development of meta-standards for internal corporate controls that help ensure the effectiveness of compliance constituencies within the organization. (Clearly, research from the point of view of corporate mangers and employees will also be helpful in understanding the impact of compliance-oriented regulation; see Parker, 1999a, 1999b.)

ABILITY TO NURTURE COMPLIANCE CAPACITY

Strategic compliance-oriented regulatory design and enforcement does not necessarily reach an audience equipped to understand or effectively respond with compliance to regulatory objectives. Innovative regulatory strategies for encouraging compliance are not likely to be effective if organizations have no capacity or expertise in how to comply with regulation. Indeed, Heimer's (1996) study of the impact of law inside neonatal intensive care units shows that

> many organisations are organized anarchies, functioning much like garbage cans into which a variety of elements are tossed. . . . Rather than decisions being made in the "rational" way that organisation charts would suggest they are . . . , decisions instead result from the episodic coupling of key

> elements that co-exist semi-autonomously in organisations. Which decisions get made depends on what participants happen to be there at the time, what is identified as a problem needing a solution, what solutions are available in the organization, and consensus that a choice point has arrived and it is time to make a decision. (p. 44)

Indeed, one of the main advantages of implementation of a compliance system from a corporate management point of view is that it will improve controls, efficiency, and the rationality of certain processes within the organization. Studies of organizational decision making and ethics have shown that organizational processes often tend to result in decisions in which the group decides on action that is more risky and unethical than any one of them individually would have chosen and that people often remain committed to group policies even when they are obviously working badly and have unintended consequences (Sims, 1994, p. 50; also see Gioia, 1992). Compliance-oriented regulatory strategy should foster "ethical intelligence" within organizational processes. Therefore, one of the more strategic things regulators can do to increase compliance is to nurture organizational capacity to comply through education, assistance, offering consultancy services, and encouraging the growth of compliance professionals with specialist expertise in the area.

SMEs are often particularly low in compliance often because they lack capacity (such as specialized staff) to comply. Assistance targeted at SMEs may therefore bear fruit. For example, OSHA's Consultation program is a broad network of occupational safety and health services that provide a free source of information and technical assistance targeted at SME employers (those with no more than 250 employees) who request help in establishing and maintaining a safe and healthful workplace. The comprehensive assistance available includes an appraisal of all mechanical systems, physical work practices, and environmental hazards of workplaces and all aspects of employer's present job safety and health programs. According to OSHA, the consultation program has helped identify and control more than 500,000 workplace safety and health hazards. The program is popular with SMEs because of the government's willingness to pay for expert services that would otherwise cost thousands of dollars. The consultation program is also completely separate from OSHA's inspection program, and the consultant pledges confidentiality provided the employer agrees to correct in a timely manner any serious hazards uncovered during the consultation visit. In an independent survey conducted for OSHA in 1995, employers who had received onsite consultation visits indicated very high levels of satisfaction with the service provided (Weinberg, 1996).

REGULATORY COMMUNITY AND COMPLIANCE PROFESSIONALISM

For targeted monitoring and enforcement, incentives for voluntary compliance, and voluntary agreements to be effective, there must be a meaningful avenue of engagement between regulator and regulatee; there must be some medium through which information can flow and dialogue can occur. Regulators must receive information about whether compliance programs put in place to stave off more harsh sanctions are effective and in line with legal standards. Regulatees must understand what regulators and communities require and why regulators have taken particular strategic enforcement decisions. They must have enough in common to understand when escalation up the pyramid will fit regulatory goals and when escalation is not necessary. Indeed, compliance-oriented regulation generally relies on the assumption that regulatory messages are communicated into a world of shared bonds and shared understandings in which companies can effectively respond to regulatory signals, and the parties deliberate effectively about their responses to them, which, in turn, creates shared commitments to regulatory goals. Regulators and regulatees need to be part of the same "community" to have continuing relationships and the same basic understanding of the meanings and goals of regulatory action (see Ayres & Braithwaite, 1992; Black, 1997, pp. 30-38; Meidinger, 1987, p. 365).

An emerging compliance profession can act as a medium of regulatory community if regulators are willing to engage with them and can also act as a pool of compliance expertise that can be translated into corporate compliance capacity. The expansion of compliance and risk management programs in corporations has opened a new professional jurisdiction in which practitioners who identify themselves as "compliance professionals" is emerging. The new occupation spans nonlawyers including human resource managers, auditors, ex-lawyers who now see themselves as compliance managers, and lawyers who specialize in compliance issues. The emergence of the new occupation is evident in a sprinkling of new professional associations and institutions that cater to their interests and concerns: the U.S. Ethics Officers Association, which was formed in 1992 and had grown from 30 to more than 500 members by 1998 (Driscoll,

Hoffman, & Murphy, 1998, p. 49; Driscoll, Hoffman, & Petry, 1995, p. 117); the compliance section of the Practising Law Institute; and the Association of Compliance Professionals for Australia (which has grown to approximately 400 members since it was established in mid-1996; Parker, 1999a). Particular areas of regulation, in which there is a history of significant regulation, have also encouraged the growth of specialist groups of compliance professionals. The Society of Consumer Affairs Professionals in Business in the United States, Australia, and Europe was set up to provide professional culture, support, and knowledge for people employed by organizations to handle consumer complaints. The Regulatory Affairs Professionals Society in the pharmaceutical industry with 4,000 members worldwide is another example of such an organization. The expansion of civil rights into the workplace has led to the creation of a whole group of human resources professionals who specialize in occupational health and safety, affirmative action, and EEO compliance (V. Braithwaite, 1992; Edelman, Erlanger, & Lande, 1993, p. 501; Parker, 1999b). Occupational health and safety regulation has also generated a professional safety engineering movement in manufacturing and mining workplaces (Rees, 1988, p. 228). Most banks and securities trading firms now have compliance divisions that are distinct from their legal departments. Compliance officers in the U.S. securities industry began to meet as early as the 1960s, with their 1996 conference having more than 2,200 participants (McCaffrey & Hart, 1998). In Britain, the introduction of a new regulatory system under the 1986 Financial Services Act encouraged most firms carrying on investment business to introduce a devoted compliance function (Weait, 1994, p. 381): The Compliance Institute and Securities Houses Compliance Officers Group were both established as professional associations for compliance managers in the finance and banking area and now have a combined membership of more than 1,000.

Some empirical evidence shows that flexible compliance-oriented programs are more likely to succeed where the regulated community includes compliance professionals who can act as a go-between for regulator and business so that business understands how to comply with regulatory goals and can communicate ideas for more innovative and flexible regulatory mechanisms back to regulators. Rees's (1988) evaluation of the Californian branch of OSHA experiment with the Cooperative Compliance Program between 1979 and 1984 found that the growth of safety management professionalism was crucial to compliance with regulatory goals. The program authorized labor-management safety committees on seven large construction sites to assume many of OSHA's regulatory responsibilities (such as conducting inspections and investigating complaints), whereas OSHA ceased routine compliance inspections and pursued a more cooperative relationship with these companies. During the program, accident rates ranged from one third lower to five times lower than comparable company projects, and the satisfaction of workers, management, and government participants with the program was high. The evaluation found that this approach succeeded mainly because it strengthened the preexistent job-site safety programs in ways that traditional regulatory strategies could not. The voluntary job-site safety programs in turn had been promoted and implemented by safety management professionals, a professional specialization promoted by the American Society of Safety Engineers. The existence of safety management professionals within the companies also allowed the labor-management and regulator-management communication necessary for the program to succeed.

An evaluation of compliance with the Australian affirmative action regime found that the degree of professionalism of EEO officers, especially their professional networking with other EEO professionals and with the EEO agency, was positively correlated with procedural and substantive compliance with the requirements of the regulation (V. Braithwaite, 1992). Similarly, in another study of corporate compliance with U.S. civil rights laws, Edelman (1990) found that an important source of diffusion of due process protections was the professionalized practices of personnel officers and the establishment of personnel departments that saw compliance as part of their professional function and therefore provided a direct channel through which models of employee rights implementation could enter the organization and created an internal constituency for the elaboration and enforcement of employee rights. McCaffrey and Faerman (1994) conclude from their study of self-regulation in the U.S. securities industry that the institutionalization of regulatory occupations within industry (in this case, financial compliance officers) is one of the main conditions in which self or "shared" regulation is most likely to be effective so long as the law strengthens the position of the compliance staff. In a completely different situation involving hospital neonatal intensive care units, Heimer (1996 p. 37) concludes that the law's shadow is likely to be "densest" within organizations when "the law's shadow largely coincides with the shadow cast by professional bodies." She goes on to argue that "professions are simultaneously the organisational participants responsible for altering the scripts or routines of organisations and the carriers of legitimacy." They legitimize organizations by acting as "sentinels" tracking the organization's external environment, including legal and regulatory messages, and adapting organizational systems to respond to those messages appropriately.

STANDARDS FOR COMPLIANCE PROGRAMS AND CORPORATE STRUCTURES

Finally, regulators and regulatees must share some common standards for voluntary compliance. Edelman's work on corporate EEO polices suggests that many companies will be highly motivated to preserve legitimacy by responding to external norms and setting up compliance programs, but these will not necessarily reflect legal norms in substance (Edelman et al., 1993). Regulators therefore need to develop some standards for compliance systems and internal corporate structures and monitor the compliance programs and functions that are being put in place; otherwise, compliance will be a sham.

One of the most significant factors influencing the effectiveness of a compliance program is whether the officer responsible for its implementation holds sufficient formal or informal clout within the organization to ensure that compliance policies are followed and ferret out breaches (J. Braithwaite & Murphy, 1993). For example, one study of the internal compliance systems of the five American coal-mining companies with the lowest accident rates for the industry showed that one of the factors they had in common was that they gave a lot of informal clout and top management backing to their safety inspectors (J. Braithwaite, 1985, p. 65). At the most basic level, this means being appointed at a senior enough level to earn respect within the hierarchical structure of the corporation. But even where formal clout is lacking or is not sufficient, savvy compliance officers find ways to appropriate clout. Clearly, the best way to achieve clout is through the direct support of the senior management, preferably the managing director himself or herself. As McCaffrey and Hart (1998) conclude from their study of internal compliance systems on Wall Street,

> anyone who looks at broker-dealer firms in any detail will be struck by how internal politics and managerial styles produce regulatory differences across them. Those working in legal and compliance offices have professional and personal stakes in being taken seriously within the firm. How successful they are in this depends on how three issues are handled. First, how well do they convince enough powerful actors in the firm that legal and compliance "adds value" to it? Second, do they establish a reputation as competent, reasonable, and respectable "insiders"? Third, how strongly does upper management support them and internal controls generally? (p. 157)

In leading corporate compliance systems, the chief compliance manager reports directly to the board or a board audit or compliance committee.

In at least one Australian company, the chief compliance manager shares the same protection in employment as the chief financial officer: The compliance manager cannot be fired or even resign voluntarily without the matter going to a meeting of the board in which directors can satisfy themselves that the firing or resignation is not occurring for the wrong reasons. Similarly, in that company the chief compliance manager must report to the board the circumstances in which any of his or her staff resign or are fired from their compliance positions.[5]

If the effectiveness of compliance officers depends on certain structural conditions within the corporation such as seniority, independence, and appropriate reporting relationships, then for compliance-oriented regulation, issues of corporate constitutionalism will be fundamental. Ensuring that a variety of different constituencies within the corporation have a voice should be an important priority because the new regulation has to rely on the ability of internal constituencies to reform corporate cultures from within. Just as various conventions have grown up to protect the independence of auditors and general counsel, so should the place of other constituencies within the corporation that might hold it to important public values be protected. This means that it is important to institutionalize, indeed constitutionalize, the compliance function through the role of general counsel, the Board Audit Committee, compliance committees, and other checks and balances. For example, in Australia the 1998 Managed Investments Act requires Australian funds managers to implement a compliance program and a compliance committee that is responsible for it. Compliance scholars could therefore connect with progressive corporate law scholarship on the democratic reform of corporate structures beyond the shareholders (see, e.g., Bottomley, 1997, 1999; Chayes, 1960).

CONCLUSION

I have argued here that compliance-oriented regulation is concerned with an outcome defined by regulatory objectives. "Compliance" has been taken to mean compliance with a regulatory goal, not compliance with a set of technical rules. As Shearing (1993) writes, "policy makers should be very wary of an approach that regards compliance with rules whether achieved through cooperation or coercion as hallmarks of sound regulatory practices. Regulatory policy should be goal rather than rule oriented" (p. 75). The paradox for business is that in one sense, compliance with a broad regulatory objective is much harder than even the toughest set of rules imposing the greatest paperwork burden because it requires thorough internalized commitment to showing regulatory responsibility in changing circumstances, not just ticking off a set of boxes. Similarly, for the regulator there is a paradox. Compliance-oriented regulation can seem weaker, perhaps less expensive, and certainly less aggressive than other styles of regulation. In fact, a truly compliance-oriented approach to regulation would include defining objectives, tailored rule design and implementation, targeted monitoring, and restoration and enforcement of compliance. It intrudes into private normative orderings in all its phases and requires understanding of and engagement with the intimate details of regulatees' characteristics, attitudes, and operations. Such a holistic-tailored approach is likely to be neither easy, cheap, nor, if effectively implemented, weak.

For both regulator and regulatee, however, there is a particular danger that compliance rhetoric will be used merely to "manage appearances." As Shearing (1993) writes,

> Therefore regulatory space is a marketplace of assurances in which multiple guarantors often compete with each other for the confidence of persons who are faced with decisions as to where and how to act. Also regulators face temptation to be content with creating appearances that will promote confidence and to be less concerned with ensuring that this confidence is actually warranted. . . . Policy should be sensitive to the danger of permitting appearance management to "capture" the regulatory process. (pp. 75-76)

Even at their best, corporate compliance systems are frequently an attempt to manage appearances and preserve legitimacy (Edelman et al., 1993) in response to public and government concerns while making as little real change as possible. The critics are correct in their analyses of the shortcomings of compliance-oriented policy and scholarship that focus on only one type of strategy among the whole of regulatory design and implementation. The evidence outlined here for a holistic approach to compliance is designed to provide a more robust basis for further research and debate.

NOTES

1. *The Netherlands: Table of Eleven Key Determinants of Compliance* (Organization for Economic Cooperation and Development, 1998); *Canada: Strategic Compliance Policies for Regulators* (Regulatory Compliance Project, 1992).

2. Nevertheless, when the Occupational Safety and Health Administration tried to expand the program, it met resistance from some employers (see Parker, 1999c).

3. See also Harrison (1995), who found that the purely cooperative Canadian approach to environmental regulation in the pulp-and-paper industry resulted in much lower compliance rates than the more adversarial regulation of the same industry in the United States.

4. Measurements of a number of other dimensions of restorative justice were made in other papers from the same study (Makkai & Braithwaite, 1993, 1994a).

5. This information is based on my own research on leading compliance systems in Australia.

REFERENCES

Aalders, M. (1993). Regulation and in-company environmental management in the Netherlands. *Law & Policy, 15*, 75-94.

Aalders, M., & Wilthagen, T. (1997). Moving beyond command-and-control: Reflexivity in the regulation of occupational health and safety and the environment. *Law & Policy, 19*, 415-443.

Affirmative Action Agency. (1998). *Facts and figures*. Sydney, Australia: Affirmative Action Agency.

Andersen, O. (1996). The Norwegian internal control system: A tool in corporate environmental management? *Eco-Management and Auditing, 3*, 26-29.

Ayres, I., & Braithwaite, J. (1992). *Responsive regulation: Transcending the deregulation debate*. New York: Oxford University Press.

Baldwin, R. (1997). Regulation after "command and control." In K. Hawkins (Ed.), *Human face of law* (pp. 65-84). Oxford, UK: Clarendon.

Bardach, E., & Kagan, R. (1982). *Going by the book: The problem of regulatory unreasonableness*. Philadelphia: Temple University Press.

Beder, S. (1997). *Global spin: The corporate assault on environmentalism*. Melbourne, Australia: Scribe.

Better Regulation Taskforce. (n.d.). *Principles of good regulation*. London: Author.

Black, J. (1997). *Rules and regulators*. Oxford, UK: Clarendon.

Bottomley, S. (1997). From contractualism to constitutionalism: A framework for corporate governance. *Sydney Law Review, 19*, 277.

Bottomley, S. (1999). The birds, the beasts, and the bat: Developing a constitutionalist theory of corporate regulation. *Federal Law Review, 27*, 243-264.

Braithwaite, J. (1985). *To punish or persuade: Enforcement of coal mine safety*. Albany: State University of New York Press.

Braithwaite, J. (1999). Restorative justice: Assessing an immodest theory and a pessimistic theory. In M. Tonry (Ed.), *Crime and justice—A review of research* (pp. 241-364). Chicago: University of Chicago Press.

Braithwaite, J. (2000). The new regulatory state and the transformation of criminology. *British Journal of Criminology, 40*, 222-238.

Braithwaite, J., & Braithwaite, V. (1995). The politics of legalism: Rules versus standards in nursing-home regulation. *Social and Legal Studies, 4*, 307-341.

Braithwaite, J., & Murphy, J. (1993, Spring). Clout and internal compliance systems. *Corporate Conduct Quarterly*, pp. 52-53.

Braithwaite, V. (1992). *First steps: Business reactions to implementing the Affirmative Action Act* (Report to the Affirmative Action Agency). Canberra: Australian National University.

Braithwaite, V. (1993). The Australian government's affirmative action legislation: Achieving social change through human resource management. *Law & Policy, 15*, 327-354.

Burby, R., & Paterson, R. (1993). Improving compliance with state environmental regulations. *Journal of Policy Analysis and Management, 12*, 753-772.

Chayes, A. (1960). The modern corporation and the rule of law. In E. Mason (Ed.), *The corporation in modern society* (pp. 25-45). Cambridge, MA: Harvard University Press.

Cragg, W. (1992). *The practice of punishment: Towards a theory of restorative justice*. London: Routledge.

Crandall, R., Rueter, F., & Steger, W. (1996). Clearing the air: EPA's self-assessment of clean-air policy. *Regulation, 4*, 35.

Driscoll, D., Hoffman, W., & Murphy, J. (1998). Business ethics and compliance: What management is doing and why. *Business & Society Review, 99*, 35-51.

Driscoll, D., Hoffman, W., & Petry, E. (1995). *The ethical edge: Tales of organizations that have faced moral crises*. New York: Mastermedia.

Edelman, L. (1990). Legal environments and organisational governance: The expansion of due process in the American workplace. *American Journal of Sociology, 95*, 1401-1440.

Edelman, L., Erlanger, H., & Lande, J. (1993). Internal dispute resolution: The transformation of civil rights in the workplace. *Law & Society Review, 27*, 497-534.

Elliott, L. (1998). *The global politics of the environment*. Houndmills, Basingstoke, Hampshire, UK: Macmillan.

Feitshans, I. (with Oliver, C.). (1997). More than just a pretty program: OSHA voluntary protection programs improve compliance by facing problems head on. *Corporate Conduct Quarterly, 5*, 69-73, 79.

Friedrichs, D. (1995). *Trusted criminals: White collar crime in contemporary society*. Belmont, CA: Wadsworth.

Fry, F. (1997). Cross-border regulatory issues achieving good compliance in an international environment. *Journal of Financial Regulation and Compliance, 5*, 346.

Galaway, B., & Hudson, J. (1990). *Criminal justice, restitution and reconciliation*. Monsey, NY: Criminal Justice Press.

Garland, D. (1997). "Governmentality" and the problem of crime: Foucault, criminology, sociology. *Theoretical Criminology, 1*, 173-214.

Geltman, E., & Skroback, A. (1998). Reinventing the EPA to conform with the new American environmentality. *Colombia Journal of Environmental Law, 23*, 1-56.

Genn, H. (1993). Business responses to the regulation of health and safety in England. *Law & Policy, 15*, 219-233.

Gioia, D. (1992). Why I didn't recognise Pinto fire hazards: How organisational scripts channel managers' thoughts and actions. Reprinted in Ermann, D., & Lundman, R. (Eds.). (1996). *Corporate and governmental deviance: Problems of organizational behavior in contemporary society*. New York: Oxford University Press.

Gordon, C. (1991). Governmental rationality: An introduction. In G. Burchell, C. Gordon, & P. Miller (Eds.), *The Foucault effect: Studies in governmentality* (pp. 1-52). Chicago: University of Chicago Press.

Grabosky, P. (1995). Using non-governmental resources to foster regulatory compliance. *Governance: An International Journal of Policy and Administration, 8*, 527-550.

Greenhouse Challenge Office. (1997). *Tackling the greenhouse challenge: Progress by Australian industry.* Canberra, Australia: Greenhouse Challenge Office.

Gruner, R. (1994). *Corporate crime and sentencing.* Charlottesville, VA: Michie.

Gunningham, N. (1998). *Environmental management systems and community participation: Rethinking chemical industry regulation.* Mimeo, Australian Centre for Environmental Law, Faculty of Law, Australian National University.

Hancher, L., & Moran, M. (1989). Organising regulatory space. In L. Hancher & M. Moran (Eds.), *Capitalism, culture and economic regulation* (pp. 271-299). Oxford, UK: Clarendon.

Harrison, K. (1995). Is cooperation the answer? Canadian environmental enforcement in comparative context. *Journal of Policy Analysis and Management, 14,* 221-244.

Harvard Law Review. (1996). Growing the carrot: Encouraging effective corporate compliance. *Harvard Law Review, 109,* 1783-1800.

Hawkins, K. (1984). *Environment and enforcement: Regulation and the social definition of pollution.* Oxford, UK: Clarendon.

Hawkins, K. (1990). Compliance strategy, prosecution policy and Aunt Sally. *British Journal of Criminology, 30,* 444-466.

Heimer, C. (1996). Explaining variation in the impact of law: Organizations, institutions and professions. *Studies in Law, Politics & Society, 15,* 29-59.

Hutter, B. (1997). *Compliance: Regulation and environment.* Oxford, UK: Clarendon.

Investment Management Regulatory Organisation. (1997). *Regulatory Plan 1996-1997.* London: Author.

Jeffcott, B., & Yanz, L. (1998). Code-breaking. *New Internationalist, 302,* 23.

Jutsen, J. (1995). Voluntary agreements with industry for reducing greenhouse gas emissions. In *Towards a sustainable future: Challenges and responses* (National Conference on Environmental Engineering, Melbourne). Barton, Australian Capital Territory: Institution of Engineers.

Levin, M. (1985, March/April). Building a better bubble at EPA. *Regulation,* p. 33.

Makkai, T., & Braithwaite, J. (1993). Praise, pride and corporate compliance. *International Journal of the Sociology of Law, 21,* 73-91.

Makkai, T., & Braithwaite, J. (1994a). The dialectics of corporate deterrence. *Journal of Research in Crime & Delinquency, 31,* 347-373.

Makkai, T., & Braithwaite, J. (1994b). Reintegrative shaming and regulatory compliance. *Criminology, 32,* 361-385.

Manning, P. (1987). Ironies of compliance. In C. Shearing & P. Stenning (Eds.), *Private policing* (pp. 293-316). Newbury Park, CA: Sage.

Marshall, T. (1985). *Alternatives to criminal courts.* Aldershot, UK: Gower.

McCaffrey, D., & Faerman, S. (1994). Shared regulation in the United States securities industry. *Administration & Society, 26,* 204.

McCaffrey, D., & Hart, D. (1998). *Wall Street polices itself.* New York: Oxford University Press.

McInerney, F., & White, S. (1995). *The total quality corporation: How 10 major companies added to profits and cleaned up the environment in the 1990s.* New York: Truman Telley/Plume.

Meidinger, E. (1987). Regulatory culture: A theoretical outline. *Law & Policy, 9,* 355-386.

Messmer, H., & Otto, H. (1992). Restorative justice: Steps on the way toward a good idea. In H. Messmer & H. Otto (Eds.), *Restorative justice on trial* (pp. 1-12). Dordrecht, the Netherlands: Kluwer.

Mitchell, R. (1994). *Intentional oil pollution at sea: Environmental policy and treaty compliance*. Cambridge: MIT Press.

Nesterczuk, G. (1996). Reviewing the National Performance Review. *Regulation, 3*, 31-39.

Occupational Safety and Health Administration. (1998). *The new OSHA: Reinventing worker safety and health* [Report published on the World Wide Web]. Washington, DC: Author. Retrieved December 6, 1998. Available: http://www.osha.gov/oshinfo/reinvent/reinvent.html

Office of Fair Trading. (1998). *Raising standards of consumer care: Progressing beyond codes of practice*. London: Her Majesty's Stationery Office.

Organization for Economic Cooperation and Development. (1997a). *The OECD report on regulatory reform Volume II: Thematic studies*. Paris: Author.

Organization for Economic Cooperation and Development. (1997b). *Public management occasional papers No. 18: Co-operative approaches to regulation*. Paris: Author.

Organization for Economic Cooperation and Development (Public Management Service). (1998). *Improving government capacity to assure high quality regulation: Draft country review of the Netherlands*. Paris: Author.

Osborne, D., & Gaebler, T. (1992). *Reinventing government: How the entrepreneurial spirit is transforming the public sector.* Reading, MA: Addison-Wesley.

Parker, C. (1999a). Compliance professionalism and regulatory community: The Australian trade practices regime. *Journal of Law & Society, 26*(2), 215-239.

Parker, C. (1999b). How to win hearts and minds: Corporate compliance policies for sexual harassment. *Law & Policy, 21*, 21-48.

Parker, C. (1999c). *The state of regulatory compliance*. Paris: OECD.

Pearce, F., & Tombs, S. (1990). Ideology, hegemony, and empiricism: Compliance theories of regulation. *British Journal of Criminology, 30*, 423-443.

Pearce, F., & Tombs, S. (1991). Policing corporate "skid rows." *British Journal of Criminology, 31*, 415-426.

Pearce, F., & Tombs, S. (1997). Hazards, law and class: Contextualising the regulation of corporate crime. *Social and Legal Studies, 6*, 79-107.

Price Waterhouse LLP. (1997). *1996 survey of corporate compliance practices*. New York: Author.

Rees, J. (1988). *Reforming the workplace: A study of self-regulation in occupational safety.* Philadelphia: University of Pennsylvania Press.

Rees, J. (1994). *Hostages of each other: The transformation of nuclear safety since Three Mile Island.* Chicago: University of Chicago Press.

Regulatory Compliance Project (Department of Justice). (1992). *A strategic approach to developing compliance policies*. Ottawa: Government of Canada.

Schmidheiny, S. (1992). *Changing course: A global business perspective on development and the environment*. Cambridge: MIT Press.

Scholz, J. (1994). Managing regulatory enforcement in the United States. In D. Rosenbloom & R. Schwartz (Eds.), *Handbook of regulation and administrative law* (pp. 423-463). New York: Marcel Drekker.

Schwartz, M. (1998). Compliance and business ethics are coming of age in Canada. *Ethikos & Corporate Conduct Quarterly, 12*, 7-9, 12.

Scott, C. (1998, June). *Analysing regulatory space: Implications for institutional design and reform*. Paper presented at the Law & Society Association annual conference, Aspen, Colorado.

Selznick, P. (1992). *The moral commonwealth.* Berkeley: University of California Press.

Shearing, C. (1993). A constitutive conception of regulation. In P. Grabosky & J. Braithwaite (Eds.), *Business regulation and Australia's future* (pp. 67-79). Canberra: Australian Institute of Criminology.

Silvani, C., & Baer, K. (1997). Designing a tax administration reform strategy: Experiences and guidelines: A working paper of the International Monetary Fund. *Tax Notes International, 15*, 375-395.

Sims, R. (1994). *Ethics and organizational decision making: A call for renewal.* Westport, CT: Quorum.

Sparrow, M. (1994). *Imposing duties: Government's changing approach to compliance.* Westport, CT: Praeger.

Sparrow, M. (1996). *Regulatory reform: Lessons from the Innovations Awards Program.* Mimeo, John F. Kennedy School of Government, Harvard University.

Still, L. (1997). *Glass floors and sticky ceilings: Barriers to the careers of women in the Australian finance industry.* Sydney, Australia: Human Rights and Equal Opportunity Commission.

Tombs, S. (1992). Stemming the flow of blood? The illusion of self-regulation. *Journal of Human Justice, 3*, 75-92.

Van Ness, D. (1986). *Crime and its victims.* Downers Grove, IL: Intervarsity.

Ward, A. (1997). Compliance surveys: Companies say better safe than sorry. *Corporate Legal Times, 62*, 1-3.

Weait, M. (1994, September). The role of the compliance officer in firms carrying on investment business. *Butterworths Journal of International Banking and Financial Law*, pp. 381-384.

Weinberg, J. (1996). OSHA consultation: A voluntary approach to workplace safety and health compliance. *Corporate Conduct Quarterly, 5*(2), 21-24.

Weinberger, A. (1990). Preventing insider trading violations: A survey of corporate compliance programs. *Securities Law Regulation Journal, 18*, 180-193.

Christine Parker is a senior lecturer in the Law Faculty at the University of New South Wales. Her current research is on best practice corporate regulatory compliance functions and the emergence of compliance professionals. She has also acted as a consultant to the Public Management Service of the OECD on regulatory compliance and regulatory reform. She has published a book, Just Lawyers: Regulation and Access to Justice *(Oxford University Press, Socio-Legal Studies Series, 1999) and numerous articles in the areas of legal ethics, the sociology of the legal profession, regulatory theory and policy, and corporate compliance in journals including the* Journal of Law and Society, International Journal of the Sociology of Law, *and* Law and Policy.

[15]

EXPLAINING VARIATION IN THE IMPACT OF LAW:

ORGANIZATIONS, INSTITUTIONS, AND PROFESSIONS

Carol A. Heimer

Sociolegal scholars are intensely concerned with questions about how influential law is, what exactly its effects are, and when its influence is larger and when smaller. Displaying a sophisticated understanding of the impact of law, sociolegal scholars have examined a wide variety of effects, including both direct and indirect effects, symbolic effects and instrumental ones, and effects on procedures as well as on substantive outcomes. Mnookin and Kornhauser (1979), for instance, ask how the law shapes divorce proceedings and conclude that divorcing couples and their lawyers bargain "in the shadow of the law," basing their offers and counteroffers on the bargaining endowments created by contemporary legal rules. Following Mnookin and Kornhauser's lead, scholars have investigated the shadow cast by law in other areas.

Studies in Law, Politics and Society, Volume 15, pages 29-59.

ISBN: 1-55938-901-X

Taking a somewhat different approach, Lempert and Sanders (1986) ask where legal intervention is especially likely to be effective—what kinds of issues are most tractable and what kinds of support from what kinds of groups increase the likelihood that new legislation will have its intended effect. In reviewing the effect of civil rights legislation, for instance, they comment that legislatures and courts can more easily undermine discrimination that is not contingent on other forms of segregation. School segregation is a particularly thorny problem, then, because it arises from residential segregation as well as from discriminatory policies of school boards. Similarly, in an examination of the effects of Supreme Court rulings on civil rights, abortion and women's rights, the environment, reapportionment, and criminal law, Rosenberg (1991) asks whether the Supreme Court is most accurately depicted as constrained or dynamic. Though he concludes that the constrained court view is more accurate, Rosenberg also discusses what the chief constraints on court action are and how they can sometimes be overcome.

Both Rosenberg (1991) and Lempert and Sanders (1986) adjust their expectations about the effect of law by taking account of the constraints faced by legal actors. Courts must wait for cases to be filed. Legislatures have less capacity to influence where people live than whether or not they will be allowed to vote. A somewhat different set of constraints is introduced by how the organizations that draft laws, process cases, and implement laws actually work. Recognizing the importance of organizational processes, Blumberg (1967) looked at defense attorneys as members of bureaucracies, Emerson (1969) examined the organizational processes of classification in the juvenile justice system, and Feeley (1979) scrutinized the working of a court of common pleas as an organization governed as much by the career imperatives and work schedules of participants as by the letter of the law.

To shed further light on questions about when legal rules have more influence and when their effect will be relatively trivial, in this paper I look at what happens inside organizations. Using primarily examples from the legal regulation of medicine, I argue that we must take seriously the articulation of new legislation with pre-existing organizational routines. In effect, legal institutions compete with medical institutions for control over medical settings. What the outcome will be depends on whether legal institutions are able to insinuate themselves into the machinery of the hospital through incorporation into hospital routines and through synchronization with medical timetables. Legal rules will have considerably more impact if legal representatives are frequently present in medical settings or if local actors function as front-line legal workers either because they are charged with that responsibility or because they themselves are empowered by enforcing the law.

The adoption and implementation of laws also raises questions about relations between organizations and their environments, though. In implementing laws, for instance in bringing hospital practices into conformity with new rules about the withdrawal of life support, an organization such as a hospital seeks to convince important elements of its environment of its legitimacy so that it can attract important resources, such as clients, skilled employees, or financial resources. The difficulty with this explanation of why an organization would bring its practices into conformity with law, or adopt practices recommended by any other important element of its environment, is that pleasing one part of the environment may alienate another group of constituents. For instance, if hospitals too strongly signal their eagerness to abide by new legislation on the withdrawal of life support, they may discourage newly minted medical professionals, concerned about professional autonomy and discretion, from applying for jobs.

But questions of legitimacy also affect what happens at a more micro level. When organizational participants haggle over which procedures to adopt or argue about how to interpret an existing policy, perceptions of the importance of problems or of the appropriateness of proposed solutions depend on the legitimacy of those groups most closely associated with them. The details of organizational decision making are inextricably intertwined, then, with questions about legitimacy, and I argue here that an examination of professions as carriers of legitimacy and of competing institutions allows us to understand why some institutions are adopted and implemented while others are not.

Organizations may modify routines or create new positions as required by law, then, but such modifications will not always end up having much effect on the daily operation of the organization. Legally-mandated modifications will have more effect when they have the support of key local participants, who function as front-line legal workers, tailoring the law to local circumstances. In addition to applying legal formulas to local circumstances, these front-line legal agents also lend the law the legitimacy of the professions or other occupations with which they are associated. If physicians support and use legal rules about medical neglect, for instance, such rules will more often seem like sensible solutions to a hospital's problems than if they are proposed as solutions only by lawyers. Institutional competitions, for instance between medicine and law, are resolved then by the acknowledgement of professional autonomy by the state and the corresponding acceptance of the rule of law by professionals. When such professional treaties are built into legislation, for instance through consultation of members of the occupations who will mainly be responsible for implementing a law, legal rules are more likely to influence the activities of organizations at an instrumental as well as a symbolic level. Variations in effects on organizational activities can be understood by looking simultaneously at institutions, professions, and organizational decision making.

To make this argument, I first discuss what law is relevant to the practice of medicine, highlighting variations in the impact of law and legal rules on hospitals and medical work. I then outline two perspectives on organizations as sites where laws are implemented. Finally, I show how the insights of these two perspectives complement one another, particularly when we identify professions and other established work groups as mechanisms that carry environmental pressures across organizational boundaries and translate variations in legitimacy with external bodies into internal support or opposition for particular decisions.

MEDICINE IN THE SHADOW OF LAW: VARIATIONS IN THE INFLUENCE OF LAW ON MEDICAL PRACTICE

The practice of medicine is shaped by civil law (e.g., medical malpractice cases), criminal law (e.g., state laws against homicide; state laws prohibiting the abuse and neglect of children and requiring the reporting of abuse and neglect), regulatory law (e.g., state law governing professional practice; state law requiring informed consent), and fiscal law (e.g., legislation specifying the details of Medicare and Medicaid coverage; federal law denying certain funds to states lacking programs to prevent medical neglect of handicapped infants).[1] But despite the existence of many federal and state laws and regulations governing medical practice, it is unclear whether and when the law fundamentally shapes how medicine is practiced, merely legitimates what medical practitioners would have done anyway, or is largely ignored by medical workers. Here I provide examples showing that each of these outcomes occurs some of the time.

Medical practice is molded, first, by ordinary civil law. Under the law of torts, medical personnel and organizations, like other actors, are accountable for harms they cause to others. Medical malpractice suits are brought against physicians, other healthcare providers, and hospitals, and insurers sell expensive policies to cover losses from malpractice suits. The standard to which a physician is held varies with the source of liability—for performance of medical tasks, the standard is negligence; for the choice of the course of treatment, the standard is usually the "standard of care" in the medical community; and for informed consent, no clear standard seems to exist (Lieberman 1981, pp. 69, 71, and 81, respectively).

Because the fundamental question in medical malpractice suits is whether the health professional could have prevented or limited harm, we should expect much effort to go into ensuring that health professionals routinely follow approved procedures and can document that they have done so. Medical malpractice insurers, like other insurers, encourage medical practitioners and hospitals to engage in a variety of loss-prevention activities. Decisions about malpractice insurance are coupled with JCAHO (Joint Commission on Accreditation of Health Care Organizations) inspections, certification of professionals, continuing education programs, development of medication and procedure protocols (the core of a "standard of care"), rules about reporting particular "incidents," rules about gowning and scrubbing, and the creation of positions for risk managers and legal counsel.

Though the effect of civil law seems quite large when described this way, we must keep in mind that the civil law is only one of several causal forces here and that civil law works through intermediate mechanisms and agents with considerable capacity to magnify or diminish its causal impact. Professional associations for instance would press for some inspections, certifications, and protocols whether or not malpractice claims made them necessary. And though physicians and nurses may complain about the drudgery of documenting their work, they typically believe that keeping records is good medical practice.

The criminal law also shapes medical practice in hospitals. Under most circumstances, ordinary citizens cannot legally cause the death of another person, and neither can physicians or other healthcare providers. Laws prohibiting murder and manslaughter are invoked to prevent physicians from withdrawing life support from (let along giving fatal injections to) patients, and though even preliminary hearings on such matters are rare, nevertheless physicians and hospital lawyers are acutely aware that such legal actions are possible. Family members also could be prosecuted for first- or second-degree murder or manslaughter for deciding to withhold medical treatment or for withdrawing support (for instance by disconnecting a ventilator) without court approval.

State laws prohibiting child abuse and neglect also govern medical care, and they are invoked more often than other criminal laws. Though they govern the behavior of both parents and hospital staff members, cases are much more commonly brought against parents than against healthcare providers or hospital social workers. In the medical context, laws prohibiting child abuse and neglect require that physicians report suspected child abuse, including drug abuse by pregnant women. Laws on medical neglect also empower physicians to take temporary custody of children to administer medically necessary treatments to which parents do not consent (Haralambie 1987, vol. 1, pp. 584-598, vol. 2, pp. 293-298).

In gauging the impact of the criminal law on medical practice, effects of the application of criminal law to patients and families must be separated from the effects of the application of law to healthcare providers. On the one hand, the likelihood of having the law applied, at least to physicians and healthcare workers, is rather remote (Nelson and Cranford 1989; Fost 1989; Zussman 1992). On the other hand, the charges, should they be made, are extremely serious. For parents, in contrast, charges are considerably more likely, though the crimes charged are typically abuse or negligence not manslaughter. Parents may have a child removed from their custody, and this can be either because the hospital or the state believes that they are truly unfit parents or instead because physicians believe that parental religious beliefs should not prevent a child from getting necessary medical treatment. The effect of law in empowering physicians (and thus threatening parents) is thus probably greater than the effect of law that works through its threat to physicians and other healthcare providers. In part, this is because an interested party, namely the physician or social worker, acts to bring parent misbehavior to the attention of the law, while parents do not ally themselves with the state against physicians.

The third category of law that impinges on medical practice in hospitals is regulatory law. The relevant regulatory law includes law about certification of health professionals and restrictions on who may practice medicine, regulation of the distribution of drugs, laws defining death, and laws requiring informed consent for medical treatment. Much of the law regulating medical practice was developed at the behest of subgroups of healthcare providers, often as a way of prohibiting competition from neighboring practitioners (Starr 1982; Abbott 1988).

Rules about informed consent illustrate how law can change more superficial aspects of medical practice without deeply altering relations between practitioners and patients. Until the mid-1970s, the rules about informed consent were developed almost entirely by the judiciary. Though the consent requirement had long been part of the common-law tradition, more recent cases, such as *Canterbury* v. *Spence* (1972) had shifted the focus from mere consent to informed consent. This shift coupled with the medical malpractice "crisis"[2] of the mid-1970s seems to have provided an impetus for medical professionals to press for statutory definition of the requirements of informed consent.[3]

The law of informed consent strikes an uneasy balance between the competing rights of the patient and family to make medical decisions and the physician to make treatment decisions. With few exceptions, the law requires that patients must be told about their medical condition, informed of the possible treatments and the risks associated with those treatments, and must give their consent prior to treatment.

Despite the apparent clarity of the law, most commentators seem to believe that the practice of informed consent is quite different than the ideal. Because decisions are worked out behind the scenes, patients and families often are consulted after staff members have agreed on a course of action. As Anspach puts it, patients and families are asked for their assent rather than their consent (1993). Though medical decisions may be presented to patients and families, other important issues, for instance about the implications of a treatment for quality of life or about the possibility that one treatment may necessitate another, are less likely to be discussed (Heimer 1992). Zussman suggests that family and patient participation becomes mostly ceremonial when a continuous decision process is treated by the law as a set of discrete decisions (1992).

Further, Zussman argues, physicians exploit this legal misunderstanding of medical decision making to preserve professional discretion.

Some observers believe the gap between ideal and reality may have increased with the routinization of informed consent procedures and with the increasing social distance between physician and patient (Faden and Beauchamp 1986; Heimer 1992; Katz 1984; Rothman 1991; Schuck 1994).[4] Rothman (1991) for instance argues that in previous generations the episodic silence of physicians on the exact nature of a person's illness occurred in the context of a strong relationship built up over a lifelong patient/physician relationship coupled with joint participation in a community; without joint biography, physician silence is considerably less acceptable. For one thing, Schuck (1994) argues, without open discussions between physician and patient, the physician will not have sufficient information to know what the patient's interest is, and so will be unable to fulfill his or her fiduciary obligation to the patient.

Regulatory laws often work in tandem with other kinds of laws. For instance, when parental consent is required for medical treatment, then parental refusal of medical treatment may constitute abuse or neglect and the hospital can petition a court for custody of the child so that it can provide the disputed treatment. Though consent procedures are important in themselves, then, they are also significant as one link in the chain of actions by which hospitals use the law to wrest control from patients and their families or by which parents use law against healthcare providers and hospitals whom they believe to have mistreated their children. Considerable institutional attention is thus focused on the consent process (see Heimer 1992) and on documentation that patients and families have been fully consulted about orders to withdraw or withhold treatment. This does not, of course, mean that all relevant information has been disclosed, or that patients and families have been made to feel comfortable asking "dumb" questions. Rules about informed consent, like other regulatory laws, surely play an important role in the life of the hospital—but they often do not mainly serve their manifest function.

Finally, what happens in hospitals is shaped by fiscal law—regulations about the expenditure of federal and state monies. Examination of fiscal law suggests considerable variation in its effect. In some instances, whole fields of medical practice depend primarily on federal financial support, and their character clearly displays their response to reimbursement rules. Medical care for those with end stage renal disease (kidney failure so advanced that either dialysis or a kidney transplant is necessary) has been funded by the federal government through Medicare since 1972. Starr argues that incentives built into the law have deeply distorted the provision of medical care in this field: "Kidney dialysis centers provide a particularly graphic example of the rise of a private industry in response to public financing and then the manipulation of public policy by the industry it originally created" (1982, p. 442). Though home dialysis is cheaper than dialysis in a clinic or hospital, typically dialysis is provided in free-standing clinics rather than at home because physician owners of such clinics earn higher fees if dialysis is done there. Further, while Medicare covered the full cost of hospital or clinic dialysis, it covered only 80 percent of the cost of home dialysis (Starr 1982, p. 443). Attempts to pass legislation encouraging home dialysis and redressing inequities in reimbursement practices failed under pressure from lobbyists representing operators of for-profit dialysis centers.

Similar distortions are found elsewhere, as is amply documented in Starr (1992). Abraham's (1994) account of the medical history of a Chicago-area family shows how the care they received depended on the rules of coverage. Visits to physicians were delayed dangerously long because transportation expenses would be paid only if the patient was sufficiently ill to require hospitalization; a CTA program to transport poor patients to their physicians would only pick up patients who were able to make it on their own to the curb.

More recently, the development of DRGs (diagnostic related groups) as a regulatory tool has led to substantial changes in hospitalization patterns. For instance, because hospitals are permitted to collect the expected cost of caring for a patient falling into a particular diagnostic category and to keep the difference should they manage to provide care more cheaply, patients are being released from the hospital more quickly. Ruggie (1992) argues that fiscal tools such as DRGs allow deeper penetration than regulators had imagined or intended, and suggests that fiscal regulation is the wedge that will permit government management of medical care to increase despite the opposition of strong professional lobbies.

In contrast, though, other groups of fiscal laws have had essentially no effect. The most notorious of these rules are the Baby Doe Regulations and the Child Abuse Amendments. Based on the 1973 rules prohibiting discrimination against the handicapped by programs receiving federal funding, the Baby Doe Regulations were initially published in a May 1982 notice from the Department of Health and Human Services. When the Baby Doe Regulations failed to pass court scrutiny, the Child Abuse Amendments were passed in 1984, and reauthorized in 1989.[5]

All hospitals receive federal funds through Medicare and Medicaid as well as through other programs, and the Baby Doe Regulations used this funding as a lever, arguing that hospitals receiving any federal funds were prohibited from discriminating against the handicapped in any of their activities, whether these activities were themselves federally funded or not. A second route, employed after the Baby Doe Regulations were struck down by the courts, used the lever of federal funding for state programs to prevent child abuse. But the enforcement mechanism is an indirect one—states receiving funds for child-abuse prevention programs are the direct target of the Child Abuse Amendments, and compliance with the federal requirements is a condition for continued funding. Hotlines, threats of investigation, pressure to set up Infant

Care Review Committees,[6] and the like, all resulted from the application of fiscal law, though some of these mechanisms quickly passed from the scene.

Though the initial effect of these laws seemed likely to be large, in practice their effect probably has been quite small. Fiscal pressure is a relatively blunt instrument here—under the Baby Doe Regulations, the federal government would have to demonstrate a pattern of discrimination before funds could be withheld; under the Child Abuse Amendments, the funds that might be withheld are relatively modest and in any case go to the state rather than to any individual hospital. Further, the pressure is being applied to the wrong problem—the bulk of cases in infant intensive care units are not "handicapped" infants but premature ones. And because the strong predisposition of physicians and parents is toward treatment rather than nontreatment in any case, there was no substantial "problem" to be corrected by the regulations and statutes.

To summarize, then, one can define law and its effects narrowly or broadly in reviewing the effect of law on the practice of medicine. Though many hospital regulations are not mandated by law, they often have been developed partly in response to law. For instance, no law requires JCAHO (Joint Commission on Accreditation of Health Care Organizations) certification. But insurers do require such certification, and hospitals and health practitioners carry malpractice insurance because of the possibility of law suits. One could argue, then, that the law casts a long shadow in medicine, but that one needs to think carefully about how the length, width, and density of that shadow varies from one area of medical practice to another. In places where the law's shadow seems densest, the cause may well be that the law's shadow largely coincides with the shadow cast by professional bodies or by some other group which itself works in the larger but lighter shadow of the law. The shadow of law is most dense, then, when legal institutions work in partnership with other institutions, and lightest when legal and other institutions work at cross purposes, as when families or physicians resist judicial intrusion. I turn now to a discussion of what makes law cast a lighter or denser, longer or shorter, shadow in some situations than in others.

"Legal considerations are, in effect, negotiable," Zussman concludes when he compares two hospitals' interpretations of the law of informed consent and on the withdrawal of life support (1992, p. 72). Ironically, though, Zussman finds that because of their resentment of legal interference in medical decision making, physicians end up magnifying the law's influence (1992, p. 185). Some legal considerations are more negotiable than others, of course, and more negotiable for some participants than for others. If the rules of informed consent seem quite maleable in the hands of physicians, they may seem considerably less flexible to other parties. If, for instance, a parent refuses consent for a blood transfusion deemed essential by a physician, the physician can take temporary custody of the child for the purposes of providing medical treatment. Patients and families would be unlikely to describe these laws as negotiable, though such an exception does provide flexibility to medical practitioners and so may look different to them.

Here in a single field—legal regulation of medical practice—we find that the effect of legislation varies a good deal. In one of these three examples, the rules about medical neglect, the law works essentially as intended. Physicians do take custody of children when they believe that parents are not providing necessary medical treatment. In the second case, rules about informed consent, the law has indeed had some effect, but though the relation between physicians and patients has been modified, patients still do not always receive full information and certainly do not participate in all of the decisions about their medical treatment. Finally, the effect of the Child Abuse Amendments has been very small. Under the original rules, many calls were received, a few led to investigations, but no cases of neglect were uncovered.

Among the elements that these cases have in common, I wish to highlight two. All of these concern activities that go on mainly in organizations—hospitals in this case—and all of them require the cooperation of non-legal professionals—primarily doctors in this instance. In this paper I argue that law is increasingly implemented in organizational settings and that high-level employees in those organizations, often themselves empowered with discretion and authority, strongly shape the ways a law or regulation is interpreted and incorporated into organizational routines. We therefore need a clearer understanding of how law functions in ongoing organizational life and how the interests, habits, and reactions of upper-level organizational members are likely to affect the effectiveness of legislation. Here I will use mainly examples from the medical field, but will suggest how my argument can be generalized to other settings.

ORGANIZATIONS—WHERE THE ACTION IS

We live increasingly in a world populated as much by organizations as by individuals (Coleman 1974, 1982; Lempert and Sanders 1986). If we are to understand how laws are interpreted and implemented, then, we need to understand the functioning of organizations. While we have long thought it naive to expect that the text of a law would tell us much about how the law was implemented, that tells us relatively little about what we might expect to find instead. An important component of an answer is an analysis of what the relevant units are, and how those units work. Here I argue that organizations and professions are among the most important units, and that we can get quite far in our understanding of how law is implemented by looking at how these key units would react to new legislation under a variety of circumstances.

It is within and by corporate bodies, especially those in which professional people dominate, that much of law is interpreted, enforced modified, or ignored. We need to ask, then, how the filter of the corporate actor, and especially that actor's professional staff, shapes the effect of law, sometimes dampening it, sometimes intensifying it, and often distorting it.

But organizations are not just law enforcement sites that modulate the effects of law. Because they have other purposes of their own, and indeed because the people who inhabit them also have their own multiple purposes, we must look at the way that these disparate purposes come together. Law then is not simply "enforced" either strongly or weakly, but can also be actively resisted when it is counter to or irrelevant to someone else's business, or used only as a tool when it is useful to someone else's project. But having said that tells us remarkably little, because we also need to know what makes law more able to retain its integrity in some instances, to be more cooptable in others. And if law is coopted into a professional project, is it more effective law (because it is not simply ignored) or less effective (because it is more easily deflected from its original purpose)?

If we can uncover key features of laws themselves and the environments into which they are injected, then we may be able to say more about when law is especially influential, when less influential. Two branches of organization theory, institutional theory and behavioral decision theory, offer different models of how law might shape the activities of organizational participants. The first suggests that organizations often will attempt to conform to the law in order to signal their legitimacy to key members of their environments with whom they must interact and from whom they get crucial resources. But a signal that conveys a message of legitimacy to one element of the environment (e.g., the medical profession at large) may not mean the same thing to another element of the environment (e.g., the courts). Organizational participants may then split over which institutions should be adopted to signal legitimacy because they care about the reactions of different elements of the environment. What happens, then, when institutions are in competition with one another, for instance when conforming to a law improves a hospital's reputation with insurers or the legal profession but hurts its reputation with physicians who feel that the hospital has too little respect for their professional expertise and is too willing to compromise their rights to make autonomous decisions?

A second view, derived from behavioral decision theory, suggests that how law shapes organizational processes depends on whether law alters the details of organizational functioning, altering organizational routines, decision timetables, the kinds of problems that are identified, the variety of solutions considered, and the rules of participation in decision making. But what this model leaves unanswered is a series of questions about what makes the participation of some actors more important than that of others, what makes some solutions seem more legitimate than others, and so forth.

In this paper I combine these two answers by arguing that professions are simultaneously the organizational participants responsible for altering the scripts or routines of organizations and the carriers of legitimacy. A solution is legitimate because it is championed by a particular profession and tied through that profession to key elements of the environment. Professions do the work of legitimating solutions by constructing bridges between organizations, importing new things from the environment, and tracking information about what signals are currently being read as important signals of legitimacy. That is, professionals are sentinels for the organization. But they play another role as well—they adapt the solutions to local environments, introducing them in forms that can be used in the organization. But whether any given professional *will* adapt a law for a local environment depends partly on what use that law is to the particular profession. If the law is useful to the professional—either in enabling him or her to work more smoothly or in improving his or her profession's situation in the organization (increasing the profession's legitimacy), then the law is more likely to be adapted for local use than if the law either is perceived as neutral or as inhibiting the work of the professional.

ORGANIZATIONS, INSTITUTIONS, AND LEGITIMACY

To do its work an organization must attract resources from outside, including financial resources, labor with particular licenses, accreditations, and skills permitting it to carry on activities, and the business and loyalty of clients or customers. Legitimacy and reputation are key elements of this equation. An organization with a good reputation has more chance of attracting resources; a disreputable one has less capacity to attract and keep key resources and so less opportunity to do a good job. Thus, the neoinstitutionalists in sociology argue, signaling legitimacy will be very important, and much of what takes place in organizations occurs not because it improves efficiency but because it confers legitimacy and so smooths interactions and transfers resources across organizational boundaries (Meyer and Rowan 1977; DiMaggio and Powell 1983, 1991). Organizations adopt routines and establish particular formal structures more to make it *look* as if the organization is behaving sensibly and reputably than actually to help it behave rationally.

The state is, of course, a key element of the environment of most organizations, and so plays a key role in the process of institutionalization. Because of its coercive qualities, because it is a common element in the environment of a variety of organizations, and because legal actors are the ones who resolve disputes over which institutions should govern particular activities, law is something of a master institution in institutional analyses. DiMaggio and Powell for instance discuss legal requirements as an example of coercive isomorphism (as distinguished from mimetic or normative isomorphism) and identify the state as one of the "great rationalizers of the second half of the twentieth century" (1983, p. 147). But though the law may be important in the process of institutionalization, institutional analysts are quick to stress that this does not mean that adopting mandated forms necessarily leads to deeper social change. In their institutional analysis of the role of law in extending civil rights into the workplace, for instance, Edelman, Erlanger, and Lande note that though legislation made attention to civil rights imperative and legitimate, organizations could avoid more basic changes by formulating organizational policies in such a way that "[t]he legal right to a nondiscriminatory workplace in effect becomes a 'right' to complaint resolution" (1993, p. 529).

If, in order to look legitimate, organizations adopt structures and practices that have been adopted by reputable peer organizations (either competitors or exchange partners) or are advocated by more powerful organizations (such as the state or regulatory bodies), organizations face two dangers. First, though adoption of new structures and practices may smooth interactions *across* organizational boundaries, it may be disruptive to the internal workings of the organization. The solution, institutionalists have argued, is decoupling. Institutions can serve a ceremonial function without disturbing existing practices if they are decoupled from other activities in the organization. In the example of the extension of civil rights into the workplace, in the short run at least, the existence of affirmative action officers and procedures alongside pre-existing employment practices and personnel departments has meant that "business as usual" was not much disrupted. A right to complaint resolution is far more superficial and entails fewer disruptions of routines than would a right to a nondiscriminatory workplace.

A second set of problems arises when multiple institutions are promulgated as solutions to a problem. The core difficulty here is that signaling an organization's legitimacy to one group may make it impossible to signal legitimacy to another group. Even with considerable decoupling, there is a limit on how many new procedures and structures can be added to an organization, and decoupling is usually not complete in any case. Someone will take the new office or new procedure seriously and insist on having the new rights honored. An organization must make choices, then, about which routines to adopt and which new positions to create.

This second set of problems is especially likely to arise under two conditions—either during periods of innovation or when multiple groups claim jurisdiction. An organization facing a new situation has to develop new routines or adapt old ones to do the new task or solve the new problem. Choices of routines are not just technical choices but also have ceremonial functions, creating alliances or severing ties. For instance, when the exploitation of North Sea oil fields began, insurers needed to modify their procedures and policies so that they could provide coverage for these new ventures (Heimer 1985). Usually insurance rates are experience-based—that is, rates depend on past losses and administrative expenses for a particular type of insurance and a particular type of policyholder. But no historical data existed for oil exploration, for the construction of oil production platforms, or for the production of oil in such a hostile environment as the North Sea. In the short run, the dependence of Norwegian insurers on the British marine insurance market led Norwegian insurers to adopt inefficient British marine insurance routines as the basis for insurance of the North Sea oil fields rather than to develop new procedures. These procedures were socially sufficient—that is, they preserved the crucial ties with British insurers who could provide reinsurance and legitimacy—but not technically sufficient, and Norwegian insurers collected additional information and made additional calculations, decoupling the official procedures from the innovations.

Only later, when ties to British insurers were less crucial in the maturing field of North Sea oil insurance, did Norwegian insurers drop the less efficient British marine insurance procedures in favor of capital-conserving innovations that expanded the size of the insurance pool but signalled a decreased willingness to bow to British preferences. Alliances with British insurers that were indispensible at the beginning became less important as Norwegian insurers became more able to function independently. As Norwegian insurers gained an independent reputation, the legitimacy of Norwegian insurers depended more on convincing insurers in other countries of the appropriateness of Norwegian rate-setting and reinsurance procedures than on British support. As Norwegian insurers developed direct ties with insurers in other countries, ties with British insurers, who had previously functioned as intermediaries, became less important. Decisions about how much weight to place on legitimacy (with the British) versus technical adequacy thus shifted as Norwegian alliances changed. Over time it became more important to seem legitimate to German and French insurers, for instance, than to British ones, and institutions evolved to support these changing alliances.

Similar problems arise when multiple groups claim jurisdiction. In neonatal intensive care units, for example, medical careproviders, the state, and families all claim the right to participate in decision making. Physicians claim the right to make decisions on the grounds of training and professional autonomy. Should a hospital too strongly signal its willingness to permit other groups to intervene in medical decision making, it would likely lose its best physicians, who would choose to practice in institutions more willing to protect professional discretion. But hospitals also face pressures from the state, and have tried to signal their respect for the rule of law. Among the recent legal changes are the diffusion of informed consent routines, the formation of Infant Care Review Committees and other general-purpose ethics committees, and more extensive consultation of the hospital legal department or risk managers by medical careproviders. Finally, families and patients claim the right to participate in decision making. Basing their claims on rights to self-determination and to family privacy, patients who can choose (usually because they are sufficiently rich) take their business to hospitals and healthcare providers who respect those rights. Hospitals signal their respect for family autonomy by advertising their routine consultation of family members, their liberal visiting hours, their openness to participation by family-chosen priests, ministers, or rabbis.

Nevertheless, when an organization must simultaneously reassure so many groups of its openness to their participation, some of these promises will seem hollow. Physicians, who must make promises to families on the hospital's behalf, are surely aware that at some points their discretion is comprised by promises that patients and families will get to participate in decision making. Offering the right to participate to too many dilutes the rights of all, though. Groups are thus in competition for organizational adoption of procedures and structures that favor them. Rather than institutionalization then smoothing interactions across organizational boundaries, during the process of institutionalization adoption of new procedures or creation of new positions can be a contested process, causing both internal disagreement and loss of legitimacy in the eyes of some external groups.

How, then, do organizational participants settle on one group of procedures rather than another, and how do they manage the public relations problems that arise from these choices? And what can we learn about the likely effectiveness of any particular law when we think about the process of implementation this way? When will legal institutions win in this institutional competition, and when will they be more likely to lose, and what does it mean to win or lose?

When the implementation of a law occurs in an organizational setting, which it often will, those who are repeat players by virtue of their employment in those organizations will be important in shaping the ultimate effect of the law, and we must focus on such actors to answer our questions about institutional competition and the ultimate effect of the introduction of new legislation. If the organization is one dominated by professionals, the professions from which the employees are drawn will be alternative sources of institutions and alternative audiences, attached to labor markets, to which organizational members will be oriented. But if key actors pick and choose among alternative institutions, this suggests that they are behaving far more instrumentally than most neoinstitutionalists suggest.[7] Thus the process of institutionalization is partly a process of strategic calculation, and even in this area that has been discussed as one where social beings *enact* scripts, we also find them choosing scripts, modifying scripts, and deviating from the text—in short, *acting* rather than enacting. And we must turn our focus to intra-organizational processes and to the role that professionals or other established occupational groups play in developing routines, making particular problems the focus of organizational attention, and legitimating particular solutions.

DECISION MAKING IN ORGANIZATIONS

An organization chart is not an adequate representation of an organization. Decisions are not made once and for all by CEOs or department heads and then implemented faithfully by their subordinates. It is therefore wildly unrealistic to expect that laws and regulations that are supposed to govern the activity of organizational participants are likely to be implemented faithfully without modification. At the very least, a law or regulation must be incorporated into organizational scripts and routines, and that necessarily entails some modification for local circumstances. Many social scientists have challenged the notion that organizations work in any "rational" way, noting that the informal system has an influence somewhat separate from that of the formal system, that organizational culture powerfully shapes action inside organizations, that the activities and responses of organizational participants are governed by scripts and routines as much as by thoughtful reactions, and that many decisions are made more for symbolic or ceremonial purposes than for instrumental ones.

If our purpose is to estimate the likely influence of a law or regulation when it must be implemented in an organizational setting, then we need to know something about how decisions are made in organizations, by whom they are made, and how a newly introduced law or regulation might be expected to work its way into the organization.

March and his colleagues (Cohen, March, and Olsen 1972; March and Olsen 1976; March 1994) answer this question by arguing that many organizations are organized anarchies, functioning much like garbage cans into which a variety of elements are tossed. Organizational decisions depend on what happens to be in the organizational garbage can and what is taken out for organizational use. Rather than decisions being made in the "rational" way that organization charts would suggest they are, they argue, decisions instead result from the episodic coupling of key elements that co-exist semi-autonomously in organizations. Which decision gets made depends on what participants happen to be there at the time, what is identified as a problem needing a solution, what solutions are available in the organization, and consensus that a choice point has arrived and it is time to make a decision.

Though we tend to think of these elements as having a logical relation to one another, Cohen, March, and Olsen would argue that we have mistaken ideology for reality. Decisions are not in fact as much governed by organizational calendars as we believe. Some decisions are actually made in backrooms and only ratified at official meetings. Others are postponed because key participants are absent or because the match between problem and solution is unsatisfactory. Similarly, it is hardly obvious when there is a problem that requires a solution. One organizational member may think the sky is falling while another urges that "if it ain't broke, don't fix it." Dissensus about what is an appropriate solution is also common. Some people will think that the cheapest solution should be accepted, others will think that approach short sighted. Some participants will offer the same solution for every problem because they have been looking for an excuse to implement that particular solution. And finally, though organization charts, job descriptions, and protocols, when they exist, make definitive statements about who is to participate in what decisions, reality is often sharply different. Rights to participate, obligations to participate, and actual participation are not the same thing. People with the most extensive rights to participate may even be especially unlikely to participate because they are vastly overcommitted. Nevertheless, meetings and other occasions when decisions might be made are likely to be organized around the schedules of those with the strongest rights to participate, with decisions being delayed until they can be present or made early to accommodate them.

Rights to participate are carefully allocated in medical decision making. Though the rights of physicians as a group have only recently been challenged, and then often the only question has been the extent to which they must consult family members or how they will bill for their services, physicians have long been concerned about *which* of them is the appropriate one to make any particular decision. Physicians were long reluctant to admit their patients to hospitals for fear that hospital staff members would take over medical decision making. In adult intensive care units, this issue has reappeared in a new guise with disputes about who is in charge of the unit's patients. In some intensive care units, unit staff take over decision making about patients admitted to the ICU; in others the admitting physician retains control over his or her own patients; in between are arrangements in which unit staff "consult" on the patients of private physicians (Devers 1994).

But not all staff members are equally privileged. Nurses, for instance, do not always feel that their views get taken seriously (Anspach 1993; Guillemin and Holmstrom 1986; Zussman 1992). Similarly, social workers, therapists, nutritionists, discharge planners, and others who are more "peripheral" to the core medical enterprise may find it difficult to get their views heard. In an attempt to redress these kinds of inequalities, other staff members sometimes organize new forums for decision making or press for the right to participate in older forums. In medical settings, a key indicator of a group's right to participate is its right or obligation to record information in the medical record. Groups that are more central to decision making have both a clear right and a clear obligation to record information. The obligation to record information is especially important because it indicates that others feel that they cannot make decisions without the information that participant might provide. In the Neonatal Intensive Care Unit (NICU), then, groups can be arranged hierarchically according to rights and obligations to write in the medical record. Physicians have both a right and an obligation, for instance, but social workers have a right to record information in the record but a much weaker obligation—some types of information must be recorded (e.g., a referral to the child welfare agency), but others are recorded at the discretion of the social worker.

Still other groups, such as parents, can get their views into the medical record only indirectly—by raising issues with the social worker, for instance, or by becoming "problems" themselves. And even then, they cannot ensure that their views are represented as they would wish. In theory patients and some family members have access to medical records, but such access is typically discouraged by such bureaucratic mechanisms as storing the record at a nursing station or insisting that the record be reviewed with a physician.

Decisions may be recorded in the medical record and may be based on information in the medical records, but they are not *made* in the medical record. Decisions are instead made in a wide variety of meetings. Some of these are regularly scheduled meetings (e.g., "rounds"), others are *ad hoc* meetings scheduled to bring together a patient's "team" for consultation or decision making. But meetings are not always sites for decision making—often they are instead a time for informing some participants of the decisions that others have already made or for laying the groundwork for decisions that will be made on other occasions. In some cases, then, participants less likely to be included in decision making call meetings in an attempt to win inclusion in decision making. Such ruses often fail, though. The "real" decision makers may not come to meetings. In two NICUs where I did research, social workers complained that physicians did not regularly attend the weekly interdisciplinary rounds at which discharge plans and family problems were discussed. Or key participants may attend meetings but treat them as informational sessions rather than as occasions for decision making. Zussman (1992) notes that most decisions are not made in discussion with patients and families but are made in separate meetings attended only by medical personnel. Once medical personnel have arrived at a consensus, that consensus is presented to the patient and family. It is no surprise, then, that patients and family members often feel disenfranchised. Though they have legal rights to participate in decision making, such rights often are not fully honored.

Variations in actual participation rights then depend not just on formal rights to participate but on access to informal gatherings in which caucusing occurs, being present at the right time, knowing when the right time is, and having the capacity to participate in the decision making.

Other decision elements similarly vary from the way they are depicted in official sources. Most physicians would be able to give detailed answers about how problems are identified, explaining the systematic review of information about patients to uncover differences between the patient's physiological state and a normal state. Vital signs and test results are compared with the standard, differences are noted, and physicians put the pieces of evidence together to form a pattern or diagnosis. Among the "problems" that physicians would identify, then, would be variations from normal on a series of indicators, the diagnosis of a medical condition (a statement that the deviations in values form a pattern), and unexpected events of a medical nature. Other "problems" might be nonmedical in nature, including difficulties locating kin for consultation, difficulties in arranging payment for medical services and medications, patient noncompliance, staffing and other personnel problems, equipment failures, or difficulties in the relations between the particular medical unit and the rest of the hospital. For these examples, though, we should expect variations in the extent to which they would be identified as problems—the condition may exist without being recognized, and once recognized it may not be identified as a problem.

Within organizations or work groups, the categorization of situations as problems or not should follow the sorts of processes that Emerson (1991) discusses for the categorization of cases. That is, categorization into a binary system of problem or not should depend on the case load and scarcity of resources, the case mix, and so forth. In addition, though, categorization of a situation as a problem is a deeply interactive process in which the participants discuss, comment, negotiate, and threaten in order to get particular situations labeled as problems worthy of sustained attention and intervention, as situations that should be monitored, or as situations that are not problems. Because problem identification is so deeply interactive, the stream of problems is clearly only partially independent of the stream of participants.

Solutions similarly have to be identified as potential matches for problems. Though we customarily think of problems as pre-dating solutions and of solutions being sought for problems, this sequence is hardly invariant. Hospitals, after all, are places where solutions are developed, tested, and refined, and where specialized personnel make matches between medical problems and medical solutions. Some solutions are used repeatedly, sometimes matched to a variety of problems, sometimes matched to a single problem that occurs with high frequency. Other solutions, used less often, are part of the active repertoire of staff members or part of the even larger inventory of solutions that are used only very occasionally. Solutions may even be stockpiled for later use, perhaps for quite different purposes than originally anticipated.[8]

Though medical staff might wish that the correspondence between problem and solution was unique and that medical solutions could always completely resolve medical problems, the match is often less than perfect, several solutions may be tried before a good match is found, and only some possible solutions are considered because others fall outside the expertise of those making the match or outside the range of what is considered legitimate in a medical setting. The perceived legitimacy of a solution will vary with the expertise and status of the person proposing it. In medical settings, solutions identified by physicians will have more legitimacy *a priori* than solutions identified by people without medical training. And, as such lay people quickly learn, one can easily disqualify a solution by attempting to bolster its legitimacy by citing support from the wrong groups. For instance in a neonatal intensive care unit, La Leche League sponsorship for some method of feeding would not make the method more reputable because the League reputation among neonatologists is for fanaticism on breastfeeding. Some solutions—*medical* solutions—are already members of the group of solutions to be considered as potential matches for a problem, and for some especially well-established solutions, consideration as potential matches does not depend on who the participants are at the time a match is made. Other potential solutions have to be introduced into consideration, and may disappear from the set being considered if particular participants are absent. In some cases this is because knowledge of the solution is possessed by only a few people. Or it may be because a particular solution is the favored solution of some participant who wishes to implement the solution whether it matches the problem well or not. This might be the case if a physician is conducting research on some particular drug or procedure, for instance. Solutions that are not native to the setting—for instance solutions associated with a religious group, an alternative medical specialty, an advocacy or support group, or an ethnic subculture—similarly are unlikely to be considered if their sponsors are absent, and will often need vigorous support to overcome opposition of regular decision makers.

Solutions and problems are matched at decision points. Some decision points exist on established organizational calendars, though even such established decision points are subject to negotiation if a key participant must be absent or if decision makers in fact make the decision in informal settings and only *present* the decision on the occasion on which the decision is officially to be made. Some medical decisions are made at regularly established decision points such as at admission, at daily rounds, or when consultants' reports are reviewed. Less routine but nevertheless common decision points are meetings with the patient and family. Even more *ad hoc* decisions are made in routine ways, through review of inscriptions in the medical record, the nursing notes, examination of the patient, and discussion with medical colleagues including peers and superiors.

Outsiders sometimes attempt to influence organizational decision making by introducing new decision points. For instance, the legal requirement of informed consent introduces a new decision point—the point at which a patient or the patient's family is informed about the medical problem, potential solutions, and asked to consent to the proposed treatment—and at the same time mandates the participation of particular people such as the patient or the patient's family. Similarly, court review of medical decisions, as occurred in several "Baby Doe" cases, in essence adds a further decision point, supplementing medical decisions with review of those decisions.

Outsiders' attempts to stall or accelerate decision making or to ensure that particular people are included in decision making may be relatively ineffective, though. Pre-existing routines are often remarkably resilient, partly because they are embedded in ongoing relationships. A decision point is not so much a formal meeting occurring at a pre-specified time as a consultation between key actors—the decision point may therefore occur at some time before or after the announced time if all of the key actors are present or have been consulted. Formal occasions are only important to those participants who are not otherwise present and who are making a point of being present to participate only in that decision. We could then measure the social distance between participants in a decision by mapping the proportion of their time when they would ordinarily be in each other's company. Attending physicians, residents, and nurses encounter one another frequently, while family members are less predictably present in the hospital, and judges are only present when they convene court in a hospital conference room (and they have only recently begun to do that).

Further, some parts of medical decision making are governed not by bureaucratic timetables or the schedules of participants but by less predictable events in the human body. Physicians and nurses are more adept at reading the signs of the human body and so can say when decisions cannot be deferred without endangering a person's life, for instance. They are also in the habit of scheduling their work and decisions to respond to birth, death, accident, illness, and so on. Routines for convening meetings at odd hours, technologies for making contact with key participants, and rules about who needs to be consulted, and when, are all already in place. Outsiders who might wish to influence medical decisions may be disadvantaged initially by being ill-adapted to medical timetables. Judges ordinarily make decisions during regular weekday working hours and convene in courtrooms. But the frustrating experience of decisions made on a legal timetable being moot because they came too late has led to some adaptation of legal personnel to medical timetables. Judges now convene court in hospital conference rooms in the middle of the night. Hot lines are available for physicians to take custody of infants and children needing immediate medical attention. Such adaptations increase the influence of law in medical settings because legal personnel and legal considerations can now shape decisions *as they are being made* rather than only commenting on such decisions after the fact. But such adaptation is not possible for everyone. Judges can insist on being called, but other participants have less capacity to *require* that their desire to participate be respected by harried medical workers.

The regularities described here—of attentive incorporation of some categories of participants but not others into organizational routine—are defining features of the relationship between professionals and organizations, and suggest that if we are to understand how institutions are adopted by organizations and why some institutions but not others are incorporated into core routines, we must look squarely at the relationship between organizations and the professionals whose work lives span organizational boundaries.

PROFESSIONS AS CARRIERS OF COMPETING INSTITUTIONS

Thus far I have presented two alternative views of how a law might shape the activities of organizational participants. In the institutionalist view, organizational procedures are adapted and positions added to bring organizational practice into conformity with the law. Organizations make these modifications because they are concerned with their legitimacy. But because they are also concerned with the efficient operation of the organization, they may try to meet legal requirements in ways that minimize disruption to parts of the organization that are functioning smoothly. To change without disrupting is difficult, and may lead to a more superficial adaptation to legal requirements than at least some legislators had in mind. The problem of appearing to conform to the wishes of a powerful group is even more difficult when an organization wishes to mollify members of several powerful groups and when the interests of these groups conflict. The institutionalist perspective then tells us that legitimacy will be a key concern, but fails to warn us that an organization may have multiple constituencies.

The alternative view, that of the organizational behavioral decision theorists, similarly rejects the notion that organizations behave "rationally," but focuses more on intra- than on interorganizational processes. What, they ask, really happens when organizational participants make decisions? Their answer is that problems, solutions, decision opportunities, and participants are all important but partially independent ingredients and that what decision will result depends on the particular mix of these ingredients on any specific day. Rather than a decision being the result of a rational and invariant process, then, decisions are highly contingent. One group of participants might choose a solution when a somewhat different group would decide that there was no problem to solve; a solution that seemed sensible and conservative to one group might seem inappropriate and crazy to another. The behavioral decision theorists thus tell us that there are multiple constituencies with diverse interests and that a wide variety of outcomes are possible. But they tell us little about what makes some solutions more attractive, some problems more compelling, and some groups especially powerful. That is, they tell us little about legitimacy.

When we juxtapose these two partial answers, we are led to look for some way to bridge the gap between external and internal, and for some mechanism that translates matters of legitimacy into ways of evaluating problems and solutions, capacity to influence organizational timetables, and variations in participant clout. It is professions that provide these bridges in organizations, I argue, and I show how an examination of the role of professions as the carriers of institutions enables us to close the gap between the neoinstitutionalists and the behavioral decision theorists.[9]

When we ask about the relative influence of legal institutions, medical institutions, familial institutions, or even the institutions of insurance in medical settings, a key question is how organized each of these alternative institutional perspectives is, and how entrenched it is in any particular organizational setting. Though there are other ways for groups to become organized, to develop ideologies, and to get their interests and purposes built into organizational routines, professions are a common one.

Professions, Abbott argues, are "exclusive occupational groups applying somewhat abstract knowledge to particular cases" (1988, p. 8). Along the way to becoming a profession, a group develops work practices that become congealed through training programs, protocols, and the like. Boundaries between nearby professions are worked out, sometimes through civilized negotiations, sometimes in less civilized ways (Halpern 1992). Such boundaries are fragile, though, because abstract knowledge can always be expanded and applied to new types of cases. New disputes develop as old professions fight over claims to new territory and as new professions arise to claim temporary vacancies. Rights to exclude others from the practice of a profession are granted by the state, but the grant of this legal authorization to pursue a profession also implies a state agreement to work through the profession on relevant matters. For instance, when rules of informed consent were being developed, state governments recognized that to have any impact those rules had to be embedded in the routines carried out by medical professionals.

The mutual recognition of professional autonomy by the state and of the rule of law by professions is in principle no different than other truces between competing institutions. Such treaties, embedded in agreements about jurisdictions and routines, then function as endowments in any work setting. Routines and protocols, like laws, are drafted from the point of view of particular people. In a hospital, routines are written with the medical hierarchy in mind. Physician discretion is written into protocols, for example, and is further protected as routines or scripts are enacted by people who hold similar cultural beliefs for instance about the appropriateness of nurse subordination to physician authority.

Such treaties are more likely when a profession or other occupation has existed for some considerable period of time and has staked a claim in a particular setting. In hospitals, agreements between older occupations such as nurses and physicians are relatively well established. But the rules of how work is to be divided between either of these occupations and newer professions such as respiratory therapy, physical therapy, occupational therapy, nutrionists, or discharge planners are still in the process of being negotiated. In infant intensive care units, for instance, social workers function as front line legal workers (Heimer and Stevens 1993) who inform physicians of the rules about taking custody of infants in cases of medical neglect. As new professions develop, they work out treaties first with adjacent occupations (Halpern 1992), and only later iron out difficulties in relations with more distant occupations. Lock (1995) for instance finds that though genetic counselors have worked out a clear division of labor with M.D. geneticists, this understanding of which tasks are appropriately performed by physicians and which by genetic counselors is local; a treaty between one medical specialty and a related ancillary profession does not define relations between that same ancillary profession and other medical specialties. Obstetricians do not seem to share geneticists' understanding of what tasks belong uniquely to genetic counselors.

Professions are important because their somewhat abstract knowledge, training and credentialling programs, work styles, territorial claims, ideologies, legal authorizations and immunities, and treaties or divisions of labor with other professions or occupations are the raw materials from which legitimacy is constructed. A proposed solution is more likely to be legitimate, then, when it is sponsored by a profession or other well-organized occupation that is well established in a particular organization. Sponsorship by a profession automatically suggests extra-organizational sources of support, cosmopolitanism rather than parochialism, while simultaneously signalling how a solution might fit into pre-existing organizational routines and who will be interested in supplying the energy to make it work.

It is professions or other established work groups, then, that import new materials including laws, scientific discoveries, or new technology into organizations in a way that incorporates them into organizational machinery. Without the sponsorship of a local agent, or at least the labor of a local worker charged with the obligation to implement it, a new rule is considerably more likely to be overlooked. The Child Abuse Amendments have had little effect because no local agent has either an interest in using them or a responsibility for ensuring compliance. In contrast, rules about medical neglect both serve the interests of physicians and are the responsibility of physicians and hospital-based social workers. When medical tradition and legal rules offer alternative solutions to a problem, legal institutions will be implemented only when legal actors pay attention to getting their solutions into the organizational machinery with the sort of sponsorship that will make them seem like legitimate solutions, at the time when they might realistically be considered, and hooked to problems that are defined by hospital staff members as real problems.

DOCTORING IN THE SHADOW OF THE LAW; JUDGING IN THE SHADOW OF MEDICINE; DOING BOTH IN THE SHADE OF THE ORGANIZATION

If we speak of "legal endowments," we can also speak of "organizational endowments," that privilege some participants over others in particular organizational settings. One can speak of legal endowments creating very specific but limited advantages, as Mnookin and Kornhauser (1979) do in their discussion of divorce, or one can speak of more general legislative endowments as Lempert and Sanders (1986) do when they show how variations in the legal competence of citizens and the orientations of legislators combine to produce laws that end up favoring one group over another. Though laws can still be interpreted neutrally or even in ways that undermine endowments created in earlier stages, nevertheless many people, recognizing which party the law favors, adjust their behavior and expectations accordingly.

Organizational endowments function in a similar way. Organizational policies are tailored to meet the needs of powerful groups. And though the rights created by organizational policy may be extended universalistically to other members of the organization, policies often create rights and privileges that are of more interest to some than others, or encode rights in ways that favor one group over others. Further, an organizational culture that honors and defers to one group will not just develop policies to favor that group but also interpret existing policies to favor it. Policies encouraging employees to get further training are more relevant to professional and managerial staff than to clerical workers, for instance, and are therefore likely to be encoded in organizations in which managerial and professional staff are powerful and clerical workers have little clout. Even when secretaries' tuition is reimbursed, secretaries are less likely to be rewarded with promotions or pay raises when they complete educational programs (Heimer 1984).

Hospitals are doctors' turf. Though physicians may feel the encroachment of hospital administrators (Starr 1992) and of the law (Zussman 1993), nevertheless hospital rules and procedures adopt the physician's perspective, respect and adjust to physicians' schedules, and protect physicians' rights to participate. Others *can* intrude, and they sometimes do succeed in shaping outcomes. But for most outsiders, and even some insiders, influencing hospital decision making is an uphill battle because the routines were not designed by them or with them in mind.

The privileged position of elite physicians in hospitals is thus the result of a professionally-based endowment, a status inequality between physicians and other groups, that has been encoded in countless routines and protocols and so structures interactions between groups, becoming in the process an organizational endowment. It is not just that physicians are respected by their hospital co-workers and by patients and their families. And it is not just that the routines, protocols, and rules favor physicians. Respect and institutionalized privilege reinforce one another in ways that are difficult to detect and difficult to overcome.

But to say that hospitals are physicians' turf is not to say that hospitals are dictatorships ruled by physicians. Physicians enjoy substantial but bounded privileges in hospitals—their rights are limited both by the realities of organizational life and by the rights and privileges accorded to others. Because medical work requires the coordinated effort of many people, it cannot occur at the whim of physicians. Rather, physicians must function as members of a team, though they may be very privileged members. In practice, organizational endowments create only limited privileges, and savvy organizational participants can learn the ropes and figure out how to make organizational routines work for them. They can learn how to manipulate timetables or how to convince others of the legitimacy of their problems and the appropriateness of their solutions. Attempts to tinker with organizational routines will be more successful if reformers recognize the importance of basing claims to legitimacy on ties to both external and internal constituencies—for instance to externally validated professions that are represented among the employees or regular participants of an organization.

In attempting to influence medical decision making, legal actors have had to work both in the shadow of medicine as a profession and in the shadow of the hospital as an organization. That is, they have had to overcome the effects of deference to respected physicians, and they have also had to contend with the disabilities they themselves faced as actors whose interests had not been taken into account in the formulation of organizational policy. Zussman (1992, p. 176) notes that though Massachusetts judges tried to increase their own influence by playing by doctors' rules, they quickly wearied of having their work and sleep interrupted so that they could rule on termination-of-treatment cases. The lower court decision requiring judicial review of all decisions to terminate treatment was quickly overruled. Hospital procedures for record keeping, consultation, decision making, and review of decisions have not been formulated for the convenience of lawyers and judges, but have instead been written to take account of the circadian and weekly rhythms of hospital life.

But though legal actors have no substantial organizational endowment in hospitals, compared with patients and their families, legal actors at least come endowed with the respect and legitimacy accorded to members of the legal profession. When judges insist that medical decisions be reviewed by the court, they are heeded. Family members may not be so effective when they attempt to insert new choice points into a crowded medical schedule. Sometimes, in fact, patient and family attempts to define something as a problem or to propose a solution backfire. With over-zealous lay support, an alleged problem may be more likely to be dismissed as trivial or a proposed solution rejected as preposterous. But the situation changes somewhat when families are able to ally themselves with legal actors. Informed consent procedures, mandated and legitimated by law, create an organizational endowment that can be used by knowledgeable and persistent patients and families.

Other cases in which social scientists characterize the law as having had a substantial effect share these features. The Environmental Impact Statements (EISs) mandated by the National Environmental Policy Act (NEPA), for instance, have been described by Taylor (1984) as a device for "making bureaucracies think." EISs are effective precisely because they simultaneously create a set of routines for collecting and evaluating a kind of information not previously collected, and create positions for environmentalists responsible for collecting the information and writing the statements.

Analyzing the controversy over the construction of Orme Dam, Espeland (1992) argues that NEPA changed the power balance between two groups in the Bureau of Reclamation. The "Old Guard" engineers first ignored, then tried to circumvent the rules when EISs failed to support previously-planned dams. The "New Guard," a loose group of biologists, economists, planners, social psychologists, sociologists, and a few engineers, most of whose jobs were created by NEPA, had a strong interest in implementing the law. Though they were initially hired to write EISs assessing projects after plans were largely complete, they hoped to increase their own power by modifying organizational routines so that environmental assessments were made much earlier as part of the regular planning process rather than as an add-on to satisfy legal requirements. It is important to note, though, that the "Old Guard" at first assumed that the new law would have little effect. Presumably the "Old Guard" anticipated that the combination of their power, pre-existing organizational routines, and the legitimacy of the engineering profession in the Bureau of Reclamation and in the culture at large would be sufficient to protect their interests. But the law was more effective than the "Old Guard" had anticipated, partly because "New Guard" members also had substantial legitimacy as professionals though they were not part of the engineering culture that dominated the Bureau of Reclamation, were able to ally themselves with legal actors, were able to insinuate themselves into federal agencies, and were able to modify at least some organizational routines.

I have shown how the influence of law is mediated by organizational processes, and I have argued that legal institutions compete with institutions associated with other professions in organizational settings. Such institutional competitions are won by whichever institution is able to function simultaneously at the macro level, increasing the legitimacy of the organization with key members of its environment, and at the micro level, shaping the day-to-day activities of organizational participants through incorporation into basic routines. Whether laws have any effect depends on whether they are incorporated into organizational machinery, shaping organizational timetables, the definition of problems, the acceptability of solutions, and the like. At the same time, though, whether new legislation is able to affect organizational routines depends on questions of legitimacy—on sponsorship by high-status professionals, on having a history in the organization, and the like. Only when we look simultaneously at the problems of gaining legitimacy and embedding in organizational decision processes can we understand when laws that must be implemented by organizations will have any substantial effect.

ACKNOWLEDGEMENTS

For helpful comments on earlier drafts of this paper, I thank Bruce Carruthers, Wendy Espeland, Richard Lempert, Arthur McEvoy, Lisa Staffen, and Arthur Stinchcombe. For very able research assistance I thank Sarah Gatson and Mitchell Stevens. The American Bar Foundation provided generous research support for the project on which this paper is based.

NOTES

1. These are analytical distinctions, of course, and in practice, laws falling into different categories typically work in tandem. For example, though statutes mandating reporting of child abuse or neglect are properly classified as criminal law, they are intertwined with regulatory law because professionals who fail to report suspected abuse or neglect are to be punished by state bodies responsible for licensing professions.

2. Lieberman (1981) concludes that the medical malpractice crisis was more a product of insurer practices than of changes in the likelihood of dissatisfied patients suing.

3. Meisel and Kabnick (1980) provide some evidence of pressure from medical organizations for legislation on informed consent and on other topics related to the malpractice crisis. In some cases informed consent statutes were drafted by attorneys for medical groups. The AMA drafted a model statute, which Meisel and Kabnick describe as "an example of the unfortunate tendency of organized medicine to view informed consent as nothing more than a legal hurdle to be surmounted by a consent form, rather than a recognition of the fundamental human rights of bodily integrity and self-determination" (1980, p. 561). Other observers tend to agree that most, though not all, medical groups have taken a defensive stance on informed consent (Katz 1984; Schuck 1994). Reviewing the statutes of the 24 states that enacted informed consent laws between 1974 and 1977, Meisel and Kabnick concluded that though on net balance the laws did not change the rules much, "they will preclude the possibility of judicial liberalization of common-law rules in a manner that might favor patients" (1980, p. 563); Faden and Beauchamp (1986, p. 140) draw the same conclusion.

4. We should be careful here to acknowledge that some important changes *have* resulted from the reform of informed consent rules. Zussman describes how the culture of rights now exists alongside the old culture of the ward, and cites research showing that while in 1961 88 percent of physicians did not level with patients about cancer diagnoses, by 1979 98 percent of physicians reported that they did inform patients that they had cancer (Zussman 1992, p. 85; Oken 1961; Novack, Plumer, Smith, Ochitill, Morrow, and Bennett 1979).

5. The story of the Baby Doe Regulations and the Child Abuse Amendments is a convoluted one involving actions by President Reagan, the Department of Health and Human Services, the Congress, the courts, and a variety of pressure groups. For a fuller account, see Bopp and Nimz

(1992); Gerry and Nimz (1987); Heimer (1993); Kopelman, Kopelman, and Irons (1992); Lyon (1985); Newman (1989); Shapiro and Barthel (1986); and Walman (1992) for discussions of these regulations and the very common mispercentions about their applicability to NICU care. The appendix of Caplan, Blank, and Merrick (1992) provides a chronology of the events in the legal history of the 1984 Child Abuse Amendments (though they have misdated the final event in the series). Lyon (1985) provides more detail than most about how key cases unfolded and what subsequently happened to families and infants.

6. See Fost (1992) for an assessment of the effectiveness of the Infant Care Review Committees.

7. Some recent neoinstitutional work (e.g., DiMaggio 1988, 1991; Powell 1991) acknowledges that actors have purposes, that ceremony coexists with instrumental purposes and indeed may have its own instrumental purpose, and that key actors may strategize about the acceptance of institutions, sifting and sorting among procedures to find the one that most suits organizational and individual purposes.

·8. See Feldman (1989) on the development of policy papers in the Department of Energy.

9. Though both DiMaggio and Powell (1983) and Edelman, Abraham, and Erlanger (1992) discuss the importance of professionals in the process of institutionalization, their approaches are somewhat different than the argument I make here.

REFERENCES

Abbott, A. 1988. *The System of Professions: An Essay on the Division of Expert Labor*. Chicago: University of Chicago Press.

Abraham, L.K. 1993. *Mama Might be Better Off Dead: The Failure of Health Care in Urban America*. Chicago: University of Chicago Press.

Anspach, R. 1993. *Deciding Who Lives: Fateful Choices in the Intensive-Care Nursery*. Berkeley: University of California Press.

Blumberg, A. 1967. "The Practice of Law as a Confidence Game: Organizational Cooptation." *Law and Society Review* 1(2):15-39.

Bopp, J., Jr., and M. Nimz. 1992. "A Legal Analysis of the Child Abuse Amendments of 1984." Pp. 73-104 in *Compelled Compassion: Government Intervention in the Treatment of Critically Ill Newborns*, edited by A.L. Caplan, R.H. Blank, and J.C. Merrick. Totowa, NJ: Humana Press.

Caplan, A.L., R.H. Blank, and J.C. Merrick, eds. 1992. *Compelled Compassion: Government Intervention in the Treatment of Critically Ill Newborns*. Totowa, NJ: Humana Press.

Cohen, M.D., J.G. March, and J.P. Olsen. 1972. "A Garbage Can Model of Organizational Choice." *Administrative Science Quarterly* 17 (March):1-25.

Coleman, J.S. 1974. *Power and the Structure of Society*. New York: Norton.

———. 1982. *The Asymmetric Society*. Syracuse, NY: Syracuse University Press.

Devers, K.J. 1994. *Triage in Adult Intensive Care Units: How Organizations Allocate Resources*. Unpublished Ph.D. dissertation, Northwestern University.

DiMaggio, P.J. 1988. "Interest and Agency in Institutional Theory." Pp. 3-22 in *Institutional Patterns and Organizations: Culture and Environment*, edited by L.G. Zucker. Cambridge, MA: Ballinger.

———. 1991. "Contructing an Organizational Field as a Professional Project: U.S. Art Museums, 1920-1940." Pp. 267-292 in *The New Institutionalism in Organizational Analysis*, edited by W.W. Powell and P.J. DiMaggio. Chicago: University of Chicago Press.

DiMaggio, P.J., and W.W. Powell. 1983. "The Iron Cage Revisited: Institutional Isomorphism and Collective Rationality in Organizational Fields." *American Sociological Review* 48:147-160.

———. 1991. "Introduction." Pp. 1-38 in *The New Institutionalism in Organizational Analysis*, edited by W.W. Powell and P.J. DiMaggio. Chicago: University of Chicago Press.

Edelman, L., S.E. Abraham, and H.S. Erlanger. 1992. "Professional Construction of Law: The Inflated Threat of Wrongful Discharge." *Law and Society Review* 26:47-83.

Edelman, L., H.S. Erlanger, and J. Lande. 1993. "Internal Dispute Resolution: The Transformation of Civil Rights in the Workplace." *Law and Society Review* 27:497-534.

Emerson, R. 1969. *Judging Delinquents*. Chicago: Aldine.

———. 1991. "Case Processing and Interorganizational Knowledge: Detecting the 'Real' Reasons for Referrals." *Social Problems* 38:198-212.

Espeland, W.N. 1992. *Contested Rationalities: Commensuration and the Representation of Value in Public Choice*. Unpublished Ph.D. dissertation, University of Chicago.

Faden, R.R., and T.L. Beauchamp in collaboration with N.M.P. King. 1986. *A History and Theory of Informed Consent*. New York: Oxford Univeristy Press.

Feeley, M. 1979. *The Process is the Punishment: Handling Cases in a Lower Criminal Court*. New York: Russell Sage.

Feldman, M.S. 1989. *Order Without Design: Information Production and Policy Making*. Stanford: Stanford University Press.

Fost, N. 1989. "Do the Right Thing: Samuel Linares and Defensive Law." *Law, Medicine and Health Care* 17:330-334.

———. 1992. "Infant Care Review Committees in the Aftermath of Baby Doe." Pp. 285-298 in *Compelled Compassion: Government Intervention in the Treatment of Critically Ill Newborns*, edited by A.L. Caplan, R.H. Blank, and J.C. Merrick. Totowa, NJ: Humana Press.

Gerry, M.H., and M. Nimz. 1987. "Federal Role in Protecting Babies Doe." *Issues in Law and Medicine* 2:339-377.

Guillemin, J.H., and L.L. Holmstrom. 1986. *Mixed Blessings: Intensive Care for Newborns*. New York: Oxford University Press.

Halpern, S. 1992. "Dynamics of Professional Control: Internal Coalitions and Cross-professional Boundaries." *American Journal of Sociology* 97:994-1021.

Haralambie, A.M. 1987. *Family Law Series*, Vols. 1 and 2. Colorado Springs, CO: Shepard's McGraw-Hill.

Heimer, C.A. 1984. "Organizational and Individual Control of Career Development in Engineering Project Work." *Acta Sociologica* 27:283-310.

———. 1985. "Allocating Information Costs in a Negotiated Information Order: Interorganizational Constraints on Decision Making in Norwegian Oil Insurance." *Administrative Science Quarterly* 30:395-417.

———. 1992. "Your Baby's Fine, Just Fine: Certification Procedures, Meetings, and the Supply of Information in Neonatal Intensive Care Units." Pp. 161-188 in *Organizations, Uncertainties, and Risks*, edited by J.F. Short and L. Clarke. Boulder, CO: Westview Press.

———. 1993. "Competing Institutions: Law, Medicine, and Family in Neonatal Intensive Care." American Bar Foundation Working Paper #9308.

Heimer, C.A. and M.L. Stevens. 1993. "Social Work, Medical Work, and an Organizational Model of Caring." American Bar Foundation Working Paper #9309.

Katz, J. 1984. *The Silent World of Doctor and Patient*. New York: Free Press.

Kopelman, L.M., A.E. Kopelman, and T.G. Irons. 1992. "Neonatologists, Pediatricians, and The Supreme Court Criticize the 'Baby Doe' Regulations." Pp. 237-266 in *Compelled Compassion: Government Intervention in the Treatment of Critically Ill Newborns*, edited by A.L. Caplan, R.H. Blank, and J.C. Merrick. Totowa, NJ: Humana Press.

Lempert, R., and J. Sanders. 1986. *An Introduction to Law and Social Science*. Philadelphia: University of Pennsylvania Press.

Lieberman, J.K. 1981. *The Litigious Society*. New York: Basic Books.

Lock, E.J. 1995. "Genetic Counselors: The Non-directive Deployment of Dangerous Knowledge." Unpublished M.A. paper, Northwestern University.

Lyon, J. 1985. *Playing God in the Nursery*. New York: Norton.

March, J.G. 1994. *A Primer on Decision Making: How Decisions Happen*. New York: Free Press.

March, J.G., and J.P. Olsen, eds. 1976. *Ambiguity and Choice in Organizations*. Bergen: Norwegian University Press.

Meisel, A., and L.D. Kabnick. 1980. "Informed Consent to Medical Treatment: An Analysis of Recent Legislation." *University of Pittsburgh Law Review* 41:407-564.

Meyer, J.W., and B. Rowan. 1977. "Institutionalized Organizations: Formal Structure as Myth and Ceremony." *American Journal of Sociology* 83:340-363.

Mnookin, R.H., and L. Kornhauser. 1979. "Bargaining in the Shadow of the Law: The Case of Divorce." *Yale Law Journal* 88:950-997.

Nelson, L.J., and R.E. Cranford. 1989. "Legal Advice, Moral Paralysis and the Death of Samuel Linares." *Law, Medicine and Health Care* 17:316-324.

Newman, S.A. 1989. "Baby Doe, Congress and the States: Challenging the Federal Treatment Standard for Impaired Infants." *American Journal of Law and Medicine* 15:1-60.

Novack, D.H., R. Plumer, R.L. Smith, H. Ochitill, G.D. Morrow, and J.M. Bennett. 1979. "Changes in Physicians' Attitudes Toward Telling the Cancer Patient." *Journal of the American Medical Association* 241:897-900.

Oken, D. 1961. "What to Tell the Cancer Patient." *Journal of the American Medical Association* 175:1120-1128.

Powell, W.W. 1991. "Expanding the Scope of Institutional Analysis." Pp. 183-203 in *The New Institutionalism in Organizational Analysis*, edited by W.W. Powell and P.J. DiMaggio. Chicago: University of Chicago Press.

Rothman, D.J. 1991. *Strangers at the Bedside: A History of How Law and Bioethics Transformed Medical Decision Making*. New York: Basic Books.

Rosenberg, G.N. 1991. *The Hollow Hope: Can Courts Bring About Social Change?* Chicago: University of Chicago Press.

Ruggie, M. 1992. "The Paradox of Liberal Intervention: Health Policy and the American Welfare State." *American Journal of Sociology* 97:919-944.

Schuck, P.H. 1994. "Rethinking Informed Consent." *Yale Law Journal* 103:899-959.

Shapiro, R.S., and R. Barthel. 1986. "Infant Care Review Committees: An Effective Approach to the Baby Doe Dilemma?" *Hastings Law Journal* 37:827-862.

Starr, P. 1982. *The Social Transformation of American Medicine: The Rise of a Sovereign Profession and the Making of a Vast Industry*. New York: Basic Books.

Taylor, S. 1984. *Making Bureaucracies Think: The Environmental Impact Statement Strategy of Administrative Reform*. Stanford: Stanford University Press.

Walman, T. 1992. "Decision Making in the Neonatal Intensive Care Unit: The Impact of the 1984 Child Abuse Amendments." Pp. 299-316 in *Compelled Compassion: Government Intervention in the Treatment of Critically Ill Newborns*, edited by A.L. Caplan, R.H. Blank, and J.C. Merrick. Totowa, NJ: Humana Press.

Zussman, R. 1992. *Intensive Care: Medical Ethics and the Medical Profession*. Chicago: University of Chicago Press.

CASE CITED

Canterbury v. *Spence*, 464 F.2d 772, 787 (D.C. Cir. 1972)

[16]

The Regulation of Contractualisation in Quasi-markets for Public Services

Peter Vincent-Jones
*Professor of Law, University of Central Lancashire**

Contractualisation may be defined as the process whereby public service functions are performed increasingly by private firms or semi-autonomous state or voluntary bodies in contractual relationships with public purchasing agencies. This process has played a major part in the radical transformation of the United Kingdom public sector over the past decade. Where bureaucratic monopolies once provided services directly, government purchasers now act on behalf of consumers in selecting providers in competitive quasi-markets for an expanding range of health, community, education, local government and other public services.[1] Contractualisation implies the replacement of bureaucratic by quasi-market forms of provision, but its future in the long term is uncertain. The negative experiences of reforms in the health and education sectors might be interpreted as indicating that quasi-market organisation is inappropriate and that provision should in future be organised more hierarchically. At the other extreme, there might be aspects of public service functions across all sectors that could better be performed through privatisation with regulation. However, New Labour has been positive towards the quasi-market inheritance since its victory in the 1997 general election. Quasi-markets in education and community care have been left almost untouched, while the NHS internal market persists in softer form with the purchaser-provider split and commissioning remaining.[2] The reform of legal aid will take an explicit quasi-market contractual form, with a new Legal Services Commission securing legal services on behalf of consumers through contracts with quality-assured providers.[3] Conservative policies designed to promote joint ventures between private and public sectors, also involving quasi-market contracting, have been adopted and extended, for example in public infrastructure projects under the Private Finance Initiative (PFI), and in the encouragement of partnerships for

* This paper is the indirect result of a project for which the support of the ESRC is gratefully acknowledged (R000 236416). I would like to thank David Campbell, David Hughes, Douglas Lewis and Colin Scott for comments on earlier drafts.

[1] J. Le Grand and W. Bartlett (eds.), *Quasi-Markets and Social Policy* (1993); W. Bartlett, C. Propper, D. Wilson, and J. Le Grand (eds.), *Quasi-Markets in the Welfare State: The Emerging Findings* (1994); W. Bartlett, J. Roberts and J. Le Grand (eds.), *Quasi-market Reforms in the 1990s: A Revolution in Social Policy* (1998).

[2] Bartlett *et al. op. cit.* (1998).

[3] Access to Justice Bill (H.L. Bill 4) December 2, 1998.

the provision of local authority services under the Public Private Partnerships Programme (Four Ps).[4]

The complexity of the multi-party relationships involved in the purchasing, provision and consumption of the public services poses major problems. The reduction in public law *accountability* accompanying the blurring of the public-private division by new public management (NPM) reforms has been much discussed by public lawyers. This paper, however, examines contractualisation from the perspective of *regulation*. If accountability refers to the duty of public managers to explain or justify their actions when things have gone wrong, and then to make amends to anyone who has suffered loss or injustice as a consequence,[5] the focus in regulation is on what institutional arrangements for service provision will maximise performance and minimise grievances, complaints and disputes. The paper demonstrates that contractualisation has a variety of regulatory dimensions (legal, economic and administrative), all of which need to be taken into account in evaluating the governance of public services. In support of this argument, the paper develops Hood and Scott's suggestion that ideas drawn from the current literature on business regulation are relevant to the analysis of recent public sector developments.[6] While the importance of state regulation of markets that have been created following privatisation has been widely acknowledged,[7] the regulation of quasi-market processes is less well understood. The analysis of such regulation will be shown to have significant implications for international debates over how public services should be delivered.[8]

Contractualisation and quasi-markets

In an ideal market organisation consumers choose to purchase goods or services from competing private producers who are subject to market incentives and sanctions. In bureaucratic organisation, by contrast, competitive market forces are absent and consumers exercise no choice: services are planned and delivered directly by state employees. Whereas private firms are financed ultimately by the proceeds of sale on the market, government bureaucracies are funded through general grants raised by taxation.[9] Government bureaucracies are different from other administrative hierarchies whose income is similarly

[4] The "Four Ps" programme involves a particular version of PFI aimed at increasing private investment in local services infrastructure. On the development of quasi-markets in broadcasting, see S. Deakin and S. Pratten, "Quasi-Markets, Transaction Costs and Trust: Institutional Change in Broadcasting", ESRC Centre for Business Research Working Paper 101, University of Cambridge, September 1998.

[5] D. Oliver and G. Drewry, *Public Service Reforms: Issues of Accountability and Public Law* (1996) at p. 134.

[6] C. Hood and C. Scott, "Bureaucratic Regulation and New Public Management in the United Kingdom: Mirror-image Developments?" [1996] 23 J.L.S. 321.

[7] See C. Veljanovski (ed.), *Regulators and the Market: An Assessment of the Growth of Regulation in the UK* (1991).

[8] See for example J. Boston (ed.) *The State Under Contract* (1995); D. Kettl, *Sharing Power: Public Governance and Private Markets* (1993).

[9] D. Beetham, *Bureaucracy* (1996).

not dependent on market sale, such as charitable bodies, in being funded by taxation rather than by voluntary subscription.[10]

The "failures" of both markets and bureaucracies have been well documented in the economics and public policy literatures.[11] Market co-ordination may lead to unfair outcomes and be incapable of satisfying certain needs, and may not even produce efficiency benefits under monopoly conditions or where there is insufficient competition. Bureaucracies, it has been argued, have a tendency to be self-serving, wasteful and inefficient.[12] The interesting feature of quasi-markets as a form of organisation is their combination of government direction with elements of market discipline, and the resulting potential for avoiding some of the deficiencies of both bureaucracies and markets. Walsh has pointed out that the recognition of market failures does not imply that "government need necessarily employ any staff or own any productive resources at all".[13] The key institutional innovation of quasi-markets is the combination of competition between providers and free access for service consumers at the point of delivery.[14] Quasi-markets may offer distinct advantages over pure market relationships in circumstances where the distribution of social goods (such as health care, education, housing, and other "public" services) cannot be left to the market for pragmatic or equity reasons, or where the interests of recipients of public services (for example as citizens) cannot be reduced to simple consumption.

Quasi-markets differ from conventional markets on both the supply side and the demand side:

> On the supply side . . . there is competition between productive enterprises or service suppliers . . . however . . . all these organisations are not necessarily out to maximise their profits, nor are they necessarily privately owned . . . On the demand side, consumer purchasing power is not expressed in money terms . . . Instead either it takes the form of an earmarked budget or "voucher" confined to the purchase of a specific service allocated to users, or it is centralised in a single state purchasing agency.[15]

Quasi-markets are but one manifestation of the revolution in public management, and contracting by public purchasers is just one mechanism of quasi-market organisation. The discussion of contractualisation in this article

[10] Beetham argues that voluntary organisations are bureaucratic despite not belonging in the strictly public sphere, whilst state owned enterprises that sell their products on the market are not technically bureaucracies; similarly, nationalised public corporations existing at arm's length from the government and enjoying considerable operational autonomy are not technically bureaucracies. Private property ownership and incentive structures remain vitally important in other respects, however.

[11] See *ibid.* pp. 22–26; P. Self, *Government by the Market? The Politics of Public Choice* (1993).

[12] D. Osborne and T. Gaebler, *Reinventing Government* (1993).

[13] K. Walsh, *Public Services and Market Mechanisms: Competition, Contracting and the New Public Management* (1995), p. 12. Other methods of dealing with market failure are possible, quasi-markets providing just one possible solution.

[14] Bartlett *et al. op. cit.* (1998) p. 1.

[15] Le Grand and Bartlett, *op. cit.* p. 10.

excludes quasi-market arrangements in which choice is exercised by consumers through the use of vouchers or other proxies for purchase and sale, rather than being concentrated in a state purchasing agency.[16] It also excludes a variety of relationships involving provision by non-state bodies where regulatory controls are not cast in contractual purchasing forms, as for example in licensing, franchising or oversight by specific regulatory agencies.[17] But our discussion will include both outsourcing and "internal" or in-house provision: in such arrangements from the viewpoint of the service consumer the function of choice is performed by the public purchaser irrespective of whether the provider is a private firm or a business unit formally within the same organisation or in an internal market relationship.[18] For present purposes, the subject also includes private-public sector partnership arrangements for local authority infrastructure or PFI projects, where a public agency is involved in selection of the partner through competitive tendering and the partnership relationship is subsequently governed by contract.

Contractualisation and accountability deficits in private and public law

Public lawyers have identified particular legal governance and accountability problems with the development of quasi-markets and contractualisation.[19] In this context the reduction in the role of the state has two aspects: the removal of certain functions from direct bureaucratic control, and the corresponding dispersal of powers of resource allocation and decision-making beyond clearly demarcated state boundaries. The new contracting forms have posed doctrinal problems within both private and public law, giving rise to the fear that contractual relationships will fail to be regulated adequately by either branch.[20] Where contractualisation has taken the form of purchaser-provider splits in internal markets *within* the state sector, as in health and local government, the lack of public law accountability is compounded by deficits in private law:

[16] The proposed reform of legal aid will involve a combination of quasi-market forms, with contracting playing a key role in conjunction with elements of franchising and the equivalent of vouchers. On the relative advantages of vouchers and contracts as quasi-market forms, see A. G. Watts, "Applying Market Principles to the Delivery of Careers Guidance Services: A Critical Review" in Bartlett *et al., op. cit.* (1998).

[17] For an analysis of the different economic conditions under which management contracts, licensing, franchising, and individual contracts subject to regulation might be most appropriate for the provision of public services, see M. Trebilcock, "Can Government Be Reinvented" in J. Boston, (ed.), *The State Under Contract* (1995).

[18] Nevertheless there are important governance differences between contracted in, and outsourced or contracted out, provision. Aronson's definition of outsourcing as "the agency process of securing another to provide goods or services directly to the public" blurs this distinction—see M. Aronson, "A Public Lawyer's Responses to Privatisation and Outsourcing" in M. Taggart (ed.) *The Province of Administrative Law* (1997).

[19] Taggart, "The Province of Administrative Law Determined?" *op. cit.*

[20] See M. Fredland, "Government by Contract and Public Law" [1994] P.L. 86 at pp. 100–104; I. Harden, *The Contracting State* (1992) pp. 74–75.

contractual legal norms control neither the relationship between purchaser/funding agency and provider, nor that between the responsible purchaser and public consumer of services. The availability of private remedies is limited by the fact that the obligations contained in the primary contract are not legally enforceable. While the claim that there are accountability deficits in internal markets needs to be tempered in the light of the existence of specific regulatory frameworks governing contracting,[21] it is nevertheless plain here that a variety of consumer, purchaser and provider interests are not protected by access to the courts whether under private or public law.

Where contractualisation has taken the form of transfer of state functions *outside* the public sector and there are legally enforceable contracts with private providers, public lawyers have been concerned at the lack of regulation of public contracting. This is in contrast to mechanisms for regulation of the privatised public utilities:

> The relationship of private organisations with the state is governed solely by contract, a relationship whose operation traditionally concerns only the contracting parties. The rapid expansion of the "contract state" raises urgently the questions as to whether the private law of contract is sufficient to ensure that public functions are properly supervised, or whether their exercise should be subject to judicial review.[22]

The claim here is that contractualisation should not be left entirely to private law, due to the essentially public nature of the interests involved. The stumbling block to the extension of judicial review in such circumstances remains the traditional distinction between public and private remedies based on whether the source of the power being exercised is of a statutory or private law nature. Despite the attempt in *Datafin*[23] to redraw the boundary of public law intervention in terms of the presence or absence of a "public element" in the function being performed,[24] more recent cases[25] may imply a "reassertion of an approach in which the only relevant factor is the source of the power".[26]

While debates over the scope of legal norms and the role of the courts in the control of contractualisation will rightly continue to preoccupy private and public lawyers, such accountability deficits need to be considered in the

[21] S. Fredman and G. Morris, "The Costs of Exclusivity: Public and Private Re-examined" [1994] P.L. 69; D. Oliver, "Judicial Review and the Shorthandwriters" [1993] P.L. 217; C. Scott, "The New Public Law", in C. Willett (ed.) *Public Service Reform and the Citizen's Charter* (1996).

[22] Fredman and Morris, *op. cit.* at p. 69.

[23] *R. v. Panel on Take-overs and Mergers, ex parte Datafin plc* [1987] 1 Q.B. 815.

[24] For discussion of the relationship between the "source of the power" and "public function" tests see Aronson, *op. cit.* pp. 45–48; M. Hunt, "Constitutionalism and the Contractualisation of Government in the United Kingdom" in Taggart, *op. cit.* pp. 27–38; J. McLean, "Intermediate Associations and the State" in *ibid.* pp. 160–166.

[25] *e.g. R. v. Lord Chancellor, ex parte Hibbitt and Saunders* [1993] C.O.D. 326.

[26] Hunt, *op. cit.* at p. 33. In *R. v. Disciplinary Committee of the Jockey Club, ex parte Aga Khan* [1993] 2 All E.R. 853 the decision of the disciplinary committee was held not subject to review because, among other reasons, the source of the committee's authority was the contract between the parties.

context of other forms of regulation that have accompanied contractualisation.[27]

Concepts of regulation: responsiveness, reflexivity, regulatory space

Judicial adjudication and the availability of legal redress are only part of the apparatus of regulation and accountability that structures economic arrangements, whether bureaucratic, market or quasi-market. The idea that privatisation and deregulation imply the complete absence of state control through the transfer of ownership to the private sector is misleading: "Markets should not be seen simply as the product of non-intervention, for they must be actively created and policed by public authorities".[28] Markets do not pre-exist regulation which intervenes in natural processes; rather regulation is constitutive of markets.[29] The regulation debate is not about a choice between regulation and non-regulation (other than at the level of rhetoric and ideology) but about the problem of designing effective regulatory institutions and processes. This section examines some general aspects of regulation, paving the way for an analysis of the regulation of contractualisation in quasi-markets.

Problems concerning the legitimacy and appropriateness of regulation stem from the transformation in the style and form of law, from a system of abstract, general and formal rules, to one of particular and substantive interventions guided by specific social and policy objectives.[30] The instrumentalisation or socialisation of law—reflecting the transition from prevention to promotion, from constitutive to regulative rules, from formal to substantive legal rationality, and from conditional programmes to purposive programmes[31]—has had a significant impact on the normative structure of law. A crisis of legitimacy is posed by the increasing potential for arbitrariness in the exercise of state power and the threat to abstract and general values and liberal market freedoms. Rather than advocating the resolution of this crisis through a Hayekian minimal state involving privatisation and deregulation, neo-evolutionary theorists have argued for the development of new forms of reflexive or responsive law,[32] which seek to maintain law's capacity to fulfil social

[27] On the limits of adjudication generally as a form of social ordering see L. Fuller, "The Forms and Limits of Adjudication" [1978] 92 *Harvard Law Review* 353; M. Eisenberg, "Participation, Responsiveness, and the Consultative Process: An Essay for Lon Fuller" [1978] 92 *Harvard Law Review* 410.

[28] T. Prosser, "Regulation, Markets and Legitimacy" in J. Jowell and D. Oliver (eds.), *The Changing Constitution* (1994) at p. 237.

[29] C. Scott, "Privatisation, Control and Accountability", in J. McCahery, S. Picciotto and C. Scott, *Corporate Control and Accountability* (1993).

[30] G. Teubner, "Substantive and Reflexive Elements in Modern Law" [1983] 17 *Law and Society Review* 239; G. Teubner, "Juridification—Concepts, Aspects, Limits, Solutions" in G. Teubner (ed.), *Juridification of Social Spheres* (1987).

[31] On the nature of this transition see M. Loughlin, *Public Law and Political Theory* (1992), p. 258.

[32] For an account of the concepts of reflexive and responsive law and governance and their interrelation, and of Teubner's interpretation of Nonet and Selznick's notion of responsiveness (P. Nonet and P. Selznick, *Law and Society in Transition; Toward Responsive Law* (1978)), see P. Vincent-Jones, "Responsive Law and Governance in Public Services Provision: A Future for the Local Contracting State" [1998] 61 M.L.R. 362.

programmes and welfare objectives whilst avoiding the harmful effects of direct and particularistic regulatory interventions.

The notion of reflexivity is implicit in the emphasis by "new public law" theorists on "regulated autonomy", drawing on Habermas's central concepts of participation and accountability.[33] There is a link between the critique of legal instrumentalism and the literature on autopoiesis, which stresses the autonomy of social systems and the limits of intervention of law and politics.[34] According to this perspective, the self-referring and self-generating nature of social systems (religion, economy, politics, law) means that *direct* control of the economy through legal norms, for example, is not possible. The economic system "will recognise as valid only economic and not legal norms . . . legal norms are external noise which it will filter and reconstruct in accordance with its own rationality of efficiency".[35] Hence legal regulation has to work *indirectly* through "reflexion structures" that encourage within other social systems self-reflection on the norms and values that guide their operation.[36] The explanation for many regulatory failures is not that those involved should have done better, but rather that direct control is not possible.[37] For the purposes of this article the interest in the concept of reflexivity lies in its capacity to increase understanding of the mechanisms of governance and help establish criteria by which to judge the effectiveness of regulatory interventions.

Research on business regulation and on self-regulation has demonstrated the ineffectiveness of traditional command and control mechanisms, and the superiority of more responsive and co-operative methods in securing compliance with the state's regulatory requirements. The purpose of state intervention may be to control harm caused by corporate actors, for example in the areas of environmental pollution, occupational health and safety, and white-collar crime. Here the studies have sought to transcend the crude opposition between punishment and persuasion, between hard and soft strategies.[38] Where the purpose of regulation is to promote positive values of efficiency, effectiveness and fairness in organisational arrangements, as in the field of corporate law and governance, the literature has focused on how the interests of consumers, employees and other stakeholders may be included in regulatory processes,

[33] See for example T. Prosser, "Towards a Critical Public Law" [1982] 9 J.L.S. 1; C. Graham, "Self-regulation" in G. Richardson and H. Genn (eds.) *Administrative Law and Government Action* (1994); N. D. Lewis, *Choice and the Legal Order* (1996); J. Black, "Constitutionalising Self-Regulation" [1996] 59 M.L.R. 24. For these authors the emphasis is mainly on the regulation of non-governmental bodies performing "public" functions that have hitherto been the direct responsibility of the State.

[34] C. Scott, "Analysing Regulatory Space: Implications for Institutional Design and Reform", paper presented to *Law and Society Association Annual Conference*, Aspen, Colorado, June 1998.

[35] J. Black, *op. cit.*

[36] Teubner, *op. cit.* (1983): "Reflexive law, in other words, will neither authoritatively determine the social functions of other subsystems nor regulate their input and output performances, but will foster mechanisms that systematically further the development of reflexion structures within other social subsystems", p. 275.

[37] Scott, *op. cit.* (1998).

[38] I. Ayres and J. Braithwaite, *Responsive Regulation: Transcending the Deregulation Debate* (1992); F. Haines, *Corporate Regulation: Beyond Punishment and Persuade* (1997).

against the traditional approach which has treated the corporation as constituted through a private contractual order.[39] According to Ayres and Braithwaite, responsive business regulation generally is distinguished by the form of response to regulatory initiatives and by what triggers that response. Effective and responsive regulation can be achieved through a variety of innovative regulatory techniques.[40] Self-regulation by corporate bodies provides a particularly attractive alternative to direct government regulation, which may be expensive and practically unworkable.[41] Under "enforced self-regulation", rules are written, monitored and enforced by companies themselves in conjunction with the government and state agencies; sanctions are applied in a graduated manner, with most effort being concentrated on persuasive activities at the base of an "enforcement pyramid", with the severest state sanctions being reserved for the relatively small number of worst regulatory failures at the pyramid's apex.[42] To the extent that state agencies retain a regulatory role, tripartism may help overcome problems of capture and corruption inherent in the bilateral regulator-regulatee relationship by involving other players (for example community or other interest groups) in regulatory processes. The responsive regulatory order is underpinned throughout by delegation and participation. This position is distinguishable from analyses that simply expose the gap between regulatory legal frameworks and the institutionalisation in practice of negotiation and bargaining "in the shadow of the law"[43] by the importance accorded to the nature of law and the design of regulatory mechanisms.

Similarly rejecting the idea of regulation as the hierarchical imposition of rules and procedures through state authority, Scott has argued convincingly for a concept of "regulatory space" in which resources including wealth, information and organisational capacities[44] are fragmented and dispersed among government departments, public agencies, private firms, pressure and interest groups, national and international organisations, and other state and non-state

[39] See L. E. Mitchell (ed.), *Progressive Corporate Law* (1995); D. Campbell, "The Role of Monitoring and Morality in Company Law: A Critique of the Direction of Present Regulation" [1997] 7 *Australian Journal of Company Law* 343; McCahery *et al.* (eds.) *op. cit.*

[40] This brief account follows Ayres and Braithwaite, *op. cit.* See also J. Braithwaite, T. Makkai, V. Braithwaite and D. Gibson, *Raising the Standard: Resident Centred Nursing Home Regulation in Australia* (1993); J. Braithwaite and V. Braithwaite, "The Politics of Legalism: Rules versus Standards in Nursing-Home Regulation" [1995] 4 *Social and Legal Studies* 307.

[41] Under self-regulation, procedures may be seen as routines with their own regulatory effect: "Organizations are more likely to comply with regulations when those regulations are closely articulated with organizational routines, when organizational actors are willing to function as 'front line regulators' because enforcing regulations serves their purposes as well as those of regulatory bodies . . ." *per* C. Heimer, "The Routinization of Responsiveness: Regulatory Compliance and the Construction of Organizational Routines", paper presented to *Law and Society Association Annual Conference*, Aspen, Colorado, June 1998. Heimer argues that responsiveness may arise from certain forms of routinisation.

[42] Ayres and Braithwaite, *op. cit.* p. 106, and pp. 35–36.

[43] See for example C. Veljanovski, "The Regulation Game" in Veljanovski (ed.). *op. cit.*

[44] For an analysis of how such resources are used by executive government to combat uncertainty and other problems of implementing policy, see T. Daintith, "The Techniques of Government" in Jowell and Oliver, *op. cit.*

bodies.[45] Solutions to regulatory problems are considered to lie not in hierarchical dictates but in complex, dynamic "horizontal relations" of negotiated inter-dependence. In this pluralistic conception, regulation consists in a variety of techniques promoting the conformity of the activities of public and private agencies with public policy objectives. The problem of regulatory design is cast in terms not of the form of incentives and sanctions emanating from discrete and independent regulatory agencies and their effectiveness and ineffectiveness, but of the configuration of interacting and inter-dependent forces and resources and their overall effect. Implying inevitable limits to law and formal processes of adjudication, this view emphasises that self-regulation and multi-agency regulation need to be at the heart of the regulatory design, harnessing and developing the resources that are likely to support the public policy objectives of the regulatory regime.[46]

The regulation of contractualisation

This general discussion of concepts of regulation may be applied to contractualisation. The regulatory space here may be expected to be particularly hotly contested.[47] Hood and Scott have observed that relatively little attention has been paid to "bureaucratic regulation"—the regulation of government bodies by other state agencies or bureaucracies.[48] Such regulation involves an increasing range of activities including standard setting, monitoring and enforcement, audit and evaluation, oversight, inspection and the adjudication of complaints and grievances. Hood and Scott examine the trend in the United Kingdom public sector, embodied in the NPM, away from traditional hierarchical controls towards devolved methods of resource allocation involving greater freedom and responsibility for public managers. While the rhetorical thrust of NPM developments has emphasised deregulation—"loosening controls, freeing managers to manage and replacing bureaucratic controls with market forms of control"[49] —from the standpoint of institutional and rule development there has been an opposite "mirror image" set of movements that may be characterised as "re-regulation". These movements involve a shift in the style of bureaucratic regulation away from general rules and policy advice towards more explicit and specific rules (for instance requiring particular forms

[45] Scott, *op. cit.* (1998); C. Scott, C. Hall and C. Hood, "Regulatory Space and Institutional Reform: The Case of Telecommunications", in P. Vass (ed.) *Regulatory Review of 1997* (1997); L. Hancher and M. Moran, "Organizing Regulatory Space", in Hancher and Moran (eds.) *Capitalism, Culture and Economic Regulation* (1989).

[46] *cf.* Aronson, *op. cit.* at p. 69: "Mixed governmental methods fracture the old dichotomy between public and private power, into a trichotomy which recognises the sharing of governmental functions between organs of the state and organisations sourced in the private sector."

[47] ". . . Regulatory space may be furiously contested. Its occupants are involved in an often ferocious struggle for advantage. Any investigation of the concept involves examining the outcomes of competitive struggles, the resources used in those struggles, and the distribution of those resources between the different involved institutions. In other words, the play of power is at the centre of this process" (Hancher and Moran, *op. cit.* at p. 277).

[48] C. Hood and C. Scott, "Bureaucratic Regulation and the New Public Management in the United Kingdom" [1996] J.L.S. 321.

[49] *ibid.* p. 341.

of contracting, accounting and auditing), more self-standing regulators, and fuller and more formal regulation generally. There may be subtle variations in how the mirror image is manifested in different regulatory contexts. In local government, tighter regulation has been accompanied by tighter management, while in other sectors (for example some of the nationalised industries) there have been movements in the direction of both looser management and looser regulation.[50]

According to the conception of regulatory space, the participation and inclusion of a range of constituencies and interests in quasi-market regulation are crucial determinants of regulatory success or failure. Consumers, purchasers and providers may have important roles to play in the setting of standards and in the monitoring and enforcement of contracts. Greater consumer involvement and the devolution of powers to consumers create incentives and pressures that may be used to beneficial effect in the regulatory design of quasi-markets. This emphasis on multi-party stakes and relationships runs counter to the individualism implicit in classical legal and neo-classical economic analysis,[51] stressing the importance of participation, inclusiveness and responsiveness in optimal regulatory design.[52]

The regulation of contractualisation will be considered with regard to the reflexivity of regulatory regimes; the use of contract by public purchasers as a regulatory mechanism; and economic regulation through the application of market forces and competition. The interests of the purchaser, provider, consumer and the general public in these dimensions of regulation will then be examined.

The reflexivity of regulatory regimes

The welfare state operates in the areas of the health, social and community care, education and local public services through regulatory frameworks that take substantive and purposive legal forms. As Freedland has pointed out in respect of the PFI, contracting in such contexts occurs as a direct result of explicit "positive policy-driven" regulation.[53] Statutory frameworks determine the powers of public agencies, the type of relationships they can and cannot enter into, the nature of access to the courts, and the type of dispute resolution available. Domestic and E.U. competition policy and public procurement rules set particular requirements for public services regarding the forms of competition and competitive tendering.[54]

[50] See C. Hood, C. Scott, O. James, G. Jones and T. Travers, *Regulation Inside Government: Waste Watchers, Quality Police and Sleazebusters* (1999).

[51] Classical law and neo-classical economies share a conception of utility-maximising individuals making discrete exchanges through legally enforceable contractual promises. Even "relational" contract scholarship remains limited in its scope by a relatively narrow focus on the interests of "the parties" in individual exchanges.

[52] See Vincent-Jones, [1998] 61 M.L.R. 362.

[53] M. Freedland, "Public Law and Private Finance—Placing the Private Finance Initiative in a Public Law Frame" [1998] P.L. 288. The PFI is considered by Freedland to be an example of *positive policy-driven regulation* promoting a particular form of contracting, as opposed to simple *regulatory control* of a process which would exist independently of the policy which encourages it (p. 297).

[54] Services Directive 92/50/EEC; Public Services Contracts Regulations (S.I. 1993 No. 3228).

Regulatory regimes may be judged according to criteria of reflexiveness and responsiveness. An ideal model of reflexive regulation of the public agencies responsible for purchasing in quasi-markets might require the following. (1) An open and democratic process of rule-making, characterised by negotiation and involvement of regulatee interests. Legitimacy would be conferred by the provision of proper opportunities for debate, by the attempt to reach consensus, and by the participation of affected bodies and interests.[55] (2) A co-operative and non-adversial relationship between regulator and regulatee, not just in the writing of rules, but in their monitoring and enforcement.[56] (3) A degree of flexibility in the rules themselves that would allow the regulatee to flesh out detail and to exercise initiative in the attainment of regulatory aims; and (as a result) conformity with the spirit as well as the letter of the law. (4) The running of the regulatory regime in an effective and efficient manner, at reasonable cost to regulator and regulatee and ultimately taxpayers. (5) The attainment of effective outcomes, with regulatory objectives being achieved at reasonable overall cost.

It is doubtful how far the welfare state reforms of the 1980s and 1990s met any of these reflexive conditions.[57] The restructuring of the health service under the National Health Service and Community Care Act 1990 was hurriedly imposed in the face of fierce opposition and with little public consultation, evaluation or debate.[58] In the area of local government, the rule-making process has been anything but open and democratic. If the political constitutionality of attacks on local authorities by the first Conservative government after 1979 was open to question,[59] then the overt attempt to weaken local authorities through the imposition of compulsory competitive tendering (CCT) aimed at reducing the role of service provision by direct labour was still more dubious.[60] Many of the key elements of CCT have been implemented through "secondary" and "tertiary" rather than "primary" governmental rules,[61] the surreptitiousness of which might be said further to weaken the claim to political legitimacy. Secondly, under CCT and related central government policy initiatives, the co-operation and mutual respect that characterised central—local relations in the immediate post-war period have

[55] See G. Richardson, "The Legal Regulation of Process" in G. Richardson and H. Genn (eds.), *Administrative Law and Government Action* (1994).

[56] Such a relationship might be expected to be characterised by "virtuous" and "moral" behaviour on the part of the regulatees and other interested parties—see F. Haines, *op. cit.*; D. Campbell, *op. cit.*

[57] Consideration of E.U. competition policy and public procurement rules is beyond the scope of this paper, but reflexive legal analysis might be applied also at the pan-European level. For general analyses see S. Arrowsmith, "Public Procurement as an Instrument of Policy and the Impact of Market Liberalisation" [1995] 111 L.Q.R. 235; C. Bovis, "The Award of Public Contracts Under the Framework of EC Public Procurement Directives" [1994] J.B.L. 615.

[58] D. Hughes, "The Reorganisation of the NHS: The Rhetoric and Reality of the Internal Market" [1991] 54 M.L.R. 88.

[59] J.A.W. Griffith, "Foreward" in M. Loughlin *et al.* (eds.) *Half a Century of Municipal Decline 1935–85* (1985).

[60] Vincent-Jones, *op. cit.* [1998].

[61] R. Baldwin, "Governing with Rules: The Developing Agenda", in Richardson and Genn *op. cit.* p. 156. The PFI is even less subject to scrutiny because the policy framework does not derive from particular legislation.

been replaced by antagonism and mistrust. Thirdly, excessive complexity and formalism have been features of the CCT rules. The problems associated with legal formalism in the design of regulatory mechanisms include ineffectiveness, game-playing and "creative compliance"[62]: "How do you control those playing by the rules? New rules simply mean new games".[63] As the CCT rules have become more complex, so the opportunities for avoidance through legal interpretation have multiplied, with CCT becoming a major field of legal practice. Fourthly, the costs of rule-making, monitoring and enforcement have been excessive under CCT. In many cases notices and directions have been contested in the courts by local authorities. Litigation is expensive and time-consuming. Finally, the extent of efficiency benefits resulting from CCT is open to question, particularly when indirect costs (redundancies and resulting economic burdens on the state, the time and expense involved in conforming to rules, the transaction costs of managing regulated contractual arrangements, and the deterioration in working conditions and pay) are taken into account.

Nevertheless, the Conservative reforms have had considerable effect in transforming management practices within local authorities. Despite the lack of reflexivity in the CCT regulatory regime, responsive contractual governance of the multi-party relationships involved in local public service provision has developed in some circumstances.[64] In the health sector, by contrast, the internal market reforms have been judged generally to have been more problematic,[65] with the form of organisation remaining fundamentally hierarchical and bureaucratic despite the introduction of some elements of contractual governance. Here the lack of reflexivity may have been expressed in the form, not so much of negative consequences for regulated organisations, as of ineffectiveness accompanied by the destruction of the political regime that attempted to implement the reforms.[66]

Regulation by contract

State agencies as public purchasers are regulated and themselves exercise regulatory functions. Just as the funding agency is subject to a regime of bureaucratic regulation through standard-setting, monitoring and enforcement by central government, so also it acts as regulator through the contractual standards it sets and the monitoring and enforcement practices it engages in with the service provider. Given this striking parallel, it is scarcely surprising that arguments as to the limits and problems of regulation and the need to

[62] Creative compliance may be described as "the process whereby those regulated avoid having to break the rules by using legal techniques to achieve non-compliance with the intention of the law without technically violating its content" (Baldwin, *op. cit.* at p. 172).

[63] D. McBarnet and C. Whelan, "The Elusive Spirit of the Law: Formalism and the Struggle for Control" [1991] 54 M.L.R. 848 at p. 873.

[64] P. Vincent-Jones and A. Harries, "Tenant Participation in Contracting for Housing Management Services: A Case Study" in D. Cowan (ed.) *Housing: Participation and Exclusion* (1998).

[65] Generally see R. Flynn and G. Williams (eds.) *Contracting for Health: Quasi-Markets and the National Health Service* (1997).

[66] See R. Laughlin and J. Broadbent, "Accounting and Law: Partners in the Juridification of the Public Sector in the UK?"[1993] 4 *Critical Perspectives on Accounting* 337.

explore extra-legal solutions should be relevant in both contexts, and reflect the main conclusions of the literature on the relative marginality of legal norms and formal judicial processes in business practice.[67]

Public purchasers may make various uses of contract as a regulatory mechanism and management tool.[68] Here a distinction is being drawn between governance (bureaucratic, legal and judicial) of contract, and governance by contract, referring to the exercise of control by public purchasers through the process of contracting. Acting within domestic and E.U. regulatory frameworks, public authorities must make choices as to internal or external providers, select amongst competing contractors, and manage the contracting process. NPM reforms have deprived health authorities, local authorities and other public agencies of the ability to deliver certain services directly under traditional bureaucratic arrangements, but in quasi-market organisation these bodies have retained the commissioning function of selecting amongst competing internal and private sector contractors, and in many cases have been able to continue to perform tasks themselves through "contractual" arrangements with competitive in-house agencies. Once contracts have been awarded, it is in the interest of public authorities to use contract as a mechanism for controlling the quality and cost of service provision. The performance of contracts is of obvious interest to public purchasers. The transaction costs of running contractual relationships in terms of monitoring, defaults, sanctions, penalties, disputes resolution and termination of contracts are likely to be critical indicators of regulatory success or failure. Empirical evidence points to the conclusion that the performance of contracts is not necessarily improved through judicial or quasi-judicial regulation, and that incentives to perform may better be secured through other mechanisms.[69]

An important dimension of regulation by contract involves the nexus of contracting and accounting processes in internal market relationships where providers are required to trade as business units and make financial rates of return, while remaining part of the same organisation as purchasers.[70] Here there may exist a close connection between contracting—the process whereby relations are managed and adjusted according to obligations specified in contract documentation—and accounting, which provides the "calculative vocabulary"[71] linking payment to performance of contractual obligations. In contracts for local authority blue collar services such as school building cleaning, the precise level of payment to the in-house provider is dependent on

[67] S. Macaulay, "Non-contractual Relations in Business: A preliminary Study" [1963] 45 *American Sociological Review* 55. For a recent example see L. Bernstein, "Opting Out of the Legal System: Extralegal Contractual Relations in the Diamond Industry" [1992] XXI *Journal of Legal Studies* 115.

[68] P. Allen, "Contracts in the National Health Service Internal Market" [1995] 58 M.L.R. 321.

[69] P. Vincent-Jones and A. Harries, "Conflict and Cooperation in Local Authority Quasi-Markets: The Hybrid Organisation of Internal Contracting under CCT" [1996] 22 *Local Government Studies* 187.

[70] The concept of the "accounting-contracting nexus" is developed in W. Seal and P. Vincent-Jones, "Accounting and Trust in the Enabling of Long-Term Relationships" [1997] 10 *Accounting, Auditing and Accountability Journal* 406.

[71] P. Miller and M. Power, "Accounting, Law and Economic Calculation" in M. Bromwich and A. Hopwood (eds.) *Accounting and Law* (1992).

the size of the task (which is subject to constant variation) and also on the degree of conformity of the DSO's performance with planned specifications, with penalty deductions being levied following the registering of defaults for defective performance. Monitoring ties together contractual obligations, performance and payment, and enables the client objectively to assess the amount the contractor should be paid under the contract. The accounting-contracting nexus is stronger in such contexts than in the health sector, due to the more developed nature of the quasi-market and the more commercial relationship between client and contractor produced by the CCT regime.[72] In the health sector there is less evidence generally of the use of contract as a management tool because contractual governance plays a relatively minor role in comparison with hierarchical planning.[73]

Local authorities particularly have attempted to use contract also as a means of ensuring that external contractors comply with the council policies, for example on local employment and equal opportunities, based on the strength of their bargaining position. Contract compliance has tended to be regarded by the Department of the Environment, Transport and the Regions (DETR) as undermining competitiveness where potential burdens are placed on private sector bidders that do not normally arise in the market and which are already built into the costs of in-house provision.[74] In other respects, however, the government has indicated that it is keen for local authorities to use contractual powers imaginatively in exploring new forms of relationship and new ways of working in partnership with the private sector.[75] A close link obviously exists between the reflexive potential of quasi-market regimes to produce effective regulatory outcomes and the ability of public agencies to perform purchasing and controlling roles through the contract mechanism. Where purchasers lack adequate powers, either generally because of restrictions on contractual capacity or more particularly due to the nature of the partnership agreement, the public benefits of quasi-market organisation are called into question. The PFI may be a good example of a form of arrangement which, beneath the rhetoric and formal justifications of value for money and risk transfer, deprives the public partner of adequate control through the delegation to private

[72] K. Walsh, N. Deakin, P. Smith, P. Spurgeon and N. Thomas, *Contracting for Change: Contracts in Health, Social Care, and Other Local Government Services* (1997), p. 20.

[73] See Allen, *op. cit.* at pp. 336–337. On the gap between the rhetoric and reality of contracting in the NHS see Hughes *op. cit.*; P. Checkland, "Rhetoric and Reality in Contracting: Research in and on the NHS" in Flynn and Williams, *op. cit.*

[74] P. Morris, "Legal Regulation of Contract Compliance" [1991] 19 *Anglo-American Law Review* 87.

[75] In addition to the specific "Four Ps" initiative, the contractual powers of local authorities generally have been clarified in the Local Government (Contracts) Act 1997. The Act is intended to allay the fears of banks and financial institutions that their investments might be lost where local authorities are held to have acted outside their legal powers. The Act introduces a certification procedure for partnership contracts establishing their lawfulness (ss.2–4), limits the circumstances in which such contracts may be argued to be unenforceable in private law proceedings (s.5), and provides for compensation to be paid to private contractors where a public law challenge is successful and the contract is set aside by the court (s.6).

contractors of decision-making powers affecting the interests and the welfare of citizens.[76]

Economic regulation through markets and competition

Economic regulation may be said to occur in quasi-markets through the incentives and pressures accompanying competition and their capacity for generating efficiency. Efficient and effective service-providing outcomes are likely to depend on the contestability of markets and the nature and degree of competition.[77] The point that market forces may themselves constitute a form of regulation has led Sir Stephen Sedley to inquire whether the market needs the rule of law or is itself a novel form of law.[78] The lack of *legal* safeguards and remedies may not be a source of regulatory failure provided that the consumer's interests in efficiency and effectiveness are met by other governance arrangements.

The point to emphasise here is that the traditional hierarchical model of control and accountability in the public sector has been replaced by a range of new control and accountability mechanisms.[79] Competition and contracting, appropriately implemented, may themselves be regarded as regulatory techniques that operate alongside more traditional mechanisms such as judicial review. Similar functions may be performed by capital markets, by performance pay and individual responsibility, and by performance targets, information and openness. According to Scott, the task for administrative lawyers might now be "to examine the effectiveness . . . of new forms of control and accountability, rather than ponder the promulgation of rules by which to check discretion".[80] From this perspective, the full regulatory implications of the NPM and in particular the introduction of contracting and competition mechanisms have yet fully to be appreciated.

In many quasi-markets there is considerable doubt as to the existence of effective competition between providers.[81] The markets may not be contestable, either because of the relative novelty of competition and the lack of competitors, or because features of the particular type of service (for example quality in health and social care) are not readily quantifiable or otherwise easily subject to competitive discipline.[82] Such arrangements may fail to deliver value for money due to a combination of ineffective competition, monopoly market conditions, and problems following the award of contracts on the basis of impossibly low bids.[83] The public benefits of PFI projects are particularly

[76] Freedland, *op. cit.* [1998] p. 307.

[77] According to economic theory market organisation may produce efficiencies, despite the absence of direct competition, where markets are "contestable"—in other words where entry barriers are low so that there exists the threat of competition from new entrants.

[78] S. Sedley, "Foreword" in Taggart, *op. cit.* p. viii.

[79] Scott, *op. cit.* (1996).

[80] *ibid.* at p. 50.

[81] Bartlett *et al.*, *op. cit.* (1998).

[82] C. Propper and W. Bartlett, "The Impact of Competition on the Behaviour of NHS Trusts", in Flynn and Williams, *op. cit.*

[83] PFI Information Technology projects have been argued to be particularly prone to failure for these reasons—see T. Phillips, *The Guardian*, November 12, 1998.

doubtful in the longer term. The need for the private sector to obtain a return on its investment means that efficiency gains in the operation of facilities may be made at the expense of service quality, and the total cost of schemes may be higher than if public bodies had been able to raise finance directly. In local government, the existence of real market contestability under CCT is open to question, given the relative lack of development of many markets and the protective attitude of most local authorities and their ability to avoid the spirit of CCT by favouring DSOs in the tendering process. Nevertheless, competitiveness has tended to be assured by the *possibility* of private sector penetration, and by the financial pressures on local authorities and the general climate of employee insecurity created by compulsory tendering.[84] In the United Kingdom as in the United States, estimated savings from market testing or competitive tendering are similar to those claimed for contracting out: " . . . Where public sector agencies are required to compete with the private sector . . . productivity differences often largely disappear".[85]

Public, purchaser, provider and consumer interests
The connections between these dimensions of regulations and the interests of the purchaser, provider, consumer and general public may now be made explicit. At the general level of regulatory design there are public and citizenship interests in the processes whereby regulatory frameworks are created, in equity and redistributional outcomes, in the capacity of regulatory structures to meet their claimed policy objectives, and in the running of the regulatory regimes in an effective and efficient manner. The extent to which these interests are satisfied depends on the reflexiveness of regulatory regimes —on the democratic processes by which they have been created and on the scope they allow public purchasers to determine quasi-market arrangements that will produce economically viable service-providing outcomes. Regulatory regimes such as CCT and the PFI may fail or succeed under different conditions on any of these reflexive criteria. It is hardly surprising that the experience of problems with some PFI projects mirrors that of contractual arrangements for service provision made under CCT, since the procurement process operates in the same manner through tightly defined competitive tendering rules, and the public "partner" is under similar pressures to give high priority to price over quality considerations.

Public purchasers have interests in the use of contract as a management tool to achieve their public service aims. Again, whether these interests are satisfied depends on the way regulatory regimes determine the parameters of contracting powers of such bodies. The ability of public purchasers to promote responsive governance arrangements through contracting depends on the reflexive qualities of the parent regulatory regime. Despite some recent clarification, there exists still considerable uncertainty over the contractual powers of public bodies.[86] In other quasi-market contexts such as the PFI, the

[84] Vincent-Jones and Harries, *op. cit.* [1996].

[85] Trebilcock, *op. cit.* at p. 20.

[86] S. Arrowsmith, "Judicial Review and the Contractual Powers of Public Authorities" [1990] 106 L.Q.R. 277.

problem may concern not so much the adequacy or clarity of contractual powers as the appropriateness of the form of institutional arrangement for service provision.

Potential contractors, whether public employees within an internal market or private firms, have interests in decisions as to the award of contracts. Procedures for the award of contracts can be designed to be open and to encourage participation of affected interests.[87] The tendering process undertaken by public purchasing agencies is heavily regulated by domestic and E.U. law. The financial interests at stake and the need for contracts to be seen to be awarded fairly in order to satisfy competition policy regulations have led to increasing judicial control of tendering processes.[88] Here the courts have a central role in encouraging transparency and the free and open flow of information.[89]

Finally, consumers of the services in question again have a variety of interests. Effectiveness and efficiency depend ultimately on the appropriateness of choice of form of provision—private, public, mixed partnership or some other hybrid arrangement—by public purchaser and how the selection has been made. The contractual specification needs to be appropriate to the needs of service users. And the management of contracts has to provide effective procedures for rectification and redress of problems with service delivery. At this point extra-legal and informal procedures have to be considered alongside legal and more formal processes. The design of appropriate governance frameworks and the role of legal, economic and administrative processes depend on how seriously and directly affected are consumer interests at the various levels and stages of the contracting process. It is trite to observe that the problems that arise in different types of service-providing situation are likely to require different remedial processes and forms of legal and extra-legal regulation. Consider the following: an elderly person is threatened with eviction from a community home; a householder's wheely-bin is not emptied; parents and children find that school buildings have not properly been cleaned; a homeless person is refused allocation of a council house; public recreational facilities are in disrepair and poorly maintained; an NHS patient is denied a particular form of treatment because it is too expensive; an operation has gone wrong and a patient considers the hospital is to blame; residents are generally unhappy with the quality of service they receive from the local authority in a particular area, or feel that they are paying too much property tax for these services.

Solutions to regulatory design problems depend on the particular public service setting. In many cases formal remedies or disputes resolution procedures may not be necessary and the interests of consumers may best be advanced through practical rectification of defective provision.[90] In such cases

[87] *cf.* Prosser, *op. cit.* (1994) p. 254.

[88] *cf. R. v. Lord Chancellor, ex parte Hibbitt and Saunders* [1993] C.O.D. 326. See *Blackpool and Fylde Aero Club Ltd v. Blackpool Borough Council* [1990] 3 All E.R. 25 on private law control.

[89] Arrowsmith, "Protecting the Interests of Bidders for Public Contracts: The Role of the Common Law" [1994] 55 C.L.J. 104; Aronson, *op. cit.* p. 58.

[90] Vincent-Jones and Harries, *op. cit.* (1998).

successful regulation is likely to depend on whether consumers are able to articulate and communicate service delivery problems, for example through complaints mechanisms,[91] and on the ability of providers and client agencies to respond appropriately. In other areas, victims of poor performance may have grievances that require administrative redress,[92] or redress and compensation through the application of law and resort to the courts. The legal accountability vacuum needs to be considered in such different contexts. In many instances the parties involved in purchasing and provision in quasi-markets may not be legally accountable, in the sense of having to make amends for the consequences of poor performance to wronged consumers. But the clarity with which their roles have been defined and distinguished, and their greater visibility and responsibility in consequence, may render them more easily accountable in other ways, administrative and legal (for example through performance on individual contracts of employment).[93] The main issue is likely often to concern what forms of sanction or incentive are necessary to facilitate performance. These may be economic, bureaucratic, administrative or operational, rather than narrowly legal or contractual. Where problems do arise with service provision requiring formal redress as opposed to rectification, recourse to the courts should generally be a last rather than a first resort, with greater regulatory pressures being concentrated towards the base of "enforcement pyramids".[94]

Issues of legal accountability are likely to be of greater importance in the health and social care sectors than in local government.[95] The interests of patients and welfare recipients are qualitatively different from those of consumers in local government, where the repetitive and mundane nature of many services calls for more attention to be paid to other aspects of regulatory design. In respect of the fundamental welfare services an interesting question for the future concerns how far the courts may be prepared to take a stronger stand in the review of resource-allocation decisions on the basis of human rights reasoning, particularly in the light of the Human Rights Act 1998.[96] The non-use of statutory dispute-settlement procedures in the health sector and the shift toward informal and largely unaccountable processes raise a question as to whether remedial procedures are meeting the needs of consumers and providers.[97]

[91] N. Lewis and P. Birkinshaw, *When Citizens Complain: Reforming Justice and Administration* (1993).

[92] Birkinshaw, *Grievances, Remedies and the State* (1994), pp. 187–245.

[93] Scott, *op. cit.* (1996) pp. 53–60.

[94] Ayres and Braithwaite, *op. cit.* pp. 35–36.

[95] Allen, *op. cit.* p. 342.

[96] Hughes *et al.* point to evidence of a shift already in the willingness of some judges, in situations where decisions as to the allocation of medical resources have life and death implications, to adopt such reasoning in the interpretation of "reasonableness"—see D. Hughes, S. McClelland and L. Griffiths " 'Cinderella' Services in the NHS Internal Market: Does Contracting Make a Difference?" [1997] 20 *Dalhousie Law Journal* 400; Lewis, *op. cit.* pp. 21–24.

[97] D. Hughes, J. McHale, and L. Griffiths, "Settling Contract Disputes in the National Health Service: Formal and Informal Pathways" in Flynn and Williams, *op. cit.*

The responsive potential of contractual governance

Responsiveness may be assessed with reference to the degree to which the regulation of quasi-markets succeeds in meeting the various interests of different constituencies affected by the process of contractualisation. Contract may be seen as a mechanism linking purchaser, provider and consumer in a manner leading to more or less responsive governance of the quasi-market relationship. In the health and welfare sectors generally the evidence as to the value of contractual management processes has been mixed. There have been particular difficulties in casting purchaser-provider relationships in contractual terms.[98] In many cases the importance of professional judgment and the relative ignorance or remoteness of consumers make it difficult to involve them in contract specification and management in a meaningful manner. In such circumstances, and in many PFI partnerships, there may be particular accountability problems that require the development of new or more effective forms of oversight and review. In local government, however, research has shown that, under the right conditions, the client-contractor split and the process of contracting for services can deliver benefits of increased transparency, efficiency, and responsiveness to consumer needs, with corresponding benefits for the authority's relationship with its local taxpayers and consumers.[99]

Towards a more reflexive regulation?

Responsive governance is likely to be attained most readily where regulatory regimes are themselves reflexive. There is some evidence that New Labour is moving towards more reflexive regulation. It may be that social democratic objectives different from those pursued by the Conservatives can be achieved by retaining quasi-markets and contractualisation, but under a more reflexive and less prescriptive regulatory umbrella.

The new government has moved most quickly to introduce reform in quasi-markets for local authority services. Here CCT is being replaced with a general requirement that local authorities demonstrate "best value" in local service provision.[1] The new framework is broader in scope and potentially more far-reaching than the CCT regime in three key respects. The duty of best value will be to provide effective as well as economic and efficient services; it will be owed to local taxpayers and customers rather than being narrowly legally defined; and it will apply simultaneously to all local authorities and all services. Councils will be required to consult with consumers, to set standards, to establish mechanisms for monitoring and evaluating service provision, to maintain trading accounts, and to allow stricter public audit and comparability with other local authority providers through benchmarking. Despite these strict requirements, the best value framework may be considered more reflexive than its predecessor. In contrast to the restrictive specification of procedure that

[98] Generally see Flynn and Williams (eds.), *op. cit.*

[99] Vincent-Jones and Harries, *op. cit.* (1998).

[1] Green Paper, *Modernising Local Government: Improving Local Services through Best Value*, 3 March 1998; White Paper, *Modern Local Government: In Touch with The People*, Ch 7, July 1998; Local Government Bill (H.C. Bill 5) November 30, 1998.

applies under CCT, there will be greater flexibility for local councils to decide how services should be provided. This form of regulation may be compared with the model of enforced self-regulation of private sector bodies described by Ayres and Braithwaite. Rather than detailed and substantive rules, there is a general prescription of *processes* of consultation, reviewing and standard-setting that must be undertaken by local authorities in establishing management frameworks and performance plans. The onus is on local authorities to challenge whether services are needed, to compare different forms of provision, and to consult on provider ambitions, targets and means.[2] Monitoring will distinguish between failures of substance and process. Failures will be dealt with through a graduated response involving a wider range of formal and informal sanctions than exists under CCT, suggesting a more subtle "pyramid" of enforcement powers. Although best value does not require quasi-markets and the associated use of contracts, it is highly likely that these institutional forms will be retained by local authorities for many services.[3]

The best value framework might be considered as scoring positively on the first three parameters of reflexivity considered above (process of rule making, process of monitoring and enforcement, and the flexibility of the rules themselves), while prospects for the final two (costs of running the regulatory system and the effectiveness of outcomes) appear promising. The greater reflexivity implicit in the best value framework suggests that, where local authorities retain a purchasing role, responsive governance of relationships is more likely to occur, more often, and at less cost. There might be expected to be a reduction in litigation under the new framework. The abolition of the primary legislation on CCT will be accompanied by the removal of many of the specific interventionist powers of the secretary of state. The monitoring functions currently performed by the DETR will be transferred to audit bodies, which will be applying more flexible and less particularistic criteria in deciding whether competitiveness and best value have been demonstrated. The secretary of state's power to issue notices and directions to individual local authorities for anti-competitive conduct or failure to meet statutory financial objectives will be replaced by more general enforcement powers exercisable by auditors and the Audit Commission. Here we appear to be witnessing a shift from "full" regulation, with powers of standard-setting, monitoring and enforcement being concentrated in the DETR, towards more "partial" regulation characterised by less direct government control and more regulatory inputs from other institutions and actors.[4]

It is too soon to judge whether this apparent movement[5] towards more reflexive regulation in local government is part of a more general trend. While

[2] Performance reviews will have to "challenge, compare and consult" as part of the process of ensuring competitiveness and demonstrating best value—White Paper, *op. cit.* para. 7.18.

[3] Vincent-Jones, "Competition and Contracting in the Transition from CCT to Best Value: Towards a More Reflexive Regulation?" [1999] *Public Administration*, forthcoming.

[4] This shift is in the opposite direction to that described by Hood and Scott in their analysis of the trend towards more specific rules and more complete regulation in the public sector generally.

[5] Much depends on the precise drafting of the best value legislation, on the manner in which powers of delegated legislation are exercised by the Secretary of State, and on the interpretation and implementation of the legislation generally.

in comparison with CCT the best value framework embodies a shift towards less specific and prescriptive regulatory control, in other areas substantive direction through policy-driven regulation is being pursued ever more forcefully, as in the PFI and the "Four Ps" programme for increasing private investment in local government services infrastructure. It appears that present regulatory developments in the public sector are complex, uneven and possibly contradictory, rather than informed by any coherent overall policy.

Responsive contractual governance

The threads of the argument as to the responsive potential of contractual governance in quasi-markets may now be drawn together. Contracting between public purchasers and internal or external providers may, *in certain sectors and under appropriate institutional forms and conditions*, contribute to effectiveness and responsiveness in public services. The benefits of contracting both within public authorities and in their relationship with external consumers and citizens derive from the reciprocal form in which the principal client-contractor relationship is cast. Contracting operates as a device for the planning and delivery of services through the allocation of responsibilities and entitlements that may serve as the basis for the subsequent management and adjustment of relationships.[6] This form of contracting offers a number of responsive governance benefits:

(1) The splitting of purchaser and provider roles opens up traditional bureaucratic processes of planning and procurement, and creates the possibility of *greater accountability* both within the organisation and to external monitoring bodies and the public generally.

(2) The separation of client and contractor responsibilities may be accompanied by the *devolution* of planning and management functions to lower levels within the organisation, with more transaction information and economic signals and hence better adaptation to environmental conditions.

(3) Contracting may provide increased opportunities for the *participation of stakeholders* or their representatives at every stage of the planning and delivery process, from service specification and contract formation through to monitoring, adjustment and problem resolution.[7]

(4) By introducing an element of competition, quasi-market contracting has the potential to include the interests of purchasers, consumers and citizens in *economy and efficiency* in a more transparent way than is possible under direct hierarchical provision.

(5) Finally, the quasi-market contracting process preserves an element of public *responsibility for*, and *control over*, how and by whom services are

[6] See Vincent-Jones, *op. cit.* [1998] p. 380.

[7] Vincent-Jones and Harries, *op. cit.* (1998). In this sense contracting may serve as a vehicle for "tripartism" in a sense analogous to Ayres and Braithwaite's terminology discussed above. This casts doubt on Aronson's blanket assertion that "it is in the nature of outsourcing that the consumer has no more say in the formation or terms of the contract than in the pre-outsourcing days when government provided the service direct" (*op. cit.* at p. 56).

> provided. Contract may serve as a instrument whereby public authorities may better achieve their legitimate objectives through contract compliance.[8]

The achievement of responsiveness in quasi-markets may depend ultimately on the degree of flexibility allowed public purchasers in their choice of procurement method. The form of contracting imposed by the previous government and encouraged by the present one typically involves the award of contracts following open competitive tendering. But contractualisation might occur in other ways, through partnerships and joint ventures developed outside particular policy-driven regulatory frameworks. Recent theoretical and empirical research on contracts and competition in both private and public sectors has stressed the complexity of competitive processes, the variety of contractual forms that exist within different contractual environments,[9] and the vital role of co-operation in long term and welfare-maximising relationships.[10] Where the decision is taken to contract out services, a fundamental issue confronting public purchasers is whether outsourcing should continue on the basis of competitive tendering, or whether more inherently relational arrangements, for example analogous to supply chains in the private sector, might be adopted.[11] The consultation paper on best value in local government explicitly acknowledged the tensions that can arise under competitive tendering, and which might be avoided through joint ventures and other forms of partnership arrangement. New regulations in this and other public service contexts need to be sufficiently flexible to avoid foreclosing choice among alternative options. Whatever the particular form of quasi-market contracting, contract will be the mechanism whereby public authorities manage their roles as purchasers of in-house or private sector provision following market testing or competitive tendering, or partners in joint ventures or other shared ownership arrangements.

Conclusion

In heeding Nonet and Selznick's warning that accountability "can suffocate institutions, paralyse energies, and hinder problem solving",[12] the regulatory design approach adopted in this paper has focused not just on legal regulation, norms, remedies and safeguards but on the overall process whereby services are delivered to citizens and public consumers. This focus responds to Oliver's call for a shift away from the traditional public law concern with decision-making

[8] Morris, *op. cit.* pp. 103–121.

[9] Generally see D. Campbell and P. Vincent-Jones (eds.) *Contract and Economic Organisation: Socio-Legal Initiatives* (1996); S. Deakin and J. Michie (eds.), *Contracts, Cooperation and Competition: Studies in Economics, Management and Law* (1997).

[10] D. Campbell and D. Harries, "Flexibility in Long Term Contractual Relationships; The Role of Cooperation" [1993] 20 J.L.S. 166.

[11] See H. Collins, "Quality Assurance and Contractual Practice" in Deakin and Michie, *op. cit.*; M. Sako, *Prices, Quality and Trust: Inter-Firm Relations in Britain and Japan* (1992).

[12] P. Nonet and P. Selznick, *Law and Society in Transition: Toward Responsive Law* (1978), p. 107.

procedures towards outcomes of decisions and actions,[13] but with a systemic rather than individual-remedial emphasis. Legal remedies and dispute resolution procedures are of undoubted significance in the majority of public service governance settings. But formal legal incentives and sanctions need to play an appropriate role in regulatory structures and be considered in the context of governance arrangements more broadly construed. It is regulatory design itself, and not just enforcement, that may be visualised in terms of a pyramid, with formal legal processes occupying a relatively small place at the apex of the pyramid's structure.

Responsive regulatory outcomes cannot be expected to occur where the form of economic organisation, whether bureaucratic, market or quasi-market, is inappropriate or inadequate to the needs of citizens and consumers. The future of quasi-market contracting looks most secure in local government, where there is evidence of effective regulation by contract and by competition. Here public management reforms may be argued to have been relatively successful and to have taken root despite the coercive manner in which they were introduced. The less prescriptive and more reflexive best value framework now being introduced may provide the conditions for experimentation with a variety of competitive and contracting forms that will facilitate responsive public services governance. In the health sector generally and in many PFI projects, however, there are significant doubts as to the benefits of quasi-markets in comparison with properly planned hierarchical provision. Where quasi-markets are retained in circumstances where there is weak or little effective economic regulation by competition and by contract, as has generally been the case in the health sector, the importance of other forms of regulation increases. Here regulatory design may have to be rethought in more imaginative ways involving more disparate institutions and actors, and greater legal accountability and access to the courts may be necessary for the protection of provider and consumer interests.[14]

The appropriateness of quasi-market organisation and the quality of regulation and its outcomes can only be assessed empirically through careful examination of the particular conditions obtaining in different institutional settings. The public purchasing of services through competitive tendering may produce benefits of increased efficiency and effectiveness for some services and for some local authorities but not for others. PFI partnerships may be appropriate for the building of roads and schools, but not for hospitals and complex IT infrastructure. Rather than prescribing particular modes of provision, central government policy should aim to maximise choice by responsible public bodies according to local environmental and institutional conditions, and to increase the level of public participation in decisions concerning the institutional framework, so that citizen and consumer interests may be adequately represented in determining optimal forms of governance. The quality and availability of information—both governmental and more

[13] Oliver, in Taggart (ed.) *op. cit.* p. 220; *ibid.* "Common Values in Public and Private Law and the Public/Private Divide" [1997] P.L. 630.

[14] Hughes *et al.* in Flynn and Williams, *op. cit.* p. 112.

generally in the markets for services—are likely to be crucial in the making of informed choices.[15] Where quasi-market organisation is adopted in preference to market or bureaucratic governance, the interests of the public and consumers should be represented in the choice of quasi-market contractor, and then in the management of contractual relationships.

The introduction of quasi-markets was originally intended by Conservative policy-makers as part of the privatisation and deregulation strategy directed at increasing market at the expense of bureaucratic provision.[16] The recent experience of contractualisation suggests, however, that quasi-market forms may be adapted to an alternative political agenda, preserving some of the redistributive features of direct state provision but with some of the advantages of markets and competition. Whether contractualisation should be welcomed in these political terms is a matter for debate. The viability of a social democratic variant on the contract state is open to question.[17] From a left perspective, the existence of private property rights and associated economic and social inequalities will be seen as imposing fundamental limits on the achievement of socialist outcomes through quasi-market organisation.[18] Nevertheless, the conclusion of this paper is that quasi-market contracting can, in properly selected cases and subject to these limitations, offer significant advantages in comparison with the form of bureaucratic organisation that until relatively recently has dominated public service provision in the United Kingdom and other capitalist societies. Under appropriate regulatory conditions, contractual governance can help provide solutions to the problem of how democratic values of openness, participation and accountability may be put into effect in arrangements for the more efficient, effective and responsive provision of public services.

[15] Lewis, *op. cit.* pp. 17–21.

[16] Kirkpatrick and Lucio stress the diverse intellectual currents in the international trend towards reorganisation of public services through contracts. While the New Right was a crucial source of ideas, it is no longer the only point of reference for government policy makers—see I. Kirkpatrick and M. M. Lucio, "The Contract State and the Future of Public Management" [1996] 74 *Public Administration* 4.

[17] *ibid.* p. 6.

[18] See the discussion in M. Robertson, "Reconceiving Private Property" [1997] 24 J.L.S. 465.

[17]

Hare and Hedgehog Revisited: The Regulation of Markets That Have Escaped Regulated Markets

by

ERICH SCHANZE *

Theories of regulation tend to look for "optimal" levels of regulation of general application. In this static model problems of rule observation are largely regarded as noise. They also refer to a diffuse normative dichotomy of market and regulation. The paper argues that a neo-institutional theory of market regulation would have to take account of the dynamics of counterreaction to the regulatory process. At the border of important markets that have typically attracted an extensive regulatory coverage we observe the work of hedgehogs, i.e. the creation of new "institutional settings" (or "markets" in the Coasean sense) escaping the conventional regime. We furthermore observe – in a comparative law perspective – that courts show "sympathy with the hedgehog" and concede a *regulatory bifurcation* as long as a superior incentive structure can be demonstrated. For promoting institutional innovation, courts resort to basic "bright-line" regulation until the new market is discovered as a target for specific regulatory coverage. But in an open constitutional setting the process does not stop here. This mechanism also affects the legal theory of interpretation. (JEL: B 4, K 2, K 4, L 0)

1. Markets and Regulation

In his Stockholm lecture, R. H. COASE [1992, 717] remarks that "it makes little sense for economists to discuss the process of exchange without specifying the institutional setting within which the trading takes place since this affects

* This paper is dedicated to Hans Joachim Mertens at the occasion of his 60th birthday on July 25, 1994. The research was, in part, made possible by the hospitality of The Law School (Boalt Hall), University of California at Berkeley, and an associated travel grant by the Niedersachsen Ministry of Science; special thanks are due to Richard Buxbaum. The written comments by Herbert Hax (Cologne) and Hans-Bernd Schäfer (Hamburg), and the communications by Stephen Guittard (Detroit), Richard Posner (Chicago), Edward Rubin (Berkeley), Ekkehart Schlicht (Munich), Alan Schwartz (Yale), and Rainer Walz (Hamburg) are specifically appreciated.

the incentives to produce and the costs of transacting." Likewise, it makes little sense for lawyers to theorize about legal arrangements which are a decisive part of the institutional setting without paying regard to the process of exchange and the related incentives. Specifically, both lawyers and economists should consider economic explanations of the regulatory process which – in a comparative perspective – would include not only the American traditional variant of regulation by agencies but *all* explicit rule making by state actors such as legislatures at various levels, the judiciary and the administrative branch (SUNSTEIN [1990]). Moreover, there are important instances in which private actors "regulate" specific conduct, thereby affecting third parties such as in variants of "regulation by consensus" (SCHANZE [1988]). Within this broader framework of "regulation," or what Coase terms "the institutional setting," we would find both (1) elements of regulation that curtail economic action in face of lucrative opportunities or would even display clearcut effects of redistribution, and (2) kinds of regulation that display "facilitative" functions (FULLER [1975]). This facilitative aspect of the institutional setting also relates to the basics of autonomous decision-making. In his assessment of the current regulatory process in the United States, Cass SUNSTEIN [1990, 40] correctly summarizes this point: "One goal of a legal system ... is not merely to ensure autonomy by allowing satisfaction of preferences, but also and more fundamentally to promote autonomy in the process of preference formation." Moreover, as will be briefly outlined with specific reference to recent work of Melvin EISENBERG [1995], the design of contractual remedies has to take account of the systematic aberrations related to cognitive dissonances. A broader, and more diffuse, issue is contained in the assertion "that sometimes regulatory programs are necessary to solve collective action and coordination problems" (SUNSTEIN [1990, 45]). Even more open to rhetoric is the theory that "some government controls commonly regarded as unjustified paternalism can be understood instead as an effort to facilitate the satisfaction of private desires" (SUNSTEIN [1990, 51]). To be sure, in the first cases mentioned (free preference formation, choice anomalies) we would hardly speak of a conflict of market transactions and regulation. They refer to rules which make meaningful transactions possible, and which economize on the search costs for viable modes of transacting.

2. New Approaches

Current theories of regulation largely imply that there is an "optimal" level of regulation. Some claim that minimal regulation is optimal (POSNER [1993]); others defend the "optimality" of current levels (SUNSTEIN [1990]). Under these theories, markets and associated "efficient" regulation are regarded as a matching pair. Given our state of sketchy knowledge about the effects of regulation this may be too ambitious an aim. Moreover, once we have adopted the view that "markets" are no economic abstractions but rather refer to "real economic settings" in which rights are traded in the Coasean sense, we arrive at a theoretical question: Is it really possible to draw an abstract borderline between "facilitative" and onerous regulation? Or rather is it up to the actors themselves to determine individually what regime will best accomplish their specific ends?[1] As a consequence we currently witness theories that are either confined to very narrow fact sets or that address partial problems or even employ explicitly partial approaches. Let us look at two important approaches of this kind before we turn to a third variant which will be elaborated in this paper.

2.1 Adapting Regulation to Cognitive Dissonances

An important move toward a more realistic understanding of the regulatory process is the explicit recognition of cognitive dissonances in the contracting process, or even more broadly, in all instances of private and public choice. It is basically a micro approach, in the sense that it looks at single transactions and concentrates on the perception of the actors, taking account of their cognitive limits. In a current paper the distinguished corporate and contract scholar Melvin EISENBERG [1995] explores the limits of contract in view of the limits of cognition. He is able to show that a number of regulatory deviations from the bargaining principle may be explained by direct reference to the experimental literature on behavioral anomalies (summary in FREY [1992]). Especially, he cites the example of mandatory social security, relating to individuals' inability to allocate appropriately their income between present and future consumption. Certain safety rules are related to anomalies in the use of information.[2]

2.2 Partial Regulation as an Alternative to All-or-Nothing Regulatory Policies

Generalizing an approach in an industry-specific study (media) by Lee BOLLINGER [1976], Ian AYRES and John BRAITHWAITE [1992] in a recent law review article advocate partial-industry regulation as a strategy of regulators in situations where all-or-nothing policies are either ineffective or infeasible. They suggest mimicking the behavior of private monopsonist consumers who will, inter alia, enter into second sourcing strategies. They demonstrate the viability of their approach in a number of examples including the destabilization of OPEC, the disparate treatment of broadcast and print media, and the regula-

---

[1] The idea of "facilitative" regimes has a significant appeal to law-and-economics scholarship. I suscribe to it but with the *caveat* that it is not a positive concept but rather packed with normative implications of standardized transacting. These have to be scrutinized.

[2] SCHANZE and HAUNHORST [1993] have taken a similar approach relating to regulation concerning security of tenure in labor relations and the choice of "new" regimes of independent contracting.

tion of long-distance telephone services. The interesting feature in the "partial" approach is its apparent contradiction to the constitutional principle of equal treatment of all persons affected by the specific regulation. The authors are able to show that courts display a fairly tolerant attitude by distinguishing the party affected by partial regulation from possible further addressees of the regulatory strategy. They quote the leading case of City of New Orleans v. Dukes[3] in which the United States Supreme Court distinguished pushcart vendors in the French Quarter of New Orleans who could show long standing from those who had just entered the market, thereby upholding a city regulation that was based on a "grandfather clause" approach. Indeed, the Court indicated in general that it would not invalidate economic regulation "solely on equal protection grounds" (427 U.S. 306). The approach taken by the Court is what may be termed a "bright-line" approach. It states that it would only invalidate a distinctive treatment if it "trammels fundamental personal rights or is drawn upon inherently suspect distinctions" (427 U.S. 306).

2.3 The Regulatory Bifurcation: The Hare and Hedgehog Paradigm

Important markets tend to attract and to host regulatory programs – in increasing scale and intensity. This paper is neither concerned with the rich literature concerning the causes, nor does it purport to explain the "correct" level of regulation. It suggests that, for a better understanding of the "systemic effects of regulatory control" (SUNSTEIN [1990, 237]), a view should be taken that is largely absent in the literature on regulation: to pay regard to the *dynamism of counterreaction* to regulation.[4]

At the border of important markets we observe the creation of new markets escaping regulation. And indeed, diligent evasion will be tolerated. In the name of private autonomy, courts concede what I may term a *regulatory bifurcation*. In this sense, regulation tends to be "partial" from the outset, and courts, wise legislators, and administrative agencies display sympathy with those who smartly escape the regulatory regime. The motivation is – as I will explain – "sympathy with the hedgehog."

Since the work of ROSEN [1988] and others, contests are increasingly used for explaining important economic phenomena. The fable of the race between the hare and the tortoise has become almost a commonplace, but, as James MARCH

[3] 427 U.S. 297 (1976).

[4] Earlier important approaches which relate implicitly to the idea of the regulatory bifurcation in different ways include MACAULAY [1963] – in ongoing business relations actors even do not resort to common law regulation but rely on private ordering; MNOOKIN and KORNHAUSER [1979] – systems of regulation work because actors bargain in the shadow of the law; and MERTENS [1982] – systems of regulation function in view of illegitimate forms of escape that are signaling that, in general, norms are respected. The approach presented here refers to a bifurcation that is explicitly tolerated by courts and administrative agencies.

[1994] noted in his Hitchcock Lectures at Berkeley, we would *not* bet on the tortoise to win if large numbers were concerned.

In contrast, the race between the Hare and the Hedgehog first reported in the 1843 edition of the collection of fairy tales of the brothers GRIMM [1843/1987] produces systematic results because, as we are told by the storyteller, "no hare has ever had the inclination to run a race again with a Buxtehude hedgehog."

The fable is set in Lower Saxony, south of Hamburg, and it concerns a fatal tournament. The hedgehog accepts the bet of the hare for a race and secretly places his wife – who looks like himself – at the end of the furrow by advising her to state firmly in Low German at the arrival of the hare (which should be understandable for all Saxon hares including those who went to Anglia): "Ik bün all hier" (Here I am already). When the astonished hare returns to the other end of the furrow the hedgehog himself repeats: "Ik bün all hier." In the 74th round the hare loses the bet and his life. Nevertheless, all children like the street-smart hedgehog who walks away with his wife, a bottle of brandy, and a Louis d'Or. Likewise, courts sympathize with the hedgehogs. They do not intervene, as will be shown in a number of examples, if smart players change the rules of the game with reference to private autonomy. Indeed, much of what lawyers do in the upper stratum of the profession – the task which I described in an earlier paper as institutional design (SCHANZE [1993 a]) – is concerned with diligent changing of the rules within the scope of legality, or emphatically termed: *institutional innovation* by utilizing the hedgehog's regulatory bifurcation.

I will present some examples of following the hedgehog's strategy before I return to regime reactions. I will show that – as an empirical matter – markets that have escaped regulated markets are likely to receive sympathetic treatment. I will then argue – as a normative matter – that this attitude is of fundamental constitutional significance for the maintenance of market economies.

3. Examples of Contracting Out-of-the-Rule

3.1 "Technological Evasion": Regulation of Small Print and the Introduction of the Computer

In some cases the hedgehogs exploit the technological characteristics of the furrow. This occurred when the German Act Concerning Standard Terms of Trade was introduced in 1976. The Act, celebrated by many as a major breakthrough for consumer protection, imposes heavy restrictions concerning the incorporation and material scope of fine print in contracting. Most of its rules would also apply to transactions between merchants (sect. 24 of the Act). Only individually negotiated contract texts are excluded from the scope of the Act (sect. 4 and 1 of the Act).

What was planned as a serious constraint on business transactions turned out to have quite moderate effects in the face of the introduction of personal computers and printers. When the law was introduced, we witnessed the simultaneous introduction of computerized documentation and printing. Most firms were about to be equipped with hardware and software to produce documents in which individual negotiation and fine print could be merged at high speed and low cost in individual documents which – on their face – had to be seen as individually negotiated contracts, and thus were outside the reach of the statute. In sect. 7 the Act explicity states that the Act is applicable in cases of contracting around the clauses of the Act. Commentators, however, agree as to the irrelevance of this special rule (see ULMER, BRANDNER and HENSEN [1990, § 7 Rdz. 1]).

3.2 Escaping to Shelters: Tax Planning and Tax Evasion

More obvious cases relate to hedgehogs' working on the design of new parallel furrows. The most visible work in this field is in the development of various tax shelters. There are innumerable variants. I will treat two of them.

Sale- and Leaseback Transactions. In sale-leaseback situations,[5] company A sells an item needed in a specific production to a leasing company B, which in turn leases the item back to A under terms of a lease that may favor both A and B by higher or deferred tax deduction on both sides, or by income after tax on one side and deductions on the other side. Such transactions are valid under both U.S. and German tax law as long as there is a reasonable relation to comparable market transactions in the sale and the lease, especially if the main risks of ownership remain with the leasing company.

In principle, taxpayers may legitimately utilize all forms of private transacting to reduce their tax load. The borderline is drawn "where the taxpayer was motivated by no business purposes other than obtaining tax benefits in entering the transaction, and that the transaction has no economic substance because no reasonable possibility of a profit exists."[6]

Financial Contract Innovation. An area in which hedgehogs are especially active is financial contract innovation. Many new financial products rely on the tax advantages caused by the distinction between fixed and contingent return assets. Although modern financial theory would suggest equal treatment, the

---

[5] For U.S. law see MOORE [1989]; for German law see SCHMIDT [1991, § 5 No. 72].

[6] Rice's Toyota World, Inc. v. Commissioner, 752 F. 2d 89 (4th Cir. 1985, 91); see also Bundesfinanzhof-Entscheidungen 147, 453 = BStBl II 87, 212. Ekkehard Schlicht and Rainer Walz, commenting on the paper, take the view that (legitimate) maneuvres to avoid taxes by using non-standard solutions create dead-weight losses which have to be borne by the economy in general. In my view generalizations at this point are dangerous. They may obscure the delicate borderline between equal treatment (which is a key issue of interpretation of legal texts) and incentive-compatible alternative institutional structures (which are advanced by the basic rule developed in this text).

relevant basic accountancy convention of the realization principle distinguishes between the situations (Warren [1993]). Only where a realized event can clearly be demonstrated is tax liability assumed. Thus the engineering of new financial products either postpones, stages, or avoids realization as far as possible. Intermediaries create, for example, synthetic shares of stock in which the investor receives two options in which put and call are technically at par. Whereas the actual share's income would be taxed on annual realization of profits, the synthetic instrument will be privileged by taxing the interest on a yield-to-maturity basis, which will likely be less onerous. The same effect is caused by "dynamic hedging" where an investor borrows money and buys a fraction of a share of stock instead of buying a call option for a specific higher stock price limit. This strategy works as a synthetic call with the advantage that taxing fixed losses (interest on debt) may (partly) offset the taxing of contingent returns.[7]

3.3 The Prohibition of Resale Price Maintenance – and Alternatives

Whereas taxes as indirect means of regulation are sticks that never challenge the arrival of the carrot, the heavy armor of regulation is presented where specific kinds of contracting are expressly prohibited. An interesting case is the *per se* prohibition of resale price maintenance (see Breit [1991]; Grimes [1992]). Vertical price fixing has long been an important target of antitrust policy. In Dr. Miles Medical Co. v. John D. Park & Sons Co.,[8] the United States Supreme Court established the rule that fixing retail prices is a conspiracy violating the Sherman Act. Only recently was the rule relaxed in the Sylvania case[9] and in the Business Electronics decision.[10] In Germany, the prohibition modelled in

[7] Edward Rubin kindly referred in addition to the creation of NOW accounts in the U.S. I quote (with his kind permission): "A particularly striking example [in the United States] is the development of the 'NOW' account. Until the 1970s, U.S. banks were forbidden to pay interest on demand deposit accounts. So the president of a small mutual savings bank in Massachusetts came up with the idea of allowing customers with interest-bearing saving accounts to issue 'negotiable orders of withdrawal,' i.e., NOWs. These previously non-existent instruments looked exactly like checks, and functioned exactly like checks, since they gave the third party to whom the account owner negotiated them the power to make a withdrawal from the account owner's account. The Massachusetts banking authority forbid this, reasoning that it was just a stratagem to circumvent the rules, so the bank went to court and won. Congressional hearings followed, in which the bank president was treated as a hero of modern capitalism. Congress then enacted legislation which specifically authorized New England banks to make use of this stratagem. Commercial banks and credit unions followed with won approval from their regulatory agencies, and Congress ultimately dismantled the entire system of restrictions."

[8] 220 U.S. 373 (1911).

[9] 433 U.S. 36 (1977).

[10] 485 U.S. 717 (1988).

accordance with the American view prevailing at its introduction in 1975 is still valid.[11] As in the U.S. there was constant activity in looking for devices which were geared as escapes from the tightly monitored prohibition.

A classic in the law-and-economics literature is the alleged price-fixing by aluminum smelters and petroleum coke producers in long-term contracts that is described and analyzed by GOLDBERG and ERICKSON [1987]. In the circumstances of the case, all tests that would relate to general market prices of petroleum coke would fail to explain the economic rationale of the pricing scheme.

Under the definition of sect. 15 of the German Act Against Restraints of Competition (GWB) the sales scheme introduced in 1981 by one of the leading German TV set producers, Telefunken, seemed to be a "clear" violation of the prohibition against price-fixing. Telefunken offered a contract to most of its retailers whereby these would operate as "commercial agents" who sold the TV sets to the customers in the name of Telefunken. Telefunken retained the full authority to determine the sales price; the agents would receive a commission on the sales effected. They had to keep an inventory of TV sets owned by Telefunken which was to be displayed in a stipulated way. The Federal Cartel Office and the Kammergericht as Court of first instance declared the scheme to be a violation of sect. 15 GWB.[12] They insisted that the scheme was designed to fix the retail price in a market in which all other producers would rely on a distribution strategy based on independent retailing.

The German Federal Court,[13] however, revised this decision, showing sympathy with the hedgehog. The Court accepted that Telefunken had chosen a way of organizing its distribution that lies outside the scope of sect. 15 GWB, specifically that is used lawfully in the distribution of other products: distribution by commission agents. As in the sale- and leaseback decisions of the tax courts, the Federal Court points to the differences in the allocation of risks, especially the risk of ownership concerning the sets displayed in the shops of the agents.

3.4 Outsourcing and Franchising

The Telefunken case exemplifies an instance in which independent firms (retailers) were vertically integrated into the producing firm by means of the

---

[11] See EMMERICH [1991, 131–154].

[12] Bundeskartellamt, WuW/E BKartA 1935; Kammergericht, WuW/E OLG 2819 "Telefunken-Partner-Vertrag I; WuW/E BKartA 2125; WuW/E OLG 3457 "Telefunken-Partner-Vertrag II" and MOESCHEL [1985].

[13] BGH Z 97, 317 (1986). Richard Posner, commenting on the paper, pointed out that the U.S. leading case of Schwinn which marks a turning point of U.S. antitrust, is essentially an alternative "price-fixing" case: U.S. v. Arnold, Schwinn & Co., 388 U.S. 365 (1967); see also U.S. v. General Electric & Co., 272 U.S. 476 (1926).

intermediate step of using commission agents.[14] The institutional option used was standardized, and well known. It only was atypical for the relevant market, and thus price fixing motives could be inferred. In contrast, we witness a rich laboratory of institutional innovation at the frontier of disintegrating the classical integrated firm. The associated catchwords are – among others – outsourcing and franchising. Both strategies have in common that the corporate link of control via capital participation and direction via employment contracts is broken, and that complex long-term contractual stipulations create the new relevant tie in the production chain.

Independent contractors. Early examples of this development of disaggregation could be observed in crafts, industries, and distribution operations where output could be easily measured and where personal monitoring of the production process was complex. Subcontracting became a common mode of organization in service operations such as newspaper distribution or other forms of dedicated collection and delivery of specific items. In the crafts, tilers disaggregated their firms by offering to their former employees independent contracts for specific tiling jobs. The same applied to the window cleaning industry. The head firm remained responsible for the acquisition of clients, the outfitting of the subcontractors and the general supervision and billing. The contractors could use the tax subsidies for starting new firms and the deductions and accounting advantages of small-scale businesses. The observation of COLLINS [1993, 763] for the U.K. and the U.S. that "this form of vertical disintegration by transforming employees into independent contractors supplying a service has been proliferating" holds for most industrialized countries. Labor courts have shown some hostility in borderline cases[15] but the overall reaction has been conducive to independent contracting.[16]

Franchising. Make-or-buy-decisions may refer (as the term suggests) to standard forms of transacting within the firm, or on the market. Since the associated standard regimes "employment" and "sale of goods" or the provision of

---

[14] The law regards the typical commission agent used in the Telefunken case as an independent firm; the next step would have been commission agents who are regarded as employees for purposes of the application of certain labor regulations.

[15] See also the account of COLLINS [1993, 766], who advances the criticism that subcontracting uses "the divergence between rates of pay between primary and secondary labor markets." As long as tax policies (which are not discussed in Collin's paper) work in the direction of independent contractors, the "attrition of the category of employees" seems to be inescapable.

[16] The much debated new decision of the European Court of Justice of April 14, 1994 (C 392/92), *Neue Zeitschrift für Arbeitsrecht*, 1994, 545–546, concerning the successful unfair dismissal claim of a cleaning person whose job was terminated based on the reason that the job was no longer available because an independent contractor would do this job in the future, is in my view no exception from the general trend of sympathy for new arrangements.

services have attracted significant regulatory coverage, innovative furrows may be ploughed in the field of "hybrid" transacting such as advanced forms of franchising. As I have shown in earlier papers (SCHANZE [1991], [1993 b]), the mere licensing of product attributes and associated processes would not merit much attention because it would be a standard mode of transfering technical design innovation from one firm to another. The same would be true of the variants of franchising in the American legal sense of the term, where independent retailers are "franchised" with opportunities of selling and servicing brand products such as automobiles.

Franchising in the narrow European meaning of the term reaches a different organizational level of a "symbiotic arrangement" where it substitutes for M-form corporate organization. Reference has been made to tightly-coordinated networks of hardware stores where the quasi-corporate policies and the blueprint of day-to-day management of the franchised "partner" are supplied and monitored by the franchisor. From an organizational perspective the franchised firm is fully integrated; though from a legal perspective it remains for almost all purposes an independent unit. Since the standard forms of organization in the corporate format, especially public corporations, have attracted substantial regulation from various directions including accounting, participation in the capital markets, labor relations, worker participation, tax treatment and antitrust supervision, symbiotic variants of advanced franchising may be understood as a form of "private deregulation" (SCHANZE [1993 b]) in the area of enterprise organization.

4. Comparing the Alternative Furrow: Regulatory Levels

4.1 Institutional Comparisons Relating to Certain Events

In most cases concerning tax planning, estimations and cost comparisons relate to (relatively) certain states. It is possible to develop realistic models of action and to compare the tax burden of the variants under scrutiny. Generalizations about the "cheapest" solution are dangerous. Especially the business administration literature abounds with simplified general advice concerning the "best" institutional options which might eventually turn out to be very costly. However, the general methodology of institutional comparisons is well developed, and general directions of outcomes may be indicated.

4.2 Comparing Institutions That Address Uncertain States

The more common if not pervasive situation in which actors select and modify institutions is defined by uncertainty concerning a number of relevant future events. Indeed, one may go further, and assume, like BARZEL [1989] following ALCHIAN [1950], that institutions as such are generated by uncertainty because they are meaningless in a Walrasian equilibrium. In Barzel's view individuals "maximize the value of their rights by delineating them in the contracting process or by selecting organizations" (BARZEL [1989, 3]). A more cautious, realistic view might even depart from the maximization analogy relating to a straightforward economic calculus, and argue that "economizing" concerning institutions is not a maximization process strictly speaking but rather an exercise in avoiding higher levels of waste.

The advantage of a fully regulated environment, even if it is burdensome, may be that there is a high degree of certainty how the environment will react if an uncertain event occurs. This is why most lawyers are fascinated by tight equity-based regulation, as in the consumer protection statutes, e.g. the law concerning standard terms. Indeed, there is a significant tradeoff between standardization of a specific transaction (assume a "consumer" contract concerning a TV set, or the tightly regulated organized package travel by tour operators) and individual institutional variety. Variety makes the assessment of contingencies more complex, and the paternalistic view can always be raised that the average actor does not comprehend what he has chosen.

An interesting "middle ground" is opened when competition of legal orders is available. For a long time, selecting Delaware as an incorporation State in the U.S. was regarded as "racing to the bottom", short of defrauding shareholders and creditors. It becomes increasingly clear, however, that Delaware is chosen because it is a "specialist" jurisdiction where we find an ambitious level of delineating the rights in all contracts relating to the corporate nexus (KÜBLER [1994]).

4.3 The Function of Base-Line Regulation

The Regulatory Equilibrium. All examples which were presented to illustrate the incidence of legitimate evasion will not escape to a legal void. They are geared to exploit the regulatory bifurcation so as to achieve lower levels of regulation. Also, the phenomena described are based on the notion that the majority of transactions remains in the standard furrow of high regulation. There is an equilibrium of standardized transacting and attempts to escape, triggered by the relative assessment of the costs of staying or leaving. Most people will travel with (regulated) tour operators, few will accept that "friends" organize the trip to Timbuctoo. The average investor will buy shares, notes, or indexed funds, some will opt for new financial products. In Buxtehude, there are obviously many hares, and few hedgehogs.

Characteristics of the Lower Standard. The typical escape from regulated contracting is guided by a general conception of contract law that is found in both civil and common law. It leads from the Law of Contracts to the Law of Contract. Modern contract teaching is concerned with the general principles of contract law and its boundaries, Law of Contract. Contract practice is marked by the division of a typology of standard transactions such as the contract of sale, of services, of employment, of lease, etc. This practical typology attracts increasing regulation over time. One of the targets of the German Statute Concerning Standard Terms was the reestablishment of the "dignity" of the balanced structure of the individual contract types in the Civil Code in the face of the challenge of "one-sided" small print. Once the typology is left, we arrive in the law of contract, i.e. the basic rules concerning the making and the execution of contracts in general. The law of contract also contains the fundamental limits to contracting. A comparative law perspective would suggest that – despite differences in technical approaches – there is a large degree of substantial compliance concerning the outcomes. One may use a modern American text on contract law for structuring the related basic rules and policies in a Civil Law context. As FARNSWORTH [1990] suggests, courts "police" agreements against unfairness by placing limits on the capacity to act, on certain means of reaching the agreement, and finally on its enforcement by looking at modification and discharge modalities. The most important limit relates to the "abuse of the bargaining process in general" (FARNSWORTH [1990, 246]) which includes coercion, and especially the variants of qualified misinformation.

In the 60's and 70's it seemed as if the basic level of disclosure in contracting would shift from *caveat emptor* (fraud and wilful deception as limits) to a general obligation to disclose all material facts that could be reasonably expected as valuable information by the contractual counterpart. There are indeed specific relations of this kind at the level of the (regulated) contract typology. In the absence of specific situations, however, courts have been unwilling to take a general step toward a higher standard of disclosure, at the base line level, in view of the diseconomies of information production in the contracting process.

A recent analysis comparing the US Supreme Court's reaction in this century concludes that the Court between 1910 and 1970 had a ... "view of contract that retained for the courts a substantial role in reviewing agreements that might in some way cause harm to third parties and that offended libertarian norms of notice and consent. The modern Court has largely abandoned these foundations and substituted an efficiency calculus drawn from law and economics ... The modern Court's public policy cases ... exhibit nothing so much as a profound skepticism regarding the ability of courts to improve on the judgements of private actors in the marketplace" (SHELL [1993, 527]; see also the highly instructive analysis of SCHWARTZ [1992]).

An assessment of the attitude of German courts would show a somewhat more interventionist picture. However, in the critical cases of non-disclosure, the standard remedy for pecuniary loss is still limited to fraud including intentional deception, plus an oscillating line sanctioning negligent non-disclosure if some form of trust relationship exists between the parties. There are indications that the current bright-line (where clear intervention can be expected by the aggrieved party) has been shifted from wilful deception to "evident" misrepresentation of material aspects of the transaction (such as the absence *ex ante* of any possibility of paying or delivering) which would then drop the subjective element of fraudulent *intent*, or at least shift the burden of proof concerning *bona fide* action if circumstantial evidence were to demonstrate the obvious.

5. Conclusion: The Merits of the Regulatory Bifurcation

The hedgehog's choice of the different furrow is not without cost. In the tax planning cases and other contracting-around situations we could even cite many practical examples where the cost of opting out could not be recovered in the new scheme. There is overplaying, estimates are wrong, or new specific regulation covers the escape earlier than anticipated. There is no sound policy reason, however, to support in general a tighter intervention by courts to foreclose the option of opting out. Rhetoric against the regulatory bifurcation will be voiced from the relatives of the hare; especially, they will claim equal treatment. The New Orleans push-cart case cited above shows that equality of treatment should be a concern of limited application. If actors present improvements in the incentive structure coping with uncertainty, courts will and, indeed, should acknowledge the difference, despite latent circumvention. Sometimes it is argued that there should be a "fair" competition between regimes which would mean that the highest level of regulation would control all transactions (see TEUBNER [1993]). But that would bar private action by those who invest in institutional innovation.

We like the hegehog, not only because he has crooked legs, but also because his attitude may be regarded as a fundamental trait of the constitution of a market economy. When the hedgehog accepts the bet he says to the hare, like David to Goliath: "Dat kummt up'n Versöök an – It's worth a trial."

References

ALCHIAN, ARMEN A. [1950], "Uncertainty, Evolution, and Economic Theory," *Journal of Political Economy*, 58, 211–221.

AYRES, IAN and JOHN BRAITHWAITE [1992], "Partial-Industry Regulation: A Monopsony Standard for Consumer Protection," *California Law Review*, 80, 13–53.

BARZEL, YORAM [1989], *Economic Analysis of Property Rights*, Cambridge University Press: Cambridge.

BOLLINGER, LEE C. [1976], "Freedom of the Press and Public Access: Toward a Theory of Partial Regulation of Mass Media," *Michigan Law Review*, 75, 1–42.

BREIT, WILLIAM [1991], "Resale Price Maintenance: What do Economists Know and When did They Know it?" *Journal of Institutional and Theoretical Economics*, 147, 72–90.

COASE, RONALD H. [1992], "The Institutional Structure of Production," *American Economic Review*, 82, 713–719.

COLLINS, HUGH [1993], "Why are There Contracts of Employment?" *Journal of Institutional and Theoretical Economics*, 149, 762–768.

EISENBERG, MELVIN A. [1995], "The Limits of Cognition and the Limits of Contract," *Stanford Law Review*, 47, forthcoming.

EMMERICH, VOLKER [1991], *Kartellrecht*, 6th ed, Beck: München.

FARNSWORTH, E. ALLAN [1990], *Contracts*, 2nd ed, Little, Brown: Boston.

FREY, BRUNO S. [1992], *Economics as a Science of Human Behaviour*, Kluwer: Boston.

FULLER, LON L. [1975], "Law as an Instrument of Social Control and Law as a Facilitation of Human Interaction," *Brigham University Law Review*, 89–96.

GOLDBERG, VICTOR P. and JOHN R. ERICKSON [1987], "Quality and Price Adjustment in Long-Term Contracts: A Case Study of Petroleum Coke," *Journal of Law & Economics*, 30, 369–389.

GRIMES, WARREN S. [1992], "Spiff, Polish, and Consumer Demand Quality: Vertical Price Restraints Revisited," *California Law Review*, 80, 815–855.

GRIMM, BROTHERS [1843/1987], *The Complete Fairy Tales of the Brothers Grimm*, Bantam: New York.

KÜBLER, FRIEDRICH [1994], "Aktienrechtsreform und Unternehmensverfassung," *Aktiengesellschaft*, 39, 141–148.

MACAULAY, STEWART [1963], "Non-Contractual Relations in Business: A Preliminary Study," *American Sociological Review*, 28, 55–69.

MARCH, JAMES G. [1994], "*Learning in Organizations*," Unpublished 2nd Hitchcock Foundation Lecture, Berkeley, April 20, 1994.

MERTENS, HANS-JOACHIM [1982], "Leges praeter legem," *Aktiengesellschaft*, 27, 29–41.

MNOOKIN, ROBERT H. and LEWIS KORNHAUSER [1979], "Bargaining in the Shadow of the Law: The Case of Divorce," *Yale Law Journal*, 88, 950–997.

MOESCHEL, WERNHARD [1985], "Absatzmittler und vertikale Preisbindung," *Betriebs-Berater*, 40 (23), 1477–1483.

MOORE, KAREN N. [1989], "The Sham Transaction Doctrine: An Outmoded and Unnecessary Approach to Combating Tax Avoidance," *Florida Law Review*, 41, 659–719.

POSNER, RICHARD A. [1993], *Economic Analysis of Law*, 4th ed, Little, Brown: Boston.

ROSEN, SHERWIN [1988], "Promotions, Elections and Other Contests," *Journal of Institutional and Theoretical Economics*, 144, 73–90.

SCHANZE, ERICH [1988], "Regulation by Consensus: The Practice of International Investment Agreements," *Journal of Institutional and Theoretical Economics*, 144, 152–171.

-- [1991], "Symbiotic Contracts: Exploring Long-Term Agency Structures Between Contract and Corporation," pp. 67–104 in: Ch. Joerges (ed.), *Franchising and the Law: Theoretical and Comparative Approaches in Europe and the United States*, Nomos: Baden-Baden.

-- [1993 a], "Legalism, Economism, and Professional Attitudes Toward Institutional Design," *Journal of Institutional and Theoretical Economics*, 149, 122-140.

-- [1993 b], "Symbiotic Arrangements," *Journal of Institutional and Theoretical Economics*, 149, 691–697.

-- and KARL HEINZ HAUNHORST [1993], "Security of Tenure in Conventional and 'Flexible' Employment Regimes," Working paper, European University Institute, Firenze, May 27–29, 1993.

SCHMIDT, LUDWIG [1991], *Einkommensteuergesetz*, 11th ed, Beck: München.

SCHWARTZ, ALAN [1992], "Relational Contracts in the Courts: An Analysis of Incomplete Agreements and Judicial Strategies," *Journal of Legal Studies*, 21, 271–318.

SHELL, RICHARD G. [1993], "Contracts in the Modern Supreme Court," *California Law Review*, 81, 431–529.

SUNSTEIN, CASS R. [1990], *After the Rights Revolution. Reconceiving the Regulatory State*, Harvard University Press: London–Cambridge, MA.

TEUBNER, GUNTHER [1993], "Piercing the Contractual Veil: Social Responsibility of Contractual Networks?" pp. 211–238 in: T. Wilhelmsson (ed.), *Perspectives of Critical Contract Law*, Dartmouth Publishing: Aldershot.

ULMER, PETER, HANS ERICH BRANDNER and HORST-DIETHER HENSEN [1990], *AGB-Gesetz. Kommentar zum Gesetz zur Regelung des Rechts der allgemeinen Geschäftsbedingungen*, 6th ed, Dr. Schmidt: Köln.

WARREN, ALVIN C. [1993], "Financial Contract Innovation and Income Tax Policy," *Harvard Law Review*, 107, 460–492.

Professor Erich Schanze
Faculty of Economics and Law
University of Oldenburg
26111 Oldenburg
Germany

Part V
Accounting for Regulation

[18]

CONSTITUTIONAL APPROACHES TO PRIVATIZATION: AN INQUIRY INTO THE MAGNITUDE OF NEO-LIBERAL CONSTITUTIONALISM

DAVID SCHNEIDERMAN*

I

INTRODUCTION

It is common in the literature on globalization to find the claim that there is an "irreducible heterogeneity" in the world today—that there is, at present, an ongoing competition between different political cultures with no predetermined structure out of which emerges a predominant winner. Roland Robertson and Frank Lechner argue, for instance, that the global scene is "highly 'pluralistic'" and that there is a "proliferation" of competing definitions of the global situation.[1] Similarly, sociologist Martin Albrow writes that there is "no axial principle underlying global institutions."[2] Rather, he argues, there is a pluralism reflecting "no theory of the greater good, simply the historic accumulation and interplay of national experiences and expertise coming to terms with each other."[3]

This view fails to account adequately for the determinate rules and structures associated with "economic globalization," the ensemble of legal rules and structures for the promotion and protection of foreign investment. These rules and structures cumulatively attempt to fashion a global vision of economic policy, property rights, and constitutionalism that institutionalizes the political project called "neo-liberalism."

This article is also available at http://www.law.duke.edu/journals/63LCPSchneiderman.

* Faculty of Law, University of Toronto.

This paper was prepared initially for the conference "Public Perspectives on Privatization" held in Geneva, July 1999, and co-sponsored by Duke University, the University of Geneva, and the University of Alberta. It was later presented at a seminar at the Faculty of Law, University of Toronto. Professor Diego López-Medina of Universidad de los Andes and Professor Luz Nagle of Stetson University College of Law furnished important and timely advice, while Moira Gracey provided excellent research assistance and translation of some key texts. Many thanks to Professor Richard Bauman for the kind invitation to present at the Geneva conference and for the comments from audiences in Geneva and Toronto.

1. Roland Robertson & Frank Lechner, *Modernization, Globalization and the Problem of Culture in World-Systems Theory*, 2 THEORY CULTURE & SOC'Y 103, 111 (1985).

2. MARTIN ALBROW, THE GLOBAL AGE 125 (1996).

3. *Id.*

In the post-1989 global scene, political alternatives seem to have narrowed in scope. The structures that influence political and economic life now are shaped by the global consensus that states must be made safe for trade and foreign investment. States are expected to remove regulatory restraints on the movement of capital, goods, and services, to divest themselves of publicly-owned enterprises—to privatize or denationalize real or financial assets—and to facilitate the private supply of certain goods and services by "contracting out" and "commercialization."[4] A number of options to achieve privatization and denationalization are available to states, but two prevailing themes emerge, each corresponding to a different vision of constitutionalism. The first is the "state capitalist" model, designed to enhance the capacity for state control and public participation.[5] The other is the "neo-liberal" model, which places legal limits on the state's regulatory capacity.[6]

This article asks whether constitutional rules in the state capitalist mode that redistribute property ownership more widely can survive the pressures generated by the neo-liberal model of constitutionalism. As a means of examining this question, this article takes up processes of privatization expressed in constitutional rules that grant ownership preference to employees of privatized state enterprises. Contemporary debates about the direction of constitutional design in an era of economic globalization are better understood in light of the interplay between these two contrasting models of constitutional thought. Contrary to Albrow's characterization,[7] there appears to be a structural tilt to the global scene generating an emerging structure with a likely winner.

Privatization programs take a variety of forms. This article considers only those programs that concern the divestiture of state assets, or denationalization through the sale of shares or assets to employees and employee associations. It neither purports to discuss the assumed benefits of privately owned over publicly owned enterprises[8] nor the benefits or pitfalls of this particular form of privatization over other methods, such as unrestricted sales to outsiders or equal-access vouchers. Among the alleged perils, it is feared that selling shares to employee "insiders" fails to bring new capital or new skills to divested companies,[9] a case of "private benefits being had at public cost."[10] This

---

4. *See* D.G. McFetridge, The Economics of Privatization, C.D. Howe Institute Benefactors Lecture 2-6 (Oct. 22, 1997) (unpublished manuscript, on file with the author).

5. *See infra* text accompanying notes 17-25.

6. *See infra* text accompanying notes 11-16.

7. *See* ALBROW, *supra* note 2, at 125.

8. *See* Carlos Vilas, *Forward Back: Capitalist Restructuring, the State and the Working Class in Latin America*, *in* WHITHER MARXISM? GLOBAL CRISES IN INTERNATIONAL PERSPECTIVE 123, 131-33 (Bernd Magnus & Stephen Cullenberg eds., 1995); JOSEPH E. STIGLITZ, WHITHER SOCIALISM? 179-81 (1994). Stiglitz argues that the case for privatization is political, not economic. *See id.* at 173. Government can "*potentially* almost always improve upon the market's resource allocation." *Id.* at 179.

9. *See* Cheryl W. Gray, *In Search of Owners: Privatization and Corporate Governance in Transition Economies*, 11 WORLD BANK RES. OBSERVER 179, 188 (1996).

10. Ronald A. Cass, *Privatization: Politics, Law, and Theory*, 71 MARQ. L. REV. 449, 514 (1988); *see* SEBASTIAN EDWARDS, CRISIS AND REFORM IN LATIN AMERICA 179 (1995).

discussion, instead, proceeds on the assumption that enabling employee access to public property is a politically valid objective to achieve in the privatization context. The pertinent question is: Can this objective survive the regime of transnational rules for the promotion and protection of foreign investment?

II

DIFFERING VISIONS OF CONSTITUTIONALISM

In an era of pervasive economic globalization, state institutions are expected to subordinate political considerations to economic ones. Jacques Donzelot has remarked that this subordination signals a shift in the role of the state "from a guarantor of progress to a manager of destiny."[11] The movement from the "social state" to "enabling state" requires a restructuring of state institutions, as well as the meta-rules that govern state institutional behavior. This change does not necessarily entail the abstention of the state, but rather activism of another sort: the creation of conditions to facilitate the smooth operation of the market. With social democracy's transformative enterprise seemingly extinct, current debates about the state's role turn on the axes of neo-liberalism (or economic liberalism) and state capitalism (or neo-social democracy). In this section, I discuss each of their respective constitutional images.

The dominant approach to constitutionalism is represented by the political project of neo-liberalism. This project advances the idea that the state should recede from the market and that limits should be placed on the redistributionist capacity of the state. Neo-liberalism is a project that disowns the compromises generated by tripartite corporatism and that treats citizens as undifferentiated consumers.

Associated with neo-liberalism is the school of constitutional thought concerned with designing institutions that place limits on the capacity of governments to intervene in the so-called "private" sphere. I have in mind here the group of theorists working within "constitutional political economy."[12] This work is premised on the economic model of methodological individualism—that of the autonomous, self-interested, and rational actor.[13]

Constitutional political economists aim to secure the gains made in the post-1989 international economic environment, such as the general tendency toward open markets and limited government, by constraining, through the force of constitutional and constitution-like limitations, the capacity of government to intervene in the market.[14] These are proposals aimed at insulating "key aspects

11. Jacques Donzelot, *The Mobilization of Society*, *in* THE FOUCAULT EFFECT: STUDIES IN GOVERNMENTALITY 169, 176 (Graham Burchell et al. eds., 1991). *See generally* NIKOLAS ROSE, POWERS OF FREEDOM: REFRAMING POLITICAL THOUGHT (1999) (discussing this shift in state functions from a neo-Foucaultian perspective).

12. James M. Buchanan, *The Domain of Constitutional Political Economy*, *in* THE ECONOMICS AND THE ETHICS OF CONSTITUTIONAL ORDER 3, 3-18 (1991).

13. *See id.*

14. *See* Stephen Gill, *Globalisation, Market Civilisation, and Disciplinary Neoliberalism*, 24 MILLENNIUM: J. INT'L STUD. 399, 412 (1995).

of the economy from the influence of politicians or the mass of citizens by imposing, internally and externally, 'binding constraints' on the conduct of fiscal, monetary, trade, and investment policies."[15]

This enterprise has a transnational dimension. It is a model of constitutional government intended primarily to facilitate the free flow of goods, services, and persons unimpeded across the borders of nation-states—a model long promoted by the leading countries of the Organization for Economic Co-operation and Development ("OECD") and by affluent minorities within developing and less-developed countries. It takes shape via instruments intended to promote and protect foreign direct investment, such as the investment chapter of the North American Free Trade Agreement ("NAFTA"), bilateral investment treaties ("BITS"), and the draft Multilateral Agreement on Investment ("MAI").

The rules and structures of this program of reform resemble domestic constitutions: They bind governments over long periods of time to constitution-like rules designed to protect the private property of individuals and firms against discriminatory treatment or takings of investment interests. These rules generate constitution-like entitlements legally enforceable before tribunals and courts.[16]

I want to contrast this neo-liberal agenda of constitutional reform with another stream of constitutional thought, one that has long been promoted by countries from the South.[17] This is one that imagines a regime of constitutional rules and structures that facilitates the exercise of government power through state building and national enterprise. This approach recognizes that constitutions give expression to great national goals and projects—that constitutions are not just about limiting government action, but about enabling self-government. This is a view of the state approximating what Robert Cox calls "state capitalism,"[18] associated with writers in the field of international political economy. It is a model of institutional design that recognizes "the indispensable guiding role of the state in the development of the nation's productive forces."[19] While state capitalism concedes the world market as the background of political choices, the project assumes that the state has a role to play in facilitating national competitiveness and in enabling the widest

15. *Id.*

16. *See* Stephen Clarkson, Somewhat Less Than Meets the Eye: NAFTA as Constitution, Address at the International Sociological Association Annual Meeting (July 27, 1998); David Schneiderman, *The Constitutional Strictures of the Multilateral Agreement on Investment*, 9 GOOD SOC'Y 90 (2000) [hereinafter Schneiderman, *Constitutional Strictures*]; David Schneiderman, *NAFTA's Takings Rule: American Constitutionalism Comes to Canada,* 46 U. TORONTO L.J. 499 (1996) [hereinafter Schneiderman, *NAFTA's Takings Rule*.].

17. For a discussion of the South as metaphor, see BOAVENTURA DE SOUSA SANTOS, TOWARD A NEW COMMON SENSE: LAW, SCIENCE AND POLITICS IN THE PARADIGMATIC TRANSITION 506-18 (1995).

18. Robert W. Cox, *The Global Political Economy and Social Choice, in* APPROACHES TO WORLD ORDER 191, 201 (Robert W. Cox & Timothy J. Sinclair eds., 1996).

19. *Id.* at 201.

distribution of wealth across the social strata of society.[20] When it takes a more "radical form," writes Cox, state capitalism tends "toward the prospect of internal socialism sustained by capitalist success in world-market competition."[21]

The state-capitalist approach to constitutionalism can take shape through various models of constitutional design, but two come primarily to mind. The first model places no substantive limits on government intervention in the market. A.V. Dicey's description of English constitutional dogma in 1885 approximates this design. According to Dicey, Parliament was supreme: It could "make or unmake any law whatever," subject to the individual rights secured by what Dicey coined "the rule of law."[22] The second model facilitating energetic government is one that specifically articulates in constitutional language the capacity of the state to intervene in the market. Latin American constitutionalism best exemplifies this use of constitutionalism for the purpose of state building.

Latin American constitutions have committed governments to certain projects, such as mandating nationalization or management of key economic sectors, that bind successive governments to the maintenance of national goals and objectives.[23] Constitutional rules may expressly enable state intervention in the market to redistribute wealth through rules permitting the expropriation or nationalization of property, subject, for instance, to the provision of "appropriate" compensation.[24] This type of constitutional project also protects national political power from the external pressures generated by foreign economic power. Indeed, the Latin American constitutional experience of the twentieth century suggests that the international economic environment has long been an influence on constitutional design.[25]

In the 1990s, state capitalism fell into disfavor. The countries of Latin America mostly abandoned the constitutional design mandating public control over the economy or enabling nationalization of key economic sectors. Only a residue of these rules remains, and one of the objectives of this article is to identify this residue in the new 1991 Colombian Constitution. The key object of the article is to track challenges to the state-capitalist form of constitutional design as it confronts the neo-liberal model—a model of constitutional design that is taking shape both inside and outside of the state.

In some ways, the dysfunctional present and past of Colombian politics makes this constitution a poor subject of inquiry. Indeed, the Colombian case points to the insufficiency of constitutional rules as a mechanism for achieving

---

20. *See id.* at 202.

21. *Id.*

22. A.V. DICEY, INTRODUCTION TO THE STUDY OF THE LAW OF THE CONSTITUTION 38, 183-84 (8th ed. 1915).

23. *See infra* text accompanying notes 34-35.

24. *See infra* text accompanying notes 49-52.

25. *See infra* text accompanying notes 41-47.

social change.[26] It is significant, though, that in 1991, Colombians massively overhauled their constitutional structure, abandoning the constitutional framework that had been in place since 1886. Because this very recent exercise in constitution-making is under pressure from the neo-liberal model, we have an opportunity to track the confrontation between old and new constitutionalism. The Colombian constitutional experience proves to be representative of the larger Latin American constitutional experience of the 1980s and 1990s, in which the neo-liberal model has gained ascendance.[27]

III

LATIN AMERICAN CONSTITUTIONALISM

A number of pressures have generated this shift in emphasis from the public to the private, and from state building to state divestiture, in Latin American constitutionalism.[28] For one, the 1980s debt crisis precipitated the adoption of structural adjustment programs under the active encouragement of the World Bank.[29] A policy of selling off state enterprises has been a central plank in the Bank's strategy.[30] Also, with the fall of the Soviet empire, there seemingly are fewer political options other than privatization available to those states wishing to improve the material conditions of their citizens and desiring to secure the political success of state managers. Moreover, numerous benefits are expected to fall upon states that take up programs of privatization, including increased foreign investment, overall efficiency gains, and technology transfers.[31] At the very least, privatizing states can anticipate a huge financial windfall, the proceeds of which could be used to pay down the public debt.[32] The shift in emphasis from public undertakings to private enterprise reflects the dominant discourse "subscribed to by corporate capital and most governments . . . that competitiveness in the world economy is the ultimate criterion of policy."[33] The formation of public policy is subordinated to this goal of enhancing the structural competitiveness of the national economy.

---

26. *But see* Martha I. Morgan, *Taking Machismo to Court: The Gender Jurisprudence of the Colombian Constitutional Court*, 30 U. MIAMI INTER-AM L. REV. 253, 262 (1999) (arguing that the new Colombian Constitution "has changed Colombian views of constitutional rights and the role of the court in protecting those rights").

27. *See infra* text accompanying notes 34-39, 107-112, 174-84.

28. Sebastian Edwards identifies "the failure of the so-called heterodox programs in Argentina, Brazil, and Peru; the experience of the East Asian economies; the advice of the multilateral institutions; and the example of Chile" as factors contributing toward this "emerging consensus." EDWARDS, *supra* note 10, at 48.

29. *See, e.g.*, THE WORLD BANK, WORLD DEVELOPMENT REPORT 1996: FROM PLAN TO MARKET 48-63 (1996).

30. *See id.*

31. *See* ALAN SHIPMAN, THE MARKET REVOLUTION AND ITS LIMITS: A PRICE FOR EVERYTHING 410-12 (1999).

32. *See id.*

33. Robert W. Cox, *Civil Society at the Turn of the Millenium: Prospects for an Alternative World Order*, 25 REV. INT'L STUD. 3, 27 (1999).

Since the late 1980s, Latin American countries have undertaken large-scale constitutional reform to relieve state agencies of the obligation of protecting the national "patrimony"—comprised of industries and public services considered vital to the future of the state, such as electric power, oil and gas development, and communication and transportation services.[34] Article 27 of the 1917 Mexican Constitution, for instance, mandates state monopoly over the hydrocarbon and petroleum industries.[35] Though these key sectors were exempted from NAFTA's scope, foreign investment rules have been relaxed to permit investment in the natural gas industry.[36] Outside the parameters of NAFTA, it is reported that the Mexican government entered into "highly complex financing transactions" in order to evade constitutional restrictions on the oil industry.[37] Other elements of Article 27 of the Mexican Constitution were amended in the lead-up to NAFTA, including provisions prohibiting the privatization of public commercial banks[38] and rules protecting *ejidos*, communal land holdings that can now be broken up into individual parcels for the purpose of commercial enterprise.[39] These amendments precipitated the Zapatista armed rebellion in the Mexican state of Chiapas on New Year's Day 1994, the same day that NAFTA took effect.[40]

This movement amounts to an abandonment of the traditional Latin American model, traceable to the work of Argentinian jurist Carlos Calvo.[41] Based on the dismal Latin American experience with interventionist international capital, Calvo argued that the countries of Latin America were entitled to the same degree of respect for their internal sovereignty as the United States of America and the countries of Europe.[42] Among Calvo's precepts is the proposition that states should be free, within reason, from interference in the conduct of their domestic policy.[43] From this premise, Calvo argued that foreign nationals could not lay claim to greater protection in their disputes with sovereign states than the citizens of those same countries.[44] Foreign nationals who chose to establish themselves within the territorial

---

34. *See* PIERRE GUISLAIN, THE PRIVATIZATION CHALLENGE: A STRATEGIC, LEGAL, AND INSTITUTIONAL ANALYSIS OF INTERNATIONAL EXPERIENCE 34-35 (1997).

35. *See id.*; CONSTITUCIÓN POLITICA DE LOS ESTADOS UNIDOS MEXICANOS [Constitution] art. 27 (Mex.) [hereinafter MEX. CONST.].

36. *See* GUISLAIN, *supra* note 34, at 247.

37. Amy Chua, *The Privatization-Nationalization Cycle: The Link Between Markets and Ethnicity in Developing Countries,* 95 COLUM. L. REV. 223, 290 (1995).

38. *See* GUISLAIN, *supra* note 34, at 35.

39. *See* Jorge A. Vargas, *NAFTA, The Chiapas Rebellion, and the Emergence of Mexican Ethnic Law,* 25 CAL. W. INT'L. L.J. 1, 13 (1994).

40. *See id.* at 14.

41. *See* M. CHARLES CALVO, LE DROIT INTERNATIONAL THEORIQUE ET PRACTIQUE (2d ed. 1870). For an English language version of Calvo's doctrine, see EDWARD M. GALLAUDET, A MANUAL OF INTERNATIONAL LAW (1879).

42. *See* DONALD R. SHEA, THE CALVO CLAUSE: A PROBLEM OF INTER-AMERICAN AND INTERNATIONAL LAW AND DIPLOMACY 19 (1955); CALVO, *supra* note 41, at 261.

43. *See* SHEA, *supra* note 42, at 19; CALVO, *supra* note 41, at 194.

44. *See* SHEA, *supra* note 42, at 19; CALVO, *supra* note 41, at 369.

confines of the host state—through direct investment, for instance—were entitled to no greater protection from state action than those nationals residing within the acting state.[45] These precepts came to be reflected in the Mexican Constitution's Calvo Clause, which prohibits foreign investors from seeking the protection of their home state in any dispute with the Mexican host state.[46] In some instances, a claim to foreign assistance can lead to the forfeiture of proprietary rights.[47] Even these rules have been abandoned by the Mexican government in the lead-up to NAFTA through a series of non-constitutional and legislative edicts.[48]

A number of Latin American constitutions took up Calvo's doctrine.[49] The 1991 Colombian Constitution draws on Calvo's precepts by declaring that "it is the duty of both citizens and of aliens in Colombia to obey the Constitution and the laws, and to respect and obey the authorities."[50] Constitutional provisions concerning the expropriation of property give expression to this doctrine.[51] One of the last vestiges of this takings rule could be found in the 1991 Colombian Constitution. The property clause authorized the legislative expropriation of property "for reasons of equity," without the payment of compensation, a determination that was not judicially reviewable.[52]

Constitutional declarations of exclusive state ownership and control also expressed this principle of the equality of states.[53] Constitutional constraints could serve both the purpose of giving expression to important national objectives and of confining successive governments from bending too easily to the pressures of foreign investors and diplomatic overtures.[54] The Calvo

45. *See* SHEA, *supra* note 42, at 19.

46. *See* MEX. CONST. art. 27(I). Calvo's principles attracted international support in the 1970s, appearing in a variety of international resolutions, including the U.N. General Assembly Resolution of 1973—declaring the New International Economic Order—and the 1974 U.N. Charter of Economic Rights and Duties of States. Article 2 of the Charter declares that laws governing nationalization and expropriation of property are those of the nationalizing state and not those of international law. *See* Justine Daly, *Has Mexico Crossed the Border on State Responsibility for Economic Injury to Aliens? Foreign Investment and the Calvo Clause in Mexico after the NAFTA.*, 25 ST. MARY'S L.J. 1147, 1186-87 (1994).

47. *See* Gloria L. Sandrino, *The NAFTA Investment Chapter and Foreign Direct Investment in Mexico: A Third World Perspective*, 27 VAND. J. TRANSNAT'L L. 259, 268 (1994). The Brazilian Constitution reserved mining exploration and production facilities to Brazilian-controlled firms. This has now been amended to permit foreign operations so long as the firm is established under Brazilian law and has its headquarters and management in Brazil. *See* CONSTITUIÇÃO FEDERAL [C.F.] art. 176 (Braz.) [hereinafter BRAZ. CONST.]; GUISLAIN, *supra* note 34, at 36.

48. *See* GUISLAIN, *supra* note 34, at 36.

49. *See* Eduardo A. Wiesner, *ANCOM: A New Attitude Toward Foreign Investment?*, 24 U. MIAMI INTER-AM. L. REV. 435-65 (1993).

50. CONSTITUCIÓN POLÍTICA DE LA REPÚBLICA DE COLOMBIA [Constitution] art. 4. (Colom.) [hereinafter COLOM. CONST.].

51. *See id.* art. 58.

52. *Id.*; *see also infra* text accompanying note 100 (concerning the recent amendment of this provision).

53. Though nationalization of material resources in Latin America, Amy Chua writes, often was precipitated by the "expropriation of political power . . . from the class against which nationalization is directed." Chua, *supra* note 37, at 272.

54. *See* SHEA, *supra* note 42, at 20.

doctrine, though, never was acceptable to the United States and other European powers.[55]

IV

THE COLOMBIAN CONSTITUTION

The Colombian Constitution is a modern text that aspires to secure important national social objectives but at the same time is encountering significant pressures to conform to new transnational norms. The Colombian model also provides an interesting case study in the insufficiency of constitutional guarantees to secure the social change necessary for peace and security. The inability to achieve these changes, however, lies beyond the scope of this paper. Instead, it focuses on the constitutional reforms of 1936 and 1991, intended to give effect to important objectives as they pertain to property rights and privatization.

A. 1936 Reforms

The reforms of 1936 have been portrayed as Colombia's "New Deal." The radical Liberal administration of President Alfonso López Pumarejo wrested control of government from the Conservatives who had held power for decades.[56] López instituted a variety of social reforms, including tax reform, agrarian reform, and the 1936 constitutional reforms, during a period known as the *Revolución en marcha*.[57] Article 26 of the Colombian Constitution was amended to enshrine the notion that "property is a social function which implies obligations."[58] It also provided that in the event of a conflict between private interests and laws passed for reasons of "public utility or social interest," the private must give way to the public.[59]

The 1936 constitutional reforms enabled the state to expropriate property for purposes of "public utility or social interest." This could be achieved under judicial supervision with the provision of prior compensation or, for reasons of equity, without compensation by a two-thirds majority vote of the Senate and House of Representatives.[60]

55. Great Britain was responsible for at least forty armed interventions in Latin America between 1820 and 1914. *See* CHARLES LIPSON, STANDING GUARD: PROTECTING FOREIGN CAPITAL IN THE NINETEENTH AND TWENTIETH CENTURIES 54 (1985).

56. *See* Richard Stoller, *Alfonso López Pumarejo and Liberal Radicalism in 1930s Colombia*, 27 J. LATIN AM. STUD. 367, 367 (1995).

57. *See id.*

58. COLOM. CONST. art. 26 (repealed 1991).

59. *Id.* art. 26.

60. *See* WILLIAM MARION GIBSON, THE CONSTITUTIONS OF COLOMBIA 367 (1948).

Article 26: Private property and other rights legally acquired in accordance with the civil laws by natural or juridic persons shall be guaranteed, nor may they be disavowed by later laws. When the enforcement of a law passed for reasons of public utility or social interest conflicts with the rights of individuals, private interests must give way to the public or social interests.

Property is a social function which implies obligations.

Recognizing that private ownership implies a degree of social obligation—that property serves a social function—is a conventional idea in post-realist legal thought.[61] The intellectual origins of this reform in Colombia often are traced back to the work of French constitutional theorist Léon Duguit.[62] Duguit outlined a theory of the state familiar to British and American progressives of the late nineteenth and early twentieth centuries: that the state is merely a body of men issuing orders.[63] The authority of the state is justified by the function it performs, and according to Duguit, that function was to provide for certain social needs.[64] Private property was justifiable to the extent that it served and was limited by this social mission.[65]

Despite its seemingly foreign origins, Kenneth Karst argues that this approach to property comports well with Latin American understandings.[66] The principle that property fulfills a social function, for instance, has doctrinal support in the notion that the underlying title to all lands lies in the state.[67] This idea was given expression in Article 27 of the 1917 Mexican Constitution and Articles 165 and 166 of the Bolivian Constitution: All private property is contingent on a transfer of title from the "Nation"—the guardian of all lands and waters.[68] Article 27 recognizes that all rights of ownership emanate from the state and, Karst writes, "properly depend[] for [their] continuance upon the satisfaction of community needs."[69] It is entirely consistent, then, to ascribe social functions to property and social obligations to property holders. A number of Latin American constitutions recognize this social function: The Venezualan constitutional guarantee of the right to private property is subject to the "public benefit or the general interest,"[70] while the Chilean Constitution declares that the social function of property includes the requirements of the

---

> For reasons of public utility or social interest, as defined by the legislature, property may be expropriated by judicial decree with prior indemnification.

Id.

61. *See* Joseph William Singer & Jack M. Beerman, *The Social Origins of Property*, 6 CAN. L.J. & JURIS. 217 (1993).

62. *See* Kenneth Karst, *Latin-American Land Reform: The Uses of Confiscation*, 63 MICH. L. REV. 327, 346 (1964); Stoller, *supra* note 56, at 391. Inspiration also was drawn from the Mexican Constitution of 1917, the Weimar Constitution of 1919, and the Spanish Constitution of 1931. *See* LUIS CARLOS SACHICA, CONSTITUCIONALISMO COLOMBIANO 263 (1989). Excerpts from Duguit's influential 1911 lecture in Buenos Aires are reproduced in ALFREDO CONSTAIN, ELEMENTOS DE DERECHO CONSTITUCIONAL 253-58 (1959).

63. *See* Harold J. Laski, Note, *A Note on M. Duguit*, 31 HARV. L. REV. 186, 187-88 (1917-18).

64. *See id.*

65. *See* LEON DUGUIT, MANUEL DE DROIT CONSTITUTIONNEL 13, 295 (4th ed. 1923).

66. *See* Karst, *supra* note 62, at 356.

67. *See id.*

68. *See* MEX. CONST. art. 27; CONSTITUCIÓN POLÍTICA DEL ESTADO [Constitution] arts. 165-66 (Bol.) [hereinafter BOL. CONST.].

69. Karst, *supra* note 62 at 356.

70. CONSTITUCIÓN DE LA REPÚBLICA DE VENEZUELA [Constitution] art. 99 (Venez.) [hereinafter VENEZ. CONST.].

nation's general interest, security, public use, health, and environmental conservation.[71]

In the Colombian context, property as a social function also gives constitutional expression to the Lockean edict that land must not remain idle but must be utilized productively.[72] Albert Hirschman, in his 1963 work on Colombian land reform, traces the lineages of this ideology in Colombian political culture.[73] The socially condoned practice of settling (or colonizing) the seemingly empty and unproductive lands of the interior of Colombia resulted in a highly inequitable concentration in the hands of large (*hacienda*) landowners.[74] Legislation giving effect to the 1936 constitutional reform (Law 200) was consistent with this ideology of productivity.[75] The law was intended to divest speculative property owners of their uncultivated rural lands by authorizing the expropriation of lands that remained uncultivated for more than ten years.[76] Law 200, wrote Hirschman, "established the fundamental principle that a presumption of private property exists in favour of those who occupy the land and make 'economic use' of it."[77]

As Hirschman shows, the agrarian reform movement of the 1930s and its successor program of the 1960s[78] made little "progress."[79] The 1936 constitutional reforms, which were seemingly radical, were never intended to be effective. Hirschman's 1963 study closed with the observation that the passage of progressive land reform laws in Colombia "may have been facilitated by the long tradition of issuing well-meaning and socially advanced laws and decrees which turn out to be ineffective because of enforcement or clever obstruction."[80]

---

71. *See* CONSTITUCIÓN POLÍTICA DE LA REPÚBLICA DE CHILE [Constitution] art. 19, ¶ 24 (Chile) [hereinafter CHILE CONST.]; Terence Daintith & Monica Sah, *Privatisation and the Economic Neutrality of the Constitution,* 1993 PUB. L. 465, 474-75; Steven E. Hendrix, *Property Law Innovation in Latin America With Recommendations,* 18 B.C. INT'L & COMP. L. REV. 1, 7-8 (1995).

72. *See* JOHN LOCKE, *The Second Treatise of Government*, *in* TWO TREATISES OF GOVERNMENT 296-97 (Peter Laslett ed., Cambridge Univ. Press, 1988) (1690).

73. *See* ALBERT O. HIRSCHMAN, JOURNEYS TOWARDS PROGRESS: STUDIES OF ECONOMIC POLICY-MAKING IN LATIN AMERICA (1965).

74. *See* Alfonso López, *Latifundismo and the Need for Agrarian Reform in Colombia, in* AGRARIAN REFORM IN LATIN AMERICA 87 (T. Lynn Smith, ed. 1965).

75. *See* HIRSCHMAN, *supra* note 73, at 107-13 (discussing the Law 200 constitutional reform of 1936).

76. *See id.*

77. HIRSCHMAN, *supra* note 73, at 150.

78. *See id.* New land reform initiatives were undertaken in the 1960s following a plebiscite in 1957 affirming the constitutional reforms of 1936. Little progress was achieved. Property was more unequally distributed by 1970 than before; larger agricultural holdings occupied even more of the national territory. *See* Harvery F. Kline, *Columbia: Building Democracy in the Midst of Violence and Drugs, in* CONSTRUCTING DEMOCRATIC GOVERNANCE: LATIN AMERICA AND THE CARIBBEAN IN THE 1990S, PART III, at 20, 39 (Jorge I. Dominguez & Abraham F. Lowenthal eds., 1996); CARLOS FELIPE JARAMILLO, LIBERALIZATION, CRISIS & CHANGE IN COLOMBIAN AGRICULTURE 51-52 (1998). The Constitutional Assembly recalled the "repugnant corruption" of forced expropriations: It was "a great business" to expropriate and to be expropriated. *See* Colombian Constitutional Court Decision No. C-358/96 (1996) at 42 (on file with author).

79. Hirshman, *supra* note 73, at 197.

80. *Id.* at 211.

Other work on the period confirms these suspicions.[81] There appears to have been no widespread belief in the 1930s that the solution to economic inequality lay in constitutional reform, or that the 1886 Constitution somehow impeded the achievement of effective social and economic change.[82] The impulse for constitutional reform in 1936, in other words, was "primarily political rather than socioeconomic."[83]

Though no meaningful land reform was realized, the 1936 constitutional changes enabled the state to undertake modest agrarian reform in the 1960s that impinged on property rights.[84] The Colombian Constitutional Court considered one such challenge to the actions of the Instituto Colombiano de Reforma Agraria ("INCORA"), the body charged with expropriating land under the 1961 agrarian law. The institute was mildly activist: By 1963, INCORA had instigated 108 lawsuits seeking revocation of title or the invalidation of claims to land.[85] Property owners were compensated by the state at market value with the provision of government bonds redeemable at some future time. Property owners, however, alleged that the state had expropriated property without "prior indemnification."[86] If the state bonds were not immediately realizable, it was argued that this did not satisfy the constitutional requirement of prior compensation in Article 26.[87]

In finding for the state, the Court reflected on the meaning of the social function of property: "The social function . . . accentuated the subordination of ownership to community interests, to the point that the guarantee given in the Constitution in favor of property rights is conditioned on the extent to which the rights correspond to the needs of the community."[88] In light of this constitutional "prevalence of social interests over private ones, in all instances and circumstances," the Court found that the provision of compensation in the form of bonds satisfied the constitutional requirement of Article 26.[89]

Karst noted in 1964 that talk about social function largely was restricted to rural land.[90] The "similar performance of social functions might, with equal reason," he wrote, "be demanded of other property."[91] The 1991 Colombian Constitution includes provisions for the privatization of public enterprise and, I argue, underlying these provisions is the principle that property serves social functions—the principle that property is subordinated to community interests.

81. *See* Stoller, *supra* note 56, at 393.

82. *See id.*

83. *Id.* at 393.

84. *See* T. LYNN SMITH, COLOMBIA: SOCIAL STRUCTURE AND THE PROCESS OF DEVELOPMENT 89 (1967).

85. *See id.*

86. KENNETH L. KARST & KEITH S. ROSENN, LAW AND DEVELOPMENT IN LATIN AMERICA 348-49 (1975).

87. *See id.*

88. *Id.*

89. *Id.* at 348.

90. *See* Karst, *supra* note 62, at 356.

91. *Id.* at 347.

B. 1991 Colombian Constitution

Colombia was one of the few Latin American countries not to have experienced severe financial turmoil in the 1980s: Until recently, Colombia had low debt ratios and only moderate fiscal deficits.[92] The relative success of the Colombian economy, however, has not spared successive governments from having to engage in some austerity initiatives, namely, International Monetary Fund-induced adjustment programs.[93]

Colombia's 1990 program of economic liberalization, *Apertura*, signaled its openness to foreign investment and commitment to a modest program of privatization.[94] According to the government's report to the World Trade Organization ("WTO") in 1996, "[t]he purpose of the privatization of public sector assets is to free the Government resources tied up in activities that could be carried out more efficiently by the private sector and to transfer them to sectors where Government intervention is essential, for example, education, health, justice and security."[95] Privatization, in other words, could increase revenue flows, reduce the deficit, and help to subsidize social reform.[96]

One of the catalysts for this program of economic and social change was the achievement of constitutional reform in 1991. This task was undertaken by a multiparty constitutional assembly, composed of seventy elected delegates widely representative of various constituencies in Colombian political life, including the Conservative and Liberal parties, labor, indigenous peoples, and four representatives of demobilized guerilla groups, including the M-19 guerilla movement.[97] The constitutional assembly has been described as the "first body in Colombia to work by seeking consensus" and its successful negotiation of a new constitution for Colombia as "stunning."[98] It was hoped that the new constitution would provide a framework for neutralizing the major sources of

92. *See* Jose Antonio Ocampo, *Crisis and Economic Policy in Colombia, 1980-85*, *in* LATIN AMERICAN DEBT AND THE ADJUSTMENT CRISIS 239, 257 (Rosemary Thorp & Laurence Whitehead eds., 1987).

93. In 1984, Colombia's adjustment program "not only involved an orthodox *macroeconomic* programme under IMF surveillance, but also World Bank interference in *sectoral*, particularly commercial, policies." *Id.* In December 1999, Colombia entered into a $2.7 billion (U.S.) loan agreement with the IMF, conditioned on increasing privatizations. *See Recovery, of Sorts*, ECONOMIST, Apr. 22, 2000, at 32.

94. *See* David J. Pascuzzi, *International Trade and Foreign Investment in Colombia: A Sound Economic Policy Amidst Crisis*, 9 FLA. J. INT'L L. 443, 449-50 (1994).

95. *Colombia*, TRADE POL'Y REV. (Gen. Agreement on Tariffs and Trade, Geneva, Switz.) 1996, at 166.

96. *See* Pascuzzi, *supra* note 94, at 468.

97. *See* Donald T. Fox & Anne Stetson, *The 1991 Constitutional Reform: Prospects for Democracy and the Rule of Law in Colombia*, 24 CASE W. RES. J. INT'L. L. 139, 145 (1992).

98. *Id.*; *see also* William C. Banks & Edgar Alvarez, *The New Colombian Constitution: Democratic Victory or Popular Surrender?*, 23 U. MIAMI INTER-AM. L. REV. 39, 45 (1991). The two remaining major armed resistance movements, the Colombian Revolutionary Armed Forces ("FARC") and the National Liberation Army ("ELN"), both refused to participate. *See* The National Organization of Indigenous Peoples of Columbia ("ONIC"), *Participation of Columbian Indigenous Peoples in the Constitutional Reform of 1991*, *in* ABORIGINAL PEOPLES 66, 72-73 (Marie Leger ed. & Arnold Bennett trans., 1994). It is said that the guerilla war reduces GDP by at least two percent per year. *See* David Swafford, *Halo of Hope*, LATIN FIN., Mar. 1999, at 45.

corruption and instability in Colombia, including continued armed resistance by Marxist guerillas and political violence instigated by the drug traffic in cocaine.

The 1991 constitution, then, amounts to a remarkable achievement by a fractious assembly in a country riven by violence and instability in all sectors of political life. The idea of *estado social de derecho*—an admixture of social state and rule of law—gives expression to the role of the state captured in the new constitution.[99] The text guarantees a variety of social and economic rights, in addition to the recognition of indigenous self-government. While the constitution gives general protection to private property, the text also envisions the democratization of property.[100] In Article 60, the constitution declares that the state "will promote access to property."[101] It also is "the duty of the state to promote the gradual access of agricultural workers to landed property in individual or associational form."[102] Aboriginal communal land rights are recognized,[103] and these lands are "inalienable, impresecriptible, and not subject to seizure."[104] Contrary to the seemingly universal tendencies in international investment law, the constitution also permitted the expropriation of property without the provision of compensation.[105] According to the Colombian Constitutional Court, the specific assignment of the *estado social de derecho* "consists in making real the social function of property."[106]

---

99. *See* Manuel José Cepeda, *Democracy, State and Society in the 1991 Constitution: The Role of the Constitutional Court*, *in* COLOMBIA: THE POLITICS OF REFORMING THE STATE 71, 86 (Eduardo Posada-Carbó ed., 1998).

100. *See* COLOM. CONST. art. 58:

> Private property and other rights acquired in accordance with civil laws may not be ignored or infringed upon by subsequent laws. When in the application of a law passed on account of public utility or social interest and recognized as essential a conflict should occur about the rights of individuals, the private interest will have to give precedence to the public or social interest.
>
> Property is a social function which implies obligations. As such an ecological function is inherent to it.
>
> The state will protect and promote associational and collective forms of property.
>
> Because of public necessity or social interest defined by the legislative, expropriation will be possible by means of a judicial determination and prior indemnification. The latter will be determined in consultation with the interests of the community and of the affected party. In cases determined by the legislative, said expropriations may be pursued by administrative means, subject to subsequent contentious administrative action at law, including with respect to price.
>
> Still, the legislative, for reasons of equity, may determine those cases in which there is no ground for indemnification through an affirmative vote of the absolute majority vote of the members of both chambers.
>
> Reasons of equity, as well as motives of public necessity or social interest invoked by the legislative, will not be judicially reviewable.

Id. The last two paragraphs were repealed by Acto Legislativo 1/99 (Aug. 4, 1999). *See* discussion *infra* Part IV.)

101. COLOM. CONST. art. 60.

102. *Id.* art. 64.

103. *See id.* art. 329.

104. *Id.* art. 63.

105. *See id.* art. 58.

106. Colombian Constitutional Court Decision No. C-037/94, § 2.2 (on file with author).

Nonetheless, a program of privatization of public sector assets and responsibilities is expressly contemplated. The 1991 constitution endorses the internationalization of economic relations[107] and permits the congress to authorize the government to "sell national assets."[108] While "public health and environmental protection" are declared to be "public services for which the state is responsible," the constitution permits "private entities . . . to exercise oversight and control over them."[109] Social security is a guaranteed "irrevocable right" that "may be provided by public or private entities."[110] Lastly, as the state is obliged to promote "access to property," when a state enterprise is privatized, it is obliged to offer employees, trade unions, pension funds, and cooperatives (*sector solidario*) shares at a minimum price and under special credit conditions.[111] Privatization in the Colombian Constitution, then, aspires to disperse property ownership to a wide stratum of the population rather than concentrating it in the hands of foreign investors or the already affluent.[112]

The Constitutional Court has halted the privatization of financial institutions because the scheme failed to comply with the requirements of Article 60.[113] As the share offering to the solidarity sector was limited to fifteen percent, and as preferential conditions also were attached to offers to current shareholders, the scheme violated the constitutional commitment to the "democratization" of public property.[114] Nevertheless, by 1996, the Colombian government had privatized approximately 100 state-owned or -controlled entities,[115] including more than six banks, savings and loan corporations, the

107. *See* COLOM. CONST. art. 277.

108. *Id.* art. 150.9.

109. *Id.* art. 49.

110. *Id.* art. 48.

111. *See* Constitutional Court Decision No. C-037/94, § 3 (on file with author); *see also* COLOM. CONST. art. 60:

> When the state sells its interest in an enterprise, it will take measures promoting democratization of the ownership of its shares and will offer its workers or the collective and worker's organizations special terms to make it possible for them to accede to the said proprietary shares.

Id.

112. According to the Colombian Constitutional Court, Article 60 is designed to prevent the privatization procedure followed "in many countries" in which privatization "is converted into the transfer of public property, for a fraction of its worth, to the richest sectors of society." Colombian Constitutional Court Decision No. C-452/95 (on file with author). Similar provisions can be found in the 1992 Paraguayan Constitution:

> Whenever the State decides to transfer a state-owned company or its shares in such a company to the private sector, it will give preferential option of purchase to the workers and sectors that are directly linked with the company. A law will regulate the way in which this option will be established.

CONSTITUCIÓN DE LA REPÚBLICA DEL PARAGUAY [Constitution] art. 111 (Para.) [hereinafter PARA. CONST.]; *see also* GUISLAIN, *supra* note 34, at 37.

113. *See* Alejandro Linares & Maristella Aldana, *Privatization Laws in Colombia,* LATIN FIN., Jan. 1997, at 23. *See generally* Cepeda, *supra* note 99; Luz Estella Nagle, *Evolution of the Colombian Judiciary and the Constitutional Court,* 6 IND. INT'L & COMP. L. REV. 59 (1995) (discussing the evolving role of the Court).

114. Colombian Constitutional Court Decision No. C-037/94 and No. C-452/95 (on file with author).

115. *See Colombia, supra* note 95, at 9.

national port authority, thermoelectric and hydroelectric plants, and railway interests.[116]

The participation of the solidarity sector in privatization has been mixed at best. Where purchases are made, it is feasible to buy only a portion of the enterprise.[117] Preferred share offerings to workers' associations and cooperatives often are sold off to the highest bidder.[118] In other instances, the privatization program has had, and likely will continue to have, little effect. Considering the low rates of unionization in Colombia (about eight percent),[119] the poorest workers will not be organized, nor will they have the fiscal capacity to purchase shares.[120]

For the disciplinarians of neo-liberalism, privatization in Colombia has moved too slowly. The majority of public services continue to be delivered by the state.[121] The current Pastrana Administration, though, has indicated that it will step up privatization: According to one report, the Administration is "rolling out the red carpet for foreign investors."[122] President Pastrana aims to privatize seventeen state-owned power companies and the state interest in a massive coal operation and also to partner with investors in new infrastructure development, such as roads, highways, and airports. The government estimates an anticipated $3.1 billion U.S. dollars in revenue from privatizations in 1999 alone.[123]

Related to the Colombian program of privatization is the relaxation of the rules for the admission of foreign investment: Investment screening has ceased, there are few restrictions on the patriation of profits, national treatment has been granted to all foreign investors, and 100% foreign ownership is permitted in almost all sectors.[124] Yet irritants to foreign investment remained in place, and they are a vestige of the notion that property performs social functions. One already has been mentioned: The constitution authorizes the state to expropriate property without the payment of compensation.[125] For "reasons of equity"—a determination not reviewable by the judiciary—the legislature, authorized by an absolute majority in both chambers of Congress, may

116. *See* Linares & Aldana, *supra* note 113, at 23.

117. In the case of the privatization of thermal electric plants, the sector was able to purchase more than a 60% interest. *See id.*

118. I am grateful to Professor Diego López-Medina for this point.

119. *See* PRS Group, *Climate for Business*, Nov. 1, 1996, *available in* LEXIS, News Library, PRS Group/IBC Market Newsletters file.

120. *See* Pascuzzi, *supra* note 94, at 476.

121. *See* Thomas Vogel, *Colombia Woos Foreign Investors in Bid to End Economic Slump*, GLOBE & MAIL, May 31, 1999, at A11.

122. *Id.*

123. *See id.* Reports in 2000 indicate a drop in privatization revenue from $2 billion (U.S.) to $830 million (U.S.) and the postponement of sales in two banks, 14 electricity distributors, and Interconexion Electrica, the national electricity grid. *See Recovery, of Sorts*, *supra* note 93, at 32.

124. *See Colombia-Investment Climate*, INT'L MARKET INSIGHT (Nat'l Trade Data Bank, Bogota, Colombia), Aug. 13, 1996, *available in* LEXIS, International Trade, Company & Financial Information, Market Reports file [hereinafter *Colombia-Investment Climate.*].

125. *See* COLOM. CONST. art. 58.

expropriate property without prior compensation.[126] Another concern is that foreign investors may be precluded from participating in the divestiture of state-owned enterprises.

How might this new constitutional regime, particularly its provisions regarding privatization and the social function of property, stack up against the new investment rules regime that reflects the neo-liberal consensus on the admission and treatment of foreign investment? I turn to this question in the next part.

V

THE TRANSNATIONAL INVESTMENT RULES REGIME

I focus here on two related instruments of transnational rule—Bilateral Investment Treaties ("BITs") and the draft Multilateral Agreement on Investment ("MAI")—and their linkages with domestic constitutional rules such as those found in the new Colombian Constitution. Privatization rules that prefer local workers or associations likely run afoul of the obligation of "national treatment" found in both investment instruments.[127] National treatment requires that there be no discrimination against foreign investors resident in the other party state, so that non-resident investors are treated as if they were residents.[128] The MAI, however, may have turned out to be a more tolerable instrument in this regard by permitting some exceptions to the blanket rule.

It is interesting to surmise whether national treatment obligations subvert or undermine constitutional commitments. International trade scholars have long argued that national treatment does not require any particular minimum standard of treatment, but only equality of treatment between local and foreign investors.[129] States, they have argued, continue to have the ability to legislate in any area. National sovereignty, then, is not impinged in any substantive way.[130] When a constitutional text authorizes or commits a state to prefer nationals, however, the national treatment rule could have the effect of negating the constitutional commitment.[131] No longer is the obligation of non-discrimination simply a version of formal equality that is neutral with regard to legislative objectives. It is this constitutional context that makes the national treatment obligation cut ever "closer to the bone of national sovereignty."[132]

126. *Id.*

127. *See infra* text accompanying notes 152-157.

128. *See* JOHN H. JACKSON, THE WORLD TRADING SYTEM: LAW AND POLICY OF INTERNATIONAL ECONOMIC RELATIONS 213-14 (2d ed. 1997).

129. *See id.* at 157.

130. *See* RICHARD G. LIPSEY ET AL., THE NAFTA: WHAT'S IN, WHAT'S OUT, WHAT'S NEXT 164 (1994).

131. *See infra* text accompanying notes 176-82.

132. Michael M. Hart, *The Mercantilist's Lament: National Treatment and Modern Trade Negotiations,* 21 J. WORLD TRADE L. 37, 55 (1987).

The terms under which foreign investment is admitted and protected have long been an issue of controversy between the countries of the North and the South, but that controversy appears to have subsided. Codification of the rules for the protection and promotion of foreign investment is being pursued in a number of arenas. These codes establish the most stringent levels of protection favorable to foreign capital. Investment protection agreements, like the draft MAI, have emerged as a priority item for international economic law.[133] An interlocking network of rules for the protection and liberalization of FDI has emerged through BITs, regional trade agreements such as NAFTA and the European Energy Charter Treaty, and at the multilateral level in the Agreement on Trade-Related Investment Measures ("TRIMs").[134] A set of non-binding investment rules was agreed to in the Asia Pacific Economic Cooperation ("APEC"), and the OECD set itself on a course of completing a multilateral agreement of which the draft MAI was the product. Taken together, these instruments of state discipline and neo-liberal principle "reflect a remarkable consensus" that the world is now safe for foreign investment.[135]

I have argued elsewhere that this web of economic rules, identifiable at the transnational, regional, and bilateral levels, exhibits some of the features and characteristics of domestic constitutions.[136] They are a form of pre-commitment strategy that binds future generations of citizens to certain pre-determined institutional forms through which politics is practiced.[137] In addition, these economic rules, like constitutions, are difficult to amend, include binding enforcement mechanisms and judicial review, and sometimes are drawn from the very language of domestic constitutions.[138]

A. The Bilateral Regime

Bilateral Investment Treaties have become a commonplace tool for investment protection and promotion. The U.N. Commission on Trade and Development reports that by the end of 1998, more than 1700 BITs had been completed involving 174 countries.[139] Two-thirds of these agreements were negotiated during the 1990s.[140] Despite adherence to aspects of the Calvo doctrine and a rigorous commitment to the principle of national sovereignty,

---

133. *See* MICHAEL J. TREBILCOCK & ROBERT HOWSE, THE REGULATION OF INTERNATIONAL TRADE 335-66 (2d ed. 1995).

134. *See* A.A. Fatouros, *Towards an International Agreement on Foreign Direct Investment?* 10 ICSID REV.—FOREIGN INVESTMENT L.J. 181, 188-89 (1995).

135. Antonio R. Parro, *The Scope of New Investment Laws and International Instruments*, *in* ECONOMIC DEVELOPMENT, FOREIGN INVESTMENT AND THE LAW 27, 31 (Robert Pritchard ed., 1996).

136. *See* Schneiderman, *Constitutional Strictures*, *supra* note 16, at 90.

137. *See id.*

138. *See* Schneiderman, *NAFTA's Takings Rule, supra* note 16, at 515.

139. *See* UNCTAD, WORLD INVESTMENT REPORT 1999: FOREIGN DIRECT INVESTMENT AND THE CHALLENGES OF DEVELOPMENT 117 (1999).

140. *See* UNCTAD, WORLD INVESTMENT REPORT 1997: TRANSNATIONAL CORPORATIONS, MARKET STRUCTURE AND COMPETITION POLICY 19 (1997).

Latin American states increasingly have become party to agreements that incorporate stringent investment protection standards.[141] At least thirty-seven BITs have been concluded between the countries of Latin America and the Caribbean.[142]

These agreements typically require state parties to adhere to a number of key disciplines, most of them organized around the principle of "non-discrimination." These disciplines include national treatment, requiring treatment no less favorable than that available to nationals within the investing state, and most favored-nation ("MFN") status, mandating treatment no less favorable than that available to investors of a third country.[143] In addition, there are substantive constraints on state parties including protection from expropriations and nationalizations (or measures having equivalent effect), the ability to enforce these obligations by foreign investors themselves, and mechanisms for the settlement and adjudication of disputes before international trade tribunals and domestic courts.[144] These same obligations are virtually replicated in NAFTA's investment chapter.[145]

It is significant that investment agreements can now be enforced by foreign investors against state parties. Ordinarily, only the contracting state parties are entitled to enforce investment agreements, so that disputes are mediated through the process of inter-state diplomatic relations. Instead, the investment rules regime purports to "depoliticize" investment disputes.[146] Investors are entitled to pursue litigation to enforce these agreements within the domestic court system of the contracting party, in addition to being entitled to submit disputes to binding investment arbitration.[147] The parties to NAFTA were the first to assent to this type of intervention, and the practice is now reproduced in the modern BIT system.[148] Kenneth Vandevelde claims that this has been "the single most important goal of the [U.S.] BIT program."[149] As has been observed in Canada, this type of intervention is license for investors to meddle significantly in public policymaking within state parties.[150]

141. *See id.* at 76-77.

142. *See id.* at 76.

143. *See* JACKSON, *supra* note 128, at 157.

144. *See* David Schneiderman, *Investment Rules and the New Constitutionalism*, 25 L. & SOC. INQUIRY 757, 769 (2000).

145. *See id.* at 769.

146. *See* Kenneth J. Vandevelde, *The BIT Program: A Fifteen-Year Appraisal, in* AMERICAN SOCIETY OF INTERNATIONAL LAW: PROCEEDINGS OF THE 86TH ANNUAL MEETING 532, 535 (1992).

147. *See id.* at 532, 538. The language of Article 8 of Colombian BITs is somewhat different. *See* Leif Weizman, *Colombia: Model Bilateral Investment Treaty of 1993*, 8 INTER-AM. LEGAL MATERIALS 111, 122-23 (1998). If no settlement is achieved following three months "using the local judiciary or any other means," the parties may submit the dispute to the "administrative courts or tribunals" of one of the parties or to arbitration or conciliation with the International Center for the Settlement of Investment Disputes ("ICSID"). *Id.* at 123.

148. *See* Vandevelde, *supra* note 146, at 534.

149. *Id.*

150. *See generally* Schneiderman, *Constitutonal Strictures*, *supra* note 16.

Parties to these agreements are entitled to list reservations, or carve-outs, for those sectors that will be exempt from the requirement of national treatment and MFN status, and there are general exceptions that typically concern such matters as national security, public order, and protection of the environment.[151] Ordinarily, no reservations or exceptions are permitted with regard to expropriations and nationalizations—these are viewed as simply beyond the pale.

BITs usually do not contain express provisions regarding processes for the divestiture of state enterprises. Typically, BIT obligations are not triggered until a foreign investor enters the host state and, in order to enter that jurisdictional space, investors must comply with all the usual laws or regulations.[152] The sale of public assets to private owners—the process of denationalization—will not ordinarily activate the national treatment obligation of non-discrimination against foreign investors unless the non-resident investor has entered the jurisdictional space of the host state. In other words, privatization schemes that impinge on foreign investor participation will not offend the national treatment rule unless the investor already is established in the country.

The OECD considered this question in 1991, asking whether the principle of national treatment, as defined in its 1976 standard investment code, should apply to the "privatisation of enterprises previously under public ownership."[153] The OECD concluded that the undertaking should come into play whenever areas

> previously under monopoly are opened up. In such cases, access to move into these areas should then be provided on a non-discriminatory basis as between private domestic and foreign-controlled enterprises *already established in the country in question*. If restrictions prohibit or impede in any way the participation of foreign-controlled enterprises vis-à-vis their domestic counterparts, then these restrictions are to be reported as exceptions to National Treatment. The objective of the instrument in this context is, therefore, to ensure access to formerly closed sectors on an equal basis.[154]

Would the constitutionally mandated privatization rule in Colombia, which requires preferential share offerings to employees, trade unions, and cooperatives, offend the principle of national treatment for those investors already established within Colombia? Leaving aside the problematic question of applying an equal rights analysis to frustrate the achievement of rational economic and political objectives,[155] the answer turns on the way in which one classifies the commitment. One option is to classify the rule as outlawing

151. *See* Ibrahim F.I. Shihata, *Recent Trends Relating to Entry of Foreign Direct Investment*, 9 ICSID REV.—FOREIGN INVESTMENT L.J. 47, 52, (1994). In the case of NAFTA, Mexico listed as non-conforming measures numerous activities protected by the Calvo Clause. *See id.* at 61.

152. *See* M. SORNARAJAH, THE INTERNATIONAL LAW ON FOREIGN INVESTMENT 85 (1994).

153. Organisation for Econ. Coop. and Dev., Main Features of the Multilateral Agreement on Investment 7 (1991) (unpublished paper, on file with author).

154. *Id.* (emphasis added)

155. *See* SORNARAJAH, *supra* note 152, at 85.

foreign investment participation and therefore discriminatory on the ground of nationality. Another is to classify the rule as preferring one economic sector over other sectors, such as employers or other potential local investors, and therefore discriminatory on the ground of employment status or some other such ground, but not on the ground of nationality. Yet another option is to consider the rule as preferring local employee and associational investors over foreign employee and other associational investors, resulting in discriminatory treatment. The first and broadest interpretation is the one adopted by the United States, as well as many international trade scholars. It would outlaw any measures that "have the intent or the effect of preventing or significantly impeding inward direct investment by non-residents."[156] According to this standard, and even according to the less broad third option, preferred share offerings to the solidarity sector likely would be inconsistent with the principle of national treatment, requiring that foreign investors be treated no less favorably than domestic enterprises and investors. The draft MAI text of April 1998 helps to shed light on this question. According to the negotiating parties, any preferential scheme would have been contrary to the broadly drafted national treatment rule.[157]

This understanding of the BIT rules suggests that the constitutionally mandated privatization rule in Colombia, which requires preferential share offerings to employees, trade unions, and cooperatives, will offend the principle of national treatment for those investors already established within Colombia. Preferred share offerings to this sector run contrary to the principle of national treatment.

Before turning to the MAI, it should be mentioned that U.S. bilateral investment treaty standards, which are incorporated increasingly into Canadian BITs, are more stringent and would increase the likelihood of conflict with the domestic constitutional regime.[158] These standards require non-discrimination in the *admission or establishment* of investments, not merely fair treatment after admission.[159] Those non-resident foreign investors who merely wish to establish a presence in the host country are entitled to equal treatment with domestic nationals even before they make any investment. Colombian constitutional requirements undoubtedly would be in conflict with this more stringent standard.

As discussed below, the Colombian Constitutional Court has shown itself to be somewhat resistant to the strictures of economic globalization. It is likely, then, that these BITs would not survive constitutional scrutiny insofar as they de-activate the constitutional obligations concerning privatization. But the material result likely would be that the Colombian government would not resist

156. Hart, *supra* note 132, at 54.

157. *See infra* text accompanying notes 164-165.

158. *See* Sornorajah, *supra* note 152, at 245.

159. *See* UNCTAD, *supra* note 139, at 77. In this way, Canadian BIT practice has ceased to be modeled after British practice. *See* ROBERT K. PATERSON ET AL., INTERNATIONAL TRADE AND INVESTMENT LAW IN CANADA 12-18 (1994).

those demands; it would submit to the disciplines of the investment rules regime by seeking an amendment to the Colombian Constitution.

B. The Multilateral Regime

How might Colombian constitutional rules fare against the terms of the draft Multilateral Agreement on Investment? The twenty-nine member countries of the OECD undertook the task of completing an enforceable agreement for the protection and promotion of foreign investment in September 1995. It was not that investment flows between these countries had been frustrated; rather, the objective was to set very high standards for the protection of investment that countries in the so-called "developing" world would be pressured to adopt.[160] The web of bilateral agreements then could be filled in by this new multilateral instrument.

Negotiations in Paris came to a halt, in part, because of resistance to the agreement in the United States Congress, the withdrawal of France from the negotiating table, and the coordinated action of citizen organizations in Canada, France, New Zealand, and elsewhere.[161] While there is little likelihood that the exercise will continue at the OECD, it is probable that negotiations will shift to other venues, like the World Trade Organization. It is worthwhile, then, to review the provisions of the MAI as they concern privatization, particularly as the draft text contains provisions that expressly contemplate rules for the treatment of foreign investors in the case of a divestiture of state assets—a proposal the OECD review had recommended back in 1991.[162]

Although a number of key issues were resolved in negotiations, it is interesting that the draft provisions concerning privatization are among the least settled.[163] In fact, the provisions concerning privatization suggest substantial disagreement between some of the negotiating parties. If the draft text signals what remained in dispute at the OECD negotiations, it also makes difficult drawing any definitive conclusions about what consensus would have emerged on this issue among the negotiating parties.

A number of matters were not in dispute, however. Because national treatment and MFN treatment would be accorded to investors in the establishment phase under Article III—the United States BIT standard—processes of privatization would ordinarily be caught by the rule. But the parties felt it desirable to spell out how these obligations applied in the privatization context. It was settled that the privatization discipline in the MAI

160. *See* JANE KELSEY, RECLAIMING THE FUTURE: NEW ZEALAND AND THE GLOBAL ECONOMY 321 (1999).

161. *See* William A. Dymond, *The MAI: A Sad and Melancholy Tale in* CANADA AMONG NATIONS 1999: A BIG LEAGUE PLAYER? 25-53 (Fen Osler Hampson et al. eds., 1999); Paul Vallely, *How the Web Saved the World*, INDEP. (LONDON), Jan. 10, 1999, at 1.

162. *See* Organisation for Econ. Coop. and Dev., *supra* note 153.

163. For a discussion of the issues that remained unresolved, including the nature of exceptions, the treatment of culture, the coverage of subnational government, and labor and environment issues, see Dymond, *supra* note 161, at 34.

would require that national treatment and MFN status be accorded to all manner of privatization "irrespective of the method of privatization chosen," such as public offering or direct sale, and to all phases of the process.[164] In dispute was the extent to which "special share arrangements," such as management/employee buy-outs, "golden shares," which are those reserved for government, and special schemes for the public, offended national treatment and MFN treatment.[165]

It was agreed that these arrangements *prima facie* offended the principle of non-discrimination; disagreement turned on the manner in which this was to be acknowledged in the text. Most delegations appeared willing to exempt special share arrangements, adopting the more restrictive definition of national treatment: So long as foreign investors are treated no less favorably than other excluded domestic investors, there is no discrimination.[166] Others preferred that the obligation of non-discrimination remain in effect, but that those states concerned about privatization in certain areas designate as reservations to the agreement special share arrangements in those sectors.[167]

The proposed text accepted by a large number of delegations would have considered special share arrangements compatible with the commitment to national treatment and MFN treatment unless they expressly offended MFN status or discriminated against investments on the grounds of "nationality or permanent residency."[168] The explanation provided by the OECD predating the April 1998 draft text is that so long as foreign investors "are not put in a more disadvantageous position than domestic investors which do not qualify for such privatisation schemes," these measures will be considered non-discriminatory.[169] Taking this interpretive clause into consideration, it may have been that, in the case of the multilateral instrument, in contrast to the BIT rules, a comprehensive code would have provided clarity for preferred share options for employees and their associations. In an environment where political alternatives are so constrained, this could have been considered the preferred alternative to an unlimited BIT national treatment rule.

A minority of delegations preferred the option of designating certain sectors as exceptions. Exempting privatization processes from MAI disciplines could also have avoided constitutional conflict. In large measure, this would have

164. "[F]our delegations reserved their position on all privatisation obligations." ORGANISATION FOR ECON. COOP. AND DEV., THE MAI NEGOTIATING TEXT 27 n.41 (1998).

165. This is the language of the draft negotiating text at ¶ 3, altern. 4, art. 7. *See id.* at 29; ANDERS AHNLID, NEW DISCIPLINES 23, 24 (OECD Working Papers, Proceedings of the Special Session on the Multilateral Inv. Agreement, Vol. V, No. 96, 23, 24 (1997)).

166. *See* AHNLID, *supra* note 165, at 24; MADALENA OLIVEIRA ESILVA, PRIVATISATION AND MONOPOLIES 33, 35 (OECD Working Papers, Multilateral Agreement on Inv. State of Play, Vol. V, No. 51 (1997)).

167. *See* AHNLID, *supra* note 165, at 24; ESILVA, *supra* note 166.

168. This was the language "supported by a large number of delegations." *See* Organisation for Econ. Coop. and Dev., *supra* note 153, at 28 (concerning ¶ 3, altern. 1, art. 4).

169. Organisation for Econ. Coop. and Dev., *supra* note 153, at 7. It is not clear whether both intentional and unintentional discrimination would be exempted. *See* ESILVA, *supra* note 166, at 33.

depended on the specificity of those reservations: Whether they were bound (in which case no new sectors could be added) or unbound (in which the reservations anticipated future sectoral exceptions).[170] The expectations of the MAI negotiators was that the agreement would "standstill" investment measures: The agreement would provide an "irreversible minimum standard" from which states could not deviate.[171] The agreement also would "rollback" reservations and exceptions, "with a view to their eventual elimination," according to a predetermined timetable, for instance.[172] Over time, then, even a list of exempted enterprises or sectors would be subject to erosion due to commitments in the MAI text or state peer pressure.

VI

CONCLUSION

The state capitalist model of constitutional design has not only fallen into disfavor, it is facing near-permanent erasure from the effects of the neo-liberal model represented by the investment rules regime. Though the draft MAI suggests a more tolerable approach to alternatives to privatization, we should remember that preferred share option schemes remain inconsistent with the key precepts of the investment rules regime and that these disciplines were intended to tighten their grip over time, so that no exceptions would be permissible.

Admittedly, the conflict outlined above is not confined to the arena of constitutional analysis. It has resonance in the context of ordinary legislative rules for the privatization of state enterprise. But the constitutional context heightens the quality of the conflict. Constitutions are intended to have a level of fixity outside of politics, that is, they are intended to standardize the enduring rules of the game. As such, they should be able to withstand the pressures generated by particular class interests within states and by the material interests of other states. But constitutions also are within politics, and so provide a focal point of real conflict about alternative futures. Constitutions, to state the obvious, both shape politics and are shaped by politics.[173]

This conflict is being felt in Colombia, where the expropriation rule in the Colombian Constitution came into direct conflict with the investment rules regime. The 1994 Colombian-United Kingdom BIT contained the usual provisions concerning national treatment, MFN treatment, and prohibitions on expropriations and nationalizations.[174] Expropriation and nationalization are prohibited unless they are for a public purpose, non-discriminatory, and accompanied by the payment of "prompt, adequate and effective

170. *See* BARRY APPLETON, NAVIGATING NAFTA 161 (1994).

171. William H. Witherell, *The OECD Multilateral Agreement on Investment*, 4 TRANSNAT'L. CORP. 1, 11 (1995).

172. *Id.*

173. *See* John Dearlove, *Bringing the Constitution Back In: Political Science and the State*, 37 POL. STUD. 521, 534 (1989).

174. *See* Bilateral Investment Treaty, Mar. 9, 1994, Col.-U.K.; Weizman, *supra* note 147, at 116.

compensation" that is fully realizable and transferable. This stringent standard of compensation, the "Hull formula," has been held up by the United States as the standard required by international law. The BIT as enacted by Law 246/95 was presented to the Colombian Constitutional Court for its certification—a constitutional requirement in Colombia.[175]

The Court held, by a six-to-three majority, that the BIT was contrary to the Colombian Constitution in two respects.[176] First, the BIT had the effect of deactivating provisions of the Colombian Constitution, such as expropriation without the payment of compensation in the interests of equity. The Government could not waive the exercise of a power delegated to it by the Constitution by conceding the payment of prompt, adequate, and effective compensation. Second, the investment treaty offended the equality provisions of the constitution by granting to citizens of British nationality preferential treatment with respect to expropriations, which was not available even to Colombian nationals. In other words, the BIT offended Calvo's edict that foreign nationals not be entitled to preferential treatment over domestic nationals.[177] The Court reached a similar conclusion in regard to a Cuba-Colombia BIT.[178]

The Colombian government, anxious to reassure foreign investors that Colombia is open to foreign investment, pledged to remove this remnant of a bygone era, though no government in modern Colombian history has expropriated foreign property, nor have investors expressed any concern that the risk of expropriation is high in Colombia.[179] Moreover, there is some doubt that any benefits will accrue to Colombia as a consequence.[180] A recent U.N. study confirms that investment protection agreements are relatively insignificant in determining amounts of Foreign Direct Investment ("FDI").[181] Other factors, including market size and growth, exchange rates, and country risks, are more important determinants of FDI.[182] Nonetheless, the Colombian government was intent on removing the offending language from the Constitution, deploying investment policy and constitutional reform to "symbolize a commitment to economic liberalism."[183] Two paragraphs of constitutional text were repealed in August 1999; the constitutional property

175. *See* COLOM. CONST. art. 241, no. 10.

176. *See* Colombian Constitutional Court Decision No. C-358/96 (on file with author).

177. *See* Weizman, *supra* note 147, at 116. One solution is to confer the same advantages on domestic nationals (though this may not satisfy the constitutional requirement) or, alternatively, on all investors regardless of nationality. According to Vandevelde, the latter option would "ensure genuine investment neutrality and create a host state constituency in support of an enduring liberal investment regime." Kenneth J. Vandevelde, *The Political Economy of a Bilateral Investment Treaty*, 92 AM. J. INT'L L. 621, 639 (1998).

178. Colombian Constitutional Court Decision No. C-379/96 (on file with author).

179. *See Colombia-Investment Climate*, *supra* note 124.

180. *See* SORNARAJAH, *supra* note 152, at 235-36.

181. *See* UNCTAD, BILATERAL INVESTMENT TREATIES IN THE MID-1990S, at 117 (1998).

182. *See id.*

183. Vandevelde, *supra* note 146, at 628.

clause no longer permits expropriation without the payment of compensation.[184] Here is a clear instance of neo-liberal constitutionalism disciplining domestic constitutional text: Interference with private property and investment rights simply is beyond the bounds of acceptability.

Terence Daintith and Monica Sah suggest that constitutions can be "economically neutral," in terms of not expressing any preference for a given system of economic relations within the state, whether public or private.[185] Perhaps removing constitutional constraints to privatization would be preferable to formal expressions of ideological precommitment. Yet the constitution-like rules that operate outside the domestic state in the transnational arena pose real constraints on domestic constitutionalism. The investment rules regime—the web of interlocking rules and structures that constrain through the force of law state treatment of foreign investment—tilts the table in favor of foreign investors. If the democratization of property and the redistribution of state assets to a wide stratum of the population are considered discriminatory, then the economic chapter of the transnational constitution is not neutral. Rather, states are bound for the foreseeable future to organize public policy in favour of the neo-liberal model.

In this environment, are domestic constitutions a reasonable resource to countervail the investment rules regime? We should keep in mind that states are the authors of this regime that limits their capacity to regulate privatizations and to intervene in the marketplace. So rather than seek to constrain state action further through constitutional limits, perhaps the better option is to loosen these binding precommitments. States perhaps should unlock themselves from the regime of investment rules, though this would be a difficult matter because most BITs remain in force for periods of up to ten years for those investments established during the time a treaty was in force. The draft MAI would have locked states into at least a twenty-year commitment.[186]

The failed MAI talks, though, should hearten those who wish to free states from a predetermined constitutional course of economic conduct. By removing themselves from the table, the French delegation was able effectively to scuttle negotiations. So rather than bypassing the state, one should better understand the ways in which states are implicated in the structuring of the investment rules

184. The amendment, by Acto Legislativo 1/99 of Aug. 4, 1999, excised the provisions concerning equitable expropriation:

> Con todo, el legislador, por razones de equidad, podrá determinar los casos en que no haya lugar al pago de indemnización, mediante el voto favorable de la mayoría absoluta de los miembros de una y otra Cámara. Las razones de equidad, así como los motivos de utilidad pública o de interés social, invocados por el legislador, no serán controvertibles judicialmente [trans: Still, the legislative, for reasons of equity, may determine those cases in which there is no ground for indemnification through an affirmative vote of the absolute majority vote of the members of both chambers. Reasons of equity, as well as motives of public necessity or social interest invoked by the legislative, will not be judicially reviewable.].

Id. (translation by Moira Gracey).

185. Daintith & Sah, *supra* note 71, at 465.

186. *See* Schneiderman, *NAFTA's Takings Rule*, *supra* note 16.

regime. Citizens, then, can aim to undo constraints, both domestic and transnational, on the democratization of property and the promotion of self-rule.

Name Index

Aalders, N. 404, 413
Abbott, A. 432, 449
Abel, R. 75, 97
Abraham, L.K. 434
Ackerman, Bruce 15
Adams, Walter 186
Adler, Max 80, 93, 96
Albrow, Martin 501, 502
Alchian, Armen A. 492
Alexander, J.C. 50
Althusser, Louis 81
Aman, Alfred C. xvii
Andersen, O. 413
Anspach, R. 432, 442
Aristotle 101
Arrow, Kenneth J. 343
Arthurs, H.W. xii
Ashby, W.R. 58
Ashton, Robert 132, 137
Assmann, H-D. 58
Atiyah, P.S. 252
Ayres, Ian xvi, xvii, 309, 394, 401, 415, 466, 478, 485

Badaracco, Joseph L. 252
Baer, K. 398
Baldwin, Robert xi, xiv, xv, xvi, 202, 204, 221–50, 266, 390, 393
Bankowski, Z. 77, 224
Bardach, Eugene xvi, 243, 252, 297, 393
Barrett, M. 97
Barzel, Yoram 492, 493
Beauchamp, T.L. 433
Beder, S. 404
Bentham, Jeremy 102, 358
Berrill, Sir Kenneth 219
Bickel, Alexander 10, 13
Billet, L. 79
Bilmes, Jack 365
Bismark, Otto von 17
Black, D. 49
Black, Julia M. xi, xii, xiv, xv, xvii, xviii, 197–200, 287–315, 415
Blackstone, Sir William 147
Blankenburg, E. 49, 50, 52, 61, 70
Blumberg, A. 428
Bobbio, N. 75
Bohannan, P. 75
Böhm, Franz 183, 184, 187, 191
Bohnert, W. 57, 60
Bollinger, Lee C. 485
Bonaparte, Napoleon 6
Bottomley, S. 419
Bradley, A.W. 224
Braithwaite, John xiv, xv, xvi, xvii, 251–85, 309, 389, 390, 393, 394, 399, 400–401, 407, 415, 418, 466, 478, 485
Braithwaite, Valerie xiv, 251–85, 407, 408, 416, 417
Brandeis, Louis 10, 19, 154, 155
Brandner, Hans E. 488
Braun, R. 130–31
Braverman, H. 97
Breit, William 489
Brenner, R. 94
Brewer, Justice 152
Bruff, Harold H. 349
Bruggemeier, G. 70
Buckley, W. 51
Bull, David 223, 224
Burawoy, Michael 94–5 *passim*
Burby, R. 398, 400, 401
Burford, Ann 346
Burrows, Paul 371

Calabresi, Guido 23
Calvo, Carlos 507–8 *passim*, 525
Carbonnier, J. 75
Carr, Justice 384
Carson, W.G. xi
Cave, Martin xi
Chamberlin, Edward 185
Charles, I, King 121, 123, 128, 132
Chayes, A. 419
Clawson, D. 97
Clegg, S. 98, 102
Clune, H. 56
Coase, Ronald H. 483
Cohen, M.D. 442
Coke, Sir Edward 125
Colbert, Jean-Baptiste 131
Coleman, J.S. 436

Collins, Hugh xvii, 491
Comte, Auguste 6, 102
Cooney, Mark xv
Coriat, B. 98
Cotterrell, Roger xii
Cox, Robert W. 504, 505
Cragg, W. 399
Craig, Paul P. xiii, 145–61, 164
Crandall, R. 404
Cranford, R.E. 431
Crew, Chief Justice 125
Crick, Francis H.C. 6
Croley, Stephen P. xiv

Dahl, Tove S. 95
Daintith, Terence xi, xiii, xvi, 526
Davis, Kenneth C. xiv, 221–31 *passim*, 232, 233, 234, 235, 237–8 *passim*, 239, 240–50 *passim*, 340
Day, Patricia 252
Deane, Phyllis 137
Del Vecchio, G. 75
Devers, K.J. 443
Dicey, Albert V. xii, xiii, xiv, 505
DiMaggio, P.J. 438–9
Diver, Colin S. xiv, 201, 202, 244, 279
Donzelot, Jacques 97, 503
Drahos, Peter xvii
Driscoll, D. 415, 416
Duguit, Léon 510
Dunkerley, D. 98, 102
Duxbury, Neil xii, xiii
Dworkin, Ronald M. 187, 224, 231

Easton, D. 58
Edelman, Lauren B. xv, 416, 417, 418, 420
Edelman, M. 60
Edward I, King 119
Edward, Corin D. 189
Edwards, James 346
Edwards, P.K. 97
Ehrlich, E. 75
Einstein, Albert 5
Eisenberg, Melvin A. 9, 17, 19, 40, 484, 485
Ekelund, Robert 129–30
Elizabeth I, Queen 121
Ellenborough, Lord 146
Elliott, L. 404
Emerson, R. 428, 445
Epstein, Richard A. xiii
Erhard, Lüdwig 183
Erlanger, H. 416
Erickson, John R. 490
Ericson, Richard V. 274

Espeland, W.N. 453
Etzioni, A. 56
Euken, Walter 183, 190, 191

Faden, R.R. 433
Faerman, S. 417
Farina, Cynthia R. 346
Farnsworth, E. Allan 494
Feeley, M. 428
Feitshans, I. 390, 411
Feyerabend, P. 50
Field, Justice 152
Fischer, T. 183
Fitzpatrick, P. 75
Foreman, Stephen E. xi
Foucault, Michel 76, 77, 93, 100–102 *passim*
Freedland, M. 468
Freeman, Jody xvi, xvii
French, Justice 383, 384, 385, 386
Frey, Bruno S. 485
Friedman, L. 49
Friedrichs, D. 393
Friendly, Henry J. 223, 230
Fry, F. 398
Frye, Timothy xvii
Fuller, Lon L. xv, 484

Gadamer, Hans 16
Gaebler, T. 392
Galanter, M. 67, 75
Galaway, B. 399
Galbraith, J.K. 185
Galligan, Dennis J. 203, 212, 229, 302, 310
Gamble, A. 78
Ganz, Gabrielle 247–8
Gardiner, John 261
Garland, D. 392
Gaudemar, J-P. 98
Geltman, E. 390, 392
Genn, H. 413
Gifford, Daniel J. 229–30 *passim*
Gioia, D. 414
Glanville, S.R. 69
Godelier, Maurice 81
Goldberg, Justice 385
Goldberg, Victor P. 490
Goodin, Robert E. 266
Gordon, C. 392
Gotthold, J. 57
Grabosky, Peter N. xv, xviii, 252, 390, 393, 402
Graham 161
Grimes, Warren S, 489
Grimm, D. 56
Grimm, Jacob 487

Grimm, Wilhelm 487
Gruner, R. 411
Guillemin, J.H. 443
Gunningham, N. 402
Günther, Eberhard 185
Gustafson, David H. 260, 261

Habermas, Jürgen xii, 46, 53, 57, 61, 62, 64, 65, 78, 97, 100, 465
Hale, Sir Matthew xiii, 146–7 *passim*, 148, 149, 151, 152, 154
Haley, John O. 252
Halpern, S. 449, 450
Hancher, Leigh xv, 391, 392
Haralambie, A.M. 431
Hargrave 146
Hart, D. 57, 416, 418
Hart, H.L.A. 373
Hartman, H. 97
Hawkins, Keith xiv, 212, 221–50, 252, 266, 280, 389, 390, 393
Hay, Douglas 95
Hayek, Friedrich A. xii, 50, 56, 57, 68, 78, 186, 189, 190, 191
Heimer, Carol A. xvi, 427–57, 440, 450, 451
Heerey, Justice 384, 385
Hegel, Gottfried W.F. 80
Heimer, C.A. 413–14, 417, 432, 433
Hejl, P.M. 51, 53, 58, 60, 65
Hensen, Horst-Diether 488
Heydebrand, W. 97
Hirschman, Albert O. 76, 100, 511
Hobsbawm, Eric 96
Hoffman, W. 416
Holmes, Oliver Wendell 154, 155
Holmstrom, L.L. 443
Hondrich, K.O. 67, 68
Hood, Christopher xv, 460, 467
Hooker, M. 75
Hoppmann, E. 57
Horn, Murray xv, 320, 321
Horwitz, Morton J. xii
Hudson, J. 399
Hunt, Alan xiii, 76
Hutter, B. 389, 393

James I, King 123, 131
James II, King 128
Jänicke. M. 76
Jeffcott, B. 402
Joerges, C. 58, 64
Jowell, Jeffrey L. 223, 239
Jutsen, J. 403

Kadish, Sanford 371, 373
Kagan, Robert A. xv, xvi, 243, 252, 297, 393
Kahn, Alfred 24
Kant, Immanuel 187
Karst, Kenneth 510, 512
Katz, J. 433
Kaysor-Jones, Jeanie 271
Keeler, Theodore E. xi
Kelman, Mark 253
Kelman, S. 252
Kennedy, Duncan 253
Keynes, Lord 158
Kirchheimer, O. 93, 96
Klein, Rudolf 252
Klitzsch, W. 57, 60
Kornhauser, Lewis 427, 451
Krause, D. 66
Krotoszynski, R.J. 252
Kübler, Friedrich 493

Ladeur, K-H. 58
Lammers, C.J. 67, 68
Lande, J. 416
Lange, Bettina xiv, xviii
Laswell, Harold 5
Lawrence, P.R. 58
Lechner, Frank 501
Lehner, F. 57
Lempert, R. 428, 436, 451
Lessig, Lawrence xvi, xvii
Levin, M. 404
Levy, Brian xiii
Lieberman, J.K. 430
Lindblom, C. 70
Llewellyn, Karl xiii
Lock, E.J. 450
Long, Susan B. 227–8
López Pumajero, Alfonso 509
Lorsch, Jay W. 58
Louis XIV, King 142
Luhmann, Niklas xii, 51, 53, 57, 58, 61, 62, 64, 66, 97

Macaulay, Lord 133
Macaulay, Stewart 67, 75
McAuslan, Patrick 226
McBarnet, Doreen xiv, 202, 203
McCaffrey, D. 416, 417, 418
McCubbins, Matthew 320, 321, 346
MacDonagh, Oliver xi
McDougall, Myers 5
Macey, Jonathan R. xv, 319–51
McInerney, F. 404
McNollgast *see* McCubbins, Noll, Weingast

Maher, Imelda xviii
Makkei, Toni 272, 400–401
Manning, P. 390, 393
March, James G. 442
Markey, Edward J. 348, 349
Marshall, Chief Justice 327
Marshall, T. 399
Marx, Karl 80, 81, 82, 88–90 *passim*, 92
Mary, Queen 127
Mashaw, Jerry L. xv, 238
Maturana, H.R. 51, 58
May, Erskin 130
Mayntz, Renate 53, 56, 57, 60, 63
Meidinger, E. 415
Melossi, D. 93
Messmer, H. 399
Mestmäcker, Ernst-Joachim 57, 186, 187, 188, 189
Meyer, J.W. 438
Miksch, Leonhard 183
Milhaupt, Curtis J. xvii
Mill, John Stuart 79
Mitchell, R. 409
Mitnick, B. 53
Mnookin, Robert H. 427, 451
Montesquieu, Charles L. de S. 43, 102
Moore, Michael 364
Moore, S. 75
Moran, Michael xv, 391, 392
Morris 365
Möschel, Wernhard xiii, 183–93
Müller-Armack, Alfred 183
Mungham, G. 77
Murphy, J. 418
Murphy, Tim xii
Murray, Andrew xvi

Nader, L. 75
Nelken, D. 224
Nelson, L.J. 431
Nesterczuk, G. 390, 392
Neves, Marcelo xii
Nichols, Glenn O. 132
Noll, Roger G. xi, 320, 321, 346
Nonet, Philippe 15, 49, 56, 62, 97, 480
Nor, K.W. 183
North, Douglass C. xiii, xv, 115–44
Nowak 157

Offe, Claus 77, 99
Ogus, Anthony xi, xvii, 371
Oliver 480
Olsen, J.P. 442
Osborne, D. 392
Otto, H. 399

Parker, Christine xvi, xviii, 389–425
Pastrana, President 516
Paterson, R. 398, 400, 401
Paulus, Ingeborg xi
Pavarini, M. 93
Pearce, F. 390, 394, 402
Petry, E. 416
Phillip IV of Spain, King 119
Phillips, Colleen 271
Picciotto, Sol xviii
Pierce, Richard J. 335
Pitschas, R. 57
Podgorecki, A. 56
Posner, Eric A. xvi
Posner, Richard A. 24, 187, 280, 378, 484
Poulantzas, N. 77, 81
Powell, W.W. 438–9
Pratt, Anna C. xiv
Presnell, L.S. 137–8
Prosser, Tony xii, xiii, 161, 163–82

Radin, Margaret J. 253
Ramsay, H. 98
Reagan, Ronald 348, 349
Rees, J. 399, 400, 416
Reich, N. 53
Reichman, Nancy xiv
Reiss, Albert J. jr 227, 228, 241
Renner, K. 93–4 *passim*
Richardson, Genevra xv, 371
Roberts, Justice 156
Robertson, Roland 501
Robinson, Joan 185
Rogoff, Kenneth 119
Rojas, F. 99
Röpke, Wilhelm 183, 187
Rose, Carol M. 253
Rose-Ackerman, Susan 324–5
Rosen, Sherwin 486
Rosenberg, G.N. 428
Rothman, D.J. 433
Rothstein, Henry xv
Rottleuthner, H. 50, 52
Rotunda 157
Rowan, B. 438
Rubin, Edward L. xii, xiv, xvii, 3–47
Rueter, F. 404
Ruggie, M. 434
Rusche, G. 93, 96
Rüstow, Alexander 183

Sabel, C. 98

Sah, Monica 526
Saint-Simon, Claude H. de R. 102
Sanders, J. 428, 436, 451
Sanford, Justice 154
Scalia, Justice 327–8
Schanze, Erich xvii, 483–97
Scharpf, F. 58
Schauer, F. 299
Schlag, Pierre 253
Schmidheiney, S. 404
Schmitter, P.C. 57
Schneiderman, David xvii, 501–27
Schoer, Ray 281
Scholz, J. 393, 394
Schorr, K-E. 61
Schuck, Peter H. 269, 433
Schwartz, Alan 494
Schwartz, M. 412
Schwartz, Thomas 320
Scott, Colin xii, xvi, xvii, 313, 391, 392, 460, 466, 467
Sedley, Sir Stephen 473
Selznick, Philip 15, 49, 50, 56, 62, 94, 97, 301–2, 306, 390, 480
Shad, John 349
Sharfman, I.L. 230
Shearing, Clifford D. xiii, xvi, 274, 391, 392, 419, 420
Shell, Richard G. 494
Shepsle, Kenneth 320, 321, 344, 350
Siegel, Stephen A. xiii
Silvani, C. 398
Simitis, S. 65
Sims, R. 414
Skroback, A. 390, 392
Slaughter, Anne-Marie xvii
Smith, Adam 6, 24, 79, 158
Smith, Gilbert 224
Smithers, Justice 386
Snare, Annika 95
Sousa Santos, Boaventura de xii, 75–112
Sparrow, M. 393, 395
Spector, William D. 262
Spencer, Herbert 158
Spiller, Pablo xiii
Stachowiak, H. 51, 52, 53, 54
Starr, P. 432, 433, 434, 451
Steger, W. 404
Stein, Lorenz von 80
Stenning, Philip C. xvi
Stevens, M.L. 450
Stewart, Richard B. 241, 334, 335
Stone, Justice 154, 155, 157
Streeck, W. 57
Suchman, Mark C. xv
Sullivan, Kathleen M. 253
Summers, Robert S. 252
Sunstein, Cass R. 329, 484, 486
Sutherland, Justice 154

Taft, Chief Justice 153
Taggart, Mike xiii
Taylor, A. 79
Taylor, S. 453
Teubner, Gunther xii, xvi, xvii, 49–74, 77, 100, 495
Thompson, E.P. 76
Titmuss, R.M. 238
Tollison, Robert 129–30
Tombs, S. 390, 394, 402
Trubek, David 102

Ulmer, Peter 488
Unger, M. 68
Unger, Roberto 97, 241, 242
Upham, Frank K. 252
Uribe, R. 58

Vanberg, Viktor J. xiii
Vandevelde, Kenneth J. 519
Van Ness, D. 399
Varela, F.J. 51, 58
Vietch, John 119
Vico, Giambattista 102
Vincent-Jones, Peter xvii, 459–82
Viner, J. 79
Vogel, David xv
Vogel, Ezra F. 252
Vogel, Steven K.
Voigt, R. 100
von Hirsch, Andrew 364
von Nell-Breuning, O. 187

Waelde, T. 56
Waite, Chief Justice 150–52 *passim*
Walker, Sir David 211
Walker, John xv
Wallerstein, I. 76, 84
Walsh, K. 461
Warren, Alvin C. 489
Warren, Chief Justice 19
Watson, James D. 6
Weait, M. 416
Weber, Max 96, 203, 281, 301
Wedderburn, K.W. 66
Weingast, Barry R. xiii, xv, 115–44, 319, 321, 346
Wellington, Duke of 6

West, Mark D. xvii
Whelan, Christopher xiv, 202, 203
White, James B. 275
White, S. 404
Wiener, Carolyn L. 271
Wiethoelter, R. 57, 70
Willgerodt, H. 183
William III, King 127, 129
Williamson, Oliver E. 118
Willke, Helmut 57, 58, 65, 66, 69, 70, 71
Wilthagen, T. 404, 413
Winter, G. 57
Wood, E. 94
Wood, Meiksins 95
Woodbury, John 365
Wright, Erik 86
Wright, Jim 348

Yanz, L. 402
Yeung, Karen xvi, 353–88
Young 157

Zeleny, M. 51, 58
Zenzy, G. 65
Ziegert, K. 49, 56
Zimmerman, David J. 262
Zussman, R. 431, 432, 433, 435, 443, 444, 451, 452